Final Report of the Thirty-third Antarctic Treaty Consultative Meeting

ANTARCTIC TREATY
CONSULTATIVE MEETING

Final Report
of the Thirty-third
Antarctic Treaty
Consultative Meeting

Punta del Este, Uruguay
3–14 May 2010

Secretariat of the Antarctic Treaty
Buenos Aires
2010

Antarctic Treaty Consultative Meeting (33rd : 2010 : Punta del Este)
  Final Report of the Thirty-third Antarctic Treaty Consultative Meeting.
  Punta del Este, Uruguay, 3–14 May 2010.
  Buenos Aires : Secretariat of the Antarctic Treaty, 2010.
  292 p.

ISBN 978-987-1515-12-7

1. International law – Environmental issues. 2. Antarctic Treaty system.
3. Environmental law – Antarctica. 4. Environmental protection – Antarctica.

DDC 341.762 5

ISBN 978-987-1515-12-7

Contents

VOLUME 1 (in hardcopy and CD)

VOLUME 2 (in CD only)

PART II. MEASURES, DECISIONS AND RESOLUTIONS (Cont.)

4. Management Plans

PART III. OPENING AND CLOSING ADDRESSES AND REPORTS

1. Statements at the Signing of the Headquarters Agreement for the Secretariat of the Antarctic Treaty

2. Reports by Depositaries and Observers

3. Reports by Experts

PART IV. ADDITIONAL DOCUMENTS FROM XXXII ATCM

1. Abstract of SCAR Lecture

2. List of documents
Working Papers
Information Papers
Secretariat Papers

3. List of Participants
Consultative Parties
Non Consultative Parties
Observers, Experts and Guests
Secretariat

Acronyms and Abbreviations

ACAP	Agreement on the Conservation of Albatrosses and Petrels
ASOC	Antarctic and Southern Ocean Coalition
ASMA	Antarctic Specially Managed Area
ASPA	Antarctic Specially Protected Area
ATS	Antarctic Treaty System or Antarctic Treaty Secretariat
ATCM	Antarctic Treaty Consultative Meeting
ATCP	Antarctic Treaty Consultative Party
CAML	Census of Antarctic Marine Life
CCAMLR	Convention on the Conservation of Antarctic Marine Living Resources and/or Commission for the Conservation of Antarctic Marine Living Resources
CCAS	Convention for the Conservation of Antarctic Seals
CEE	Comprehensive Environmental Evaluation
CEP	Committee for Environmental Protection
COMNAP	Council of Managers of National Antarctic Programmes
EIA	Environmental Impact Assessment
HCA	Hydrographic Committee on Antarctica
HSM	Historic Site and Monument
IAATO	International Association of Antarctica Tour Operators
ICG	Intersessional Contact Group
ICSU	International Council for Science
IEE	Initial Environmental Evaluation
IHO	International Hydrographic Organization
IMO	International Maritime Organization
IOC	Intergovernmental Oceanographic Commission
IP	Information Paper
IPCC	Intergovernmental Panel on Climate Change
IPY	International Polar Year
IPY-IPO	IPY Programme Office
IUCN	International Union for Conservation of Nature and Natural Resources
RFMO	Regional Fishery Management Organisation
SATCM	Special Antarctic Treaty Consultative Meeting
SCAR	Scientific Committee on Antarctic Research

SCALOP	Standing Committee for Antarctic Logistics and Operations
SC-CAMLR	Scientific Committee of CCAMLR
SP	Secretariat Paper
SPA	Specially Protected Area
UNEP	United Nations Environment Programme
UNFCCC	United Nations Framework Convention on Climate Change
WG	Working Group
WMO	World Meteorological Organization
WP	Working Paper
WTO	World Tourism Organization

PART I
Final Report

1. Final Report

Final Report of the Thirty-third Antarctic Treaty Consultative Meeting

Punta del Este, May 3–14, 2010

(1) Pursuant to Article IX of the Antarctic Treaty, Representatives of the Consultative Parties (Argentina, Australia, Belgium, Brazil, Bulgaria, Chile, China, Ecuador, Finland, France, Germany, India, Italy, Japan, the Republic of Korea, the Netherlands, New Zealand, Norway, Peru, Poland, the Russian Federation, South Africa, Spain, Sweden, Ukraine, the United Kingdom of Great Britain and Northern Ireland, the United States of America, and Uruguay) met in Punta del Este from 3 to 14 May 2010, for the purpose of exchanging information, holding consultations and considering and recommending to their Governments measures in furtherance of the principles and objectives of the Treaty.

(2) The Meeting was also attended by delegations from the following Contracting Parties to the Antarctic Treaty which are not Consultative Parties: Canada, the Czech Republic, Monaco and Romania. A delegation from Malaysia was present by invitation of ATCM XXXII to observe the Meeting.

(3) In accordance with Rules 2 and 31 of the Rules of Procedure, Observers from the Commission for the Conservation of Antarctic Marine Living Resources (CCAMLR), the Scientific Committee on Antarctic Research (SCAR) and the Council of Managers of National Antarctic Programs (COMNAP) attended the Meeting.

(4) In accordance with Rule 39 of the Rules of Procedure, Experts from the following international organisations and non-governmental organisations were invited to attend the Meeting: the Secretariat of the Agreement on the Conservation of Albatrosses and Petrels (ACAP), the Antarctic and Southern Ocean Coalition (ASOC), the International Association of Antarctica Tour Operators (IAATO), the International Hydrographic Organization (IHO), the International Maritime Organization (IMO), the Intergovernmental Oceanographic Commission (IOC),

15

the International Union for the Conservation of Nature (IUCN), the World Tourism Organization (WTO), the World Meteorological Organization (WMO) and the United Nations Environment Programme (UNEP).

(5) The Host Country fulfilled its information requirements towards the Contracting Parties, Observers and Experts through Secretariat Circulars, letters and a website, which included both public and restricted areas.

Item 1: Opening of the Meeting

(6) The Meeting was officially opened on 3 May 2010. On behalf of the Host Government, in accordance with Rules 5 and 6 of the Rules of Procedure Mr Albert Lluberas called the meeting to order and proposed the candidacy of the distinguished Dr Roberto Puceiro Ripoll as Chair of ATCM XXXIII. The proposal was accepted.

(7) The Chair warmly welcomed all Parties to Punta del Este. He recalled the long history of exploration that led to the presence of Parties in Antarctica. In particular, he noted early views of the continent as an inaccessible, isolated place. As countries began to further explore and conduct research, they recognised the need to coexist in Antarctica and to agree to principles for working together for peaceful purposes. The resulting Antarctic Treaty addresses and continues to evolve with regards to environmental protection, the management of living marine resources and guidelines for tourism.

(8) Dr Luis Almagro, the Uruguayan Minister of Foreign Affairs, Mr Luis Rosadilla, the Uruguayan Minister of Defence, and Ing. María Simon, the Vice Minister of Education and Culture, officially welcomed delegates to the Meeting. Dr Luis Almagro noted the growing challenges of climate change, thawing ice caps and the thinning of the ozone layer, and the rapid growth of technological change and research in new areas, like bioprospecting. He noted that these emphasise the importance of the work of the Parties together to achieve environmental protection and sustainability in Antarctica.

(9) The Chair thanked the Ministers for their moving words and noted that their remarks would guide the Meeting.

Presidential Address to Plenary

(10) The President of the Oriental Republic of Uruguay, Mr José Mujica, addressed a plenary session of the XXXIII Antarctic Treaty Consultative

Meeting, extending a warm welcome to participating delegations and underlining that the Antarctic Treaty is a great example of international cooperation. He also signalled the importance for the future of protecting the wilderness of the Antarctic. The Chair of ATCM XXXIII thanked the President for his welcome remarks and for finding time in his schedule to show his support for the work of the Meeting. The Meeting expressed its warm appreciation of the President's remarks.

Signing of the Headquarters Agreement

(11)   On 12 May 2010, pursuant to the entry into force of Measure 1(2003), the Minister of Foreign Affairs of the Republic of Argentina, Jorge Taiana and Dr Roberto Puceiro Ripoll, Chair of ATCM XXXIII, signed the Headquarters Agreement for the Secretariat of the Antarctic Treaty. The Foreign Minister welcomed the confidence expressed by the Treaty Parties in deciding to base its Secretariat in Argentina. The Chair of ATCM XXXIII thanked Argentina for the facilities given by this Headquarters Agreement. The Meeting expressed its appreciation for the Foreign Minister's remarks.

(12)   A signed copy of the Agreement is attached to this Report (see page 229). The texts of speeches by Minister Taiana and Dr Puceiro Ripoll are can be found in Volume 2, Part III, section 1.

Item 2: Election of Officers and Creation of Working Groups

(13)   Mr Ariel Mansi, Representative of Argentina (Host Country of ATCM XXXIV) was elected Vice-chair. In accordance with Rule 7 of the Rules of Procedure, Dr Manfred Reinke, Executive Secretary of the Antarctic Treaty Secretariat, acted as Secretary to the Meeting. Mr Albert Lluberas, head of the Host Country Secretariat, acted as Deputy Secretary. Dr Neil Gilbert, Representative of New Zealand, acted as Chair of the Committee for Environmental Protection for his final year.

(14)   Three Working Groups were established:

- Working Group on Legal and Institutional Affairs;
- Working Group on Tourism and Non-governmental Activities;
- Working Group on Operational Matters.

(15)   The following Chairs of the Working Groups were elected:

- Legal and Institutional Affairs Working Group: Mr Richard Rowe of Australia;
- Operational Matters Working Group: Dr José Retamales of Chile;
- Tourism and Non-governmental Activities Working Group: Mr Evan Bloom of the United States of America.

Item 3: Adoption of the Agenda and Allocation of Items

(16)   The following Agenda was adopted:

1. Opening of the Meeting
2. Election of Officers and Creation of Working Groups
3. Adoption of the Agenda and Allocation of Items
4. Operation of the Antarctic Treaty System: Reports by Parties, Observers and Experts
5. Operation of the Antarctic Treaty System: General Matters
6. Operation of the Antarctic Treaty System: Review of the Secretariat's Situation
7. Report of the Committee for Environmental Protection
8. Liability: Implementation of Decision 1 (2005)
9. Safety and Operations in Antarctica
10. The International Polar Year 2007-08
11. Tourism and Non-Governmental Activities in the Antarctic Treaty Area
12. Inspections under the Antarctic Treaty and the Environment Protocol
13. Science Issues, Including Climate-related Research, Scientific Cooperation and Facilitation
14. Operational Issues
15. Education Issues
16. Exchange of Information
17. Biological Prospecting in Antarctica
18. Development of a Multi-Year Strategic Work Plan
19. Preparation of the 34th Meeting
20. Any Other Business
21. Adoption of the Final Report

(17)   The Chair referred to the request by some Parties to amend the proposed agenda of the Meeting (SP 1 rev. 1) to add an item specifically on climate change. It was noted that a specific emphasis on climate change in the agenda would be consistent with a recommendation of the Antarctic Treaty Meeting of Experts (ATME) on Climate Change held in Svolvær, Norway 6-9 April 2010, that the ATCM address climate change as a separate agenda item.

(18)   The Meeting agreed that its consideration of climate change was not a matter of considering climate change policy, which is within the purview of the United Nations and other bodies, but agreed to take up the issue for purposes of a focused discussion of the effects and implications of climate change on Antarctica within the context of the Treaty. The Meeting agreed to discuss this further under agenda item 18.

(19)   The Meeting adopted the following allocation of agenda items:
- Plenary: Items 1, 2, 3, 4, 7, 18, 19, 20, 21;
- Legal and Institutional Working Group: Items 5, 6, 8, 17, and review of draft measures of CEP report, item 7;
- Tourism Working Group: Items 9, 11;
- Operational Matters Working Group: Items 9, 10, 12, 13, 14, 15, 16;
- Item 9 containing safety and operational issues would be discussed in a joint meeting of the Tourism Working Group and the Operational Matters Working Group.

(20)   The Meeting decided to allocate draft instruments arising out of the work of the Committee for Environmental Protection and the Working Groups on Operational Matters and Tourism to the Legal and Institutional Working Group for consideration of their legal and institutional aspects.

Item 4: Operation of the Antarctic Treaty System: Reports by Parties, Observers and Experts

(21)   Pursuant to Recommendation XIII-2, the Meeting received reports from: The United States in its capacity as Depositary of the Antarctic Treaty and the Protocol; the United Kingdom in its capacity as Depositary of the Convention for the Conservation of Antarctic Seals (CCAS); Australia in its capacity as Depositary of the Convention on the Conservation of Antarctic Marine Living Resources (CCAMLR) and Depositary of the Agreement on the Conservation of Albatrosses and Petrels (ACAP); the Commission for

the Conservation of Antarctic Marine Living Resources (CCAMLR); the Scientific Committee on Antarctic Research (SCAR); and the Council of Managers of National Antarctic Programs (COMNAP).

(22) The United States, in its capacity as Depositary Government, reported on the status of the Antarctic Treaty and the Protocol on Environmental Protection to the Antarctic Treaty, noting that Portugal had acceded to the Treaty on 29 January 2010, and Monaco had acceded to the Protocol on 1 July 2009, concluding that there were now 48 Parties to the Antarctic Treaty and 34 Parties to the Protocol. (see Vol. 2, Part III, section 2 for the complete report).

(23) The United States noted that Measure 1 (2003) had been approved by all Consultative Parties and became effective on 6 October 2009. The United States also noted that in April 2010 three Parties requested an extension with regard to approving Measure 16 (2009). Measure 16 (2009) would become effective after all three Parties had approved it. It also urged prompt action to approve pending Recommendations, Measures, Decisions, and Resolutions and emphasised the necessity of this for the health of the Treaty system.

(24) Australia, in its capacity as Depositary for the Convention for the Conservation of Antarctic Marine Living Resources, reported that there had been no new accessions to the Convention since ATCM XXXII (see Vol. 2, Part III, section 2).

(25) The United Kingdom, as Depositary for the Convention on the Conservation of Antarctic Seals, reported that there had been no accessions to the Convention since ATCM XXXII. No seals were killed during the period between March 2007 and February 2008. The United Kingdom expressed its appreciation to Parties to the Convention in meeting the 30 June yearly deadline for reporting the information referenced in paragraph 6 of the Annex to the Convention to SCAR and the Contracting Parties (see Vol. 2, Part III, section 2).

(26) Australia, in its capacity as Depositary for the Agreement on the Conservation of Albatrosses and Petrels, reported that there had been no new accessions to the Agreement since ATCM XXXII (see Vol. 2, Part III, section 2).

(27) The CCAMLR observer presented IP 4 *Report by the CCAMLR Observer to the Thirty-Third Antarctic Treaty Consultative Meeting,* a report on the outcomes of CCAMLR XXVIII which was held at Hobart, Australia in November 2009. He highlighted measures to support improved monitoring of the krill fishery and resolutions relating to the Salvage Convention, climate

change and best available science. He noted on-going efforts by CCAMLR to protect vulnerable marine ecosystems and the designation of 94,000km² in the South Orkney Islands region as an MPA and the establishment of a fund to support capacity building in science. He noted Dr Denzil Miller's contribution to CCAMLR and the ATS over many years and looked forward to continuing the close relationship between CCAMLR and the ATCM particularly in respect of the outcomes of the 2009 SC-CAMLR-CEP Workshop.

(28) The United Kingdom thanked CCAMLR for its report, welcomed the new Executive Secretary, and echoed thanks to former Executive Secretary, Dr Denzil Miller. The United Kingdom emphasised the particular interest of the Committee in CCAMLR's work with regard to climate change, spatial management and best available science. It also highlighted WP 44 rev. 1 *Complementary protection for Marine Protected Areas designed by CCAMLR.*

(29) The President of the Scientific Committee on Antarctic Research introduced the SCAR Report (see Vol. 2, Part III, section 2), which included the main activities of SCAR from 2009, also covered in other agenda items. SCAR released a report in December 2009 on "Antarctic Climate Change and the Environment (ACCE)", which was received internationally with great interest. This report also contributed to the Antarctic Treaty Meeting of Experts (ATME) on Climate Change held in Svolvær, Norway 6-9 April. SCAR will continue to provide annual updates to this report. In 2009, SCAR also underwent an external review and will adopt a six-year strategic plan in 2010. SCAR was pleased to announce the first recipient of the Martha Muse Prize for Policy, Professor Steven Chown of South Africa, who would receive the prize at the International Polar Year Conference in June 2010. The SCAR President further noted that Dr Michael Sparrow is SCAR's new Executive Director following the retirement of Dr Colin Summerhayes, and Dr Renuka Badhe is the new Executive Officer. He recalled that the SCAR's next Open Science Conference would be held in Buenos Aires 3-6 August 2010. To this end, he noted Monaco had applied for membership to SCAR, which would be considered at the SCAR meeting.

(30) The Executive Secretary of the Council of Managers of National Antarctic Programs introduced the COMNAP Report (see Vol. 2, Part III, section 2), and made particular mention of its newly agreed constitution, the election of the new Executive Secretary, the existing new location, and the new way of working. She expressed gratitude to Australia as the previous host

of the COMNAP Secretariat and to the present host, Christchurch, New Zealand. COMNAP looked forward to strengthening partnerships with other organisations. COMNAP introduced IP 78 as a report of the second Search and Recue (SAR) Workshop, and announced its work on a five-year strategic plan in consultation with the CEP work plan and ATCM requests. COMNAP also underlined an outreach group for young people to continue engagement and interest in Antarctica.

(31) In relation to Article III-2 of the Antarctic Treaty, the Meeting received reports from the International Hydrographic Organization (IHO), the Antarctic and Southern Ocean Coalition (ASOC), and the International Association of Antarctica Tour Operators (IAATO). These reports can be found in Vol. 2, Part III, section 3.

(32) The representative of the International Hydrographic Organization introduced IP 51, the IHO report *Cooperation in Hydrographic Surveying and Charting of Antarctic Waters*. He highlighted the outcome of the seminar on Hydrography at the Annual Meeting of COMNAP held in Punta Arenas, Chile in August 2009, where two initiatives were proposed and adopted by COMNAP. IHO emphasised the convenience of addressing environmental and scientific issues in addition to safety of navigation issues and noted that only 67 out of 102 International Nautical Charts have been so far produced. IHO recalled that, despite the willingness expressed by Antarctic Treaty representatives at different meetings, hydrographic surveys and production of nautical charts of Antarctica were not, in practice, being given the required priority. This was reflected in the reports analysed at the last HCA meeting where only 7 out of 23 HCA Members reported that some systematic hydrographic surveys were conducted in the last season. He referred also to the IHO contribution to the ATME held in New Zealand in December 2009. Finally he noted that the 10th Meeting of the HCA would be held from 20-22 September 2010, in Cambridge, United Kingdom.

(33) While thanking IHO for its Report, Argentina noted that South Georgia should not be included in Annex B since that territory is not within the Antarctic Treaty Area.

(34) The United Kingdom stated that it considered that the focus for hydrographic work must remain on the needs of mariners for safe operation, but certainly agreed that there is room for greater coordination on hydrographic and scientific information on Antarctica as highlighted in WP 11 *Forwarding of hydrographic data collected during the IPY*.

(35) New Zealand acknowledged IHO's important contributions at the Antarctic Treaty Meeting of Experts (ATME) on Ship-borne Tourism in the Antarctic Treaty Area. Chile noted the lack of priority and rapid fulfilment of nautical chart priorities by Parties.

(36) The representative of the Antarctic and Southern Ocean Coalition introduced the ASOC report (IP 114). ASOC noted that it had participated in several meetings this year, including both ATMEs, and expressed support for recommendations coming from these meetings. ASOC emphasised the need for the ATCM to adopt a polar vessel code for all vessels navigating in the Southern Ocean, and to ensure substantial regulation and control of tourism. ASOC also drew attention to issues of hydrocarbon pollution, the implementation of Annex VI, and overall environmental protection. ASOC also expressed its surprise at the lack of response to Recommendation 2 of Resolution 7 (2005) on biological prospecting.

(37) The representative of the International Association of Antarctica Tour Operators introduced IAATO's Annual Report (IP 12). He noted that tourism activities continued to decline during the 2009-10 season due to the global economy crisis. Through its participation at two Antarctic Treaty Meetings of Experts, COMNAP, IHO-HCA and IMO meetings, IAATO expressed its commitment to its mission of safe and environmentally responsible tourism, and the need for continued collaboration with national programmes, NGOs and scientific bodies. He expressed concern about non-IAATO visits to Antarctica by groups that may not be aware of the Environmental Protocol and the value of strong competent authority processes. He also welcomed the representatives of Treaty Parties to the IAATO 21st Annual Meeting to be held the week of 20 June 2010 in Torino, Italy.

(38) IAATO noted there were two tourist-related evacuations from the South Pole and thanked the United States for its assistance during those events.

ATME Results

(39) New Zealand introduced WP 1 *Chairs' Report - Antarctic Treaty Meeting of Experts on the Management of Ship-borne Tourism in the Antarctic Treaty Area* held in Wellington, New Zealand from 9 to 11 December 2009. It noted that the seventeen recommendations of the ATME would be discussed in the appropriate working groups. Seventy-two delegates from nineteen Consultative Parties participated, together with fourteen representatives from international organisations including ASOC, COMNAP, IAATO, IHO, IMO

and WTO. Thirty-one papers were submitted and presented to the ATME. New Zealand thanked the Chairs and Vice-chairs of the ATME and the Antarctic Treaty Secretariat and Executive Secretary for their assistance.

(40) Norway presented the Chair's report from the Antarctic Treaty Meeting of Experts (ATME) on Implications of Climate Change for Antarctic Management and Governance. This ATME was held in Svolvær, Norway from 6 to 9 April 2010. It noted the very helpful and constructive previous discussions on climate change as a separate agenda item at Consultative Meetings and indicated strong support for climate change discussions at future Meetings. Thirty-six representatives from fifteen Consultative Parties participated, along with eight invited experts and one representative from the Antarctic Treaty Secretariat. A total of three working papers and thirteen information papers were submitted and used as a basis for discussions. Norway underlined the SCAR report and its key findings as important tools to the work at the ATME. Norway expressed gratitude to the United Kingdom for co-hosting the ATME in Norway, and thanked SCAR and the CEP Chair for their contributions to the meeting.

(41) Norway underlined that the recommendations from the ATME would be discussed in the appropriate working groups, but were summarised briefly as follows:

- Recommendations 1-3 highlighted the importance of climate change in Antarctica;
- Recommendations 4-6 discussed emissions and energy efficiency in Antarctica;
- Recommendations 7-9 looked at impacts on human activities in Antarctica;
- Recommendations 10-17 discussed research needs and monitoring;
- Recommendations 18-25 focused on nature management;
- Recommendations 26-29 examined ATS cooperation between the ATCM and CCAMLR;
- Recommendation 30 suggested having a separate ATCM agenda item on climate change.

(42) The United Kingdom and the United States thanked both New Zealand and Norway for hosting these ATMEs. They recognised the meetings as a considerable undertaking and investment for host countries and attendees, along with the intersessional work. They encouraged those who could not take part in the ATME to look at the recommendations of the reports and

concurred with comments made on the importance of issues, particularly with regard to climate change and the importance of a polar code.

(43) ASOC echoed the comments by the United Kingdom and the United States. It noted the high quality of the intersessional organisation and the need for this Meeting to follow up on the ATME recommendations.

Marine Spatial Protection and Management

(44) The United Kingdom and Belgium introduced WP 44 rev. 1 *Complementary Protection for Marine Protected Areas Designated by CCAMLR*, proposing a mechanism that would prohibit discharges and dumping of any type of waste by all non-fishing vessels in the South Orkney Islands southern shelf Marine Protected Area (MPA). The paper also proposed one option to streamline future joint ATCM and CCAMLR work in respect of the designation of a network of marine protected areas by 2012. The United Kingdom explained that the aim of the paper was to highlight the need to develop a mechanism for the ATCM and CCAMLR to adopt a harmonised approach to the protection of the marine environment.

(45) Several Parties strongly expressed their support for the designation of the South Orkney Islands southern shelf as an MPA by CCAMLR, recognising it as an important first step towards the development of a representative network of MPAs.

(46) The United States said that it shared the desire to promote the development of marine protected areas in the Southern Ocean, and had supported the South Orkney Islands MPA initiative at CCAMLR. However, it had some key concerns with respect to the approach taken in WP 44 rev. 1. It indicated its view that IMO was the primary venue for regulating shipping, especially with respect to discharge from vessels under MARPOL, and noted that IMO could set rules for ships of all flags, not just those flagged to Antarctic Treaty Parties. In addition, the United States said it would be desirable for the ATCM to receive advice from CEP on whether extending environmental restrictions to non-fishing vessels was warranted before the Meeting takes such a decision. The United States also expressed a number of legal concerns with the draft proposed Measure.

(47) IAATO noted the adoption of the South Orkneys MPA as a milestone for CCAMLR. While it understood the intent of the paper, IAATO asked for clarification on the process for stakeholder consultation regarding adoption of any future MPAs by CCAMLR that could include restrictions that Parties

consider applicable to non-fishing vessels, either directly through CCAMLR measures, or subsequently through the ATCM.

(48) Some Parties expressed concern that the process outlined in the proposed Measure in WP 44 rev. 1 would extend the provisions of CCAMLR MPAs to all non-fishing vessels within designated areas, comprising vessels of non-Treaty Parties, without a review by the International Maritime Organization (IMO). Other Parties considered that to proceed independently of an IMO review could raise legal issues.

(49) Additionally, some Parties suggested that the proposed Measure be submitted to the CEP for its review. As such, the CEP review would address the issues associated with discharges and dumping of waste by non-fishing vessels as matters of environmental protection. It was noted that it would not be a review of the environmental merit of the MPA designated by CCAMLR.

(50) Japan expressed its appreciation to the UK and Belgium for their efforts to put together WP 44 rev. 1. It drew Parties' attention to the point that the Environment Protocol provides for ASPA (Art. 3 of Annex V to the Protocol) and ASMA (Art. 4 of Annex V to the Protocol) and that this was the statutory basis of the designation of any area for environmental protection by the ATCM. Emphasising that there was no definition of a "marine protected area" in the Antarctic Treaty or the Environment Protocol, Japan stated that any consideration by the ATCM should be based on the legal basis mentioned above. In this context, it expressed deep concern that the proposed Measure would be a significant deviation from the statute and practice governing the ATCM.

(51) Japan also expressed concerns about the formulation of the proposed Measure. For example, while giving due regard to development of cooperation between CEP and CCAMLR, Japan pointed out that it was the CEP who should take the initiative and advise the ATCM for approval of ASPA and ASMA, after appropriately taking into account the comments made by CCAMLR, and not *vice versa*.

(52) Parties supporting the proposed Measure stressed the need to capitalise on the momentum achieved by CCAMLR in designating an MPA and lent their support to using the Measure as a means to do so.

(53) Following informal consultations, the United Kingdom noted there remained much to be discussed in relation to the important issue of MPAs. It expressed its regret that it was not possible to pursue the proposal in WP 44 rev. 1, due to reservations raised by some delegations. The United Kingdom welcomed

the work of CCAMLR in relation to the designation of the South Orkney Islands as an MPA. The United Kingdom further noted its commitment to the development of a harmonised marine approach.

(54) Several Parties noted their endorsement of the work of CCAMLR in this regard and expressed their disappointment that agreement could not be reached on this matter at this Meeting. Some Parties welcomed the designation of the South Orkneys as a first step for a network of MPAs, and urged the ATCM to recognise the need for a streamlined approach on the designation of MPAs within the Treaty system.

Item 5: Operation of the Antarctic Treaty System: General Matters

Rules governing the participation of experts in meetings of the ATCM bodies

(55) France introduced WP 45 *Rules governing the participation of experts in meetings of ATCM bodies,* which identified a need for procedures to allow participation in meetings of ATCM bodies by experts from non-party States, non-governmental bodies or by independent experts to present information within their competence and areas of expertise. France noted that its proposal would not change the procedure for extending invitations. The paper proposed amendments to Rules 40 and 42 of the Rules of Procedure for the ATCM and revision of the title of Rule 39.

(56) France recalled the difficulties which arose at ATCM XXXII in formally receiving a presentation by a representative of the Government of Liberia on the investigation conducted following the sinking of the Liberian-flagged vessel *M/S Explorer* in 2007. Under the existing Rules of Procedure, even though it had been invited by the ATCM to present its findings to the Meeting, Liberia, as a non-party State, could not formally address the Meeting. As a result, Liberia made a presentation during an informal session to the meeting, which could not be noted in the report of ATCM XXXII.

(57) Many Parties supported the intent of this proposal, with some Parties noting that only technical edits to the proposed amendments were required, while other Parties indicated that as participation for such experts would only be on an exceptional basis, they did not see a need to amend the Rules of Procedure and encouraged the consideration of alternative measures.

(58) In supporting the proposal, the United Kingdom also noted that in the example of ATCM XXXII, the difficulties also related to the timing of the

invitation, which was not in line with the 180 day timeline set out in Rule 40 of the Rules of Procedure.

(59)   In support of the proposal from France and as a way of advancing the debate, the Netherlands proposed alternative wording that would result in a new Rule:

Other experts

"46 (bis) Other experts may be invited to attend a meeting during consideration of a specified item. Rules 36-46 apply *mutatis mutandis*."

(60)   Further discussion indicated initial support by many Parties for this revised proposal but informal consultations carried out by France showed that no consensus text could be agreed during ATCM XXXIII. Many Parties encouraged France to continue its work on this topic. France indicated its willingness to carry on its efforts to reach a consensus text on this topic at ATCM XXXIV.

Review of ATCM Recommendations

(61)   Uruguay introduced WP 20 *Forwarding of recommendations on operational matters to COMNAP*, proposing that the ATCM use the facilities of COMNAP for confirming the status of measures on operational matters as outlined in the Secretariat's analysis of the status of ATCM recommendations (SP 6).

(62)   Noting that Argentina and Germany would be introducing WP 51, a broader proposal to continue the review of ATCM recommendations, Uruguay suggested that the Meeting conduct its discussion of the issue on the basis of WP 51.

(63)   Argentina and Germany introduced their joint WP 51 *A proposal to continue review of ATCM recommendations*. The paper proposed the establishment of an Intersessional Contact Group (ICG) to review SP 5 *Review of the Status of ATCM Recommendations on Protected Areas and Monuments*, SP 6 *Review of the Status of ATCM Recommendations on Operational Matters*, and SP 7 *Review of the Status of ATCM Recommendations on Environmental Issues other than Area Protection and Management*. The ICG would report back to ATCM XXXIV with details of its work.

(64)   The Assistant Executive Secretary introduced SP 5, SP 6 and SP 7, noting that these papers had previously been submitted to ATCM XXXII.

(65) Netherlands suggested that an Antarctic Treaty Meeting of Experts, held in Argentina immediately prior to ATCM XXXIV, might more expeditiously address the legal and technical issues involved in clarifying the status of the recommendations adopted since 1961. Chile indicated that, while supporting the effort to clarify the status of ATCM recommendations, it was important to maintain an archive of all recommendations adopted by the ATCM for future consultation and as a means for understanding the context of past ATCM decision-making.

(66) There was general support for both an ICG and, alternatively or additionally, an ATME. Argentina agreed to convene an ICG and the Meeting agreed to the following Terms of Reference:

1) To examine and review the status of recommendations on:
   - Protected Areas and Monuments
   - Operational Matters
   - Environmental Issues other than Area Protection and Management

   Observers, as indicated in Rule 2 of the Rules of Procedure and invited experts to the ATCM, as indicated in Rule 39 of the Rules of Procedure and the Final Report from ATCM XXXII (paragraph 333), would be invited to participate.

   Consideration will be given to the work undertaken by the Secretariat and presented in SP 5, SP 6 & SP 7;

2) To elaborate a work plan to undertake consideration of each of the above referenced topics;

3) To provide an initial status report to ATCM XXXIV with a proposal as to which recommendations could be designated as no longer current, and include any suggestion to seek the advice of the CEP.

The Handbook of the Antarctic Treaty System

(67) The Executive Secretary noted that Measure 1 (2003) directed the Secretariat, under the guidance of the ATCM, to take responsibility for maintaining and updating the Antarctic Treaty System Handbook. He introduced SP 8 *The Handbook of the Antarctic Treaty System*, which provided an outline draft for Volume 1. This outline had been circulated during the intersessional period. Comments received from the four Parties that responded to the

Secretariat were divergent in their views, including questioning whether there was a need for a new edition of the Handbook.

(68)   The Executive Secretary noted that the proposed structure of the Handbook would differ from earlier versions in no longer functioning as the repository of all measures. ATCM Recommendations, Measures, Decisions and Resolutions would instead be accessible through the Secretariat's website.

(69)   While thanking the Secretariat for SP 8, Argentina noted that the inclusion in Appendix 1 of both historical background and introductory comments may contribute to generating either disagreement or divergent interpretations. For example, in its view the fourth paragraph in Chapter I .1 was contradictory and the first paragraph of Chapter III. 1 contained incorrect information of an historic and legal nature. In addition Argentina recalled that commercial activities by sealers from the Río de la Plata had already taken place in the South Shetland Islands well before 1819.

(70)   Chile introduced WP 66 *Considerations of Chile on the Antarctic Treaty System Handbook*, affirming that the Handbook was valuable in assisting in the understanding of how the Antarctic Treaty operated. Chile noted that it had distributed the first edition of a manual in Spanish entitled "Handbook of the Theory and Practice of the Antarctic System" to Consultative Parties during ATCM XVI (Bonn, 1991). Chile proposed that the ATCM Handbook be revised using the 1991 manual as a general model.

(71)   Chile suggested that a new ATCM Handbook could be entitled "Handbook of the Theory and Practice of the Antarctic System" and include four volumes organised by topic. The Handbook would be practical and provide a means to better understand the history and context of the Antarctic Treaty system and the ATCM. Chile proposed that all Recommendations, Measures, Decisions and Resolutions as well as extracts from the ATCM Final Report be listed according to each of the four topic areas. It further suggested that the costs for publishing the Handbook could be reduced by publishing it only electronically through the website, leaving it to Parties to print and distribute hard copies at their discretion.

(72)   Chile advised that it would prepare a version of a pilot pocket Handbook on Tourism for consideration at ATCM XXXIV.

(73)   Some Parties expressed the view that there was no need for a Handbook as the Secretariat's website constituted a comprehensive database of Antarctic material. Concern was expressed by several Parties about the possible difficulty in arriving at mutually agreed historical references. Parties also discussed

the intended audience for the Handbook, production costs, and limitations of Secretariat resources in producing a text of significant size and quality that could include ATCM Measures, Decisions and Resolutions, with extracts of past ATCM reports associated with the adoption of each Measure.

(74)   The Netherlands did not see a real need for a Handbook on the scale proposed in WP 66. It proposed instead a "Compilation of Key Documents of the Antarctic Treaty System", a small, practical, pocket-sized reference booklet consisting of Basic Texts, Rules of Procedure, Financial Regulations, Staff Regulations and Lists of Treaty Parties. The booklet would be inexpensive to produce and could be made available for purchase by Parties. It could also be accessed on the Secretariat's website.

(75)   Argentina noted that should it be decided to undertake a compilation, the electronic version on the website should include the legal texts adopted by the Antarctic Treaty bodies. Argentina also proposed that "the legislative record" of proceedings in the ATCM and CEP, as contained in the documentation, should be included on the Secretariat's website. The latter may be of great use as it illustrates the evolutionary process undergone to arrive at current norms. Publicity of such content contributes to more in-depth knowledge and transparency, in contrast with certain situations which occur in other fora in which certain parts of the documentation permanently remained with restricted access. Support for the "legislative record" proposal was expressed by several Parties.

(76)   Chile differentiated between the content of a Handbook, which was Chile's proposal, and what had been proposed by the Netherlands, which in fact referred to a Compendium of basic texts. Chile added that it had several Compendia on different subjects which it would make available to the Secretariat.

(77)   The United States and several Parties expressed support for a pocket-sized compilation and useful reference document. Some Parties also noted the value of a more comprehensive handbook envisioned by Chile. Other Parties queried the need to produce the Handbook given the comprehensive information available on the website.

(78)   Japan said it would encourage the Secretariat to enhance the information on the website. It also said Japan would join the emerging consensus around the proposal by the Netherlands. At the same time it stated that, in Japan's view, the cost of printing hard copies, if borne by the Secretariat's budget,

should be absorbed within the current proposed budget, and that the utility of printing hard copies could be reviewed by the ATCM in the future.

(79) Australia asked for confirmation that the material contained in the Compilation in printed format would be identical to the corresponding material on the website. The Meeting confirmed that this should be the case.

(80) Following further discussion, the Netherlands and the United States proposed a draft decision on "Compilation of Key Documents of the Antarctic Treaty System", which was adopted as Decision 1 (2010).

(81) Argentina made the following statement: "With regard to incorrect references to the territorial status of the Malvinas Islands, South Georgias and South Sandwich Islands made in documents available at this Antarctic Treaty Consultative Meeting, Argentina rejects any reference to these islands as being a separate entity from its national territory, thus giving them an international status that they do not have. Furthermore, it rejects the shipping register operated by the alleged British authorities thereof and any other unilateral act undertaken by such colonial authorities, which are not recognised by Argentina. The Malvinas, South Georgias and South Sandwich Islands and the corresponding maritime areas are an integral part of the Argentine national territory, are under illegal British occupation and are the subject of a sovereignty dispute between the Argentine Republic and the United Kingdom of Great Britain and Northern Ireland."

(82) In response, the United Kingdom stated that it had no doubt about its sovereignty over the Falkland Islands, South Georgia and the South Sandwich Islands and their surrounding maritime areas, as is well known to all delegates. In that regard, the United Kingdom has no doubt about the right of the government of the Falkland Islands to operate a shipping register for UK-flagged vessels.

(83) Argentina rejected the statement by the United Kingdom and reaffirmed its legal position.

Item 6: Operation of the Antarctic Treaty system: Review of the Secretariat's situation

Secretariat Report 2009/10

(84) The Executive Secretary thanked Argentina, as host country of the Antarctic Treaty Secretariat, for its ongoing support. He also expressed appreciation to

his predecessor, Jan Huber, and to the Parties, for their support and advice regarding his appointment.

(85)   The Executive Secretary provided a short overview of the Secretariat's work over the past year (SP 2 rev. 1 *Secretariat Report 2009/10*). He commented on the activities that had taken place, in particular drawing attention to the reduction of budgetary costs. He further noted that progress had been made concerning the updating of the delegates' manual, translation of guidelines, provision of technical support to three ATCM and four CEP intersessional contact groups (ICGs), and the support extended to Norway and New Zealand as the hosts of the two Antarctic Treaty Meetings of Experts (ATMEs).

(86)   The Executive Secretary noted that 15 Consultative Parties fully utilised the Electronic Information Exchange System (EIES). He reported on the implementation of a new advance reporting feature, as requested by several Parties.

(87)   The United Kingdom highlighted the value to Parties of a regularly updated database of Recommendations, Measures, Decisions and Resolutions.

(88)   The Executive Secretary noted the entry into force of Measure 1 (2003) on 6 October 2009, which enabled the Antarctic Treaty Secretariat to be fully functioning rather than provisional. He noted he had the honour of receiving the President of the Norwegian Parliament at the Secretariat on 16 April 2010.

Financial Matters

(89)   The Executive Secretary noted there had been issues concerning the Secretariat's book-keeping in the period 2008/2009 and 2009/2010, due to a change in personnel.

(90)   The Executive Secretary presented the audited financial report 2008/09 (attached to SP 2 rev. 1) which stated in its conclusion:

"In our opinion, …, the financial statements present fairly, in all material respects, the financial position of Antarctic Treaty Secretariat as of March 31th, 2009, and its financial performance for the period then ended in accordance with International Accounting Standards and the specific rules of Antarctic Treaty Consultative Meetings."

(91)   The Executive Secretary reported the difficulty in presenting a fully audited report to ATCM XXXII and ATCM XXXIII due to the proximity of the end

of the respective financial years to these Meetings. He hoped this would not be a problem in 2011 due to the later date proposed for ATCM XXXIV.

(92)	The Executive Secretary drew attention to the Auditor's report, attached to SP 2 rev. 1, and stated his intention to improve the handling of the finances in line with the auditor's comments.

(93)	The Executive Secretary noted that in the Final Report 2009/2010, the provisional report indicated a lower budgetary expenditure, despite several deviations from the budget line. He expressed his appreciation to Parties for taking note of the word limitation placed on the submission of papers, as required by paragraph 2 of Decision 3 (2009). Observance of this provision significantly contributed to the reduction of printing costs.

(94)	The Executive Secretary noted that the last page of the report recorded that the contributions had been received from all Parties, except Ukraine, Brazil and Chile. Chile, Ukraine and Brazil stated their contributions would be paid in the near future.

(95)	The Meeting expressed its appreciation to the Executive Secretary for his efforts on financial issues and his resolve to keep costs to a minimum.

Progress of the Secretariat

(96)	The Executive Secretary introduced the key elements of SP 3 rev. 2 *Draft Secretariat Programme 2010/11* related to ATCM/CEP support, information exchange, documentation, public information, management and finances. He reported that progress had been made in all of these areas.

(97)	The Executive Secretary stated that the Secretariat was still seeking to complete its archives and thanked Australia for the provision of a 1964 document. The Executive Secretary emphasised that research documents provided by Parties improved the collection and that the Secretariat was happy to receive copies in electronic form. The Executive Secretary added that the Secretariat hoped to receive more official documents in the three Treaty languages other than English.

(98)	The Executive Secretary, commenting on Staff Regulation 10.4, noted the need for accuracy in auditing procedures, and stressed the need for corresponding information explaining the non-payment of the former Executive Secretary's separation payment. According to the Regulation, Executive staff members upon separation of service are compensated at a rate of one month for every year of service, beginning with the second year. Apparently an understanding had been reached between the previous Executive Secretary and the Meeting that for personal reasons he would not receive such a payment; however, this agreement was not documented. Because there was no documentation that the former Executive Secretary had waived his entitlement to this payment, the Meeting suggested that written clarification on this matter would be helpful. The Executive Secretary agreed, for auditing purposes, to contact the former Executive Secretary in this regard and confirm in writing his decision to waive a separation payment.

(99) There was an ambiguity in Staff Regulation 10.4, namely whether a separation payment should include a month's salary for the first year of service or only for every year thereafter. The Regulation was similar to that of CCAMLR. CCAMLR in practice adopted the first interpretation. In accordance with Regulation 12.1 the Executive Secretary requested guidance from the ATCM.

(100) After carefully considering the issue and noting minor variations in the different language versions of the Staff Regulations, the ATCM agreed that the entitlement to payments under Regulation 10.4 vested after one full year of service, and for the purposes of calculation, included the first year. Further, following the first year, the calculation of payment for any period of less than a full year was to be done on a *pro rata* basis. Moreover, the ATCM agreed that Regulation 10.4 applied to all departures from service of executive staff, subject to the specific caveats set out in Regulation 10.

(101) The Executive Secretary expressed his wish to renew the contract of the Assistant Executive Officer. The Executive Secretary also raised the desirability of upgrading the position of the Secretariat book-keeper to that of financial officer because the downgrade was temporary and this position now covered not only cash flow, but also budgeting, fiscal law and other responsibilities.

(102) The Meeting confirmed its confidence in the Assistant Executive Officer and welcomed the Executive Secretary's intention to renew his contract for a further three years. One Party noted that this further three year contract for the Assistant Executive Secretary would mean his tenure would end in the same year as the Executive Secretary's first term of office.

(103) The Meeting also supported the Executive Secretary's request to upgrade the Book-keeper from G3 to G2 and to revise the title for the position to "Finance Officer".

(104) The Executive Secretary noted that with Measure 1 (2003) entering into force, the budget for 2010/11 would be higher than in previous years due to the Secretariat assuming the Meeting's translation and interpretation costs which were previously borne by the host government.

Draft Secretariat Programme 2010/11

(105) Referring to the Electronic Information Exchange System (EIES), the United Kingdom asked whether there were barriers preventing full utilisation of the newly implemented online system. The Executive Secretary noted that with more users, feedback and information submitted on the system, the accessibility and efficiency of the system would continue to increase. The Executive Secretary encouraged use of the system by Parties and noted that it was currently functional for all users. The Executive Secretary asked for feedback from EIES users. The Executive Secretary specifically pointed to the usefulness of the system for tourism-related information, as well as for non-tourism issues.

(106) France welcomed efforts to make regulations, laws and other guidelines governing Antarctica more available and accessible to the public. It suggested establishing links from the Secretariat website to Treaty Party national websites so that all visitors to the Antarctic could be made aware more easily of their obligations. France offered to assist the Secretariat in this endeavour.

Proposed Budget 2010/11, Forecast Budget 2011/12 and Forward Financial Planning

(107) The Executive Secretary noted that a tender process would be put into place regarding the engagement of translators. He said he wished to have the highest quality translation and interpretation available for the Meetings. The process would start immediately after ATCM XXXIII and would be finalised during the southern autumn, with the intention of ensuring that transparency and maximum value for money was obtained.

(108) The Meeting noted with appreciation the Executive Secretary's resolve to keep costs low. Japan indicated that the 2011/12 budget should remain at the same level as 2010/11, except for the increase caused by the entry into force of Measure 1 (2003).

(109) Peru suggested that the Secretariat might secure outside sources of funding so that it did not rely solely on the contributions of Treaty Parties. Peru considered NGOs and private sector interests as possible funding options. It

further noted that while this could enable a decrease in Party contributions, the budget could, nevertheless, increase.

(110) The Executive Secretary responded that, bearing in mind the importance of maintaining the independence of the Secretariat and the ATCM, he would need clear guidance from the ATCM before considering such an option.

(111) Bulgaria proposed that technical amendments to the guidelines for the submission, translation and distribution of documents for the ATCM and the CEP would reduce the cost of translation of Information Papers. While several Parties supported this proposal, some Parties thought this matter should be given further consideration.

(112) The Meeting took note and approved the audited budget for the financial year 2008/09. Following discussion in an informal open-ended contact group, the revised budget for 2010/11 and the Forecast Budget for 2011/12 presented in SP 3 rev. 2 were approved and the Meeting adopted Decision 2 (2010). SP 3 rev. 2 also contained the Executive Secretary's projection for an estimated budget for 2012/13.

(113) The Meeting requested that the Secretariat produce for ATCM XXXIV a multi-year forward budget profile which aimed to flatten out the predictable elements within the budget over a five year period. This would help underpin further discussion among the Parties about the potential use of the working capital fund to manage fluctuations in those elements of the budget, for example, travel. The United Kingdom encouraged the Secretariat to submit this forward budget in line with the recommended deadline for papers requiring translation.

Item 7: Report of the Committee for Environmental Protection

(114) Dr Neil Gilbert, Chair of the Committee for Environmental Protection, introduced the report of CEP XIII (see page 115). The CEP considered 48 Working Papers, 69 Information Papers and 4 Secretariat Papers (the full list of papers is at Annex I to the Report of CEP XIII).

Strategic Discussions on the Future Work of the CEP (CEP Agenda Item 3)

(115) The CEP highlighted the continuing value of its prioritised five-year work plan as an effective means of guiding its work and managing its workload and encouraged the ATCM to draw on its experience when considering a multi-year strategic plan for the ATCM.

(116) The United States and the United Kingdom noted the utility of the CEP's five-year work plan and the subsequent improvement in the quality and efficiency of the CEP's work.

Operation of the CEP (CEP Agenda Item 4)

(117) The Secretariat reported on the Electronic Information Exchange System (EIES) (web-based) developed as a mechanism for exchanging information between the Parties in accordance with the requirements of Article 17 of the Protocol. The Committee noted that between CEP XII and CEP XIII only 60% of Parties had contributed information. The CEP Chair had urged Parties to ensure 100% usage by ATCM XXXIV.

(118) The United Kingdom noted its concern that the EIES was not being fully utilised by the Parties and urged full compliance in the use of the EIES in the next year.

(119) The CEP had examined its Rules of Procedure. The Meeting agreed to revise Rule 15 of the CEP's Rules of Procedure and adopted Decision 3 (2010) (see page 317).

Environmental Impact Assessment (EIA) (CEP Agenda Item 6)

(120) The CEP had considered a report from Russia updating the CEP on the Lake Vostok drilling project, including Russia's responses to comments made on the draft CEE for this project considered at CEP VI.

(121) At the request of the ATCM, the CEP considered the Report of the ATME on Ship-borne Tourism, paying particular attention to Recommendations 11, 12, 13 and 14 in that Report. The CEP endorsed the assessment of environmental aspects of Ship-borne Tourism referred to in ATME Recommendation 11 (Attachment A to WP 28 (Australia)) and agreed to refer it to the CEP's tourism study with a suggestion that it be expanded to identify the level of risk associated with the various environmental aspects. On Recommendation 12, the CEP noted the range of data sets that were being prepared through its tourism study and would provide more information to the ATCM on this when presenting the study to ATCM XXXIV. With regard to Recommendations 13 and 14, the CEP noted the importance of cooperation among Parties and National Programmes in attempting to develop contingency plans to respond to large-scale marine environmental incidents, in fulfilment of Article 15 of the Protocol.

(122) New Zealand welcomed the CEP's recommendations and noted specifically the importance of developing contingency plans for major incidents such as oil spills arising from maritime incidents.

(123) In response to a comment by the United Kingdom, the Chair clarified that work planned by the CEP to further develop the assessment in attachment A to WP 28 would be applicable to shipping generally and not just in the context of the CEP's tourism study.

(124) The CEP had reviewed progress on the CEP's tourism study, noting that the complexity of the project, and the significant challenges in obtaining reliable data and information on which to base the study (particularly with regard to non-IAATO tourism), had prevented its completion by CEP XIII. The paucity of information on yachting activity in Antarctica was noted. While yachts account for a small proportion of operators in Antarctica, many yachts enter Antarctic waters without authorisation and the CEP noted that their impact (albeit rarely) may be substantial. Parties were urged to provide information on yachting activity to assist the CEP's tourism study. The CEP gratefully accepted New Zealand's offer to continue to lead the study.

(125) The United States thanked New Zealand for its efforts coordinating the CEP tourism study.

(126) The CEP considered draft guidelines to minimise light pollution from stations and ships aimed at minimising bird strike, noting that IAATO has guidelines in place to minimise seabirds landing on its ships. Parties had been invited to voluntarily test or implement the guidelines through their National Programmes and to consider gathering bird strike data to allow for further consideration of the issue.

Area Protection and Management Plans (CEP Agenda Item 7)

(127) The Committee had reviewed 15 revised protected or managed area management plans. One of these had been subject to review by the Subsidiary Group on Management Plans (SGMP) and 14 revised management plans had been submitted directly to CEP XIII.

(128) Accepting the CEP's advice, the Meeting adopted the following Measures on Protected and Managed Areas:

- Measure 1 (2010): Antarctic Specially Protected Area No 101 (Taylor Rookery, Mac.Robertson Land): Revised Management Plan

- Measure 2 (2010): Antarctic Specially Protected Area No 102 (Rookery Islands, Holme Bay, Mac.Robertson Land): Revised Management Plan
- Measure 3 (2010): Antarctic Specially Protected Area No 103 (Ardley Island and Odbert Island, Budd Coast, Wilkes Land): Revised Management Plan
- Measure 4 (2010): Antarctic Specially Protected Area No 105 (Beaufort Island, McMurdo Sound, Ross Sea): Revised Management Plan
- Measure 5 (2010): Antarctic Specially Protected Area No 106 (Cape Hallett, Northern Victoria Land, Ross Sea): Revised Management Plan
- Measure 6 (2010): Antarctic Specially Protected Area No 119 (Davis Valley and Forlidas Pond, Dufek Massif): Revised Management Plan
- Measure 7 (2010): Antarctic Specially Protected Area No 139 (Biscoe Point, Anvers Island, Palmer Archipelago): Revised Management Plan
- Measure 8 (2010): Antarctic Specially Protected Area No 155 (Cape Evans, Ross Island): Revised Management Plan
- Measure 9 (2010): Antarctic Specially Protected Area No 157 (Backdoor Bay, Cape Royds, Ross Island): Revised Management Plan
- Measure 10 (2010): Antarctic Specially Protected Area No 158 (Hut Point, Ross Island): Revised Management Plan
- Measure 11 (2010): Antarctic Specially Protected Area No 159 (Cape Adare, Borchgrevink Coast): Revised Management Plan
- Measure 12 (2010): Antarctic Specially Protected Area No 163 (Dakshin Gangotri Glacier, Dronning Maud Land): Revised Management Plan
- Measure 13 (2010): Antarctic Specially Protected Area No 164 (Scullin and Murray Monoliths, Mac.Robertson Land): Revised Management Plan
- Measure 14 (2010): Antarctic Specially Managed Area No 7 (Southwest Anvers Island and Palmer Basin): Revised Management Plan

(129) Noting that substantial changes were proposed to the management plan for ASPA 126 Byers Peninsula, the CEP decided to refer the management plan

to the Subsidiary Group on Management Plans (SGMP) for intersessional review.

(130) The CEP considered the report from the SGMP on its work, in accordance with its fourth Term of Reference, to improve management plans and the process for their intersessional review. In accordance with a commitment made at CEP XI (2008), the CEP had reviewed the effectiveness of the SGMP and agreed that the group had been highly effective in providing advice on management plans referred for intersessional review and on improvements to management plans more generally and the process for their intersessional review.

(131) The CEP adopted a long-term goal of *'ensuring that all ASPA and ASMA management plans contain adequate content, and are clear, consistent, and likely to be effective'* and, accordingly, had expanded the SGMP's Terms of Reference to add a function of developing and suggesting procedures that would assist in achieving this long-term goal (Appendix 1 to the Report of CEP XIII). The CEP endorsed the SGMP's proposed work plan (Appendix 2 to the Report of CEP XIII), which included work over the next two years to revise the Guide to the preparation of management plans.

(132) The United Kingdom noted the improved efficiency of the CEP facilitated by the work completed by the SGMP, and emphasised that the SGMP benefits from broad participation by Treaty Parties.

(133) Accepting the CEP's advice, the Meeting agreed to add one new site to the list of Historic Sites and Monuments held under Measure 3 (2003) and adopted Measure 15 (2010) (see page 275):

> Antarctic Historic Sites and Monuments: Plaque Commemorating the PM-3A Nuclear Power Plant at McMurdo Station.

(134) The CEP approved four new Site Guidelines for Torgersen Island, Danco Island, Damoy Point and Seabee Hook and forwarded them to the Meeting for adoption, noting that once adopted, Site Guidelines and / or national operator procedures would be in place for the 20 most frequently visited tourist landing sites in Antarctica.

(135) The United Kingdom echoed this sentiment and thanked the CEP for this work.

(136) The Meeting adopted Resolution 1 (2010) (see page 333).

(137) The CEP reviewed the work of an Intersessional Contact Group (ICG) established to review the generic guidance for visitors, including that

contained in Recommendation XVIII-1. The CEP recognised that further consideration of the issue was needed and appointed Australia as convener of a new ICG. The terms of reference are contained in the CEP Report.

(138) The United Kingdom encouraged all Parties to work to bring Recommendation XVIII-1 (1994) into force.

(139) The CEP reviewed a methodology to assess cumulative impacts from national operator activities in Antarctica, as well as means to assess the concept of human footprint in Antarctica. The CEP agreed that this was an important issue and encouraged its Members to work together during the intersessional period to bring further papers to CEP XIV that might assist in developing a better understanding of the term "human footprint", as well as on data and information that might be used to characterise human impacts in Antarctica.

(140) The CEP recognised SC-CAMLR´s timetable for action towards developing a network of marine areas by the 2012 deadline, and mirrored the timetable in the CEP´s five-year work plan, noting that it would nominate observers to CCAMLR meetings and workshops as appropriate. The CEP further welcomed CCAMLR´s progress in affording protection to a marine area in the South Orkney Islands and encouraged further areas to be identified in the 11 priority areas endorsed by both SC-CAMLR and the CEP.

(141) Japan stated that this issue had been discussed under Agenda Item 4. Japan noted that, in its view, it is SC-CAMLR that CEP encouraged to work on in order to identify further areas. It further noted that the word "endorse" had not appeared in the Final Report of ATCM XXXII in the context of the relations between 11 priority areas on the one hand and SC-CAMLR and the CEP on the other, and that this paragraph or the entire section of the Advice did not mean that the ATCM formally recognised "marine protected areas" because of fundamental legal issues. In this context, Japan drew attention of Parties to the first bullet point of paragraph 171 of CEP XII Report, Advice to the ATCM, which says, "Develop a strategy and work towards the establishment of effective, representative and coherent spatial protection of marine biodiversity within the Antarctic Treaty Area within the next three years, through the designation of Antarctic Specially Protected Areas (ASPAs) and Antarctic Specially Managed Areas (ASMAs) under Annex V of the Protocol on Environmental Protection."

(142) The United Kingdom emphasised the importance of cooperation between CEP and SC-CAMLR to achieve SC-CAMLR's goal of a network of MPAs

by 2012, noted that the CEP had lent its endorsement to the 11 priority areas and therefore endorsed the consideration of SC-CAMLR's work plan in the formulation of CEP's five-year work plan.

(143) The United States and Australia welcomed CEP's endorsement of SC-CAMLR's work on MPAs and noted the importance of such measures for the protection of biodiversity.

(144) The CEP considered SCAR's assessment as to the extent to which the CEP's environmental domains analysis (EDA, which is based on spatially explicit physical data) corresponded to patterns found in spatially explicit biodiversity data. SCAR's assessment concluded that the EDA was a useful first order assessment of likely systematic variation in biodiversity for ice free areas of Antarctica.

(145) The CEP considered the implications of climate change for the Antarctic protected areas system, noting in particular the recommendations from the ATME on climate change, held in Norway (April 2010), in particular ATME recommendations 24, 25 and 26. The CEP had discussed ways in which it would address these issues in its future work.

Conservation of Antarctic Flora and Fauna (CEP Agenda Item 8)

(146) The CEP had noted that the issues of non-native species in Antarctica remained a priority 1 issue on its five-year work plan. The CEP reviewed the work of an ICG established at CEP XII and convened by France. The ICG had developed initial draft text for a non-native species manual, draft text for objectives and key guiding principles, and a proposed list of prioritised measures to reduce the risk of introductions.

(147) The Committee had commented on several aspects of the ICG's report, offered overall support, and reiterated the importance of managing this issue and the priority of this work in the five-year work plan. New Zealand had been appointed as the ICG convener for the next intersessional period (Terms of Reference were agreed and are shown in the CEP Report).

(148) The United States and the United Kingdom welcomed the ongoing operation of the ICG, and noted the continuing importance of including SCAR and COMNAP in the efforts of this group, particularly with regard to the development of a guidance manual where the expertise of national operators would be instrumental.

(149) The CEP Chair welcomed the extremely useful advice from SCAR and COMNAP.

(150) The CEP further reviewed other recommendations from the ATME on climate change related to Annex II to the Protocol, noting in particular recommendations 17 and 20.

Environmental Monitoring and Reporting (CEP Agenda Item 9)

(151) The CEP had a substantive debate on the issue of climate change in the Antarctic context, based on the outcomes to and recommendations from the climate change ATME held in Svolvær, Norway (April 2010). The CEP acknowledged the importance of SCAR's ACCE report (published in 2009), used as the basis for the ATME in Norway.

(152) The CEP undertook a comprehensive review of the report and recommendations from the ATME on Climate Change and the Antarctic Environment, noting that the implications of climate change cut across many of the issues on the CEP's agenda. It concluded that much of its current work programme addressed many of the issues raised during the ATME. It agreed to place climate change as a high priority issue on its agenda.

(153) Many Parties and ASOC thanked Norway for hosting the ATME on Climate Change and described this as an area of importance, noting the ATME was an excellent first step to mainstreaming Treaty-level consideration of climate change. Parties also welcomed the inclusion of climate change on the CEP agenda as a separate item encouraging the unique forum the CEP offers for dialogue between science and policy.

(154) Many Parties looked forward to addressing carefully all thirty recommendations made by the ATME while the United States, with general support from other Parties and ASOC, suggested consideration of an additional recommendation (31) to address ocean acidification in the Southern Ocean that would encourage research to establish baseline information for this region and examine the potential ecological impacts of acidification.

(155) China reminded the Meeting that efforts should concentrate on the implications of climate change as related to the Antarctic Treaty. Japan suggested that the Recommendations should be prioritised in order of importance.

Inspection Reports (CEP Agenda Item 10)

(156) The CEP considered the Inspection Report from Norway (WP 57 and IP 30). A number of Parties provided comments on the report and information on progress made with aspects highlighted by the report, since the inspections had been carried out in 2009. The CEP Chair noted that this report would also be considered under ATCM Agenda Item 12.

(157) The CEP noted additional Inspection Reports would be forthcoming from Australia and Japan at CEP XIV.

Cooperation with Other Organisations (CEP Agenda Item 11)

(158) The SC-CAMLR Observer to CEP and the CEP Observer to SC-CAMLR provided a report on the twenty-eighth meeting of the Scientific Committee to CCAMLR, 26–30 October 2009, focusing on those issues agreed to be of common interest by the joint CEP/SC-CAMLR Workshop held in April 2009.

(159) The CEP noted the positive and growing relationship between the two committees. It had also noted SC-CAMLR´s planned review of its Ecosystem Monitoring Programme and the opportunity this offered for both SC-CAMLR and CEP to consider their respective monitoring needs. The CEP welcomed a proposed joint CEP/SC-CAMLR meeting on monitoring perhaps to be held in 2012, and encouraged contribution of biodiversity and monitoring information to be submitted to its next meeting to enable it to prepare for such a workshop.

(160) The CEP thanked Dr George Watters (United States), convener of the WG-EMM, who offered to act as CEP representative to SC-CAMLR's WG-EMM and to report back to the CEP following the 2010 WG-EMM meeting. The CEP had further thanked Dr Polly Penhale (United States) who offered to take on the role of CEP Observer to SC-CAMLR.

(161) At the invitation of SCAR, the Committee had accepted with appreciation the offer of Dr Rasik Ravindra (India) to represent the CEP at, and provide a short presentation to, the next SCAR Delegates Meeting (Buenos Aires, Argentina, August 2010).

(162) The United Kingdom highlighted the utility of CEP co-ordination with these other groups.

General Matters (CEP Agenda Item 12)

(163) At the request of the ATCM, the CEP considered the implications of running its meeting from mid-week to mid-week. Whilst there was no agreed CEP conclusion to these discussions a number of matters were raised relating to the efficiency with which the CEP manages its own workload and the implications of change to the timing of the meeting.

(164) CEP Members noted the CEP continues to review the efficiency of its work and also receives the majority of papers submitted to ATCMs. Regarding a potential change of timing of its meetings, CEP Members noted additional costs and translation concerns might ensue with parallel sessions. It thought consideration might be given to separating the CEP and ATCM meetings, though these views were not shared by all.

Election of Officers (CEP Agenda Item 13)

(165) The CEP elected Dr Yves Frenot of France to the position of CEP Chair for the next two years. The CEP warmly congratulated Dr Frenot on his election, recalling his significant contributions to the work of the CEP in his past role as Vice-chair.

(166) The CEP also re-elected Mr Ewan McIvor from Australia as Vice-chair for his second two-year term, noting also the ongoing and significant contributions of Mr McIvor to the work of the CEP.

(167) The Meeting expressed its sincere gratitude to Dr Neil Gilbert for his exceptional work during two terms as Chair of the CEP.

Preparation for Next Meeting (CEP Agenda Item 14)

(168) The CEP adopted the agenda for CEP XIV contained in Appendix 4 to the CEP report and updated its five-year work plan contained in Appendix 5 to the CEP report.

Item 8: Liability: Implementation of Decision 1 (2005)

(169) Several Parties (New Zealand, United Kingdom, the Russian Federation, the United States and Chile) reported on progress since ATCM XXXII in implementing into domestic law Annex VI to the Protocol on Environmental Protection relating to Liability arising from Environmental Emergencies.

(170) The Meeting noted that a decision was required as per paragraph 2 of Decision 1 (2005). In Decision 1 (2005), the Consultative Parties decided:

"1. to evaluate annually, from the adoption of Annex VI to the Protocol, progress towards its becoming effective in accordance with Article IX of the Antarctic Treaty, and what action may be necessary and appropriate to encourage Parties to approve the Annex in a timely fashion;

2. not later than five years from the adoption of the Annex, in light of the evaluation pursuant to paragraph 1 above, to take a decision on the establishment of a time-frame for the resumption of negotiations, in accordance with Article 16 of the Protocol, to elaborate further rules and procedures as may be necessary relating to liability for damage arising from activities taking place in the Antarctic Treaty area and covered by the Protocol."

(171) The Netherlands noted that no papers had been submitted on the issue of remedial measures, and suggested that the next five years be used to collect information on scientific and technical issues relating to measures needed to remediate and repair the damaged environment. Chile, while supporting the need for delegations to prepare papers regarding restoration work, considered five years until the resumption of negotiations too long since Article 16 of the Protocol directed the Parties to protect the Antarctic Environment and dependent and associated ecosystems and Decision 1 (2005) had set a deadline from the adoption of Annex VI.

(172) Following consultations, the Netherlands and Chile proposed a draft Decision on "Liability arising from Environmental Emergencies", which was adopted as Decision 4 (2010).

Item 9: Safety and Operations in Antarctica

(173) The Meeting considered Recommendation 5 of the ATME on Ship-borne tourism held in Wellington in 2009: *That the Treaty Parties should continue to contribute to the continuation and improvement of sea ice services in the Antarctic Treaty Area.*

(174) The Meeting endorsed ATME Recommendation 5, noting the importance of gathering ice information important to safe navigation in Antarctic waters.

(175) The Meeting considered ATME Recommendation 8: *That all crew on vessels planning to navigate in Antarctic waters should be required to undertake relevant training appropriate to the conditions expected to be encountered, and where appropriate in accordance with Chapter 14 of the IMO's Guidelines for Ships Operating in Polar Waters.*

(176) Norway noted that it had been working with the United States and Denmark to develop mandatory training measures for navigators working in the Arctic and in the Antarctic.

(177) New Zealand suggested that Recommendation 8 might be taken up by Parties in work on the mandatory Polar Code, which should include provision for training standards. It noted the Liberian report on the investigation of the *Explorer* incident indicated that a lack of training was a contributing factor.

(178) Argentina informed the Meeting of IP 116 *Antarctic Navigation Course*, detailing a course taught every year at the National Nautical School in Buenos Aires. Argentina noted that this course includes aspects of ice navigation in all kinds of ice-covered waters in Antarctica. Attendance is encouraged for all members of the crew.

(179) Uruguay and Argentina noted that relevant training appropriate to Antarctic conditions should also be undertaken by staff in charge of passengers, who are not listed as crew members.

(180) IAATO noted the importance of relevant training, and referenced the work currently being done at IMO International Convention on Standards of Training, Certification and Watchkeeping for Seafarers (STCW) on this issue. IAATO thanked Chile and Argentina for offering their ice navigation courses, and also emphasised the importance of practical experience.

(181) ASOC supported the strong recognition of the need for appropriate training for ice navigation and noted that this is in line with the Republic of Liberia's recommendation following the investigation into the sinking of the *M/S Explorer*. ASOC proposed that a requirement for suitable qualified crew including an Ice Master on vessels should be addressed too.

(182) The Meeting endorsed ATME Recommendation 8.

(183) France presented WP 46 *Improving the coordination of maritime search and rescue in the Antarctic Treaty area*, noting that, in line with Resolution 6 (2008), and according to the similar conclusions of the COMNAP SAR workshops held in 2008 in Viña del Mar and in 2009 in Buenos Aires, and

of the ATME on Ship-borne tourism held in 2009 in Wellington, growth in maritime traffic in the Antarctic will undoubtedly lead to the continued need to ensure safety of ship traffic in the Antarctic Treaty area. France proposed that Parties recognize the importance of SAR efforts by adopting a Resolution.

(184) France noted its view that the guidelines currently in place for tourism vessels should be extended to all vessels operating within Antarctic Treaty waters. France also noted that newly proposed information sharing mechanisms should not create a new level of hierarchy or redundancy that would overlap with existing data mechanisms (CCAMLR, COMNAP and IAATO).

(185) Chile thanked France and noted the work done by the ATME on Ship-borne Tourism and it emphasised the importance of including yachts within the scope of this Resolution.

(186) The Russian Federation and Norway expressed concerns regarding the application of reporting procedures to all vessels operating within Antarctic Treaty waters; whether new data reporting would be redundant or whether it would supersede existing mechanisms. Russia was also concerned about the definition of "regular reporting" of positions and the security of sensitive data reported to the system.

(187) France responded to Chile, Norway, and Russia's comments by noting that it viewed all vessels as potentially subject to the Resolution; that data reporting noted herein would neither be redundant nor supersede existing mechanisms; and that France shares concerns about the sensitivity of data, providing relevant protections through the language: "in accordance with their national laws" (such that yachts may be included), and "giving due consideration to the sensitivity of position data for certain vessels."

(188) The United Kingdom noted that several workshops have been held among Maritime Rescue Coordination Centres (MRCCs), COMNAP and IAATO in an attempt to improve upon the collection and exchange of relevant position data, such as in accordance with Resolution 6 (2008). It further referred to Recommendation 9 of the ATME on Ship-borne Tourism report, recognizing that there has been great impetus to move forward this valuable endeavour. The United Kingdom also recalled Measure 4 (2004) and Resolution 4 (2004), which call for vessels operating in Antarctic Treaty waters to be self-sufficient with regards to search and rescue.

(189) Uruguay and ASOC expressed support for WP 46, noting that the Resolution it contains would be important for safety and other reasons, and also useful to identify ships in emergency situations.

(190) The Meeting adopted Resolution 6 (2010). This Resolution contains a recommendation that Governments recognise the importance of ensuring the effectiveness of search and rescue efforts by:

1. placing on the Antarctic Treaty Secretariat ("the Secretariat") website regular and up-to-date search and rescue related information, using the most appropriate technical means (eg, through the Electronic Information Exchange System – EIES), of coastal stations facilities as well as the availability of sea and air assets in the Antarctic Treaty area;

2. making available in advance vessel schedules of national Antarctic programmes and tourist operators to the Secretariat (eg, through the EIES) which then would be available to all MRCC to access; and

3. encouraging national Antarctic programmes and operators of tourist vessels not participating in the COMNAP and IAATO vessel tracking schemes to report the positions of their vessels regularly to the relevant regional MRCC.

(191) The Meeting considered Recommendation 9 of the ATME on Ship-borne tourism: *The Antarctic Treaty Parties should continue to encourage tourist and non-governmental organisations' vessels not participating in the IAATO or COMNAP vessel monitoring schemes to report their positions regularly to the relevant MRCC. All tourist and NGO vessels should closely follow the IMO's 'Enhanced contingency planning guidelines for passenger ships operating in areas remote from SAR facilities' in accordance with ATCM Resolution 6 (2008).*

(192) New Zealand noted that all passenger vessels, including yachts under their authority are already advised to report their locations as appropriate to the MRCC.

(193) Japan noted that Resolution 6 (2010) effectively responds to this Recommendation.

(194) The Meeting endorsed ATME Recommendation 9.

(195) COMNAP introduced IP 76, *Towards Improved Search and Rescue in the Antarctic*, reporting on the Workshop on Improved Search and Rescue Coordination and Response in the Antarctic, held in November 2009 in Buenos Aires, Argentina. COMNAP noted that the Final Report of the 2009

workshop was annexed to IP 76. In particular, COMNAP emphasised three key recommendations. Recommendation 1 urges National Antarctic Programmes to stress the importance to their Antarctic vessel operators of reporting their positions on a regular basis through the COMNAP Ship Position Reporting System (SPRS) or the IAATO vessel tracking scheme or directly to the relevant Search and Rescue (SAR) authority. This recommendation applies equally to government-operated vessels and non-governmental organisation-operated vessels. Recommendation 2 suggests that National Antarctic Programmes include in their national papers to the IMO information on Antarctic SAR issues from workshops such as the one in Buenos Aires. Recommendation 8 suggests that National Antarctic Programmes express to their governments the need for SAR contingency planning to be outlined in all permit or authorization applications or advance notifications before they are considered.

(196) Argentina thanked COMNAP for its support, noted the importance of the workshop, and urged Parties to become more involved in COMNAP's work improving coordination in SAR.

(197) ASOC welcomed the COMNAP report and the workshop. ASOC noted the important recommendations from the workshop and looked forward to discussing them in further detail.

(198) IAATO also thanked Argentina and COMNAP and noted the importance to IAATO of the recommendations on vessel reporting and training.

(199) Chile recalled to the Meeting that the first workshop on SAR was held in Chile in 2008 and was reported to ATCM XXXII as WP 47. Chile reiterated the importance of this topic and noted that it intended to continue to participate in efforts to improve SAR in the Antarctic. Chile expressed the hope that COMNAP would convene additional SAR workshops.

(200) Chile noted that ship traffic in the Antarctic has increased significantly and highlighted the importance of Recommendation 3 of the Final Report of the Workshop, that vessel operators be specifically trained for the Antarctic. Chile noted that Argentina and Chile have facilitated courses on navigation in the Antarctic. Chile also stressed the particular importance of the contingency planning recommended by the COMNAP workshop and added that Argentina and Chile were actively engaged in cooperation to this end.

(201) China introduced IP 39 *Report on the Evacuation of an Injured Expeditioner at Zhongshan Station,* noting an incident on 8 January 2010 in which a member of the CHINARE 26 team had an accident during construction work at Zhongshan Station. Due to the limited medical resources available

51

at Zhongshan, help from Progress Station (Russia) was sought. The patient was first treated at Zhongshan Station and then taken to Progress Station, where he was operated on by doctors from China, the Russian Federation and Australia's Davis Station. The patient was later taken to Hobart, Australia where he was treated at the Royal Hobart Hospital, and from there travelled back to China. China expressed its gratitude to Russia and Australia, citing their efforts as an embodiment of cooperation in the Antarctic.

(202) Australia expressed its appreciation for IP 39, noting that this activity was one example of the close collaboration emerging between Parties active in Prydz Bay.

(203) India expressed its appreciation of the quick response from Australia and Russia to the emergent situation and informed that India had put its helicopter crew and medical doctors available on board the expedition ship near Larsemann Hills, on high alert and stand-by for any need that might have emerged.

(204) Ecuador noted its appreciation for help from station personnel at Frei Base and Arturo Prat Base in evacuating an accident victim from its station.

(205) France thanked Australia for its help in an incident involving an evacuation from Concordia Base at the end of the summer season during which time SAR equipment was less available. France noted that medical and accident evacuations were facilitated by strong solidarity and pragmatism among the Parties on such operations, but noted the need for an international instrument addressing land rescues in Antarctica. France mentioned IP 76 tabled by COMNAP, which recognises the challenges of land SAR, which unlike maritime and aeronautical SAR, is not covered by any existing international arrangements.

(206) COMNAP noted that the COMNAP Workshop had identified limited resources and large distances between bases as some of the greatest difficulties of land rescue.

(207) Argentina agreed with France on the need for an agreement and the importance of cooperation on the issue at the ATCM. In this respect, the Combined Antarctic Naval Patrol carried out four medical evacuations. Argentina noted that COMNAP had completed an analysis of medical skills and facilities at each Antarctic base, and that the same work was carried out at the meetings of Latin American countries. Argentina suggested there be guidelines for how to proceed with medical evacuations and suggested that

the matter be addressed within COMNAP, with input from medical groups, to make recommendations to the ATCM.

(208) Australia thanked France for its suggestion and agreed on the need to formalize ongoing discussions on SAR within COMNAP.

(209) IAATO noted its members' resources could be used as needed for search and rescue operations.

(210) IP 35, *Report of a Joint Oil Spill Exercise: RV Laurence M. Gould at Rothera Research Station*, submitted under this agenda item, was not introduced and was taken as read.

Item 10: The International Polar Year 2007-2008

(211) Uruguay introduced WP 11 *Forwarding of hydrographic data collected during the IPY*. Uruguay noted the importance of the work of the Hydrographic Commission on Antarctica (HCA) of the International Hydrographic Organization (IHO) with respect to improving the collection of hydrographic data and charting in the Antarctic region. Uruguay also noted that the IMO and other organisations, including SCAR and COMNAP, had also called for improved hydrographic and bathymetric data in the Antarctic region. Uruguay proposed that the ATCM adopt a Resolution urging governments to ensure that hydrographic and bathymetric data collected during the IPY be forwarded by the National Antarctic Programmes to the national hydrographic services using formats developed to this end by the HCA, and to give the HCA access to the inventory of relevant data so that it can be considered for producing international nautical charts.

(212) Sweden urged Consultative Parties that have collected hydrographic and bathymetric data in the Antarctic Treaty area as part of the preparation of their submissions to the UN Commission on the Limits of the Continental Shelf (CLCS) to make such data available and also to convey relevant data from such surveys to the HCA.

(213) Several Parties noted that the request should be limited to data relevant to the work of the HCA.

(214) COMNAP noted that it had been working with the HCA on data submission guidelines and referred Parties to IP 51 *Report by the International Hydrographic Organization (IHO) on "Cooperation in hydrographic surveying and charting of Antarctic waters"*. Annex B to this IP included the

IHO Collection and Rendering of Hydrographic Data Form, which Parties might find useful for the submission of data by ships of opportunity.

(215) The United States thanked Uruguay for its work on promoting hydrographic information sharing. As a strong proponent of navigational safety of operations in the Antarctic, the United States supported the recommendation. The United States also noted the importance of standardization between scientific data and hydrographic mapping.

(216) Several Parties and ASOC also supported the proposal by Uruguay. After some discussion on the kind of data to be submitted, and stressing the importance of using a common format for reporting hydrographic and bathymetric data to the HCA, the Meeting adopted Resolution 2 (see page 337).

(217) The Meeting considered Recommendation 4 of the ATME on Ship-borne Tourism: *That the Treaty Parties should continue to contribute to hydrographic surveying and charting information and consider advising vessels intending to operate in the Antarctic Treaty area that many areas have not been surveyed to modern standards,* and ATME Recommendation 17: *The IHO-HCA should continue to be invited to annual ATCMs to report the status of hydrographic survey and nautical chart production in Antarctic waters. Parties also agreed that, as appropriate, the ATCM should be represented at IHO-HCA meetings. Where an IHO-HCA meeting was to be held in a country that was also a Consultative Party, then that Consultative Party should consider attending the HCA meeting.*

(218) The United Kingdom noted the relevance of Recommendations 4 and 17 to hydrographic charting and the provision of data. The United Kingdom considered it was important for the HCA to continue to be invited to attend the ATCM. The United Kingdom further noted that the HCA will meet in Cambridge, UK in September 2010.

(219) COMNAP informed the Meeting that it has and will continue to send observers if invited to the IHO-HCA meetings, consistent with Recommendation 17.

(220) New Zealand noted that in Antarctica less than one percent of the sea area within the 200 metre contour, which includes the areas most frequently visited by those passenger ships which make landings, had been adequately surveyed to meet the needs of contemporary shipping.

(221) The Meeting endorsed ATME Recommendations 4 and 17, noting the majority of the Southern Ocean remains unsurveyed.

(222) Uruguay reiterated that the data contained in its WP 11 contribute to regional safety, SAR, environmental protection and scientific exploration, noting IAATO operators also make a worthwhile contribution when submitting data in the IHO agreed format.

(223) Japan introduced IP 64 *Japan in IPY 2007-2008* reporting on IPY activities and noting the legacy of IPY for outreach programmes for young generations in Japan.

(224) Romania introduced IP 100 *Romania contribution in IPY 2007-2008*, noting IPY activities in cooperation with Bulgaria, Estonia and India, and highlighting outreach activities in Romanian universities and institutes.

(225) The Republic of Korea noted that it will host Arctic Science Summit Week (ASSW), with the theme of "The Arctic: New Frontiers for Global Science" from March 28 – April 1, 2011 in Seoul, Korea. The meeting will include interdisciplinary sessions on response to climate change. Information on the meeting can be found at *www.assw2011.org.*

(226) ASOC noted the continuation of its IPY-endorsed project on the Environmental Legacy of the IPY, and drew attention to the session on human impacts and management implications at the IPY conference in Oslo in June this year that will be co-sponsored by ASOC.

Item 11: Tourism and Non-Governmental Activities in the Antarctic Treaty Area

i. Overview of the Antarctic tourist activity in the 2009/2010 season

(227) IAATO introduced IP 113 *IAATO Overview of Antarctic Tourism: 2009-10 Season and Preliminary Estimates for 2010-11 and Beyond* providing a report of tourist activity in Antarctica during the last season, as well as an overview of Antarctic tourism trends. IAATO informed the Meeting that estimated figures showed that the total number of visitors for the 2009–2010 season for IAATO members was around 36,900, including over-flights and cruise-only voyages, noting that this number was about three percent below the 37,900 visitors for the 2008–2009 season. IAATO noted that its membership continued to incorporate the majority of recognized Antarctic private-sector tour operators and that all commercial ship-based operators conducting tourism activities in the Antarctic Treaty area are members of IAATO at the present time.

(228) IAATO noted that overall visitation to the Antarctic has declined in 2009-10 from its peak in 2007-08 due primarily to the poor global economy in recent years. The only category of visitation that increased in 2009-10 compared with 2008-09 was that of cruise-only vessels carrying more than 500 passengers, which increased by 41% and reached its peak to-date in this last season. IAATO predicted a sharp decline in the number of passengers in the category of cruise-only vessels carrying more than 500 passengers due to the IMO ban on ships carrying heavy fuel oil in Antarctic waters.

(229) Parties thanked IAATO for its report and its on-going collection of tourism data.

(230) The United Kingdom also noted that the IAATO information did not provide the complete picture of tourism and non-governmental activities in Antarctica.

ii. Management of Ship-borne Tourism

(231) New Zealand introduced WP 1 *Chairs' Report – Antarctic Treaty Meeting of Experts on the Management of Ship-borne Tourism in the Antarctic Treaty Area*, informing the Meeting on the results of the ATME held in Wellington in December 2009. New Zealand noted that it was a very successful meeting, attended by 86 representatives of 19 Parties and 6 expert organisations, and over 30 valuable papers were considered.

(232) The ATME, based on the terms of reference agreed at ATCM XXXII, discussed a wide range of issues concerning ship-borne tourism in Antarctica, such as trends in ship-borne tourism over the past 10 years, including maritime incidents and future projections; developments in the IMO relating to ship-borne tourism in the Antarctic Treaty area; maritime safety; environmental protection; vessels flagged to non-Parties and cooperation between the ATCM and the IMO and IHO. New Zealand informed the Meeting that the ATME had agreed on 17 recommendations to the ATCM, covering a wide range of issues concerning ship-borne tourism in Antarctica.

(233) The Meeting thanked New Zealand for having conducted a very well run and productive ATME. New Zealand observed that the ATME had proved timely as the previous week the IMO had adopted the Polar Guidelines. In February 2010 the IMO had commenced work at the 53rd meeting of its subcommittee on Design and Equipment (DE53) on the mandatory Polar Code. New Zealand had presented a paper to DE53 reporting on the ATME. The IMO was currently conducting an intersessional process

under the chair of Norway in preparation for DE54 which would be held from 25 to 29 October 2010, and where the mandatory Polar Code would be further discussed. In addition, the IMO had adopted the prohibition on heavy grade oil in the Antarctic in March 2010. New Zealand emphasised that it was important for the Treaty Parties to contribute to the development of the mandatory Polar Code. It noted that the ATME had usefully brought together a mix of Antarctic and maritime experts and had served to promote dialogue between these groups, including within national administrations. The experts had offered a range of views about the content of the mandatory Polar Code.

iii. Supervision and Management of Tourism

(234) Argentina presented WP 48 *Supervision of Antarctic Tourism*, recalling that at ATCM XXXII several Parties and IAATO commented on mechanisms for ensuring more appropriate supervision of tourism on board cruise ships, and that the ATCM had adopted Resolution 7 (2009) on General Principles for Antarctic Tourism. Argentina noted that Parties had currently three mechanisms for supervising various aspects of tourist activities on board cruise ships: Inspections conducted under Article VII of the Treaty; National Antarctic Programmes deploying observers on cruise ships flying the Party's flag or whose operator has a legal address on their territory; and deploying observers at sites regularly visited by tourist cruise ships.

(235) New Zealand noted that it required observers to be carried on all tourist vessels departing its ports for Antarctica, under its legislation implementing the Environmental Protocol. The role of the observers was to monitor compliance by the tour operators with the EIA and any permits that had been issued.

(236) Argentina proposed the establishment of an Intersessional Contact Group to discuss possible additional tools, or modifications to existing tools, that would serve to ensure better supervision of the management of Antarctic tourism on board cruise ships.

(237) Several Parties endorsed the establishment of the ICG proposed by Argentina in WP 48.

(238) Several Parties felt that the supervision of small vessels and yachts often represented a more difficult challenge than larger commercial cruise vessels and those yachts already under the auspices of IAATO and that the scope of the ICG should be expanded to include such smaller vessels.

(239) While several Parties noted the demonstrated benefit of official observers on board cruise vessels, other Parties cautioned that such an observation programme would be highly resource intensive and that any programme of observers should consider the practical challenges involved. It was also observed that it would be desirable to develop an improved vessel inspection checklist. Norway and Japan said that Article VII of the Treaty stipulates that "ships (...) at points of discharging or embarking cargoes or personnel in Antarctica, shall be open at all times to inspection by any observers (...)". Any suggestion to change this mandate for inspections must be discussed within the ATCM in future meetings as a separate agenda point. The Meeting noted that any new checklist would need to take account of varying conditions across Antarctica.

(240) The Meeting agreed to establish an Intersessional Contact Group, based on the ATCM Discussion Forum on the Secretariat website. The ICG will be led by Argentina, with the following Terms of Reference:

- Considering recommendation 2 from the ATME on ship-borne tourism and drawing on existing checklists for inspections set out in Resolution 5 (1995) and Resolution 4 (2008) and any relevant practical experience, consider the development of a separate checklist to support inspections under Art. VII of the Antarctic Treaty and Article 14 of the Madrid Protocol, regarding tourism and non-governmental activities;
- Identify any issues related to the inspection of tourism and non-governmental activities, under Art. VII of the Antarctic Treaty and Article 14 of the Madrid Protocol, and suggest likely ways to facilitate more such inspections in the future;
- Gather and analyse information about existing and previous tourism and non-governmental "observer programmes" in the Antarctic Treaty area, and examine the need and identify potential options to enhance the observation of tourism and non-governmental activities in Antarctica; and
- Submit a report to ATCM XXXIV (Buenos Aires, 2011).

(241) Observers, as indicated in Rule 2 of the Rules of Procedure and invited experts to the ATCM, as indicated in Rule 39 of the Rules of Procedure and the Final Report of ATCM XXXII (Paragraph 333), would be invited to participate.

(242) Argentina introduced WP 49 *Proposal for the drafting of guidelines for bases that receive visitors*, noting considerations given in Resolution 7

(2009) on General Principles of Antarctic Tourism and in the guidelines contained in the *IAATO Field Operations Manual*. Argentina proposed that the ATCM encourage Parties to draft guidelines for regulating tourist visits to the Antarctic national bases.

(243) Argentina indicated that during the 2008-09 season, tourist vessels visited a total of 17 Antarctic bases of 11 Consultative Parties and that only four bases had internal tourism management procedures that were included in the IAATO Field Operations Manual. Consequently, in its view, the majority of tourist visits to Antarctic bases are not subject to formal regulation, leaving the manner in which visits take place to be agreed unofficially between the bases and the vessels.

(244) Argentina proposed if possible that such guidelines be drafted using the same format as the Visitor Site Guidelines, facilitating tourist vessel expedition crew comprehension and use. However, it noted that it was not proposing that these guidelines should be submitted for consideration by the ATCM since it is understood that each Party is free to establish national procedures for managing tourism at its Antarctic bases. Norway referred to WP 57, *The 2009 Norwegian Antarctic Inspection under Article VII of the Antarctic Treaty* and said that the Norwegian inspection team had noted that it would be a clear advantage for stations and national programmes if they were to have clearly stated policies with respect to the level of availability of infrastructure and personnel to cater for tourism activities.

(245) Many Parties supported the idea that bases should have written policies related to visitors, although many indicated that the format could not be uniform and should be up to the Parties that operate the bases, and that rules for visitors would vary depending on the circumstances of each station. Some Parties further noted the need to keep any guideline structure clear and concise.

(246) Noting that the first objective of national programme bases is science, some Parties noted that their stations did not encourage tourists and expressed the concern that visit guidelines may encourage tourist visits to national stations and thus suggested that care be taken that these guidelines not promote the expectation that the tour operators have the right to visit the national bases.

(247) The United States and the United Kingdom noted that visits by tourists can provide an opportunity to educate the public about environmental protection in Antarctica.

(248) To this end, the Meeting agreed to encourage Parties to prepare policies related to visitors at Antarctic stations and to keep the ATCM and IAATO informed where appropriate on such policies, in order to ensure a broader access to them.

(249) Russia introduced WP 61 *Queen Maud Land – a new center of non-governmental activity in the Antarctic* recalling to the Meeting that the "Dronning Maud Land Air Network" (DROMLAN) is an international aviation programme in the Dronning Maud Land area, agreed by eleven Parties in 2003, to provide aviation support for national Antarctic expeditions on a corporate financial basis. Russia informed the Meeting that since 2006-07, DROMLAN had transported 195 passengers from Cape Town, South Africa to the Novolazarevskaya airstrip to participate in non-governmental activities and mentioned that Russia had not been involved in organising these activities. Russia raised its concerns that use of the DROMLAN by non-governmental activities was placing increased pressure on its National Programme. It considered that Parties involved in DROMLAN should officially co-ordinate non-governmental activities with national operators, as owners of the Antarctic expedition infrastructure, before issuing their national permits for non-governmental activities.

(250) Many Parties expressed support for Russia's conclusion that there was a need to effectively regulate non-governmental activities, in Dronning Maud Land and elsewhere. In addition, some Parties suggested there was a need to develop a clear, coordinated permitting procedure for non-governmental activities using DROMLAN. Some Parties expressed concerns in respect of the growth of land-based tourist activities through the use of science infrastructure.

(251) Many Parties agreed with Russia on the need for greater cooperation among operators located in Dronning Maud Land, and welcomed the information that the upcoming COMNAP meeting in August 2010 would be used by DROMLAN participants to discuss the issue further.

(252) In response to questions related to permitting of non-governmental activities, South Africa informed the Meeting that it did not have all necessary regulations in place, but it was working to address that problem. It also informed the Meeting that DROMLAN's South African service provider, The Antarctic Company (TAC), had applied for IAATO membership and that a South African representative had accompanied last year's IAATO inspection of TAC operations at the Novo airstrip.

(253) IAATO informed the Meeting that TAC had recently become an associate member of IAATO. It also noted that, following its inspection of TAC operations of the Novo airstrip last year, IAATO had shared results of its observer report with Russia, South Africa and United Kingdom and hoped that this would assist efforts to co-ordinate the regulation of non-governmental activities in Dronning Maud Land.

(254) ASOC thanked Russia for WP 61, which brought clarity about tourism uses of the DROMLAN airstrip. ASOC echoed the comments by the Netherlands that sustainable tourism is essentially ship-borne tourism, and expressed the view that encouraging land-based tour operators to join IAATO was helpful, but was not in itself a solution to the issue of land-based tourism, which required strategic environmental planning.

(255) The United Kingdom suggested that, given the volume and nature of activities being undertaken in the region being discussed, it might be a suitable candidate for area protection in the form of an ASMA. It also informed the Meeting that IAATO had requested the United Kingdom to make contact with a tourist operator based in the Dronning Maud Land area in order to consider undergoing UK permitting arrangements for its activities.

(256) The United Kingdom, on behalf of the authors, introduced WP 25 *Report of an incident at Wordie House (HSM No 62)* (United Kingdom, France and Ukraine), providing details of an incident during January 2010 which resulted in some damage to HSM 62. It reported that the United Kingdom Antarctic Heritage Trust had found two French citizens from two yachts moored nearby, sleeping in the hut. Some damages were found in the door and window of the refuge as they had been forced.

(257) The United Kingdom informed the Meeting that French authorities had confirmed that neither of the two vessels involved in the incident had applied to the relevant French administration for authorisation nor had been granted approval to proceed to Antarctica. The United Kingdom also highlighted the difficulty of regulating the conduct of small yacht activity in Antarctica, and the need to better inform yacht operators of the requirements for Antarctic travel.

(258) France expressed gratitude for the cooperation regarding this incident, and noted that though the incident was not especially serious, it could be used as a case study on how to respond to other situations of non-compliance. It noted the difficulty in determining whether a citizen of their country had

received authorisation from another country, and the need to ensure that small yacht operators are aware of relevant regulations so that they cannot claim ignorance and avoid punishment. It informed the Meeting that legal action was being taken against the two individuals involved, and that the outcome would be shared with the ATCM.

(259) Consequently, the Meeting encouraged national authorities to consider ways in which to raise awareness of the requirements of the Antarctic Treaty and the Protocol, in particular to highlight the need for prior authorisation or declaration to enter Antarctica and compliance with the Protocol's environmental principles and protection of Historic Sites and Monuments.

(260) Germany highlighted the importance of the yachting issue. It asked for a comparison between the amount of non-IAATO yachting activity versus IAATO activity in the Antarctic. It also suggested that this data should not only be collected in a tourism study, but that the ATCM should find a mechanism to enter and regularly update that information into an ATS database or discussion forum for information exchange.

(261) IAATO noted that WP 25 raised important issues and that similar incidents related to yachts had occurred in the past. IAATO referred to IP 75, which contained information on the encounters between IAATO vessels and other visitors, largely non-IAATO vessels, in Antarctica. It stated that a strong authorisation process with communication was a good teaching mechanism for visitors. In IP 75, IAATO highlighted the importance of planning and encouraging yachts to go through the authorisation process.

(262) With regard to WP 25, Argentina noted that the text at the end of paragraph 7 is not consistent with the applicable site guidelines. In Argentina´s view the wording of both texts makes this quite clear. The United Kingdom responded that in its view it did not consider that WP 25 was inconsistent with the Site Guidelines for Wordie House.

(263) Argentina pointed out that in this context it is a matter of simply reading and comparing text and not a matter of interpretation.

(264) The United States introduced WP 52 *Data Collection and Reporting on Yachting Activity in Antarctica* (United States and United Kingdom) noting that, in the framework of the tourism study being conducted by the CEP, considerable difficulties were encountered in collecting data on yachting activities in Antarctica.

(265) The United Kingdom noted that relatively complete records on yacht tourism exist for Port Lockroy, where it had been administering an extensive visitor monitoring scheme for all vessels and visitors over the last 14 seasons. However, the United Kingdom noted that additional information was necessary before an assessment of the potential environmental risks associated with Antarctic yachting could be undertaken.

(266) The Meeting accepted the recommendation in WP 52 that information additional to the data provided in Appendix A of WP 52 be gathered, and noted that Dr Neil Gilbert of New Zealand had agreed to steward this information in the context of the CEP's Tourism Study. Parties agreed that any additional information they had to contribute to the current CEP study could be provided to New Zealand (Dr Gilbert):

- Construction material (eg, metal, wood, fibreglass);
- Whether operated as a charter or private expedition;
- If a charter, who was the operator;
- Indication if IAATO member or not; and
- The seasons during which the yacht operated in Antarctica.

(267) Chile welcomed the suggestion for more information exchange and noted its readiness in providing all information that its maritime institutions had for vessel activities, particularly those started in Chile as point of departure.

(268) IAATO endorsed WP 52 and informed that it would provide the requested information for IAATO yachts that is not already included annually in the IAATO overview of Antarctic tourism information paper. IAATO added that it looks forward to the compilation of information in the future report.

(269) The Netherlands agreed that small vessels in the Antarctic were an important issue, especially in view of WP 25. It noted that the five yachts flagged from Netherlands in the paper had all followed the proper authorisation process from the Netherlands. It encouraged the use of a strong authorisation process and noted the difficulties of this.

(270) Chile introduced WP 68 rev. 1, *Recommendations for controlling yachts under a third flag navigating in the Antarctic Chilean SAR area*, which included a list of 20 vessels navigating in the Antarctic. It believed that some Flag States had not fulfilled their responsibility to instruct small vessels of their duty to follow Antarctic Treaty rules when entering Antarctic waters. It noted that the majority of yachts monitored by Chilean maritime authorities carried short range communication equipment, and the risk of yachts heading

into Antarctic waters without proper communication and safety equipment. Chile highlighted the need for port states to be more vigilant and promoted the idea of strengthening the port state authority to be applied in the case of small vessels that are unsuitable for navigation in Antarctica.

(271) The United Kingdom agreed with Chile's recommendation for full implementation of Resolution 3 (2004) on information exchange between competent authorities. The United Kingdom noted that it is doing more to educate its yacht owners but noted there are difficulties in tracking Antarctic-bound yachts, particularly if the yacht's decision to go to Antarctica is made on short notice or en route. The United Kingdom therefore requested that port states and national authorities notify the United Kingdom if they receive requests from UK registered yachts to visit Antarctica, which are not already in possession of a United Kingdom permit.

(272) Brazil noted its concern with yacht activity and how to better deal with the issue. It further noted that the expeditions mentioned in WPs 52 and 68 were not authorised by the Brazilian government, and agreed that the information exchange system, which would have information on authorised activities, should be a starting point to work on the issue of exchange of information among Parties regarding private expeditions and yachts.

(273) The United States noted that not all the yachts referenced in the paper were without prior authorisation, including the U.S. vessel *The Seal*, which was an IAATO member that had submitted an environmental impact assessment prior to its departure. The United States suggested that the contact database of the ATS website could enable Parties to reach each other regarding yachting activities and that advance notifications listed on the ATS website contain information about yachts that have been regulated by Parties. The United States suggested that further clarification of this website and more evident links to Parties' websites could further facilitate this communication.

(274) Australia welcomed discussion on approaches to ensuring those planning non-governmental activities in Antarctica were aware of the requirements for visits. It noted that the lists of yachts in WP 52 and WP 68 included Australian-flagged yachts which were duly authorised and for which advance notification had been provided. Australia noted that the EIES was the best way of collecting and managing information on activities, and that duplication of reporting systems may not be desirable. Australia further noted that the list of national points of contact existed to assist Parties in consulting with each other with respect to planned activities. In addition, Australia expressed its appreciation for incident reports it received from

IAATO and its members, and commented that where appropriate, such reports were addressed.

(275) IAATO commented that IAATO yachts are authorised and currently carry the equipment referenced in recommendation 1 of WP 68. IAATO noted it would be pleased to contribute to discussions on the recommendations during the intersessional period.

(276) Chile suggested the IMO's facilitation committee could be a useful mechanism for improving current procedures to authorise yacht visits to Antarctica. It noted that the issue of documentation and authorisation could be resolved by adding an appendix to the required IMO record-keeping process of crew registers and port records. This appendix would require yachts to document when they plan to travel to Antarctica, and if they have met the requirements to do so. Chile noted that such an appendix would be an easy way to incorporate documentation into the international regime.

(277) The United Kingdom noted, in reference to suggestions made in WP 68 rev. 1, that it was very important that yacht-authorisation procedures take into account compliance with the Antarctic Treaty and Environmental Protocol.

(278) Following on from discussion on safety equipment aboard yachts, Norway supported the idea of consulting IMO for clarification on how to take this issue forward.

(279) The Meeting agreed that the issues of enhanced safety practices for yachts warranted further discussion. The United Kingdom, the United States, France, Chile, and others expressed their will to cooperate informally on these matters during the intersessional period.

(280) The Meeting considered recommendation 10 from the Wellington ATME on tourism: *That those Antarctic Treaty Parties that have not yet done so should consider approving Measure 4 (2004) on Insurance and Contingency Planning for Tourism and Non-governmental Activities in the Antarctic Treaty Area as a matter of priority.*

(281) There was strong support in the Meeting for Parties to finish their domestic approval processes for Measure 4 (2004), although it was noted that many Parties had yet to act and it had been some years since the adoption of this Measure.

(282) New Zealand noted the importance of making progress on the implementation of the Measure which had the effect of reducing the burden placed on

National Programmes to provide SAR response for non-governmental activities.

(283) The United Kingdom noted that Measure 4 (2004) has led to beneficial changes in the manner in which non-governmental activities have been planned. Japan also supported the need for each Party to finish its domestic approval process of Measure 4 (2004), and, in this connection, also drew attention to the fact that very few Parties had approved Measure 15 (2009).

(284) The Meeting then considered recommendation 12 from the Wellington ATME: *The meeting recommended that Parties and those involved in non-governmental activities be encouraged to provide spatial and temporal data in support of future studies and syntheses for discussion by the CEP and ATCM.*

(285) There was strong support from the Meeting for ATME recommendation 12.

(286) The United States and IAATO submitted IP 2 *Spatial Patterns of Tour Ship Traffic in the Antarctic Peninsula Region*, which provided for consideration by Parties a paper reviewing the pattern of tour ship traffic in the Antarctic Peninsula region using 19 years of passenger landing statistics and five years of reconstructed itineraries from 2003-04 to 2007-08 seasons. The paper provides a discussion of human impacts in the Peninsula region, makes a prioritisation of sites for monitoring programmes, and analyses strategic approaches to the development of future management tools and review of current management tools. The United States welcomed receiving other data, especially non-IAATO data, so that it can be incorporated into the study.

(287) Several Parties noted the utility of collecting spatial and temporal data on tourism activities as reflected in IP 2 and the ongoing activities of the CEP tourism study.

(288) The Parties encouraged full compliance with the EIES but noted that the EIES does not currently require the same level of information as the post-visit report form as provided in Resolution 5 (2005) which underpinned the analysis presented in IP 2 by the United States and IAATO. Parties were therefore encouraged to send all appropriate available post-visit report data to the United States and New Zealand to support the CEP tourism study.

(289) Chile noted the importance of publicizing the request that operators and others provide data for these purposes to relevant authorities.

(290) IAATO submitted IP 75 *Non-IAATO Tourism and Visitation in Antarctica*, informing the Parties that IAATO operators encounter non-IAATO tourism and visitation at sites each season, particularly around the Peninsula area,

where a proportion of those involved are either unaware or unwilling to follow ATCM guidelines or best practices. IAATO indicated that it had put in place initiatives to lessen this problem including educational outreach to promote awareness and, when serious incidents occur, reporting information to appropriate national authorities. IAATO said that it would welcome advice from ATCM on both the usefulness of these efforts and on any additional work that can be undertaken to improve the outreach and education regarding non-IAATO tourism and visitation.

(291) Parties thanked IAATO for its offer to provide information to Parties on activities it sees in Antarctica that appear to be in breach of ATCM guidelines, and indicated that they would welcome such reports.

(292) IAATO submitted IP 25 *IAATO Online Field Staff Assessment & Logbook* on the initiatives it had taken to improve field staff training. The paper describes how during the past two years IAATO prepared the IAATO Field Operations Manual (FOM), the IAATO Expedition Staff Logbook and how it had established an online field staff assessment scheme designed to augment the training and test the knowledge of field staff on the contents of the Field Operations Manual. IAATO noted that the online assessment scheme will be available for the 2010-11 season where initially all ship-based expedition leaders will be asked to take part.

(293) The United States submitted IP 26 *Antarctic Site Inventory: 1994-2010*. The Antarctic Site Inventory is a monitoring programme that has collected biological data and site-descriptive information in the Antarctic Peninsula since 1994.

(294) IAATO submitted IP 62 *Report on IAATO Member use of Antarctic Peninsula Landing Site and ATCM Visitor Site Guidelines* noting that, because of timing reasons, it reported only on IAATO Member landing information for 2008-09 season. IAATO indicated that Antarctic tourism continued to be primarily focused on traditional ship-based tourism in the Antarctic Peninsula, representing over 95% of landed activity. IAATO informed that the landing activities decreased as result of the decrease in Antarctic tourism during the reporting period because of the global economic downturn. Most of the landing sites were covered by site specific management, either through ATCM Site Guidelines or through National Programme management through their proximity to stations.

(295) ASOC made a presentation summarizing the following contributions:

- IP 70 *Comparison of Three Antarctic Treaty Meeting of Experts on Shipping and Tourism*. The document compared the ATME held in December 2009 with previous ATMEs on shipping in 2000 and on tourism in 2004. ASOC noted that Antarctic Treaty Parties had made progress on the regulation of both shipping and tourism (and the interface of these two activities) with respect to the situation in 2000 and 2004. However, ASOC considered that progress has been relatively slow, and forced by shipping incidents and tourism developments.

- IP 79 *Tourism and Land-based Facilities in Antarctica: Analysis of a Questionnaire Distributed to Antarctic Treaty Parties at XXXII ATCM*. ASOC indicated that eight Parties operating twelve facilities answered the questionnaire and they noted that none of the respondents provides support to tourism other than free basic hospitality. Most respondents opposed the notion of Parties being involved in tourism operations. No Party reported being aware of land-based facilities from other Parties being used for tourism purposes in their area of operations. ASOC said it would appreciate the inputs of all Parties that had not yet done so to respond to the questionnaire.

- IP 81 *Coastal Hydrocarbon Pollution: A Case Study from Deception Island, Antarctica* on monitoring activities conducted in 2001-02 which identified detectable hydrocarbon concentrations at a number of Deception Island coastal sites. ASOC said that the results suggested that regular and effective monitoring should take place to allow assessment of the impacts of ongoing activities at Deception Island as well as at other Antarctic sites where high levels of shipping are frequent.

- IP 82 *Antarctic Ship-borne Tourism and Inspections under Article VII of the Antarctic Treaty and Article 14 of the Protocol on Environmental Protection*. ASOC noted that tourism has become a major Antarctic activity in terms of the number of people, ships, and sites involved, hence it is natural that tourism has become the focus of increasing inspections. ASOC suggested that some official inspections should focus primarily on inspecting tourism vessels, activities and landing sites rather than primarily on research stations as has been the practice so far and that those inspections should be as detailed and critical, where applicable, as those of National Antarctic Programme facilities. ASOC noted that the existing inspection checklists can be used for the time being, but purpose-made checklists for tourism may eventually be required.

(296) Chile introduced WP 65 *Report of the Intersessional Contact Group on Marathons and other large – scale Sporting Activities in Antarctica* on the results of discussions of the ICG established at ATCM XXXII. Chile informed the Meeting that several Parties and experts participated in the discussions that were based on a questionnaire that it circulated for consideration by participants.

(297) Chile commented that the majority of comments received suggested the need for more effective compliance with the existing provisions under the Environmental Protocol. The participants also stressed the importance of the exchange of information and advance notification of such activities. Despite the many valuable comments received during the intersessional period, Chile did not feel the information gathered was sufficient to produce a draft resolution regarding these activities.

(298) Parties noted the importance of discussing this matter. Some Parties indicated that due to the timing of the ICG, they had had insufficient time to participate. Some Parties, including France, Argentina and India, considered that the effective implementation of existing tools, such as prior notification of activities, the EIA process and effective exchange of information, were sufficient and critical to ensuring that marathons and large-scale sporting activities were conducted with minimal impact on the Antarctic environment and on national research priorities. China encouraged Parties to co-operate to enhance implementation of existing tools and continue consideration of these issues to find out whether additional tools might be required.

(299) Other Parties, including Germany, considered that the development of additional tools with which to assess large-scale activities might be required. The Netherlands expressed the view that the subject of marathons illustrates the difficulties that competent authorities may experience in assessing whether certain types of activities should be considered appropriate in the Antarctic. A number of Parties said tourism activities should be considered primarily in terms of their environmental impact.

(300) France highlighted the pivotal role of the Parties in charge of the process of authorisation in supervising marathons and similar activities, especially in the context of preparation of EIAs. Argentina added that operators should make EIA reports on proposed marathons available to the host national programmes well in advance of the event to better enable such programmes to safeguard against potential environmental and logistical impacts.

(301) ASOC thanked Chile for its co-ordination work and expressed the view that marathons are a novel form of tourism distinct from traditional tourism activities, and that arguably there is no compelling reason for the conduct of Antarctic marathons.

(302) Chile and IAATO commented that a recent marathon in the Antarctic had demonstrated a marked improvement in the way marathons were organised and that this has been documented in an independent observer report on the marathon that had been distributed to those Parties involved and IAATO. IAATO considered this positive outcome to be a result of strengthened communication between Parties and operators.

(303) The Meeting agreed that the ICG on marathons and other large-scale sporting activities in Antarctica should continue its work, convened by Chile and based on the ATCM Discussion Forum on the Secretariat website, with the following revised Terms of Reference:

- Conduct an analysis of the management of large-scale sporting and marathon running events; and gather more information about large-scale events which took place and are planned to take place in Antarctica.
- Review existing tools and mechanisms to regulate and manage large-scale sporting events and consider whether any additional mechanisms, such as regulations, site specific instruments or checklists, are necessary.
- Noting Resolution 3 (2004), to consider whether additional procedures for prior communication and exchange of information between Parties are needed. Share examples of helpful communication and information exchange between Parties and provide advice on possible improvements.

(304) Observers, as indicated in Rules of Procedure Paragraph 2, and invited experts to the ATCM, as indicated in Rules of Procedure Paragraph 39 and the Final Report from ATCM XXXII (Paragraph 333), would be invited to participate.

(305) Ecuador expressed concern as to the definition of the meaning of large-scale events.

iv. Long-term considerations in tourism policy

(306) The Meeting considered Recommendation 6 from the ATME on Ship-borne Tourism: *That the Treaty Parties proactively apply to tourist vessels bound*

for the Antarctic Treaty area the existing regime of port State control (PSC), through PSC memoranda of understanding or agreements if appropriate, so that they can meet all applicable legally binding international standards.

(307) New Zealand introduced WP 37 *The Enhancement of Port State Control for Passenger Ships Departing to Antarctica*, recalling Recommendation 6 from the ATME on Ship-borne Tourism which proposed Parties proactively apply Port State Control (PSC) to tourist vessels bound for the Antarctic Treaty area through PSC memoranda of understanding or agreements if appropriate, so that they can meet all applicable legally binding international standards. Noting the high percentage of vessels bound for the Antarctic Treaty area flagged by non-Party countries and the number of recent incidents involving passenger vessels, port States should proactively and regularly conduct inspections according to the existing international framework to ensure that vessels departing for Antarctic waters meet the necessary standards.

(308) New Zealand noted that existing port State control regimes had introduced targeted inspections based upon simple risk indicators that have proven to be valid through many hundreds of inspections, and that a high priority status for passenger ships could help to ensure they were inspected at a maximum of three monthly intervals by at least one Party, using common inspection guidelines. New Zealand also recommended that the Parties encourage the secretariats of the various PSC memoranda of understanding to share information on inspections of vessels departing to Antarctica.

(309) Argentina felt that the prioritized port State inspections should be expanded so as to include not only the last port prior to departure for the Antarctic, but also ports visited prior, so that any changes in itinerary would not cause ships to miss port State inspection.

(310) The United States thanked New Zealand for its paper and expressed support for the three recommendations contained in the paper and for the use of focused port State control under existing measures to ensure both the safety of ships and the protection of the marine environment. It further noted its view that the regulation of shipping safety and environmental protection from ships in areas beyond port or coastal state jurisdiction is the primary responsibility of the Flag State. Furthermore, in its view, the combination of Flag State and focused existing Port State Control scheme measures to enforce IMO instruments relevant to polar waters should be adequate to increase ship safety and help increase protection of Antarctic waters from pollution from ships.

(311) South Africa noted that the language in Recommendation 6 referred only to tourist vessels and questioned why other vessels were excluded. Several Parties noted that the mandate of ATME was focused on tourism, and thus only passenger vessels were discussed.

(312) The United Kingdom, Chile, and Sweden expressed a desire to see consistent port state control and inspection mechanisms for all vessels bound for Antarctica. Based on several existing port state control measures, it was noted that no agreement established exceptions for a port state to board third-party flag ships and conduct inspections.

(313) China noted that the existing port State control regime does not apply to government vessels. The United States shared the concerns expressed by China, especially with regard to sovereign immune vessels. Japan agreed to the points made by China and the United States.

(314) New Zealand recalled that the topic of the ATME was ship-borne tourism and not other forms of shipping. It reminded the Meeting that its proposal was to indicate that the ATCM thought it was important for Parties to give priority to passenger vessels bound for the Antarctic Treaty area when conducting port State control.

(315) Argentina, Russia, Uruguay, and Japan supported New Zealand. Argentina and Russia noted that applying port state control to all ships would be difficult. Japan stated that the issue being addressed was ship-borne tourism because it was the growth of ship-borne tourism which prompted Parties to begin deliberation in the first place, and thus should appropriately remain the focus. Uruguay noted that all vessels are urged to go through port State control measures regardless of the proposal, and broadening the language would lose the intent to prioritize passenger vessels.

(316) The Meeting adopted Resolution 7 (2010), The Enhancement of Port State Control for Passenger Vessels Bound for the Antarctic Treaty Area.

(317) ASOC noted that IP 80 *Making Tangible Progress on a Strategic Vision for Antarctic Tourism* reports that there are relatively few legally binding instruments addressing tourism and recommends that a regulatory regime should be consolidated by means of legally binding instruments, including those that have been approved and are not yet effective (including Measure 4 (2004), Measure 15 (2009), and Annex VI to the Protocol), and by new instruments implementing the general principles of Resolution 7 (2009). In addition, existing environmental management tools (EIAs, ASMAs and ASPAs) could be applied proactively as tourism management tools. ASOC

argued that Parties should consider tourism in the context of other activities and processes (such as climate change) but avoid losing focus from tourism in order to improve its management. While acknowledging the problems caused by yachts, ASOC also recalled the sinking of the *M/S Explorer* in 2007 and the risks of cumulative impacts posed by mainstream forms of tourism, which in its view raised far more significant issues.

(318) Several Members welcomed ASOC's IP 80 and thanked ASOC for its work on a strategic vision for Antarctic tourism. Many Members noted the need to continue to work on such a strategic vision, bearing in mind Resolution 7 (2009).

(319) IAATO stressed the need for continued communication among interested Parties in the development of a strategic vision for Antarctic tourism in preparation for a resumption of growth in the tourism industry, and highlighted the establishment of an annual roundtable discussion of Antarctic tourism as introduced in IP 84.

v. Other Matters

(320) IAATO introduced IP 60 *Developing a Risk Assessment Framework for IAATO Passenger Vessels* informing the ATCM on a presentation made to the 53rd meeting of the Design and Equipment Subcommittee of the IMO's Marine Safety Committee. The aim of this work is to provide IAATO operators with a framework for voyage planning and assist in the application of the current IMO Guidelines for Ships Operating in Polar Waters. The study is in its initial phase and IAATO, through Cruise Lines International Association (CLIA) will be submitting the preliminary report to the D&E correspondence group working in the Mandatory Polar Code and through this mechanism looks forward to feedback on the study.

(321) The United Kingdom said it was looking forward to IAATO's full report, noting that the study is a responsible reaction to the ongoing work and topics related to shipping in the Antarctic region.

(322) New Zealand noted it would be important to determine the effectiveness of attempting to apply different regulations to shipping in the Antarctic on a regional basis as opposed to taking a uniform approach to the Treaty Area as a whole which was its firm preference. New Zealand noted that the environmental sensitivity of the Treaty Area and risk factors such lack of charting, extremes of weather and remoteness of SAR facilities supported the latter approach.

(323) The Meeting considered Recommendation 3 from the ATME on Ship-borne Tourism: *That the Treaty Parties make use as appropriate of the views expressed in discussions amongst experts about the proposed IMO mandatory Polar Code in their preparations for the upcoming meetings of the IMO Sub-Committee on Ship Design and Equipment and the ATCM, and discuss at the ATCM how the Treaty Parties might best input into the IMO discussions.*

(324) The Meeting endorsed ATME Recommendation 3.

(325) The United States introduced WP 53 *Public Availability of Information Concerning Life-saving Appliances Onboard Passenger Ships*, proposing that additional steps should be taken to help address continuing concerns over the adequacy of life-saving appliances (LSA) onboard commercially operated ships and thus, contribute to passenger safety in Antarctica. The United States, noting its suggestion at ATCM XXXII that open lifeboats (OLB) not be permitted on any passenger ships operating in the Antarctic Treaty area, proposed that the ATCM call upon all commercial tour operators to take steps to ensure prospective passengers are aware of the LSAs provided onboard their ships operating in the Treaty area. The United States considered that such action would provide a heightened level of transparency for members of the public helping them make informed decisions when choosing among options for ship-borne tours of Antarctica.

(326) A number of Parties and ASOC supported WP 53, recalling the sinking of the *M/S Explorer* in 2007, and noting this sort of transparency will help promote safety in the Treaty area.

(327) The United Kingdom indicated that in its view the public were not in a position to make an informed judgement about the level of life-saving appliances (LSA) on a vessel and that this is a matter for the regulators. In the view of the UK, the safety level of the ship cannot be judged via LSA provision alone, but that the ice class, damage stability, and competence of the crew will all contribute to the likelihood of an abandon ship situation arising and that these are dealt with via international regulations. Whilst the UK is supportive of the desire to prevent vessels from operating in Antarctic regions with open lifeboats it is not felt that encouraging the public to 'vote with their feet' is the correct way to do so, rather the IMO is the proper forum for this.

(328) Norway supported the concerns raised by the United Kingdom and said that it also shared the United States' concerns but that this sort of issue should be handled by the IMO.

(329) Germany agreed with publication of information related to which lifeboats are used by passenger vessels, but was more reserved about whether to publicize other LSA's.

(330) ASOC noted that it had produced a pamphlet called *Know before you go* which informs tourists about what they can do before, during and after their Antarctic trip. Basic information about the life saving appliances available onboard passenger ships may be available in EIA documents, which ASOC recommends tourists examine before departure. ASOC considered that the U.S. proposal is sensible in terms of supporting the ability of the public to make informed choices.

(331) IAATO noted its operators' desire to be open and transparent and appreciated the intent of the paper, but shared concerns of UK and Norway regarding this proposal. IAATO endorses Parties efforts to encourage tour operators to use only partially or totally enclosed lifeboats.

(332) The Meeting agreed that passenger safety for ship-borne tourism in Antarctica was of the highest importance and that it was desirable that information relating to passenger safety for ship-borne tourism be readily available. In addition, the Meeting, recalling the *IMO Guidelines for Ships Operating in Polar Waters* (A 26/Res. 1024, adopted on 2 December 2009), agreed that, for use in the conditions of Antarctica, all lifeboats should be either of the partially or totally enclosed type. In this regard, the Meeting encouraged Parties to pay particular attention to the question of lifeboats in regulating tour ship cruises to the Antarctic Treaty Area.

(333) The Meeting considered Recommendation 7 from the ATME on Ship-borne Tourism: *The Meeting agreed that the five Parties with Search and Rescue coordination responsibility in the Antarctic area should share their plans and further coordinate with national programmes, and IAATO.*

(334) The Meeting endorsed ATME Recommendation 7, noting mechanisms by which this type of information sharing is already occurring.

(335) The Meeting considered ATME Recommendation 15: *The meeting agreed that enhanced coordination between the Antarctic Treaty Parties with respect to Antarctic-related matters within IMO may be valuable in some*

circumstances, and noted that mechanisms for coordination should be considered by ATCM XXXIII.

(336) With reference to Recommendation 15 of the ATME on Ship-borne tourism, Australia introduced WP 22 *Enhanced co-ordination of Antarctic Treaty proposals within the IMO*, recalling that the ATCM had referred a number of proposals to the IMO for consideration and implementation in seeking to ensure maritime safety and environmental protection in Antarctica. Australia, recognizing the ATCM and associated fora as the primary place to deal with matters pertaining to Antarctica, noted the role of the IMO in shipping safety and environmental protection including the Antarctic region is also well recognized. Australia therefore considered that a coordinated and consistent approach by Parties who are also members of the IMO was desirable to advance on these proposals within IMO fora.

(337) Australia recalled that the ATME on Ship-borne tourism had agreed Recommendation 15 on enhancing cooperation between ATCPs and the IMO and implementing mechanisms for such coordination. Australia therefore proposed that Parties should:

- identify simple methods that they can use to track, discuss, and, if required, coordinate views on proposals referred from the ATCM to the IMO as they proceed through IMO fora; and
- agree that Parties making proposals, Parties active in the IMO, and/or Parties otherwise interested, should seek to keep Antarctic Treaty Parties collectively informed of progress in the IMO of Antarctic-related issues, using those methods as appropriate.

(338) Australia suggested that interactions by the Parties on these matters could be undertaken using the existing communication mechanisms.

(339) The Meeting discussed Recommendation 15 in the context of WP 22 and endorsed the Recommendation. One Party emphasised that there should be flexibility in the coordination that is carried out.

(340) The Meeting thanked Australia for its paper and highlighted the importance of taking a proactive and innovative approach to shipping issues in the Antarctic within the mandate of the ATCM. The Meeting agreed that strengthened cooperation between the ATS and the IMO was an important and urgent matter particularly in regards to the development of the Polar Code. The Meeting adopted Resolution 5 (2010) Coordination Among Antarctic Treaty Parties on Antarctic Proposals under Consideration in the IMO.

(341) The Meeting agreed the Secretariat should establish a web-based forum immediately after ATCM XXXIII to provide for informal exchanges of views among the Parties, Observers, and Experts on the development of the IMO mandatory Polar Code.

(342) The Meeting considered ATME Recommendation 16: *Recognising the usefulness of having the IMO present and the valuable contributions the IMO representative made, the meeting encouraged IMO's attendance at the next ATCM. The meeting recommended that ways to enhance the cooperative working relationship between the ATCM and IMO should be further considered at ATCM XXXIII.*

(343) The Meeting endorsed Recommendation 16, noting that IMO attendance at the ATCM is encouraged and may be facilitated by consultation and coordination with IMO when scheduling ATCM dates. The view of the Meeting in this regard was also reflected in Resolution 5 (2010).

(344) Argentina introduced IP 129, *Report on Antarctic tourist flows and cruise ships operating in Ushuaia during the 2009/2010 austral summer season*, and IP 130, *The Antarctic voyage experience and visitors' satisfaction for the 2009/2010 season*. ASOC thanked Argentina for IP 129 since it provided a different perspective on the tourist flows to Antarctica, while IAATO thanked Argentina for IP 130 which brought a refreshing and innovative approach about visitors' perspectives of Antarctica.

(345) The United States presented IP 92 *Amundsen-Scott South Pole Station, South Pole Antarctic Specially Managed Area (ASMA No 5) 2010 Management Report*, summarising the continuing challenges in managing diverse scientific research efforts in a remote and extreme environment in which tourism and non-governmental activities are conducted. The United States identified an increase in visitor interest in visiting the South Pole via air, vehicle or on skis.

(346) Noting that co-ordination is essential in this ASMA to facilitate effective management and minimal risk to participants, the United States discussed how it engaged in discussions with participants in tourism and non-governmental activities in the relocation of visitor camping areas and encouraged non-governmental organisations and other visitors to include questions related to altitude sickness in their medical screening process prior to deployment. The United States also requested information from Parties regarding upcoming activities at the South Pole, especially those related to

upcoming historic anniversaries in 2011. The United States noted the revised version of the ASMA will be available for review in 2012.

(347) ASOC asked if the camp described in IP 92 was a permanent or seasonal feature. The United States responded that the tents and associated camping material are set up and removed each season by the various tourism and non-governmental groups that visit the South Pole.

(348) Norway and the United Kingdom informed the Meeting of upcoming activities to commemorate the 100th year anniversary of the Amundsen and Scott expeditions, noting they will liaise with the United States on forthcoming celebrations that could involve visits to the South Pole.

(349) Similarly, India informed the Parties about an upcoming expedition from Maitri to the South Pole, also in celebration of the centennial of the expeditions.

(350) New Zealand introduced IP 11 *International requirements for ships operating in polar waters*, noting that the paper provided the contribution of the IMO to the ATME on Ship-borne tourism via its representative (Heike Deggim) to the meeting. New Zealand further noted that subsequent to the drafting of IP 11, the IMO adopted regulation on the prohibition on the use or carriage of heavy fuel oil in Antarctic waters.

(351) Norway thanked New Zealand for the submission of this paper on behalf of the IMO and the ATME and urged that this paper be kept as a reference for future work.

(352) The United Kingdom voiced its appreciation of this paper and recommended that the ATCM formally welcome the IMO's agreement on the prohibition of the use and carriage of heavy fuel oil in the Antarctic Treaty area.

(353) The Meeting considered ATME Recommendation 13: *The Treaty Parties should exchange information on contingency planning undertaken in fulfilment of Article 15, for responding to incidents with potential adverse impacts on the Antarctic environment.*

(354) The Meeting endorsed ATME Recommendation 13. The Meeting agreed to further discuss the inclusion of sharing information on contingency planning on the ATCM Operations Working Group agenda.

(355) New Zealand introduced IP 7 *Marine oil spills in the Antarctic Treaty Area – Environmental considerations*, regarding oil spill behaviour and potential for impacts. IP 7 discussed the risks and the potential impacts of a marine oil spill in Antarctic waters. New Zealand considered that an oil spill in the

seas surrounding Antarctica could significantly impact on a range of biota and may result in long-term impacts on shorelines, and that a response to a large-scale marine oil spill in the Antarctic would be extremely difficult.

(356) New Zealand also introduced IP 8 *Oil Spill Response*, which discussed the special requirements and restrictions that mounting a response to a marine-based spill in the Antarctic Treaty area can pose. New Zealand noted that undertaking a response in the Antarctic to a minor incident relies on the vessel having the ability to recover spilled oil from the environment using homogenous assets and crew in sub zero temperatures. However, a response to a catastrophic incident would require a lot more planning and effort and could involve a decision on whether a response should occur balanced over the safety of personnel, logistics and practicalities of minimizing damage to the Antarctic environment. New Zealand recommended that the Antarctic Treaty Parties should consider the development of an oil spill contingency plan for the Antarctic Treaty area with an operational focus on response issues and listing assets and resources to be used if a catastrophic incident occurs.

(357) The Meeting considered ATME Recommendation 14: *That the ATCM consider developing guidelines for responding to large-scale marine oil spills in the Antarctic Treaty area.*

(358) In their consideration of this Recommendation, several Parties commented that contingency plans for an oil spill in the Antarctic Treaty area would be most appropriately considered in the Operations Working Group.

(359) Several Parties highlighted the expertise of COMNAP in contingency planning for oil spills and emphasised the utility in soliciting advice from COMNAP in future work by the CEP and the ATCM on this issue.

(360) Chile noted that its joint Antarctic naval patrol with Argentina included qualified personnel and response equipment that may be usefully deployed in the event of an oil spill, but cautioned that other Parties should also prepare a response in the case that its own capacity for response was overwhelmed by a large-scale disaster.

(361) SCAR reminded the Treaty Parties that it has an "Action Group on Antarctic Fuel Spills" consisting of oceanographers, ecologists and other specialists to respond to requests from the Antarctic Treaty Secretariat and/or Antarctic Treaty Parties for assistance or advice in this matter.

(362) ASOC noted that it strongly supported Recommendation 14, and noted the extensive experience that exists within the ATS and other bodies. ASOC

said it would welcome contributing to the development of such guidelines. ASOC also noted that following some recent incidents involving spills the response was not always effective, there was no clean up attempted and no ongoing monitoring of subsequent impacts.

(363) Argentina noted the willingness of the Parties to work together and share resources, as has happened in the SAR workshops conducted in Chile and Argentina, in addition to the scientific monitoring in areas where large spills occurred. Argentina has scientific research which is based on the bioremediation of soils with native bacteria from Antarctica and includes these concepts in spill contingency plans.

(364) The Meeting endorsed ATME Recommendation 14.

(365) The Meeting considered ATME Recommendation 1: *Incidents involving tourist vessels in the Antarctic Treaty Area should be considered by the Antarctic Treaty Parties for the Antarctic specific lessons they may provide for the avoidance of similar incidents in the future. Parties with relevant links to such incidents (especially flag or authorising States) should be asked to provide information to assist such considerations.*

(366) The Meeting endorsed ATME Recommendation 1.

(367) The Meeting considered ATME Recommendation 2: *Drawing on the checklists currently available for other Antarctic operations, the Treaty Parties should consider the development of a specific checklist for Antarctic Treaty inspections of tourist vessels and tourist activities in Antarctica.*

(368) New Zealand, the United Kingdom, Chile, ASOC and IAATO supported ATME Recommendation 2 and noted that an ICG would consider this during the coming year. The United States noted that non-mandatory tourist vessel checklists could help guide Parties.

(369) Chile echoed the importance of checklists to help analyse impacts, monitor and control the activities of tour vessels.

(370) Norway noted that priority should be given to ensure that vessels operating in Antarctica meet IMO standards and if needed adopt new IMO standards as appropriate, to reduce the likelihood of incidents.

(371) The Meeting endorsed ATME Recommendation 2.

(372) The Meeting considered ATME Recommendation 11: *The meeting recommended that the relevant committees and groups of the ATCM (such as the CEP and the Operations Working Group) give further consideration*

to how the assessment of the environmental aspects and impacts of Antarctic ship-borne tourism in WP 8 (Appendix A) could be drawn on to inform their discussions regarding the management of ship-borne tourism and shipping generally.

(373) Australia introduced WP 28 *Environmental Aspects of Antarctic Ship-Borne Tourism*, which was a modified version of the Australian working paper submitted to the ATME on Ship-borne Tourism and referenced in ATME Recommendation 11. Appendix A to the paper provided an assessment of the ways in which ship-borne tourism can interact with the Antarctic environment, and which of those interactions (environmental aspects) are addressed in existing regulations and guidelines. Australia noted that WP 28 had been considered by the CEP, which agreed to consider Appendix A within the ongoing tourism study with the suggestion that a risk assessment be undertaken on the various aspects identified in the assessment (CEP Report, paragraphs 74-81). Australia recalled the ATME's agreement that the assessment was also applicable to Antarctic shipping generally, and should also be considered by relevant Working Groups of the ATCM.

(374) Several Parties, including the United States, New Zealand, the United Kingdom, the Netherlands and Chile, as well as IAATO, supported ATME Recommendation 11 and thanked Australia for its work, noting the importance of keeping the information from Appendix A of WP 28 readily available to the ATCM.

(375) The Netherlands recalled Paragraph 79 of the CEP Report, in which the Committee agreed to further consider how Appendix A might be appended to EIA guidelines.

(376) ASOC expressed support for ATME Recommendations 1, 2, and 11, and welcomed WP 28 as well as the idea of including the table appended to WP 28 in the EIA process. In addition, ASOC recalled the presentation of the Liberian registry at the last ATCM, which made some 20 different findings and recommendations. ASOC asked how Parties were to consider the range of recommendations on a wide range of issues and problems identified in the Liberian report, in order to learn from past experiences.

(377) IAATO introduced IP 61 *IAATO further recommendations to tourism vessel operators to enhance marine safety guidelines for small boat operations in the vicinity of ice*, recalling that a similar version of this paper was presented at the ATME on Ship-borne Tourism. IAATO also recalled previous comments from ASOC about the importance of incorporating recommendations made

in the Liberian report on the *M/S Explorer*, presented at ATCM XXXII, emphasizing that IP 61 represents some of the work IAATO has undertaken to consider these recommendations.

(378) Chile reminded the Meeting of IP 111 *Antarctic Waters Operations Course 2010*, noting their marine instruction training course to be held on October 19 - 20, 2010, which is required for deck officers sailing under the Chilean flag, but is also critically important for all crew. An invitation was extended to this free course, which is conducted in Spanish and English, recommending Parties and ship operators to send representatives. Chile added that their instructional content includes simulator exercises presenting a myriad of plausible situations likely to be encountered when navigating Antarctic Treaty waters.

(379) South Africa informed the Meeting that one of their senior officers benefited greatly from the course offered by Chile and confirmed its plans to send other officers on the course.

Item 12: Inspections under the Antarctic Treaty and the Environment Protocol

(380) Australia introduced WP 21 *Australian Antarctic Treaty and Environmental Protocol inspections, East Antarctica, 2010*. In January 2010, Australia conducted inspections of Syowa station (Japan), Druzhnaya IV and Soyuz stations (Russian Federation), and Mount Harding (ASPA 168). As provided for under Article VII (4) of the Antarctic Treaty, Australian observers also conducted an aerial observation of Molodezhnaya station (Russian Federation). Australia expressed its gratitude to Japan and the Russian Federation for the hospitality and support provided to the team in the conduct of the inspection activity. Australia noted that the inspection team travelled to Antarctica and the inspected stations by air, which, as well as being a new mode of operations for Australian inspections, meant that the support provided by the inspected Parties was particularly important. Australia noted that its inspection team included members fluent in the languages of each station being inspected, which helped ensure a full understanding of all facets of the operations of the stations visited. Australia also noted its intention to present its final inspection report to Parties at ATCM XXXIV.

(381) Argentina commended Australia for including inspection team members capable of speaking the language of stations visited as this leads to more successful inspections.

(382) Norway presented WP 57 *The 2009 Norwegian Antarctic Inspection under Article VII of the Antarctic Treaty.* During February 2009, Norway inspected Princess Elisabeth Antarctica (Belgium), Halley (United Kingdom), Novo runway (Russian Federation) and Antarctic Logistics Centre International (ALCI) Airbase.

(383) Norway expressed its gratitude for the spirit of commitment and dedication encountered at all the sites visited, by the openness and friendliness shown to the inspection team and it added that most of the recommendations of the report have since been addressed. The full report of the inspections was provided in IP 30 *Report of the Norwegian Antarctic Inspection under Article VII of the Antarctic Treaty. February 2009.*

(384) Norway reported that inspection checklist A "Permanent Antarctic Stations and Associated Installations", appended to Resolution 5 (1995) had been useful and helped make the inspections consistent, as well as providing a basis for comparison. Norway also noted that the inspection team found it helpful when an already completed checklist was provided on arrival, as was the case at Halley V. Norway recommends that all stations and installations have relevant information available in such a format both for the purposes of inspections and other instances where such information could be useful.

(385) Norway highlighted the innovative, creative and cutting edge design of Belgium's Princess Elisabeth Antarctica station and it reported that good procedures and practices were in place to ensure environmentally well-founded operations at the United Kingdom's Halley V station. Norway was impressed by the commitment at Halley to maintaining a long-term approach to monitoring and research, and noted that energy efficiency had been a priority in the design of the new Halley VI station, soon to replace Halley V.

(386) Norway noted that there is a potential shift with respect to ownership, financing and objectives associated with Antarctic science operations and related activities. The Parties might want to consider such issues in order to ensure the most appropriate management of Antarctic activities within the framework of the objectives of the Antarctic Treaty. Norway also noted it may be appropriate to consider what driving forces define the research planned for new research stations, ie, whether long term, coordinated and

unique, scientific motives are the relevant drivers. Norway noted that changes seem to be happening, and that the Antarctic Treaty Parties may want to consider implications at an early stage.

(387) Norway also noted that the number of scientists at two of the inspected research stations was low compared to the total number of occupants. This could easily be explained for both stations as they were in a period of heavy construction. Norway considered this is a general tendency in Antarctic operations and potentially an issue worth discussion. Norway reported that no military activities were observed in any of the stations.

(388) Norway noted that stations and national programmes may benefit from clearly stated policies regarding tourism and the level of station infrastructure and personnel available to cater for tourism activities. It also noted that the operations at Novo Runway/ALCI Airbase provide a platform for unregulated tourism to Dronning Maud Land. Norway recommended that all involved Parties clarify their responsibilities and obligations for permitting and notification of the activities at ALCI airbase in accordance with Antarctic Treaty obligations.

(389) The inspection team did not have sufficient time or appropriate expertise to consider the element of safety sufficiently during the inspection. However, considering the importance of safety in the context of large-scale flight operations, the inspection team did find that it could be useful if DROMLAN, through COMNAP, could report to the ATCM on safety management procedures at Novo Runway/ALCI Airbase.

(390) Many Parties thanked Norway for its excellent inspection report.

(391) The UK noted that the Norwegian inspection team had found it very useful on their arrival at Halley V station to be presented with an already filled out checklist. The UK agreed with Norway that all stations should have relevant information, including the checklist, ready for visiting inspection teams.

(392) Several Parties disagreed that there was a general tendency at Antarctic stations to reduce the number of scientists, compared to technical support staff. The UK explained that the opposite would happen at the new Halley VI station where there would be more scientists and fewer support personnel compared to Halley V.

(393) The United States also noted that the research community is engaging in scientific projects with increasingly industrial components such as drilling and heavy construction, which change the ratio of science to support personnel.

(394) Argentina agreed with the United States that there was a need to have logistic and technical staff and at the same time indicated that there has been an increase in the number of scientists involved in their programme.

(395) The United Kingdom also commended Norway on the effort taken to incorporate comments from all Parties whose stations had been inspected. The United Kingdom further commented on the value of an external inspection team providing a new and outside perspective. It noted that the inspection report may further provide useful recommendations for other stations and Parties not involved in this inspection.

(396) ASOC congratulated Norway on its excellent report and felt it was one of the most thorough and important inspection reports presented to the ATCM to date. ASOC strongly supported the suggestion of establishing long-term strategic scientific priorities at stations in light of the increasing trend away from government-led activities and towards control by private entities, which are more loosely responsible to the ATS. ASOC noted its concern regarding operations at Novo Runway/ALCI Airbase as a platform for unregulated tourism to Dronning Maud Land. ASOC looks forward to future discussions and actions.

(397) Poland noted that Norway's well-balanced report should serve as a model for future reports and that Poland aims to emulate such comprehensive analyses internally.

(398) India complimented Norway for its detailed inspection report and asked for additional details about non-governmental activities, such as the 'White Desert Company' in very close vicinity of the Maitri Station.

(399) The UK responded to India's question, noting that the UK was aware that White Desert Company's role in this area had evolved. Thus, the UK is working closely with White Desert Company and IAATO to ensure the company's activities in Dronning Maud Land are fully regulated in accordance with the requirements of the Antarctic Treaty and the Environmental Protocol.

(400) Belgium informed the Meeting of some new developments relating to Princess Elisabeth Antarctica since the completion of Norway's inspection report. With respect to ownership of the station, Belgium noted that as of 31 March 2010 ownership of the station had been transferred from the private International Polar Foundation (IPF) to the Belgian Federal Science Policy Office and that the building was now almost exclusively owned by the Belgian state. Belgium further informed the Meeting of the recent

establishment of the Polar Secretariat, a cooperative structure formed by the Belgian Federal Science Policy Office and the IPF. In response to a reference in IP 30 to a weakness in the station's communication system, Belgium noted that the station's communication facility had not been completed at the time of the inspection. In addition, Belgium informed the Meeting that the installation was now complete and fully in line with current technology.

(401) The Russian Federation thanked Norway for their report and its importance given the role that Novo airfield plays on operations in the region.

(402) IAATO welcomed Norway's inspection report and agreed with many of the comments from other Parties. This useful paper was noted as helping better to understand the difficulties of operating in the DROMLAN region. IAATO also noted that The Antarctic Company applied for IAATO membership last year. IAATO has observed the company's operation and will be considering the Observer's report during its next annual meeting.

(403) COMNAP referred to section 2.4 (safety) within WP 57 and commented that the DROMLAN group will be meeting on the margins of the upcoming COMNAP annual meeting. The WP 57 request for a report will be conveyed to the DROMLAN group at that time.

(404) Argentina introduced WP 26 *Final Report of the Intersessional Contact Group on the revision of List A "Permanent Antarctic Stations and Associated Installations" appended to Resolution 5 (1995)*. Argentina highlighted that the first revision step was to increase efficiency of inspections and to assist inspectors in making data collection procedures clearer. Argentina further reminded the Meeting that this checklist is a starting point and that other checklists may be revised in the future. Argentina also highlighted the importance of Parties providing information within the EIES as it relates to inspections.

(405) Argentina expressed its thanks to Parties and Experts for their contributions and cooperation in drafting and seeking consensus on the ICG report. Argentina also identified three main changes to the report relating to a reduction in questions and sections of checklist; the inclusion of references to sources of information relating to the Antarctic, such as on-site and off-site inspections to facilitate the work of inspectors; and editorial changes to improve the meaning and scope of questions, provision of examples for inspectors, enhanced reflection of agreed provisions and reservations. Argentina highlighted that these changes aimed to avoid misunderstanding in translation, and enhance consistency.

(406) Many Parties further commented on the value of the checklist as an instrument to assist in focusing on particular priorities at stations, as well as the use of the checklist internally to improve management and performance.

(407) Japan noted the value of having the checklist edited by one person to enhance consistency, and added that the provision of links to websites is beneficial.

(408) The Republic of Korea commented that having the final ICG discussion paper with the checklist on the Secretariat website would make it more easily understood to Parties.

(409) Parties highlighted that the checklist is a guide only, and that it does not replace the work done by inspectors in the field. Rather, the checklist is a tool for inspections or internal reviews by which National Programmes may measure their own compliance and management. Checklists should be viewed within the context of operations and be flexible. Situations, such as weather, may require that checklists be added to or subtracted from on a case-by-case basis.

(410) The United States commented that the right to conduct inspections and the obligation to submit to inspection are key tenets of the Antarctic Treaty. While it is helpful to make checklists as useful and relevant as possible, they are a recommendatory tool, and cannot substitute for active and spontaneous dialogue between those conducting an inspection and those being inspected. The long-recognized purpose of inspections is to verify through observation. Questions contained on inspection checklists may be clear and comprehensive, but they cannot replace full, candid, and unscripted interaction between inspectors and station personnel. Thus, the checklists must not be seen as in any way limiting the scope of inspections carried out under the Treaty.

(411) The United States supported editorial changes and revisions to WP 26. However, the United States noted that, as originally submitted, the checklist was too long and suggested formatting changes to shorten the document. The United States thanked Argentina for their cooperation in shortening the original checklist.

(412) The Meeting welcomed the work done by the ICG and adopted Resolution 3 (2010) (see page 339).

(413) Japan introduced IP 5, *Inspection undertaken by Japan in accordance with Article VII of the Antarctic Treaty and Article XIV of the Protocol on Environmental Protection.* From 29 January to 10 February 2010 Japan

undertook inspections to six stations in Dronning Maud Land: Maitri Station, Neumayer III Station, Novolazarevskaya Station, Princess Elisabeth Station, SANAE IV Base and Troll Station. Japan expressed its gratitude to those who received the inspection team at the stations as well as those in the capitals who enabled the visit. The inspection report is currently being compiled. The draft report will be sent to inspected Parties for their comments. Then, the full report will be submitted to ATCM XXXIV.

(414) IP 6, *Update on the Comprehensive Environmental Evaluation (CEE) of New Indian Research Station at Larsemann Hills, Antarctica (India)*,submitted under this agenda item, was already presented at CEP and taken as read.

Item 13: Science issues, including climate-related research, scientific cooperation and facilitation

Climate Change

(415) The Russian Federation introduced WP 60 *Current tendencies of climate changes based on data of Russian studies in the Antarctic*, a review of the SCAR Antarctic Climate Change and the Environment (ACCE) report, in which it expressed its support for the main points of the report. Russia suggested, however, that earlier SCAR reports on ice cover should be considered in the ACCE, and that further analysis on permafrost and modelling is required. Russia added that climate data should be complimented with data on flora, especially as related to the sub-Antarctic region. Russia suggested that future ACCE reports would benefit if the national expertise of Antarctic Treaty Parties is included in them. Russia commented on the difficulties of language barriers and that work conducted in non-Treaty languages is useful to include. Russia hoped that future ACCE reports would be more comprehensive, and proposed that a similar document be presented by SCAR in 10 years time, to see whether there have been any changes in the trends.

(416) SCAR thanked Russia for its comments and added that SCAR agreed that more permafrost studies were required and that improved modelling studies were needed. SCAR clarified that the link between the ozone hole and the increase in the winds circulating Antarctica (and therefore isolating the continent from much of the effects of global warming) is well established by several studies. SCAR looked forward to working with Russia and other Parties on future updates to the ACCE report.

(417) With regard to WP 60, Argentina congratulated Russia and underscored the importance of having SCAR include scientific documents in languages other than English. In this regard, the Parties should contribute by submitting to SCAR the aforementioned studies. Argentina suggested that within the Meeting of Administrators of Latin American Antarctic Programs (RAPAL) documents in Spanish be sent to SCAR.

(418) SCAR indicated it would have welcomed the inclusion of peer-reviewed studies not available in English had they been available and looked forward to including such studies in the future.

ATME on Climate Change

(419) Norway referred to WP 63 *Report from Antarctic Treaty Meeting of Experts on Implications of Climate Change for Antarctic Management and Governance* and the recommendations from the ATME held in Svolvær, Norway, in April 2010.

(420) Norway noted that because of time constraints it might not be possible to discuss in detail the following 18 recommendations during this ATCM:

Recommendation 1: T*he ATME recommends that the ATCM acknowledge and welcome the SCAR ACCE report as an important resource for its own deliberations and as an input to the wider global climate negotiations, e.g. the UNFCCC.*

Recommendation 2: *The ATME recommends that the ATCM considers developing an Antarctic climate change communication plan to bring the findings of the ACCE report to the attention of other decision makers, the general public and the media.*

Recommendation 3: *The ATME recommends that the ATCM consider how best to provide information about Antarctic climate change to fora discussing and negotiating global climate change.*

Recommendation 4: *The ATME recommends that Parties be requested to:*

- acknowledge and encourage continuing efforts in developing and exchanging experience of energy efficiency and alternative energy practices so as to promote reduction of the carbon footprint of activities in Antarctica and cut fossil fuel use from stations, vessels, ground transportation and aircraft;
- solicit from COMNAP a report on progress on the implementation of its Best Practice for Energy Management – Guidance and

Recommendations (endorsed by CEP X in Delhi), and ask for an update including details of best practices on energy efficiency and alternative energy deployment; and

- welcome the efforts of IAATO in working towards developing best practice towards reducing the carbon footprint of its tour ships.

Recommendation 5: *Recognizing the importance of emission cuts in Antarctica and their symbolic value in the global context, the ATME recommends that the ATCM encourage COMNAP to work with national programmes to use consistent methods to quantify and publish savings made by energy efficiencies, and which contribute to both (a) reducing carbon footprint, and (b) reducing fuel consumption and operating costs.*

Recommendation 6: *The ATME recommend that Parties be advised to use atmospheric models to evaluate the wind regimes around their individual stations, to determine the potential for wind power as a means of cutting fuel costs and greenhouse gas emissions.*

Recommendation 7: *Welcoming the risk assessment approach taken by Australia to identify potential climate change implications for current and future Antarctic infrastructure, logistics and environmental values, the ATME recommends that Parties be encouraged to undertake and report on appropriate risk assessment processes.*

Recommendation 8: *In developing EIAs for new facilities, the ATME recommends that Parties be requested to take climate change considerations into account.*

Recommendation 9: *Noting that the WMO Executive Council Panel of Experts on Polar Observations, Research and Services, promotes and coordinates relevant programs carried out in the polar regions, the ATME recommends that the Panel and others be urged to increase the refinement of Antarctic climate models, and the WMO be invited to provide regular reports to the ATCM to update Parties on progress with outcomes of the Committee's activities.*

Recommendation 10: *The ATME recommends that Parties be advised to expand research that will refine and enhance our ability to predict future climate change with increasing accuracy on various temporal and geographical scales; and to encourage steps to link scientific research efforts to the activities of operational agencies involved in providing climate services and other related activities.*

Recommendation 11: *Given that the IPY has been very successful in significantly increasing the volume and interdisciplinary character of polar research, especially in relation to understanding climate change, the ATME recommends that national agencies be urged to maintain the momentum of that research as a key contribution to the IPY legacy.*

Recommendation 12: *The ATME recommends that Parties be requested to encourage the collaboration required to develop comprehensive and advanced integrated Earth System models capable of producing outputs at decadal scales and regional scales that can be used to assess the likelihood, timing and amplitude of climate change.*

Recommendation 13: *The ATME recommends that Parties be requested to encourage the space agencies to continue coordinated observations of the Antarctic region from space, in the context of improving the operation of observing systems for climate change, and to attend a future ATCM to give a demonstration of the use of modern space-based technologies for observing the Antarctic region in the context of climate change.*

Recommendation 14: *The ATME recommends that Parties be requested to continue to strongly encourage collaboration and development of sustained integrated observing systems using in situ, air and space-based techniques.*

Recommendation 15: *Recognizing that Parties are obliged under the Treaty to share scientific data and information, and that there is a great deal to be gained from working more closely together on the collection of observations of climate change and its effects, the ATME recommends that Parties be requested to encourage greater collaboration in such collections, and to support access to such data through the Antarctic Master Directory.*

Recommendation 16: *The ATME recommends that Parties be requested to encourage national operators and SCAR to seek close cooperation and synergies with existing climate observing and assessment initiatives such as the Global Climate Observing System (GCOS) and the IPCC.*

Recommendation 17: *The ATME recommends that the ATCM encourages SCAR to incorporate identification of key regions, habitats and species at greatest risk from climate change effects into its research programmes.*

Recommendation 18: *The ATME recommends that ATCM and CEP give consideration to taking a more regional approach in the application of environmental management tools, in addition to the current continent-wide approach.*

(421) The Meeting supported that the ATME recommendations which were not given full consideration at this meeting should be considered at the next ATCM.

(422) Sweden lent its support to Norway's proposal but believed at least Recommendation 1 (possibly more) was worthy of attention at this ATCM, pointing out that this was the first report from SCAR on climate change. In an effort to address SCAR's report as soon as possible (noting the report was published in 2009), Sweden suggested that the ATCM take action on Recommendation 1 from the ATME on climate change already this year.

(423) The United Kingdom agreed that it was important to address these topics at this ATCM and highlighted the relevance of several recommendations, including four and five, to COMNAP.

(424) Sweden proposed the Meeting to adopt a Resolution and a Decision on SCAR's report Antarctic Climate Change and the Environment (ACCE) in order to address recommendation one from the ATME. The Resolution would acknowledge and welcome the SCAR ACCE report as an important resource for further ATCM deliberations and as an input to the wider global climate negotiations, for example, the United Nations Framework Convention on Climate Change (UNFCCC). The Decision would task to the Chairman of the ATCM with the sending of letters to those international bodies that deal with Antarctic related issues.

(425) With regards to IP 46 *Antarctic Climate Change and the Environment – An Update* (SCAR), SCAR reminded the Delegates that SCAR will provide regular updates to the ACCE report and will actively seek input from the SCAR Members and other interested parties.

(426) After some discussion among Parties and SCAR, the Meeting adopted Decision 5 (2010) *Letters to UNFCCC, IPCC, WMO and IMO* and Resolution 4 (2010) *SCAR Antarctic Climate Change and the Environment Report.*

(427) COMNAP commented that Recommendation 4 from the ATME on climate change was added to the CEP 5-Year Work Plan and that it will be further discussed at the upcoming COMNAP meeting. In relation to Recommendation 5 of the ATME on climate change, COMNAP has an expert group which discusses and encourages cooperation on energy issues. It also drew attention to the COMNAP workshop to be held on 8 August 2010 on energy management and technology and the COMNAP Symposium

on 11 August 2010 with the theme "Responding to change through new approaches." COMNAP noted that the symposium is an open event and encouraged participation.

(428) Australia presented IP 105 *Management implications of climate change in the Antarctic region – an initial Australian assessment.* The paper notes that in preparation for Australia's participation in the ATME on Climate Change and Implications for Antarctic Management and Governance, the Australian Antarctic Division (AAD) held a workshop to undertake a preliminary Antarctic climate risk assessment. The workshop followed a standard risk assessment process and highlighted a range of implications for existing and future infrastructure, logistics and environmental values.

(429) The Meeting welcomed Australia's approach and, consistent with Recommendation 7 from the Meeting of Experts, recommended that Parties be encouraged to undertake and report on appropriate risk assessments.

(430) New Zealand introduced IP 37, *Ross Island Wind Energy Project: Sustainability through collaboration* (New Zealand, United States) reporting that the New Zealand and United States Antarctic Programmes have cooperated on the establishment of a three turbine wind farm that will provide up to 70% of the electrical requirements for Scott Base and McMurdo Station. New Zealand noted the value of the collaborative approach taken, the joint commitment to a more sustainable approach to operations on Ross Island, and looked forward to ongoing cooperation with the United States.

(431) The United States noted that the Ross Island Wind Energy project is a collaboration in the context of the joint logistics pool with New Zealand, and that the project has resulted in a shared power grid between McMurdo Station and Scott Base. Further work on the power grid will be carried out during the 2010-2011 season as the United States completes long term upgrades to the McMurdo power plant.

(432) ASOC noted the usefulness of IP 37 on the Ross Island wind project and thanked New Zealand and the United States for the informative paper, which reflects recommendations in ASOC IP 73 on key climate change actions in Antarctica. The US-NZ project clearly demonstrates the opportunity for emissions reductions in Antarctica. ASOC noted that the NZ-US efforts are in line with Recommendation 4 from the ATME on climate change, which requests the Parties "acknowledge and encourage" efforts to develop and share energy efficiency practices. This is an important recommendation and ASOC encouraged Parties to think of ways to implement it.

(433) ASOC introduced IP 73, *Key Climate Change Actions in Antarctica: Emissions Reduction, Adaptation and Science.*

(434) The Russian Federation thanked New Zealand and the United States for IP 37 and inquired if the wind energy project environmental impact studies had identified issues with the impacts of infrasound on living organisms, in particular humans.

(435) New Zealand reported that it had conducted a thorough initial environmental evaluation for the project, including an assessment of potential impacts on science in the area, as well as on flora and fauna. This assessment was followed up by three seasons of monitoring.

(436) The United States further informed the Meeting that the environmental impact assessment considered the impacts of infrasound on scientific instrumentation. The environmental impact assessment also considered sound audible to humans and noted that is not possible to hear the turbines at either McMurdo Station or Scott Base.

(437) Argentina reminded the Meeting that this topic would also be discussed at the next COMNAP meeting in addition to many other fora. It also pointed out that many Parties are interested in the impacts from infrasound on the human population in Antarctica.

(438) Argentina presented IP 108, *XXXI SCAR Meeting – XXII COMNAP Meeting Buenos Aires – 2010. Argentine invitation for participants.* Argentina extended a warm invitation to the XXXI SCAR Meeting and its Open Science Conference (OSC) as well as the XXII meeting of COMNAP, to take place in Buenos Aires between July 30 and August 12, 2010. The Open Scientific Conference (OSC), titled *"Antarctica – Witness to the Past and Guide to the Future,"* is SCAR's first major scientific meeting after the finalization of the field and observation activities undertaken as part of the IPY.

(439) Argentina presented IP 109, *Grants program to attend SCAR-OSC 2010* and noted that it has awarded fellowships to all of the 124 young scientists and researchers from 18 countries who applied to attend the OSC. Argentina indicated that although the deadline to apply for a fellowship had passed, it would continue to receive applications and asked Parties to make this known within their countries.

(440) Romania congratulated Argentina on its announcement and its support of young polar scientists and researchers from many nations that work in polar regions.

(441) The Republic of Korea presented IP 55, *Scientific and Science-related Collaborations with Other Parties During 2009-2010.* These collaborations were on Hydroacoustic monitoring in the Bransfield Strait (United States); International collaboration on the study of Antarctic oscillation and its impact on mid-latitude climate (China); International collaborative marine and Quaternary geosciences research on abrupt environmental change in the Larsen Ice Shelf system (United States); the 16th International Symposium on Polar Sciences (held in Korea in June 2009) and the 17th International Symposium on Polar Sciences (in May 26-28, 2010); and the first year of the Korea-UK Focal Point Project. The Republic of Korea noted it anticipates the projects with scientists from the United States, China and UK to continue for a number of years.

(442) Japan introduced IP 63 *Preliminary Plan for Installation and Operation of the PANSY Atmospheric Radar System at Syowa Station.* The plan calls for the installation of an antenna system and associated facilities at Syowa station, to help understand the atmospheric system through the measurement of wind and plasma parameters from the surface up to 500km and to contribute to improving global atmospheric models for better forecasting the future global climate. Japan noted that SCAR and several other academic associations have endorsed the project. The system will be one of the largest such systems in the world and the first in Antarctica. The measurement is planned to continue for at least twelve years to cover one cycle of solar activity. After completion of observations, this antenna system will be removed and the environment will be restored to its original condition.

(443) ASOC congratulated Japan for its PANSY paper, including its plan to remove everything when the project is finished.

(444) China introduced IP 38 *The Meeting Report of the 10th AFoPS.* China noted that the 10th Asian Forum of Polar Science was held from July 9 to 10, 2009 in Shanghai, China, hosted by the Polar Research Institute of China. The AFoPS is a polar summit meeting held to promote communication and cooperation on polar science among Asian national Programme leaders and scientists. AFoPS countries are encouraged to invite young scientists from non-polar Asian countries to carry out field work in their research agencies and stations. The 11th AFoPS will be held in June 2010 in Shanghai.

(445) Romania introduced IP 97 *European and International Partnership in Polar Climate Science*, noting the participation of Australia, Bulgaria, Czech Republic, Denmark, Estonia, India, Italy, Poland, Romania, Russian Federation, Spain and Ukraine in the INTER-HEMISPHERE project.

Romania noted that the project will address the structure and dynamics of polar ecosystems through inter-hemispheric comparisons of micro, macroflora and biogeochemical processes in relation to climate change. This project will apply the recommendations from the ATME on climate change.

(446) Romania also introduced IP 101 *Scientific Activities in the Law-Racovita Station with Logistic Support of India January-February 2009*. Romania thanked India for its logistic support of research activities conducted by scientists from India, Estonia and Australia. The preliminary results of the research will be presented at the IPY Oslo Science Conference in June 2010.

(447) Bulgaria introduced IP 103 *The Bulgarian Antarctica Project about Multimedia Installation*, reporting that the project comprises an installation that will combine sculpture, photography, and video productions with a collection of scientific data, logistical devices, and ordinary objects from the St Kliment Ohridski station on Livingston Island. The project is intended to develop a parallel between art and science and will focus on the work of Bulgarian scientists within the landscape and climate of Antarctica. The final installation will be exhibited in 2010-2011 at Sofia University and at the gallery of the National Academy of Fine Arts in Bulgaria, as well at Wright State University in Ohio, United States.

(448) Chile introduced IP 87 *Two recent International Climate Change Scientific Events held in Chile*, noting that both events gathered important groups of international scientists. The two events were: The International Colloquium "Climate Change in Magellan and Antarctic Regions: Evidence for the Future" and the International Glaciological conference "Ice and Climate Change: A View from the South" (VICC 2010). The colloquium included a wide audience of local authorities, decision makers, academics, students and the general public. The objectives of the conference were to present new results and discuss ongoing cryospheric and climate changes in the Southern Hemisphere and their impacts and consequences on society and the environment.

(449) ASOC introduced IP 83 *Rising to the challenge: Key steps to deliver a Comprehensive and Representative Marine Protected Areas Network in the Southern Ocean by 2019*. ASOC had presented this paper to the CEP.

(450) ASOC also introduced IP 77 *The Case for Inclusion of the Ross Sea Continental Shelf and Slope in a Southern Ocean Network of Marine Reserves*, again noting that the paper had been presented and discussed at the CEP.

(451) Ecuador introduced IP 119 *Estimación del balance de masa sobre el Glaciar Quito en Punta Fort William,* reporting on studies comparing work on Antarctic glaciers with tropical glaciers in Ecuador; IP 120 *Ejes de Investigación del Instituto Antártico Ecuatoriano,* presenting an overview of four main fields of research activities; IP 121 *Estimación de riesgo al cambio climático y la variabilidad climática, en los ecosistemas terrestres circundantes y en la infraestructura física de la Estación Científica Maldonado,* discussing risk assessments of climate change and climate variability on the land systems surrounding Ecuador's station; and IP 123 *Desarrollo de robots submarinos autónomos no tripulados para exploración antártica,* noting an interesting programme on the use of autonomous robots.

(452) Ecuador also introduced IP 126 *Informe del V Simposio Latinoamericano sobre Investigaciones Antárticas y II Simposio Ecuatoriano de Ciencia Polar, Ecuador 2009,* reporting on the 5th Latin American Symposium on Antarctic Research and the 2nd Ecuadorian Symposium on Polar Science held in August 2009 to commemorate the 50th Anniversary of the signing of the Antarctic Treaty, the bicentenary of the first Call for Independence in Latin America and the bicentenary of the birth of Charles Darwin. Ecuador noted that close to 200 participants from seven Latin American countries participated in the symposia, clearly demonstrating progress in all Antarctic activities by Latin American scientists and researchers. Ecuador also noted the availability of the final report of the symposia, including availability on CD for all interested Parties.

(453) The Russian Federation introduced IP 90 *Results of Russian studies of subglacial lake Vostok in the season 2009-2010.* Russia gave a brief account of drilling activities at Vostok station in the 2009-2010 season, including the deflection of a faulty borehole and resumption of drilling in a new branch of the borehole starting at the depth of 3590m. Russia reported that the new ice cores contained mineral inclusions, consistent with drilling in the original branch of the borehole, but at higher concentrations than thought to be present. The ice cores also contained other minerals not previously identified. Russia noted information on seismic studies by method of reflected waves of the deep geological structure of the valley where Lake Vostok is located. Russia and Germany will conduct joint research in the future.

(454) Romania noted that the results of Russia's research with respect to drift direction and speed of glacial movement represents new data valuable for continuing research. Romania also noted its gratitude to Russia and Australia

97

for its field support to Romania and welcomed cooperation and assistance from other Parties in continuing Romania's Antarctic activities. Romania highlighted its gratitude for assistance in developing the European and international project "Inter-hemisphere" which is coordinated by Romania and monitored by the European Science Foundation and the European Polar Board, respectively.

(455) Russia introduced IP 91 *Russian Research in the Antarctic in 2009*. Russia noted its studies in 2009 on climate change, the bio-productivity of Antarctic waters in the main commercial fishing areas, an analysis of the bird populations in the vicinity of Bellingshausen station, and other activities.

(456) SCAR briefly introduced IP 50 *The Southern Ocean Observing System (SOOS)*, noting that the SOOS plan presents a community view of the need for, relevance of and feasibility of a sustained observing system in the Southern Ocean, which has direct relevance to both climate and ecosystem studies. A version of the SOOS plan is currently being finalised. This will be made available for comment to interested Parties before a final version of the plan is produced. SCAR has agreed to provide the full plan for the next ATCM.

(457) China noted that copies of the National Annual Report on Polar Program of China highlighting recent Chinese scientific activity had been placed in each Party's pigeon hole. Parties wishing additional copies should contact the Chinese delegation.

(458) The following papers submitted under this agenda item were not introduced and were taken as read:

- IP 3 *The SCAR Lecture Psychrophiles: a challenge for life* (SCAR)
- IP 17 *1ˢᵗ India-Brazil-South Africa (IBSA) Dialogue Forum Seminar on Antarctica: exchange amongst Antarctic programs* (Brazil, India, South Africa)
- IP 47 *Census of Antarctic Marine Life* (CAML) (SCAR, Australia)
- IP 65 *Japan's Antarctic Research Highlights in 2009-2010* (Japan)
- IP 66 *SCAR Data and Information Strategy (DIMS)* (SCAR)
- IP 73 *Key Climate Change Actions in Antarctica: Emissions Reduction, Adaptation and Science* (ASOC)

- IP 117 *Biodiversidad Microbiológica y Aplicaciones Biotecnológicas* (Ecuador)

Item 14: Operational Issues

(459) ASOC introduced IP 68, *Working Towards a Polar Vessel Code* which addressed both recent developments in elaborating a Polar Code and also provided a follow-up to the Wellington ATME. ASOC noted that work on the mandatory Polar Code at the IMO has now commenced and is making fairly rapid progress – with a Correspondence Group up and running and its report due to be completed over the next 3 – 4 months. ASOC highlighted two recommendations in IP 68 pertinent to the development of the Polar Code:

- The urgent need for the ATCM to consider the essential elements for inclusion in the Polar Code and to ensure this is input to the IMO's Correspondence group and subsequent meetings. Some work was undertaken by an informal contact group at the Wellington ATME and could be forwarded to the Correspondence Group.
- The need for the ATCM to consider the detail of a Polar Code as it is developed. Annex II of IP 68 sets out ASOC's views on the detailed elements of a Polar Code, and in summary ASOC highlighted the need for a broad scope to the Polar Code which addresses all vessels operating in the Southern Ocean; the need for mandatory provisions for all vessels as far as possible; the need to consider all aspects of safety, environmental protection, and infrastructure support including search & rescue, environmental response, traffic monitoring and port state control.

ASOC reiterated its view that the Polar Code be a "one-stop" shop for polar vessels, urging that ATCM decides and agrees on how to ensure that the needs of vessels operating in Antarctic waters are met through the mandatory Polar Code.

(460) France welcomed ASOC's paper, noting many states were supporting the IMO's development of the Polar Code. France noted the importance of maintaining consistency in regulations among the Arctic and Antarctic regions. France stressed the need for the ATCM to be flexible, and was supportive of a forum on the ATS website for members to express views and exchange ideas. France noted it had some concern with the suggestions

in IP 68, noting that in its view, a Memorandum of Understanding (MOU) between the IMO and the ATCM would be too formal.

(461) Norway supported maintaining the momentum gained by the ATCM in cooperating with the IMO, and noted its support for development of a mandatory Polar Code. When discussing the differences between the Arctic and Antarctic regions, Norway pointed to similarities in navigating in ice covered waters.

(462) Other Parties considered that the Polar Code should apply universally to the Arctic and Antarctic regions. The United Kingdom noted that whilst the development of the mandatory Polar Code within IMO's Design and Equipment subcommittee was an important place setter for the management of Antarctic ship traffic, it was also important to consider inputs into other IMO committees such as the Marine Environment Protection Committee (MEPC) regarding other relevant ATCM issues.

(463) The Russian Federation indicated its support for a mandatory Polar Code. It drew on its experience and history in the polar regions, noting its view that ice conditions between the Arctic and Antarctic areas are vastly different, and further noting that the Arctic was a region characterised by a network of ports, facilities, permanent satellites and aircraft-based observations for which there is no equivalent in Antarctica. Russia explained that these regions require different vessel design, crew training, and search and rescue capabilities.

(464) Argentina and Uruguay emphasised the need to take into account Antarctica's unique nature in the development of a Polar Code.

(465) The United States presented IP 27 rev. 1, *Energy Management Strategies for U.S. Antarctic Research Stations*. The United States provided a presentation highlighting the approach to managing the reduction of fuel consumption and energy production at its research stations. This approach includes the recovery of waste heat from conventional generators for building heating, computerised "Smart Grid" power management systems, and the integration of alternative energy from wind into the Ross Island power grid through a joint programme with New Zealand. The United States also noted other improvements in energy efficiency from the South Pole overland traverse and a future project to develop modular, multi-purpose solar modules for accommodations and laboratory space in the field.

(466) Many Parties and ASOC congratulated the United States for its paper.

(467) France congratulated the United States for their presentation and noted that it had experience in replacing fossil fuels with natural energy sources like wind energy, but had found that the reduction in the consumption of conventional fuels is not proportionate to the amount of wind energy fed into the network, due to threshold effects related to the conventional production of power.

(468) The United States thanked France for its support and concurred that wind energy is an intermittent resource and therefore cannot fully replace conventional power generation at larger stations. The United States also concurred that the challenge is to find the appropriate threshold of power generation and to use operational techniques and Smart Grid power management systems to allow demand to be met by a combination of conventional and alternative energy systems for maximum efficiency. This may also include the use of smaller "peaking" generators designed to meet small, short term energy demands which cannot be eliminated or met by alternative systems.

(469) The United States further commended France for its significant efforts to promote energy conservation at Dome Concordia and noted that the United States was implementing many of the same technological solutions at McMurdo and other stations.

(470) Chile indicated it is constantly involved in efforts to reduce the fuel consumption required by its presence throughout the entire year in the Antarctic. Chile noted that it has experimented with wind energy and has one vertical wind turbine in operation at one of its bases. The wind turbine is used such that it minimises disruption of fauna.

(471) ASOC noted that the U.S. papers shows what can be done when a Party 'rolls up its sleeves' to find ways to save energy, reduce CO2 emissions, and save money, which can be used to support science. ASOC noted that this is relevant to ATME Recommendation 5 on Climate Change, which requests COMNAP to work with Parties on "consistent methods to quantify and publish savings made by energy efficiencies".

(472) The Republic of Korea congratulated the United States and agreed with ASOC's suggestion that the United States' energy management strategy should be discussed at the next COMNAP symposium.

(473) Argentina noted that it is also working on alternative energy approaches and will present them at the COMNAP symposium.

(474) Romania noted that some of the technologies employed require large and comprehensive engineering solutions.

(475) Argentina introduced IP 23, *Report of clean-up efforts by the Argentinian National Antarctic Program in the area of the Neko Harbour refuge (north-west coast of the Antarctic Peninsula)*. Argentina provided details on the clean-up operation to remove the remains of a hut at Neko Harbour, on the west side of the Antarctic Peninsula. The refuge was completely destroyed by a gale during the 2008/09 season, likely after the door to the refuge was left open by a visitor. After collecting the debris, Argentina has placed a plaque at the site commemorating the refuge. Argentina could reconstruct the hut in the near future. Argentina noted that it was informed of the destruction by IAATO.

(476) ASOC presented IP 74 *Energy Efficiency and Renewable Energy Under Extreme Conditions: Case Studies From Antarctica*. Years of successful operation of energy efficiency and renewable energy at different stations demonstrate that these can substantially reduce energy use and save money. ASOC urged Parties to follow up on the recommendations from the ATME on Climate Change, especially recommendations 4 and 5, to reinforce and build a supportive environment which would further foster such innovations.

(477) Several Parties thanked ASOC.

(478) Australia noted that it had undertaken a range of initiatives to improve the energy efficiency of its stations, including installing wind turbines, energy efficient lighting, energy efficient refrigeration, variable speed drives and building monitoring control systems (BMCS). These actions had reduced the cost and environmental risks associated with the handling, transport and storage of fuel.

(479) Several Parties noted the importance of an integrated approach to energy efficiency as identified in the U.S. paper, and stressed both the environmental and economic value of installing and maintaining up to date technology at Antarctic stations.

(480) India noted that bipolar perspectives on these issues are useful to enrich discussion.

(481) The Republic of Korea introduced IP 56 *The First Antarctic Expedition of Araon*, informing the Meeting that the Korean icebreaker *Araon* was completed and embarked for Antarctica last season. In Korea's work to identify a site for a second station, Korean scientists conducted in depth

surveys at two candidate sites using *Araon*. The Republic of Korea thanked the Russian Federation and New Zealand for their support.

(482) The Russian Federation congratulated the Republic of Korea on the success of their voyage to Antarctica.

(483) The following papers submitted under this agenda item were taken as read:

- IP 54 *The Republic of Korea's contribution to Antarctic science by installing a new permanent station in Terra Nova Bay, Ross Sea* (Korea)
- IP 106 *New state of the art polar research and supply vessel for South Africa* (South Africa)
- IP 110 *Dismantling and subsequent use of Neumayer Station II for SANAP Summer Station and Russian Antarctic Expedition* (Germany and South Africa)

Item 15: Education Issues

(484) SCAR presented IP 28 *The Association of Polar Early Career Scientists (APECS): Shaping the Future of Polar Research*. SCAR informed Parties that, established during the planning stages of the International Polar Year, APECS has evolved into the pre-eminent international organisation supporting polar researchers in the beginning or early stages of their careers. APECS provides a strong voice for young researchers, enabling information sharing between early-career and more established professionals, promoting and organizing science, education and outreach events, and being actively involved with other polar organizations in the support of polar research. APECS has signed Memoranda of Understanding with both SCAR and the International Arctic Science Committee (IASC). SCAR recommended that Parties interact with APECS on educational and other related issues.

(485) Chile introduced IP 85 *The Chilean Antarctic scientific program: A leap forward*, noting two changes: the introduction of an open competitive system for project selection; and a significant increase in national project funding, which resulted in a leap in the number of accepted projects, and an increase in logistical support for these projects.

(486) Chile next introduced IP 86 T*hree strategies to talk about Antarctic and science when nobody knows what you're talking about*, commenting on the development of three strategies relating to scientific events that promote the dissemination of scientific information amongst youth in Chile.

(487) Chile also presented IP 124 *Activities carried out in Chile to commemorate the Fiftieth Anniversary of the signing of the Antarctic Treaty*. Chile noted that a series of articles devoted to Antarctica were published in two issues of the Diplomacy Journal of Chile.

(488) Argentina noted its reserve with some of the contents of IP 124 submitted by Chile, due to lack of time to read all documents.

(489) Uruguay drew attention to IP 29 *The Uruguayan Antarctic Institute's educational and awareness-raising activities in 2009-2010*, commenting on the range of national interactive activities and programmes developed by Uruguay aimed at promoting Antarctica to school children.

(490) The Republic of Korea introduced IP 57 *Highlight of Korean Outreach Programmes 2009-2010*, commenting on national initiatives aimed at enhancing scientific spirit within the wider community. The Republic of Korea also expressed its desire to further discussion on the issue of joint programmes among Parties.

(491) The Russian Federation introduced IP 89 *Training and education center at Bellingshausen station*. The Russian Federation noted the initiative is aimed at young scientists, students and academics, and highlighted the success of a two week course at Bellingshausen which dealt with important issues such as climate change. The Russian Federation further noted that a course in satellite geodesy in Antarctica is planned for 2012 in partnership with the Technical University of Dresden, and noted the reconstruction of buildings at Bellingshausen for educational purposes.

(492) The Republic of Korea thanked the Russian Federation for its paper and offered its support of potentially providing lectures at Bellingshausen courses in the future.

(493) Romania highlighted the importance of scientific integration and cooperation, particularly concerning the development of programmes aimed at supporting young scientists and information exchange in Antarctica.

(494) The following paper was submitted under this agenda item was taken as read:

- IP 95 *Management Report of Narębski Point, ASPA No 171 (2009-2010)* (Korea)

Item 16: Exchange of Information

(495) The Secretariat introduced SP 9 *Electronic Information Exchange System (EIES): Report on the 2nd operational season and summary information examples*. The Secretariat informed the Meeting that as of 1 March, 2010, fifteen of the twenty-eight Consultative Parties and two Non Consultative Parties had supplied pre-season information for 2009/2010 in any way. Two Parties have reported by sending a document to the Secretariat or linking to their website while the others used the EIES. Other three Consultative Parties have supplied data to the system but have not yet completed a pre-seasonal report.

(496) The Secretariat noted that this was the first season in which Parties could upload their annual report. The Secretariat further noted that requests to improve the system had been adopted where technically feasible. The Executive Secretary informed the Meeting that the Secretariat is not in a position to assess the completeness or quality of the data, since each Party is responsible for the content of the data which it submits.

(497) The Meeting thanked the Secretariat for its considerable effort and excellent work in reporting on the EIES and upgrading the system over the last year.

(498) Germany commented on the importance of the EIES as an informative tool, and introduced WP 41 *Antarctic Treaty Information Exchange via the Electronic Information Exchange System (EIES): Current state and improvements for a consistent use*. Germany noted different ways in which "scientific activities of the previous year" in the annual report can be interpreted and some limitations in the pre-season report. Germany noted further that there seems to be no consensus between Parties on presenting the required information. While several Parties follow the requirements of the regulations, others seem to have difficulties in submitting their data for exchange. Germany proposed the convening of an ICG to discuss ways of improving the system, and expressed its desire to discuss the issue further at the next ATCM.

(499) Several Parties thanked Germany for their paper.

(500) The United States, United Kingdom and Norway suggested that the focus of the EIES should be on promoting information exchange, and that the Meeting should allow the Secretariat to continue its work at this time without the need for setting up an ICG to look at information system requirements.

(501) Some Parties noted with regret that although CEP XII had encouraged Members to achieve 100 per cent usage of the EIES during the intersessional period, this request was not fulfilled.

(502) The UK also noted that the CEP had recommended that the Secretariat should send out a reminder to the Parties that the new EIES was available and that they should now use it for information exchange.

(503) The Meeting and ASOC expressed deep concern at the fact that only fifteen Parties had provided information to the EIES in any form. The Meeting noted the legal obligation of Parties to participate in the EIES and urged all Parties to act accordingly to ensure 100 percent participation in the system.

Item 17: Biological Prospecting in Antarctica

(504) SCAR introduced WP 2 *Biological Prospecting in the Antarctic region: a conservative overview of current research*. It had reviewed the most recent published research, which may have involved biological prospecting in the Antarctic, provided an assessment of these efforts, and conducted a survey of ongoing biological prospecting research being undertaken within the SCAR community. The review had concluded that "bio-prospecting research in the Antarctic region and/or involving Antarctic organisms is extensive and widespread." SCAR also noted that there were varying perspectives on the definition of bio-prospecting.

(505) Belgium introduced IP 96 *The Role of Ex-Situ Collections in Antarctic Bioprospecting*, a joint paper with UNEP. It highlighted the importance of *ex situ* collections in biological prospecting and for the study, conservation and use of Antarctic biodiversity. The annex to IP 96 was a preliminary list of *ex situ* collections, and Belgium, noting that other collections would be a welcome addition to the list, called for enhanced sharing of information amongst Parties.

(506) The Netherlands introduced WP 13 *Report of the ATCM Intersessional Contact Group to Examine the Issue of Biological Prospecting in the Antarctic Treaty Area*. It thanked the Secretariat for its assistance as well as participants of the ATCM Discussion forum, and noted that all 13 sub-issues were addressed by participants (13 consultative parties and ASOC).

(507) The Netherlands also introduced WP 24 *Principles for the Access to and Use of Biological Material in the Antarctic Treaty Area*, based on Resolution 9 (2009), that the ATS "is the appropriate framework for managing the

collection of biological materials in the Antarctic Treaty area and for considering its use". The ten principles in WP 24 aimed to identify policy options for the regulation of access to, and use of, Antarctic biological material. The Netherlands also stated a desire to see harmonisation of international agreements on bioprospecting as much as possible, noting that a bio-prospecting regime within the ATS could set an example for any future global regime.

(508) Several Parties thanked SCAR, Belgium, and the Netherlands for their work and the Netherlands for hosting the ICG. While some Parties considered the concepts in WP 24 might provide a basis for future discussion, others thought they were neither sufficiently defined nor was there consensus on the concepts to allow for an agreement based on these points.

(509) Chile acknowledged the progress made in the ICG and reported in WP 13, and encouraged Parties to set boundaries or a scope for bio-prospecting. Sweden suggested the formulation of clear rules for bio-prospecting with particular reference to the needs of industry for security of patents and also to potential options for benefit sharing. The United Kingdom noted that the papers highlighted differences in the definition of biological prospecting, especially if reports under Resolution 7 (2005) are compared with the results in WP 2. Japan also noted the absence of definition and expressed its concern that benefit sharing might discourage scientific research and innovation in Antarctica. It also noted that the ATCM, not other fora, is the appropriate body to deal with this issue.

(510) Australia noted the rich diversity of views on the subject of bio-prospecting and reaffirmed the common consensus that the Antarctic Treaty System is the appropriate framework for managing bio-prospecting in Antarctica. Several other Parties agreed. Australia recalled the comprehensive framework under the Treaty and the Protocol for managing the environmental aspects of bio-prospecting and cautioned against making assumptions that bio-prospecting necessarily caused environmental damage. It queried the justification for taxing only one kind of scientific research or commercial activity. Given the lack of consensus on many aspects of bio-prospecting, it was hesitant to launch into a full discussion of the proposed principles in WP 24.

(511) The United States noted that WP 13 showed the diversity of views among the Parties and that consensus was still lacking on the way forward.

(512) ASOC congratulated the authors for their papers and noted that the information from WP 2 should help move the ATCM forward in regard

to bio-prospecting. It also requested more information about the lack of compliance with Resolution 7 (2005), noting the importance of current information being shared.

(513) The Netherlands noted that according to the mandate of the ICG, WP 13 did not contain recommendations. It also noted that the term "biological materials" and the information for the first principle in WP 24 were taken from Resolution 9 (2009). WP 24 was the Netherlands' national contribution to encourage discussion and further consideration of the issue in the spirit of Resolution 9 (2009). The Netherlands said it would consider preparing a further paper elaborating on the ten principles contained in WP 24 for consideration at ATCM XXXIV.

(514) Italy suggested that the ATCM should not disregard the fact that normative development might take place in other fora. Italy also strongly emphasised its view that Antarctic could not in theory be excluded from other regimes. Therefore, Italy believed that it is important to adopt specific Antarctic provisions on bioprospecting.

(515) China indicated the need to inform other relevant fora of the adoption of Resolution 9 (2009) and called for actions to be taken to that end.

(516) On this point, Japan expressed its view that this could be done by Parties communicating internally within their respective governments and by drawing attention to Resolution 9 (2009) in those other fora. The Meeting strongly supported Japan's proposal.

(517) CCAMLR noted that given the reference to CCAMLR in Resolution 9 (2009), that should the ATCM consider engaging CCAMLR in discussions on bio-prospecting, it requested early advice of possible areas CCAMLR might be invited to contribute to.

(518) Several Parties felt it important to retain bio-prospecting on the agenda. They supported the idea of encouraging Members to put forward working papers on this subject as had been done in the past. The Netherlands, while supportive of a general request for working papers at ATCM XXXIV, stated that would probably not be sufficient for obtaining new material on bio-prospecting. The Netherlands indicated its willingness to chair a third ICG on the subject but requested Terms of Reference that would encourage new views, ideas, and ways forward from the ICG. Some Parties questioned the value of establishing a further ICG and noted that they did not have the resources to participate in such a process.

Item 18: Development of a Multi-Year Strategic Work Plan

(519) The Chairman asked the Meeting for its advice on how to address the agenda item on the Multi-year Strategic Plan since no working paper or information paper had been submitted. A number of Parties noted that this issue had received extensive debate at ATCM XXXII and suggested that the report of this debate and associated materials should enable the Meeting to discussion strategic priorities for the ATCM.

(520) Norway introduced a proposal under the agenda item on a Multi-year Strategic Work Plan to organize the work of the ATCM. Norway noted that it was important for the ATCM to improve its efficiency and that it would be important to consider ways to make the meeting shorter. Based on lessons learned and considering the effort, time and resources that went into the Antarctic Treaty Consultative Meetings, it felt that the time had come for a thorough assessment of whether the meetings could be organised in a shorter and more efficient manner.

(521) Recognising the importance of the work carried out at the meetings and the effective functioning of the ATCM, further improvements may be made by:

- Shortening the meetings at both ends, eg, starting on Wednesday in the first week, (with the meeting of the Heads of Delegation on Tuesday evening) and ending the ATCM by lunch on Thursday in the following week. This would give 6.5 effective meeting days (compared to today's 10), with the opportunity to consider utilising days of the weekend in between if necessary.

(522) Some initiatives would have to be considered to allow for a shortening of the total time allocated for the meeting, eg:

- A general review and update of the agenda, including consideration of whether some of the ATCM agenda items could be merged or replaced by new items, or removed from the agenda; or
- Whether there may be agenda items that could be handled every second year instead of on an annual basis.
- Time used for presentation could be significantly reduced by assuming that IPs had been read in advance of the meeting, and that IPs were presented to the meetings only when considered necessary to inform the discussions at hand. Some IPs may be circulated intersessionally with no need to be considered at the ATCM. Some papers provided by experts who could not provide WPs to the Meeting might need presentation;

- For specific questions that may require more in depth discussions substantial time for consideration may be provided by holding expert meetings (or other relevant fora). Furthermore, more extensive use of ICGs could also be considered in this context. The latter had been proven to work successfully for clearly identified specific issues.

(523) In addition to shortening the length of the meeting, Norway felt that consideration could be given to how more time could be allocated to the ATCM for discussion of overarching/holistic issues.

(524) The proposal was welcomed by the Meeting, and it was agreed that work on this subject should proceed as a matter of priority. There was general agreement to reduce the length of the meeting. Some Parties indicated acceptability of starting on Tuesday afternoon and ending at noon on Thursday the following week.

(525) Some suggestions put forward by Parties for consideration included:

- The need to focus on the quality of the agenda/meeting by giving higher priority to fundamental issues such as science, environmental protection, impacts of climate change in Antarctica, tourism, coordination of ATS with other bodies.
- A need to look closely at how to organise the meeting in a more efficient way.
- Shortening the meeting should have positive budget implications.
- Some issues should be given higher priority than others.
- Need for long-term strategic planning.
- Consideration of the structure of Working Groups.
- Urge Parties to submit WPs jointly with other Parties, in order to increase consultation and build support for proposals before Meetings.
- Agreement that IPs normally should not be presented at meetings, but could be presented intersessionally. The exception could be that experts/observers who were not authorised to present WPs would be allowed to present IPs.
- In order to keep the meetings within the time limits suggested, evening and weekend meetings/informal contact groups without interpretation might be used, if required.
- Working towards paperless meetings, for example, starting from not printing those ATCM papers posted on the website in advance of an ATCM.

- A decision to be made in Buenos Aires and implemented for future meetings as soon as possible, taking into account the need to allow the host country sufficient time to alter administrative arrangements.
- The holding of intersessional expert meetings.
- The importance of brief presentations.

It was recognised that this was an indicative list only, not exhaustive, of points which could be the subject of consideration.

(526) Regarding the CEP:

- Explore whether the timing of the CEP Meeting could also be revised, taking into account the need to ensure sufficient time to complete its agenda.
- Safeguarding translation of the CEP report in time for the ATCM meeting.
- The importance of intersessional work as a means of diminishing the workload in the CEP meeting itself.

(527) Norway offered to prepare, by 1 September 2010, for circulation by the Secretariat, a draft decision paper including a model draft ATCM agenda and a model draft schedule, and invited Parties to submit their written views on the proposal by 1 December, 2010. Taking into account the comments of Parties, Norway would then prepare a paper, containing a draft decision which it would submit for consideration at ATCM XXXIV.

Science Issues in the Multi-Year Work Plan

(528) Sweden introduced a proposal, co-authored by 11 Parties, suggesting two new agenda items for ATCM XXXIV to ensure that Climate Change in Antarctica was particularly identified in the agenda. These would replace the existing Agenda item 13: Science Issues, Including Climate-related Research, Scientific Cooperation and Facilitation, and Agenda item 10: The International Polar Year 2007-2008.

(529) Several Parties supported the need to prioritise the work of the ATCM for the future and to develop a multi-year work plan along the lines of that developed by the CEP.

(530) India thanked Sweden for clarifying the issues involved in revising the agenda on the lines proposed. It noted that the CEP would be taking climate change implications for the Antarctic environment as a separate agenda item, in

support of the recommendations of the ATME. Accordingly, there was a need to include a similar agenda item on climate change for within the ATCM.

(531) Several Parties expressed concern about the potential ambiguity in the term "governance" included in the proposed agenda item. Following discussion, it was decided that the proposed agenda items should be:

- XX. Science Issues, Scientific Cooperation and Facilitation, including the Legacy of the International Polar Year 2007-2008
- YY. Implications of Climate Change for Management of the Antarctic Treaty Area

White Book

(532) Chile announced that a White Book will be presented to ATCM XXXIV in Buenos Aires, Argentina as a strictly academic work that is non-binding on the Consultative Parties on the meaning of the 50th anniversary of the entry into force of the Antarctic Treaty.

(533) Some Parties expressed their support for such endeavour. The U.S. stated that the result of such an academic work would not be representative of the position of the Antarctic Treaty Parties. Instead, it would be an individual exercise of the contributing Parties. Argentina reiterated its willingness to participate in the preparation of the White Book.

Item 19: Preparation of the 34th Meeting

a. Date and place

(534) The Meeting welcomed the kind invitation of the Government of the Republic of Argentina to host ATCM XXXIV in Buenos Aires from 20 June to 1 July 2011.

(535) For future planning, the Meeting took note of the following likely timetable of upcoming ATCMs:

- 2012: Australia
- 2013: Belgium

(536) The Meeting welcomed the intention of the Government of Australia to host the 35th ATCM in Hobart.

(537) Further to paragraph 526 with a view to continuing to improve the efficiency of its proceedings, the Meeting agreed that ATCM XXXV should be held over a period of eight working days. It was also therefore agreed that ATCM XXXIV would consider the modalities for holding ATCM XXXV within an eight day timeframe, including a general review and update of the agenda.

(538) As far as the subsequent ATCMs are concerned, the Meeting further agreed that the appropriate length of ATCMs would be kept under review.

b. Invitation of international and non-governmental organisations

(539) In accordance with established practice, the Meeting agreed that the following organisations having scientific or technical interest in Antarctica should be invited to send experts to attend ATCM XXXIV: the ACAP Secretariat, ASOC, IAATO, IHO, IMO, IOC, the Intergovernmental Panel on Climate Change (IPCC), IUCN, UNEP, WMO and WTO.

c. Invitation to Malaysia

(540) The Chair reported on informal contact with the Delegation of Malaysia in the margins of ATCM XXXIII. Recalling that Malaysia had been invited to observe the ATCM on several occasions, the Meeting looked forward to Malaysia's early decision on accession to the Treaty and thus its formal participation in the Antarctic Treaty system. The Meeting invited Malaysia to observe ATCM XXXIV in Buenos Aires.

d. Preparation of the agenda for ATCM XXXIV

(541) The Meeting approved the Preliminary Agenda for ATCM XXXIV (see page 241) noting that current Agenda items 13: *Science Issues, Including Climate-related Research, Scientific Cooperation and Facilitation, and 10: The International Polar Year 2007-2008* are removed. Furthermore, the Preliminary Agenda will include two new agenda items:

Science Issues, Scientific Cooperation and Facilitation, including the Legacy of the International Polar Year 2007-2008;

and

Implications of Climate Change for Management of the Antarctic Treaty Area.

e. Organisation of ATCM XXXIV

(542) Pursuant to Rule 11, the Meeting decided as a preliminary matter to propose the same working groups at ATCM XXXIV as at this Meeting.

f. The SCAR Lecture

(543) Taking into account the valuable series of lectures given by SCAR at a number of ATCMs, the Meeting decided to invite SCAR to give another lecture on scientific issues relevant to ATCM XXXIV.

Item 20: Any Other Business

(544) There was no other business.

Item 21: Adoption of the Final Report

(545) The Meeting adopted the Final Report of the 33rd Antarctic Treaty Consultative Meeting.

(546) The Chair of the Meeting, Dr Roberto Puceiro Ripoll made closing remarks.

(547) The Meeting was closed on Friday, 14 May 2010 at 14:42.

2. CEP XIII Report

Report of the Committee for Environmental Protection (CEP XIII)

Punta del Este, May 3–7, 2010

Item 1: Opening of the Meeting

(1) The CEP Chair, Dr Neil Gilbert (New Zealand), opened the meeting on Monday 3 May 2010 and thanked Uruguay for arranging and hosting the meeting in Punta del Este.

(2) On behalf of the Committee, the Chair warmly welcomed Monaco to membership of the CEP following its accession to the Environmental Protocol on 31 July 2009. Monaco's accession to the Protocol brings the number of Committee Members to 34.

(3) The Chair summarised the work undertaken during the intersessional period as a result of actions and activities agreed at CEP XII, including an intersessional contact group (ICG) on non-native species, an ICG on general guidance for visitors to Antarctica, the CEP's tourism study and issues related to Area Protection and Management through the Subsidiary Group on Management Plans (SGMP). In addition the Antarctic Treaty Parties had held two Antarctic Treaty Meetings of Experts. The Chair noted that the outcomes of these groups and meetings would be dealt with during the course of CEP XIII.

Item 2: Adoption of the Agenda

(4) The Committee adopted the following agenda and confirmed the allocation of papers to Agenda Items:

1. Opening of the Meeting
2. Adoption of the Agenda
3. Strategic Discussions on the Future Work of the CEP
4. Operation of the CEP

5. Progress to the International Polar Year

6. Environmental Impact Assessment (EIA)

   a. Draft Comprehensive Environmental Evaluations

   b. Other EIA Matters

7. Area Protection and Management Plans

   a. Management Plans

   b. Historic Sites and Monuments

   c. Site Guidelines

   d. Human Footprint and Wilderness Values

   e. Marine Spatial Protection and Management

   f. Other Annex V Matters

8. Conservation of Antarctic Flora and Fauna

   a. Quarantine and Non-native Species

   b. Specially Protected Species

   c. Other Annex II Matters

9. Environmental Monitoring and Reporting

   a. Climate Change

   b. Other Environmental Monitoring and Reporting Matters

10. Inspection Reports

11. Cooperation with Other Organisations

12. General Matters

13. Election of Officers

14. Preparation for Next Meeting

15. Adoption of the Report

16. Closing of the Meeting

(5) The Committee considered 48 Working Papers, 69 Information Papers and four Secretariat Papers (Annex 1).

Item 3: Strategic Discussions on the Future Work of the CEP

(6)   No Working Papers were submitted under this agenda item.

(7)   The Committee noted the utility of the Five-year Work Plan in prioritising its workload. The Committee agreed that the Five-year Work Plan should be reviewed and updated at the end of each meeting and, as well as being appended to the Report of CEP XIII, should be published on the CEP website, as well as being submitted to future CEP meetings as a Working Paper.

(8)   Australia noted that the ATCM intended to hold discussions on strategic planning and suggested that it would be useful to highlight the approach taken and lessons learned by the CEP in developing and implementing its work plan. The Committee agreed with this suggestion.

Advice to the ATCM

(9)   The CEP highlighted the continuing value of its prioritised five-year work plan as an effective means of guiding its work and managing its workload, and encouraged the ATCM to draw on its experience in developing and implementing that plan, as appropriate, when considering a multi-year strategic plan for the ATCM.

---

(10)   A number of Members drew attention to the significant number of papers submitted for consideration by CEP XIII and raised concerns about the limited time available to consider such a large number of papers. Several Parties suggested options to address the issue including:

- urging Members to provide clear recommendations in their Working Papers;

- limiting the amount of time spent on Information Papers during meetings, including time available for addressing individual Information Papers, and potentially having Information Papers available only in electronic format, and,

- careful consideration as to how many ICGs can realistically be established in any one year.

(11)   The Committee agreed that this issue should be considered further in preparation for future meetings.

Item 4: Operation of the CEP

(12) The Secretariat introduced SP 9 *Electronic Information Exchange System (EIES): Report on the 2nd operational season and summary information examples,* noting that 60% of the Parties had contributed information to the electronic information exchange system. The Secretariat noted that all technical changes to the EIES that had been proposed by Parties had been addressed to the extent that the suggested changes complied with Appendix 4 of the Final Report of ATCM XXIV and other relevant Measures. At the request of CEP XII, and following discussions at the ATCM XXXII, the Secretariat had developed two example data reports to demonstrate the utility of the EIES: one on Area Protection and Management and one on Ship Based Operations.

(13) Several Members and ASOC thanked the Secretariat for its intersessional work on the EIES and for the illustrative report, noting that the EIES has potential to be an exceptionally useful tool to support the CEP's work.

(14) However, it was noted by several Members that the utility of the EIES is dependent upon the extent to which the required data and information is provided by Parties. The Committee agreed that there is an urgent need to ensure that all Parties are fulfilling all information exchange requirements of the Treaty and Article 17 of the Environmental Protocol.

(15) Following a suggestion by France the Secretariat agreed to issue a reminder in advance of deadlines for the submission of information, to facilitate improved use of the EIES.

(16) ASOC noted that from a non-governmental organisation (NGO) perspective it was difficult to determine the extent to which the EIES was being used by Parties as the information could not be publicly accessed.

(17) The Secretariat noted that individual Party reports against each of the Pre-season, Annual and Permanent information categories are made publicly available via the Secretariat website once submitted by the Parties.

(18) Based on the conclusions of this document, Argentina suggested that it may be timely to review the information exchange requirements, in particular due to the fact that these were agreed before the Secretariat was established and the Electronic Information Exchange System was implemented.

(19) Pertinent to the discussion, Germany introduced WP 41 *Antarctic Treaty Information Exchange via the Electronic Information Exchange System (EIES): Current state and improvements for a consistent use*, recommending that Members establish an ICG to review the success of the EIES with regard to utilization, standards of information exchange and availability of the advance notice according to Article VII (5).

(20) Receiving no comment on the issue of reviewing the information exchange requirements, the Chair noted that WP 41 would be further considered by the ATCM. In concluding the discussions the Chair echoed comments from Members and strongly urged all Members to provide information to the EIES to ensure 100 per cent participation by ATCM XXXIV.

(21) Other papers submitted under this Agenda item were:

- IP 72 *Annual Report Pursuant to Article 17 of the Protocol on Environmental Protection to the Antarctic Treaty* (Ukraine)

- IP 78 *Annual Report Pursuant to Article 17 of the Protocol on Environmental Protection to the Antarctic Treaty* (Italy)

- IP 127 *Informe Anual del Ecuador de acuerdo con el Artículo 17 del Protocolo al Tratado Antártico sobre Protección del Medio Ambiente- Expedición 2009-2010* (Ecuador)

(22) The Chair reminded all Members that the submission of such Information Papers was no longer required given that submission of information to the EIES is now the preferred mechanism.

(23) Chile proposed a revision to the election procedure for Vice-chairs noting that the most experienced Vice-chair, serving in their second two-year term, should automatically become the first Vice-chair, with the most recently elected Vice-chair assuming the role of second Vice-chair. This would mean that in the event of the first Vice-chair having to stand in for the Chair in his/her absence, the role would be assumed by the most experienced Vice-chair.

(24) The Committee agreed with Chile's suggestion and proposed an amendment to Rule 15 of the Rules of Procedure of the CEP.

Advice to the ATCM

(25)   The Committee reviewed a proposal for revised CEP Rules of Procedure and forwarded a revised version to the ATCM for consideration and adoption by means of a Decision.

Item 5: International Polar Year

(26)   Uruguay introduced WP 11 *Forwarding of hydrographic data collected during the IPY* and noted that with increasing maritime traffic, the value of collected hydrographic data during the IPY - through improved bathymetric surveying - for reasons of scientific research, environmental protection as well as maritime safety cannot be understated. Uruguay noted that it was essential for data collected by national programmes during the IPY to be made freely available as soon as possible to national hydrographic agencies. Uruguay offered a draft Resolution to this effect for consideration by the Committee.

(27)   Many Members as well as IAATO agreed that it was essential to ensure that all hydrographic and bathymetric data was made available for the purposes of improving maritime charts in Antarctic waters.

(28)   SCAR agreed and noted the valuable contribution such data would also make to a Southern Ocean Observing System. SCAR noted that it has made several recommendations to its Members to ensure the collection and submission of hydrographic and bathymetric data.

(29)   Whilst agreeing in principle with the approach, the UK noted the importance of ensuring that submitted data was high quality data that could be used by charting agencies.

(30)   France also agreed with the principle, but with regard to the draft Resolution appended to WP 11, France and Argentina suggested that the forwarding of data should not be limited only to data collected during IPY, but should be an ongoing obligation of national operators and other vessel operators in Antarctica.

(31)   Australia noted the environmental benefits of collecting hydrographic data and adequate charting, as outlined in Resolution 5 (2008).

(32)   The Chair noted that WP 11 and the attached draft Resolution would be further considered by ATCM XXXIII.

(33)   SCAR introduced IP 50 *The Southern Ocean Observing System (SOOS)* noting that, despite the unique and critical role that the Southern Ocean plays in both driving global climate and supporting diverse biological communities, it has been poorly monitored. SCAR informed the Committee that the SOOS project is a partnership of several organisations (SCAR, SCOR, CAML, GOOS, WCRP, and POGO with involvement also from COMNAP and IAATO). SCAR noted that the project meets the requirements of ATCM Resolution 3 (2007), that it is one of the key recommendations from the Antarctic Climate Change and the Environment Report (Turner et al., 2009), and that it is a significant legacy of IPY. Finally, SCAR noted that to succeed, a SOOS Secretariat will be required and requested support from the Parties for this initiative.

(34)   In response to a question SCAR clarified that the SOOS plan, once finalised, will be circulated to interested parties, and will be made available to the Committee at its next meeting.

(35)   Romania presented IP 99 *Young Scientists Fully Aware of the Importance of Antarctic Environment*, noting the education of students from more than ten countries with respect to climate change and general polar science.

Item 6: Environmental Impact Assessment

6a) Draft Comprehensive Environmental Evaluations

(36)   No draft CEEs were circulated in advance of CEP XIII.

(37)   Russia introduced WP 59 *Answers to comments on CEE for "Water Sampling the Sub-glacial Lake Vostok."* The paper was presented in response to concerns raised during ATCM XXVI in Madrid, Spain, in 2003 (Appendix 2 to the Report of CEP VI refers).

(38)   Russia reminded the Committee of the history of the activity and the further drilling work that it had completed since the draft CEE had been circulated. Russia noted that some of the concerns raised by the Committee in 2003 could only be answered after resuming drilling in borehole 5G-1 in order to obtain new data on ice composition and structure above the sub-glacial lake.

Drilling operations had recommenced in 2004, and by 28 October 2007, the borehole depth was 3668m. However a technical accident resulted in the loss of the drill at the bottom of the borehole. Attempts were made to extract the drill in the seasons of 2007-08 and 2008-09, but were unsuccessful. In January 2009 it was decided to bypass the accident segment by borehole deflection from the vertical. The deflection was started from a depth of 3590m, 1.5m from the accident segment. By late January 2010, the depth of borehole 5G-2 was 3650m.

(39) Glaciological data obtained from this further drilling would allow Russia to respond to the concerns raised by the Committee. However, Russia noted that the drilling results needed for the completion of a final CEE had not been available in time for submission of the final CEE to CEP XIII. Russia anticipated finalising the CEE to allow it to circulate the document at CEP XIV.

(40) Based on its experience and other ice drilling technologies used in Greenland and elsewhere in Antarctica, Russia informed the Committee that:

- Ice crystals in excess of 1.5m, with minimal inter-crystal spacing, suggest ice composition that is unlikely to result in drilling fluid spreading unpredictably throughout the ice. Such ice structure above the lake reduces the risk of contamination by drilling fluid at Lake Vostok. Drilling with a kerosene-freon mixture is likely to be the most environmentally "clean" drilling technique. Using similar technology, work undertaken on sub-glacial aquatic systems in Greenland suggests that frozen water that has risen upward in to the borehole is contaminated by drilling fluid only in the uppermost 10cm of the "fresh frozen" ice in the borehole. The lower layers of this Greenland core did not have any traces of contamination. Furthermore, this drilling fluid mixture is less dense than water and is hydrophobic, minimizing the risk of accidental contamination of lake waters. Thus, it seems to provide fewer environmental and logistical issues than several other methods that were evaluated.

- A further alternative hot water drilling solution had also been assessed. However, this technology cannot be applied at Vostok Station, as the required power for a constant hot water circulation in the ice borehole with a temperature of about +90°C far exceeds what is available at Vostok Station.

- Knowledge gaps noted in 2003 about the ice/water interface conditions and the chemical and microbiological composition of surface water of Lake Vostok had been the subject of assessment by Russia for the past 7 years. Data on the hydrochemical properties of ice from the lower horizons of borehole 5G-1 had been presented at different international forums and published in scientific journals. Microbiological analyses of ice from the lower part of borehole 5G-1 showed the concentration of living cells to be low, comprising 1 to 10 cells in 1ml suggesting an extremely low biological activity in the surface water layer of Lake Vostok. These results had also been presented at different international forums and published in scientific journals.

(41) The UK thanked Russia for this update noting the significant period of time since submission of the draft CEE in 2003. In finalising its CEE, the UK urged Russia to take account of new knowledge and information available since 2003 including the National Academy of Sciences study of sub-glacial aquatic systems and the soon to be published SCAR code of conduct on sub-glacial research. The UK also urged Russia to take account of the energy requirements of the drilling activity, which in its view should be standard considerations in all EIAs. The UK considers hot water drilling to be a clean technology that would afford protection to the sub-aquatic environment. The UK also urged all Parties to submit draft and final CEEs in a timely manner.

(42) France thanked Russia for the information provided and noted its concern over the length restrictions on Working Papers. Such a restriction prevents the possibility to submit detailed information, which would have been more useful in a complex case such as this. In this context, France noted its interest in seeing further information in the final CEE, particularly on the suggestion that Lake Vostok is isolated from other sub-glacial aquatic systems. France congratulated Russia for exploring the possibility of drilling the ice at low pressure and encouraged Russia to undertake reliable and continuous monitoring of the pressure at the bottom of the borehole.

(43) The United States thanked Russia for its paper and noted that it would welcome further dissemination of scientific information with regards to work from Lake Vostok thus far, in order that this knowledge may be applied to future drilling projects.

(44) Germany congratulated Russia on the comprehensive work undertaken since 2003 and noted that the sampling of sub-glacial lakes in Antarctica was a big scientific goal.

(45) Romania and India also congratulated Russia noting that any such activity had to balance environmental concerns against the scientific benefits.

(46) India appreciated the technical expertise developed by Russia in the field of ice-core drilling and expressed that the project should be encouraged considering the scientific results expected.

(47) SCAR responded to a question from Argentina about the current status of the SCAR code of conduct on sub-glacial lakes, commenting that environmental stewardship has always been a high priority for SCAR. Within SCAR there is a history of producing codes of conduct, which are produced by SCAR Members for SCAR Members. SCAR noted that these Codes of Conduct are guidelines only. The code of conduct for sub-glacial lakes has been reviewed by SCAR Members and national operators through COMNAP. The code of conduct for sub-glacial lakes has been put forward for approval by the SCAR delegates in August 2010 and, if approved, will be submitted as an IP to the next CEP meeting.

(48) ASOC thanked Russia for the information it had provided. Expressing concern about the use and potential spillage of drilling fluids, ASOC encouraged the use of a precautionary approach in the continuation of the Lake Vostok drilling project. It requested confirmation from Russia that, to the extent possible based on the information available, the completion of the drilling into Lake Vostok would not result in the uncontrolled release of drilling fluid into the lake.

(49) New Zealand thanked Russia for the update, and also noted the significant period of time that had elapsed since the circulation of the draft CEE. New Zealand, supported by the Netherlands and Germany, questioned whether such a time gap may merit re-circulation of an updated draft CEE for comment.

(50) The Committee noted that neither the Protocol, nor its own operating guidelines currently made any provision on the time gap between circulation of a draft CEE and the final version.

(51) Russia assured the CEP that it would fulfil the environmental impact assessment requirements of Annex I to the Protocol and that penetration of Lake Vostok would not take place until the final CEE had been submitted to the relevant Russian authorities for approval and circulated to the CEP.

(52) India presented IP 6 *Update on the Comprehensive Environmental Evaluation (CEE) of New Indian Research Station at Larsemann Hills, Antarctica* informing the Meeting that during 2009 and 2010 international meetings were held to finalize the design of the proposed new station and to discuss and define a strategy for transportation of various basic construction machines and for the development of an approach path from the landing site to the construction site at Larsemann Hills. India announced that basic construction equipment had been transported to the site over fast ice and an emergency shelter hut was placed at the site. It also informed the Committee that water and biological samples were collected from the site in order to monitor environmental impacts. India noted its plans to submit the final CEE by December 2010. The construction of the new station will commence in austral summer 2010/11.

(53) Romania noted that it is important to keep the Larsemann Hills ASMA Management Plan in consideration in the further development of this project.

6b) Other EIA Matters

(54) New Zealand introduced WP 1 *Chairs' Report - Antarctic Treaty Meeting of Experts on the Management of Ship-borne Tourism in the Antarctic Treaty Area*. New Zealand noted that the ATME, held in Wellington in December 2009, was a very successful meeting, attended by representatives of 19 Parties and six international organisations, and that a number of valuable papers had been considered. New Zealand noted this meeting had been held to accelerate the Treaty Parties' consideration of the management of ship-borne tourism in Antarctica, not least to minimise the risks of a humanitarian and environmental disaster occurring in Antarctica as the result of a maritime casualty.

(55) New Zealand noted that the ATME had considered a range of issues under the broad topics of maritime safety and environmental protection, and had agreed 17 recommendations for the ATCM to consider. New Zealand highlighted four of these recommendations that it considered of particular relevance to the CEP:

Issues related to Environmental Safeguards

- Recommendation 11: The meeting recommended that the relevant committees and groups of the ATCM (such as the CEP and the Operations Working Group) give further consideration to how assessment of the environmental aspects and impacts of Antarctic ship-borne tourism in ATME WP 8 - Appendix A could be drawn on to inform their discussions regarding the management of ship-borne tourism and shipping generally.

- Recommendation 12: The meeting recommended that Parties and those involved in non-governmental activities be encouraged to provide spatial and temporal data in support of future studies and syntheses for discussion by the CEP and ATCM.

Issues related to Emergency Response Action (Article 15 of the Protocol on Environmental Protection to the Antarctic Treaty)

- Recommendation 13: The Treaty Parties should exchange information on contingency planning undertaken in fulfilment of Article 15, for responding to incidents with potential adverse impacts on the Antarctic environment.

- Recommendation 14: That the ATCM consider developing guidelines for responding to large-scale marine oil spills in the Antarctic Treaty area.

(56) New Zealand noted that improved collaboration with the International Maritime Organization (IMO) had been a highlight of the ATME. New Zealand noted IMO's ongoing work in developing a mandatory Polar Shipping Code and that it had been asked to consider how the Code might be used to provide guidance on fuel spill response in the Antarctic Treaty area.

(57) New Zealand noted that it would be submitting a paper on environmental issues including fuel spill response to the next meeting of IMO's Design and Equipment Sub-Committee (October 2010), within which the Polar Shipping Code was being developed.

(58) In this regard New Zealand also intended to give further consideration to Recommendation 14 from the ATME and would provide a further paper on the matter to ATCM XXXIV.

(59) The Committee, IAATO and ASOC thanked New Zealand for introducing the paper and offered congratulations for an excellent ATME.

(60) With regard to Recommendation 12, the United States made note of its IP 2 *Spatial Patterns of Tour Ship Traffic in the Antarctic Peninsula Region* as an example of collaborative work with IAATO to report and analyse Antarctic maritime traffic. The United States noted the importance of such data to assess the efficacy of management, and that it would be happy to continue and expand such collaborations in the future to collect and assess spatial and temporal data.

(61) IAATO echoed the comments of the United States noting the importance of collecting data from all maritime operators.

(62) The United Kingdom expressed their continued commitment to work with the United States, IAATO and other organisations on data and information collection. The United Kingdom noted the importance of collecting data to facilitate a more complete picture of all maritime activities, both governmental and non-governmental.

(63) In this regard COMNAP noted its existing ship position reporting system that includes both governmental and non-governmental participation and is used principally for search and rescue.

(64) New Zealand also drew attention to the list of databases in WP 36 *Environmental Aspects and Impacts of Tourism and Non-governmental Activities in Antarctica: Project Report,* which had been compiled during the CEP's tourism study.

(65) The Committee agreed that it would be important to continue to compile such data so as to support informed policy discussions and management decisions, though the collection, storage and management of such data represented a significant challenge.

(66) With regard to Recommendations 13 and 14 from the ATME (WP 1), Chile and Argentina noted their longstanding cooperative agreements and joint naval patrols designed to provide a joint search and rescue response, including to environmental emergencies.

(67) The UK also highlighted the importance of cooperation in such matters and noted that it frequently held joint oil spill response exercises as reported in

IP 35 *Report of a Joint Oil Spill Exercise: RV Laurence M. Gould at Rothera Research Station.*

(68) Argentina also recalled the significant work being undertaken by COMNAP to improve coordination on emergency response action and search and rescue including improved coordination among national Marine Rescue Coordination Centres in the framework of IMO. Any further work on these areas should take into account this framework.

(69) Romania requested that ATMEs be numbered to reflect the number of ATMEs that have occurred on a given topic.

(70) New Zealand observed that the Wellington ATME was the third over the past decade to consider aspects of shipping in Antarctica and reflected the ATCM's interest in the considerable expansion of ship-borne tourism in Antarctica including its concerns over incidents such as the sinking of the *M/S Explorer* in 2007.

(71) New Zealand noted that the comments from Chile and Argentina provided an excellent example of maritime collaboration, and highlighted that the severe and extreme conditions in Antarctica would require broad coordination among multiple Parties in the event of a maritime incident. New Zealand noted the provisions of Article 15 of the Protocol and suggested the consideration of contingency plans could be a task taken up by the CEP.

(72) COMNAP noted that its members had prepared guidelines for developing contingency plans and that many plans were lodged with the COMNAP Secretariat. Those plans are usually site-specific, so that further consideration was needed as to how national operators and Parties might respond in the event of a large-scale environmental emergency.

(73) Argentina suggested that a CEP representative could attend the search and rescue workshops being held by COMNAP.

(74) With regard to ATME Recommendation 11, Australia presented WP 28 *Environmental Aspects of Antarctic Ship-borne Tourism*, noting that it was a revised version of an Australian paper submitted to the ATME. The attachment provided an assessment of the ways in which ship-borne tourism can interact with the Antarctic environment, and which of those interactions are addressed in existing regulations and guidelines. Australia noted that an

important next step would be to evaluate the significance of the identified interactions through a risk analysis. Consistent with ATME Recommendation 11, Australia welcomed discussion on this type of approach and on how the assessment could be drawn on to inform the CEP's work to understand and address the environmental aspects of ship-borne tourism and shipping generally.

(75) The Committee, IAATO and ASOC thanked Australia for this comprehensive work.

(76) The United States noted that this table might usefully be addressed to the CEP's ongoing tourism study.

(77) New Zealand, supported by the UK, agreed with the United States' proposal and suggested that a risk assessment be undertaken on the basis of the table and that such a table might also be added as an appendix to the EIA guidelines.

(78) ASOC noted the usefulness of WP 28 to further work in the CEP tourism study and elsewhere. ASOC noted that while all activities may contribute to cumulative impacts, it is important to isolate the impact of tourism as a way to assess and manage this activity.

(79) The Committee agreed to consider the environmental aspects table appended to WP 28 within the ongoing tourism study with the suggestion that a risk assessment be undertaken on the various aspects identified in the table. The Committee also agreed to further consider how the environmental aspects table might be appended to the EIA guidelines.

Advice to the ATCM

(80) At the request of the ATCM, the Committee considered the Report of the ATME on ship-borne tourism, paying particular attention to Recommendations 11, 12, 13 and 14 in that Report.

(81) The Committee endorsed the assessment of environmental aspects of ship-borne tourism referred to in ATME Recommendation 11 (Attachment A to Working Paper 28 (Australia)) and agreed to refer it to the CEP's tourism study with a suggestion that it be expanded to identify the level of risk associated with the various environmental aspects.

(82) With regard to Recommendation 12, the Committee noted the range of data sets that were being prepared through its tourism study and will provide more information to the ATCM on this when presenting the study to ATCM XXXIV.

(83) With regard to Recommendations 13 and 14, the Committee noted the importance of cooperation among Parties and National Programs in attempting to develop contingency plans to respond to large-scale marine environmental incidents, in fulfilment of Article 15 of the Protocol.

(84) New Zealand introduced WP 36 *Environmental Aspects and Impacts of Tourism and Non-governmental Activities in Antarctica: Project Report.* New Zealand recalled that CEP XII had accepted a proposal by Australia, France and New Zealand to undertake a comprehensive assessment of the environmental aspects and impacts of Antarctic tourism. The study was initiated in May 2009, and 12 Members, IAATO and ASOC indicated their desire to support the work through participation in the Project Management Group through the CEP Discussion Forum. In December 2009 a small workshop had been held in Christchurch, New Zealand, to review progress with the study and to identify the work still to be concluded.

(85) New Zealand indicated that excellent progress had been made with the study, but insufficient time was available ahead of CEP XIII to allow for completion. New Zealand noted that a draft of Part 1 of the study report, focussing on an analysis of the current status and observed trends of Antarctic tourism, was available on the CEP discussion forum. Part 2, which focuses on an assessment and discussion of potential environmental impacts resulting from tourism and non-governmental activities in the Antarctic, required further work and additional input, especially from scientists involved in impact-related research projects.

(86) New Zealand thanked the Project Management Group members for their support and expertise, and IAATO for its support and provision of data. New Zealand invited the views of the CEP on the progress made thus far and matters that should be included in Part 2 of the study. New Zealand noted it would be happy to continue to lead this project with the support of Project Management Group and anticipated submitting a full report to CEP XIV.

(87) Many Members, IAATO and ASOC thanked New Zealand and the Project Management Group and other contributors for this progress report.

(88) France highlighted the complexity of the issues and data on this topic, noting that while IAATO members are compliant with the request for data, there is a paucity of non-IAATO member data.

(89) Romania echoed the comments of France, and noted the importance of ensuring the data sets listed in the paper could be further developed over time to allow for ongoing assessments of tourism impacts.

(90) ASOC underlined the need to collect information on all forms of tourism activities. In response to a question from ASOC New Zealand noted that it did not have sufficient data to assess the proportion of non-IAATO member tourism in Antarctica.

(91) Australia noted the considerable work undertaken to date, including the commencement of a range of useful discussions on better understanding the interactions between tourism and the Antarctic environment. It noted that the continuation and completion of this work would greatly assist the overall aim of providing a sound and objective basis for future discussions regarding the environmental management of Antarctic tourism.

(92) The United States noted the importance of including other data and information so as to place tourism impacts in the broader context of a changing Antarctic environment. Such information might be derived from national research programmes, long-term data sets including CCAMLR's ecosystem monitoring programme and Oceanites' Antarctic Site Inventory project as reported in IP 26 *Antarctic Site Inventory: 1994-2010*.

(93) Germany suggested that the EIES may be considered as a data management tool to facilitate and broaden the CEP's database on tourism activities.

(94) The Committee noted the ongoing nature of this work and welcomed the support of other Members in providing data and information to support the study, particularly with regard to non-IAATO tourism activities, and broader environmental monitoring or research studies on tourism or human impacts in Antarctica. The Committee gratefully accepted New Zealand's offer to continue to lead the study.

(95) The United States introduced WP 52 *Data Collection and Reporting on Yachting Activity in Antarctica* (United States and United Kingdom) noting that, in the framework of the tourism study being conducted by the CEP,

considerable difficulties were encountered in collecting data on yachting activities in Antarctica. Gaps were most significant among non-IAATO related yachts. Such yachts likely account for a small proportion of operators in the Antarctic, but their impact may be substantial as in the case of the recent event at Wordie House. The United States noted that the list of vessels attached to the paper was far from exhaustive.

(96) The United States recommended that, in addition to completing the table provided in WP 52 to the extent possible, Parties contribute additional relevant yacht information to the current CEP study.

(97) Relevant information can be sent to Dr Neil Gilbert *n.gilbert@antarcticanz. govt.nz* who is coordinating the CEP tourism study.

(98) Romania thanked the UK and US for their paper and emphasised the need to comply with such requests for data to ensure the tourism study is as complete as possible.

(99) France echoed appreciation for this paper and noted its support for New Zealand's complementary work on the tourism study. France also noted that several vessels on the list attached to WP 52 are operating under the French flag and have not received approval from the French authorities.

(100) The UK noted that this was not an exhaustive list and welcomed all efforts to complete the information. The UK also drew attention to its ongoing efforts to raise awareness among the UK yachting community about regulatory requirements in Antarctica, including training courses, and would be pleased to share such information with interested Parties.

(101) The Russian Federation expressed gratitude to the authors of this document and noted the significant data gaps. Russia further noted gaps in effective national regulations and the regular use of flags of convenience among vessels operating in the Antarctic. To improve consistency among Parties, all authorising governments must have sound domestic regulations for control and monitoring of their operators.

(102) Chile agreed that there was a particular problem in managing this type of vessel in Antarctica, and noted that it had submitted a paper to the ATCM on the issue of yachts travelling under flags of convenience.

(103) ASOC thanked the UK and US and noted that while there appear to be limited data about yachts, there are records of all known yachts that sailed to the Antarctic up until the early 1990s in the academic literature, and furthermore noted that there are only a few gateway locations from where yachts would depart to the Antarctic and where they would normally be required to report their departure and the next port of call. With the help of Parties in gateway locations it would be possible to close the information gap about current yacht activity in Antarctica.

(104) Argentina agreed with other delegations regarding the lack of data and the need for improved information, though noted that its monitoring efforts in Argentina have revealed that many vessels do not disclose their intentions to enter Antarctic waters. This may be intentional or due to a lack of understanding regarding requirements, permits, and necessary reporting.

(105) IAATO agreed with Russia on the need for strong competent authority processes to regulate yachting and other NGO activities in Antarctica, and noted that the majority of non-IAATO operators which had gone through a strong competent authority process are responsible and well-prepared. IAATO drew attention to its IP 75 *Non-IAATO tourism and visitation in Antarctica*, noting its outreach efforts to inform non-IAATO operators on proper operating procedures in Antarctic waters. IAATO agreed with Argentina that many vessels travel undetected and unreported but hopes that through outreach efforts, such as described in IP 75, non-IAATO vessels will be reached and appropriately educated. IAATO noted that it would continue to report any violations by non-IAATO visitors to the appropriate national authorities.

(106) France recommended that such violations be reported to the CEP and the ATCM and recalled that implementation of the existing regulations is the responsibility of the Parties.

(107) Australia, France and the United Kingdom welcomed IAATO's outreach work and its support in providing data and reports on tourism activities and of possible infringements. All such information was highly valued.

(108) Argentina reported that it has established a tourism observation programme that will place trained observers at key visitor sites in Antarctica. The programme will result in reliable data collection on tourist activities.

(109) ASOC thanked IAATO and suggested that, with respect to collecting data about tourism behaviour, Parties rather than IAATO were primarily responsible to monitor the conduct of tourism and suggested that a simple format for standard reporting of tourism incidents could be agreed on so that anyone witnessing tourism related incidents could report them to national authorities.

(110) ASOC introduced IP 79 *Tourism and Land-based Facilities in Antarctica: Analysis of a Questionnaire Distributed to Antarctic Treaty Parties at XXXII ATCM* that summarizes the results of a questionnaire on tourism use of land-based facilities operated by Antarctic Treaty Parties distributed at ATCM XXXII, which had a response rate of c. 25% among Parties. The respondents were representative of all Antarctic Treaty Parties that run facilities in all parts of the Antarctic region. None of the respondents provides any support to tourism other than free basic hospitality. Most respondents opposed the notion of Parties being involved in tourism operations.

(111) ASOC noted that no Party reported being aware of land-based facilities from other Parties that were used for tourism purposes in their area of operations. Two of the eight respondents indicated that one or more National Antarctic Programs (other than the respondents) possibly transport and/or accommodate tourists, which is consistent with some observations made in the official inspection reports presented under agenda item 10. These activities might have an environmental impact that is not necessarily considered in for example EIAs or in the CEP tourism study. ASOC requested the Parties that have not yet done so to respond to the questionnaire attached to IP 79.

(112) The United Kingdom presented WP 12 *Guidelines on Minimising the Impact of Pollution by Light at Antarctic Stations and Ships* noting that pollution by light is recognized as an environmental concern, which can result in loss of scientific data and mortality of seabirds, but that there was no Treaty-wide endorsed procedure for controlling light pollution from bases and vessels. In addition, whilst stations in the Antarctic clearly require outdoor lighting for safety reasons, light pollution mitigation procedures are not consistently adopted.

(113) The United Kingdom had developed and implemented the proposed guidelines for use within its own operations to minimize the impacts of light pollution and the guidelines were recognised as an example of best practice by the British Astronomical Association. The UK also drew attention to its web-based bird strike log and indicated that it would be willing to share

the software with interested Parties. The UK suggested that the Committee consider developing a single set of guidelines for wider use in Antarctica, perhaps by integrating similar guidelines from other Parties.

(114) IAATO presented IP 24 *IAATO Guidelines to Minimize Seabirds Landing on Ships*. IAATO reported that it had developed these guidelines, primarily for sub-Antarctic waters, working with Birdlife International and that bird strikes by tour vessels had been reduced as a result of their implementation. IAATO would welcome any comment on the guidelines from the Committee.

(115) South Africa, France, Ecuador, Australia, and Germany offered their support for the United Kingdom's proposal and indicated that they would be willing to participate in further discussions towards the development of a single set of guidelines for adoption at the ATCM.

(116) Argentina noted that it had not encountered any bird strike on its stations or ships, though it did try and reduce external lighting as much as possible. Argentina suggested further scientific study might be required to assess the extent of the problem, and perhaps Parties may simply chose to implement the suggested guidelines if they wish to do so.

(117) Whilst supporting the principle of minimising bird strike and pollution from artificial light, COMNAP noted the importance of not compromising safety on stations and ships and noted that light pollution was often managed by the need to reduce energy use and to protect scientific values.

(118) India questioned what data might be available to characterise the extent of the problem.

(119) The UK noted that it had collected two years of data through its web-based bird strike log.

(120) The Committee thanked UK for its initiative. The Committee recognized that these guidelines can be useful and invited Parties to voluntarily test or implement them through their National Programmes and to consider gathering bird strike data to allow for further consideration of the issue.

(121) IAATO presented IP 25 *IAATO Online Field Staff Assessment & Logbook* on the initiatives it had taken to improve field staff training. IAATO noted that during the past two years it prepared the IAATO Field Operations Manual (FOM), the IAATO Expedition Staff Logbook and that it had also

established an online field staff assessment scheme designed to augment the training and test the knowledge of field staff on the contents of the FOM. IAATO also noted that the online assessment scheme will be rolled out for the 2010/11 season where initially all ship based Expedition Leaders will be asked to take part.

(122) Argentina emphasised the importance of such efforts and that they be performed in other languages as well as English, offering to help in translation of materials. IAATO welcomed this offer.

(123) The Republic of Korea presented IP 54 *The Republic of Korea's contribution to Antarctic science by installing a new permanent station in Terra Nova Bay, Ross Sea* reminding the Committee that in 2006 the Korean government had announced a plan to build a new research station in the Antarctic in order to enhance the Republic of Korea's scientific and collaborative capabilities in Antarctica. The Republic of Korea informed the Committee that, after visiting ten candidate sites, Terra Nova Bay, Northern Victoria Land, was considered the most suitable place to build the new station and to undertake a range of atmospheric, marine and climate change related research in the Pacific Ocean sector of Antarctica.

(124) The Republic of Korea reported that its new station would embrace modern energy efficiency standards and provide 3000m^2 of floor space for scientists and support staff. With the establishment of the new research station the Republic of Korea looked forward to making a significant contribution to international scientific collaboration and the effective management and conservation of the Antarctic environment. A draft Comprehensive Environmental Evaluation (CEE) for the new station is to be prepared and circulated in advance of CEP XIV.

(125) In response to an inquiry by the Netherlands as to the need for a new station as opposed to working through existing stations, the Republic of Korea explained that its proposal for a year-round station will allow for greater monitoring of climate change in this area, where year-round data are not currently collected.

(126) Italy congratulated the Republic of Korea for the interesting presentation on its new base in Terra Nova Bay and welcomed Korean colleagues in relation to the scientific and logistic collaboration at the Italian base Mario Zucchelli. Italy is ready to work with Korean scientists on environmental

and ecological issues and on the Italian proposal on marine protected areas that is in advanced study in the Ross Sea area.

(127) Many Parties congratulated the Republic of Korea on its proposed new research station and recognized the valuable scientific contribution that the station will make for Antarctic ecology, geophysics and geology, marine science and climate change research.

(128) Japan welcomed the initiative of the Republic of Korea to install a new wintering station at Terra Nova Bay area. The year-round station will be indispensable to monitor climate change, especially in the atmosphere and ocean, on the Pacific side of the Antarctic.

(129) Germany, supported by the US, noted that the new Korean research and resupply vessel *Araon* may need to frequently travel through the Bellingshausen Sea area if transiting between the two Korean bases. It highlighted the unique opportunity presented to the Republic of Korea in conducting marine science while transiting the Bellingshausen and Amundsen Seas with its icebreaker.

(130) Australia welcomed the Republic of Korea's advice regarding its plans for the new station and its intention to bring forward an appropriate environmental impact assessment to CEP XIV. Australia noted that it has developed a decadal science strategy, and would welcome discussion with the Republic of Korea and others on science cooperation, particularly with respect to climate science and oceanography.

(131) Romania also congratulated the Republic of Korea and recognized the important science contribution the new station would make, though Romania wondered if the proposed size of the station exceeded its capacity needs.

(132) The Committee looked forward to receiving the draft CEE during the intersessional period, noting that this would trigger its procedures for intersessional consideration of draft CEEs.

(133) In presenting IP 63, *Preliminary Plan for Installation and Operation of the PANSY Atmospheric Radar System at Syowa Station*, Japan informed the Committee that, in order to improve understanding of the atmospheric system from the surface up to 500km and to contribute to improving the global atmospheric model for better forecasting the future global climate, it will

install a large radar system at Syowa Station and operate for at least 12 years. Japan noted that, after completion of observations, this antenna system and associated facilities will be removed and the environment will be restored to its original condition. Japan announced that the Initial Environmental Evaluation document for this proposed activity will be submitted to the Japanese authorities for assessment this year.

(134) Germany presented IP 13 *Continued operation of Kohnen Base as a summer base in Dronning Maud Land including maintenance of a lab in the deep ice by the Alfred Wegener Institute* focusing on the permit, which has now been issued. In line with Article 2, paragraph 1, sub paragraph d) of Annex III to the Protocol on Environmental Protection, the Federal Environment Agency of Germany (UBA) concluded that the drilling liquid and densifier are wastes which have to be removed from the Antarctic as soon as the activities are finished. Germany noted that here are two problems: on the one hand, there is no alternative to the used drilling liquid and on the other hand, there is no tested technology to remove the drilling liquid from the drilling hole. Therefore, the new permit stipulates that the Alfred Wegener Institute (AWI) must investigate possible technologies for the removal of such drilling liquid. As soon as such technology has been identified, the AWI is obliged to remove the drilling liquid. Since use and continuance of the used drilling liquid Exxol® D40 (pure kerosene) and of the densifier (HCFC 141b) in the Antarctic are still controversial, the paper was intended to stimulate a debate on possible ways of developing reasonable alternatives to this drilling liquid and of developing and testing technologies for the complete removal of drilling liquids from the Antarctic.

(135) On the issue of drilling fluid removal from ice boreholes, the United Kingdom agreed with Germany on the need to debate the use of drill fluids and recalled that certain technologies already exist, as presented in IP 54 at CEP XI.

(136) Other papers submitted under this Agenda item were:

- IP 1 *Initial Environmental Evaluation for Development of Approach Path at Proposed New Indian Research Station at Larsemann Hills, East Antarctica* (India)

- IP 104 *An Environmental Management System for the Brazilian Antarctic Station "Comandante Ferraz"* (Brazil)

- IP 122 *Informe preliminar del Estudio de Impacto Ambiental ex – post de la Estación Científica Pedro Vicente Maldonado* (Ecuador)

- SP 11 *Annual List of Initial Environmental Evaluations (IEE) and Comprehensive Environmental Evaluations (CEE) prepared between April 1ˢᵗ 2009 and March 31ˢᵗ 2010*

Item 7: Area Protection and Management Plans

7a) Management Plans

    i. *Draft management plans which had been reviewed by the Subsidiary Group on Management Plans*

(137) In its capacity as convenor of the *Subsidiary Group on Management Plans (SGMP)*, Australia introduced WP 58 *Subsidiary Group on Management Plans – Report on Terms of Reference #1 to #3: Review of Draft Management Plans*. It noted that during the 2009/10 intersessional period the SGMP had included nineteen participants who communicated via the CEP Discussion Forum and email. Australia thanked all participants for their hard work.

(138) Australia noted that no draft management plans submitted to CEP XII were referred for intersessional review during the 2009/10 intersessional period, but the SGMP had continued its review, coordinated by the United Kingdom, of the draft management plan for ASPA 106: Cape Hallett, Northern Victoria Land, Ross Sea, which had been referred by CEP XI for intersessional review. In response to the SGMP's initial comments in March 2008, the United States had undertaken further fieldwork during the 2009/10 season, and had forwarded a revised version of the management plan to the SGMP.

(139) The SGMP recognised the significant amount of work undertaken by the United States to revise the management plan, as described in IP 59 *Review of management plans under the Protocol: an example at Cape Hallett*. In considering the revised plan, the SGMP had sought further clarification from the proponent on a small number of issues, including: whether the Area boundary could be modified slightly to allow safe and environmentally sensitive access by visitors to adjacent areas outside the ASPA; possible biosecurity issues arising from the presence within the Area of a frozen body of a dog; possible benefits of adding a marine component to the ASPA to

protect foraging areas used by the penguin colony; and the basis for allowing poultry products to be taken (but not released) into Area. The United States had provided a written response to the SGMP's comments, together with a further revision to the draft management plan.

(140) Australia informed the Committee that the SGMP had concluded that the issues raised during its reviews of the draft management plan had been adequately addressed by the proponent. Accordingly, the SGMP suggested that the CEP approves the revised Management Plan for ASPA 106.

(141) The Committee endorsed the SGMP's recommendation and agreed to forward the revised management plan for ASPA 106 (Cape Hallett) to the ATCM for adoption.

(142) The Committee also congratulated the United States on the thoroughness of the review process for the management plan, as outlined in IP 59.

(143) New Zealand thanked the SGMP for its extensive intersessional work and noted that the reduced time required in Committee to address management plans demonstrated the efficacy and key role of the SGMP.

   ii. *Draft revised management plans which had not been reviewed by the Subsidiary Group on Management Plans*

(144) The Committee considered revised management plans for the following Antarctic Specially Protected Areas (ASPAs) and Antarctic Specially Managed Areas (ASMAs) under this category:

   • WP 18 *Revision of maps and text for the Management Plan for Antarctic Specially Managed Area No 7: Southwest Anvers Island and Palmer Basin* (United States)

   • WP 19 rev. 1 *Revised Management Plan for ASPA No 119: Davis Valley and Forlidas Pond, Dufek Massif, Pensacola Mountains* (United States)

   • WP 27 *Revised Management Plan for Antarctic Specially Protected Area No 139: Biscoe Point, Anvers Island, Palmer Archipelago* (United States)

   • WP 31 *Revision of Management Plan for Antarctic Specially Protected Area (ASPA) No 105: Beaufort Island, Ross Sea* (New Zealand)

- WP 32 *Revision of Management Plan for Antarctic Specially Protected Area (ASPA) No 155: Cape Evans, Ross Island* (New Zealand)

- WP 33 *Revision of Management Plan for Antarctic Specially Protected Area (ASPA) No 157: Backdoor Bay, Cape Royds, Ross Island* (New Zealand)

- WP 34 *Revision of Management Plan for Antarctic Specially Protected Area (ASPA) No 158: Hut Point, Ross Island* (New Zealand)

- WP 35 *Revision of Management Plan for Antarctic Specially Protected Area (ASPA) No 159: Cape Adare, Borchgrevink Coast* (New Zealand)

- WP 38 *Review of Management Plans for Antarctic Specially Protected Areas (ASPAs) 101, 102, 103 and 164* (Australia)

- WP 43 *Management Plan for Antarctic Specially Protected Area No 126: Byers Peninsula, Livingston Island, South Shetland Islands* (United Kingdom, Chile and Spain)

- WP 55 *Review of Management Plan for Antarctic Specially Protected Area (ASPA) No 163: Dakshin Gangotri Glacier, Dronning Maud Land* (India)

(145) In introducing its revised management plans for ASMA 7, ASPA 139, and ASPA 119, the United States noted that:

- substantial increases in number of breeding pairs of gentoo penguins on Biscoe Point had necessitated the inclusion of a Helicopter Access Zone for ASPA 139 (Biscoe Point), with consequent changes to a map in the management plan for ASMA 7 (Southwest Anvers Island and Palmer Basin);

- the management plan for ASPA 119 (Davis Valley and Forlidas Pond) had been updated with input from the Russian Federation and United Kingdom. A notable change was the inclusion of a provision to allow visits to the Area for compelling educational reasons; and

- other minor changes to the text and maps of these plans were outlined in the corresponding Working Papers.

(146) In response to a query from ASOC, the United States advised that educational visits would allow the outstanding features of the Area to be documented for the purpose of informing a wider audience about the Area and its value in the global context. It had no plans at present for such an expedition, but in its view the potential for limited and strictly controlled visits for these purposes should not be prohibited in the future.

(147) In presenting the revised management plans for ASPA 105 (Beaufort Island), ASPA 155 (Cape Evans), ASPA 157 (Backdoor Bay), ASPA 158 (Hut Point), and ASPA 159 (Cape Adare) New Zealand noted that:

- the fast ice portion of the boundary to ASPA 105 had been revised and enlarged to account for the movement of the breeding area of emperor penguins; and

- minor modifications had been made to promote consistency between the management plans for the four ASPAs in the Ross Sea region which are designated to protect heroic era historic huts.

(148) The United Kingdom endorsed the proposed revisions to the management plans for ASPAs 155, 157, 158 and 159 and noted its strong interest in these Areas, given that all of these historic huts were associated with previous British expeditions.

(149) In presenting the revised management plans for ASPAs 101 (Taylor Rookery), 102 (Rookery Islands), 103 (Ardery Island and Odbert Island), and 164 (Scullin and Murray Monoliths), Australia noted that:

- only minor amendments to each of the management plans were required; and

- the provisions of the management plan for ASPA 102 had been modified to encourage the conduct of a census at the Giganteus Island southern giant petrel colony (situated within a Restricted Zone) at least once every five years, consistent with the recommendations arising from Resolution 5 (2009) on Protection of the Southern Giant Petrel.

(150) In presenting the revised management plan for ASPA 163 (Dakshin Gangotri Glacier), India noted that few observational visits had been made to the Area since its designation in 2005, and no significant changes had been introduced to the management plan.

(151) On behalf of the co-authors of WP 43, the United Kingdom noted that, following a visit to the Area in January 2010, the management plan for ASPA 126 (Byers Peninsula) had been revised and updated. Substantive changes included:

- the addition of Spain as a co-sponsor;

- the establishment of an International Coordination Committee to oversee implementation of the management plan;

- a requirement that no more than twelve people can be in the Area at any one time, due to the environmental sensitivity of the Area;

- redefining the boundary of the Area such that newly exposed ice-free ground resulting from the retreat of Rotch Dome would automatically be considered within the ASPA;

- the designation of Ray Promontory and recently de-glaciated areas along Rotch Dome ice front as restricted areas.

(152) The Committee agreed with the proponents' proposal that this draft revised management plan should be referred to the SGMP for intersessional review.

(153) The Committee agreed to refer all other revised management plans to the ATCM for adoption.

iii. New draft management plans for protected/managed areas

(154) There were no draft management plans submitted for proposed new ASPAs or ASMAs.

Advice to the ATCM

(155) The Committee had before it 15 revised protected or managed area management plans. One of these had been subject to review by the Subsidiary Group on Management Plans (SGMP) and 14 revised management plans had been submitted directly to CEP XIII.

(156) In reviewing the advice of the SGMP, and following the Committee's assessment of those plans that had not been subject to intersessional review, the Committee agreed to forward the following 14 management plans to the ATCM for adoption:

#	Name
ASMA 7	Southwest Anvers Island & Palmer Basin
ASPA 101	Taylor Rookery, Mac.Robertson Land
ASPA 102	Rookery Islands, Holme Bay, Mac.Robertson Land
ASPA 103	Ardery Island and Odbert Island, Budd Coast
ASPA 105	Beaufort Island, McMurdo Sound, Ross Sea
ASPA 106	Cape Hallett, Northern Victoria Land, Ross Sea
ASPA 119	Davis Valley and Forlidas Pond, Dufek Massif, Pensacola Mountains
ASPA 139	Biscoe Point, Anvers Island, Palmer Archipelago
ASPA 155	Cape Evans, Ross Island
ASPA 157	Backdoor Bay, Cape Royds, Ross Island
ASPA 158	Hut Point, Ross Island
ASPA 159	Cape Adare, Borchgrevink Coast
ASPA 163	Dakshin Gangotri Glacier, Dronning Maud Land
ASPA 164	Scullin and Murray Monoliths, Mac.Robertson Land, East Antarctica

(157) Noting that substantial changes were proposed to the management plan for ASPA 126 Byers Peninsula, the Committee decided to refer the management plan to the SGMP for intersessional review.

iv. Other matters relating to management plans for protected/managed areas

(158) As convenor of the SGMP, Australia introduced WP 30 *Subsidiary Group on Management Plans – Report on Term of Reference #4: Improving Management Plans and the Process for their Intersessional Review.* Australia noted that during the 2009/10 intersessional period the SGMP had addressed the tasks outlined in the work plan agreed by CEP XII.

(159) The Committee considered the draft suggested standard wording and template for ASPA management plans developed by the SGMP and presented in Attachment A to WP 30. These products were intended to promote consistency between management plans. The SGMP had again emphasised the need for management plans to contain sufficient details about the special features of the area in question and requirements for access and management, to ensure that people planning visits and national authorities responsible for issuing permits are able to do so in a manner consistent with the purpose for designation. Accordingly, the suggested standard wording and template were not intended to discourage proponents from developing and implementing

site-specific or creative and innovative approaches to area protection and management.

(160) The Committee noted that the SGMP had considered but did not reach a conclusion on the suitability of standard wording regarding taking poultry products into ASPAs. The Chair recalled that this issue had been raised in past meetings though never resolved. The Committee encouraged Members to seek further advice on this topic and provide advice to the SGMP or CEP as appropriate.

(161) Emphasising the importance of ensuring that the process for developing management plans does not become automated, the Committee endorsed the SGMP's proposal that the standard wording and template be completed and incorporated into a revised version of the *Guide to the Preparation of Management Plans for Antarctic Specially Protected Areas* (the Guide), which the SGMP would prepare during the 2010/11 intersessional period.

(162) The Committee next considered the SGMP's work coordinated by Norway on developing an approach to reviewing management plans not referred by the CEP for intersessional review. It was noted that the CEP had established a functional manner in which to review ASPA and ASMA management plans before adopting them, utilizing the function of the SGMP in that process. However, certain types of plans may not be subject to consideration by the SGMP, including:

- Type 1: Management plans in Annex V format that were adopted before the SGMP was established and which undergo such small changes (or none) during the five-year review and that the CEP advises the ATCM to adopt directly.

- Type 2: Management plans in Annex V format that are overdue for five-yearly review. Likely there is a process underway for the review of many of these management plans that may be delayed for various reasons, but some of these may not reappear in front of the CEP for a number of years.

- Type 3: Management plans in Annex V format that have undergone the five-yearly review, but have been determined by the proponent to not require revision, and thereby not put in front of the CEP for consideration.

- Type 4: Management plans that have not yet been adopted in Annex V format.

(163) The Committee agreed with the SGMP's recommendations on:

- establishing a long-term goal of ensuring that all ASPA and ASMA management plans contain adequate content, and are clear, consistent, and likely to be effective;

- adding an additional Term of Reference to provide a basis for the SGMP to suggest mechanisms for achieving this goal, as follows: *'Develop and suggest procedures that would assist in achieving a long-term goal aiming at ensuring that all ASPA and ASMA management plans contain adequate content, and are clear, consistent and likely to be effective'*; and

- agreeing that the SGMP should invite those Parties responsible for Type 2, 3 and 4 plans to provide information about the review status and timeframe, as a basis for further prioritisation.

(164) Noting that there are currently no guidelines for the preparation of ASMA management plans, the SGMP also brought forward a proposal by the United Kingdom suggesting that it would be useful to exchange best practice and produce guidelines for preparing management plans, perhaps by convening an ASMA workshop.

(165) The United States noted the importance of holding this workshop as soon as practical, due to the fact that three ASMA management plans are to be revised within the next two years.

(166) The Committee endorsed the idea of an ASMA workshop and noted that it remained necessary to identify a suitable date and venue for such a workshop, as well as options for funding the attendance of experts. In that respect, the Committee warmly welcomed an offer by Uruguay to host a workshop prior to CEP XIV, but noted that further discussions with the hosts of CEP XIV (Argentina) would take place during the intersessional period before any arrangements for a workshop could be finalised. The Committee noted that the objectives and themes identified in section 6 of WP 30 would provide a good basis for such a workshop.

(167) As agreed at ATCM XXXI (2008), the Committee reviewed the effectiveness of the SGMP over the previous two-year period and the suitability of its suggested work plan for the 2010/11 intersessional period. It agreed that the SGMP had been highly effective in advising the CEP on the matters

addressed in the group's Terms of Reference and that, as discussed earlier, the group's Terms of Reference should be expanded to include the function of providing advice on achieving the long-term goal of ensuring that all ASPA and ASMA management plans contain adequate content, and are clear, consistent and likely to be effective (Appendix 1).

(168) The Committee noted that several papers presented to the meeting raised issues that would be worth considering in the SGMP's work to review the Guide and, accordingly, endorsed a modified version of the forward work plan appended to WP 30 (Appendix 2).

(169) The Committee looked forward to receiving the outputs of the SGMP's future activities, and thanked Mr McIvor from Australia for his ongoing work to coordinate the SGMP.

Advice to the ATCM

(170) The Committee considered the report from the Subsidiary Group on Management Plans (SGMP) on its work, in accordance with its fourth Term of Reference, to improve management plans and the process for their intersessional review.

(171) In accordance with a commitment made at CEP XI (2008), the CEP reviewed the effectiveness of the SGMP and agreed that the group had been highly effective in providing advice on management plans referred for intersessional review and on improvements to management plans more generally and the process for their intersessional review.

(172) The Committee adopted a long-term goal of 'ensuring that all ASPA and ASMA management plans contain adequate content, and are clear, consistent, and likely to be effective' and, accordingly, expanded the SGMP's Terms of Reference to add a function of developing and suggesting procedures that would assist in achieving this long-term goal (Appendix 1).

(173) The Committee endorsed the SGMP's proposed work plan (Appendix 2), which includes work over the next two years to revise the *Guide to the Preparation of Management Plans for Antarctic Specially Protected Areas*, to plan further for a possible ASMA workshop, and to seek information from Members with a view to identifying options for achieving the long-term goal.

(174) The United States introduced WP 10 *Guidelines for the Application of Management Zones within Antarctic Specially Managed Areas and Antarctic Specially Protected Areas* which identified the wide range of zones used in existing ASMAs and ASPAs. It proposed a core set zones, and accompanying guidelines, which would help promote consistency between areas. This would assist not only those drafting management plans, but also people visiting ASMAs and ASPAs. The United States proposed that the draft guidelines could be referred to the SGMP for consideration as part of its work to review the *Guide to the Preparation of Management Plans for Antarctic Specially Protected Areas* (the Guide).

(175) In response to a question from the Netherlands, the United States clarified that Visitor Zones would only apply to ASMAs, not to ASPAs.

(176) The United Kingdom noted its agreement with the suggestion in the paper that the development of a core set of zones should not preclude the development of new zone categories as necessary.

(177) ASOC agreed that zoning can be a very useful management tool, and noted that zones need to be strategically chosen, taking into account impacts of human activities and the values to be protected. In its view, zoning should not be used as a tool to simply reinforce continuing existing uses.

(178) The Committee thanked the United States for the extremely useful framework, and agreed that WP 10 should be forwarded to the SGMP for consideration in its work to revise the Guide.

(179) Argentina introduced WP 50 *Use of the Guidelines for the designation of Protected Areas* proposing that a number of additional elements be included in Resolution 1 (2008) "Guide to the Presentation of Working Papers Containing Proposals for ASPAs, ASMAs or HSMs", to allow for confirmation that Resolution 1 (2000) *Guidelines for Implementation of the Framework for Protected Areas* (the Guidelines) were being implemented effectively.

(180) The Committee welcomed Argentina's objective of promoting the use of the Guidelines appended to Resolution 1 (2000). However some Members expressed the view that requiring proponents to present supporting information, as proposed, would create an additional administrative burden,

and that management plans themselves should contain sufficient information about the reasons for designation.

(181) While recognising concerns regarding the potential burden of this proposed additional paperwork, Argentina reiterated the crucial need to reinforce the use of the Guidelines in designating protected areas.

(182) Norway supported the intention of Argentina's proposal, and highlighted the value of Members providing early information to the Committee when considering the designation of a new area, such as in IP 33 *Blood Falls, Taylor Valley, Victoria Land: an initiative towards proposal of a new Antarctic Specially Protected Area* (United States).

(183) Australia noted that the Guidelines appended to Resolution 1 (2000) had been adopted after the Guide to the Preparation of Management Plans for Antarctic Specially Protected Areas, and that in the SGMP's work to review the Guide it could be useful to include cross references to the Guidelines, as one means of further promoting their use.

(184) The Committee agreed in principle on the benefit of following a process when developing protected area proposals and pursuing a systematic approach to the protected areas system. The Chair noted that the Committee might wish to keep under consideration other options for promoting the use of the guidelines, and the possible need to review and update them as necessary.

(185) The United States briefly introduced IP *33 Blood Falls, Taylor Valley, Victoria Land: an initiative towards proposal of a new Antarctic Specially Protected Area*, encouraging interested Members to participate in an ongoing discussion on whether and how to afford protection to this area.

(186) The following papers were also submitted under this agenda item:

- IP 16 *Deception Island Antarctic Specially Managed Area (ASMA) Management Group report* (Argentina, Chile, Norway, Spain, US & UK)

- IP 18 *Bird populations on Deception Island* (Spain)

- IP 19 *Volcanic risk on Deception Island* (Spain)

- IP 31 *Revision of Maps for Antarctic Specially Managed Area No 2 McMurdo Dry Valleys, Victoria Land* (United States)

- IP 40 *Report of the Larsemann Hills Antarctic Specially Managed Area (ASMA) Management Group* (Australia, China, India, Romania and Russia)

- IP 92 *Amundsen-Scott South Pole Station, South Pole Antarctic Specially Managed Area (ASMA No 5) 2010 Management Report* (United States)

- IP 95 *Management Report of Narębski Point, ASPA No 171 (2009-2010)* (Korea)

- IP 115 *Revisión del ASMA N° 4. Isla Decepción. Bibliografía científica española* (Spain)

- SP 10 *Register of the status of Antarctic Specially Protected Area and Antarctic Specially Managed Area Management Plans* (Secretariat)

7b) Historic Sites and Monuments

(187) The United States introduced WP 5 *Proposed addition of the Plaque Commemorating the PM-3A Nuclear Power Plant at McMurdo Station to the List of Historic Sites and Monument* proposing the plaque commemorating the PM-3A nuclear power plant at McMurdo station for addition to the List of Historic Sites and Monuments. The US noted that the plaque commemorates the significant technical achievement of safely installing, operating, and removing the first, and only, nuclear power plant in Antarctica.

(188) The Russian Federation supported the proposal, noting that the plaque commemorates a memorable achievement, and represents a tribute to those involved.

(189) The Committee endorsed the proposal and agreed to recommend to the ATCM the inclusion of the plaque on the list of Historic Sites and Monuments.

(190) The United Kingdom and France presented WP 25 *Report of an incident at Wordie House (HSM No 62)* (United Kingdom, France and Ukraine), for the information of the Committee, and in accordance with Article 13 of the Protocol. The United Kingdom briefly described an incident which resulted in some damage to Wordie House (HSM 62), believed to be caused by individuals from two yachts understood to originate from France. While there had been damage to the hut, and a risk to the safety of the

individuals concerned, there were fortunately no injuries and the damage was subsequently repaired by a team from the United Kingdom Antarctic Heritage Trust which was working on the site.

(191) The United Kingdom noted that this incident raised concern about the behaviour of a small minority of visitors, and also about the effectiveness of authorisation processes, and suggested there is a need to raise the awareness of the requirements of the Antarctic Treaty and the Protocol.

(192) France thanked the United Kingdom and Ukraine for their assistance in launching an investigation into this event. France noted two potential breaches in this incident: entering Antarctica without authorisation; and forced entry into the historic site. France noted that investigations are ongoing, and made reference to a range of legal issues that may arise in relation to any legal proceedings.

(193) The United Kingdom and France outlined their approaches to disseminating information on visit requirements to the yachting community, including through websites, yacht clubs and publications, and recommended that the Committee discuss strategies to communicate and enforce the provisions of the Protocol.

(194) Ukraine echoed the concerns expressed by the United Kingdom and France, noting that the incident occurred in a regularly visited area, close to Vernadsky Station. Ukraine stated the individuals involved were not Ukrainian, and encouraged the Parties to expand their efforts to ensure that potential visitors were made aware of the requirements of the Protocol.

(195) IAATO thanked the United Kingdom, France and Ukraine for raising awareness of these issues, and drew the attention of the Committee to its outreach efforts, designed to inform non-IAATO yacht and small boat operators of the requirements for visiting Antarctica.

(196) The Russian Federation expressed its profound concern with this incident, and reminded the Committee of previous incidents involving its facilities, where it experienced similar difficulties in taking legal proceedings. The Russian Federation also noted that it is taking action to endow its station managers with law enforcement powers to facilitate the function of primary investigation.

(197) Argentina echoed the concerns expressed, and noted it had experienced some similar incidents involving its own facilities. Argentina suggested that the advertising of adventure activities may encourage similar poor behaviour.

(198) The United Kingdom welcomed the cooperation between Parties in responding to and investigating the incident but also highlighted that the vast majority of visitors to the Antarctic behaved responsibly.

(199) The Committee expressed its concern at the incident, in particular the damage to a listed historic site, and noted that the proposals in WP 25 will be considered by the ATCM.

(200) Argentina introduced WP 47 *Proposal for the discussion of aspects related to the management of Historic Sites and Monuments*. Argentina considered that further work is needed to develop practical, specific tools to ensure the protection of Historic Sites and Monuments. Argentina also referred to IP 22, *Additional information for the discussion of issues associated with the management and operation of Historic Sites and Monuments* which forms an appendix for WP 47 and contains a summary of current HSM management tools, as well as a brief analysis of the entries on the List of Historic Sites and Monuments.

(201) Argentina suggested discussion of a change in the strategy for dealing with historic sites and monuments, both to evaluate the concept of what is considered to be "historic", and to include the more holistic concept of 'enhancement', which encompasses protection, conservation and dissemination. Argentina proposed that the Committee establish an ICG for further discussion of these issues.

(202) Chile welcomed Argentina's work, noting that in its view 'enhancement' was an important concept that should underlay the approach to HSM's.

(203) Noting the large intersessional workload for Members, the Committee welcomed Argentina's offer to lead informal discussions in the intersessional period, supported by the CEP web-based forum, with a view to reporting to CEP XIV.

(204) Chile introduced WP 67 *Proposed Modification to Historic Site Nº 37*, which outlines a proposal for protection of additional elements associated with the historic site and the former General Bernardo O'Higgins Base.

(205) Noting that additional time would be required by some Parties to consult appropriate experts, the meeting welcomed Chile's offer to work with Parties on the proposal during the intersessional period, with an opportunity for more detailed consideration at CEP XIV and any improvement which may be required for approval of this document.

(206) Uruguay introduced IP 67 *Actualización del estudio de los restos históricos del naufragio de Punta Suffield*, an update on the status of the investigations of a shipwreck near Artigas station. Uruguay anticipated bringing forward a proposal for the inclusion of the shipwreck on the list of Historic Sites and Monuments in the future.

Advice to the ATCM

(207) The Committee recommends that the ATCM approves the addition of the following new site to the list of Historic Sites and Monuments held under Measure 3 (2003):

- Plaque Commemorating the PM-3A Nuclear Power Plant at McMurdo Station.

7c) Site Guidelines

(208) Proposals for five new Visitor Site Guidelines were presented to the Committee.

(209) The United States introduced WP 17 *Antarctic Treaty Visitor Site Guide for Torgersen Island, Arthur Harbor, Southwest Anvers Island* noting that the area had long been of considerable interest for tourist visits because of its high biological diversity, its accessibility and its proximity to Palmer Station, which allows visitors to observe both Antarctic wildlife and scientific research operations. The United States noted that although activities at Torgersen Island are covered by the Management Plan for ASMA 7, it was important to present information in a format that was easily accessible to tour operators, guides and visitors.

(210) The United Kingdom introduced WP 39 *Site Guidelines for Danco Island, Errera Channel, Antarctic Peninsula* (United Kingdom, United States and IAATO). The United Kingdom informed the Committee that the island was the site of the former British Base "O". It also has a colony of gentoo

penguins and is frequently visited by tour operators, private yachts, and occasionally national Antarctic programmes.

(211) Recalling its revision of the management plan for ASPA 106 Cape Hallett (WP 58), the United States presented WP 42 *Antarctic Treaty Visitor Site Guidelines for Seabee Hook, Cape Hallett, Northern Victoria Land, Ross Sea*. The United States noted that controlled tourist visitation to the Adélie penguin colony on Seabee Hook, which had previously been allowed in accordance with the provisions for a Management Zone contained within ASPA 106, was more appropriately addressed through the framework of a Visitor Site Guideline. Following recent surveys, analyses and consultations, the Management Plan for ASPA 106 had been substantially revised and, as part of that process, two separate areas on Seabee Hook were assessed as suitable for continued tourist access, such that the values for which ASPA 106 was designated would not be compromised.

(212) The United Kingdom presented WP *56 Site Guidelines for Damoy Point, Wiencke Island, Antarctic Peninsula* (United Kingdom and Argentina). The area contains the Damoy Hut, a British air transit facility established in 1975 and designated as HSM 84 in 2009, and the Argentine Bahía Dorian Hut, established in 1953. The United Kingdom advised that Damoy Point is visited frequently by tour operators, private yachts and by national Antarctic programmes. It noted that the adoption of Visitor Site Guidelines for Danco Island and Damoy Point would mean that Site Guidelines and/or national operator procedures would be in place for the twenty most frequently visited tourist landing sites in Antarctica and that this was a significant achievement for the Committee.

(213) France questioned whether the asbestos warning in the proposed Visitor Site Guidelines for Damoy Point was relevant given the short period of potential exposure during brief tourist visits.

(214) The United Kingdom noted that other Visitor Site Guidelines include information about hazards and that any asbestos in the Damoy Hut was being managed.

(215) Chile introduced WP 64 *Site Guidelines for the Northeast beach of Ardley Peninsula (Ardley Island), King George Island* (25 de Mayo Island), South Shetland Islands (Argentina and Chile). The paper contained a revised version of the draft Visitor Site Guidelines presented to CEP XII, modified

to incorporate comments received during the intersessional period. Chile and Argentina highlighted the importance of Visitor Site Guidelines due to the close proximity of the site to ASPA 150 Ardley Island and the diverse biological values contained therein.

(216) After making minor changes to the Site Guidelines for Danco Island and Damoy Point related to wildlife distances, the Committee approved these guidelines.

(217) A number of Parties raised queries regarding provisions in the proposed Visitor Site Guidelines for Ardley Peninsula, including in relation to the provisions limiting access to only 40 visitors per day, and allowing visits by station personnel only on weekends.

(218) Following further discussions during the meeting, it was not possible to reach agreement on the Site Guidelines as presented. The proponents agreed to consult with interested Parties during the intersessional period, with a view to submitting a final revised version for approval at CEP XIV. Chile and Argentina look forward to the adoption of these guidelines to afford protection to ASPA 150 next year.

(219) The Committee agreed to present the Site Guidelines for Torgersen Island, Danco Island, Seabee Hook and Damoy Point to the ATCM for adoption.

Advice to the ATCM

(220) The Committee approved the guidelines for Torgersen Island, Danco Island, Damoy Point, and Seabee Hook, and agreed to forward them to the ATCM for adoption by means of a Resolution.

(221) The United States briefly introduced IP 26 *Antarctic Site Inventory: 1994-2010* (United States), noting that the Antarctic Site Inventory continued to collect biological data and site-descriptive information in the Antarctic Peninsula, a project that had been underway since 1994. The Chair noted the utility of the data from the Antarctic Site Inventory and thanked Oceanites for its valuable contribution to the CEP's ongoing study into the environmental aspects and impacts of Antarctic tourism.

(222) The Netherlands expressed its view that tourism should have no more than a minor or transitory impact, and that Site Guidelines should be enforced

in a strict manner and might be linked to national processes of licenses and environmental impact assessments. It felt that, while Site Guidelines are a useful tool, additional measures are needed to control the impacts of tourism. ASOC expressed its support for these views.

(223) IAATO presented IP 62 *Report on IAATO Member use of Antarctic Peninsula Landing Site and ATCM Visitor Site Guidelines.*

(224) Several Parties noted the importance of having up-to-date information on tourism and thanked IAATO for its work to provide regular reports to the Committee.

(225) The Chair recalled that CEP XII had established an ICG to discuss 1) the development of generic guidelines to go alongside site specific guidelines and 2) the process for reviewing site guidelines.

(226) Several Members thanked Chile for leading the ICG, which had made useful progress during the intersessional period but had not completed its work. The Committee welcomed the offer by Australia (Dr Phillip Tracey) to leading the continuing work of the ICG during the coming intersessional period.

(227) The Committee agreed the following Terms of Reference for the ICG:

   i. Review the environmental elements of Recommendation XVIII-1 (1994) Guidance for Visitors to the Antarctic, and Guidance for Those Organising and Conducting Tourism and Non-governmental Activities in the Antarctic and other advice to visitors including in Site Guidelines, Recommendations and Resolutions;

   ii. Develop revised and updated guidance for visitors based on Recommendation XVIII-1 in a format that can also be used as a generic cover to accompany site specific guidelines;

   iii. Consider options for how the CEP might most effectively assess new site guidelines and periodically review existing guidelines; and

   iv. Report to CEP XIV on the outcomes of this work.

7d) *Human footprint and wilderness values*

(228) Australia presented IP 48 *Topic Summary: Footprint* informing the Committee that, in order to facilitate the CEP's work to develop an agreed understanding

of the term 'footprint', it had reviewed CEP meeting reports and meeting papers since 1998 referring to that concept. Australia also recalled that the topic had received more detailed consideration as part of the Committee's recent strategic planning discussions. From its review, Australia observed that several categories of 'footprint' have been identified over time, most of them considering footprint as a measure of the spatial extent of physical disturbance related to national programmes activities, although tourism is mentioned in some papers. The concept is also referred to in several CEEs. Other papers considered by the CEP in the past had discussed ways to measure, monitoring and reduce the footprint of various activities.

(229) The Committee thanked Australia for preparing this topic summary which helpfully synthesised the CEP's past consideration of this issue.

(230) The United Kingdom introduced WP 23 *Assessing cumulative environmental impacts: identifying the distribution and concentration of national operator activities in Antarctica* describing a method to estimate the spatial extent and chronology of human activities in Antarctica using information derived from a number of science and mapping databases. The activities of the United Kingdom within the Antarctic Peninsula region were shown as an example. The UK noted that science and survey work had been performed by Treaty Parties at sites dispersed throughout Antarctica for at least the last 65 years, and though reliable data on precise location of past activities is not always readily available, the spatial extent and chronology of national operator activities in Antarctica can be generated using location data held in existing science and mapping databases.

(231) The UK suggested that the CEP endorses the use of existing systems in the collation of information relating to the location of past science, survey and logistic activities, in order to provide a holistic perspective of human impact across Antarctica, which could be used to inform future environmental policy and management. The UK further suggested that the CEP considers other methods to determine human activity at a regional and continent-wide scale.

(232) The Committee thanked the UK for their paper and several Members noted the importance of this kind of work to integrate different sources of data to help in characterising human footprint in Antarctica.

(233) Russia welcomed such a constructive approach to understanding human impact in Antarctica noting that human beings are now part of the Antarctic environment.

(234) Argentina cautioned that Parties interested in undertaking such work explore this, as well as other likely approaches that may also be applicable.

(235) The UK agreed and explained this was the approach recommended in the paper.

(236) The United States suggested that Parties share ideas on how cumulative impacts may be assessed through a range of approaches. The US drew attention to its McMurdo Station monitoring programme which it would report on at CEP XIV, as well as a GIS it had developed to help manage activities in the McMurdo Dry Valleys.

(237) COMNAP offered assistance through its data management expert group to examine other methods to determine human activity at a regional/continent-wide scale. Several Parties thanked COMNAP for their offer of assistance.

(238) Australia recalled the CEP's obligations with regard to advising the ATCM on the state of the Antarctic environment and noted that approaches such as the one demonstrated by the UK would greatly assist in characterising human pressure on the Antarctic environment.

(239) ASOC recalled the obligations under Article 8(3) of Annex III to the Protocol requiring Parties to prepare an inventory of sites of past activity. ASOC suggested that Members submit examples of such inventories to the Committee as a further means of assessing human footprint.

(240) Germany supported ASOC's suggestion and noted that a centralised means of holding information of all sites of past activity in Antarctica would be extremely useful.

(241) New Zealand welcomed the UK initiative noting that it was undertaking a similar exercise for its own national programme activities in the Ross Sea region. New Zealand also drew attention to its WP 29 T*he concept of Human Footprint in the Antarctic* and supporting IP 49, with the same name. New Zealand noted that there was considerable overlap of issues including the concepts of wilderness, footprint, and human impacts and suggested that

the Committee may need to develop an agreed understanding of such terms. New Zealand suggested that the study of human impacts in Antarctica be retained on the CEP's agenda and on its five-year work plan and looked forward to working with the UK and others in developing such initiatives in the intersessional period.

(242) Argentina agreed that the CEP may need to define the term "footprint" and recalled that the CEP's EIA Guidelines include the term "output" which may be associated with the concept of footprint. Argentina also suggested that "Human Footprint" be moved on the CEP's agenda to item 6 on EIA matters due to the fact that its scope under Area Protection may be limited.

(243) ASOC drew attention to its poster in the coffee area that explores the concept of footprint and welcomed comments and further collaboration on the subject.

(244) The Committee agreed that this was an important issue and encouraged Members to work together during the intersessional period and to bring further papers to CEP XIV that might assist in developing a better understanding of the term "human footprint", as well as on data and information sources on human activities in Antarctica, including examples of inventories of sites of past activity, and examples of analytical methods that might be used to characterise human impacts in Antarctica.

(245) The Committee agreed that it would consider where the issue of human footprint should sit on its agenda at its next meeting.

(246) ASOC presented IP 81 *Coastal Hydrocarbon Pollution: A Case Study from Deception Island, Antarctica* on monitoring activities conducted in 2001/02 which identified detectable hydrocarbon concentrations at a number of Deception Island coastal sites. ASOC said that the results suggested that regular and effective monitoring should take place to allow assessment of the impacts of ongoing activities at Deception Island as well as at other Antarctic sites where high levels of shipping occur.

(247) Spain's IP 20 *Possible human impact on Deception Island* describing tourist activities in Deception Island and detected impacts on the local environment was noted by the Committee.

7e) Marine Spatial Protection and Management

(248) New Zealand introduced IP 107 *Bioregionalisation and Spatial Ecosystem Processes in the Ross Sea Region* informing the Committee of the outcomes to a Workshop on Bioregionalisation and Spatial Ecosystem Processes in the Ross Sea Region, held in Wellington, New Zealand in June 2009. The aim of the workshop was to contribute to the identification and potential designation of marine protected areas. The workshop was well attended by international experts. New Zealand noted that the outputs from the workshop included a fine-scale benthic/demersal bioregionalisation of the Ross Sea region, a fine-scale pelagic bioregionalisation of the Ross Sea region, as well as an agreed list of spatially bounded ecosystem processes of particular importance in the regional ecosystem, and which may be amenable to protection using spatial management tools.

(249) New Zealand noted that it intended to submit the workshop report to the next meeting of SC-CAMLR's Working Group on Ecosystem Monitoring and Management (WG-EMM).

(250) The SC-CAMLR Observer thanked New Zealand for introducing the report and reminded the Committee that CCAMLR had in place a well developed programme for working towards a network of marine protected areas by the 2012 deadline. Through its own Southern Ocean bioregionalisation exercise CCAMLR had identified 11 priority areas for action, which had also been endorsed by the CEP (Appendix 4 of the report of CEP XII refers). In 2009 SC-CAMLR had also agreed a timetable of action to work towards the 2012 deadline. This timetable is referred to in WP 7 and IP 12.

(251) The SC-CAMLR Observer noted that in taking this forward CCAMLR would be looking to draw on expertise elsewhere, in particular within SCAR and CEP. In that regard the SC-CAMLR Observer invited a CEP Observer to attend WG-EMM in July 2010, as well as the planned CCAMLR workshop in 2011. During both of these meetings, work will be undertaken to synthesize relevant data from multiple sources. Thus, the Committee was invited to facilitate submission of such information to WG-EMM.

(252) The US noted CCAMLR's timetable for action on marine spatial protection and suggested that this might be reflected in the CEP's five year work plan, noting the invitation for a CEP Observer to attend WG-EMM and the 2011 workshop.

(253) Italy introduced IP 45 *Terra Nova Bay – Wood Bay Marine Protected Area inside a wider proposal for a Ross Sea MPA* recalling that the establishment of spatial protection for marine biodiversity had been identified as a priority issue by both the CEP and SC-CAMLR. Italy informed the Committee that the aim of the proposed MPA was to conserve and protect the unique and outstanding environment of the Terra Nova Bay region by regulating the activities within the area. The area would require special management to ensure that the important values are protected and sustained in the long-term, especially the extensive scientific data sets collected over the last 25 years. The Committee also noted that the Republic of Korea and Italy will be holding a workshop on Terra Nova Bay Marine Protected Area at the end of May in Rome.

(254) Italy noted that it would also send the paper and possibly a report from the joint Italy - Republic of Korea workshop to SC-CAMLR's WG-EMM in July 2010 for further consideration alongside other spatial marine management papers, including the outcomes to New Zealand's Ross Sea bioregionalisation workshop.

(255) Australia, supported by the United Kingdom, suggested that the CEP should welcome and support the action taken by CCAMLR, including to afford protection to the South Orkneys Islands marine area and to establish a timetable for actions to develop a marine protected areas system. Australia recalled that the joint CEP/SC-CAMLR workshop had recognised that the issue of marine spatial protection and management is best led by SC-CAMLR, and that the CEP had previously stressed the need to constructively engage in and support SC-CAMLR's work in this area. Australia noted that it would be useful to establish a suitable mechanism to ensure such engagement takes place.

(256) Argentina noted its support for any measures to improve marine conservation in the Southern Ocean, but noted that the CEP and ATCM needed to give attention as to how they might also take action to achieve this.

(257) Belgium recorded its support for the priority attention being paid to marine protection mechanisms in the Ross Sea region so as to make good progress by the 2012 deadline.

(258) The Netherlands strongly supported the priority being given to a marine protected area network, noting that a lot needs to be done before the 2012

deadline. It further noted that establishing such a network becomes all the more important because of climate change.

(259) The Committee welcomed CCAMLR's efforts to afford protection to this marine area in the South Orkney Islands.

(260) ASOC introduced IP 77 *The Case for Inclusion of the Ross Sea Continental Shelf and Slope in a Southern Ocean Network of Marine Reserves*. ASOC noted the significant biological diversity of the Ross Sea and the extent of baseline ecological data and urged that comprehensive protection be afforded to the Ross Sea.

(261) France, New Zealand and the US thanked ASOC for their valuable contribution to the discussion on Marine Protected Areas.

(262) ASOC also presented IP 83 *Rising to the Challenge: Key steps to deliver a Comprehensive and Representative Marine Protected Areas Network in the Southern Ocean by 2012* on the important milestones for the next several years necessary to achieve a comprehensive and representative network of marine protected areas and marine reserves across the Southern Ocean by 2012.

(263) The Committee thanked ASOC for this paper.

(264) The Committee welcomed SC-CAMLR's work on marine protected areas and expressed its desire to remain closely involved in SC-CAMLR's work and remain abreast of developments in this area of mutual interest. The Chair noted that the ASMA workshop proposed by the SGMP intends to address the issue of how the ASMA mechanism might usefully be applied to the concept of marine protected areas, and that this might also assist SC-CAMLR's further deliberation on this issue.

(265) In response to a suggestion by the United Kingdom, the Secretariat agreed to consider preparing a summary of the work that the CEP has done on marine protected areas as a contribution to SC-CAMLR's efforts.

Advice to the ATCM

(266) The Committee welcomed the evolving cooperation with SC-CAMLR and, noting that the issue of spatial marine management will be discussed in detail,

accepted SC-CAMLR's invitation to send an observer to SC-CAMLR's WG-EMM meeting in July 2010. The Committee nominated Dr George Watters (US) as its observer to WG-EMM.

(267) The Committee recognised SC-CAMLR's timetable for action towards developing a network of marine protected areas by the 2012 deadline, and mirrored the timetable in the CEP's five-year work programme, noting that it would nominate observers to CCAMLR meetings and workshops as appropriate.

(268) The Committee further welcomed CCAMLR's progress in affording protection to a marine area in the South Orkney Islands and encouraged further areas to be identified in the 11 priority areas endorsed by both SC-CAMLR and CEP.

(269) Uruguay introduced IP 32 *Identificación y evaluación de la acción antrópica de grupos poblacionales de mamíferos marinos pinnípedos en áreas de la costa del Estrecho de Drake*, which referred to fishing activity debris and pinniped populations on such beaches.

(270) An additional paper submitted under this Agenda item was:

- IP 58 *Designation of a new Marine Protected Area for the South Orkney Islands southern shelf* (United Kingdom)

7f) Other Annex V Matters

(271) SCAR introduced WP 3 *Biodiversity-based Evaluation of the Environmental Domains Analysis* recalling that, at ATCM XXX, it had agreed to undertake an assessment of the extent to which the outcome of the Environmental Domains Analysis (EDA) corresponds with patterns found in spatially explicit biodiversity data for the region compiled in the SCAR Biodiversity Database. SCAR noted that the use of abiotic environmental variables as surrogate measures of diversity is a well-established approach used for other continental regions. It informed the Committee that the EDA provided a useful and important measure of environmental variation across Antarctica that, in terms of the ice-free domains, can be considered essential as a first order assessment of likely systematic variation in biodiversity.

(272) SCAR suggested that for meaningful analysis at the finer spatial scales typically used in protected area designation, the EDA must be supplemented with biodiversity data, which not only reflect current conditions but, importantly, historical processes that cannot in many instances be captured by modern environmental data.

(273) The Committee welcomed this comprehensive and useful work by SCAR. Noting that more comprehensive terrestrial biodiversity information would increase the ability to undertake detailed and thorough analyses, the Committee agreed that Members should strongly encourage national scientific programmes to collect further biodiversity data and make such data available via the SCAR Biodiversity Database maintained by the Australian Antarctic Division. The Committee noted that such action was also encouraged by the ATME on Climate Change (Recommendation 20). The Committee also noted that the EDA was one tool to assist with further developing the protected areas system, but that it was important to draw effectively on all available tools.

(274) Australia noted that SCAR's assessment might also usefully serve as the basis for an interim biodiversity assessment or baseline for state of the Antarctic environment reporting.

(275) India informed the Committee that a monograph of lichens has already been published.

(276) Australia introduced WP 54 *Enhancing the Antarctic Protected Areas Database to help assess and further develop the protected areas system.* It recalled that at CEP XII the Committee endorsed the SGMP's suggestions on: including additional information in the protected areas database; and promoting the use of global positioning systems (GPS) to accurately define protected area boundaries. Australia proposed that the Committee consider expanding the protected areas database to incorporate additional information, including the primary reason for designation, values being protected, an accurate indication of the size of the area and the environmental domain(s) represented. It also proposed that the Committee consider encouraging proponents of ASPAs and ASMAs to submit area boundaries in a suitable digital format. Collectively, these actions would assist the CEP to assess how existing or proposed protected areas represent the environmental domains and the suite of values identified by Annex V for protection in ASPAs.

(277) Many Members and ASOC supported the proposals, noting the benefits of making such data and information centrally available through the Secretariat website. Other Members supported the proposals in principle but noted a need to further consider the detail of some elements, including regarding a consistent approach to describing geospatial data.

(278) Australia thanked the Committee for these remarks and invited comments from interested parties during the intersessional period, with a view to possibly bringing an updated proposal to the next meeting. Australia also indicated that it would discuss these ideas further with the Secretariat.

(279) The United Kingdom introduced WP 16 T*he Implications of Climate Change for the Antarctic Protected Areas System.* It noted that climate change is likely to have significant implications for terrestrial, freshwater and marine ecosystems, and for ASPAs protecting these environments, in particular in areas where regional climate warming is established (for example, the Antarctic Peninsula). The United Kingdom also noted that ASPAs should become an increasingly important tool in mitigating the impacts of climate change, by ensuring that other pressures are minimised.

(280) The United Kingdom proposed that the CEP consider:

- How to ensure a more strategic approach to ASPA selection and designation. Such an approach should consider the implications of climate change, particularly in regions of rapid change (eg, Antarctic Peninsula). It should be evidence-based, dynamic and flexible enough to fast-track the protection of important new sites and facilitate the de-listing of sites for which the principal values no longer exist;

- Developing a methodology for classifying existing ASPAs continent-wide according to their potential vulnerability to regional climate change;

- Whether particular attention should be given to ASPAs which contain, or whose boundaries comprise, ice-fronts. In some cases, automatic temporary protection might be afforded to newly-exposed ground following ice retreat;

- Giving newly-exposed marine habitats protection following the collapse of ice-shelves to allow scientific research to establish baseline information and monitor further change;

167

- Whether further spatial protection for species that are particularly vulnerable to climate change (eg, Adélie and emperor penguins) is appropriate to minimise other impacts that might limit their survival in marginal locations;

- Reviewing the need for further or continued site-protection of species whose abundance or range has increased substantially under climate warming;

- Whether it would be appropriate to use the ASPA system to protect natural colonisation and establishment events on the basis of their importance to science, and their uniqueness or rarity.

(281) The Committee noted that this paper had also been submitted to the ATME on Climate Change, and that some of these proposals were reflected in the recommendations outlined in the ATME report (WP 63), particularly including:

- *Recommendation 24*: The ATME recommends that CEP review the means of applying protected and managed area management tools to ensure sufficient flexibility to account for climate change effects. Such a review should consider:

    - the need to ensure that climate change effects are assessed during each five-yearly review of management plans, including for example, the need to establish protected and managed area boundaries that are climate change resilient; and

    - the potential to delist sites at which the original values to be protected have been lost or degraded.

- *Recommendation 25*: The ATME recommends that the CEP consider a systematic approach to protected or managed areas to:

    - protect species, or habitats identified to be of particular risk to climate change consequences (cf. Recommendation 18);

    - accommodate areas that have potential to be environmental or climate refuges;

    - set aside areas for future climate change related research, including reference areas.

- *Recommendation 26*: The ATME recommends, recognising the responsibilities of and need to coordinate with CCAMLR, that the CEP consider, and advise the ATCM accordingly, as to means by which automatic interim protection might be afforded to newly exposed areas, such as marine areas exposed through ice-shelf collapse.

(282) The United Kingdom indicated its intention to undertake work to classify protected areas according to their vulnerability to climate change, and to report back to CEP XIV.

(283) Argentina and France agreed that climate change needs to be considered in the management of Antarctica and the designation of ASPAs and ASMAs, but noted that it was important to consider candidate areas on a case-by-case basis rather than designate areas automatically. Argentina also emphasised the importance of using existing tools for selecting protected areas (eg, Resolution 1 (2000)) and drawing on other available management tools as appropriate (eg, specially protected species designation).

(284) ASOC noted that the concept of interim protection was not new and cited the example of new islands' protection under Recommendation VI-11.

(285) The United States emphasised the importance of including climate change in future planning as opposed to responding to changes as they happen. It suggested that the forward-looking paper (WP 16) be submitted to CCAMLR and WG-EMM for their consideration.

(286) Australia noted that the protected areas system is a fundamental environmental management tool, including for maximising the resilience of the Antarctic environment and ecosystems to climate change. It also noted that climate change may have implications for the continuing protection of values within existing protected areas. These are each important issues for the CEP's attention when developing advice to the ATCM on protection of the Antarctic environment and on managing the protected areas system. Australia noted that it would be important to revisit the paper's recommendations in conjunction with the climate change recommendations.

(287) The Netherlands noted its support for the United Kingdom's proposals and in particular, the fifth recommendation on affording protection to key vulnerable species.

(288) Norway emphasised that discussion of these recommendations should be added to the Committee's five-year work plan, and underscored its interest in continuing discussion of these issues informally during the intersessional period.

(289) The Committee welcomed the United Kingdom's initiative, and noted that the protected areas system was an important tool to management the implications of climate change. The Committee also welcomed the United Kingdom's offer to take forward work on classifying existing protected areas according to their vulnerability to climate change. It agreed to consider the issues raised in WP 16 in its forward planning through the five-year work plan, and to make the paper available to the SGMP and to WG-EMM for consideration.

(290) Germany introduced WP 40 *Third Progress Report on the Discussion of the International Working Group about Possibilities for Environmental Management of Fildes Peninsula and Ardley Island* (Chile and Germany) summarising the actions of the International Working Group (IWG) established to consider a management scheme for the Fildes Peninsula region. It noted that an IWG meeting held in July 2009 in Punta Arenas had discussed the need to establish and to further define a Facilities Zone in the area. Germany also advised that a revised draft management plan for Fildes Peninsula had been produced during the intersessional period.

(291) Germany noted that while some progress had been made on developing a management framework for the Fildes Peninsula region, the following aspects should be taken into consideration in future discussions:

- the spatial synthesis of the different requirements concerning a possible Facilities Zone, on the basis of the maps submitted by the countries with stations in the area;

- the proposed revised management plan and its relationship with the existing and any proposed ASPA in the region;

- any missing requirements, either in the information already provided by stations, or in other matters requiring coordination and enhancing or contributing to the justification for a Fildes Peninsula ASMA.

(292) Other participants in the IWG thanked Chile and Germany for their leadership of the group.

(293) Uruguay noted that the IWG would continue intersessional work on developing a system of Codes of Conduct for the environmental protection of the region. It cited the discussion of Ardley Island as an example of the development of this system.

(294) Argentina emphasised the importance of collaboratively managing this sensitive area, and expressed its hope for an expedient process in developing guidelines.

(295) The Russian Federation highlighted the difficulty of developing a management plan for the region, given the geographic extent, the number of stations, and the multi-national nature of the human presence in this area. It noted that the Working Group was moving in the right direction to address these challenges.

(296) Chile and Germany expressed their gratitude to all members of the Working Group and welcomed additional participants and feedback. They also informed the meeting that the international working group will continue its work intersessionally at the web-based discussion forum as discussed at the informal meeting of the IWG held on 5 May in Punta del Este.

(297) The Committee commended the IWG for its progress to develop a cooperative international management framework for the Fildes Peninsula region.

(298) The United States presented IP 2 *Spatial Patterns of Tour Ship Traffic in the Antarctic Peninsula Region*, which introduced a joint paper by *Oceanites Inc.*, the US and IAATO that reviewed the pattern of tour ship traffic along the Antarctic Peninsula. The paper discussed human impacts in the Peninsula region, established a prioritisation of sites for monitoring programmes, analysed strategic approaches to the development of future management tools and reviewed current management tools. The paper had been submitted to the ATME on ship-borne tourism and was also submitted for discussion under ATCM Agenda Item 11.

(299) The United States expressed its interest in collection of all relevant data and in collaboration with any interested parties. Ukraine and IAATO noted the value of such collaborative efforts.

(300) The Committee commended the authors of the paper, which would be a useful reference for the ongoing CEP tourism study.

(301) Ukraine introduced IP 71 *Progress on Designation of Broad-scale Management System in the Vernadsky Station Area* and emphasised its appreciation to Germany for its methodological support and full-scale consultation during the previous intersessional period. Ukraine indicated that it would welcome any comments on this paper during the coming intersessional period.

Item 8: Conservation of Antarctic Fauna and Flora

8a) Quarantine and non-native species

(302) The United Kingdom introduced IP 42 *Colonisation status of known non-native species in the Antarctic terrestrial environment*, summarising information on non-native species that have been recorded in the Antarctic terrestrial environment, and providing details of their colonisation status. It reported that all of the recorded non-native species have been found close to research stations or field huts, that species from a range of biological groups are capable of colonising Antarctica, and that two non-native species in Antarctica were expanding their distribution. The United Kingdom noted that the issue of non-native species introductions has surpassed theoretical concerns, and is an issue already requiring management.

(303) France introduced WP 9 *Open-ended Intersessional Contact Group on "Non-Native Species" (NNS) - 2009-2010 Report*, updating the Committee on the results of the first year of discussions by the ICG that was established at the CEP XII. France informed that thirteen Members, Observers and Experts had participated in the discussions based on the agreed terms of reference, and that those discussions produced the following outputs:

- An introductory text and a glossary of terms were drafted to support the Committee's work on non-native species in the Antarctic context and to be appended to a future quarantine manual.

- A draft text defining the overall objective and key guiding principles for Parties' actions to address non-native species concerns. Twelve guiding principles were proposed and categorised according to the three major components of a non-native species management framework (prevention, monitoring and response).

- A proposed set of measures to minimise the risk of introduction of non-native species, (where 'introduction' includes the transfer of species to Antarctica and between sites in Antarctica). These measures, collectively, would be used to form the basis of a future quarantine manual. The measures were ranked by the ICG according to the extent to which they were easily applicable and able to be generalised to all Parties. It was noted that the ranking was only used to assist the ICG process.

- The ICG identified particular aspects of Antarctic operations for which further work might be required in order to develop specific guidance, as well as suggested priorities and potential stakeholders. The ICG noted that it would be important to regularly review priorities as work on this subject develops.

(304) France, on behalf of the ICG participants, invited the Committee:

- to comment on the conclusions of the report;

- to endorse the outputs from this period of intersessional work (introductory text, glossary, overall objective, key principles);

- to consider incorporating actions required to provide specific guidance in the CEP five-year work plan;

- to provide indications to the ICG for the continuation of the work, namely the development of specific aspects of a manual, in line with the most applicable measures identified by the ICG; and

- to encourage all the Parties, Observers and Experts to participate in the next steps of the ICG, recognising that such a manual will be useful only if elaborated by the largest group of "users".

(305) The Committee, IAATO, COMNAP and SCAR noted their support for this urgent and high priority work and commended the ICG, France and Dr Yves Frenot as the ICG convener, for their work.

(306) The United Kingdom reminded the Committee of existing guidelines applicable to the issue of non-native species that the ICG could draw on to include in a manual, for example, the Ballast Water Guidelines. The United

Kingdom emphasised the importance of applying a precautionary approach to the issue of non-native species, particularly in the absence of baseline scientific data.

(307) Several Members highlighted the word 'prevention' in the overall objective (as drafted in WP 9), noting that it was an absolute term, and that terms like 'minimising' or 'reducing' risks might be more appropriate. France noted that the ICG discussed this matter, and the majority of participants recognised that in practice the measures would minimise the risk of non-native species introduction but that the overall objective should be prevention, which is a higher standard, consistent with the principles of the Protocol.

(308) Argentina also noted that the meaning of 'species' in this context might need further definition as, for example, application of this word to micro-organisms is limited. France agreed, noting that further work is needed to clarify the language.

(309) The Committee agreed that the quarantine manual could be more appropriately named the 'non-native species manual' or something similar, as the word 'quarantine' did not resonate for all Members.

(310) Argentina indicated some concern over development of requirements and operational procedures. Australia recalled that the purpose of the work on a manual was to assist Parties to meet the requirements of Annex II.

(311) The United States noted the emphasis on terrestrial non-native species and suggested that the work might be expanded to include consideration of marine non-native species and non-human vectors.

(312) The Committee offered overall support for the ICG's work, and reiterated the importance of managing this issue, and the priority of this work in the five-year work plan.

(313) The Committee accepted the offer by New Zealand (Jana Newman) to convene the Group, and agreed the following Terms of Reference:

    i.   Continue the discussion on the overall objective and key guiding principles for Parties' actions to address risks posed by non-native species.

    ii. Continue the development of a suggested set of generally applicable measures (practical measures, tools or procedures), to prevent or minimise the risk of the introduction of non-native species, and to monitor and to respond to any introductions (including the transfer of species between sites in Antarctica). The ICG will consider the recent work presented by several Parties at CEP XIII, the relevant recommendations from the ATME on the implications of climate change, and the existing guidelines endorsed by the ATCM or those used by other bodies (eg, COMNAP, SCAR, IAATO, IMO) for inclusion in a manual.

iii. Continue the identification of particular aspects of Antarctic operations for which further work might be required in order to develop specific guidance.

iv. Report to CEP XIV on progress with the above.

(314) SCAR presented WP 4 *Preliminary Results from the International Polar Year Programme: Aliens in Antarctica* noting that the CEP had recognised non-native species as a major concern in Antarctica. SCAR reported that, as part of the International Polar Year, the Aliens in Antarctica project was an international effort to assess propagule pressure and pathways in an integrated way.

(315) SCAR reported on the preliminary analyses of data on vascular plant seeds carried by visitors to the region. A total of 850 people travelling on 23 different ships and aircraft were sampled. These preliminary analyses suggested that the personnel posing the highest risks of non-native species propagule transfer (specifically plant seeds) are those from national Antarctic programmes, tourist support personnel, and tourists travelling with national Antarctic programmes or on small vessels. SCAR advised that final analyses will emerge over the next few years.

(316) COMNAP noted there will be a COMNAP-SCAR workshop on non-native species in Buenos Aires in August 2010.

(317) The United Kingdom welcomed WP 4 and noted that non-native species would be discussed during upcoming meetings of the IPY and COMNAP. The United Kingdom highlighted the relevance of these discussions to the CEP and suggested that results from each meeting be presented to CEP XIV.

(318) Australia noted that the findings reported in WP 4 usefully identify the relative risks associated with types of visitor and types of equipment, and demonstrate the need to develop and implement practical preventive measures, consistent with Recommendation 23 from the ATME on Climate Change.

(319) Dr Yves Frenot of France informed the Committee that he would be attending the IPY and COMNAP meetings and offered to report the meetings' conclusions to the next CEP. The Committee thanked Dr Frenot for his offer and looked forward to his reports.

(320) Argentina noted that SCAR had invited the CEP to its upcoming meeting in Buenos Aires and highlighted the opportunity this presented to the CEP to circulate information on this issue.

(321) The Committee thanked SCAR for the report, noted the relevance of climate change to the issue of non-native species, and looked forward to seeing the full results of the study when they become available.

(322) SCAR presented WP 6 *Current knowledge for reducing risks posed by terrestrial non-native species: towards an evidence-based approach* (SCAR and Australia) noting that the primary objective of the document was to provide an overview of how further to consider the risks associated with non-native species, in keeping with global conservation best practice and the developing framework for such management in the region.

(323) SCAR noted three major challenges: the introduction of non-native species not indigenous to the area south of 60°S (extraregional introduction); the movement and further establishment of indigenous species among different regions of Antarctica (extralimital introduction); and the introgression of populations, constituting the movement of individuals (by humans) among populations that are genetically distinct (genetic homogenization).

(324) Several Members thanked SCAR and Australia for their work and noted similar work being conducted by their own national programmes. New Zealand informed the Committee that it was currently developing a risk-based approach to its work on reducing introduction of non-native species and looked forward to sharing its results with the CEP.

(325) New Zealand noted the diversity of Working Papers on the subject of non-native species, highlighted the need for taking a strategic risk-based

approach and noted the importance of both understanding native systems, and implementing simple practical procedures.

(326) ASOC thanked SCAR and Australia for WP 6 and encouraged Members to act on the key conclusions of the paper, particularly conducting baseline biodiversity surveys and developing survey protocols for detection and response in highly visited areas, especially those that are showing rapid change.

(327) The UK informed the Committee that IP 44 outlined its framework for scientists attempting to determine the colonisation status of newly discovered terrestrial or freshwater species within the Antarctic Treaty area.

(328) Russia informed the Committee that it had commenced its non-native species monitoring programme in 2004. Russia expressed its willingness to share data from this monitoring programme with interested Members.

(329) The Chair suggested that the ICG on non-native species take into account the conclusions of this paper into their work.

(330) The United Kingdom presented WP 14 *Intra-regional transfer of species in terrestrial Antarctica* noting that with ongoing human activities in Antarctica, human mediated intra-regional transfer of species will continue, with the result that over time Antarctica's unique biological assemblages and scientific research opportunities may be compromised. It also noted that Antarctic species indigenous to one region are likely to have pre-adaptation to cold environments found in the other areas of Antarctica, therefore increasing the likelihood of survival and establishment of intra-regionally transferred species. The United Kingdom also considered that, given the lack of information of baseline biodiversity in some areas, a precautionary approach might be appropriate until adequate biodiversity information is available.

(331) The United Kingdom, therefore, recommended that the Committee:

- encourage the on-going synthesis of available knowledge on the biogeography, bioregionalisation and endemism within Antarctica by SCAR;

- discuss the spatial scale at which biosecurity measures aimed at reducing the risk of intra-regional species transfer might be practicably applied; and

- consider the precautionary approach of intra-regional transfer biosecurity measures between major biogeographical zones, where detailed biodiversity surveys are incomplete.

(332) Many Members, SCAR and ASOC congratulated the United Kingdom on its paper, noting the importance of the work.

(333) The Committee expressed general support for the sentiment of the paper and the recommendations, saw this as a thought provoking paper and noted more work on this issue would be useful.

(334) The United Kingdom presented WP 8 *Draft procedures for vehicle cleaning to prevent transfer of non-native species into and around Antarctica* reminding the Meeting that a first proposal on these procedures had been presented at CEP XII. It noted that the proposed procedures had been created to reduce the risk of biological material being transported by vehicles into and around Antarctica.

(335) Grateful for the excellent input during the intersessional period, the United Kingdom recommended the revised guidelines be endorsed by the Committee and inserted into the upcoming non-native species manual.

(336) Many Members and IAATO thanked the United Kingdom for these guidelines, noting they represent an excellent example of measures to prevent non-native introduction.

(337) IAATO noted it would adopt these guidelines until the more comprehensive manual from the work of the ICG is available.

(338) The Committee welcomed the guidelines in WP 8 and agreed to send the recommendations on to the ICG on non-native species for further consideration of how best to incorporate these into the non-native species manual. In the meantime, Parties were invited to consider using these guidelines to help protect the environment from the impacts of non-native species introductions.

(339) The United Kingdom presented WP 15 *Guidance for visitors and environmental managers following the discovery of a suspected non-native species in the terrestrial and freshwater Antarctic environment*, stressing that preventing the introduction of non-native species must continue to be the primary means of protection. The United Kingdom also noted that,

as it is difficult to predict the level of invasiveness of a newly introduced non-native species, the 'precautionary principle' should be applied, and a confirmed introduced species should be assumed to be highly invasive and therefore if practicable, eradicated or contained as soon as possible.

(340) The UK further identified IP 44 *Suggested framework and considerations for scientists attempting to determine the colonisation status of newly discovered terrestrial or freshwater species within the Antarctic Treaty Area* that accompanied WP 15.

(341) The United Kingdom introduced IP 43 *Eradication of a vascular plant species recently introduced to Whalers Bay, Deception Island* (United Kingdom and Spain), stating it was this event that stimulated the production of the draft practical guidance within WP 15 and IP 44.

(342) The United Kingdom recommended that the draft guidance proposed in WP 15 and IP 44 be considered by the CEP, and invited comment during the intersessional period. The Committee supported that approach, and supported the goal of inclusion, following appropriate revision and review, into the manual proposed by the ICG on non-native species.

(343) The Committee and IAATO thanked the United Kingdom for the instructive information in WP 15 and IP 44, and noted their request that Parties use the procedures on a trial basis over the next year to guide intersessional comment.

(344) The following paper was also submitted under this agenda item:

- IP 14 T*he Role of Human Activities in the Introduction of Non-Native Species into Antarctica and in the Distribution of Organisms Within the Antarctic* (Germany)

8b) Specially protected Species

(345) No papers were submitted under this agenda item.

8c) Other Annex II Matters

(346) Australia presented IP 41 *Southern giant petrel monitoring in ASPA 167, Hawker Island, using automated cameras* noting that, consistent with Resolution 5

(2009) Protection of the Southern Giant Petrel, it is trialling the use of digital automated cameras to monitor the breeding colony of southern giant petrels in ASPA 167, Hawker Island. Australia invited interested Members to contact the project manager identified in the paper.

(347) The Committee recalled that the following recommendations from the ATME on Climate Change (WP 63) were of relevance to this agenda item:

- *Recommendation 17*: The ATME recommends that the ATCM encourages SCAR to incorporate identification of key regions, habitats and species at greatest risk from climate change effects into its research programmes.

- *Recommendation 20*: The ATME recommends that the ATCM and CEP encourage national Antarctic programmes to undertake marine and terrestrial biodiversity surveys and to submit, as a matter of urgency, all relevant biodiversity data to appropriate databases (eg, the Biodiversity Database). In conducting such surveys, priority attention should be paid to regions considered to be at high risk of climate change impacts as well as to existing protected areas established to protect biological values.

(348) SCAR noted that many existing research programmes address the issues raised in these recommendations, and that they will be encouraged to continue to the extent possible.

(349) The Committee supported the ATME recommendations, welcomed the valuable contributions being made by SCAR, and encouraged the continuation of such work.

(350) The following papers were also submitted under this agenda item:

- IP 47 *Census of Antarctic Marine Life (CAML)* (SCAR and Australia)

- IP 117 *Biodiversidad Microbiológica y Aplicaciones Biotecnológica*s (Ecuador)

- IP 118 *Aislamiento e Identificación de Bacterias Antárticas Capaces de Biodegradar Hidrocarburos* (Ecuador)

Item 9: Environmental Monitoring and Reporting

9a) Climate Change

(351) Norway introduced WP 63 *Report from Antarctic Treaty Meeting of Experts on Implications of Climate Change for Antarctic Management and Governance*. Norway noted that the ATME on Climate Change and Implications for Management and Governance of the Antarctic Region had been held in Svolvær, Norway in April 2010. Norway noted that it had been a very successful meeting attended by representatives of 15 Treaty Parties, as well as experts and invited organisations.

(352) Norway recalled that the ATME had been established by the ATCM under Decision 1 (2009) which required the ATME to:

- examine key scientific aspects of climate change and consequences of such change to the Antarctic terrestrial and marine environment;

- the implications of climate change to management of Antarctic activities;

- the need for monitoring, scenario planning and risk assessments;

- the outcomes of the Copenhagen negotiations relevant for the Antarctic, and

- the need for further consideration of any of the above issues and manners in which this can be achieved.

(353) Norway noted that the Meeting particularly emphasised the importance of the SCAR report on Antarctic Climate Change and the Environment (ACCE), as a fundamental source of scientific information and the importance that the findings and recommendations of the report will play in further consideration of climate change issues in the Antarctic.

(354) Norway also noted that the Meeting agreed that Antarctic climate change and the implications for governance and management in Antarctica is both a relevant and important topic to discuss under the Antarctic Treaty system and emphasised the importance of continuing the discussions on climate change issues in Antarctica.

(355) Norway informed the CEP that the ATME had agreed 30 recommendations (Appendix 3) covering a range of issues for consideration by the ATCM and CEP. Norway drew attention in particular to those recommendations that were of particular relevance to the work of the CEP, notably: ATME Recommendations 1, 4, 7, 8, 10, 11, 14, 15, 17, 18, 19, 20, 21, 22, 23, 24, 25, 26, 27, 28, 29 and 30.

(356) The Committee congratulated Norway and the UK for hosting the Meeting of Experts. The Committee noted that climate change was an important topic, that it spanned many CEP agenda items, and that it warranted on-going consideration by the CEP. It also acknowledged the importance of SCAR's ACCE Report as a guide to discussion at the Meeting and as a valuable tool for further understanding the Antarctic environment.

(357) New Zealand noted that it was critical for the CEP to take account of the drivers and effects of climate change in managing human activity in Antarctica. New Zealand noted the important role the CEP has to play in contributing to the pool of knowledge on climate change implications for Antarctica and to advising the ATCM on the state of the Antarctic environment under Article 12(1)(j) of the Environmental Protocol.

(358) Germany endorsed the outcomes to the ATME, noting in particular the recommendation to place climate change as a separate item on the CEP's agenda (Recommendation 30) and for the CEP to develop a climate change work programme (Recommendation 19).

(359) The UK noted the large number of recommendations from the ATME and suggested that these would need to be prioritised and handled in the short, medium and long-term. The UK also emphasised the need to take a comprehensive ecosystem approach to managing the implications of climate change, which would require cooperation with other bodies both inside and outside the Antarctic Treaty system.

(360) The Netherlands also supported the recommendations from the ATME especially the recommendation to protect species vulnerable to climate change (Recommendation 25). It also stressed the importance of climate change research in Antarctica.

(361) Sweden also supported the recommendation to place climate change as a separate item on the agenda and emphasised the importance of

Recommendations 21 and 22 relating to climate change related data management and non-native species, respectively.

(362) Argentina, supported by Ecuador, congratulated SCAR on its excellent ACCE report, and agreed that the issue should be placed as a separate item on the CEP agenda. Argentina also urged the CEP to consider the environmental implications of climate change. Argentina noted that it would carefully consider the recommendations from the ATME including consulting with its scientists.

(363) Russia reminded Members that references to climate change should refer to long-term changes and, in accordance with WMO standards, should not only consider data observations collected after 1962 but also consider all relevant historical data. It also highlighted the importance of differentiating the impact of climate changes on Antarctica from the role of Antarctica in global climate change trends.

(364) ASOC drew attention in particular to ATME Recommendations 19, 26, 27 and 28. ASOC also encouraged the CEP to consider a formal mechanism for ensuring that the ATME report could be conveyed to SC-CAMLR, to ensure consideration of the recommendations in that body.

(365) India also noted the reduction of the carbon footprint of human activities in Antarctica as a high priority for the CEP.

(366) France, supported by the US, noted that many of the recommendations from the ATME could be readily incorporated into the CEP's current programme of work given that the Committee is already addressing a number of the issues highlighted by the ATME recommendations.

(367) The United States noted that recommendations from the ATME might ultimately lead towards consideration of other topics. For example, much as climate change has raised concern about potential impacts from non-native species (resulting, for example, in Recommendation 22), climate change is also raising concern about possible extinctions (for example, through the impacts of ocean acidification).

(368) The SC-CAMLR Observer noted that CCAMLR has climate change on its agenda, and that the matter had been recognised as one of common interest to both Committees at the joint CEP/SC-CAMLR workshop in

2009. CCAMLR's particular focus related to understanding the impacts of climate change on its ability to manage the Southern Ocean fishery and to attempt to distinguish the effects of climate change from the effects of fishing. The SC-CAMLR Observer noted that the Scientific Committee had agreed to review its Ecosystem Monitoring Programme (CEMP) to ensure it was addressing these two objectives. In this regard an opportunity existed to work with the CEP on broader monitoring issues.

(369) The Committee agreed to prioritise the ATME recommendations and to consider how they might be taken forward. The Committee endorsed Norway's suggestion as to which of the ATME recommendations were pertinent to the CEP and allocated several of these to the relevant CEP agenda items (Appendix 3).

(370) For those ATME recommendations allocated to agenda item 9a, the Committee discussed these and agreed the following:

Recommendation 4: The ATME recommends that Parties be requested to:

- acknowledge and encourage continuing efforts in developing and exchanging experience of energy efficiency and alternative energy practices so as to promote reduction of the carbon footprint of activities in Antarctica and cut fossil fuel use from stations, vessels, ground transportation and aircraft;

- solicit from COMNAP a report on progress on the implementation of its Best Practice for Energy Management – Guidance and Recommendations (endorsed by CEP X in Delhi), and ask for an update including details of best practices on energy efficiency and alternative energy deployment; and

- welcome the efforts of IAATO in working towards developing best practice towards reducing the carbon footprint of its tour ships.

(371) Consistent with the action in the CEP's five-year work plan, the Committee agreed to request a report from COMNAP on the implementation of its Best Practice Energy Management Guidance.

Recommendation 7: Welcoming the risk assessment approach taken by Australia to identify potential climate change implications for current and future Antarctic infrastructure, logistics and environmental values, the

ATME recommends that Parties be encouraged to undertake and report on appropriate risk assessment processes.

(372) The Committee welcomed the Australian risk assessment approach (reported to CEP XIII in IP 105 *Management implications of climate change in the Antarctic region – an initial Australian assessment)* and recommended that Parties consider undertaking similar exercises.

Recommendation 18: The ATME recommends that ATCM and CEP give consideration to taking a more regional approach in the application of environmental management tools, in addition to the current continent-wide approach.

(373) The Committee took note of the recommendation and agreed to consider this further at a future meeting.

Recommendation 19: The ATME recommends that the CEP consider developing a climate change response work programme. Such a work programme should attempt to incorporate, *inter alia*:

- The need to continue to afford a high priority to the management of non-native species;

- A classification of existing protected areas according to climate change vulnerability;

- The need for more sophisticated and coordinated ecosystem monitoring, including the need for increased collaboration between CEP and SC-CAMLR;

- A review of existing management tools to assess their continuing suitability in a climate change context (eg, EIA guidelines (particularly with regard to planned long-term activities), Specially Protected Species guidelines, the guide to the preparation of management plans).

(374) The Committee agreed to place the issue of a climate change work programme on its five-year work plan for attention at a future meeting.

Recommendation 29: The ATME recommends that the CEP remain alert to the development of climate change related conservation tools elsewhere in the world that may also have application in an Antarctic context (eg, climate change adaptation plans, risk assessment tools and mechanisms for assisted translocation of endangered species).

(375) The Committee took note of this recommendation.

Recommendation 30: The ATME recommends that Parties consider making climate change a separate agenda item on the ATCM and CEP agendas.

(376) The Committee agreed with the recommendation, noting that it would address the matter under agenda item 14.

(377) Romania introduced WP 62 *Environmental Monitoring and Ecological Activities in Antarctica* informing the Committee that through the Romanian Polar Research Institute it is participating in the European and International Joint Research Project INTERHEMISPHERE - an interdisciplinary bipolar project involving 12 countries. Romania informed that the principal scientific objectives of the joint research project are related to polar microbiology and ecology, permafrost and polar pedobiology, polar ecology, vegetation and ecological monitoring. Romania informed the CEP that the project will: expand polar monitoring capability of Arctic and Antarctic ecosystem parameters; aid the establishment of databases, and the design of realistic models of polar ecosystems under climate change.

(378) The Committee congratulated Romania on this initiative and looked forward to learning more of the science outcomes.

(379) SCAR introduced IP 46 *Antarctic Climate Change and the Environment - An Update*, noting that it intends to provide regular updates on the Antarctic Climate Change and the Environment (ACCE) report.

(380) The Committee thanked SCAR for its paper and looked forward to further update reports, noting the importance of a regular flow of information on climate research and the implications for the Antarctic environment to support the ongoing work of the Committee.

(381) ASOC introduced IP 73 *Key Climate Change Actions in Antarctica: Emissions Reduction, Adaptation and Science*, commenting on the significance of adaptation strategies, and the associated benefits of establishing 'concrete action' especially from recommendations 4, 5 and 29.

(382) The following additional IPs were submitted under this agenda item:

- IP 34 *Southern Ocean Sentinel: An international Program to assess climate change impacts on marine ecosystems* (Australia)

- IP 98 *Climate Processes of Ocean, Ice and Atmosphere ERICON AB Icebreaker FP7 project* (Romania)

Advice to the ATCM

(383) The Committee undertook a comprehensive review of the report and recommendations from the ATME on Climate Change and Implications for Management and Governance of the Antarctic Region.

(384) The Committee recognised that the implications of climate change cut across many of the issues on the CEP's agenda. The Committee concluded that much of its current work programme addresses many of the issues raised during the ATME.

(385) The Committee agreed to place climate change as a high priority issue on its agenda, and allocated the relevant recommendations from the ATME to the relevant items on the CEP agenda.

(386) The CEP also gave recognition to the need for ongoing work on this issue, in the CEP five year work plan.

9b) Other Environmental Monitoring and Reporting Matters

(387) For those Climate Change ATME recommendations allocated to agenda item 9b (recommendations 14, 15, 21, 27 and 28), the Committee agreed to return to all of these at its next meeting and encouraged Members to give consideration as to how they might be taken forward.

(388) New Zealand noted that the CEP may want to give urgent attention to ATME Recommendation 27 (on the need for biodiversity assessments) noting that a number of papers, such as WP 3 and SCAR's ACCE report, had highlighted the urgent need for fundamental biodiversity surveys to support environmental management activities in Antarctica.

(389) The United States drew attention to the information contained in IP 27 rev. 1 *Energy Management Strategies for U.S. Antarctic Research Stations* and noted that it will be presented during the Working Group on Operations.

(390) Uruguay presented IP 69 *Benthic Marine Invertebrates as a Tool for the Monitoring of Fuel Transfer from Transport Ships in King George Island* and referred to the monitoring of the re fuelling activity by using benthic marine invertebrates as bio indicators aiming to develop an index of biological integrity for the coastal zone of Base Artigas.

(391) The following papers were also submitted under this agenda item:

- IP 35 *Report of a Joint Oil Spill Exercise: R/V Laurence M. Gould at Rothera Research Station* (United Kingdom and United States)

- IP 66 SCAR *Data and Information Strategy (DIMS)* (SCAR)

- IP 121 *Estimación de riesgo al cambio climático y la variabilidad climática, en los ecosistemas terrestres circundantes y en la infraestructura física de la Estación Científica Maldonado* (Ecuador)

Item 10: Inspection Reports

(392) Norway introduced WP 57 *The 2009 Norwegian Antarctic Inspection under Article VII* of the Antarctic Treaty.

(393) During February 2009, Norway conducted its fourth inspection programme under Article VII of the Antarctic Treaty in Dronning Maud Land and Coats Land, inspecting Princess Elisabeth Antarctica (Belgium), Halley Station (United Kingdom), Novolazarevskaya airfield (Russian Federation) and ALCI Airbase (Antarctic Logistics Centre International (ALCI)). The full report of the inspections was provided in IP 30 *Report of the Norwegian Antarctic Inspection under Article VII of the Antarctic Treaty. February 2009.*

(394) Norway reported that inspection Checklist "A" Permanent Antarctic Stations and Associated Installations, appended to Resolution 5 (1995) had proven very useful, and helped make the inspections consistent, as well as providing a basis for comparison. Norway also noted that the inspection team found it very helpful when a pre-completed checklist was provided on arrival.

(395) Norway's inspection activity had focussed on operations, permitting, safety, scientific research, environment, military activities and tourism. Norway

drew the Committee's attention to those issues pertaining to environmental observations.

(396) In reporting on its inspection of Belgium's Princess Elisabeth Antarctica station, Norway drew the Committee's attention to the innovative, creative and cutting edge design. Norway commented that the station set a precedent in planning and designing an environmentally conscious station in Antarctica.

(397) Norway reported that good procedures and practices were in place to ensure environmentally well-founded operations at the United Kingdom's Halley V station. Norway noted that energy efficiency had been a priority in the design of the new Halley VI station, soon to replace Halley V. The provision of a pre-completed inspection checklist was very beneficial to the inspection team's work.

(398) Norway expressed the overall satisfaction of the inspection team with respect to environmental aspects of Novo Runway and ALCI Airbase. Norway noted some potential weaknesses in environmental routines and procedures including waste handling, training and EIA procedures. Norway noted that it had been informed by ALCI, following the inspection, that steps were being taken at ALCI Airbase to address these issues.

(399) Norway expressed its gratitude for the spirit of commitment and dedication encountered at all the stations visited, and by the openness and friendliness shown to the inspection team.

(400) France warmly congratulated Norway for this report on the inspection of three contrasting types of operation, including: 1) a station run by a national programme that had been in place for a long time; 2) a new station built to high environmental standards with a complex ownership structure; and 3) a third facility providing a platform for unregulated tourism to Dronning Maud Land. France considered that the inspection report illustrated the nature of new developments in Antarctica and raised some concerns about the consequences of these new developments on environmental and scientific issues.

(401) Belgium informed the Committee of some new developments relating to Princess Elisabeth Antarctica since the completion of Norway's inspection report. With respect to ownership of the station, Belgium noted that, as of 31 March 2010, ownership of the station had been transferred from the

private International Polar Foundation (IPF) to the Belgian Federal Science Policy Office and that the building was now almost exclusively owned by the Belgian State. Belgium further informed the Committee of the recent establishment of the Polar Secretariat, a cooperative structure formed by the Belgian Federal Science Policy Office and the IPF. In response to a reference in IP 30 to a weakness in the station's communication system, Belgium noted that the station's communication facility had not been completed at the time of the inspection. In addition, Belgium informed the Committee that the installation was now complete and fully in-line with current technology.

(402) South Africa shared the concerns expressed by the inspection team regarding permitting obligations and safety implications in terms of the activities inspected in the DROMLAN area. The service providers were encouraged to obtain IAATO membership and in doing so their activities were appraised by both an IAATO and a South African National Antarctic Programme representative during the past summer season. South Africa is working closely with IAATO in this regard and a meeting with Parties to discuss and review findings will be held in the near future. Given the complexities surrounding this operation, as it also involves the interests of 11 Treaty Parties who utilize the DROMLAN Network, these issues and concerns will be further discussed at the DROMLAN Meeting in Buenos Aires later this year. A Working Paper may be drafted for discussion at the next ATCM.

(403) IAATO welcomed the Norwegian report as a useful contribution to understanding the complexities of issues in the DROMLAN area. Last year ALCI's sister company, The Antarctic Company (TAC), which deals with tourism activities applied to join IAATO. IAATO welcomed this approach as this provided an opportunity for IAATO to understand the tourist activities taking place in the area. As part of the IAATO Membership assessment IAATO sent an observer to Novo area during the 2009-10 season. An observer's report, with a series of recommendations, had been submitted to IAATO Members for consideration at the next IAATO Annual Meeting after which Members will vote on TAC's Membership status. IAATO noted with appreciation their discussions with South Africa, Russia and the UK as they work towards achieving clarity on the complexities of this operation and attempt to resolve issues, and appreciates the opportunity for additional discussions going forward.

(404) The UK congratulated Norway for its reports and was pleased to host the inspection team. Discussion of science at Halley was timely as data gathered

there contributed to the discovery of the ozone hole, the 25ᵗʰ Anniversary of which is observed this week. The UK thanked Norway for their comments on Novo Base as it highlighted the need for close cooperation between Treaty Parties to ensure the proper regulation of activities.

(405) In response to concerns raised over ownership structures at Novo Runway and ALCI Airbase, Russia reminded the Committee that Dronning Maud Land Air Network (DROMLAN) involved a consortium of eleven national programmes and connected Cape Town with Novo Air Base, close to the Russian Novolazarevskaya station. Russia commented that many of these National Programmes relied on logistical support from Novolazarevskaya station which, as a result, appropriated additional environmental pressure and waste. Russia noted that many projects in the Dronning Maud Land region, including the construction of Princess Elisabeth Antarctica, relied on Russia's support.

(406) ASOC commended Belgium and the United Kingdom on the strong focus they had placed on the environmental design of their new stations. ASOC welcomed the commitment to environmental protection demonstrated by some stations inspected by Norway. While observing that there appeared to be no major environmental concerns identified in Norway's inspection report, ASOC noted that several practices observed were common in Antarctica many years ago.

(407) The Committee thanked Norway for its report and highlighted the value of inspections conducted under the provisions of the Treaty and Protocol.

(408) Australia introduced WP 21 *Australian Antarctic Treaty and Environmental Protocol inspections, East Antarctica, 2010.* In January 2010, Australia conducted inspections of Syowa station (Japan), Druzhnaya IV and Soyuz stations (Russian Federation), and Mount Harding (ASPA 168). As provided for under Article VII (4) of the Antarctic Treaty, Australian observers also conducted an aerial observation of Molodezhnaya station (Russian Federation).

(409) Australia expressed its gratitude to Japan and the Russian Federation for the hospitality and support provided to the team in the conduct of the inspection activity. Australia noted that the inspection team travelled to Antarctica and the inspected stations by air, which, as well as being a new mode of operations for Australian inspections, meant that the support provided was

particularly important. Australia noted that its inspection team included members fluent in the languages of each station being inspected, which helped ensure a full understanding of all facets of the operations of the stations visited. Australia also noted its intention to present its final inspection report to Parties at ATCM XXXIV.

(410) Argentina commended Australia for including inspection team members capable of speaking the language of national programme bases as this leads to more successful inspections.

(411) ASOC introduced IP 82 *Antarctic Ship-borne Tourism and Inspections under Article VII of the Antarctic Treaty and Article 14 of the Protocol on Environmental Protection*. ASOC asserted that an increase in official inspections under Article VII is warranted, as tourism has become a major Antarctic activity in terms of the number of people, ships, and sites involved.

(412) ASOC suggested that inspections might focus on tourism vessels, activities, and landing sites rather than primarily on research stations. ASOC further noted that a similar level of scrutiny should be applied in inspections of tourism vessels, activities, and sites, as is applied to national programme facilities. In ASOC's view, existing inspection checklists could be used for the time being, but checklists specific to tourism may eventually be required.

(413) On this topic, ASOC drew the attention of the Committee to Recommendation 2 from the ATME on the Management of Ship-borne Tourism, in which the ATME participants recommended that the Treaty Parties should consider the development of a specific checklist for Antarctic Treaty inspections of tourist vessels and tourist activities in Antarctica.

(414) The Committee thanked ASOC for its paper, noting that it will be considered further under ATCM Agenda Item 11.

(415) Argentina drew the Committee's attention to work conducted in the intersessional period on the review of inspection Checklist "A" Permanent Antarctic Stations and Associated Installations, appended to Resolution 5 (1995), which will be considered under ATCM Agenda Item 12 (WP 26).

(416) The other paper submitted under this Agenda item was:

• IP 5 *Inspection undertaken by Japan in accordance with Article VII of the Antarctic Treaty and Article XIV of the Protocol on Environmental Protection* (Japan)

Item 11: Cooperation with Other Organisations

(417) The SC-CAMLR Observer introduced IP 12 *Report by the SC-CAMLR Observer to the Thirteenth Meeting of the Committee for Environmental Protection* and noted the parallel report WP 7 *Report of the CEP Observer to the twenty-eighth meeting of the Scientific Committee to CCAMLR; 26 – 30 October 2009*. The SC-CAMLR Observer drew the Committee's attention to several matters arising from SC-CAMLR XXVIII, in particular those issues agreed to be of common interest by the joint CEP/SC-CAMLR Workshop held in April 2009 including:

• Climate change

• Biodiversity and non-native species

• Species requiring special protection

• Marine spatial management and protection

• Ecosystem and environmental monitoring

(418) The SC-CAMLR Observer welcomed the positive relationship with the CEP and drew attention to some key issues of common interest, noting in particular, SC-CAMLR's review of its CEMP and the opportunity this offered for both SC-CAMLR and CEP to consider their respective monitoring needs. In this regard the SC-CAMLR Observer noted the potential to consider a second Joint CEP/SC-CAMLR workshop and arising from informal discussion between the Chairs, suggested the CEP consider whether such a workshop might be scheduled for 2012 on the theme of monitoring – a subject that is of undoubted interest to the work of both committees and where potential synergies exist.

(419) The Committee thanked the SC-CAMLR Observer for his report, noting that cooperation with SC-CAMLR will provide the CEP with access to a vast range of expertise and data and that Parties should encourage more participation from the broader scientific community.

(420) The United States requested that CCAMLR make available on their website a list of areas where CEMP research is currently undertaken.

(421) Following some discussion the Committee welcomed the suggestion of a joint CEP/SC-CAMLR meeting on monitoring, and encouraged proposals regarding biodiversity and monitoring to be submitted to its next meeting to enable it to prepare for such a workshop. The Committee welcomed the close relationship with SC-CCAMLR, and looked forward to working together in the future.

(422) Argentina stressed the need to have this workshop in conjunction with an existing meeting of one of these Committees.

(423) Dr George Watters (United States), convener of the WG-EMM, volunteered to report back to the CEP following the 2010 WG-EMM meeting.

(424) Dr Polly Penhale (United States) volunteered to take on the role as the CEP Observer to SC-CAMLR.

(425) The Committee accepted with appreciation the offers of Dr Watters and Dr Penhale.

(426) An additional paper submitted under this agenda item was:

- IP 88 *Council of Managers of National Antarctic Programs (COMNAP) Report to ATCM XXXIII* (COMNAP)

Item 12: General Matters

(427) Germany introduced IP 110 *Dismantling and subsequent use of Neumayer Station II for SANAP Summer Station and Russian Antarctic Expedition* (Germany and South Africa), updating the Committee on the dismantling Neumayer Station II in March, 2010. Germany noted that this endeavour represents a joint effort between Germany, Russia, and South Africa. Germany also noted that special attention was paid to carbon emissions during these operations, which had been greatly reduced.

(428) South Africa thanked Germany for its assistance in providing equipment, technical expertise and support.

2. CEP XIII Report

(429) Germany further informed that there is now an established route between the German and South African bases, which allowed for a quick and successful response to an injury earlier in the week.

(430) ASOC welcomed IP 110 and noted that a number of recent EIAs include plans to remove infrastructure at the end of their lifetime, and noted that it was encouraging to see such actions today.

(431) Japan thanked Germany and South Africa for their paper and expressed its hope that other Parties will use it as an example for the future. Japan noted that it had participated in an inspection in the Neumayer area and commended Germany for its careful handling of containers and materials. Japan noted that the activities outlined in the paper further demonstrated the importance and benefits of saving resources and energy.

(432) An additional paper submitted under this agenda item was:

- IP 9 *Belgian Antarctic Research Expedition BELARE 2009-2010*

(433) The Committee noted that it had been asked by the ATCM to consider the implications of running its meeting from mid-week to mid-week, following the ATCM's consideration as to how it might improve the efficiency of the meetings.

(434) In discussing the matter, Members raised several issues related to how the efficiency with which CEP meetings are run and managed. Among the points raised it was noted:

- The CEP has over time given significant attention to the way it conducts its business and has already implemented a number of means to increase its efficiency and effectiveness. Such measures include the development of a prioritised five-year work plan, use of intersessional contact groups, development and implementation of an on-line discussion forum, use of workshops ahead of CEP meetings to deal with specific topics, as well as regularly reviewing its agenda and removing or adding issues as appropriate.

- The CEP receives a large number of papers each year on a range of substantive matters and currently deals with the vast majority of material submitted to any one Antarctic Treaty meeting.

- Further opportunities to improve the efficiency of the CEP meetings can be considered including the manner in which Information Papers are handled and the amount of time that might be devoted to their consideration (noting that IPs from invited Experts may fall into a different category), and the need to ensure that WPs have clear recommendations for the CEP to consider, ensuring that all papers meet the deadline for submission and deciding not to consider any papers received after this date.

(435) On the specific matter of the timing of the CEP meetings and whether the Committee could meet from Wednesday to Tuesday, with a weekend break, the following observations were made:

- It was noted that if this resulted in having more sessions in parallel, costs could be increased if this requires additional interpretation support;

- It is normal practice for the CEP report to be translated in advance of its presentation to the ATCM, and an altered timing of the CEP meeting may not allow this to happen. Some Members noted that translation of the report assists in the dialogue between the CEP and the ATCM. Others suggested that this was not essential provided it was translated immediately after the meeting.

- It is not essential, though it is useful, for the CEP and the ATCM to meet in conjunction. Consideration might be given to separating the meetings, though not all Members shared this view.

Item 13: Election of Officers

(436) Dr Yves Frenot from France was elected to the position of CEP Chair and he was warmly congratulated on his election. The outgoing Chair noted Dr Frenot's significant contributions to the CEP in his past role as Vice-chair. Dr Frenot thanked the Committee and the Chair for their support and kind words.

(437) The Committee expressed its sincere gratitude and appreciation to the outgoing Chair, Dr Neil Gilbert from New Zealand, for his commitment and enthusiasm, which resulted in excellent guidance for the work of the Committee during the last four years.

(438) The Committee also re-elected Mr Ewan McIvor from Australia as Vice-chair for a new two-year term. The Chair noted the significant contributions of Mr McIvor to the Committee throughout his last term.

Item 14: Preparation for CEP XIV

(439) The Committee adopted the provisional agenda for CEP XIV (Appendix 4).

(440) The Committee made further changes and updates to its prioritised five-year work plan in accordance with the outcomes to CEP XIII (Appendix 5).

Item 15: Adoption of the Report

(441) The Committee adopted its Report.

Item 16: Closing of the Meeting

(442) The Chair closed the meeting on Friday 7 May 2010.

ANNEX 1

CEP XIII Agenda and Final List of Documents

Paper No	*Title*	*Submitted By*

Item 1: Opening of the Meeting

SP 1 rev 2	ATCM XXXIII - CEP XIII Agenda and Schedule	ATS

Item 3: Strategic Discussion on the Future Work of the CEP

Item 4: Operation of the CEP

IP 72	Annual Report Pursuant to Article 17 of the Protocol on Environmental Protection to the Antarctic Treaty	Ukraine
IP 78	Annual report pursuant to Article 17 of the Protocol on Environmental Protection to the Antarctic Treaty	Italy
SP 9	Electronic Information Exchange System (EIES): Report on the 2nd operational season and summary information examples	ATS

Item 5: Progress to the International Polar Year

WP 11	Forwarding of hydrographic data collected during the IPY	Uruguay
IP 50	The Southern Ocean Observing System (SOOS)	SCAR
IP 99	Young Scientists Fully Aware of the Importance of Antarctic Environment	Romania

Item 6: Environmental Impact Assessment (EIA)

6a) Draft Comprehensive Environmental Evaluations

WP 59	Answers to comments on CEE for "Water Sampling the Subglacial Lake Vostok"	Russian Federation
IP 6	Update on the Comprehensive Environmental Evaluation (CEE) of New Indian Research Station at Larsemann Hills, Antarctica	India

6b) Other EIA Matters

WP 1	Chairs Report - Antarctic Treaty Meeting of Experts on the Management of Ship-borne Tourism in the Antarctic Treaty Area	New Zealand
WP 12	Guidelines on Minimising the Impact of Pollution by Light at Antarctic Stations and Ships	United Kingdom
WP 28	Environmental Aspects of Antarctic Ship-borne Tourism	Australia

Paper No	Title	Submitted By
WP 36	Environmental Aspects and Impacts of Tourism and Non-governmental Activities in Antarctica: Project Report	New Zealand
WP 52	Data Collection and Reporting on Yachting Activity in Antarctica	United States United Kingdom
IP 1	Initial Environmental Evaluation for Development of Approach Path at Proposed New Indian Research Station at Larsemann Hills, East Antarctica	India
IP 13	Continued operation of Kohnen Base as a summer base in Dronning Maud Land including maintenance of a lab in the deep ice by the Alfred Wegener Institute for Polar and Marine Research (AWI)	Germany
IP 24	IAATO Guidelines to Minimize Seabirds Landing on Ships	IAATO
IP 25	IAATO Online Field Staff Assessment & Logbook	IAATO
IP 54	The Republic of Korea's contribution to Antarctic science by installing a new permanent station in Terra Nova Bay, Ross Sea	Korea (ROK)
IP 63	Preliminary Plan for Installation and Operation of the PANSY Atmospheric Radar System at Syowa Station	Japan
IP 75	Non-IAATO Tourism and Visitation in Antarctica	IAATO
IP 79	Tourism and Land-based Facilities in Antarctica: Analysis of a Questionnaire Distributed to Antarctic Treaty Parties at XXXII ATCM	ASOC
IP 104	An Environmental Management System for the Brazilian Antarctic Station "Comandante Ferraz"	Brazil
IP 122	Informe preliminar del Estudio de Impacto Ambiental ex – post de la Estación Científica Pedro Vicente Maldonado	Ecuador
SP 11 rev 1	Annual list of Initial Environmental Evaluations (IEE) and Comprehensive Environmental Evaluations (CEE) prepared between April 1st 2009 and March 31st 2010	ATS

Item 7: Area Protection and Management Plans

7a) Management Plans

WP 10	Guidelines for the Application of Management Zones within Antarctic Specially Managed Areas and Antarctic Specially Protected Areas	United States

200

Paper No	Title	Submitted By
WP 18	Revision of maps and text for the Management Plan for Antarctic Specially Managed Area No 7: Southwest Anvers Island & Palmer Basin	United States
WP 19 rev 1	Revised Management Plan for ASPA No 119 Davis Valley and Forlidas Pond, Dufek Massif, Pensacola Mountains	United States
WP 27	Revised Management Plan for Antarctic Specially Protected Area No 139 Biscoe Point, Anvers Island, Palmer Archipelago	United States
WP 30	Subsidiary Group on Management Plans – Report on Term of Reference #4: Improving Management Plans and the Process for their Intersessional Review	Australia
WP 31	Revision of Management Plan for Antarctic Specially Protected Areas (ASPA) No 105: Beaufort Island, Mc Murdo Sound, Ross Sea	New Zealand
WP 32	Revision of Management Plans for Antarctic Specially Protected Areas No 155: Cape Evans, Ross Island	New Zealand
WP 33	Revision of Management Plans for Antarctic Specially Protected Areas (ASPA) No 157: Backdoor Bay, Cape Royds, Ross Island	New Zealand
WP 34	Revision of Management Plans for Antarctic Specially Protected Areas (ASPA) No 158: Hut Point, Ross Island	New Zealand
WP 35	Revision of Management Plans for Antarctic Specially Protected Areas (ASPA) No 159: Cape Adare, Borchgrevink Coast	New Zealand
WP 38	Review of Management Plans for Antarctic Specially Protected Areas (ASPAs) 101, 102, 103 and 164	Australia

7b) Historic Sites and Monuments

Paper No	Title	Submitted By
WP 5	Proposed addition of the Plaque Commemorating the PM-3A Nuclear Power Plant at McMurdo Station to the List of Historic Sites and Monument	United States
WP 25	Report of an incident at Wordie House (HSM No 62)	United Kingdom France Ukraine
WP 47	Proposal for the discussion of aspects related to the management of Historic Sites and Monuments	Argentina
WP 67	Proposed Modification to Historic Site N° 37	Chile
IP 21	Enhancement activities for HSM 38 "Snow Hill"	Argentina

Paper No	Title	Submitted By
IP 22	Additional information for the discussion of aspects related to the management of Historic Sites and Monuments	Argentina
IP 67	Actualización del estudio de los restos históricos del naufragio de Punta Suffield	Uruguay
IP 93	Conservation and Management of Mawson's Huts, Cape Denison, King George V Land, ASPA 162, ASMA 4 and HSM 77	Australia

7c) Site Guidelines

Paper No	Title	Submitted By
WP 17	Antarctic Treaty Visitor Site Guide for Torgersen Island, Arthur Harbor, Southwest Anvers Island	United States
WP 39	Site Guidelines for Danco Island, Errera Channel, Antarctic Peninsula	United Kingdom United States
WP 42	Antarctic Treaty Visitor Site Guidelines for Seabee Hook, Cape Hallett, Northern Victoria Land, Ross Sea	United States
WP 56	Site Guidelines for Damoy Point, Wiencke Island, Antarctic Peninsula	United Kingdom Argentina
WP 64	Site Guidelines for the Northeast beach of Ardley Peninsula (Ardley Island), King George Island (25 de Mayo Island), South Shetland Islands	Argentina Chile
IP 26	Antarctic Site Inventory: 1994-2010	United States
IP 62	Report on IAATO Member use of Antarctic Peninsula Landing Site and ATCM Visitor Site Guidelines - 2008-09 Season	IAATO

7d) Human footprint and wilderness values

Paper No	Title	Submitted By
WP 23	Assessing cumulative environmental impacts: identifying the distribution and concentration of national operator activities in Antarctica	United Kingdom
WP 29	The concept of Human Footprint in the Antarctic	New Zealand
IP 20	Possible human impact on Deception Island	Spain
IP 48	Topic Summary: Footprint	Australia
IP 49	The concept of Human Footprint in the Antarctic	New Zealand
IP 81	Coastal Hydrocarbon Pollution: A Case Study From Deception Island, Antarctica	ASOC

Paper No	*Title*	*Submitted By*

7e) Marine Spatial Protection and Management

IP 32	Identificación y evaluación de la acción antrópica de grupos poblacionales de mamíferos marinos pinnípedos en áreas de la costa del Estrecho de Drake	Uruguay
IP 45	Terra Nova Bay – Wood Bay Marine Protected Area inside a wider proposal for a Ross Sea MPA	Italy
IP 58	Designation of a new Marine Protected Area for the South Orkney Islands southern shelf	United Kingdom
IP 77	The Case for Inclusion of the Ross Sea Continental Shelf and Slope in a Southern Ocean Network of Marine Reserves	ASOC
IP 83	Rising to the challenge: Key steps to deliver a Comprehensive and Representative Marine Protected Areas Network in the Southern Ocean by 2012	ASOC
IP 107	Bioregionalisation and Spatial Ecosystem Processes in the Ross Sea Region	New Zealand

7f) Other Annex V Matters

WP 3	Biodiversity-based Evaluation of the Environmental Domains Analysis	SCAR
WP 16	The Implications of Climate Change for the Antarctic Protected Areas System	United Kingdom
WP 40	Third Progress Report on the Discussion of the International Working Group about Possibilities for Environmental Management of Fildes Peninsula and Ardley Island	Chile Germany
WP 54	Enhancing the Antarctic Protected Areas Database to help assess and further develop the protected areas system	Australia
IP 2	Spatial Patterns of Tour Ship Traffic in the Antarctic Peninsula Region	United States IAATO
IP 71	Progress on Designation of Broad-scale Management System in the Vernadsky Station Area	Ukraine

Paper No	*Title*	*Submitted By*

Item 8: Conservation of Antarctic Flora and Fauna

8a) Quarantine and non-native species

WP 4	Preliminary Results from the International Polar Year Programme: Aliens in Antarctica	SCAR
WP 6	Current knowledge for reducing risks posed by terrestrial non-native species: towards an evidence-based approach	SCAR Australia
WP 8	Draft procedures for vehicle cleaning to prevent transfer of non-native species into and around Antarctica	United Kingdom
WP 9	Open-ended Intersessional Contact Group on "Non-Native Species" (NNS) - 2009-2010 Report	France
WP 14	Intra-regional transfer of species in terrestrial Antarctica	United Kingdom
WP 15	Guidance for visitors and environmental managers following the discovery of a suspected non-native species in the terrestrial and freshwater Antarctic environment	United Kingdom
IP 14	Research Project "The role of human activities in the introduction of non-native species into Antarctica and in the distribution of organisms within the Antarctic"	Germany
IP 42	Colonisation status of known non-native species in the Antarctic terrestrial environment	United Kingdom
IP 43	Eradication of a vascular plant species recently introduced to Whaler's Bay, Deception Island	United Kingdom Spain
IP 44	Suggested framework and considerations for scientists attempting to determine the colonisation status of newly discovered terrestrial or freshwater species within the Antarctic Treaty Area	United Kingdom

8b) Specially Protected Species

8c) Other Annex II Matters

IP 41	Southern giant petrel monitoring in ASPA 167, Hawker Island, using automated cameras	Australia
IP 47	Census of Antarctic Marine Life (CAML)	SCAR Australia
IP 117	Biodiversidad Microbiológica y Aplicaciones Biotecnológicas	Ecuador

Paper No	*Title*	*Submitted By*
IP 118	Aislamiento e Identificación de Bacterias Antárticas Capaces de Biodegradar Hidrocarburos	Ecuador

Item 9: Environmental Monitoring and Reporting

9a) Climate Change

WP 62	Environmental Monitoring and Ecological Activities in Antarctica, 2010-2012	Romania
WP 63	Report from Antarctic Treaty Meeting of Experts on Implications of Climate Change for Antarctic Management and Governance. Co-chairs' executive summary with advice for actions	Norway United Kingdom
IP 34	Southern Ocean Sentinel: an international program to assess climate change impacts on marine ecosystems	Australia
IP 46	Antarctic Climate Change and the Environment – An Update	SCAR
IP 73	Key Climate Change Actions in Antarctica: Emissions Reduction, Adaptation and Science	ASOC
IP 98	Climate Processes of Ocean, Ice and Atmosphere - ERICON AB Icebreaker FP7 Project	Romania
IP 105	Management implications of climate change in the Antarctic region – an initial Australian assessment	Australia

9b) Other Environmental Monitoring and Reporting Matters

IP 27 rev 1	Energy Management Strategies for U.S. Antarctic Research Stations	United States
IP 35	Report of a Joint Oil Spill Exercise: RV Laurence M. Gould at Rothera Research Station	United Kingdom United States
IP 66	SCAR Data and Information Strategy (DIMS)	SCAR
IP 69	Benthic Marine Invertebrates as a Tool for the Monitoring of Fuel Transfer from Transport Ships in King George Island	Uruguay
IP 121	Estimación de riesgo al cambio climático y la variabilidad climática, en los ecosistemas terrestres circundantes y en la infraestructura física de la Estación Científica Maldonado	Ecuador

Paper No	*Title*	*Submitted By*

Item 10: Inspection Reports

WP 21	Australian Antarctic Treaty and Environmental Protocol inspections, East Antarctica, 2010	Australia
WP 57	The 2009 Norwegian Antarctic Inspection under Article VII of the Antarctic Treaty	Norway
IP 5	Inspection undertaken by Japan in accordance with Article VII of the Antarctic Treaty and Article XIV of the Protocol on Environmental Protection	Japan
IP 30	Report of the Norwegian Antarctic Inspection under Article VII of the Antarctic Treaty. February 2009	Norway
IP 82	Antarctic Ship-borne Tourism and Inspections Under Article VII of the Antarctic Treaty and Article 14 of the Protocol on Environmental Protection	ASOC

Item 11: Cooperation with Other Organisations

WP 7	Report of the CEP Observer to the twenty-eighth meeting of the Scientific Committee to CCAMLR; 26 – 30 October 2009	New Zealand
IP 12	Report by the SC-CAMLR Observer to the Thirteenth Meeting of the Committee for Environmental Protection	CCAMLR
IP 88	Council of Managers of National Antarctic Programs (COMNAP) Report to ATCM XXXIII	COMNAP

Item 12: General Matters

IP 9	Belgian Antarctic Research Expedition BELARE 2009-2010	Belgium
IP 110	Dismantling and subsequent use of Neumayer Station II for SANAP Summer Station and Russian Antarctic Expedition	Germany South Africa

Item 13: Election of Officers

Item 14: Preparation for Next Meeting

Item 15: Adoption of the Report

Item 16: Closing of the Meeting

Appendix 1

Revised Terms of Reference for the Subsidiary Group on Management Plans

The CEP's proposal to establish a Subsidiary Group on Management Plans (SGMP) was approved by ATCM XXXI in 2008 (Final Report paragraph 94) and the SGMP's Terms of Reference were outlined in Appendix 3 to the CEP XI Report. At that time it was agreed that the CEP should review the effectiveness of the SGMP after a two-year period, and revise the terms of reference as necessary. CEP XIII conducted such a review, and determined that SGMP had been effective in its carrying out its role of developing advice to the CEP on draft management plans referred for intersessional review and on improving management plans and the process for their intersessional review. Following a proposal by the SGMP (outlined in ATCM XXXIII/WP 30), CEP XIII agreed to include an additional Terms of Reference for the group, as follows.

Terms of Reference

1) Examine any draft new or revised Management Plan to consider, in consultation with relevant experts if appropriate:

   - whether it is consistent with the provisions of Annex V to the Protocol, particularly Articles 3, 4 and 5[1], and with relevant CEP guidelines;[2]
   - its content, clarity, consistency and likely effectiveness; [3]
   - whether it clearly states the primary reason for designation;[4] and
   - whether it clearly states how the proposed Area complements the Antarctic protected areas system as a whole.[5]

2) Advise proponents of suggested amendments to the draft Management Plan to address issues in relation to 1) above.

3) Submit a Working Paper to the CEP with recommendations for the adoption or otherwise of each new or revised draft Management Plan, identifying where the Plan reflects comments received by Members, and where they have not been, the reasons

---

[1] Modified from "Terms of Reference for an Intersessional Contact Group to Consider draft Management Plans" ToR #2 (CEP VII Report, Annex 4).

[2] Currently including – for ASPAs – Resolution 2 (1998) *Guide for the Preparation of Management Plans for Antarctic Specially Protected Areas and Resolution 1 (2000) Guidelines for Implementation of the Framework for Protected Areas set forth in Article 3, Annex V of the Environmental Protocol.*

[3] From "Guidelines for CEP Consideration of New and Revised Draft ASPA and ASMA Management Plans" paragraph 8 (CEP VI Report, Annex 4), and "Terms of Reference for an Intersessional Contact Group to Consider draft Management Plans" ToR #2 (CEP VII Report, Annex 4).

[4] Agreement at CEP VIII (Report paragraph 187).

[5] Agreement at CEP VIII (Report paragraph 187).

for not doing so. The Working Paper is to include all revised Management Plans and the information required by the ATCM's Legal and Institutional Working Group.

4) Provide advice to the CEP as necessary for the purpose of improving Management Plans and the process for their intersessional review.

5) Develop and suggest procedures that would assist in achieving a long-term goal aiming at ensuring that all ASPA and ASMA management plans contain adequate content, and are clear, consistent and likely to be effective.[6]

---

[6] Term of Reference added at CEP XIII (Report paragraph162).

Appendix 2

Subsidiary Group on Management Plans (SGMP) Work Plan

Terms of Reference (ToR)	2010/11 intersessional period	2011/12 intersessional period (provisional tasks)
ToR 1 to 3	Review draft management plan for ASPA 126 Byers Peninsula (see ATCM XXXIII/WP 43) and provide advice to proponents and the CEP	Review draft management plans referred by CEP for intersessional review and provide advice to proponents and the CEP
ToR 4	Review and update SGMP work plan	Review and update SGMP work plan
	Finalise suggested standard wording and template for management plans	
	Review and commence revision of *Guide to the Preparation of Management Plans for Antarctic Specially Protected Areas*, including to incorporate: • suggested standard wording and template for management plans (see ATCM XXXIII/WP 30); • guidelines for the application of management zones (see ATCM XXXIII/WP 10); • cross-references to the guidelines appended to Resolution 1 (2000) (see ATCM XXXIII/WP 51); • guidance regarding climate change considerations for management plans (see ATCM XXXIII/WP 63, Recommendation 19); • guidance on preventing the introduction of non-native species (see ATCM XXXIII/WP 9, Annex III, Item 3); and • other appropriate modifications.	Complete revision of *Guide to the Preparation of Management Plans for Antarctic Specially Protected Areas.*
	Further planning for workshop to share best practice in ASMA management and develop *Guide to the Preparation of Management Plans for Antarctic Specially Managed Areas*	
ToR 5	Invite those Parties responsible for Type 2, 3 and 4 plans to provide information about the review status and timeframe, as basis for further prioritization	Commence review of management plans overdue for five-yearly review
Working Papers	Prepare report for CEP against SGMP ToR 1 to 3	Prepare report for CEP against SGMP ToR 1 to 3 and ToR 5
	Prepare report for CEP against SGMP ToR 4 and 5*	Prepare report for CEP against SGMP ToR 4

Appendix 3

Recommendations from the Antarctic Treaty Meeting of Experts on Climate Change

ATME Recommendation	Agenda
Recommendation 1: The ATME recommends that the ATCM acknowledge and welcome the SCAR ACCE report as an important resource for its own deliberations and as an input to the wider global climate negotiations, eg, the UNFCCC.	
Recommendation 2: The ATME recommends that the ATCM considers developing an Antarctic climate change communication plan to bring the findings of the ACCE report to the attention of other decision makers, the general public and the media.	
Recommendation 3: The ATME recommends that the ATCM consider how best to provide information about Antarctic climate change to fora discussing and negotiating global climate change.	
Recommendation 4: The ATME recommends that Parties be requested to: • acknowledge and encourage continuing efforts in developing and exchanging experience of energy efficiency and alternative energy practices so as to promote reduction of the carbon footprint of activities in Antarctica and cut fossil fuel use from stations, vessels, ground transportation and aircraft; • solicit from COMNAP a report on progress on the implementation of its Best Practice for Energy Management – Guidance and Recommendations (endorsed by CEP X in Delhi), and ask for an update including details of best practices on energy efficiency and alternative energy deployment; and • welcome the efforts of IAATO in working towards developing best practice towards reducing the carbon footprint of its tour ships.	CEP 9a
Recommendation 5: Recognizing the importance of emission cuts in Antarctica and their symbolic value in the global context, the ATME recommends that the ATCM encourage COMNAP to work with national programmes to use consistent methods to quantify and publish savings made by energy efficiencies, and which contribute to both (a) reducing carbon footprint, and (b) reducing fuel consumption and operating costs.	

ATME Recommendation	Agenda
Recommendation 6: The ATME recommend that Parties be advised to use atmospheric models to evaluate the wind regimes around their individual stations, to determine the potential for wind power as a means of cutting fuel costs and greenhouse gas emissions.	
Recommendation 7: Welcoming the risk assessment approach taken by Australia to identify potential climate change implications for current and future Antarctic infrastructure, logistics and environmental values, the ATME recommends that Parties be encouraged to undertake and report on appropriate risk assessment processes.	CEP 9a
Recommendation 8: In developing EIAs for new facilities, the ATME recommends that Parties be requested to take climate change considerations into account.	CEP 6b
Recommendation 9: Noting that the WMO Executive Council Panel of Experts on Polar Observations, Research and Services, promotes and coordinates relevant programmes carried out in the polar regions, the ATME recommends that the Panel and others be urged to increase the refinement of Antarctic climate models, and the WMO be invited to provide regular reports to the ATCM to update Parties on progress with outcomes of the Committee's activities.	
Recommendation 10: The ATME recommends that Parties be advised to expand research that will refine and enhance our ability to predict future climate change with increasing accuracy on various temporal and geographical scales; and to encourage steps to link scientific research efforts to the activities of operational agencies involved in providing climate services and other related activities.	
Recommendation 11: Given that the IPY has been very successful in significantly increasing the volume and interdisciplinary character of polar research, especially in relation to understanding climate change, the ATME recommends that national agencies be urged to maintain the momentum of that research as a key contribution to the IPY legacy.	CEP 5
Recommendation 12: The ATME recommends that Parties be requested to encourage the collaboration required to develop comprehensive and advanced integrated Earth System models capable of producing outputs at decadal scales and regional scales that can be used to assess the likelihood, timing and amplitude of climate change.	

ATME Recommendation	Agenda
Recommendation 13: The ATME recommends that Parties be requested to encourage the space agencies to continue coordinated observations of the Antarctic region from space, in the context of improving the operation of observing systems for climate change, and to attend a future ATCM to give a demonstration of the use of modern space-based technologies for observing the Antarctic region in the context of climate change.	
Recommendation 14: The ATME recommends that Parties be requested to continue to strongly encourage collaboration and development of sustained integrated observing systems using *in situ*, air and space-based techniques.	CEP 9b
Recommendation 15: Recognizing that Parties are obliged under the Treaty to share scientific data and information, and that there is a great deal to be gained from working more closely together on the collection of observations of climate change and its effects, the ATME recommends that Parties be requested to encourage greater collaboration in such collections, and to support access to such data through the Antarctic Master Directory.	CEP 9b
Recommendation 16: The ATME recommends that Parties be requested to encourage national operators and SCAR to seek close cooperation and synergies with existing climate observing and assessment initiatives such as the Global Climate Observing System (GCOS) and the IPCC.	
Recommendation 17: The ATME recommends that the ATCM encourages SCAR to incorporate identification of key regions, habitats and species at greatest risk from climate change effects into its research programmes.	CEP 8c
Recommendation 18: The ATME recommends that ATCM and CEP give consideration to taking a more regional approach in the application of environmental management tools, in addition to the current continent-wide approach.	CEP 9a

ATME Recommendation	Agenda
Recommendation 19: The ATME recommends that the CEP consider developing a climate change response work programme. Such a work programme should attempt to incorporate, *inter alia*: • The need to continue to afford a high priority to the management of non-native species; • A classification of existing protected areas according to climate change vulnerability; • The need for more sophisticated and coordinated ecosystem monitoring, including the need for increased collaboration between CEP and SC-CAMLR; • A review of existing management tools to assess their continuing suitability in a climate change context (eg, EIA guidelines (particularly with regard to planned long-term activities), Specially Protected Species guidelines, the guide to the preparation of management plans).	CEP 9a
Recommendation 20: The ATME recommends that the ATCM and CEP encourage national Antarctic programmes to undertake marine and terrestrial biodiversity surveys and to submit, as a matter of urgency, all relevant biodiversity data to appropriate databases (eg, the Biodiversity Database). In conducting such surveys, priority attention should be paid to regions considered to be at high risk of climate change impacts as well as to existing protected areas established to protect biological values.	CEP 8c
Recommendation 21: The ATME recommends that the CEP give consideration as to means for improving climate change related data and information management to support its environmental management responsibilities.	CEP 9b
Recommendation 22: The ATME recommends that the CEP consider: • using established methods of identifying a) Antarctic environments at high risk from establishment by non-natives and b) non-native species that present a high risk of establishment in Antarctica; • implementing non-native species monitoring protocols at areas of high risk, as well as at protected areas; • developing decision making tools to aid responses to identified establishments of non-native species.	CEP 8a

214

ATME Recommendation	Agenda
Recommendation 23: The ATME recommends that Parties be encouraged to comprehensively and consistently implement management measures to respond to the environmental implications of climate change, particularly measures to avoid introduction and translocation of non-native species, and to report on their effectiveness.	CEP 8a
Recommendation 24: The ATME recommends that CEP review the means of applying protected and managed area management tools to ensure sufficient flexibility to account for climate change effects. Such a review should consider: • the need to ensure that climate change effects are assessed during each five-yearly review of management plans, including for example, the need to establish protected and managed area boundaries that are climate change resilient; and • the potential to delist sites at which the original values to be protected have been lost or degraded.	CEP 7f
Recommendation 25: The ATME recommends that the CEP consider a systematic approach to protected or managed areas to: • protect species, or habitats identified to be of particular risk to climate change consequences (cf. Recommendation 18); • accommodate areas that have potential to be environmental or climate refuges; • set aside areas for future climate change related research, including reference areas.	CEP 7f
Recommendation 26: The ATME recommends, recognising the responsibilities of and need to coordinate with CCAMLR, that the CEP consider, and advise the ATCM accordingly, as to means by which automatic interim protection might be afforded to newly exposed areas, such as marine areas exposed through ice-shelf collapse.	CEP 7f,
Recommendation 27: The ATME recommends that the CEP and SC-CAMLR be encouraged to ensure that sufficiently frequent biodiversity surveys and adequate monitoring programmes are established to provide an understanding of climate change induced responses in species distribution and abundance.	CEP 9b
Recommendation 28: The ATME recommends that CEP and SC-CAMLR continue to develop means for collecting and sharing data and information on the status and trends of species of interest to both bodies (eg, seals, penguins and seabirds), including the need to cooperate with other experts bodies such as SCAR and ACAP.	CEP 9b

ATME Recommendation	Agenda
Recommendation 29: The ATME recommends that the CEP remain alert to the development of climate change related conservation tools elsewhere in the world that may also have application in an Antarctic context (eg, climate change adaptation plans, risk assessment tools and mechanisms for assisted translocation of endangered species).	CEP 9a
Recommendation 30: The ATME recommends that Parties consider making climate change a separate agenda item on the ATCM and CEP agendas.	CEP 9a

Appendix 4

Provisional Agenda for CEP XIV

1. Opening of the Meeting
2. Adoption of the Agenda
3. Strategic Discussions on the Future Work of the CEP
4. Operation of the CEP
5. Climate Change Implications for the Environment: Strategic approach
6. Environmental Impact Assessment (EIA)

    a. Draft Comprehensive Environmental Evaluations
    b. Other EIA Matters

7. Area Protection and Management Plans

    a. Management Plans
    b. Historic Sites and Monuments
    c. Site Guidelines
    d. Human Footprint and Wilderness Values
    e. Marine Spatial Protection and Management
    f. Other Annex V Matters

8. Conservation of Antarctic Flora and Fauna

    a. Quarantine and Non-native Species
    b. Specially Protected Species
    c. Other Annex II Matters

9. Environmental Monitoring and Reporting
10. Inspection Reports
11. Cooperation with Other Organisations
12. General Matters
13. Election of Officers
14. Preparation for Next Meeting
15. Adoption of the Report
16. Closing of the Meeting

Appendix 5

CEP Five Year Work Plan

Issue / Environmental Pressure Actions	CEP Priority	Inter-sessional Period	CEP XIV 2011	Inter-sessional Period	CEP XV 2012	Inter-sessional Period	CEP XVI 2013	Inter-sessional Period	CEP XVII 2014	Inter-sessional Period	CEP XVIII 2015
Introduction of non-native species **Actions:** 1. Develop practical guidelines / standards / norms for all Antarctic operators. 2. Advance recommendations from climate change ATME	1	ICG to continue as per revised work plan	Consider report from the ICG and progress with NNS manual Consider revised guidance Tourism	Progress with further work requirements identified by ICG		Progress with further work requirements identified by ICG		Progress with further work requirements identified by ICG				Review non-native species manual
Tourism and NGO activities **Actions:** 1. Provide advice to ATCM as requested. 2. Advance recommendations from ship-borne tourism ATME	1	Tourism study overseen by project management group	study reviewed and forwarded to the ATCM Ongoing consideration of ATME outcomes under relevant agenda items		Ongoing consideration of ATME outcomes under relevant agenda items							
Global Pressure: Climate change **Actions:** 1. Consider implications of climate change for management of Antarctic environment 2. Advance recommendations from climate change ATME	1		Ongoing consideration of ATME outcomes under relevant agenda items		Ongoing consideration of ATME outcomes under relevant agenda items		Standing agenda item		Standing agenda item		Standing agenda item

Timetable for actions to be addressed at CEP meetings and during the Intersessional periods (subject to annual review)

Issue / Environmental Pressure Actions	CEP Priority	Inter-sessional Period	CEP XIV 2011	Inter-sessional Period	CEP XV 2012	Inter-sessional Period	CEP XVI 2013	Inter-sessional Period	CEP XVII 2014	Inter-sessional Period	CEP XVIII 2015
Processing new and revised protected / managed area management plans:	1	SGMP conducts work as per agreed work plan (ref CEP XIII Final report)	Consideration of SGMP report	SGMP / conducts work as per agreed work plan	Consideration of SGMP / report	SGMP / conducts work as per agreed work plan	Consideration of SGMP / report	SGMP / conducts work as per agreed work plan	Consideration of SGMP / report	SGMP / conducts work as per agreed work plan	
Actions: 1. Refine the process for reviewing new and revised management plans. 2. Update existing guidelines. 3. Advance recommendations from climate change ATME											
Marine spatial protection and management	1	1. Send relevant papers to WG EMM (26 Jul-3 August, Cape Town). 2. CEP Observer to attend WG-EMM 3. CEP ASMA workshop to consider application of ASMA	Review CEP Observer reports to WG-EMM and SC-CAMLR	1. Send relevant papers to SC-CAMLR MPA workshop (Jul or Aug 2011). 2. CEP Observer to attend MPA Workshop and WG-EMM	Review CEP Observer reports to WG-EMM, MPA workshop and SC-CAMLR						
Actions: 1. Cooperate with CCAMLR on Southern Ocean bioregionalisation. 2. Identify processes for MPA designation. 3. Advance recommendations from climate change ATME.											

		Timetable for actions to be addressed at CEP meetings and during the Intersessional periods (subject to annual review)									
Issue / Environmental Pressure Actions	CEP Priority	Inter-sessional Period	CEP XIV 2011	Inter-sessional Period	CEP XV 2012	Inter-sessional Period	CEP XVI 2013	Inter-sessional Period	CEP XVII 2014	Inter-sessional Period	CEP XVIII 2015
Operation of the CEP and Strategic Planning	**1**										
Actions:											
1. Keep the 5 year plan up to date based on changing circumstances and ATCM requirements.			Standing item		Standing item		Standing item		Standing item		Standing item
2. Identify opportunities for improving the effectiveness of the CEP.			Review and revise work plan as appropriate		Review and revise work plan as appropriate		Review and revise work plan as appropriate		Review and revise work plan as appropriate		Review and revise work plan as appropriate
3. Consider long-term objectives for Antarctica (50-100 years time)											
Human footprint / wilderness management	**2**										
Actions:											
1. Develop an agreed understanding of the terms "footprint" and "wilderness".		Consideration by Interested Parties	Review future actions based on intersessional work Secretariat summary report of information exchanged on inventory of past activities				Agreement on terms 'footprint' and 'wilderness'				

221

Timetable for actions to be addressed at CEP meetings and during the Intersessional periods (subject to annual review)

Issue / Environmental Pressure Actions	CEP Priority	Inter-sessional Period	CEP XIV 2011	Inter-sessional Period	CEP XV 2012	Inter-sessional Period	CEP XVI 2013	Inter-sessional Period	CEP XVII 2014	Inter-sessional Period	CEP XVIII 2015
Maintain the list of Historic Sites and Monuments	2										
Actions:											
1. Maintain the list and consider new proposals as they arise.		Intersessional discussion of HSM 37	Standing item		Standing item		Standing item		Standing item		Standing item
Monitoring and state of the environment reporting	2										
Actions:											
1. Identify key environmental indicators			Report from SCAR regarding SC-ADM support for CEP work								
2. Establish a process for reporting to the ATCM											
3. Advance recommendations from climate change ATME											

Timetable for actions to be addressed at CEP meetings and during the Intersessional periods (subject to annual review)

Issue / Environmental Pressure Actions	CEP Priority	Inter-sessional Period	CEP XIV 2011	Inter-sessional Period	CEP XV 2012	Inter-sessional Period	CEP XVI 2013	Inter-sessional Period	CEP XVII 2014	Inter-sessional Period	CEP XVIII 2015
Exchange of Information	2										
Actions: 1. Assign to the Secretariat.		Commence 100% use of EIES	Secretariat Report		Secretariat Report		Secretariat Report		Secretariat Report		Secretariat Report
Biodiversity knowledge	2										
Actions: 1. Maintain awareness of threats to existing biodiversity. 2. Advance recommendations from climate change ATME											
Site specific guidelines for tourist-visited sites	2										
Actions: 1. Review site specific guidelines as required. 2. Provide advice to ATCM as required.		Continue ICG to review Recommendation XVIII-1	Review ICG work. Make recommendations to ATCM — Plan future work on basis of ICG work								

223

Timetable for actions to be addressed at CEP meetings and during the Intersessional periods (subject to annual review)

Issue / Environmental Pressure Actions	CEP Priority	Inter-sessional Period	CEP XIV 2011	Inter-sessional Period	CEP XV 2012	Inter-sessional Period	CEP XVI 2013	Inter-sessional Period	CEP XVII 2014	Inter-sessional Period	CEP XVIII 2015
Implementing and improving the EIA provisions of Annex I	3	Establish ICG to review draft CEEs as required	Consideration of ICG report on draft CEE, as required	Establish ICG to review draft CEEs as required	Consideration of ICG report on draft CEE, as required	Establish ICG to review draft CEEs as required	Consideration of ICG report on draft CEE, as required	Establish ICG to review draft CEEs as required	Consideration of ICG report on draft CEE, as required	Establish ICG to review draft CEEs as required	Consideration of ICG report on draft CEE, as required
Actions: 1. Refine the process for considering CEEs and advising the ATCM accordingly. 2. Develop guidelines for assessing cumulative impacts. 3. Keep the EIA Guidelines under review. 4. Consider application of strategic environmental assessment in Antarctica. 5. Advance recommendations from climate change ATME											
Specially protected species	3										
Actions: 1. Consider listing / de-listing proposals as required.											
Overview of the protected areas system / EDA	3									Discuss possible implications of an updated gap analysis based on EDA		
Actions: 1. Apply the Environmental Domains Analysis (EDA) to enhance the protected areas system. 2. Advance recommendations from climate change ATME											

Timetable for actions to be addressed at CEP meetings and during the Intersessional periods (subject to annual review)

Issue / Environmental Pressure Actions	CEP Priority	Inter-sessional Period	CEP XIV 2011	Inter-sessional Period	CEP XV 2012	Inter-sessional Period	CEP XVI 2013	Inter-sessional Period	CEP XVII 2014	Inter-sessional Period	CEP XVIII 2015
Emergency response action and contingency planning	3										
Actions: 1. Advance recommendations from ship-borne tourism ATME			Review outcomes of ATCM XXXIII consideration of ATME report								
Updating the Protocol and reviewing Annexes	3										
Actions: 1. Prepare a prioritized timetable for the review of the remaining annexes.							Requires CEP discussion on the need and aims for reviewing Protocol annexes				
Inspections (Article 14 of the Protocol)	3										
Actions: 1. Review inspection reports as required.			Standing item		Standing item		Standing item		Standing item		Standing item

Timetable for actions to be addressed at CEP meetings and during the Intersessional periods (subject to annual review)

Issue / Environmental Pressure Actions	CEP Priority	Inter-sessional Period	CEP XIV 2011	Inter-sessional Period	CEP XV 2012	Inter-sessional Period	CEP XVI 2013	Inter-sessional Period	CEP XVII 2014	Inter-sessional Period	CEP XVIII 2015
Energy management	4										
Actions: 1. Develop best-practice guidelines for energy management at stations and bases.					COMNAP report presented to CEP – dedicated time for discussion						
Outreach and education	4								Dedicated time for discussion		
Actions: 1. Review current examples and identify opportunities for greater education and outreach.											
Waste	5										
Actions: 1. Develop guidelines for best practice disposal of waste including human waste.									COM-NAP report requested		COMNAP report presented to CEP – dedicated time for discussion
Clean up of sites of past activity	5										
Actions: 1. Establish Antarctic-wide inventory of sites of past activity.			Secretariat summary report of information exchanged on inventory of past activities								Secretariat requested to develop and maintain an inventory COMNAP report on best practice requested
2. Develop guidelines for best practice approach to clean up.											

3. Appendices

Headquarters Agreement

HEADQUARTERS AGREEMENT

FOR THE SECRETARIAT OF THE ANTARCTIC TREATY

The Antarctic Treaty Consultative Meeting (ATCM) and the Argentine Republic,

Convinced of the need to strengthen the Antarctic Treaty system;

Bearing in mind the special legal and political status of Antarctica and the special responsibility of the Antarctic Treaty Consultative Parties to ensure that all activities in Antarctica are consistent with the purposes and principles of the Antarctic Treaty and its Protocol on Environmental Protection;

Having regard to Decision 1 (2001) of the XXIV ATCM and Measure 1 (2003) of the XXVI ATCM on the Secretariat of the Antarctic Treaty in Buenos Aires, Argentina;

Desiring to enable the Secretariat as an organ of the ATCM fully and efficiently to fulfill its purposes and functions; and

Desiring to define the legal capacity of the Secretariat as an organ of the ATCM as well as its privileges and immunities and those of the Executive Secretary and other staff members in the territory of the Argentine Republic;

Have agreed as follows:

Article 1
Definitions

For the purpose of this Agreement:

a. "Antarctic Treaty" or "the Treaty" means the Antarctic Treaty done at Washington on 1 December 1959;
b. "Appropriate Authorities" means the national, provincial or local authorities of the Argentine Republic in accordance with the laws of the Argentine Republic;
c. "Archives" means all correspondence, documents, manuscripts, photographs, computer data storage, films, recordings and any other records, in paper, electronic or any other form, belonging to or held by the Secretariat;

d. "Committee for Environmental Protection" or "CEP" means the Committee established under Article 11 of the Protocol;
e. "Delegates" means Representatives, Alternate Representatives, Advisers and any other persons who represent the States Parties;
f. "Executive Secretary" means the Executive Secretary appointed by the ATCM to head the Secretariat according to the instrument establishing the Secretariat;
g. "Expert" means a person engaged to perform short term or temporary projects on behalf of the Secretariat or participate in the work of or perform a mission on behalf of the Secretariat without necessarily receiving remuneration from the Secretariat, but does not include staff members;
h. "Government" means the Government of the Argentine Republic;
i. "Headquarters" means the premises, including buildings or parts of buildings and any land ancillary thereto, irrespective of ownership, occupied by the Secretariat for the performance of its Official Activities;
j. "Official Activities" means all activities undertaken pursuant to the Treaty and the Protocol including the Secretariat's administrative activities;
k. "Protocol" means the Protocol on Environmental Protection to the Antarctic Treaty done at Madrid on 4 October 1991;
l. "Secretariat" means the Secretariat of the Antarctic Treaty, established as a permanent organ of the ATCM;
m. "Staff member" means the Executive Secretary and all other persons appointed for employment with the Secretariat and subject to its Staff Regulations, but does not include persons recruited locally and assigned to hourly rates of pay; and
n. "States Parties" means the States Parties to the Antarctic Treaty.

Article 2
Legal capacity

The Secretariat as an organ of the ATCM has legal personality and capacity to perform its functions in the territory of the Argentine Republic. It has, in particular, the capacity to contract, to acquire and dispose of movable and immovable property, and to institute and be a party to legal proceedings. The Secretariat may exercise its legal capacity only to the extent authorized by the ATCM.

Article 3
Headquarters

1. The Headquarters shall be inviolable and shall be under the full authority of the Secretariat.

2. The Government shall provide premises rent-free, in Buenos Aires, suitable as the Headquarters.

3. The Government shall take all appropriate steps to protect the Headquarters against any intrusion or damage and to prevent any impairment of its dignity.

4. The Government shall arrange for the Headquarters to be supplied by the appropriate authorities with available public services, such as electricity, water, sewerage, gas, mail, telephone, telegraph, drainage, garbage collection and fire protection, on terms no less favourable than those enjoyed by diplomatic missions in Argentine Republic.

5. Through the ATCM, the Secretariat shall make known to the Government the need for any changes to the location or extent of its permanent premises or archives and of any temporary occupation of premises for the performance of its Official Activities. Where any premises other than those provided under paragraph 2 above are used or occupied by the Secretariat for the performance of its Official Activities, such premises shall, with the concurrence of the Government, be accorded the status of official premises of the Secretariat. Where any permanent or temporary changes are made to the premises of the Secretariat in accordance with this paragraph, any additional premises occupied by the Secretariat shall not necessarily be provided by the Government rent-free.

6. Without prejudice to the terms of this Agreement, the Secretariat shall not permit the Headquarters to become a refuge from justice for persons avoiding arrest or service of legal process or against whom an order of extradition or deportation has been issued.

7. The Appropriate Authorities may enter the Headquarters to carry out their duties only with the consent of the Executive Secretary and under the conditions agreed by him/her. The Executive Secretary's consent shall be deemed to have been given in the case of fire or other exceptional emergencies which require immediate protective action.

Article 4
Immunities

1. Subject to what is provided for in the Treaty, the Protocol or this Agreement, the activities of the Secretariat in the Argentine Republic shall be governed by Argentine domestic law consistent with international law.

2. Within the scope of its Official Activities, the Secretariat as an organ of the ATCM and its property, premises and assets shall have immunity of jurisdiction in judicial and administrative proceedings except:

    a) to the extent that the ATCM expressly waives such immunity;

b) in respect of any contract for the supply of goods or services and any loan or other transaction for the provision of finance and any guarantee or indemnity in respect of any such transaction or of any other financial obligation;

c) in respect of a civil action by a third party for death, damage or personal injury arising from an accident caused by a motor vehicle belonging to, or operated on behalf of, the Secretariat to the extent that compensation is not recoverable from insurance;

d) in respect of a motor vehicle offence involving a motor vehicle belonging to, or operated on behalf of, the Secretariat;

e) in the event of a claim for salaries, wages or other emoluments owed by the Secretariat;

f) in respect of a counter-claim directly connected with proceedings initiated by the Secretariat;

g) in respect of claims made on real estate situated in the Argentine Republic; and

h) in respect of actions based on the Secretariat's status as heir or beneficiary of property situated in the Argentine Republic.

3. The Secretariat's property, premises and assets shall have immunity from any form of restrictions or controls such as requisition, confiscation, expropriation or attachment. They shall also be immune from any form of administrative or judicial constraint provided that motor vehicles belonging to or operated on behalf of the Secretariat shall not be immune from administrative or judicial constraint when temporarily necessary in connection with the prevention of, and investigation into, accidents involving such motor vehicles.

4. Nothing in this Agreement shall impair, or shall be construed as a waiver of, immunity that States enjoy in the territory of other States.

Article 5
Objective and waiver of privileges and immunities

1. Privileges and immunities provided for in this Agreement are granted to ensure the unimpeded functioning of the ATCM and the Secretariat and the complete independence of the persons to whom they are accorded. They are not granted for the personal benefit of the individuals themselves.

2. Except as provided in paragraph 3 below, the privileges and immunities provided in this Agreement may be waived by the ATCM. They should be waived in a particular case where the privilege and immunity in question would impede the course of justice and can be waived without prejudice to the purpose for which they are accorded.

3. In the case of Delegates, their privileges and immunities provided in this Agreement may be waived by the States Parties which they respectively represent.

Article 6
Archives

The Archives shall be inviolable.

Article 7
The Treaty flag and emblem

The Secretariat shall be entitled to display the Treaty flag and emblem on the premises and means of transport of the Secretariat and of the Executive Secretary.

Article 8
Exemption from direct taxes

Within the scope of its Official Activities, the Secretariat, its property, premises and assets, and its income (including contributions made to the Secretariat as the result of any agreement arrived at by the States Parties) shall be exempt from all direct taxes including income tax, capital gains tax and all State taxes. The Secretariat shall be exempt from municipal taxes with the exception of those which constitute payment for specific services rendered in accordance with paragraph 4 of Article 3 above.

Article 9
Exemption from customs and excise duties and value added tax

1. The property used by the Secretariat necessary for its Official Activities (including the ATCM publications, motor vehicles and items for official entertainment purposes) shall be exempt from all customs and excise duties.

2. The Secretariat shall be exempt from any value added tax or similar taxes for services and goods, including publications and other information material, motor vehicles and items for official entertainment purposes, if the services and goods so purchased by the Secretariat are necessary for its official use.

Article 10
Exemption from restrictions and prohibitions

Goods imported or exported for the Official Activities of the Secretariat shall be exempt from any prohibitions or restrictions applicable to such goods on grounds of national origin.

Article 11
Re-sale

Goods which have been acquired or imported by the Secretariat to which exemptions under Article 9 above apply and goods acquired or imported by the Executive Secretary or other staff members to which the exemptions under Article 16 or Article 17 below apply, shall not be given away, sold, lent, hired out or otherwise disposed of in the Argentine Republic, except under conditions agreed in advance with the Government.

Article 12
Currency and exchange

The Secretariat shall be exempt from any currency or exchange restrictions, including those in respect of funds, currency and securities received, acquired, held or disposed of. The Secretariat may also operate without restrictions bank or other accounts for its official use in any currency, and have them transferred freely within the Argentine Republic or to any other country.

Article 13
Communications

1. With regard to its official communications and the transfer of all its documents, the Secretariat shall enjoy treatment not less favourable than that generally accorded by the Government to any other government, including the latter's diplomatic mission, in the matter of priorities, rates and taxes on mails and all forms of telecommunications.

2. The Secretariat may employ any appropriate means of communication, including encrypted messages. The Government shall not impose any restriction on the official communications of the Secretariat or on the circulation of its publications.

3. The Secretariat may install and use radio transmitters with the consent of the Government.

4. Official correspondence and other official communications of the Secretariat are not subject to censorship and shall enjoy all the guarantees established by Argentine domestic law.

Article 14
Publications

The importation and exportation of the Secretariat's publications and other information material imported or exported by the Secretariat within the scope of its Official Activities shall not be restricted in any way.

Article 15
Privileges and immunities of delegates

1. Delegates of the States Parties shall enjoy, during their stay in the Argentine Republic for exercising their official functions, the privileges and immunities of diplomatic agents as established in the Vienna Convention on Diplomatic Relations of 18 April 1961.

2. The provisions of paragraph 1 above shall be applicable irrespective of the relations existing between the governments which the persons referred to represent and the Government, and are without prejudice to any additional immunities to which such persons may be entitled in the Argentine Republic.

3. The privileges and immunities described in paragraph 1 above shall not be accorded to any delegate of the Government or to any national or permanent resident of the Argentine Republic.

4. The Government shall treat Delegates with all due respect and shall take all necessary measures to prevent encroachment on their person, freedom and dignity. Where it appears that an offence may have been committed against a Delegate, steps shall be taken in accordance with Argentine legal procedures to investigate the matter and to ensure that appropriate action is taken with respect to the prosecution of the alleged offender.

Article 16
Executive Secretary

In addition to the privileges, immunities, exemptions and facilities provided for in Article 17 below, the Executive Secretary, unless he or she is a national or a permanent resident of the Argentine Republic, shall enjoy the privileges, immunities, exemptions and facilities to which a diplomatic agent in the Argentine Republic is entitled, including privileges, immunities, exemptions and facilities in respect of the members of their family which form a part of the household, unless they are nationals or permanent residents of the Argentine Republic.

Article 17
Staff members

1. Staff members of the Secretariat:

a) shall have, even after the termination of their service with the Secretariat, immunity from suit and any other legal or administrative proceedings or judicial request in respect of acts and things done by them in the exercise of their official functions, including words written or spoken;

b) immunities set out in the sub-paragraph above shall not, however, apply in the case of a motor vehicle offence committed by such a staff member or the Executive Secretary nor in the case of civil or administrative proceedings arising out of death, damage or personal injury caused by a motor vehicle belonging to or driven by him or her to the extent that compensation is not recoverable from insurance;

c) shall be exempt from any obligations in respect of military service and all other kinds of mandatory service, unless they are nationals or permanent residents of the Argentine Republic;

d) shall be exempt from the application of laws relating to the registration of aliens and immigration;

e) unless they are nationals or permanent residents of the Argentine Republic, they shall be accorded the same exemption from currency and exchange restrictions as is accorded to an official of comparable rank from an international agency in the Argentine Republic;

f) unless they are nationals or permanent residents of the Argentine Republic, they shall when taking up their post in the Argentine Republic for the first time, be exempt from customs duties and other such charges (except payments for services) in respect of import of furniture, motor vehicles and other personal effects in their ownership or possession or already ordered by them and intended for their personal use or for their establishment. Such goods shall be imported within six months of a staff member's first entry into the Argentine Republic but in exceptional circumstances an extension of this period shall be granted by the Government. Goods which have been acquired or imported by staff members and to which exemptions under this sub-paragraph apply shall not be given away, sold, lent, hired out, or otherwise disposed of except under conditions agreed in advance with the Government. Furniture and personal effects may be exported free of duties when leaving the Argentine Republic on the termination of the official functions of the staff member;

g) shall be exempt from all taxes on income received from the Secretariat. This exemption shall not apply to staff members who are nationals or permanent residents of the Argentine Republic;

h) shall have similar repatriation facilities as are accorded to representatives of international agencies in times of international crisis; and

i) shall have personal inviolability with respect to any form of personal arrest or detention or seizure of their personal baggage unless they are nationals or permanent residents of the Argentine Republic.

2. Privileges and immunities applicable to a staff member in accordance with sub-paragraphs c), d), e), f), h) and i) of paragraph 1 above shall also apply to the members of his or her family forming a part of the household, unless they are nationals or permanent residents in the Argentine Republic.

Article 18
Experts

In the exercise of their functions experts shall enjoy the following privileges and immunities to the extent necessary for the carrying out of their functions, including while traveling in the Argentine Republic to that effect:

a) immunity from suit and any other legal or administrative proceedings or judicial request in respect of acts and things done by them in the exercise of their official functions, including words written or spoken. This immunity shall not, however, apply in the case of a motor vehicle offence committed by such experts nor in the case of civil or administrative proceedings arising out of death, damage or personal injury caused by a motor vehicle belonging to or driven by him or her to the extent the compensation is not recoverable from insurance. Such immunity shall continue after the expert's function in relation to the Secretariat has ceased;

b) inviolability for all their official papers and documents as well as other official materials, which are related to the performance of the functions of the Secretariat;

c) unless they are nationals or permanent residents of the Argentine Republic, the same exemption from currency and exchange restrictions as is accorded to a representative of a foreign Government on a temporary mission in Argentina on behalf of that Government; and

d) unless they are nationals or permanent residents of the Argentine Republic, immunity from personal arrest and detention and from attachment of personal luggage.

Article 19
Visas

1. All persons having official business with the Secretariat, namely Delegates and members of their families forming a part of the household, staff members of the Secretariat and any members of their families forming a part of the household, and the experts referred to in Article 18 above, shall have the right of entry into, stay in and exit from the Argentine Republic.

2. The Government shall take all measures necessary to facilitate the entry into the Argentine Republic, the sojourn on that territory and the exit therefrom of all persons mentioned in paragraph 1 above. Visas, where required, shall be granted without wait or delay, and without fee, on production of a certificate that the applicant is a person described in paragraph 1 above. In addition, the Government shall facilitate travel for such persons within the territory of the Argentine Republic.

Article 20
Cooperation

The Secretariat shall co-operate fully at all times with the appropriate Authorities in order to prevent any abuse of the privileges, immunities and facilities provided for in this Agreement. The Government reserves its sovereign right to take reasonable measures to preserve security. Nothing in this Agreement prevents the application of laws necessary for health and quarantine or, with respect to the Secretariat and its officials, laws relating to public order.

Article 21
Notification of appointments, identity cards

1. The ATCM shall notify the Government of the appointment of an Executive Secretary and the date when he or she is to take up or relinquish the post.

2. The Secretariat shall notify the Government when a staff member takes up or relinquishes his or her post or when an expert starts or finishes a project or mission.

3. The Secretariat shall twice a year send to the Government a list of all experts and staff members and the members of their families forming a part of the household in the Argentine Republic. In each case the Secretariat shall indicate whether such persons are nationals or permanent residents of the Argentine Republic.

4. The Government shall issue to all staff members and experts as soon as practicable after notification of their appointment, a card bearing the photograph of the holder and identifying him or her as a staff member or expert as the case may be. This card shall be accepted by the appropriate Authorities as evidence of identity and appointment. The members of their families forming a part of the household shall also be issued with an identity card. When the staff member or expert relinquishes his or her duties, the Secretariat shall return to the Government his or her identity card together with identity cards issued to members of his or her family forming a part of the household.

Article 22
Consultation

The Government and the Secretariat as an organ of the ATCM shall consult at the request of either of them concerning matters arising under this Agreement. If any such matter is not promptly resolved, the Secretariat shall refer it to the ATCM.

Article 23
Amendment

This Agreement may be amended by agreement between the Government and the ATCM.

Article 24
Settlement of disputes

Any dispute arising out of the interpretation or application of this Agreement shall be settled by consultation, negotiation or any other mutually acceptable method, which may include resort to binding arbitration.

Article 25
Entry into force and termination

1. This Agreement shall enter into force upon signature.

2. This Agreement may be terminated by written notification by either Party. Termination shall take effect two years after receipt of such notification unless otherwise agreed.

Done in Punta del Este, on the tenth day of May, two thousand and ten, in two originals, in the Spanish, English, French and Russian languages, both being equally authentic.

For the Argentine Republic

For the Antarctic Treaty
Consultative Meeting

Jorge Enrique Taiana
Minister of Foreign Affairs, International
Trade and Worship

Roberto Puceiro Ripoll
Chairman of the XXXIII rd. Antarctic
Treaty Consultative Meeting

Preliminary Agenda for ATCM XXXIV

1. Opening of the Meeting

2. Election of Officers and Creation of Working Groups

3. Adoption of the Agenda and Allocation of Items

4. Operational of the Antarctic Treaty System: Reports by Parties, Observers and Experts

5. Operation of the Antarctic Treaty System: General Matters

6. Operation of the Antarctic Treaty System: Review of the Secretariat's Situation

7. Report of the Committee for Environmental Protection

8. Liability: Implementation of Decision 1 (2005)

9. Safety and Operations in Antarctica

10. Tourism and Non-Governmental Activities in the Antarctic Treaty Area

11. Inspections under the Antarctic Treaty and the Environment Protocol

12. Science Issues, Scientific Cooperation and Facilitation, including the Legacy of the International Polar Year 2007-2008

13. Implications of Climate Change for Management of the Antarctic Treaty Area

14. Operational Issues

15. Education Issues

16. Exchange of Information

17. Biological Prospecting in Antarctica

18. Development of a Multi-Year Strategic Work Plan

19. Preparation of the 35th Meeting

20. Any Other Business

21. Adoption of the Final Report

PART II

Measures, Decisions and Resolutions

1. Measures

Antarctic Specially Protected Area No 101
(Taylor Rookery, Mac.Robertson Land):
Revised Management Plan

The Representatives,

Recalling Articles 3, 5 and 6 of Annex V to the Protocol on Environmental Protection to the Antarctic Treaty, providing for the designation of Antarctic Specially Protected Areas ("ASPA") and the approval of Management Plans for those Areas;

Recalling

- Recommendation IV-I (1966), which designated Taylor Rookery, Mac. Robertson Land as Specially Protected Area ("SPA") No 1;

- Recommendation XVII-2 (1992), which adopted a Management Plan for the Area;

- Decision 1 (2002), which renamed and renumbered SPA 1 as ASPA 101;

- Measure 2 (2005), which adopted a revised Management Plan for ASPA 101;

Recalling that Recommendation XVII-2 (1992) has not become effective, that the Management Plan for ASPA 101 attached to it was withdrawn by Measure 2 (2005) and that the other Management Plans attached to it (in respect of ASPA 102, 103 and 116) have also already been withdrawn (by Measure 2 (2005) and Measure 1 (2006));

Noting that the Committee for Environmental Protection has endorsed a revised Management Plan for ASPA 101;

Desiring to replace the existing Management Plan for ASPA 101 with the revised Management Plan;

Recommend to their Governments the following Measure for approval in accordance with paragraph 1 of Article 6 of Annex V to the Protocol on Environmental Protection to the Antarctic Treaty:

That:

1. the revised Management Plan for Antarctic Specially Protected Area No 101 (Taylor Rookery, Mac.Robertson Land), which is annexed to this Measure, be approved;

2. the Management Plan for ASPA 101 annexed to Measure 2 (2005) shall cease to be effective; and

3. Recommendation XVII-2 (1992), which is not yet effective, be withdrawn.

Antarctic Specially Protected Area No 102
(Rookery Islands, Holme Bay, Mac.Robertson Land): Revised Management Plan

The Representatives,

Recalling Articles 3, 5 and 6 of Annex V to the Protocol on Environmental Protection to the Antarctic Treaty, providing for the designation of Antarctic Specially Protected Areas ("ASPA") and the approval of Management Plans for those Areas;

Recalling

- Recommendation IV-2 (1966), which designated Rookery Islands, Holme Bay as Specially Protected Area ("SPA") No 2;

- Recommendation XVII-2 (1992), which adopted a Management Plan for the Area;

- Decision 1 (2002), which renamed and renumbered SPA 2 as ASPA 102;

- Measure 2 (2005), which adopted a revised Management Plan for ASPA 102;

Recalling that Recommendation XVII-2 (1992) has not become effective, that the Management Plan for ASPA 102 attached to it was withdrawn by Measure 2 (2005) and that the other Management Plans attached to it (in respect of ASPA 101, 103 and 116) have also already been withdrawn (by Measure 2 (2005) and Measure 1 (2006));

Noting that the Committee for Environmental Protection has endorsed a revised Management Plan for ASPA 102;

Noting that Measure 1 (2010) withdraws Recommendation XVII-2 (1992);

Desiring to replace the existing Management Plan for ASPA 102 with the revised Management Plan;

Recommend to their Governments the following Measure for approval in accordance with paragraph 1 of Article 6 of Annex V to the Protocol on Environmental Protection to the Antarctic Treaty:

That:

1. the revised Management Plan for Antarctic Specially Protected Area No 102 (Rookery Islands, Holme Bay, Mac.Robertson Land), which is annexed to this Measure, be approved; and

2. the Management Plan for ASPA 102 annexed to Measure 2 (2005) shall cease to be effective.

Antarctic Specially Protected Area No 103
(Ardery Island and Odbert Island, Budd Coast, Wilkes Land): Revised Management Plan

The Representatives,

Recalling Articles 3, 5 and 6 of Annex V to the Protocol on Environmental Protection to the Antarctic Treaty providing for the designation of Antarctic Specially Protected Areas ("ASPA") and approval of Management Plans for those Areas;

Recalling

- Recommendation IV-3 (1966) which designated Ardery Island and Odbert Island, Budd Coast as Specially Protected Area ("SPA") No 3;

- Recommendation XVII-2 (1992), which adopted a Management Plan for the Area;

- Decision 1 (2002), which renamed and renumbered SPA 3 as ASPA 103;

- Measure 2 (2005), which adopted a revised Management Plan for ASPA 103;

Recalling that Recommendation XVII-2 (1992) has not become effective, that the Management Plan for ASPA 103 attached to it was withdrawn by Measure 2 (2005) and that the other Management Plans attached to it (in respect of ASPA 101, 102 and 116) have also already been withdrawn (by Measure 2 (2005) and Measure 1 (2006));

Noting that the Committee for Environmental Protection has endorsed a revised Management Plan for ASPA 103;

Noting that Measure 1 (2010) withdraws Recommendation XVII-2 (1992);

Desiring to replace the existing Management Plan for ASPA 103 with the revised Management Plan;

Recommend to their Governments the following Measure for approval in accordance with paragraph 1 of Article 6 of Annex V to the Protocol on Environmental Protection to the Antarctic Treaty:

That:

1. the revised Management Plan for Antarctic Specially Protected Area No 103 (Ardery Island and Odbert Island, Budd Coast, Wilkes Land), which is annexed to this Measure, be approved; and

2. the Management Plan for ASPA 103 annexed to Measure 2 (2005) shall cease to be effective.

Antarctic Specially Protected Area No 105
(Beaufort Island, McMurdo Sound, Ross Sea): Revised Management Plan

The Representatives,

Recalling Articles 3, 5 and 6 of Annex V to the Protocol on Environmental Protection to the Antarctic Treaty, providing for the designation of Antarctic Specially Protected Areas ("ASPA") and the approval of Management Plans for those Areas;

Recalling

- Recommendation IV-5 (1966), which designated Beaufort Island, Ross Sea as Specially Protected Area ("SPA") No 5;

- Measure 1 (1997), which annexed a Management Plan for the Area;

- Decision 1 (2002), which renamed and renumbered SPA 5 as ASPA 105;

- Measure 2 (2003), which adopted a revised Management Plan for ASPA 105;

Recalling that Measure 1 (1997) has not become effective;

Noting that the Committee for Environmental Protection has endorsed a revised Management Plan for ASPA 105;

Desiring to replace the existing Management Plan for ASPA 105 with the revised Management Plan;

Recommend to their Governments the following Measure for approval in accordance with paragraph 1 of Article 6 of Annex V to the Protocol on Environmental Protection to the Antarctic Treaty:

That:

1. the revised Management Plan for Antarctic Specially Protected Area No 105 (Beaufort Island, McMurdo Sound, Ross Sea), which is annexed to this Measure, be approved;

2. Recommendation IV-5 (1966) and the Management Plan for ASPA 105 annexed to Measure 2 (2003) shall cease to be effective; and

3. Measure 1 (1997), which is not yet effective, be withdrawn.

Antarctic Specially Protected Area N° 106
(Cape Hallett, Northern Victoria Land, Ross Sea): Revised Management Plan

The Representatives,

Recalling Articles 3, 5 and 6 of Annex V to the Protocol on Environmental Protection to the Antarctic Treaty, providing for the designation of Antarctic Specially Protected Areas ("ASPA") and the approval of Management Plans for those Areas;

Recalling

- Recommendation IV-7 (1966), which designated Cape Hallett, Victoria Land as Specially Protected Area ("SPA") No 7;

- Recommendation XIII-13 (1985), which revised the description and boundaries of SPA 7;

- Decision 1 (2002), which renamed and renumbered SPA 7 as ASPA 106;

- Measure 1 (2002), which adopted a Management Plan for the Area;

Noting that the Committee for Environmental Protection has endorsed a revised Management Plan for ASPA 106;

Desiring to replace the existing Management Plan for ASPA 106 with the revised Management Plan;

Recommend to their Governments the following Measure for approval in accordance with paragraph 1 of Article 6 of Annex V to the Protocol on Environmental Protection to the Antarctic Treaty:

That:

1. the revised Management Plan for Antarctic Specially Protected Area No 106 (Cape Hallett, Northern Victoria Land, Ross Sea), which is annexed to this Measure, be approved; and

2. Recommendation IV-7 (1966), Recommendation XIII-13 (1985) and the Management Plan for ASPA 106 annexed to Measure 1 (2002) shall cease to be effective.

Antarctic Specially Protected Area No 119
(Davis Valley and Forlidas Pond, Dufek Massif, Pensacola Mountains): Revised Management Plan

The Representatives,

Recalling Articles 3, 5 and 6 of Annex V to the Protocol on Environmental Protection to the Antarctic Treaty, providing for the designation of Antarctic Specially Protected Areas ("ASPA") and the approval of Management Plans for those Areas;

Recalling

- Recommendation XVI-9 (1991), which designated Forlidas Pond and Davis Valley Ponds as Specially Protected Area ("SPA") No 23 and annexed a Management Plan for the Area;

- Decision 1 (2002), which renamed and renumbered SPA 23 as ASPA 119;

- Measure 2 (2005), which adopted a revised Management Plan for ASPA 119;

Recalling that Recommendation XVI-9 (1991) has not become effective, and that the Management Plan for ASPA 119 attached to it was withdrawn by Measure 2 (2005);

Noting that the Committee for Environmental Protection has endorsed a revised Management Plan for ASPA 119;

Desiring to replace the existing Management Plan for ASPA 119 with the revised Management Plan;

Recommend to their Governments the following Measure for approval in accordance with paragraph 1 of Article 6 of Annex V to the Protocol on Environmental Protection to the Antarctic Treaty:

That:

1. the revised Management Plan for Antarctic Specially Protected Area No 119 (Davis Valley and Forlidas Pond, Dufek Massif, Pensacola Mountains), which is annexed to this Measure, be approved;

2. the Management Plan for ASPA 119 annexed to Measure 2 (2005) shall cease to be effective; and

3. Recommendation XVI-9 (1991), which is not yet effective, be withdrawn.

Antarctic Specially Protected Area No 139
(Biscoe Point, Anvers Island, Palmer Archipelago): Revised Management Plan

The Representatives,

Recalling Articles 3, 5 and 6 of Annex V to the Protocol on Environmental Protection to the Antarctic Treaty, providing for the designation of Antarctic Specially Protected Areas ("ASPA") and the approval of Management Plans for those Areas;

Recalling

- Recommendation XIII-8 (1985), which designated Biscoe Point, Anvers Island, Palmer Archipelago as Site of Special Scientific Interest ("SSSI") No 20 and annexed a Management Plan for the site;

- Resolution 3 (1996), which extended the expiry date of SSSI 20 to 31 December 2000;

- Decision 1 (2002), which renamed and renumbered SSSI 20 as ASPA 139;

- Measure 2 (2004), which adopted a revised Management Plan for ASPA 139;

Recalling that ASPA 139 is located within Antarctic Specially Managed Area No 7;

Noting that the Committee for Environmental Protection has endorsed a revised Management Plan for ASPA 139;

Desiring to replace the existing Management Plan for ASPA 139 with the revised Management Plan;

Recommend to their Governments the following Measure for approval in accordance with paragraph 1 of Article 6 of Annex V to the Protocol on Environmental Protection to the Antarctic Treaty:

That:

1. the revised Management Plan for Antarctic Specially Protected Area No 139 (Biscoe Point, Anvers Island, Palmer Archipelago), which is annexed to this Measure, be approved; and

2. all prior Management Plans for ASPA 139, namely those annexed to:

   • Recommendation XIII-8 (1985); and

   • Measure 2 (2004)

   shall cease to be effective.

Antarctic Specially Protected Area No 155
(Cape Evans, Ross Island): Revised Management Plan

The Representatives,

Recalling Articles 3, 5 and 6 of Annex V to the Protocol on Environmental Protection to the Antarctic Treaty, providing for the designation of Antarctic Specially Protected Areas ("ASPA") and the approval of Management Plans for those Areas;

Recalling

- Measure 2 (1997), which designated the Cape Evans Historic Site and its environs as Specially Protected Area ("SPA") No 25 and annexed a Management Plans for the Area;

- Decision 1 (2002), which renamed and renumbered SPA 25 as ASPA 155;

- Measure 2 (2005), which adopted a revised Management Plan for ASPA 155;

- Measure 12 (2008), which adopted a revised Management Plan for ASPA 155;

Recalling that Measure 2 (1997) has not become effective and that all Management Plans for the Area ceased to be effective in accordance with Measure 12 (2008);

Noting that the Committee for Environmental Protection has endorsed a revised Management Plan for ASPA 155;

Desiring to replace the existing Management Plan for ASPA 155 with the revised Management Plan;

Recommend to their Governments the following Measure for approval in accordance with paragraph 1 of Article 6 of Annex V to the Protocol on Environmental Protection to the Antarctic Treaty:

That:

1. the revised Management Plan for Antarctic Specially Protected Area No 155 (Cape Evans, Ross Island), which is annexed to this Measure, be approved;

2. the Management Plan for ASPA 155 annexed to Measure 12 (2008) shall cease to be effective; and

3. Measure 2 (1997), which is not yet effective, be withdrawn.

Antarctic Specially Protected Area No 157
(Backdoor Bay, Cape Royds, Ross Island): Revised Management Plan

The Representatives,

Recalling Articles 3, 5 and 6 of Annex V to the Protocol on Environmental Protection to the Antarctic Treaty, providing for the designation of Antarctic Specially Protected Areas ("ASPA") and the approval of Management Plans for those Areas;

Recalling

- Measure 1 (1998), which designated the Cape Royds site as Specially Protected Area ("SPA") No 27 and annexed a Management Plan for the Area;

- Decision 1 (2002), which renamed and renumbered SPA 27 as ASPA 157;

- Measure 1 (2002), which adopted a revised Management Plan for ASPA 157;

- Measure 2 (2005), which adopted a revised Management Plan for ASPA 157;

Recalling that Measure 1 (1998) has not become effective;

Noting that the Committee for Environmental Protection has endorsed a revised Management Plan for ASPA 157;

Desiring to replace the existing Management Plan for ASPA 157 with the revised Management Plan;

Recommend to their Governments the following Measure for approval in accordance with paragraph 1 of Article 6 of Annex V to the Protocol on Environmental Protection to the Antarctic Treaty:

That:

1. the revised Management Plan for Antarctic Specially Protected Area No 157 (Backdoor Bay, Cape Royds, Ross Island), which is annexed to this Measure, be approved;

2. the prior Management Plans for ASPA 157, namely those annexed to:

   • Measure 1 (2002); and

   • Measure 2 (2005)

   shall cease to be effective; and

3. Measure 1 (1998), which is not yet effective, be withdrawn.

Antarctic Specially Protected Area No 158
(Hut Point, Ross Island): Revised Management Plan

The Representatives,

Recalling Articles 3, 5 and 6 of Annex V to the Protocol on Environmental Protection to the Antarctic Treaty, providing for the designation of Antarctic Specially Protected Areas ("ASPA") and the approval of Management Plans for those Areas;

Recalling

- Measure 1 (1998), which designated the Hut Point Historic Site as Specially Protected Area ("SPA") No 28 and annexed a Management Plan for the Area;

- Decision 1 (2002), which renamed and renumbered SPA 28 as ASPA 158;

- Measure 2 (2005), which adopted a revised Management Plan for ASPA 158;

Recalling that Measure 1 (1998) has not become effective;

Noting that the Committee for Environmental Protection has endorsed a revised Management Plan for ASPA 158;

Noting that Measure 9 (2010) withdraws Measure 1 (1998);

Desiring to replace the existing Management Plan for ASPA 158 with the revised Management Plan;

Recommend to their Governments the following Measure for approval in accordance with paragraph 1 of Article 6 of Annex V to the Protocol on Environmental Protection to the Antarctic Treaty:

That:

1. the revised Management Plan for Antarctic Specially Protected Area No 158 (Hut Point, Ross Island), which is annexed to this Measure, be approved; and

2. the Management Plan for ASPA 158 annexed to Measure 2 (2005) shall cease to be effective.

Antarctic Specially Protected Area No 159
(Cape Adare, Borchgrevink Coast): Revised Management Plan

The Representatives,

Recalling Articles 3, 5 and 6 of Annex V to the Protocol on Environmental Protection to the Antarctic Treaty, providing for the designation of Antarctic Specially Protected Areas ("ASPA") and the approval of Management Plans for those Areas;

Recalling

- Measure 1 (1998), which designated the Cape Adare Historic Site and its environs as Specially Protected Area ("SPA") No 29 and annexed a Management Plan for the Area;

- Decision 1 (2002), which renamed and renumbered SPA 29 as ASPA 159;

- Measure 2 (2005), which adopted a revised Management Plan for ASPA 159;

Recalling that Measure 1 (1998) has not become effective;

Noting that the Committee for Environmental Protection has endorsed a revised Management Plan for ASPA 159;

Noting that Measure 9 (2010) withdraws Measure 1 (1998);

Desiring to replace the existing Management Plan for ASPA 159 with the revised Management Plan;

Recommend to their Governments the following Measure for approval in accordance with paragraph 1 of Article 6 of Annex V to the Protocol on Environmental Protection to the Antarctic Treaty:

That:

1. the revised Management Plan for Antarctic Specially Protected Area No 159 (Cape Adare, Borchgrevink Coast), which is annexed to this Measure, be approved; and

2. the Management Plan for ASPA 159 annexed to Measure 2 (2005) shall cease to be effective.

Antarctic Specially Protected Area No 163
(Dakshin Gangotri Glacier, Dronning Maud Land): Revised Management Plan

The Representatives,

Recalling Articles 3, 5 and 6 of Annex V to the Protocol on Environmental Protection to the Antarctic Treaty, providing for the designation of Antarctic Specially Protected Areas ("ASPA") and the approval of Management Plans for those Areas;

Recalling Measure 2 (2005), which designated Dakshin Gangotri Glacier, Dronning Maud Land as ASPA 163 and annexed a Management Plan for the Area;

Noting that the Committee for Environmental Protection has endorsed a revised Management Plan for ASPA 163;

Desiring to replace the existing Management Plan for ASPA 163 with the revised Management Plan;

Recommend to their Governments the following Measure for approval in accordance with paragraph 1 of Article 6 of Annex V to the Protocol on Environmental Protection to the Antarctic Treaty:

That:

1. the revised Management Plan for Antarctic Specially Protected Area No 163 (Dakshin Gangotri Glacier, Dronning Maud Land), which is annexed to this Measure, be approved; and

2. the Management Plan for ASPA 163 annexed to Measure 2 (2005) shall cease to be effective.

Antarctic Specially Protected Area No 164
(Scullin and Murray Monoliths, Mac.Robertson Land): Revised Management Plan

The Representatives,

Recalling Measure 2 (2005), which designated Scullin and Murray Monoliths, Mac.Robertson Land, East Antarctica as ASPA No 164 and annexed a Management Plan for the Area;

Noting that the Committee for Environmental Protection has endorsed a revised Management Plan for ASPA 164;

Desiring to replace the existing Management Plan for ASPA 164 with the revised Management Plan;

Recommend to their Governments the following Measure for approval in accordance with paragraph 1 of Article 6 of Annex V to the Protocol on Environmental Protection to the Antarctic Treaty:

That:

1. the revised Management Plan for Antarctic Specially Protected Area No 164 (Scullin and Murray Monoliths, Mac.Robertson Land), which is annexed to this Measure, be approved; and

2. the Management Plan for ASPA 164 annexed to Measure 2 (2005) shall cease to be effective.

Antarctic Specially Managed Area No 7
(Southwest Anvers Island and Palmer Basin):
Revised Management Plan

The Representatives,

Recalling Articles 4, 5 and 6 of Annex V to the Protocol on Environmental Protection to the Antarctic Treaty, providing for the designation of Antarctic Specially Managed Areas ("ASMA") and the approval of Management Plans for those Areas;

Recalling

- Measure 1 (2008), which designated Southwest Anvers Island and Palmer Basin as Antarctic Specially Managed Area No 7 and annexed a Management Plan for the Area;

- Measure 2 (2009), which adopted a revised Management Plan for ASMA 7;

Noting that the Committee for Environmental Protection has endorsed a revised Management Plan for ASMA 7;

Noting Measure 7 (2010) concerning Antarctic Specially Protected Area ("ASPA") No 139 (Biscoe Point, Anvers Island), which is located within ASMA 7;

Desiring to replace the existing Management Plan for ASMA 7 with the revised Management Plan;

Recommend to their Governments the following Measure for approval in accordance with paragraph 1 of Article 6 of Annex V to the Protocol on Environmental Protection to the Antarctic Treaty:

That:

1. the revised Management Plan for Antarctic Specially Managed Area No 7 (Southwest Anvers Island and Palmer Basin), which is annexed to this Measure, be approved; and

2. Measure 2 (2009) shall cease to be effective.

Antarctic Historic Sites and Monuments: Plaque Commemorating the PM-3A Nuclear Power Plant at McMurdo Station

The Representatives,

Recalling the requirements of Article 8 of Annex V to the Protocol on Environmental Protection to the Antarctic Treaty to maintain a list of current Historic Sites and Monuments, and that such sites shall not be damaged, removed or destroyed;

Recalling Measure 3 (2003), which revised and updated the "List of Historic Sites and Monuments", as subsequently amended;

Desiring to add a further historic monument to the List of Historic Sites and Monuments;

Recommend to their Governments the following Measure for approval in accordance with paragraph 2 of Article 8 of Annex V to the Protocol on Environmental Protection to the Antarctic Treaty:

That the following historic monument be added to the "List of Historic Sites and Monuments" annexed to Measure 3 (2003):

"No 85: Plaque Commemorating the PM-3A Nuclear Power Plant at McMurdo Station

The plaque is approximately 18 x 24 inches, made of bronze and secured to a large vertical rock at McMurdo Station, the former site of the PM-3A nuclear power reactor. It is approximately half way up the west side of Observation Hill. The plaque text details achievements of PM-3A, Antarctica's first nuclear power plant.

Location: 77° 51' S, 166° 41' E

Original proposing Party: USA

Party undertaking management: USA"

2. Decisions

Compilation of Key Documents of the Antarctic Treaty System

The Representatives,

Desiring to enhance the efficiency of the functioning of the Antarctic Treaty system;

Conscious of the benefits that a compilation of key documents of the Antarctic Treaty system could bring in that regard;

Decide:

1. to task the Antarctic Treaty Secretariat ("the Secretariat") to compile, produce and distribute a "Compilation of Key Documents of the Antarctic Treaty System" ("the Compilation");

2. that the Compilation will be a practical, pocket-sized, low cost, soft cover reference booklet containing the following texts:

   • the Antarctic Treaty ("AT"), the Environmental Protocol to the AT, including its Final Act and its six Annexes, the Convention on the Conservation of Antarctic Marine Living Resources ("CCAMLR") including its Final Act, and the Convention on the Conservation of Antarctic Seals ("CCAS");

   • the Rules of Procedure of the Antarctic Treaty Consultative Meeting ("ATCM") and of the Committee for Environmental Protection ("CEP");

   • the Headquarters Agreement of the Secretariat in Buenos Aires;

   • the Staff Regulations, Financial Regulations and mandate of the Secretariat, which is contained in Measure 1 (2003); and

   • Decision 1 (1995) on Measures, Decisions and Resolutions;

3. that the Secretariat will also produce and distribute an insert for the Compilation including the following information:

   - a list of Parties to the AT and its Environmental Protocol, CCAS and CCAMLR, with information on dates on accession, ratification, and entry into force; and

   - a list of ATCMs, Special ATCMs, Antarctic Treaty Meetings of Experts and CEP meetings and their dates and locations;

4. that the Compilation will not contain other items or introductory and/or explanatory materials;

5. that the Compilation will be produced in the four official languages of the AT;

6. that the production of the Compilation will be without prejudice to any action with regard to a "Handbook of the Antarctic Treaty System". However, the Secretariat is not required to take any action under Article 2, paragraph 2(k), of Measure 1 (2003) until so requested by the ATCM;

7. that the Compilation will be produced in time for distribution at ATCM XXXIV; and

8. that the Secretariat may produce updated versions of the Compilation and its insert when so requested by the ATCM.

Secretariat Reports, Programme and Budgets

The Representatives,

Recalling Measure 1 (2003) on the establishment of the Secretariat of the Antarctic Treaty ("the Secretariat");

Bearing in mind the Financial Regulations for the Secretariat annexed to Decision 4 (2003);

Decide:

1. to approve the audited Financial Report for 2008/09 annexed to this Decision (Annex 1);

2. to take note of the Secretariat Report 2009/10 (SP 2 rev. 1) which includes the Estimate of Income and Expenditures 2009/10 and which is annexed to this Decision (Annex 2);

3. to support the intention of the Executive Secretary to renew the contract for the Assistant Executive Secretary and approve the Executive Secretary's proposal to upgrade the position of the Book-keeper (level G3) to Finance Officer (level G2); and

4. to approve the Secretariat Programme 2010/11 (SP 3 rev. 2) which includes the Budget for 2010/11 and the Forecast Budget for 2011/12 which is annexed to this Decision (Annex 3).

Buenos Aires

MR. EXECUTIVE SECRETARY:

SINDICATURA GENERAL DE LA NACIÓN, as independent external auditor, has performed the audit of the Antarctic Treaty Secretariat Financial Statements corresponding to the fiscal year ended March 31, 2009. The Independent Auditor Report thereof is hereby attached as Annex I.

In addition to the abovementioned audit, we made observations and recommendations on accounting-administrative and internal control matters that we consider report you and for your interval to the XXXIII Antarctic Treaty Consultative Meeting 2009 for knowledge and future action. The described task is summarized in a document attached hereto as Annex II.

Financial Report 2008/09
Statement of Income and Expenditure for All Funds
for the Period 1 April 2008 to 31 March 2009

INCOME	Budget	Prov. Report	Def. Report
Contributions prior years (Note 1.2 & 7)	$ 111,571	$ 138,317	$ 138,317
Contributions current year (Note 1.2 & 7)	$ 394,567	$ 404,118	$ 404,118
Other income (Note 2)	$ 2,200	$ 11,300	$ 13,517
TOTAL INCOME	**$ 508,338**	**$ 553,735**	**$ 555,952**
EXPENDITURES			
Salaries			
Executive Staff	$ 220,318	$ 220,318	$ 220,320
General Staff	$ 144,486	$ 144,486	$ 146,843
Total Salaries	**$ 364,804**	**$ 364,804**	**$ 367,163**
Goods and Services			
Audit	$ 14,370	$ 7,185	$ 14,946
Data entry	$ 3,500	$ 2,000	$ 3,931
Documentation services	$ 0	$ 2,100	$ 543
Legal advice	$ 5,400	$ 5,000	$ 3,300
Miscellaneous	$ 6,626	$ 8,000	$ 6,989
Office expenses	$ 10,000	$ 14,600	$ 14,547
Postage	$ 6,600	$ 3,400	$ 3,836
Printing	$ 26,000	$ 28,500	$ 37,249
Representation	$ 3,000	$ 3,000	$ 3,172
Telecommunications	$ 9,600	$ 9,600	$ 13,029
Training	$ 600	$ 2,000	$ 2,021
Translation	$ 212,300	$ 235,033	$ 232,554
Travel	$ 67,700	$ 43,000	$ 59,653
Total Goods and Services	**$ 365,696**	**$ 363,418**	**$ 395,770**
Equipment			
Documentation	$ 1,000	$ 1,000	$ 1,056
Furniture	$ 4,500	$ 5,000	$ 5,246
IT Equipment	$ 14,500	$ 22,600	$ 17,769
Development	$ 11,000	$ 21,000	$ 23,527
Total Equipment	**$ 31,000**	**$ 49,600**	**$ 47,598**
Fund Appropriation			
Staff Replacement Fund	$ 0	$ 0	$ 0
Staff Termination Fund (Note 1.5)	$ 0	$ 0	$ 9,415
Working Capital Fund (Note 1.6)	$ 0	$ 14,149	($ 6,866)
Total Fund Appropriation	**$ 0**	**$ 14,149**	**$ 2,549**
TOTAL EXPENDITURES	**$ 761,500**	**$ 788,471**	**$ 813,080**
(Deficit) / Surplus	**($ 253,162)**	**($ 234,736)**	**($ 257,128)**

This statement should be read in conjunction with NOTES 1 to 7 attached.

ASSETS	Prior Year	Current Year
Current assets		
Cash and cash equivalents (Note 3)	$ 966,891	$ 959,231
Credits (Note 4)	$ 8,760	$ 48,421
Total	**$ 975,651**	**$ 1,007,652**
Non-current assets		
Plant and equipment (Note 5)	$ 61,991	$ 62,196
Total	**$ 61,991**	**$ 62,196**
Total Assets	**$ 1,037,642**	**$ 1,069,848**
LIABILITIES		
Current liabilities		
Payables (Note 6)	$ 53,629	$ 91,630
Unearned income (Note 1.2 & 7)	$ 134,925	$ 379,605
Salaries payable	$ 0	$ 4,103
Total	**$ 188,554**	**$ 475,339**
Non-current liabilities		
Staff Termination Fund (Note 1.5)	$ 13,704	$ 23,119
Staff Replacement Fund	$ 50,000	$ 50,000
Total	**$ 63,704**	**$ 73,119**
Total Liabilities	**$ 252,258**	**$ 548,458**
NET ASSETS	**$ 785,384**	**$ 521,390**

This statement should be read in conjunction with NOTES 1 to 7 attached.

Represented by Funds	Net Assets 01-04-2008	Operations 2008/09	Decision 2 (2008)	Net Assets 31-03-2009
General Fund	$ 251,601	($ 257,128)	$ 40,578	$ 35,051
Working Capital Fund	$ 133,783	($ 6,866)		$ 126,917
Future Meeting Fund	$ 400,000		($ 40,578)	$ 359,422
Net Assets	**$ 785,384**	**($ 263,994)**	**$ 0**	**$ 521,390**

This statement should be read in conjunction with NOTES 1 to 7 attached.

Notes to and forming part of the Financial Statements
31 March 2009

Note 1: Summary of significant accounting principles and policies

1.1   Historical Cost

The accounts are drawn up in accordance with the convention of historical costs, except where otherwise indicated, and therefore do not reflect changes in purchasing power of money or current valuation of non-monetary assets.

1.2   Accrual Basis

The Secretariat Statement of Income and Expenditure, Statement of Financial Position and Statement of changes in Net Assets are prepared on an accrual basis in accordance with International Accounting Standards, except for current and prior year contributions that are recorded on a cash basis.

1.3   Currency

All transactions in the financial statements are presented in United States currency.

1.4   Premises

The use of the Secretariat offices is provided rent-free by the Ministry of Foreign Affairs, International Trade and Worship of the Argentine Republic, as are the expenses related to use and upkeep of the building.

1.5   Staff Termination Fund

The Secretariat is using a restrictive interpretation of Regulation 10.4 of the Staff Regulations "… executive staff members shall be compensated at a rate of one month base pay for each year of service, beginning the second year…", and no accrual for the Executive Secretary has been set up.

1.6   Working Capital Fund

In accordance to the Financial Regulations 6.2 (a), the fund was adjusted to one-sixth (1/6) of the budget of the financial year.

Note 2. Other Income

	Prov. Report	Def. Report
Bank interest	$ 2,000	$ 2,082
Exchange rate adjustment	$ 9,120	$ 11,254
Value Added Tax recovery	$ 180	$ 181
	$ 11,300	$ 13,517

Note 3. Cash and cash equivalents

Cash	$ 1,141
BNA US Dollar account	$ 922,491
BNA Argentine Peso account	$ 35,599
Total	$ 959,231

Note 4. Credits

Prepayments to suppliers	$ 35,972
VAT to be reimbursed	$ 11,930
Salary advance	$ 500
Turnover tax to be reimbursed	$ 19
Total	$ 48,421

Note 5. Plant and equipment

Plant and equipment 01-4-2008	$ 65,805
Disbursements 2008/09	$ 528
Books	$ 3,240
Depreciation	($ 7,377)
Plant and equipment 31-3-2009	$ 62,196

Note 6. Payables

Provision for social security & income tax refund ex Reg. 5.6 of the Staff Regulations	$ 67,800
Accounts payable	$ 23,830
	$ 91,630

Note 7. Contributions

The breakdowns of contributions received by corresponding budget year are as follows:

Financial Year Received	2006/07 2008/09	2007/08 2008/09	2008/09 2007/08	2008/09 2008/09	2009/10 2008/09
Argentina				$ 14,948	
Australia				$ 14,948	$ 36,404
Belgium		$ 23,222		$ 9,905	
Brazil				$ 9,905	
Bulgaria				$ 8,449	$ 20,534
Chile				$ 11,453	
China				$ 11,388	
Ecuador				$ 8,421	
Finland				$ 9,949	
France			$ 22,289		
Germany			$ 20,461		
India				$11,439	
Italy				$12,948	
Japan				$14,948	
Korea				$9,949	
Netherlands				$11,449	
New Zealand			$ 14,936		$ 36,404
Norway			$ 14,918		
Peru		$ 19,688			
Poland				$ 10,061	
Russia			$ 18,343		
South Africa		$ 26,756		$ 17,055	$ 27,859
Spain				$ 26,756	
Sweden			$11,449		
Ukraine	$ 22,217	$ 23,212			
United Kingdom			$ 14,948	$ 32,000	$ 36,404
United States			$ 17,581		$ 222,000
Uruguay		$ 23,222		$23,222	
TOTAL	$ 22,217	$ 116,100	$ 134,925	$ 269,193	
		$ 138,317		$ 404,118	$ 379,605

289

Annex I

Independent auditor's report
XXXIII Antarctic Treaty Consultative Meeting 2010,
Punta del Este, Uruguay

1. Report on the Financial Statements

We have audited the Financial Statements of the Antarctic Treaty Secretariat attached hereto, which comprise the Statement of Revenues and Expenditures, the Statement of Financial Position and other explanatory notes for the period started at April 1st, 2008 and ended at March 31th, 2009.

2. Management's Responsibility for the Financial Statements

The Antarctic Treaty Secretariat is responsible for the preparation and fair presentation of these Financial Statements according to the International Financial Reporting Standards and specific regulations of the Antarctic Treaty Consultative Meetings. This responsibility includes: designing, implementing and maintaining internal control relevant to the preparation and fair presentation of financial statements so that they are free from material misstatement, whether due to fraud or error; selecting and applying appropriate accounting policies; and making accounting estimates that are reasonable for the circumstances.

3. Auditor's Responsibility

Our responsibility is to express an opinion on these Financial Statements based on our audit. We conducted our audit in accordance with the International Standards on Auditing and the Annex to Decision 3 of the XXXI Antarctic Treaty Consultative Meeting which describes the tasks to be carried out by the external audit.

Those standards require that we comply with ethical requirements and plan and perform the audit to obtain reasonable assurance whether the financial statements are free from material misstatement.

An audit involves performing procedures to obtain audit evidence about the amounts and disclosures in the Financial Statements. The procedures selected depend on the auditor's judgment, including the assessment of the risks of material misstatement of the financial statements, whether due to fraud or error. In making those risk assessments, the auditor considers internal control relevant to the entity's preparation and fair presentation of the financial statements in order to design audit procedures that are appropriate in the circumstances.

An audit also includes evaluating the appropriateness of accounting policies used and the reasonableness of accounting estimates made by management, as well as evaluating the overall presentation of the Financial Statements.

We believe that the audit evidence we have obtained is sufficient and appropriate to provide a basis for our audit opinion.

4. Explanatory notes prior to the auditor opinion

As explained in Note 1.5 to the Financial Statements stated in item 1, the Secretariat has applied the restrictive criterion as regards the interpretation of Regulation 10.4 of the Staff Regulations —Decision 3 (2003) and the compensation corresponding to the Executive Secretary whose separation took place 08/31/2009 has not been included. (See Annex II, Internal Control Report as of 03/31/1009. Item 3.3 Staff, from the current fiscal year).

5. Opinion

In our opinion, and subject to the incidence that may occur on the Financial Statements audited according to what has been stated in 4 above, the financial statements present fairly, in all material respects, the financial position of Antarctic Treaty Secretariat as of March 31th, 2009, and its financial performance for the period then ended in accordance with International Accounting Standards and the specific rules of Antarctic Treaty Consultative Meetings.

Dr. Edgardo De Rose
Contador Público
T°182 F° 195 CPCECABA

Buenos Aires, 5th April, 2010

Sindicatura General De La Nación
Av. Corrientes 381 Buenos Aires
República Argentina

Annex II

External audit Antarctic Treaty Secretariat Internal control report 03.31.2009

1. Objective

To state briefly the main findings and recommendations arising from the external audit of the Antarctic Treaty Secretariat carried out for the fiscal year ended 31 March 2009.

2. Task performed

The following activities were performed:

- Accounting analysis.
- Financial statements audit.
- Assessment of present situation and evaluation of information technology activities.
- Evaluation of tasks performed by the Antarctic Treaty Secretariat; verification fulfillment thereof with rules and regulations in full force and effect.

3. Relevant Aspects

Until the issuance of this report the assessment performed showed relevant aspects which are hereinbelow mentioned. They are of different nature and include recommendations on matters which may affect the entity's Financial Statements and/or Internal Control System. During the assessment on the observed aspects hereinbelow stated, oral recommendations have been made.

Accounting Performance

3.1 Funds turnover

From previous fiscal years:

- Lack of rules and procedures as regards the Secretariat's usual activities established as Section 9, subsection 9.1 (a) of the Financial Regulations.
- Pursuant to Section 9 subsection 9.1 (c) some officials have been appointed entitled to receiving funds, fulfilling obligations and tendering payments on behalf of the Secretariat. Such appointments entitle them to manage only small amounts. This fact could adversely affect the adequate Secretariat's performance.

- In general, the procurement procedures and other procedures stated in Section 9 subsection 9.4 of the Financial Regulations are not completely fulfilled. It is particularly relevant the contract of employment made by and between the Secretariat and Mr Bernard Ponette due to the fact that it represents 20 % of the total expenses corresponding to the Secretariat's fiscal year. It has been specifically observed that said contract has been entered into without fulfilling the requirement of asking for three budgets before contracting. It has not been verified, as regards exceptions to this rule:

  (a) the fact of being only one supplier available (being thus ratified by the Executive Secretary).

  (b) the fact of being either an emergency or that the rules hereinbefore mentioned not being the most convenient ones for the Secretariat from the financial viewpoint.

- Receipts issued by the Secretariat are not pre-printed neither pre-numbered nor issued in duplicate.

- It has been verified the payment of Secretariat's debts out of a personal credit card of a staff member.

- In some cases, lack of the original invoice corresponding to expenses was observed.

- It has been found vouchers not fulfilling essential requirements to be considered as invoices and on which significant payments have been made.

From the current fiscal year:

- From the analysis of the Petty Cash accounting proceedings, payments of services that may not be considered minor and/or urgent expenses were found. Due to their regularity those payments should have been made by checks (telephone and internet charges, water charges, papers and magazines, etc.).

- From the analysis carried out on the usual services paid by the Secretariat, it has been detected that in the case of the cleaning and fumigation firm, no contract has been performed clearly stating terms and conditions of said service and the rights and duties of the parties concerned.

Recommendations

From previous fiscal years:

In order to perform minimum internal control rules, it is hereby recommended:

To issue a Procedures Manual on Secretariat's main payment circuits and usual activities.

To entitle the corresponding officials to make payments for the necessary amounts for a better Secretariat performance.

To comply with the Financial Regulations, and in pursuant thereof, to ask for three budgets in cases of procurement or, if not, to state the reasons of said failure.

To issue pre-printed, pre-numbered and in duplicate receipts.

To avoid making payments out of funds not belonging to the Secretariat's own account.

That the Secretariat shall refrain from making payments without the original expense or provision invoice issued to the order of the Secretariat.

From the current fiscal year:

- To use Petty Cash funds to pay minor and/or urgent expenditures.
- Whenever possible, to perform contracts in order to legitimate commercial relationships so that be clearly stated the terms and conditions of services and the rights and duties of the parties concerned.

3.2 Accounting

From previous fiscal years:

- Accounting is recorded in delay giving origin to the following internal control deficiencies:
- Expenses are not allocated when the invoices are received but when they are paid.
- Lack of updated accounting books.
- The Secretariat does not have an approved general inventory of goods, technological equipment and information technology resources, based on a formalized procedure that involves the uniform label of all goods and a list where any changes thereof could be formally registered.

Recommendations

From previous fiscal years:

To adequate the accounting records in order to reflect activities reliably and in due time. Thus it can be used as a tool for the decision making process.

To record debts and expenses when the act that gives origin to the payment obligation is perfected (i.e.: invoice reception).

To comply with in force regulations as regards books of accounts.

To keep an updated and valued General Inventory.

3.3 Personnel

From previous fiscal years:

- The Staff Regulations approved by Decision 3/2003, sets some rules which are less favourable to workers than those in full force in the Argentine Republic.

From the current fiscal year:

- Subsection 10.4, Staff Regulations for the Secretariat of the Antarctic Treaty, Decision 3 (2003) states that "In the event of separation from service with the Secretariat, executive staff members shall be compensated at a rate of one month base pay for each year of service, beginning the second year, unless"... . According to Decision 1 (2006), ATCM directed the Secretariat to establish a Staff Replacement Fund to be used to defray the expenses to be paid according to what was hereinabove stated. From the analysis carried out it appears that:

  - According to the rule interpretation it is not clear if it is necessary to have stayed more than one year in office in order to collect the compensation for the total amount of service years or whether the amount to be collected is calculated directly as from the second year. The criterion used by the Secretariat for the Fund provision, has been —according to this audit— the restricted one, i.e. calculated as from the second year.
  - The compensation corresponding to the Executive Secretary whose separation took place 08/31/2009 is not included in the amount calculated as 03/31/2009. The amount to be added corresponding to the Executive Secretary, calculated using the method described in the previous paragraph, is USD 43,390.32 (forty-three thousand, three hundred and ninety US Dollars and thirty-two cents).

Recommendations

From previous fiscal years:

To prepare a document supplementing the Staff Regulations according to Argentine labour law. This would enable the Secretariat to know and assess the budgetary and legal impact of the decisions it makes as regards hired personnel.

From the current fiscal year:

According to what was hereinabove stated, the Secretariat should ask ATCM for further advice as regards the way the Fund should be estimated.

The Secretariat should obtain documentation supporting the reasons why the compensation corresponding to the former Executive Secretary was not included in the Fund estimates.

3.4 Financial Obligations

From previous fiscal years:

- Secretariat has not performed as tax withholding agent with tax providers pursuant to what is stated in rules in full force and effect.

From the current fiscal year

It has been observed that during December 2008, the salary of General Service workers corresponding to January 2009 was paid in advance. Likewise, during the month of January 2009, it was paid in advance 50% of the salary corresponding to February 2009. The reasons of said behaviour are not stated in writing and it does not comply with the rules in force. Said practice could, therefore, distortion the income tax estimation which must be paid by the staff as well as the advances estimation that Secretariat should withhold for such a concept.

Recommendations

From previous fiscal years:

To act according to what is stated in the legislation in force.

From the current fiscal year:

To pay the staff salaries according to law or otherwise document exceptions made to said rule.

Information Technology Performance

The following aspects have been observed during previous fiscal years. During the current period several measures have been adopted by the Secretariat which allowed for the improvement of information technology controls. Notwithstanding what is hereinabove mentioned, there are still some weaknesses that need security measures and controls to be implemented, as the case may be.

3.5 Information Technology Security Policy

- Pursuant to a SIGEN recommendation, the Secretariat has prepared a document corresponding to Information Technology Security Policy. This fact constitutes a significant progress in the definition of controls and specifications of information technology security measures because it supports the decisions adopted on this subject matter.
- It is worth mentioning that, although the development of this Policy becomes a very important first step, it does not consider some detailed aspects that SIGEN recommended which —according to what has been informed— will be included in future stages.

Recommendation

To plan the preparation of documents which allow for the completion of the Information Technology Security Policy, by adopting definitions on the following items:

- A procedure related to the mechanisms designed to restore operating continuity in case of contingencies.

- Security procedures related to systems development and maintenance which include activities related to the programs promotion to the production environment (it is related to another finding herein described).
- Security and control mechanisms on outsourced services.
- Further procedures or explanations on approved uses as regards:
    - Mobile equipments security (users' responsibilities, taking out insurances etc.)
    - Logs or transaction records implementation (subjects to be recorded, back up frequency and revision procedures),
    - Antivirus defense measures,
    - Information transfers and international communication (encrypts, digital signatures, international communications)
    - The Secretariats' assets control and registry. References to the hardware and software inventory general procedure. To consider specifications when obtaining licenses.

3.6 Systems Implementation

- As it has already been stated in previous reports, several information technology systems are processed through its web site. Said systems are developed by external consultants through contract for services. During the audited period, a second server has been implemented which constitutes an intermediate environment to solve a deficiency informed by SIGEN as regards external developers access permissions for the production environment. Accordingly, at present developers can have access to that second server to store the programs created together with automated instructions (script) for the programs promotion to the production environment. According to what has been analyzed, programs promotion to the production environment is carried out by the Secretariat staff after the corresponding program tests on the alternative server.
- The abovementioned described practice constitutes an improvement compared to the previous situation. However, control procedures for the systems implementation is neither documented nor approved; tests and releases approvals are not formalized and programs promotion to the production environment either.

Recommendation

To continue improving the systems development and implementation process, documenting the procedure and establishing formal control points that secure tests on programs and approval of software releases implemented on the production environment.

It must be taken into account detailed procedures for:

- The detailed requirement documents for new systems procurement or for changes to the existing ones.
- The controls to implement in case of emergency systems changes.

- The performance of sufficient tests, in a specific environment representative of the future operative environment and different from the production environment.
- The promotion of the approved system from the test/development environment to the production environment.
- The control of software releases.
- The preparation of systems documents.

3.7 Outsourcing sensible functions

The Secretariat is operatively managed according to an Operation Plan annually agreed at the Treaty Meeting. Up to now, Secretariat adopted the decision of outsourcing several information technology services.

Recommendation

To adopt all the necessary steps tending to document the information technology strategy in the long term, by making provisions to the integration and coordination of the existing and future foreseen systems and services either locally or via Internet.

It is hereby repeated the suggestion of analyzing the possibility of reducing the outsourcing as regards information technology services, specially in those services related to information technology security management.

3.8 Back up Procedures

- The back up procedure is documented and integrated to the Security Policy. During this period, it has been implemented a remote back up mechanism tending to regularize a situation stated by SIGEN in a previous report. Said mechanism consists on creating back up through the service rendered by a firm via Internet.

Recommendation

To generate periodic tests as regards already generated back ups in order to secure an adequate functioning of recovery mechanisms in case of contingency.

From the current fiscal year:

3.9 Analysis of security vulnerabilities

- From the analysis of the vulnerabilities report carried out by the firm Rack2 —as agreed in the contract executed by the Secretariat and this firm— there appeared an item of Medium Risk level and several of low risk level. The medium risk level is caused by the lack of technology updating of certificates providing remote access to e-mail accounts of the Secretariat staff. Said aspect is being analyzed in search of solution.

- There is no evidence of periodic vulnerabilities analysis on servers of the Data Center.

Recommendation

It is recommended to carry out a formal procedure for the revision of the vulnerabilities analysis periodically performed by the hired firm in order to verify its timely execution and the analysis of results. Its results, the conclusions thereof and the measures tending to solve eventual vulnerabilities should be kept in a file.

To analyze the feasibility and technical and economic convenience of implementing measures tending to solve vulnerabilities detected during the analysis, in particular that ranked as medium risk level.

To consider asking the firm Rack2 a vulnerability analysis on Data Center servers.

3.10 Uses

As from data resulting from the survey carried out on the analysis of the main Secretariat applications, it appeared that there are still no Users' Manuals for the Legal Antarctic Treaty Database—AT Database, in use as of march 2009 and for the Protected Areas Information System —APA, in development as from January 2009.

Recommendation

To promote the development of users' manuals corresponding to all the systems in use in the Secretariat.

3.11 Software licenses and technology updating

According to our analysis, the Secretariat computers are using different releases of the office software products.

Recommendation

To analyze the feasibility and convenience of homogenizing software products of the different Secretariat equipments.

Dr. Edgardo De Rose
Contador Público
T°182 F° 195 CPCECABA
Buenos Aires, march 6th, 2010
Sindicatura General De La Nación

Estimate of Income and Expenditure for all Funds for the Period 1 April 2009 to 31 March 2010

	Budget 2008/9	Budget 2009/10	Estimate 2009/10
INCOME	*$189,611*		
Previous FY contributions	$138,317	$32,613	$32,613
Current FY contributions	$404,118	$808,124	$808,124
Other	$13,517	$1,400	$1,292
TOTAL	**$555,952**	**$842,137**	**$842,029**
EXPENDITURES			
SALARIES			
Executive Staff	$220,320	$232,425	$232,425
General Staff	$146,843	$161,905	$167,876
Over Hours			
Auxliary Staff			
Total Salaries	**$367,163**	**$394,330**	**$400,301**
GOODS AND SERVICES			
Audit	$14,948	$7,185	$7,813
Data entry	$3,931	$2,000	$0
Doc. Services	$543	$2,000	$3,062
Legal advice	$3,300	$5,900	$3,600
Miscellaneous	$6,989	$8,000	$9,344
Office expenses	$14,547	$15,200	$10,604
Postage	$3,836	$7,700	$1,798
Printing	$37,249	$23,100	$13,981
Representation	$3,172	$3,300	$2,927
Telecom	$13,029	$10,700	$11,479
Training	$2,021	$1,400	$4,101
Translation (Contract Ponette)	$232,554	$248,500	$233,376
Travel	$59,653	$43,000	$58,538
Total Goods & Services	**$395,770**	**$377,985**	**$360,622**
EQUIPMENT			
Documentation	$1,056	$1,100	$1,633
Furniture	$5,246	$4,400	$8,805
IT Equipment	$17,769	$21,400	$20,878
Development	$23,527	$15,000	$12,390
Total equipment	**$47,598**	**$41,900**	**$43,706**
Total Appropriations	**$810,531**	**$814,215**	**$804,630**
Future Meeting Fund		$13,001	$13,001
Staff Replacement Fund			
Staff Termination Fund	$9,415	$7,900	$7,900
Working Capital Fund	-$6,866	$2,475	$2,475
Total Funding	**$2,549**	**$23,376**	**$23,376**
EXPENDITURES	**$813,080**	**$837,591**	**$828,006**
Surplus / (deficit)	-$257,128	$4,546	$14,024

	Budget 2008/9		Budget 2009/10	Estimate 2009/10
Summary of Funds	**31/03/2008**		**31/03/2010**	**31/03/2010**
General Fund	$35,052		$39,598	$49,076
Future Meeting Fund	$359,422		$372,423	$372,423
Staff Replacement Fund	$50,000			$0
Staff Termination Fund	$23,119		$21,604	$31,019
Working Capital Fund	$126,917		$129,392	$129,392

Secretariat Programme 2010/11

Introduction

This work programme outlines the activities proposed for the Secretariat in the Financial Year 2010/11 (1 April 2010 to 31 March 2011). The main areas of activity of the Secretariat are treated in the first three chapters, which are followed by a section on management and a forecast of the programme for the financial year 2010/11. The draft budget for 2010/11, the forecast budget for 2011/12 and the accompanying contribution and salary scales are included in the appendices.

The Secretariat asks for several decisions of the Meeting related to personnel; the use of the Working Capital Fund to cover a deficit in translation and interpretation costs; an interpretation of Staff Regulation 10.4 on Staff Termination Fund; and a modification of the appropriation lines. Most of these matters, which are discussed in different sections of this paper, will influence the Secretariat budgets of the upcoming years.

The programme and the accompanying budget figures for 2010/11 are based on the Forecast Budget for 2010/11 (Decision 4 (2009), Appendix 1).

The Programme focuses on the regular activities, such as preparation of the ATCM XXXIV, publication of Final Reports and the various specific tasks assigned to the Secretariat under Measure 1 (2003).

Contents

1. ATCM/CEP support

ATCM XXXIII

The Secretariat will support the ATCM XXXIII by gathering and collating the documents for the meeting and publishing them in a restricted section of the Secretariat website. The Delegates section will also provide online registration for delegates and an up to date list of delegates to download.

The Secretariat will support the functioning of the ATCM through the production of Secretariat Papers, a Manual for Delegates, as well as annotated agendas for the ATCM, the CEP and the Working Groups.

The Secretariat already maintains close contact with the Government of Argentina in connection with the preparation of the ATCM XXXIV in 2011, and will maintain contact with the Government of Australia in connection with the preparation of the ATCM XXXV.

Review of ATCM Recommendations

The Secretariat has submitted three Secretariat papers concerning the Review of ATCM Recommendations (Secretariat Papers 5, 6 and 7). Depending on the decisions taken by the ATCM XXXIII on this subject, the Secretariat will produce revised or new resource papers for next meeting.

Coordination and contact

Aside from maintaining constant contact per email, telephone and other means with the Parties and international institutions of the Antarctic Treaty system, attendance at meetings is an important tool to maintain coordination and contact.

The Executive Secretary is attending the ATME on Climate Change in Svolvær, Norway from 6 to 9 April 2010. The Secretariat is providing data and administrative services as needed to the Meeting.

COMNAP XXIII will take place in connection with the XXXI SCAR and its Open Science Conference in Buenos Aires from 9 August to 12 August. Attendance at the meeting will provide an opportunity to further strengthen the connections and interaction with COMNAP and brief the NAPs about the issues to be faced in the operational phase of the EIES. Another issue on which contact with COMNAP may be necessary is the review of the status of recommendations on operational matters.

The staff of the Secretariat is already in close co-operation with Argentina authorities as the host government secretariat of ATCM XXXIV. The staff will be strengthened during the meeting with staff members contracted *ad hoc*. Since the ATCM XXXIV will take place in Buenos Aires only travel costs for auxiliary staff will be needed.

The travels to be undertaken are as follows:

The other travel to be undertaken is as follows:

–	IPY JC	Oslo, Norway	7 to 12 June 2010

On instruction from the ATCM, the former Executive Secretary has been attending the IPY Joint Committee meetings as one of the two observers (the other observer being from the Arctic Council) and providing reports to the ATCM.

–	CCAMLR	Hobart	25 October to 5 November 2010

The CCAMLR meeting, which takes place roughly midway between succeeding ATCMs, provides a good opportunity for the Secretariat to brief the ATCM Representatives, many of whom attend the CCAMLR meeting, on developments in the Secretariat's work. Liaison with the CCAMLR Secretariat is also important for the Antarctic Treaty Secretariat, as many of its regulations were modeled after those of the CCAMLR Secretariat.

Development of the Secretariat website

The website will see some medium sized updates to make it more concise and easier in using, increasing the visibility of the most relevant sections and information. The reporting facilities of the website databases, especially the Antarctic Treaty database, will be further developed. The Secretariat will keep incorporating meeting documents from previous ATCM and SATCM. Insofar as these documents are not available in digital form, this involves scanning, proofreading and data entry printed documents. The new Protected Areas Database will be enhanced by including new fields and geographical information.

Support of intersessional activities

During the last years both the CEP and the ATCM produced an important amount of intersessional work mainly through intersessional contact groups (ICG). The Secretariat will give technical support for the online establishment of the ICGs agreed at the ATCM XXXIII and CEP XIII and by producing specific documents if required by the ATCM or the CEP.

The Secretariat will update the website with the measures adopted by the ATCM and with the information produced by the CEP and the ATCM.

Printing

The Secretariat will publish and distribute the Final Report and its Annexes of the ATCM XXXIII in the four Treaty languages within six months of the end of the meeting. The text of the Final Report will be printed while the annexes will be published as CD attached to the printed report.

2. Information Exchange

General

The Secretariat will continue to assist Parties in posting their information exchange materials, as well as integrating information on EIAs in the EIA database.

Electronic Information Exchange System

During the third operational season and depending on the decisions of the ATCM XXXIII the Secretariat will, on one hand, make any adjustments necessary to facilitate the use of the electronic system for the Parties, and on the other hand, develop tools to compile and present summarized reports.

3. Records and Documents

Documents of the ATCM

The Secretariat will continue its efforts to complete its archive of the Final Reports and other records of the ATCM and other meetings of the Antarctic Treaty System in the four Treaty languages. Assistance from the Parties in searching their archives will be essential in achieving a complete archive.

Antarctic Treaty database

The database of the Recommendations, Measures, Decisions and Resolutions of the ATCM is at present complete in English and almost complete in Spanish and French, although the Secretariat is still lacking a few copies of Final Reports in those languages to get the authentic texts of those measures. In Russian, more Final Reports are lacking, and materials that have been received are being converted into electronic formats and proofread.

Antarctic Treaty Handbook

On August 2009 the Secretariat distributed a draft Volume I of the 10th Edition of the Handbook of the Antarctic Treaty System in Circular 18/2009. It consists of the texts of the Antarctic Treaty and the subsidiary Antarctic agreements and short factual introductions. The Secretariat is presenting Secretariat Paper 8 to the ATCM XXXIII summarizing the comments of Parties and asks the Meeting for instructions how to proceed with edition of the Handbook.

4. Public Information

The Secretariat and its website will continue to function as a clearinghouse for information on the Parties' activities and relevant developments in Antarctica as well as specific information related to the follow up and heritage of the International Polar Year (IPY, 2007-9).

5. Management

Personnel

On January 1, 2010, the Secretariat staff consisted of the following personnel:

Executive staff

Name	Nationality	Position	Rank	Since
Manfred Reinke	Netherlands	Executive Secretary	E1	1-9-2009
José Maria Acero	Argentina	Assistant Executive Officer	E3	1-1-2005

General staff

José Luis Agraz	id.	Information Officer	G2	1-4-2005
Diego Wydler	id.	Information Technology Officer	G1	1-2-2006
Roberto Alan Fennell	id.	Accountant (part time)	G3	1-12-2008
Pablo Wainschenker	id.	Editor	G3	1-2-2006
Ms Violeta Antinarelli	id.	Librarian (part time)	G3	1-4-2007
Ms Gloria Fontan	id.	Office Manager	G5	1-4-2004
Ms Karina Gil	id.	Data Entry Assistant (part time)	G6	1-4-2007

After the dismissal of the former accountant the ES appointed Mr Alan Fennell on 1.12.2008. The responsibility of the post was temporarily reduced from a Finance Officer to a Book Keeper (level G2 to G3). The experience from this last one and a half year shows that for a proper functioning the Secretariat needs a Finance Officer who has to fulfil tasks that exceed the responsibilities of a mere book keeper. Now that Measure 1 (2003) has come into force, budgeting and cash flow controls are even much more relevant. The responsibilities now include: financial matters, salaries, taxation, budgeting, cash flow, internal controls procedures and accounting. Mr Alan Fennell has the formal and personal qualities to fulfil these tasks. The ES asks the Meeting to upgrade Mr Alan Fennell from Level G3 to Level G2 as from 1 April 2010.

On December 31, 2010 the second term of the AES, José Maria Acero, will end. Mr Acero has demonstrated a high commitment and efficiency in his tasks during the last five years and it is the intention of the ES to continue with his assistance for one more period. To this end, the ES made an unofficial communication to all Parties by e-mail and found a strong support for the renewal of his contract. Staff Regulation 6.3 (e) reads: *(e) for executive staff the period of appointment, which shall not exceed four years, and which may be renewed in consultation with the ATCM.* The ES will take a decision after further consultation during the ATCM XXXIII.

Financial matters

Securitizing the Forecast Budget for the FY 2010/2011 (Appendix 1) two major deficiencies had been detected in the appropriation lines for Translation and Interpretation and Salaries.

Further on, the auditor SIGEN recommends a clarification from the Meeting on the Staff Termination Fund funding in relation to Regulation 10.4 of the Staff Regulations.

Translation and interpretation

Measure 1 (2003) entered into effect on October 6, 2009, after ratification by Brazil. As a direct consequence, the responsibility for the interpretation and translation of the annual ATCM, which had been borne by the respective Host Countries, will be now taken over by the Secretariat. This will mean that the budget, which is now less than US$900,000, will rise to around US$1,410,000 in the Financial Year 2011/12. Decision 7 (2005) and Decision 4 (2009) had set up a Future Meeting Fund of US$ 350,000 for defraying the expenses of interpretation and translation of the first Antarctic Treaty Consultative Meeting to be held after the entry into effect of Measure 1 (2003).

On October 15, 2009 the ES reported through a communication according to Rule 46 of the rules of procedure (Circular 27/2009) that the budget for the FY 2010/11 was not securing the expected expenditures for translation and interpretation on the Meeting after the coming into force of Measure 1 (2003).

In consultation with the Secretariat's external Auditor, SIGEN, the Secretariat had developed a proposal for this new situation, which was accepted by the Parties:

> *"The Secretariat signs a contract for translation of documents before the meeting, and translation and interpretation services during the meeting, which including the costs of travel and accommodation for interpreters and translations amounts to US$ 596,330. This amount is largely covered by the Forecast Budget of the FY 2010/2011 and the established Future Meeting Fund.*
>
> *The contract leaves open the translation and edition of the Final Report (US$ 133,450).*
>
> *The XXXIII Meeting can decide whether to use the Working Capital Fund to finance the translation and edition of the Final Report or use an alternative solution that has to be defined (Circular 27/2009)."*

The ES reported about the result of the consultation in Circular 32/2009.

The ES renegotiated the contract for translation and interpretation. The costs could be considerably reduced by using remote translators saving costs for travel and accommodation. The ES signed a contract with Mr Bernard Ponette amounting to US$ 430,093, which did not include the costs of the air tickets (ca. US$ 70,000). The costs for translation and proof-reading of the final report are estimated at US$ 120,000 (it will depend on the amount of text to be translated). The total estimated costs for translation and interpretation amounts to US$ 620,093. The forecast budget allotted US$ 564,500.

The ES asks the Meeting to authorize him to sign a contract for translation and proof reading of the Final Report of the ATCM XXXIII.

Salaries

Salaries for the Secretariat staff have been recalculated to take into account the increase of the IVS (Salary Variation Index provided by the Argentine National Office of Statistics and Census) adjusted for the devaluation of the Argentine Peso during the same period. This method was explained by the ES and agreed at ATCM XXXII (Final Report p. 238). Since in the year 2009 the IVS rose 16.7% and the rate ARG Peso/US$ Dollar changed from $0.29 to $0.26 the resulting rise for 2010/2011 is 7.9%.

In the year 2008/2009 the former ES temporarily reduced the working hours of the part time staff due to the financial problems of the Secretariat. He restored them to the former level in August 2009. Both factors had not been considered in the Forecast Budget of the salaries 2010/11.

The Secretariat always contracts two or three persons for the support during the Meetings according to Staff Regulation 11. In the past the Secretariat had booked their salaries, accommodation and travels under the budget line "Translation and Interpretation". In the Draft Budget 2010/2011 their salaries appear under the budget line "Salaries: Auxiliary Staff" and their travel and accommodation costs under the budget line "Travel" to achieve more transparency.

Regulation 5.10 of the Staff Regulations requires compensating general staff members in the general category when they have to work more than 40 hours during on week. Over time is requested during the ATCM Meetings.

The Draft Budget lists therefore US$ 466,419 instead of US$ 410,505 in the Forecast Budget for the salaries taking into account factors described above.

Funds

Staff Termination Fund

An unclear situation exists how to apply Regulation 10.4 of the Staff Regulations. Regulation 10.4 reads:

> *In the event of separation from service with the Secretariat, executive staff members shall be compensated at a rate of on month base pay for each year of service, beginning with the second year, unless the cause of termination has been gross dereliction of duties imposed in Regulation 2.*

The CCAMLR Staff Regulations, which had been a 'blue print' for the Staff Regulations of the Secretariat, have under their Regulation 10.4 the wording:

> *In the event of separation from service with the Secretariat, staff members shall be compensated at a rate of on month base pay for each year of service, beginning with the second year, unless the cause of termination has been gross dereliction of duties imposed in Regulation 2.*

The Secretariat had asked CCAMLR about the implementation of this regulation. The answer from Ed Kremzer, the Administration and Finance Officer of CCAMLR, is attached in Appendix 4.

In CCAMLR the intent of the fund is to include the first year of service in the payout but to exclude any person who departs before completing at least one year of service. If ie, a staff member departed CCAMLR after one year plus one day of service CCAMLR's calculation of the payout would be on the basis of one month's base salary for the completed year of service plus 1/365 of one month's base salary for the additional day.

In 2006 Ed Kremzer completed a report to the Secretariat following his visit to the AT Secretariat. The report which was tabled at the 2006 ATCM included advice that staff termination payouts were on the basis of one month's salary for each year of service with no mention of any qualifying period or payment.

The Secretariat's auditor SIGEN advised the Secretariat to ask the Meeting for a clarification according to Regulation 12.1 whether its Regulation 10.4 should be applied in the same way as in CCAMLR.

Staff Replacement Fund

50% of the Staff Replacement Fund has to be refilled to cover the costs of an international filling of the job for the Assistant Executive Secretary (AES).

Working Capital Fund

The deficit in the budget will be covered by the Working Capital Fund, which according to the Financial Regulation 6.2 (a) has to be maintained at 1/6 of the Secretariat's budget. It has to be filled up to in several steps to ca. US$ 222,000 in the upcoming years.

Further Details of the Draft Budget 2010/11

The allocation to the appropriation lines has been adjusted according to the expected expenses of the financial year 2009/2010.

- *Category Goods and Services:* The total budget for this category equals the total budget in the forecast budget 2010/11 without considering the appropriation line "translation and interpretation", but it was necessary to make some adjustments in between the appropriation lines. The forecast amount for the appropriation line *"Travel"* was under estimated. The travel costs for the ATCM XXXIII in Punta del Este amounts US$ 51,500. The ATME in Norway (April 2010) amounts US$ 4,720. Foreseen are travels to the IPY JC and IPY conference in Norway 7-12 June 2010 (US$ 5,790) and CCAMLR (US$ 5,800). The SCAR Open Science Conference and the COMNAP XXIII Meeting will take place in Buenos Aires. Only registration costs are due (US$ 900). Considerably less is allocated for *"Printing"*, *"Office expenses"* and *"Postage"*. The line *"Data entry"* is not longer used.

- *Category Equipment:* The appropriation line *"Documentation"*, together with the abovementioned "Data entry" had been used for trainees and miscellaneous expenditures; therefore, it is not longer used as a discrete appropriation line.

Appropriation Lines

In cooperation with the external auditor SIGEN the Secretariat has been considering to adequate the appropriation lines to better demonstrate in what the Secretariat spend the contributions assessed and for what purpose.

Right now the appropriation lines reflect items where the Secretariat spends money but without informing exactly how it spend the contributions. The idea is to classify the Secretariat's expenditure by dollar importance, work programme and specific expense category. The total spent will be the same dollar amount as before the change but it would be shown in a different manner.

The Secretariat suggests having the following appropriation lines:

- *Salaries:* this would include not only the salaries approved in the budget for ATS direct staff but also those who assist us in the meetings and the over time for the general staff during the ATCM.
- *Translation:* all moneys for translation before, during and after the ATCM yearly meeting (includes air fares, lodging and sundry).
- *Information technology:* all the investments in equipment, software, programmes development and IT maintenance and security.
- *Printing, editing and copying:* for the Final Report in paper and electronic support.
- *General services:* all local support services, such as audit, legal, banking, training.
- *Communications:* includes telephone, internet, WEB hosting, postage.
- *Office:* stationary, books, insurance, maintenance.
- *Administrative:* local transport, supplies.
- *Financing*: net translation gain or loss.

This, together with recognizing the contributions on an accrual basis, will make it easier to understand the ATS functioning, financial position, especially now that Decision 1 (2003) has come into force.

The Secretariat will implement the new appropriation lines during FY 2010/11 and will present the Report of FY 2010/11 and the forecast budget of FY 2011/12 in both schemes. It will ask the ATCM XXXIV for a decision how to proceed.

6. Forecast Programme 2011/12 and 2012/13

It is expected that most of the ongoing activities of the Secretariat will be continued in 2011/12 so, unless the programme undergoes major changes, no change in the staff complement is foreseen for 2011/12.

The Forecast Budget 2011/12 has been compiled on the basis of the draft budget for 2011/12 with some correction for inflation, using the figures from the Argentine National Office for Statistics and Census and the IMF World Economic Outlook. The travel costs will be considerably lower in 2011 since the Meeting will take place in Buenos Aires. The ES proposes to add a certain amount in 2011 to keep the 2012/13 budget stable. The Secretariat will issue a call for tender later this year for translation and interpretation at the ATCM XXXIV in 2011.

The budget and thus the contributions in FY 2010/11 and in the following years will be much higher to provide for the translation and interpretation expenses of the ATCM. The contributions in FY 2011/12 will rise to US$ 1,339,600. In FY 2012/13 the Secretariat expects contributions to increase to US$ 1,426,000.

Appendix 1

Provisional Report 2009/10, Budget 2010/11 and Forecast 2011/12

	Prov. Report 2009/10	Forecast 2010/11	Budget 2010/11	Forecast 2011/12
INCOME				
Previous FY contributions	$32,613			
Current FY contributions	$808,124	$899,942	$899,942	$1,339,600
Other	$1,292	$2,500	$1,000	$1,000
TOTAL	**$842,029**	**$902,442**	**$900,942**	**$1,340,600**
EXPENDITURES				
SALARIES				
Executive Staff	$232,425	$233,560	$247,974	$270,291
General Staff	$167,876	$176,945	$193,543	$210,962
Over Hours			$8,038	$8,761
Auxliary Staff			$16,864	$16,864
Total Salaries	**$400,301**	**$410,505**	**$466,419**	**$506,879**
GOODS AND SERVICES				
Audit	$7,813	$7,800	$9,360	$9,360
Data entry	$0	$2,200	$0	$0
Doc. Services	$3,062	$2,200	$0	$0
Legal advice	$3,600	$6,400	$4,200	$4,490
Miscellaneous	$9,344	$8,500	$8,500	$8,500
Office expenses	$10,604	$16,700	$11,700	$12,520
Postage	$1,798	$8,500	$2,500	$2,680
Printing	$13,981	$24,900	$11,500	$12,310
Representation	$2,927	$3,600	$2,000	$2,000
Telecom	$11,479	$11,500	$13,000	$13,910
Training	$4,101	$1,500	$4,100	$4,100
Translation (Air tickets)			$35,000	
Translation (Contract Ponette)	$233,376	$214,500	$430,093	$585,093
Translation Final Report			$120,000	
Travel	$58,538	$46,500	$68,800	$42,508
Total Goods & Services	**$360,622**	**$354,800**	**$720,753**	**$697,471**

	Prov. Report 2009/10	Forecast 2010/11	Budget 2010/11	Forecast 2011/12
EQUIPMENT				
Documentation	$1,633	$1,300	$1,900	$1,500
Furniture	$8,805	$5,600	$5,000	$5,000
IT Equipment	$20,878	$23,600	$23,600	$25,000
Development	$12,390	$15,100	$15,100	$16,000
Total equipment	**$43,706**	**$45,600**	**$45,600**	**$47,500**
Total Appropriations	**$804,630**	**$810,905**	**$1,232,772**	**$1,251,850**
Future Meeting Fund	$13,001	$7,577	$0	$0
Staff Replacement Fund		$13,000	$8,333	$16,667
Staff Termination Fund	$7,900	$8,700	$25,974	$27,084
Working Capital Fund	$2,475	$62,260	$62,260	$45,000
Total Funding	**$23,376**	**$91,537**	**$96,567**	**$88,750**
EXPENDITURES	**$828,006**	**$902,442**	**$1,329,339**	**$1,340,600**
Surplus / (deficit)	$14,024	$0	($428,397)	$0
FINANCING				
General Fund			$49,076	
Future Meeting Fund			$372,423	
Working Capital Fund			$6,898	
			$428,397	

Summary of Funds	31/03/2010	31/03/2011	31/03/2011	31/03/2012
General Fund	$49,076	$49,076	$0	
Future Meeting Fund	$372,423	$30,000	$0	$0
Staff Replacement Fund	$0	$13,000	$8,333	$25,000
Staff Termination Fund	$31,019	$30,304	$56,993	$84,076
Working Capital Fund	$129,392	$191,652	$184,754	$229,754

Appendix 2

Contribution Scale 2011/12

2011/12	Cat.	Mult.	Variable	Fixed	Total
Argentina	A	3.6	$36,424.17	$23,921.43	$60,346
Australia	A	3.6	$36,424.17	$23,921.43	$60,346
Belgium	D	1.6	$16,188.52	$23,921.43	$40,110
Brazil	D	1.6	$16,188.52	$23,921.43	$40,110
Bulgaria	E	1	$10,117.82	$23,921.43	$34,039
Chile	C	2.2	$22,259.21	$23,921.43	$46,181
China	C	2.2	$22,259.21	$23,921.43	$46,181
Ecuador	E	1	$10,117.82	$23,921.43	$34,039
Finland	D	1.6	$16,188.52	$23,921.43	$40,110
France	A	3.6	$36,424.17	$23,921.43	$60,346
Germany	B	2.8	$28,329.91	$23,921.43	$52,251
India	C	2.2	$22,259.21	$23,921.43	$46,181
Italy	B	2.8	$28,329.91	$23,921.43	$52,251
Japan	A	3.6	$36,424.17	$23,921.43	$60,346
Korea	D	1.6	$16,188.52	$23,921.43	$40,110
Netherlands	C	2.2	$22,259.21	$23,921.43	$46,181
New Zealand	A	3.6	$36,424.17	$23,921.43	$60,346
Norway	A	3.6	$36,424.17	$23,921.43	$60,346
Peru	E	1	$10,117.82	$23,921.43	$34,039
Poland	D	1.6	$16,188.52	$23,921.43	$40,110
Russia	C	2.2	$22,259.21	$23,921.43	$46,181
South Africa	C	2.2	$22,259.21	$23,921.43	$46,181
Spain	C	2.2	$22,259.21	$23,921.43	$46,181
Sweden	C	2.2	$22,259.21	$23,921.43	$46,181
Ukraine	D	1.6	$16,188.52	$23,921.43	$40,110
United Kingdom	A	3.6	$36,424.17	$23,921.43	$60,346
United States	A	3.6	$36,424.17	$23,921.43	$60,346
Uruguay	D	1.6	$16,188.52	$23,921.43	$40,110
		66.2	$669,800.00	$669,800.00	**$1,339,600**

Budget amount	$1,339,600
Base rate	$10,118

Appendix 3

Salary Scale 2010/11

2010/11 Level		I	II	III	IV	V	VI	VII	VIII	IX	X	XI	XII	XIII	XIV	XV
									STEPS							
1	A	$111,577	$113,652	$115,728	$117,806	$119,881	$121,957	$124,033	$126,110							
1	B	$139,471	$142,066	$144,660	$147,257	$149,852	$152,447	$155,042	$157,638							
2	A	$93,954	$95,721	$97,488	$99,254	$101,020	$102,786	$104,552	$106,319	$108,086	$109,852	$111,618	$111,818	$113,561		
2	B	$117,442	$119,651	$121,860	$124,067	$126,275	$128,482	$130,690	$132,899	$135,108	$137,315	$139,523	$139,773	$141,952		
3	A	$78,347	$80,051	$81,756	$83,461	$85,165	$86,869	$88,574	$90,279	$91,983	$93,686	$95,391	$95,754	$97,436	$99,117	$100,797
3	B	$97,934	$100,063	$102,195	$104,326	$106,457	$108,586	$110,718	$112,849	$114,978	$117,108	$119,239	$119,693	$121,795	$123,897	$125,997
4	A	$64,965	$66,543	$68,124	$69,698	$71,278	$72,855	$74,431	$76,011	$77,590	$79,166	$80,745	$81,185	$82,742	$84,298	$85,854
4	B	$81,206	$83,179	$85,155	$87,122	$89,098	$91,069	$93,038	$95,014	$96,988	$98,957	$100,931	$101,482	$103,427	$105,372	$107,317
5	A	$53,862	$55,275	$56,686	$58,098	$59,509	$60,919	$62,332	$63,740	$65,153	$66,565	$67,973	$68,430			
5	B	$67,327	$69,094	$70,857	$72,622	$74,386	$76,149	$77,914	$79,675	$81,441	$83,206	$84,967	$85,537			
6	A	$42,639	$43,996	$45,351	$46,709	$48,064	$49,420	$50,778	$52,134	$53,488	$54,313	$54,845				
6	B	$53,299	$54,995	$56,688	$58,386	$60,080	$61,774	$63,472	$65,167	$66,860	$67,892	$68,557				

Level	I	II	III	IV	V	VI	VII	VIII	IX	X	XI	XII	XIII	XIV	XV
								STEPS							
1	$44,200	$46,261	$48,324	$50,386	$52,535	$54,776									
2	$36,833	$38,551	$40,270	$41,988	$43,779	$45,646									
3	$30,693	$32,125	$33,557	$34,990	$36,483	$38,040									
4	$25,579	$26,772	$27,965	$29,158	$30,403	$31,700									
5	$21,130	$22,117	$23,102	$24,089	$25,118	$26,191									
6	$17,320	$18,127	$18,936	$19,744	$20,587	$21,466									
7															
8															

Revised Rules of Procedure for the Committee for Environmental Protection

The Representatives,

Recalling Decision 2 (1998), which established the Rules of Procedure for the Committee for Environmental Protection and Decision 6 (2009) which revised those Rules;

Desiring to update the Rules of Procedure;

Decide:

1. that the Revised Rules of Procedure for the Committee for Environmental Protection (2010) annexed to this Decision shall replace the Revised Rules of Procedure for the Committee for Environmental Protection (2009) attached to Decision 6 (2009); and

2. that Decision 2 (1998) and Decision 6 (2009) are no longer current.

Revised Rules of Procedure for the Committee for Environmental Protection (2010)

Rule 1

Where not otherwise specified the Rules of Procedure for the Antarctic Treaty Consultative Meeting shall be applicable.

Rule 2

For the purposes of these Rules of Procedure:

(a) the expression "Protocol" means the Protocol on Environmental Protection to the Antarctic Treaty, signed in Madrid on 4 October, 1991;

(b) the expression "the Parties" means the Parties to the Protocol;

(c) the expression "Committee" means the Committee for Environmental Protection as defined in Article 11 of the Protocol;

(d) the expression "Secretariat" means the Secretariat of the Antarctic Treaty.

Part I. Representatives and Experts

Rule 3

Each Party to the Protocol is entitled to be a member of the Committee and to appoint a representative who may be accompanied by experts and advisers with suitable scientific, environmental or technical competence.

Before each meeting of the Committee each member of the Committee shall, as early as possible, notify the Host Government of that meeting of the name and designation of each representative, and before or at the beginning of the meeting, the name and designation of each expert and adviser.

Part II. Observers and Consultation

Rule 4

Observer status in the Committee shall be open to:

(a) any Contracting Party to the Antarctic Treaty which is not a Party to the Protocol;

(b) the President of the Scientific Committee on Antarctic Research, the Chairman of the Scientific Committee for the Conservation of Antarctic Marine Living

Resources and the Chairman of the Council of Managers of National Antarctic Programmes, or their nominated Representatives;

(c)   subject to the specific approval of the Antarctic Treaty Consultative Meeting, other relevant scientific, environmental and technical organisations which can contribute to the work of the Committee.

Rule 5

Before each meeting of the Committee each observer shall, as early as possible, notify the Host Government of that meeting of the name and designation of its representative attending the meeting.

Rule 6

Observers may participate in the discussions, but shall not participate in the taking of decisions.

Rule 7

In carrying out its functions the Committee shall, as appropriate, consult with the Scientific Committee on Antarctic Research, the Scientific Committee for the Conservation of Antarctic Marine Living Resources, the Council of Managers of National Antarctic Programmes and other relevant scientific, environmental and technical organisations.

Rule 8

The Committee may seek the advice of experts as required on an *ad hoc* basis.

Part III. Meetings

Rule 9

The Committee shall meet once a year, generally and preferably in conjunction with the Antarctic Treaty Consultative Meeting and at the same location. With the agreement of the ATCM, and in order to fulfill its functions, the Committee may also meet between annual meetings.

The Committee may establish informal open-ended contact groups to examine specific issues and report back to the Committee.

Open-ended contact groups established to undertake work during intersessional periods shall operate as follows:

(a)   where appropriate, the contact group coordinator shall be agreed by the Committee during its meeting and noted in its final report;

(b) where appropriate, the terms of reference for the contact group shall be agreed by the Committee and included in its final report;

(c) where appropriate, the modes of communication for the contact group, such as e-mail, the online discussion forum maintained by the Secretariat and informal meetings, shall be agreed by the Committee and included in its final report;

(d) representatives who wish to be involved in a contact group shall register their interest with the coordinator through the discussion forum, by e-mail or by other appropriate means;

(e) the coordinator shall use appropriate means to inform all group members of the composition of the contact group;

(f) all correspondence shall be made available to all members of the contact group in a timely manner; and

(g) when providing comments, members of the contact group shall state for whom they are speaking.

The Committee may also agree to establish other informal sub-groups or to consider other ways of working such as, but not limited to, workshops and video-conferences.

Rule 10

The Committee may establish, with the approval of the Antarctic Treaty Consultative Meeting, subsidiary bodies, as appropriate.

Such subsidiary bodies shall operate on the basis of the Rules of Procedure of the Committee as applicable.

Rule 11

The Rules of Procedure for the preparation of the Agenda of the Antarctic Treaty Consultative Meeting shall apply with necessary changes to Committee meetings.

Before each meeting of any subsidiary body the Secretariat, in consultation with the Chairperson of both the Committee and of the subsidiary body, shall prepare and distribute a preliminary annotated Agenda.

Part IV. Submission of Documents

Rule 12

Members of the Committee and Observers should follow the procedures for submission of documents for the Antarctic Treaty Consultative Meeting and Committee meetings as agreed by the Antarctic Treaty Consultative Meeting and promulgated by the Secretariat.

Observers referred to in Rule 4(c) may only submit documents for distribution to the meeting as Information Papers.

Part V. Advice and Recommendations

Rule 13

The Committee shall try to reach consensus on the recommendations and advice to be provided by it pursuant to the Protocol.

Where consensus cannot be achieved the Committee shall set out in its report all views advanced on the matter in question.

Part VI. Decisions

Rule 14

Where decisions are necessary, decisions on matters of substance shall be taken by a consensus of the members of the Committee participating in the meeting. Decisions on matters of procedure shall be taken by a simple majority of the members of the Committee present and voting. Each member of the Committee shall have one vote. Any question as to whether an issue is a procedural one shall be decided by consensus.

Part VII. Chairperson and Vice-chairs

Rule 15

The Committee shall elect a Chairperson and two Vice-chairs from among the Consultative Parties. The Chairperson and the Vice-chairs shall be elected for a period of two years and, where possible, their terms shall be staggered.

The Chairperson and the Vice-chairs shall not be re-elected to their post for more than one additional two-year term. The Chairperson and Vice-chairs shall not be representatives from the same Party.

The Vice-chair who has been a Vice-chair for the longer period of time (in total, counting any previous term of office) shall be first Vice-chair.

In the event that both Vice-chairs are appointed for the first time at the same meeting, the Committee shall determine which Vice-chair is elected as first Vice-chair.

Rule 16

Amongst other duties the Chairperson shall have the following powers and responsibilities:

(a) convene, open, preside at and close each meeting of the Committee;

(b) make rulings on points of order raised at each meeting of the Committee provided that each representative retains the right to request that any such decision be submitted to the Committee for approval;

(c) approve a provisional agenda for the meeting after consultation with Representatives;

(d) sign, on behalf of the Committee, the report of each meeting;

(e) present the report referred to in Rule 22 on each meeting of the Committee to the Antarctic Treaty Consultative Meeting;

(f) as required, initiate intersessional work; and

(g) as agreed by the Committee, represent the Committee in other forums.

Rule 17

Whenever the Chairperson is unable to act, the first Vice-chair shall assume the powers and responsibilities of the Chairperson.

Whenever both the Chair and first Vice-chair are unable to act, the second Vice-chair shall assume the powers and responsibilities of the Chairperson.

Rule 18

In the event of the office of the Chairperson falling vacant between meetings, the first Vice-chair shall exercise the powers and responsibilities of the Chairperson until a new Chairperson is elected.

If the offices of both the Chairperson and first Vice-chair fall vacant between meetings, the second Vice-chair shall exercise the powers and responsibilities of the Chairperson until a new Chairperson is elected.

Rule 19

The Chairperson and Vice-chairs shall begin to carry out their functions on the conclusion of the meeting of the Committee at which they have been elected.

Part VIII. Administrative Facilities

Rule 20

As a general rule the Committee, and any subsidiary bodies, shall make use of the administrative facilities of the Government which agrees to host its meetings.

Part IX. Languages

Rule 21

English, French, Russian and Spanish shall be the official languages of the Committee and, as applicable, the subsidiary bodies referred to in Rule 10.

Part X. Records and Reports

Rule 22

The Committee shall present a report on each of its meetings to the Antarctic Treaty Consultative Meeting. The report shall cover all matters considered at the meeting of the Committee, including at its intersessional meetings and by its subsidiary bodies as appropriate, and shall reflect the views expressed. The report shall also include a comprehensive list of the officially circulated Working and Information Papers. The report shall be presented to the Antarctic Treaty Consultative Meeting in the official languages. The report shall be circulated to the Parties, and to observers attending the meeting, and shall thereupon be made publicly available.

Part XI. Amendments

Rule 23

The Committee may adopt amendments to these rules of procedure, which shall be subject to approval by the Antarctic Treaty Consultative Meeting.

Liability arising from Environmental Emergencies

The Representatives,

Considering the adoption of Measure 1 (2005);

Recalling the undertaking in Article 16 of the Protocol on Environmental Protection to the Antarctic Treaty;

Recalling Decision 3 (2001) regarding the elaboration of an Annex on the liability aspects of environmental emergencies, as a step in the establishment of a liability regime in accordance with Article 16 of the Protocol;

Decide:

1) to continue to evaluate annually the progress made towards Annex VI to the Protocol on Environmental Protection to the Antarctic Treaty becoming effective in accordance with Article IX of the Antarctic Treaty, and what action may be necessary and appropriate to encourage Parties to approve Annex VI in a timely fashion;

2) that ten years from the adoption of Annex VI, in light of the evaluation pursuant to paragraph 1 above, to take a decision on the establishment of a time-frame for the resumption of negotiations, in accordance with Article 16 of the Protocol, to elaborate further rules and procedures as may be necessary relating to liability for damage arising from activities taking place in the Antarctic Treaty area and covered by the Protocol;

3) to request the Committee for Environmental Protection to consider environmental issues related to the practicality of repair or remediation of environmental damage in the circumstances of Antarctica, in order to assist the ATCM in adopting an informed decision in 2015 related to the resumption of the negotiations; and

4) that Decision 1 (2005) is no longer current.

Letters to UNFCCC, IPCC, WMO and IMO on the SCAR ACCE Report

The Representatives,

Recognising the role of the Antarctic region in global climate processes;

Considering the relevance of SCAR's Antarctic Climate Change and the Environment (ACCE) Report (2009) for the work of other international bodies involved in global climate change science;

Decide:

to ask the Chair of the ATCM to send the attached letter forwarding the SCAR Antarctic Climate Change and the Environment Report to:

- the Executive Secretary of the United Nations Framework Convention on Climate Change (UNFCCC) for conveyance to the President of the Conference of the Parties to the UNFCCC;

- the Executive Secretary of the Intergovernmental Panel on Climate Change Secretariat (IPCC);

- the Secretary General of the World Meteorological Office (WMO); and

- the Secretary General of the International Maritime Organization (IMO).

Letters to UNFCCC, IPCC, WMO and IMO

Dear Mr Yvo de Boer (Executive Secretary UNFCCC) / Dr Renate Christ (IPCC) / Mr Michel Jarraud (WMO) / Mr Efthimios E. Mitropoulos (IMO)

As part of their work at the 33rd Antarctic Treaty Consultative Meeting (ATCM XXXIII) in Punta del Este, Uruguay from 3 to 14 May 2010, the Antarctic Treaty Consultative Parties considered the implications of climate change for the Antarctic region.

To assist that work, ATCM XXXIII had before it the full version of the Antarctic Climate Change and the Environment (ACCE) report prepared by the Scientific Committee on Antarctic Research (SCAR).

In light of the relevance of the SCAR ACCE report also to the work of the United Nations Framework Convention on Climate Change (UNFCCC) / IPCC / WMO / IMO, I have the honor to convey to you a copy of the report, and respectfully request that you provide it to [the President of the Conference of the Parties to the UNFCCC], [relevant IPCC working groups] etc as appropriate.

Yours sincerely,

Mr Roberto Puceiro

Chairman of ATCM XXXIII

3. Resolutions

Site Guidelines for visitors

The Representatives,

Recalling Resolution 5 (2005), Resolution 2 (2006), Resolution 1 (2007), Resolution 2 (2008) and Resolution 4 (2009) which adopted lists of sites subject to Site Guidelines;

Believing that Site Guidelines enhance the provisions set out in Recommendation XVIII-1 (Guidance for those organising and conducting tourism and non-Governmental activities in the Antarctic);

Desiring to increase the number of Site Guidelines developed for visited sites;

Confirming that the term "visitors" does not include scientists conducting research within such sites, or individuals engaged in official governmental activities;

Noting that the Site Guidelines have been developed based on the current levels and types of visits at each specific site, and aware that the Site Guidelines would require review if there were any significant changes to the levels or types of visits to a site;

Believing that the Site Guidelines for each site must be reviewed and revised promptly in response to changes in the levels and types of visits, or in any demonstrable or likely environmental impacts;

Recommend:

1. that the list of sites subject to Site Guidelines that have been adopted by the Antarctic Treaty Consultative Meeting ("ATCM") be extended to include a further four new sites. The full list of sites subject to Site Guidelines is annexed to this Resolution;

2. that the Antarctic Treaty Secretariat place the texts of such "Site Guidelines", as adopted by the ATCM, on the website of the Secretariat;

3. that any proposed amendment to existing Site Guidelines be discussed by the Committee for Environmental Protection ("CEP") which should advise the ATCM accordingly. If such advice is endorsed by the ATCM then the Secretariat should make the necessary changes to the texts of Site Guidelines on the website;

4. that the Governments urge all those intending to visit such sites to ensure that they are fully conversant with, and adhere to, the advice in the relevant Site Guidelines as published by the Secretariat; and

5. that the Secretariat post the texts of Resolution 5 (2005) and Resolution 4 (2009) on its website in a way that makes clear that they are no longer current.

List of Sites subject to Site Guidelines

1.   Penguin Island (Lat. 62° 06' S, Long. 57° 54' W);

2.   Barrientos Island, Aitcho Islands (Lat. 62° 24' S, Long. 59° 47' W);

3.   Cuverville Island (Lat. 64° 41' S, Long. 62° 38' W);

4.   Jougla Point (Lat 64° 49' S, Long 63° 30' W);

5.   Goudier Island, Port Lockroy (Lat 64° 49' S, Long 63° 29' W);

6.   Hannah Point (Lat. 62° 39' S, Long. 60° 37' W);

7.   Neko Harbour (Lat. 64° 50' S, Long. 62° 33' W);

8.   Paulet Island (Lat. 63° 35' S, Long. 55° 47' W);

9.   Petermann Island (Lat. 65° 10' S, Long. 64° 10' W);

10.   Pleneau Island (Lat. 65° 06' S, Long. 64° 04' W);

11.   Turret Point (Lat. 62° 05' S, Long. 57° 55' W);

12.   Yankee Harbour (Lat. 62° 32' S, Long. 59° 47' W);

13.   Brown Bluff, Tabarin Peninsula (Lat. 63° 32' S, Long. 56° 55' W);

14.   Snow Hill (Lat. 64° 22' S, Long. 56° 59' W);

15.   Shingle Cove, Coronation Island (Lat. 60° 39' S, Long. 45° 34' W);

16.   Devil Island, Vega Island (Lat. 63° 48' S, Long. 57° 16.7' W);

17.   Whalers Bay, Deception Island, South Shetland Islands (Lat. 62° 59' S, Long. 60° 34' W);

18.   Half Moon Island, South Shetland Islands (Lat. 60° 36' S, Long. 59° 55' W);

19.   Baily Head, Deception Island, South Shetland Islands (Lat. 62° 58' S, Long. 60° 30' W);

20.   Telefon Bay, Deception Island, South Shetland Islands (Lat. 62° 55' S, Long. 60° 40' W);

21.   Cape Royds, Ross Island (Lat. 77° 33' 10.7" S, Long. 166° 10' 6.5" E);

22.   Wordie House, Winter Island, Argentine Islands (Lat. 65° 15' S, Long. 64° 16' W);

23.   Stonington Island, Marguerite Bay, Antarctic Peninsula (Lat. 68° 11' S, Long. 67° 00' W);

24.   Horseshoe Island, Antarctic Peninsula (Lat. 67° 49' S, Long. 67° 18' W);

25.   Detaille Island, Antarctic Peninsula (Lat. 66° 52' S, Long. 66° 48' W);

26. Torgersen Island, Arthur Harbour, Southwest Anvers Island (Lat. 64° 46' S, Long. 64° 04' W);

27. Danco Island, Errera Channel, Antarctic Peninsula (Lat. 64° 43' S, Long. 62° 36' W);

28. Seabee Hook, Cape Hallett, Northern Victoria Land, Ross Sea, Visitor Site A and Visitor Site B (Lat. 72° 19' S, Long. 170° 13' E);

29. Damoy Point, Wiencke Island, Antarctic Peninsula (Lat. 64° 49' S, Long. 63° 31' W);

The contribution of the IPY to hydrographic knowledge of waters of the Antarctic Treaty area

The Representatives,

Considering the appeal made by the Hydrographic Commission on Antarctica (HCA) of the International Hydrographic Organization (IHO) with respect to improving collection of hydrographic data and charting in the Antarctic region;

Noting the increase in scientific expeditions in the Southern Ocean in the Antarctic Treaty area, as part of the International Polar Year (IPY) 2007 – 2008;

Noting also other relevant charting surveys of the Southern Ocean in the Antarctic Treaty area;

Considering that vessels of the National Antarctic Programmes and others linked to the IPY are being urged to compile, whenever possible, hydrographic and bathymetric data on all Antarctic voyages;

Acknowledging that access to and management of observations and data collected during the IPY is fundamental to ensuring the legacy of the IPY;

Taking into account the fact that new forms of data forwarding have been developed since the publication of Resolution 5 (2008);

Taking into account also Recommendation No 4 of the Antarctic Treaty Meeting of Experts on Management of Ship-borne Tourism in the Antarctic Treaty Area, which was held in Wellington, New Zealand on 9-11 December 2009, to continue contributing to the information about hydrographic survey and cartography;

Recommend that their Governments:

1. Support and promote contacts and liaison between National Antarctic Programmes and national hydrographic offices;

2. Endeavour to ensure that hydrographic and bathymetric data collected by the National Antarctic Programmes' ships and others linked with their activity in the Antarctic, be forwarded by the National Antarctic Programmes, or by other means, to the national hydrographic services using the IHO Collection and Rendering of Hydrographic Data Form;

3. Encourage National Antarctic Programmes to work with their national hydrographic offices to assist the HCA in producing a full inventory of hydrographic data so that they can be considered for use in the production of international nautical charts under the international charting scheme coordinated by the HCA;

4. Promote liaison and cooperation between national hydrographic offices and the HCA to ensure the legacy of the IPY in the field of hydrography, thereby contributing to the improvement of nautical charts and the safety of navigation in waters of the Antarctic Treaty area, which in turn will help safeguard life at sea, protect the Antarctic environment, and further support scientific activities; and

5. Continue contributing to the report of hydrographic and bathymetric data, using appropriate instruments of their hydrographic services or offices and the IHO Collection and Rendering of Hydrographic Data Form to ensure a timely production of Antarctic nautical charts.

Revised Antarctic inspection Checklist "A"

The Representatives,

Taking into account Resolution 5 (1995) "Antarctic inspection checklists" which proposes a number of checklists to guide the planning and conduct of inspections under Article VII of the Antarctic Treaty, including, among others, Checklist "A" *Antarctic Stations and Subsidiary Installations*;

Considering the extensive use made of the checklists since the adoption of Resolution 5 (1995), which has made it possible to evaluate their practical implementation;

Noting the evolution of the Antarctic Treaty system since the adoption of Resolution 5 (1995), including, *inter alia*, the entry into force of the Protocol on Environmental Protection to the Antarctic Treaty and the establishment of the Antarctic Treaty Secretariat and its Electronic Information Exchange System;

Reaffirming that inspection checklists are useful as guidelines for those planning and conducting inspections under Article VII of the Antarctic Treaty and in assessing implementation of the provisions of the Protocol on Environmental Protection to the Antarctic Treaty;

Noting that inspection checklists are not mandatory and are not to be used as a questionnaire;

Desiring to update Checklist "A" to simplify the inspection process and make it more effective;

Recommend:

That the Consultative Parties adopt the revised Checklist "A" attached, replacing the original Checklist "A", contained in Resolution 5 (1995).

Checklist "A"
Antarctic Stations and Subsidiary Installations

This checklist could also be used to help prepare for, and guide, inspections of remote camps and refuges that are not subsidiary facilities of a station. Some items on the checklist may not be relevant to the inspection of such remote camps and refuges. When planning inspections, the checklist should be examined and adapted for the particular facility to be inspected

INDEX

Section 1 – General information

1.1. Name of station visited

Off site sources

- ATS Electronic Information Exchange System (EIES), as agreed by Resolution 6 (2001), Appendix 4. Available at www.ats.aq, section "Information Exchange".
- COMNAP website (*www.comnap.aq*)

1.2. Operating nation(s)

Off site sources

- EIES- Permanent Information (Operational information-Stations)
- COMNAP website (*www.comnap.aq*)

1.3. Responsible agencies or ministries

Off site sources

- Contact National Authority for detailed information

On site sources

- Interview, if applicable

1.4. Location

Off site sources

- EIES- Permanent Information (Operational information-Stations)
- COMNAP website (*www.comnap.aq*)

1.5. Date established

Off site sources

- EIES- Permanent Information (Operational information-Stations)
- COMNAP website (*www.comnap.aq*)

On site sources

- Interview, if applicable

1.6. Station current and past status ("year-round", "seasonal", "temporarily closed", "closed", "no longer exists-clean up activities in progress")

Off site sources

- EIES- Permanent Information (Operational information-Stations)
- COMNAP website (*www.comnap.aq*)

On site sources

- Interview, if applicable

1.7. Operational language(s) of the station

On site sources

- Interview

1.8. Main uses of the station

Off site sources

- EIES

On site sources

- Interview

1.9. Plans for future use of the station

Off site sources

- Contact National Authority for detailed information

On site sources

- Interview (it should be born in mind that this is information that station staff may not always have exhaustive knowledge of. That is why such information should also be checked with the National Authority).

1.10. International logistic cooperation

Off site sources

- Contact National Authority for detailed information

On site sources

- Interview

Section 2 – Inspection details

2.1. Date

On site sources

- To be filled by the inspection team

2.2. Time of visit

On site sources

- To be filled by the inspection team

2.3. Duration of visit

On site sources

- To be filled by the inspection team

2.4. Last inspection (nation(s), date)

Off site sources

- ATS website (a list of past inspections and their reports, when available, can be found in *http://www.ats.aq/e/ats_governance_listinspections.htm*)

On site sources

- Interview + document verification (copies of previous inspection reports available)

Section 3 – Station personnel

3.1. Name of person in charge of station

Off site sources

- EIES Pre-season information

On site sources

- Interview

3.2. Total number of personnel on station at the moment of the inspection. Average and maximum population on station

Off site sources

- COMNAP website (*www.comnap.aq*)

On site sources

- Interview

3.3. Number of science personnel on station at the moment of the inspection. Average and maximum number of science personnel on station

On site sources

- Interview

3.4. Number of over-wintering personnel, if applicable

On site sources

- Interview

3.5. Nominal/Optimal capacity of station

Off site sources

- EIES Permanent Information (Operational information-Stations)

On site sources

- Interview

3.6. General training - including on: fuel management, waste management, first aid, SAR activities, medical evacuation procedures, fire fighting, etc.

On site sources

- Interview

3.7. Training focused on the requirements of the Antarctic Treaty and the Environmental Protocol.

On site sources

- Interview

Section 4 – Physical description of the station

- The National Program's website may contain additional details

4.1. Area covered by station (surface area of station footprint)

On site sources

- Interview

4.2. Number and type of buildings, including their purpose

On site sources

- Interview + field verification

4.3. Age and state/condition of buildings

On site sources

- field verification

4.4. Construction works currently in progress or recently completed

On site sources

- Interview + field verification

4.5. Map(s) of station showing buildings, services and other major structures and facilities

On site sources

- Interview + document verification

4.6. Description of major aerial systems (antennas)

On site sources

- Interview + field verification

4.7. Description of other major –on or under ground– services (power, water, sewage, etc.)

On site sources

- Interview + field verification

4.8. Port or dock facilities (wharf, craft landing site, anchorage) Description and condition

On site sources

- Interview + field verification

4.9. Roads (length, type of surface, condition)

On site sources

- Interview + field verification

4.10. Airstrips. Status (active/not active), length, type of surface (snow, ice, gravel) and landing gear suitability (wheel, ski, both). Methods and frequence of maintenance. Period of operation

Off site sources

- COMNAP's Antarctic Flight Information Manual (AFIM).

On site sources

- Interview + field verification (inspectors should check, through observation on site, the information provided by AFIM to find out the degree of concordance and the need for likely update of AFIM's information).

4.11. Helipads (diameter, surface and condition)

Off site sources

- COMNAP's Antarctic Flight Information Manual (AFIM). Manuals and subscriptions to revisions of the AFIM are available through the COMNAP Secretariat

On site sources

- Interview + field verification (inspectors should check, through observation on site, the information provided by AFIM to find out the degree of concordance and the need for likely update of AFIM's information).

4.12. Subsidiary facilities (camps, refuges, depots, etc.). Status (active/not active), purpose, location and accessibility (by vehicle, by air, on foot).

Off site sources

- EIES Permanent Information (Operational information-Stations)

On site sources

- Interview

Section 5 – Scientific activities

5.1. Major scientific programmes supported by the station during the season in which the inspection takes place, and the following winter-over, if applicable

Off site sources

- Contact National Authority for detailed information
- EIES- Annual report (Scientific Information / Forward plans)

On site sources

- Interview

5.2. Dedicated permanent scientific facilities and other major scientific equipment on the station and subsidiary facilities

Off site sources

- EIES Permanent information (although EIES includes only information about "automatic recording stations/observatories")
- Contact National Authority for more detailed information

On site sources

- Interview

5.3. Number and nationality of science personnel from other National Antarctic Programs

On site sources

- Interview

5.4. Advance notice, use and control of radio-isotopes

Off site sources

- EIES (information exchange on the use of radio-isotopes is required by ATCM VI-6 ,Tokyo 1970)

On site sources

- Interview

Section 6 – Tourist and non-governmental activities

6.1. Visits to the station by tourists or non-governmental expeditions. Frequency, method (cruise ships, yachts, aircraft), numbers, availability of visit records (type of information included)

Off site sources

- EIES Pre-season information (Non-governmental expeditions) include data on proposed sites of tour operations)
- Contact National authority for more detailed information

On site sources

- Interview + document verification

6.2. Procedures developed to facilitate or control tourist and non-governmental activities (advance permission, maximum allowed length of the stay, restrictions on schedules, etc.)

On site sources

- Interview + document verification, if appropriate

6.3. Operational problems for the station caused by visitors (for example, unannounced visits, behaviour of visitors, etc.)

On site sources

- Interview

6.4. Environmental impact of visitors at the station or nearby

On site sources

- Interview (it was noted that inspectors should contact either the environmental officer or scientists at the station to properly answer this question).

6.5. Describe any other NGO activity carried out at the station.

Off site sources

- EIES Pre-season information (Non-governmental expeditions) can include information on NGO activities.

On site sources

- Interview

Section 7 – Logistics and operations

7.A. Communications

7.A.1. Communication facilities. Types of links (HF, VHF, Internet, satellite, other) and methods of communication (voice, fax, e-mail, web, video conferencing/telemedicine, etc.)

Off site sources

- EIES Permanent Information (Communication facilities and frequencies)

- COMNAP's AFIM and ATOM (Antarctic Telecommunications Operators Manual). Updated versions of COMNAP's ATOM can be downloaded from *www.comnap.aq* (Members only/password required)
- Contact National Authority for more detailed information

On site sources

- Interview + document verification

7.B. Transport

7.B.1. Number and type of ground vehicles

On site sources

- Interview + field verification

7.B.2. Number and type of small boats

On site sources

- Interview + field verification

7.B.3. Number and type of fixed and rotary wing aircraft

Off site sources

- EIES Pre-season information (Aircraft / Type of aircraft, planned number of flights, periods of flights or planned departure dates, routes and purpose)

On site sources

- Interview + field verification

7.B.4. Number of aircraft movements per year

Off site sources

- EIES Pre-season information (Aircraft / Type of aircraft, planned number of flights, periods of flights or planned departure dates, routes and purpose)
- Contact National Authority for more detailed information

On site sources

- Interview

7.B.5. Frequency and methods of resupply

Off site sources

- Contact National Authority for more detailed information

On site sources

- Interview

7.C. Fuel storage / usage

7.C.1. Fuel Contingency Plans / Fuel Management Plans. Availability and format

Off site sources

- EIES Permanent Information (Contingency Plans)

On site sources

- Interview + document verification

7.C.2. Types, amount and use of fuel (diesel, petrol, aviation fuel, etc.)

On site sources

- Interview + document verification

7.C.3. Types, number and capacity of station storage containers, including type of containment system(s) available

On site sources

- Interview + field verification

7.C.4. Monitoring of fuel pumping systems and storage tanks (method)

On site sources

- Interview + field verification + document verification

7.C.5. General description of fuel pipelines

On site sources

- Interview + field verification + document verification

7.C.6. Methods to transfer bulk fuel

On site sources

- Interview + document verification

7.C.7. Methods of emptying fuel pipelines (gravity, compressed air, etc.)

On site sources

- Interview

7.C.8. Field fuel depots (for example, quantity, type of fuel, type of containers, geographic location and distance to the station, and proximity to environmental values, such as freshwater systems, wildlife concentrations, etc.).

On site sources

- Interview

7.C.9. Responsibility for fuel management

On site sources

- Interview

7.C.10. Oil and other spills. Describe any spills over 200 litres (50 gallons) that have occurred during the past five years.

Off site sources

- COMNAP Accidents, Incidents and Near Misses Reporting System (AINMR)

On site sources

- Interview + document verification

7.D. Power generation and management

7.D.1. Electrical power and heat sources from fuel. Number, type and capacity of generation systems

On site sources

- Interview + field verification

7.D.2. Annual fuel consumption in generators and heaters (litres, m^3 or metric tonnes)

On site sources

- Interview

7.D.3. Efficiency of the generation system. Average load (in kW) or output (in kW/h) of the station.

On site sources

- Interview

7.D.4. Methods of energy conservation (strategies, procedures, equipment and/or infrastructure to conserve energy at the station)

On site sources

- Interview + document verification

7.D.5. Renewable energy sources (eg, wind turbines, photovoltaic, solar hot water systems), purpose, and share of energy supplied.

On site sources

- Interview + field verification

7.D.6. Filtering and monitoring of emissions from generators and heaters (parameters measured, method, frequency and availability of records)

On site sources

- Interview + field verification + document verification

7.E. Water system

7.E.1. Availability and quality of water supply

On site sources

- Interview + document verification

7.E.2. Methods to supply and store water. Availability and quality of water supply.

On site sources

- Interview + field verification

7.E.3. Consumption of water per person/day. Distinguish between different water types, if appropriate

On site sources

- Interview

7.E.4. Methods of water conservation

On site sources

- Interview + field verification (if appropriate).

Section 8 – Management of dangerous elements

8.A. Hazardous chemicals

8.A.1. Types and quantities of chemicals

On site sources

- Interview + field verification

8.A.2. Storage and monitoring arrangements

On site sources

- Interview + field verification + document verification

8.A.3. Protection against leaks and spills

On site sources

- Interview + field verification

8.B. Firearms / explosives

8.B.1. Number, type and purpose of firearms and ammunition

Off site sources

- EIES Pre-season information (Military) includes an item on Armaments

On site sources

- Interview + field verification

8.B.2. Amount, type and use of explosives

On site sources

- Interview + field verification

8.B.3. Storage of explosives and method of disposal

On site sources

- Interview + field verification

Section 9 – Medical capabilities

9.1. Medical facilities (X ray, Anaesthetic equipment, surgery, dental suites, etc)

On site sources

- Interview + field verification

9.2. Medical personnel (general practitioner, nurse, paramedics, surgeon, dentist, other specialists) and specific training.

On site sources

- Interview + field verification

9.3. Number of patient beds

On site sources

- Interview + field verification

Section 10 – Emergency response capability

10.1. General - a) Search and rescue capability (SAR teams, vehicles, aircraft, positioning systems), including types of scenarios covered and undertaking of SAR drills (frequency and relevant records)

On site sources

- Interview + field verification + document verification

10.2. General - b) Accidents and incidents in the last year resulting in human death, significant injuries, significant damage to station facilities or to the environment

On site sources

- Interview

10.3. General - c) Method of reporting accidents, incidents or near-misses

Off site sources

- COMNAP Accident, Incident and Near-Miss Reporting –AINMR- system

On site sources

- Interview + document verification

10.4. Medical - a) Mobile medical emergency response capability

On site sources

- Interview + field verification

10.5. Medical - b) Evacuation plan for medical emergencies

On site sources

- Interview + document verification, if appropriate

10.6. Fire - a) Fire emergency plan. Latest update

On site sources

- Interview + document verification, if appropriate

10.7. Fire - b) Fire fighting equipment

On site sources

- Interview + field verification

10.8. Fire - c) Training of personnel for fire fighting

On site sources

- Interview

10.9. Fire - d) Fire fighting exercises (frequency, personnel involved, scenarios covered and relevant records available)

On site sources

- Interview + document verification

10.10. Pollution (oil and chemical spills) - a) Risk assessment for spills

On site sources

- Interview

10.11. Pollution (oil and chemical spills) - b) Training of personnel to deal with spills

On site sources

- Interview

10.12. Pollution (oil and chemical spills) - c) Spill response exercises (frequency, personnel involved, scenarios covered and relevant records available)

On site sources

- Interview + document verification

10.13. Pollution (oil and chemical spills) - d) Mobile spill response capability (boomers, adsorbent substances, pumps, centrifuge, other)

On site sources

- Interview + field verification

Section 11 – Matters related to the Madrid Protocol

11.A. Environmental Impact Assessment (EIA)

11.A.1. Degree of awareness of station management personnel of the requirement to conduct an EIA for all new activities

On site sources

- Interview

11.A.2. Availability of record/copies of EIAs for activities carried out in/by the station

Off site sources

- ATS website (note that only records of CEEs and IEEs are available at such a website)

On site sources

- Interview + document verification

11.A.3. Environmental monitoring of indicators of possible environmental impacts of the station or associated activities (parameters measured, method, frequency and availability of records)

Off site sources

- EIES annual report (Environmental Information-Monitoring activities report)

On site sources

- Interview + document verification

11.B. Conservation of flora and fauna

11.B.1. Methods of making station personnel aware of the rules relating to the conservation of Antarctic flora and fauna

On site sources

- Interview

11.B.2. Wildlife or plant sites near the station

On site sources

- Interview + field verification

11.B.3. Activities undertaken in/through the station during the past year requiring taking and/or harmful interference permits. Details of any damage or harm caused to flora and fauna. Availability of permits on station.

Off site sources

- EIES Annual report (Permit information)

On site sources

- Interview + document verification

11.B.4. Non-native species. a) Measures taken to minimize introductions of non-native species (awareness programs, operational procedures, monitoring/surveillance programs), including relevant records; b) Are non-native species present?; c) If so, was the introduction managed in accordance with a permit?; d) For unintended introductions, what is known about the source and status and what actions have been / will be taken in response?

Off site sources

- EIES Annual report (Permit information)

On site sources

- Interview + document verification + field verification

11.B.5. Problems with station personnel or visitors not observing the provisions of Annex II.

On site sources

- Interview

11.B.6. Local guidelines controlling human activities close to concentrations of wildlife, including use of aircraft, vehicle operations, hiking, etc.

On site sources

- Interview + document verification

11.C. Waste management

11.C.1. Availability of a Waste management plan for the separation, reduction, collection, storage and disposal of wastes. Adequacy and compliance with Annex III provisions.

Off site sources

- EIES Annual report (Environmental information-Waste management plans)

On site sources

- Interview + document verification

11.C.2. Responsibility for waste management on the station.

On site sources

- Interview

11.C.3. Availability of waste production reports. Type of information included.

On site sources

- Interview + document verification

11.C.4. Waste classification system(s) at the station.

On site sources

- Interview + field verification

11.C.5. Methods of making station personnel aware of the provisions relating to waste management, including training and the need to minimize the impact of wastes on the environment.

On site sources

- Interview + field verification

11.C.6. Methods of treating and disposing of wastes at the station and subsidiary camps/refuges/depots, including use of landfill or ice pit.

On site sources

- Interview + field verification

11.C.7. Methods to store hazardous wastes until removal from the station.

On site sources

- Interview + field verification

11.C.8. Solid waste management facilities (eg, incinerator, containers, transportation, etc).

On site sources

- Interview + field verification

11.C.9. Use of incineration; Disposal of ash; Control and monitoring of emissions.

On site sources

- Interview + document verification

11.C.10. Treatment and disposal of sewage and domestic liquid wastes; Monitoring of effluent (parameters measured, method, frequency and availability of records).

On site sources

- Interview + document verification

11.C.11. Methods of waste recycling.

On site sources

- Interview + field verification

11.C.12. Measures taken to prevent wastes which are to be removed from the Treaty area being dispersed by wind or accessed by scavengers.

On site sources

- Interview + field verification

11.C.13. Inventory of past subsidiary facilities (abandoned camps or refuges, old fuel depots, etc.), including information reported and latest update.

Off site sources

- EIES (Permanent information) may contain data on non-active refuges

On site sources

- Interview + document verification

11.C.14. Clean-up of the effects of past activities and future plans, if applicable.

On site sources

- Interview

11.C.15. Problems with station personnel, station activities/infrastructure or visitors in relation to the provisions related to wastes. Measures taken in response (if applicable).

On site sources

- Interview

11.D. Management of protected areas (ASPAs, ASMAs and HSMs)

11.D.1. Methods of making station personnel aware of the provisions relating to ASPAs, ASMAs and Historic Sites and Monuments.

On site sources

- Interview

11.D.2. ASPAs, ASMAs and Historic Sites and Monuments in the vicinity of, or containing, the station (type, name, site number)

Off site sources

- An updated database on protected areas can be found at the AT Secretariat's website, under section "Environmental protection" *(http://www.ats.aq/e/ep_protected.htm)*

On site sources

- Interview

11.D.3. Relevant management plans and maps of protected areas held on the station.

On site sources

- Interview + document verification

11.D.4. Entry by station personnel to ASPAs within the past year; Issue of permits and reasons for their issue.

Off site sources

- EIES Annual report (Permit information)

On site sources

- Interview + document verification

11.D.5. Problems with station personnel or visitors not observing the provisions of protected areas.

On site sources

- Interview

11.D.6. Marking of the protected area(s) in the vicinity of, or containing, the station.

On site sources

- field verification

11.D.7. Monitoring or management of protected areas

On site sources

- Interview

11.D.8. Additional steps that should be taken to protect the areas

On site sources

- Interview

Section 12 – Other matters

12.A. Military support activities

12.A.1. Describe any military support to the station

Off site sources

- EIES Pre-season information (Military) includes an item on Military equipment

On site sources

- Interview + field verification

12.A.2. Details of military equipment held at station

On site sources

- Interview + field verification

12.B. Antarctic Treaty legislation

12.B.1. Availability of Antarctic Treaty documentation on station

On site sources

- Interview + document verification

SCAR Antarctic Climate Change and the Environment Report

The Representatives,

Recognising that the Antarctic region offers a unique environment for the study of climate change;

Recalling the Washington Ministerial Declaration on the fiftieth anniversary of the signing of the Antarctic Treaty, in which Ministers from all Antarctic Treaty Consultative Parties noted their concern over the implications of global environmental change, in particular climate change, for the Antarctic environment and dependent and associated ecosystems and confirmed their intention to work together to better understand changes to the Earth's climate and to actively seek ways to address the effects of climate and environmental change on the Antarctic environment and dependent and associated ecosystems;

Welcoming the report on Antarctic Climate Change and the Environment (ACCE) by the Scientific Committee on Antarctic Research (SCAR) as a first step in compiling a comprehensive assessment of scientific information on the climate system in the Antarctic region;

Concerned by the findings of the ACCE report that effects of climate change are already occurring in the Antarctic region;

Recommend that their Governments:

1. forward copies of the SCAR ACCE report to their respective departments and agencies engaged in climate change negotiations;

2. encourage dissemination of the findings of the SCAR ACCE report and of ongoing Antarctic climate change research to the general public and the media;

3. forward copies of the SCAR ACCE report to their national Antarctic science and research bodies, and encourage them to consider fully the findings and recommendations from the report; and

4. welcome regular updates by SCAR on Antarctic climate change and its implications.

Co-ordination among Antarctic Treaty Parties on Antarctic proposals under consideration in the IMO

The Representatives,

Noting the steps taken by the Antarctic Treaty Parties to promote the safety of life at sea and environmental protection in the Antarctic Treaty area;

Acknowledging the role of the International Maritime Organization ("IMO") in aspects of maritime safety and security and the prevention of pollution from ships in the Antarctic Treaty area;

Recalling previous cooperation between the IMO and the Antarctic Treaty Consultative Meeting ("ATCM"), including requests by the ATCM for the IMO to take steps relating to Antarctic maritime matters;

Emphasising the desirability of IMO attendance at the ATCM and recalling the ATCM's regular invitations to the IMO to attend as an expert;

Welcoming the adoption by the IMO of *Guidelines for Ships Operating in Polar Waters* and the work initiated in the IMO to develop a mandatory code for polar shipping and emphasising the valuable contribution the Parties can make to its development and expeditious conclusion;

Welcoming the adoption by the IMO of a ban on the use and carriage by vessels of heavy grades of oil in the Antarctic Treaty area, following requests by the ATCM;

Noting the desire of the Parties to ensure that regulatory actions relating to shipping in the Antarctic Treaty area are consistent with the objectives of the Antarctic Treaty and its Protocol on Environmental Protection and take into account the conduct of Antarctic activities including, *inter alia*, operations of national Antarctic programmes, in light of the specific circumstances of the Antarctic environment;

Emphasising the importance of representatives to the ATCM working closely with their national IMO representatives on matters relating to the Antarctic Treaty area;

Noting the desirability of timely consideration within the IMO of proposals relating to the Antarctic Treaty area;

Recommend:

That when a Party or group of Parties initiates a proposal to the ATCM that results in a referral by the ATCM to the IMO concerning matters relevant to the Antarctic Treaty area, the initiating Party or group of Parties:

1. report to the ATCM on the anticipated timeline for consideration of the matter referred by the ATCM, including the schedule of IMO meetings and processes;

2. report to the ATCM on the progress of the matter referred by the ATCM within the IMO, including key issues or changes that may arise in IMO deliberations;

3. report intersessionally to the Parties through the Secretariat or other suitable mechanism (eg, web-based discussion forum), where appropriate, after IMO meetings where the matter referred by the ATCM is considered; and

4. inform the ATCM when further action may need to be considered in order to further the objectives of the ATCM.

Improving the co-ordination of maritime search and rescue in the Antarctic Treaty area

The Representatives,

Aware of the increase in vessel traffic, in particular passenger vessel traffic, in the Antarctic Treaty area;

Concerned about the possible risk of accidents involving these ships and the resulting harm to both persons and the environment;

Recalling the work of the International Maritime Organization (IMO) in the field of maritime safety and rescue;

Recalling the key outcomes and recommendations from the COMNAP Antarctic SAR Workshop I (Valparaíso, 2008) and the COMNAP Antarctic SAR Workshop II (Buenos Aires, 2009);

Recalling the work of the Antarctic Treaty Meeting of Experts on Management of Ship-borne tourism (Wellington, 2009);

Recalling Measure 4 (2004) and Resolution 6 (2008);

Recognising the value and importance of the search and rescue systems and procedures established under the auspices of the IMO, in particular as regards the network of Search and Rescue Regions and the corresponding Maritime Rescue Coordination Centres (MRCC);

Noting that these MRCCs have systems able to maintain the confidentiality of information transmitted by vessels and collected by the Centres;

Wishing to improve the coordination of maritime search and rescue efforts in the Antarctic Treaty area;

Recommend:

That their Governments recognise the importance of ensuring the effectiveness of search and rescue efforts by:

1. placing on the Antarctic Treaty Secretariat ("the Secretariat") website regular and up-to-date search and rescue related information, using the most appropriate technical means (eg, through the Electronic Information Exchange System – EIES), of coastal stations facilities as well as the availability of sea and air assets in the Antarctic Treaty area;

2. making available in advance vessel schedules of national Antarctic programmes and tourist operators to the Secretariat (eg, through the EIES) which then would be available to all MRCC to access; and

3. encouraging national Antarctic programmes and operators of tourist vessels not participating in the COMNAP and IAATO vessel tracking schemes to report the positions of their vessels regularly to the relevant regional MRCC.

Enhancement of port State control for passenger vessels bound for the Antarctic Treaty area

The Representatives,

Recalling Resolution 8 (2009) regarding a Mandatory shipping code for vessels operating in Antarctic waters;

Welcoming the start of work by the International Maritime Organization in February 2010 on a mandatory International Code of safety for ships operating in polar waters (Polar Code);

Acknowledging the duties of the flag State as set out in article 94 of the United Nations Convention on the Law of the Sea which include *inter alia* the taking of such measures for vessels flying its flag as are necessary to ensure safety at sea;

Noting articles 218 and 219 of the United Nations Convention on the Law of the Sea regarding Enforcement by port States and Measures relating to seaworthiness of vessels to avoid pollution;

Recalling the requirements of the International Convention on the Safety of Life at Sea (SOLAS) 1974; the International Convention for the Prevention of Pollution from Ships 1973, as modified by the Protocol of 1978 relating thereto (MARPOL); the International Convention on Standards of Training, Certification and Watchkeeping for Seafarers (STCW) 1978; and the Protocol on Environmental Protection to the Antarctic Treaty;

Conscious that many passenger vessels operating in the Antarctic Treaty area are not flagged to States which are Parties to the Antarctic Treaty or to its Protocol on Environmental Protection;

Concerned about recent incidents involving passenger vessels in the Antarctic Treaty area;

Recommend:

That the Parties proactively apply, through their national maritime authorities, the existing regime of port State control to passenger vessels bound for the Antarctic Treaty area.

1. Amb. Ingo Winkelmann (Germany)
2. Amb. Ora Meres-Wuori (Finland)
3. Dr Valerii Lytvynov (Ukraine)
4. Mr Yo Osumi (Japan)
5. Mr Vassily Titushkin (Russian Federation)
6. Mr Key Cheol Lee (Republic of Korea)
7. Ms Penny Richards (Australia)
8. Dr Manfred Reinke (Secretariat of the Antarctic Treaty)
9. Amb. Helena Ödmark (Sweden)
10. Mr Henry Valentine (South Africa)
11. Mr Albert Lluberas (Host Country Secretariat)
12. Mr Ariel Mansi (Argentina)
13. Mr Evan Bloom (USA)
14. RA Leonardo Alonso (Uruguay)
15. Mr Serge Segura (France)
16. Amb. Jorge Berguño (Chile)
17. Mr Chris vanden Bilcke (Belgium)
18. Mr Jian Zhou (China)
19. Mr Trevor Hughes (New Zealand)
20. Mr Karsten Klepsvik (Norway)
21. Mr Vincent van Zeijst (Netherlands)
22. Ms Patrizia Vigni (Italy)
23. Min. Fábio Vaz Pitaluga (Brazil)
24. Mr Luis Sandiga Cabrera (Peru)

Volume 2 (in CD only)

PART II

**Measures, Decisions
and Resolutions (Cont.)**

4. Management Plans

Management Plan for Antarctic Specially Protected Area No. 101

TAYLOR ROOKERY, MAC.ROBERTSON LAND

Introduction

Taylor Rookery is an emperor penguin (*Aptenodytes forsteri*) colony located on the east side of Taylor Glacier, Mac.Robertson Land (67°27'S; 60°53'E, Map A). The site was originally designated as Specially Protected Area No. 1, through Recommendation IV-I (1966), after a proposal by Australia. In accordance with Resolution XX-5 (1996) the site was redesignated and renumbered as Antarctic Specially Protected Area (ASPA) No. 101. A management plan for the Area was adopted under Recommendation XVII-2 (1992) and revised under Measure 2 (2005). Taylor Rookery is designated as an ASPA to protect the largest known colony of emperor penguins located entirely on land.

1. Description of values to be protected

Of the 40-plus known emperor penguin colonies around Antarctica only three are land-based while all others are located on fast ice. For many years, the only known land-based colonies were at Emperor Island, Dion Islands, Antarctic Peninsula (67°52'S, 68°42'W) and at Taylor Glacier. Because of this uncommon characteristic both colonies were designated as Specially Protected Areas in 1966. A third land-based colony was discovered in Amundsen Bay, East Antarctica, in 1999.

The emperor penguin colony at Taylor Glacier was discovered in October 1954. It is the largest known land-based colony (Map B) and as such is of outstanding scientific importance. The Australian Antarctic program has carried out population monitoring at the Taylor Glacier colony since 1957, including annual photographic censuses since 1988 which have resulted in counts with high levels of accuracy. The number of adults at the colony has ranged from 2462 in 1989 to 3307 in 1990 and has averaged approximately 3000 over 15 years from 1988 to 2002. Similar long term records are available only for one other location, the colony near Dumont d'Urville (Pointe-Géologie Archipelago, ASPA 120, 66°40'S, 140°01'E) and a number of colonies in the Ross Sea region. However, the records of the latter are not continuous. Only a limited number of visits are made each year to Taylor Glacier, and the colony is ideal for census work, being surrounded by small rocky hills which make it possible to observe the penguins without entering the breeding area. Thus, the disturbance to the colony, especially since 1988, has been very low and direct human interference can be excluded as a potential factor influencing the health of this population.

2. Aims and Objectives

Management of Taylor Rookery aims to:

- avoid degradation of, or substantial risk to, the values of the Area by preventing unnecessary human disturbance;
- allow research on the ecosystem and physical environment, particularly on the avifauna, provided it is for compelling reasons which cannot be served elsewhere;
- minimise the possibility of introduction of pathogens which may cause disease in bird populations within the Area;
- minimise the possibility of introduction of alien plants, animals and microbes to the Area;

- allow for the gathering of data on the population status of the emperor penguin colony on a regular basis and in a sustainable manner; and
- allow visits for management purposes in support of the aims of the management plan.

3. Management Activities

The following management activities will be undertaken to protect the values of the Area:

- visits shall be made to the Area as necessary (preferably not less than once every five years) to assess whether the Area continues to serve the purposes for which it was designated and to ensure that management activities are adequate; and
- the Management Plan shall be reviewed at least every five years and updated as required.

4. Period of Designation

Designated for an indefinite period.

5. Maps

Map A: Antarctic Specially Protected Area No. 101, Taylor Rookery, Mawson Coast, Mac.Robertson Land, East Antarctica. The inset map indicates the location in relation to the Antarctic continent.

Map B: Antarctic Specially Protected Area No. 101, Taylor Rookery: Topography and Emperor Penguin Colony.

Map C: Antarctic Specially Protected Area No. 101, Taylor Rookery: Vehicle and Helicopter Approach and Landing Site.

All map specifications: Horizontal Datum: WGS84; Vertical Datum: Mean Sea Level

6. Description of the Area

6(i) Geographical co-ordinates, boundary markers and natural features

The Taylor Rookery ASPA consists of the whole of the northernmost rock exposure on the east side of Taylor Glacier, Mac.Robertson Land (67°27'S, 60°53'E, Map B). There are no boundary markers delimiting the site.

The emperor penguin colony is located on a low lying rock outcrop in the south-west corner of a bay formed by Taylor Glacier to the west, the polar ice cap to the south and the islands of the Colbeck Archipelago to the east. The Area is surrounded by sea ice to the north and east. The Area is some 90 kilometres west of Mawson station. There is ice-free terrain adjacent to the glacier on the western boundary and to the south the rock rises steeply to meet the ice of the plateau. The rock itself forms a horseshoe around a central flat area of exposed rock and moraine. This Area is covered with snow in winter and is occupied by the emperor penguins. A couple of small melt lakes form in late spring and a small stream exits to the north-east. The sides of the horseshoe are rounded ridges of rock which are bare and smoothed by ice. Otherwise the terrain is rough and dissected with cracks and fissures. The average height of the ridges is about 30 metres.

The Area also has a raised beach which is typical of several found along the coast of Mac.Robertson Land. The beach is composed of locally derived pebbles, cobbles and boulders between 1cm and 1m across. It

2

slopes upwards from the shoreline to a well defined platform several metres broad and 3 to 6m above sea level. The Area is readily defined by its natural features.

Climate

Limited data exist for the meteorology of the Area. Conditions are probably similar to those of the Mawson station area, approximately 90km to the east, where the mean monthly temperatures range from +0.1°C in January to -18.8°C in August, with extreme temperatures ranging from +10.6°C to -36.0°C. The mean annual wind speed is 10.9m per second with frequent prolonged periods of strong south-easterly katabatic winds from the ice cap with mean wind speeds over 25m per second and gusts often exceeding 50m per second. Local sections of the coast vary in their exposure to strong winds and it is possible that slightly lower mean wind speed may exist at Taylor Rookery. Other characteristics of the weather are high cloudiness throughout the year, very low humidity, low precipitation and frequent periods of strong winds, drifting snow and low visibility associated with the passage of major low pressure systems.

Environmental domains analysis

Based on the Environmental Domains Analysis for Antarctica (Resolution 3(2008)) Taylor Rookery is located within Environment D *East Antarctic coastal geologic*.

Geology and Soils

The rocks at Taylor Rookery are metamorphic and probably formed from ancient metamorphic sedimentary rocks. They are mapped as garnet-biotite-quartz-felspar gneiss, granite and migmatite. The metamorphic rocks are intruded by charnockite which has yielded an isotopic age of 100 million years, thus defining a minimum age for the metamorphic rocks. Numerous shear zones intersect the banded metamorphic rocks and there are recognised traces of an old erosion surface at about 60m altitude.

Vegetation

The flora of Taylor Rookery consists of at least ten species of lichen (Table 1) and an unknown number of terrestrial and freshwater algae. No mosses have been recorded from the Area. Twenty six species of lichen and three species of moss can be found in the region, 20 of which are found on nearby Chapman Ridge and 16 from Cape Bruce on the western side of Taylor Glacier. The rock types are not conducive to colonization by lichens. Most of the lichens occurring at Taylor Rookery grow on the higher outcrops at the southern end where weathering is least.

LICHENS

Pseudephebe minuscula	*Lecidea phillipsiana*
Buellia frigida	*Physcia caesia*
Caloplaca citrina	*Xanthoria elegans*
Candelariella flava	*Xanthoria mawsonii*
Rhizoplaca melanophthalma	*Lecanora expectans*

Table 1. Plants recorded from Taylor Rookery.

Birds

Emperor penguins

The breeding site of the emperor penguins is a north-facing amphitheatre formed by the tongue of the Taylor Glacier to the west and rocky hills to the east. The penguins breed mainly on a saucer shaped depression of rock and gravel to the south of the headland, and to a lesser extent on the surface of a frozen melt lake at the northern side. Both areas are level and for most of the breeding season are covered with snow.

First hatchlings have been observed in mid July which suggests mid May as the onset of laying. Fledglings depart the colony from mid December to mid January, usually leaving during the day when the weather is the warmest and the katabatic wind has subsided. Adult birds and fledglings head in a N-NE direction towards a polynya about 62km from the colony. This ice edge reduces to approximately 25km by mid January. The polynya appears to be a permanent feature of the Mawson Coast.

The size of the adult population appears to have remained relatively stable during the counting period. Numbers of adults ranged from 2462 in 1989 to 3307 in 1990 and averaged 3019 ± 267 over the 15 years from 1988 to 2002. Data obtained from more recent census work will be analysed and published within the term of this management plan.

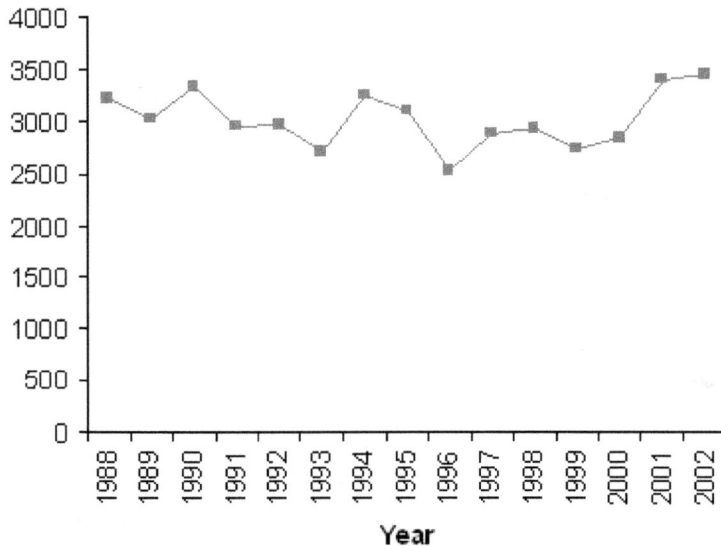

Figure 1. Numbers of adult emperor penguins present in the colony during winter at Taylor Glacier, 1988-2002. Vertical axis shows number of individual birds. Horizontal axis shows bird count year.

Skuas

Skuas are often observed near the penguin colony. It is not known whether these birds breed in this location.

6(ii) Access to the Area

Access to the Area is covered under section 7(ii) of this plan.

6(iii) Location of structures within and adjacent to the Area

There are no structures within the Area. A four-berth refuge is located in the Colbeck Archipelago, approximately five kilometres to the north-east of the Area (see Map B). Mawson station (67°36' S, 62°53' E) is approximately 90 kilometres to the east.

6(iv) Location of other protected areas in the vicinity

ASPA 102 Rookery Islands, Mac.Robertson Land (67°36'36.7" S and 62°32'06.7" E) is located approximately 80 kilometres east of Taylor Rookery.

6(v) Special zones within the Area

There are no special zones within the Area.

7. Terms and conditions for entry permits

7(i) General permit conditions

Entry into the Area is prohibited except in accordance with a permit issued by an appropriate national authority. Conditions for issuing a permit to enter the Area are that:

- it is issued only for compelling scientific reasons that cannot be served elsewhere, in particular for scientific study of the avifauna and ecosystem of the Area, or for essential management purposes consistent with plan objectives, such as inspection, management or review;
- the actions permitted will not jeopardise the values of the Area;
- the actions permitted are in accordance with the management plan;
- the permit, or an authorised copy, shall be carried within the Area;
- a visit report shall be supplied to the authority named in the permit;
- permits shall be issued for a finite period; and
- the appropriate national authority shall be notified of any activities or measures undertaken that were not included in the authorised permit.

7(ii) Access to and movement within or over the Area

Travel to the Area may be by vehicle over sea ice, which is generally only possible during the period 1 May to 25 December, or by aircraft.

Whenever possible, vehicle access to the Area should be from sea ice to the east of Colbeck Archipelago, to avoid crossing the penguin's pathways from the rookery to the sea (see Map B). Vehicle entry to the Area is prohibited. Vehicles used for transport to the Area are to be left outside the Area, to the east, and entry to the Area must be by foot. The approach route for vehicles is marked on Map C.

The following conditions apply to the use of aircraft:

- disturbance of the colony by aircraft shall be avoided at all times;
- overflights of the colony are prohibited, except where essential for scientific or management purposes. Such overflights are to be at an altitude of no less than 930m (3050ft) for single-engined helicopters and fixed-wing aircraft, and no less than 1500m (5000ft) for twin-engined helicopters;
- fixed wing aircraft are not permitted to land inside the Area.
- fixed wing aircraft used to approach the Area shall not land or take off within 930m (3050ft) or fly within 750m of the colony;
- helicopters shall approach the Area from the east over the sea ice and preferably, where sea ice conditions permit, land outside the Area, with access to the Area being by foot (see Map C);
- when landing outside the Area, single-engined helicopters should not land or take off within 930m (3050ft) or fly within 750m of the colony, and twin-engined helicopters should not land, take off or fly within 1500m (5000ft) of the colony;
- if landing inside the Area is essential due to unsuitable sea ice conditions, only singled-engined helicopters may land in the north-east of the Area at the point marked "H" on Map C, where a headland to the south obscures the colony from view and noise;
- single-engined helicopters approaching to land in the Area should fly at the lowest safe height over the sea ice to avoid disturbing the colony; and
- refuelling of aircrafts is not permitted within the Area.

There are no marked pedestrian routes within the Area. Unless disturbance is authorised by permit, pedestrians should keep well away from the colony area and give way to departing and arriving penguins. Pedestrians moving in and around the Area should avoid crossing the access routes of the birds if possible, or cross quickly without obstructing penguin traffic.

7(iii) Activities which are or may be conducted within the Area, including restrictions on time and place

The penguins are particularly sensitive to disturbance during the following periods:

- from mid-May to mid-July, when they are incubating eggs; and
- from mid-July to mid-September, when adults are brooding chicks.

As penguins may be in the area in most months, restrictions shall apply year-round.

The Area may be accessed to conduct censuses of the emperor penguin colony. The colony is ideal for census work because it can be done without any disturbance to the birds. The best vantage point for viewing and photographing the penguins in winter is a rocky headland which runs adjacent to Taylor Glacier, on the western side of the colony. The ideal time for a census of adults is from 22 June to 5 July, since during this time most birds present are incubating males, each representing one breeding pair.

Other activities which may be conducted in the Area:

- compelling scientific research which cannot be undertaken elsewhere and which will not jeopardise the avifauna or the ecosystem of the Area;
- essential management activities, including monitoring; and
- sampling, which should be the minimum required for the approved research programmes.

7(iv) Installation, modification or removal of structures

Any structures erected or installed within the Area are to be specified in a permit. Scientific markers and equipment must be secured and maintained in good condition, clearly identifying the permitting country, name of principal investigator and year of installation. All such items should be made of materials that pose minimum risk of harm to fauna and flora or of contamination of the Area.

A condition of the permit shall be that equipment associated with the approved activity shall be removed on or before completion of the activity. Details of markers and equipment temporarily left *in situ* (GPS locations, description, tags, etc. and expected "use by date") shall be reported to the permitting authority. Temporary field huts, if permitted, should be placed well away from the penguin colony at the point to the north-east of the Area, where a headland to the south obscures the colony from view.

7(v) Location of field camps

A four-berth refuge is located in the Colbeck Archipelago, approximately 5 kilometres to the north-east of the Area.

Camping is permitted within the Area and should be well away from the penguin colony, at the point to the north-east of the Area where a headland to the south obscures the colony from view.

7(vi) Restrictions on materials and organisms which may be brought into the Area

- No poultry products, including dried food containing egg powder, are to be taken into the Area.
- No depots of food or other supplies are to be left within the Area beyond the season for which they are required.

- No living animals, plant material or microorganisms shall be deliberately introduced into the Area and precautions shall be taken against accidental introductions.
- No herbicides or pesticides shall be brought into the Area. Any other chemicals, including radio-nuclides or stable isotopes, which may be introduced for scientific or management purposes specified in a permit, shall be removed from the Area at or before the conclusion of the activity for which the permit was granted.
- Fuel is not to be stored in the Area unless required for essential purposes connected with the activity for which the permit has been granted. All such fuel shall be removed at the conclusion of the permitted activity. Permanent fuel depots are not permitted.
- All material introduced shall be for a stated period only, shall be removed at or before the conclusion of that stated period, and shall be stored and handled so as to minimise the risk of environment impacts.

7(vii) Taking of, or harmful interference with, native flora and fauna

Taking of or harmful interference with native flora and fauna is prohibited, except in accordance with a permit. Where taking or harmful interference with animals is involved this should, as a minimum standard, be in accordance with the SCAR Code of Conduct for the Use of Animals for Scientific Purposes in Antarctica.

Ornithological research on the breeding birds present within the Area shall be limited to activities that are non-invasive and non-disruptive. If the capture of individuals is required, capture should occur outside the Area if at all possible to reduce disturbance to the colony.

7(viii) Collection and removal of anything not brought into the Area by the permit holder

Material may be collected or removed from the Area only in accordance with a permit and should be limited to the minimum necessary to meet scientific or management needs.

Material of human origin likely to compromise the values of the Area, and which was not brought into the Area by the permit holder or otherwise authorised, may be removed unless the impact of the removal is likely to be greater than leaving the material *in situ*: if this is the case the appropriate Authority must be notified and approval obtained.

7(ix) Disposal of waste

All wastes, including all human wastes, shall be removed from the Area.

7(x) Measures that may be necessary to continue to meet the aims of the Management Plan

- Permits may be granted to enter the Area to carry out biological monitoring and Area inspection activities, which may involve the collection of samples for analysis or review; the erection or maintenance of scientific equipment and structures, and signposts; or for other protective measures.
- Any specific sites of long-term monitoring shall be appropriately marked and a GPS position obtained for lodgement with the Antarctic Data Directory System through the appropriate national authority.
- Visitors shall take special precautions against the introduction of alien organisms to the Area. Of particular concern are pathogenic, microbial or vegetation introductions sourced from soils, flora or fauna at other Antarctic sites, including research stations, or from regions outside Antarctica. To minimise the risk of introductions, before entering the Area, visitors shall thoroughly clean footwear and any equipment to be used in the Area, particularly sampling equipment and markers.

7(xi) Requirements for reports

Visit reports shall provide detailed information on all census data; locations of any new colonies or nests not previously recorded, as texts and maps; a brief summary of research findings; copies of relevant photographs taken of the Area; and comments indicating measures taken to ensure compliance with permit conditions.

The report may make recommendations relevant to the management of the Area, in particular as to whether the values for which the Area was designated are being adequately protected and whether management measures are effective.

The report shall be submitted as soon as practicable after the visit to the ASPA has been completed, but no later than six months after the visit has occurred. A copy of the report shall be made available to the permit issuing authority and the Party responsible for development of the Management Plan (if different) for the purposes of reviewing the management plan in accordance with the Antarctic Treaty system requirements. Such reports should include, as appropriate, the information identified in the Visit Report form contained in Appendix 4 of the Guide to the Preparation of Management Plans for Antarctic Specially Protected Areas appended to Resolution 2 (1998). Parties should maintain a record of such activities and, in the Annual Exchange of Information, should provide summary descriptions of activities conducted by persons subject to their jurisdiction, which should be in sufficient detail to allow evaluation of the effectiveness of the Management Plan.

7(xii) Emergency provision

Exceptions to restrictions outlined in the management plan are in an emergency as specified in Article 11 of Annex V of the Protocol on Environmental Protection to the Antarctic Treaty (the Madrid Protocol).

8. Supporting Documentation

Budd, G.M. (1961): The biotopes of emperor penguin rookeries. In: *Emu, 61, 171-189.*

Budd, G.M. (1962): Population studies in rookeries of the emperor penguin *Aptenodytes forsteri. Proceedings of the Zoological Society, London 139, 365-388.*

Crohn, P.W. (1959): A contribution to the geology and glaciology of the western part of the Australian Antarctic Territory. *Bull. Bur. Miner. Resour. Geol. Geophys., Aust., No. 32.*

Filson, R.B. (1966): The lichens and mosses of Mac.Robertson Land. Melbourne: Dep. Ext. Affairs, Australia (Antarc. Div.).

Fretwell, P.T. and Trathen, P.N. (2009): Penguins from space: faecal stains reveal the location of emperor penguin colonies. *Global Ecology and Biogeography, No 18:543-552*

Horne, R.S.C. (1983): The distribution of penguin breeding colonies on the Australian Antarctic Territory, Heard Island, the McDonald Islands and Macquarie Island. *ANARE Res. Notes No. 9.*

Kirkwood, R. and Robertson, G. (1997): Seasonal change in the foraging ecology of emperor penguins on the Mawson Coast, Antarctica. *Marine Ecology Progress Series 156: 205-223.*

Kirkwood, R. and Robertson, G. (1997): The energy assimilation efficiency of emperor penguins, *Aptenodytes forsteri*, fed a diet of Antarctic krill, *Euphausia superba. Physiological Zoology 70: 27-32.*

Kirkwood, R. and Robertson, G. (1997): The foraging ecology of female emperor penguins in winter. *Ecological Monographs 67: 155-176.*

Kirkwood, R. and Robertson, G. (1999): The occurrence and purpose of huddling by Emperor penguins during foraging trips. *Emu 99: 40-45.*

Longton, R. E. (1988): Biology of polar bryophytes and lichens, Cambridge University Press, Cambridge, *307-309.*

Melick, D. R., Hovenden, M. J., & Seppelt, R. D. (1994): Phytogeography of bryophyte and lichen vegetation in the Windmill Islands, Wilkes Land, Continental Antarctica. *Vegetation 111: 71-87.*

Morgan, F., Barker, G., Briggs, C. Price, R. and Keys, H (2007): Environmental Domains of Antarctica, Landcare Research New Zealand Ltd

Øvstedal, D. O., and Lewis Smith, R. I. (2001): Lichens of Antarctica and South Georgia: A guide to their identification and ecology, Cambridge University Press, Cambridge.

Robertson, G. (1990): Huddles. *Australian Geographic, 20: 76-94.*

Robertson, G. (1992): Population size and breeding success of emperor penguins *Aptenodytes forsteri* at the Auster and Taylor Glacier Colonies, Mawson Coast, Antarctica. *Emu. 92: 62-71.*

Robertson, G. and Newgrain, K. (1992): Efficacy of the tritiated water and 22Na turnover methods in estimating food and energy intake by Emperor penguins *Aptenodytes forsteri. Physiological Zoology, 65:933-951.*

Robertson, Graham G. (1994): The foraging ecology of emperor penguins (*Aptenodytes forsteri*) at two Mawson Coast Colonies, Antarctica. *PhD Thesis, University of Tasmania.*

Robertson, G., Williams, R. Green, K. and Robertson, L. (1994): Diet composition of emperor penguin chicks *Aptenodytes forsteri* at two Mawson Coast colonies, Antarctica. *Ibis, 136: 19-31*

Robertson, G. (1995): The foraging ecology of emperor penguins *Aptenodytes forsteri* at two Mawson Coast colonies, Antarctica. *ANARE Reports 138, 139.*

Schwerdtfeger, W. (1970): The climate of the Antarctic. In: *Climates of the Polar Regions (ed. S. Orvig), pp. 253-355.*

Schwerdtfeger, W. (1984): Weather and climate of the Antarctic. In: *Climates of the Polar Regions (ed. S. Orvig), p. 261.*

Streten, N.A. (1990): A review of the climate of Mawson– a representative strong wind site in East Antarctica. *Antarctic Science 2, 79-89.*

Trail, D.S. (1970): ANARE 1961 Geological traverses on the Mac.Robertson Land and Kemp Land Coast. *Rept. Bur. Miner. Resour. Geol. Geophys. Aust. No. 135.*

Trail, D.S., McLeod, I.R., Cook, P.J., and Wallis, G.R. (1967): Geological investigations by the Australian National Antarctic Research Expeditions 1965. *Rept. Bur. Miner. Resour. Geol. Geophys. Aust. No. 118.*

Wienecke, B., Kirkwood, R., Robertson, G. (2004): Pre-moult foraging trips and moult locations of emperor penguins at the Mawson Coast. *Polar Biology 27: 83-91.*

Wienecke, B. C. and Robertson, G. (1997): Foraging space of emperor penguins *Aptenodytes forsteri* in Antarctic shelf waters in winter. *Marine Ecology Progress Series 159: 249-263.*

Wienecke, B., Robertson, G., Kirkwood, R., Lawton, K. (2007): Extreme dives by free-ranging emperor penguins. *Polar Biology 30:133-142.*

Wienecke, B., Kirkwood, R., Robertson, G. (2004): Pre-moult foraging trips and moult locations of emperor penguins at the Mawson Coast. *Polar Biology 27. 83-91*

Wienecke, B. (2009): Emperor penguin colonies in the Australian Antarctic Territory: how many are there?. *Polar Record 45:304-312.*

Wienecke, B. (2009): The history of the discovery of emperor penguin colonies, 1902-2004. *Polar Record (in press) doi:10.1017/S0032247409990283.*

Willing, R.L. (1958): Australian discoveries of Emperor penguin rookeries in Antarctica during 1954-57. *Nature, London, 182, 1393-1394.*

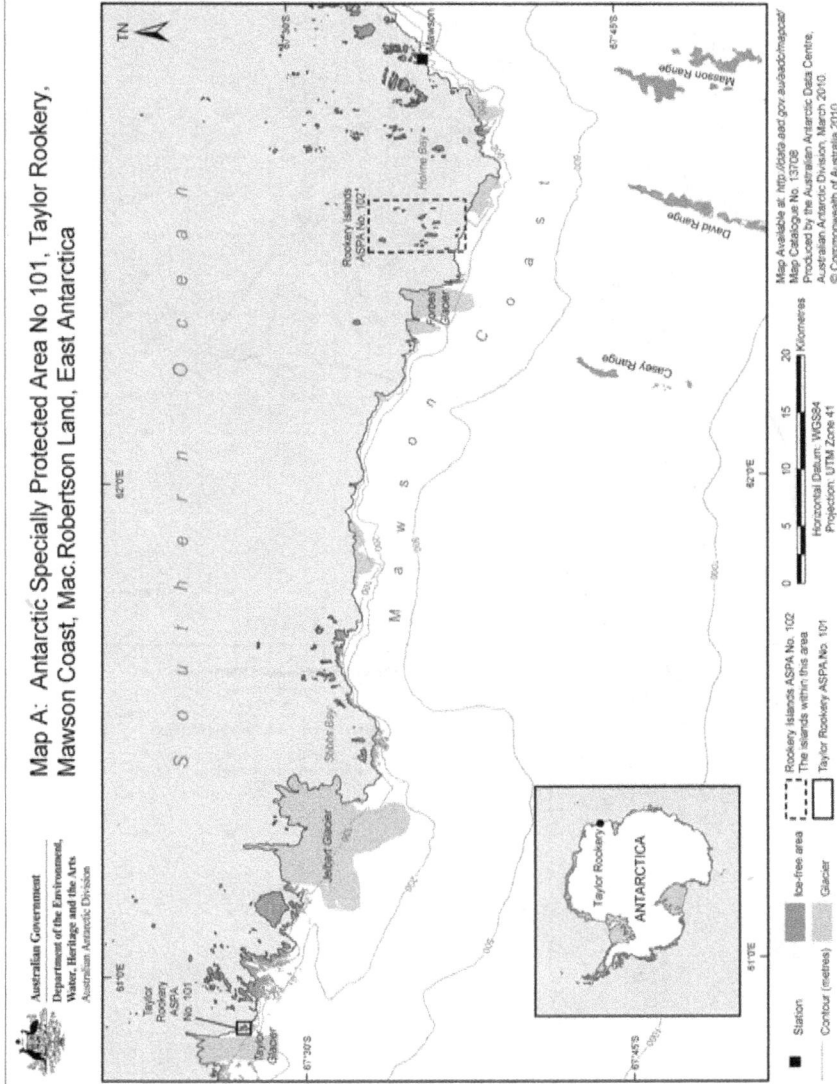

Map A: Antarctic Specially Protected Area No 101, Taylor Rookery, Mawson Coast, Mac.Robertson Land, East Antarctica

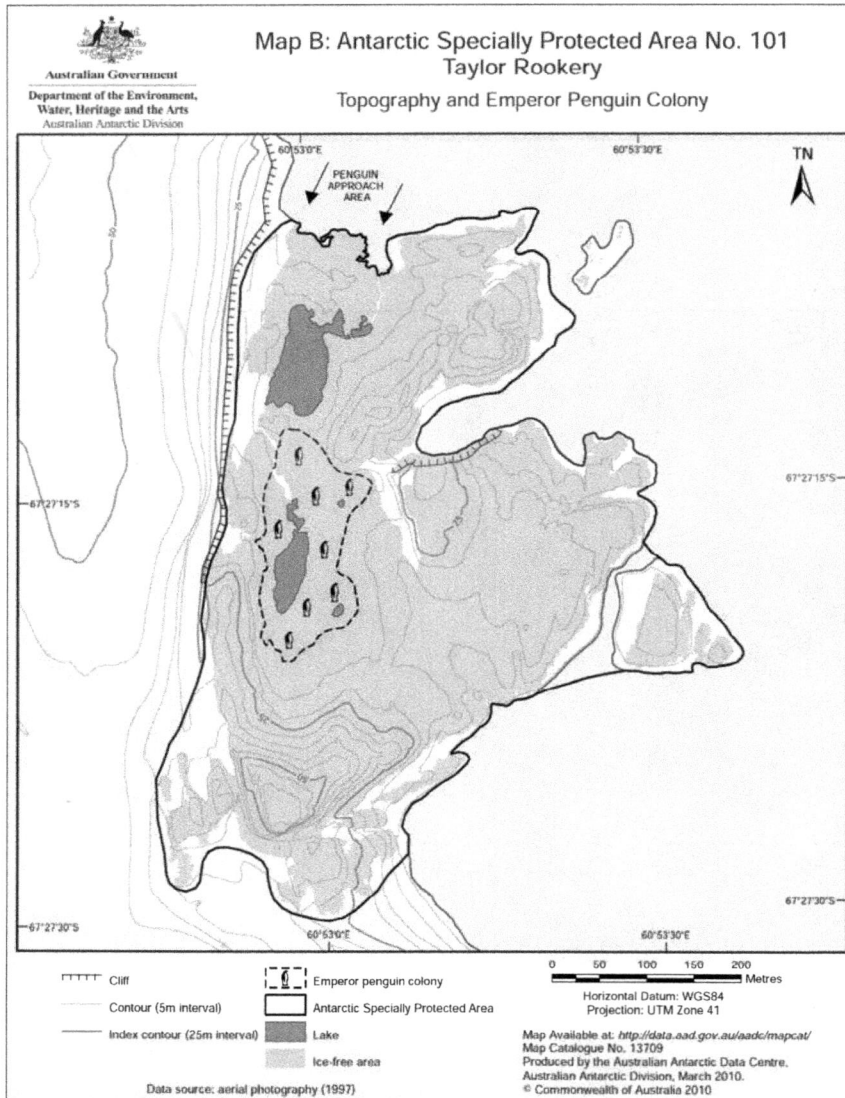

Map B: Antarctic Specially Protected Area No. 101
Taylor Rookery
Topography and Emperor Penguin Colony

Map C: Antarctic Specially Protected Area No. 101, Taylor Rookery
Vehicle and Helicopter Approach and Landing Site

Australian Government

Department of the Environment,
Water, Heritage and the Arts
Australian Antarctic Division

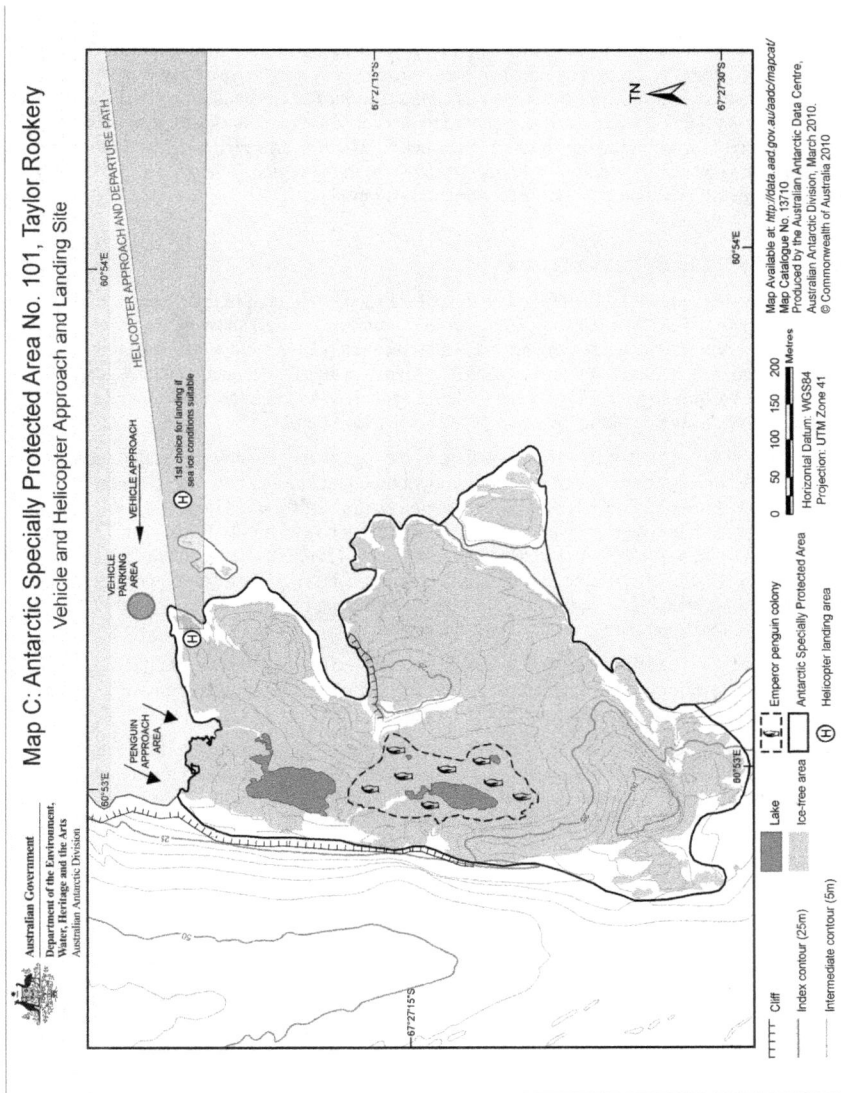

HELICOPTER APPROACH AND DEPARTURE PATH

VEHICLE APPROACH

VEHICLE PARKING AREA

1st choice for landing if sea ice conditions suitable

PENGUIN APPROACH AREA

TN

60°53'E

60°54'E

67°27'15"S

67°27'30"S

Cliff

Index contour (25m)

Intermediate contour (5m)

Lake

Ice-free area

Emperor penguin colony

Antarctic Specially Protected Area

Helicopter landing area

0   50   100   150   200
Metres

Horizontal Datum: WGS84
Projection: UTM Zone 41

Map Available at: http://data.aad.gov.au/aadc/mapcat/
Map Catalogue No. 13710
Produced by the Australian Antarctic Data Centre,
Australian Antarctic Division, March 2010.
© Commonwealth of Australia 2010

Management Plan for Antarctic Specially Protected Area No. 102

ROOKERY ISLANDS, HOLME BAY, MAC.ROBERTSON LAND

Introduction

The Rookery Islands are a group of small islands and rocks in the western part of Holme Bay, lying to the north of the Masson and David Ranges in Mac.Robertson Land, East Antarctica (67°36'36.7" S, 62°32'06.7" E, Map A and Map B). The Rookery Islands were originally designated as Specially Protected Area No. 2 through Recommendation IV-II (1966), after a proposal by Australia. In accordance with Resolution XX-5 (1996), the site was redesignated and renumbered as Antarctic Specially Protected Area (ASPA) No. 102. A management plan for the Area was adopted under Recommendation XVII-2 (1992) and revised under Measure 2 (2005). The Area is designated to protect breeding colonies of possbly six bird species resident in the region, including the southern giant petrel (*Macronectes giganteus*) and the Cape petrel (*Daption capensis*) which are not known to occur elsewhere in the region. The Area is one of only four known southern giant petrel breeding colonies on continental Antarctica.

1. Description of values to be protected

The Rookery Islands contain breeding colonies of up to six bird species resident in the Mawson region, including: Adélie penguin (*Pygoscelis adeliae*), Cape petrel (*Daption capense*), snow petrel (*Pagodroma nivea*), southern giant petrel (*Macronectes giganteus*), Antarctic skua (*Catharacta maccormicki*) and probably Wilson's storm petrel (*Oceanites oceanicus*). The Area is primarily designated to safeguard this unusual assemblage of six bird species. The Rookery Islands also provide a representative sample of the near-shore island habitats occurring along the coast of Mac.Robertson Land.

The southern giant petrel is not known to breed elsewhere in the region, and the colony located on Giganteus Island in the Rookery Islands group is one of only four known breeding sites on continental Antarctica. The other three continental colonies are located near the Australian stations of Casey (Frazier Islands, ASPA 160, 66°14'S 110°10'E, approximately 250 pairs), and Davis (Hawker Island, ASPA 167, 68°35'S, 77°50'E, approximately 25 pairs), and near the French station Dumont d'Urville (Pointe-Géologie Archipelago, ASPA 120, 66°40'S, 140°01'E, 12-15 pairs).These four breeding colonies comprise less than one per cent of the global breeding population, which is approximately 54,000 breeding pairs, approximately 11,000 of which are found south of 60°S, mostly in the Antarctic Peninsula region.

Currently there are relatively few published data available that allow robust analyses of southern giant petrel population trends. Some locations have experienced a decrease that appears to be stabilising or to have reversed in recent years. Small increases have occurred at other locations.

Southern giant petrels are widespread in more northerly latitudes, breeding on islands in the north-west region of the Antarctic Peninsula and on islands of the Scotia Ridge. However, it is important that the species is protected at the southern limit of its breeding range and the Antarctic Treaty parties have committed to minimise human disturbance and encourage regular population counts at all breeding sites in the Antarctic Treaty area.

2. Aims and Objectives

Management of the Rookery Islands aims to:

- avoid degradation of, or substantial risk to, the values of the Area by preventing unnecessary human disturbance to the Area;
- allow scientific research on the ecosystem, particularly on the avifauna, and physical environment, provided it is for compelling reasons which cannot be served elsewhere;

- minimise the possibility of introduction of pathogens which may cause disease in bird populations within the Area;
- minimise the possibility of introduction of alien plants, animals and microbes to the Area;
- minimise human disturbance to southern giant petrels on Giganteus Island;
- allow Giganteus Island to be used as a reference area for future comparative studies with other breeding populations of southern giant petrels;
- preserve Giganteus Island, henceforth, as a highly restricted area by limiting human visitation to the island during the southern giant petrel breeding season;
- allow for the gathering of data on the population status and related demography of the bird species on a regular basis; and
- allow visits for management purposes in support of the aims of the management plan.

3. Management Activities

The following management activities shall be undertaken to protect the values of the Area:

- information on the location of the Area (stating special restrictions that apply), and a copy of this Management Plan shall be kept available at adjacent operational research/field stations and will be made available to ships visiting the vicinity;
- where practicable the Area shall be visited as necessary (preferably no less than once every five years), to assess whether it continues to serve the purposes for which it was designated and to ensure that management activities are adequate;
- where practicable, at least one research visit should be conducted to census the southern giant petrels at Giganteus Island and other seabird populations in each five year period, to enable assessment of breeding populations.
- the Management Plan shall be reviewed at least every five years.

4. Period of Designation

Designation is for an indefinite period.

5. Maps

Map A:Antarctic Specially Protected Area No 102, Rookery Islands, Holme Bay, Mac.Robertson Land. The inset map indicates the location in relation to the Antarctic continent.

Map B: East Antarctica, Mac.Robertson Land, Rookery Islands Antarctic Specially Protected Area No 102. Distribution of nesting seabirds on the Rookery Islands

Map C: East Antarctica, Mac.Robertson Land, Rookery Islands Antarctic Specially Protected Area No 102. Topography and distribution of nesting seabirds on Giganteus Island (Restricted Zone).

Specifications for all Maps:

Horizontal Datum: WGS84   Projection: UTM Zone 49.

6. Description of the Area

6(i) Geographical co-ordinates, boundary markers and natural features

The Rookery Islands comprise a small group of approximately 75 small islands and rocks in the south-west part of Holme Bay, Mac.Robertson Land, about 10km to the west of the Australian station Mawson. The Area comprises those rocks and islands lying within a rectangle enclosed by following coordinates: 62°28'01"E, 67°33'45"S; 62°34'37"E, 67°33'47"S; 62°28'02"E, 67°38'10"S; 62°34'39"E, 67°38'11"S (Map B).

There are no boundary markers delimiting the site.

The Rookery Islands range in size from small rocks which barely remain above water at high tide to the larger members of the group which include Giganteus Island (approximately 400 m long, 400 m wide and 30 m high) and Rookery Island, the highest of the group, with an altitude of 62 m, and of similar area, but slightly more elongate. Raised beaches are evident on Giganteus Island.

Climate

Limited data exist for the meteorology of the Area. Conditions are probably similar to those of the Mawson station area where the mean monthly temperature ranges from +0.1°C in January to -18.8°C in August, with extreme temperatures ranging from +10.6°C to -36.0°C. The mean annual wind speed is 10.9 m per second with frequent prolonged periods of strong south-easterly katabatic winds from the ice cap at mean speeds over 25 m per second and gusts often exceeding 50 m per second. Mean wind speed decreases seaward with distance from the icecap, but is unlikely to be much lower at the Rookery Islands which lie quite close to the coast. Other general characteristics of the coastal Antarctic climate to which these islands are likely to be subjected are high cloudiness throughout the year, very low absolute humidity, low precipitation and frequent periods of intensified winds, drifting snow and low visibility associated with the passage of major low pressure systems.

Environmental domains analysis

Based on the Environmental Domains Analysis for Antarctica (Resolution 3 (2008)) the Rookery Islands are located within Environment D *East Antarctic coastal geologic*.

Geology and soils

The Rookery Islands are outcrops of the Mawson charnockite, a rock type which occurs over an area of at least 2000 square kilometres along the coast of Mac.Robertson Land. The charnockites of the Rookery Islands are the fine grained variant and are comparatively poor in the mineral hypersthene but rich in garnet and biotite. The charnockites enclose abundant bands and lenses of hornfels, garnetiferous quartz and felspar-rich gneisses. There are also a number of pegmatic dykes which cut across the charnockite rocks.

Vegetation

No mosses or lichens have been recorded from any of the Rookery Islands. There are some terrestrial algae but no taxonomic identifications have been made. Most of the smaller islands and rocks are covered with sea spray in summer and are sometimes scoured by rafted sea ice in winter and spring. It is considered unlikely that species of moss or lichen could become established.

Inland waters

There are no freshwater bodies on the Rookery Islands.

Birds

Six species of birds are thought to breed on the Rookery Islands: Adélie penguin (*Pygoscelis adeliae*), Cape petrel (*Daption capensis*), snow petrel (*Pagodroma nivea*), southern giant petrel (*Macronectes giganteus*), Wilson's storm petrel (*Oceanites oceanicus*) and the south polar skua (*Catharacta maccormicki*).

The southern giant petrels nest on Giganteus Island (Map C). The colony is currently marginal but has been stable at 2-4 breeding pairs since the 1960s. A total of 16 incubating birds were recorded in 1958 and 13 in 1967. However, only two nests were present in 1972, four in 1973, two in 1977, one in 1981, two in 1982, and three in 2001. During the most recent count in 2007, four nests were counted on two separate occasions, with two pairs and two lone birds at first count (27th November) and three pairs and one lone bird on an egg (therefore assumed to have an absent partner) at second count (10th December). The nests are shallow mounds of stones and are built on broad gravel patches on the raised beaches. The area has many old nests and several may be rebuilt each year but there is no evidence that each regularly contains eggs.

Cape petrels breed on Rookery Island and a small island known as Pintado Island, located 300 m north-west of Rookery Island. There were seven nests on Rookery Island and 12 nests on Pintado Island in 1958. No systematic counts of nests with eggs have been made since 1958, although the numbers of adults present

3

recorded subsequently are 69 in 1977, 48 in 1981, and 28 in 1982. On 24 December 2007, there were at least 123 nests observed on Pintado Island many with eggs but these were not systematically assessed. Approximately 10 nests were observed on Rookery Island. Larger breeding colonies of Cape petrels occur along the rock outcrops near Forbes Glacier 8km to the west, and on Scullin and Murray Monoliths (ASPA 164) approximately 100km to the east.

Snow petrels nest throughout the Rookery Islands and in greatest concentration on Rookery Island. Wilson's storm petrels are frequently seen flying around the islands and probably breeds on a number of the larger islands in the group, although no nests have been recorded.

Adélie penguins breed on 14 of the islands. The largest populations occur on Rookery and Giganteus Islands (4850 pairs in December 1971). On 17 December 1972, 33,000 adults were present on 10 of the islands. In December 2007, a population survey for all 14 islands with Adelie penguin colonies estimated a breeding population of 78,682 to 104,420 nests. Of these, approximately 31,800 nests were counted on Rookery Island and approx 10,000 nests on Giganteus Island.

6(ii) Access to the Area

The Area can be accessed by oversnow vehicles or boats (depending on sea ice conditions). There are no designated landing sites (also see 7(ii)).

6(iii) Location of structures within and adjacent to the Area

There are no structures within or adjacent to the Area.

6(iv) Location of other protected areas in the vicinity

ASPA 101 Taylor Rookery, Mac.Robertson Land (67°26'S; 60°50'E) is located approximately 80 kilometres to the west.

6(v) Special zones within the Area

Giganteus Island is designated as a Restricted Zone to afford a high level of protection to southern giant petrels (Map B, Map C). Entry is restricted and may only be permitted in accordance with the purposes and conditions detailed elsewhere in this management plan.

7. Terms and conditions for entry permits

7(i)   General conditions

Entry into the Area is prohibited except in accordance with a permit issued by an appropriate national authority. Conditions for issuing a permit to enter the Area are that:

- it is issued only for compelling scientific that cannot be served elsewhere, in particular for scientific study of the avifauna and ecosystem of the Area, or for essential management purposes consistent with plan objectives, such as inspection, maintenance or review;
- the actions permitted will not jeopardise the values of the Area;
- the actions permitted are in accordance with the management plan;
- the permit, or an authorised copy, shall be carried within the Area;
- a visit report shall be supplied to the authority named in the permit;
- permits shall be issued for a stated period;
- the appropriate national authority shall be notified of any activities/measures undertaken that were not included in the authorised permit.

Entry to the Giganteus Island Restricted Zone is only permitted in accordance with conditions outlined below.

- Permits to enter the Giganteus Island Restricted Zone during the southern giant petrel breeding period (1 October to 30 April) may only be issued for the purpose of conducting censuses. Other research may be conducted outside the breeding period in accordance with a permit.

- Wherever practicable, censuses should be conducted from outside the southern giant petrel colony using vantage points from which the nesting birds may be counted.
- Access to the Restricted Zone should be limited to the minimum amount of time reasonably required to undertake the census.
- Visits to conduct censuses should be made by a team including at least one bird biologist associated with a national Antarctic program or someone with relevant scientific skills and experience. Other personnel should remain at the shoreline.
- Persons shall not approach closer than is necessary to obtain census data or biological data from any nesting southern giant petrels, and in no case closer than 20m.
- Overflights of Giganteus Island are prohibited.

7(ii) Access to, and movement within or over the Area

Travel to the Area may be accessed by boat, by vehicle over sea ice, or by aircraft.

Vehicles are prohibited on the islands, and vehicles and boats must be left at the shoreline. Movement on the islands is by foot only. Vehicles used to access the islands over sea ice must be taken no closer than 250m from concentrations of birds.

Access to Giganteus Island is prohibited except in accordance with the provisions elsewhere in this Plan.

If access to the islands is not possible by boat or by vehicle over sea ice, then fixed wing aircraft or helicopters may be used subject to the following conditions:

- disturbance of the colonies by aircraft shall be avoided at all times
- sea ice landings shall be encouraged (where practicable);
- aircraft landings on Giganteus Island during the breeding season are prohibited;
- as aircraft may provide the only viable access to the other islands when sea and sea ice access is not possible, single-engined helicopters may land on the islands during the breeding season where it is possible to maintain a distance of at least 500m from bird colonies. Permission to land an aircraft may be granted for essential scientific or management purposes only if it can be demonstrated that disturbance will be minimal. Only personnel who are required to carry out work in the Area should leave the helicopter;
- when accessing Giganteus Island by aircraft outside the breeding season sea ice landings are preferred, following separation distances mentioned below;
- at all other times, single-engined helicopters and fixed wing aircraft must not land or take off within 930 m (3050 ft) or fly within 750m of bird colonies, and twin-engined helicopters must not land, take off or fly within 1500 m of bird colonies;
- overflights of the islands during the breeding season is prohibited, except where essential for scientific or management purposes. Such overflights are to be at an altitude of no less than 930m (3050ft) for single-engined helicopters and fixed-wing aircraft, and no less than 1500m (5000ft) for twin-engined helicopters;
- refuelling of aircraft is prohibited within the Area.

7(iii) Activities which are or may be conducted within the Area, including restrictions on time and place

The following activities may be conducted within the Area as authorised in a permit;

- scientific research consistent with the Management Plan for the Area which cannot be undertaken elsewhere and which will not jeopardise the values for which the Area has been designated or the ecosystems of the Area;
- essential management activities, including monitoring; and
- sampling, which should be the minimum required for approved research programmemes.

7(iv) Installation, modification, or removal of structures

- Permanent structures or installations are prohibited.
- Other structures or installations shall not be erected within the Area except as specified in a permit.
- Small temporary refuges, hides, blinds or screens may be constructed for the purpose of scientific study of the avifauna.
- Installation (including site selection), removal, modification or maintenance of structures shall be undertaken in a manner that minimises disturbance to breeding birds.
- All scientific equipment or markers installed within the Area must be clearly identified by country, name of the principal investigator and year of installation.
- Markers, signs or other structures erected within the Area for scientific or management purposes shall be secured and maintained in good condition and removed when no longer required. All such items should be made of materials that pose minimal risk of harm to bird populations or of contamination of the Area. Permits will require the removal of specific structures, equipment or markers before the permit expiry date.

7(v) Location of field camps
- Camping is prohibited within the Area except in an emergency.

7(vi) Restrictions on materials and organisms that may be brought into the Area
- No poultry products, including dried food containing egg powder, are to be taken into the Area.
- No depots of food or other supplies are to be left within the Area beyond the season for which they are required.
- No living animals, plant material or microorganisms shall be deliberately introduced into the Area and precautions shall be taken against accidental introductions.
- No herbicides or pesticides shall be brought into the Area. Any other chemicals, including radio-nuclides or stable isotopes, which may be introduced for scientific or management purposes specified in a permit, shall be removed from the Area as far as possible at or before the conclusion of the activity for which the permit was granted.
- Fuel is not to be stored in the Area unless required for essential purposes connected with the activity for which the permit has been granted. Permanent fuel depots are not permitted.
- All material introduced shall be for a stated period only, shall be removed at or before the conclusion of that stated period, and shall be stored and handled so as to minimise the risk of environmental impact.

7(vii) Taking of, or harmful interference with, native flora and fauna
- Taking of, or harmful interference with, native flora and fauna is prohibited, except in accordance with a permit. Where taking or harmful interference with animals is involved this should, as a minimum standard, be in accordance with the *SCAR Code of Conduct for the Use of Animals for Scientific Purposes in Antarctica*.
- Ornithological research shall be limited to activities that are non-invasive and non-disruptive to the breeding seabirds present within the Area. Surveys, including aerial photographs for the purposes of population census, shall have a high priority.
- Disturbance of southern giant petrels shall be avoided at all times.

7(viii) Collection or removal of anything not brought into the Area by the permit holder
- Material may only be collected or removed from the Area as authorised in a permit and shall be limited to the minimum necessary to meet scientific or management needs.
- Material of human origin likely to compromise the values of the Area, which was not brought into the Area by the permit holder or otherwise authorised, may be removed unless the impact of the removal is likely to be greater than leaving the material *in situ*. If such material is found, the appropriate Authority must be notified and approval obtained prior to removal.

7(ix) Disposal of waste
- All wastes, including human wastes, shall be removed from the Area.

7(x) Measures that may be necessary to continue to meet the aims of the Management Plan

- Permits may be granted to enter the Area to carry out biological monitoring and Area inspection activities, which may involve the collection of samples for analysis or review; the erection or maintenance of scientific equipment and structures, and signposts; or for other protective measures.

- Any specific sites of long-term monitoring shall be appropriately marked and a GPS position obtained for lodgement with the Antarctic Data Directory System through the appropriate national authority.

- To help maintain the ecological and scientific values of the Area, visitors shall take special precautions against introductions of non-indigenous organisms. Of particular concern are pathogenic, microbial or vegetation introductions sourced from soils, flora and fauna at other Antarctic sites, including research stations, or from regions outside Antarctica. To minimise the risk of introductions, before entering the Area visitors shall thoroughly clean footwear and any equipment, particularly sampling equipment and markers to be used in the Area.

- Where practical, a census of southern giant petrels on Giganteus Island shall be conducted at least once in every five year period. Censuses of other species may be undertaken during this visit provided no additional disturbance is caused to the southern giant petrels.

- To reduce disturbance to wildlife, noise levels including verbal communication is to be kept to a minimum. The use of motor-driven tools and any other activity likely to generate noise and thereby cause disturbance to nesting birds is prohibited within the Area during the breeding period (1 October to 30 April).

7(xi) Requirements for reports

Parties shall ensure that the principal permit holder for each permit issued submits to the appropriate national authority a report on activities undertaken. Such reports should include, as appropriate, the information identified in the Visit Report form contained in Appendix 4 of the Guide to the Preparation of Management Plans for Antarctic Specially Protected Areas appended to Resolution 2 (1998). Parties should maintain a record of such activities and, in the Annual Exchange of Information, should provide summary descriptions of activities conducted by persons subject to their jurisdiction, which should be in sufficient detail to allow evaluation of the effectiveness of the Management Plan.

Parties shall, wherever possible, deposit originals or copies of such original reports in a publicly accessible archive to maintain a record of usage, to be considered in any review of the Management Plan and in organising the use of the Area. A copy of the report should be forwarded to the Party responsible for development of the Management Plan (Australia) to assist in management of the Area, and the monitoring of bird populations. Visit reports shall provide detailed information on census data, locations of any new colonies or nests not previously recorded, a brief summary of research findings and copies of photographs taken of the Area.

7(xi) Emergency provision

Exceptions to restrictions outlined in the management plan are in emergency as specified in Article 11 of Annex V to the Protocol on Environmental Protection to the Antarctic Treaty (the Madrid Protocol).

8. Supporting Documentation

Australian Antarctic Division: Environmental Code of Conduct for Australian field activities, *Australian Antarctic Division.*

Cowan, A.N. (1981): Size variation in the snow petrel. *Notornis 28: 169-188.*

Cowan, A.N. (1979): Giant petrels at Casey. *Australian Bird Watcher 8: 66-67.*

Crohn, P.W. (1959): A contribution to the geology and glaciology of the western part of the Australian Antarctic Territory. *Report for the Bureau for Mineral Resources, Geology and Geophysics Australia No. 52.*

Croxall, J.P., Steele, W.K., McInnes, S.J., Prince, P.A. (1995): Breeding Distribution of the snow petrel *Pagodroma nivea. Marine Ornithology 23: 69-99.*

Environment Australia (2001): Recovery Plan for albatrosses and giant petrels. *Prepared by Wildlife Scientific Advice, Natural Heritage Division in consultation with the Albatross and Giant Petrel Recovery Team, Canberra.*

Garnett, S.T., Crowley, G.M. (2000): The action plan for Australian birds 2000. *Commonwealth of Australia, Environment Australia, Canberra*

Horne, R.S.C. (1983): The distribution of penguin breeding colonies on the Australian Antarctic Territory, Heard Island, the McDonald Island, and Macquarie Island. *ANARE Research Notes, No. 9.*

Kizaki, K. (1972): Sequence of metamorphism and deformation in the Mawson Charnockite of East Antarctica. In Antarctic Geology and Geophysics (ed. R.J. Adie), pp. 527-530. Oslo: Universitetsforlaget,

Lynch, H.J. Naveen, R., Fagan, W.F. (2008): Censuses of penguin, blue-eyed shag *Phalacrocorax atriceps* and southern giant petrel *Macronectes giganteus* populations on the Antarctic Peninsula, 2001-2007. Marine Ornithology 36:83-97.

Ingham, S.E. (1959): Banding of giant petrels by the Australian National Antarctic Research Expeditions, 1955-58. *Emu 59: 189-200.*

Jouventin, P., Weimerskirch, H. (1991): Changes in the population size and demography of southern seabirds: management implications. In: *Perrins, C.M., Lebreton, J.-D. and Hirons, G.J.M. Bird population studies: Relevance to conservation and management. Oxford University Press: 297-314.*

Orton, M.N. (1963): Movements of young giant petrels bred in Antarctica. *Emu 63: 260.*

Patterson D.L., Woehler, E.J., Croxall, J.P., Cooper, J., Poncet, S., Peter, H.-U., Hunter, S., Fraser, W.R. (2008): Breeding distribution and population status of the northern giant petrel *Macronectes halli* and the southern giant petrel *M. giganteus. Marine Ornithology* 36:115-124.

Scientific Committee on Antarctic Research (2008): Status of the Regional, Antarctic Population of the Southern GianT Petrel – Progress. *Working Paper 10 rev.1 to the 31st Antarctic Treaty Consultative Meeting, Ukraine, 2008.*

Sheraton, J.W. (1982): Origin of charnockitic rock of Mac.Robertson Land. In: *Antarctic Geoscience (ed. C.C. Craddock), pp. 487-489.*

Stattersfield, A.J., Capper, D.R. (2000): Threatened birds of the world. *Birdlife International, Lynx Publications.*

Trail, D.S. (1970): ANARE 1961 Geological traverses on the Mac.Robertson and Kemp Land Coast. *Report for the Bureau for Mineral Resources, Geology and Geophysics Australia No 135.*

Trail, D.S., McLeod, I.R., Cook, P.J. & Wallis, G.R. (1967): Geological investigations by the Australian National Antarctic Research Expeditions 1965. *Report for the Bureau for Mineral Resources, Geology and Geophysics Australia . No. 118.*

van Franeker, J.A., Gavrilo, M., Mehlum, F., Veit, R.R., Woehler, E.J. (1999): Distribution and abundance of the antarctic petrel. *Waterbirds 22: 14-28.*

Wienecke, B., Leaper, R., Hay, I., van den Hoff, J. (2009) Retrofitting historical data in population studies: southern giant petrels in the Australian Antarctic Territory. *Endangered Species Research* 8:157-164

Woehler E.J., Croxall J.P. (1997): The status and trends of Antarctic and subantarctic seabirds. *Marine Ornithology 25: 43-66.*

Woehler, E.J., Johnstone, G.W. (1991): Status and conservation of the seabirds of the Australian Antarctic Territory. In: *Croxall, J.P. (ed.) Seabird Status and Conservation: A Supplement. ICBP Technical Publication No.11: 279-308.*

Woehler, E.J., Riddle, M.J. (2001): Long-term population trends in southern giant petrels in the Southern Indian Ocean. *Poster presented at 8th SCAR Biology Symposium, Amsterdam.*

Woehler, E.J., Riddle, M.J., Ribic, C.A. (2001): Long-term population trends in southern giant petrels in East Antarctica. *Proceedings 8th SCAR Biology Symposium, Amsterdam.*

Woehler, E.J., Johnstone, G.W., Burton, H.R. (1989): The distribution and abundance of Adelie penguins, *Pygoscelis adeliae*, in the Mawson area and at the Rookery Islands (Antarctic Specially Protected Area 102), 1981 and 1988. *ANARE Research Notes 71.*

Woehler, E.J., Cooper, J., Croxall, J.P., Fraser, W.R., Kooyman, G.L., Miller, G.D., Nel, D.C., Patterson, D.L., Peter, H-U, Ribic, C.A., Salwicka, K., Trivelpiece, W.Z., Wiemerskirch, H. (2001): A statistical assessment of the status and trends of Antarctic and subantarctic seabirds. *SCAR/CCAMLR/NSF, 43.*

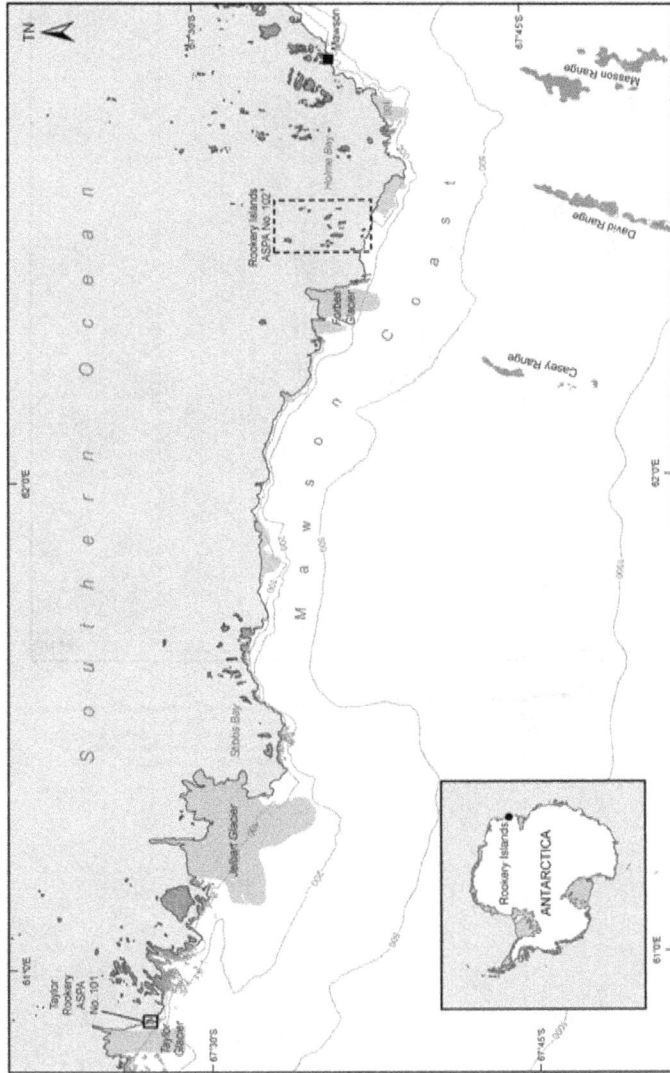

Map A: Antarctic Specially Protected Area No 102, Rookery Islands, Holme Bay, Mac.Robertson Land, East Antarctica

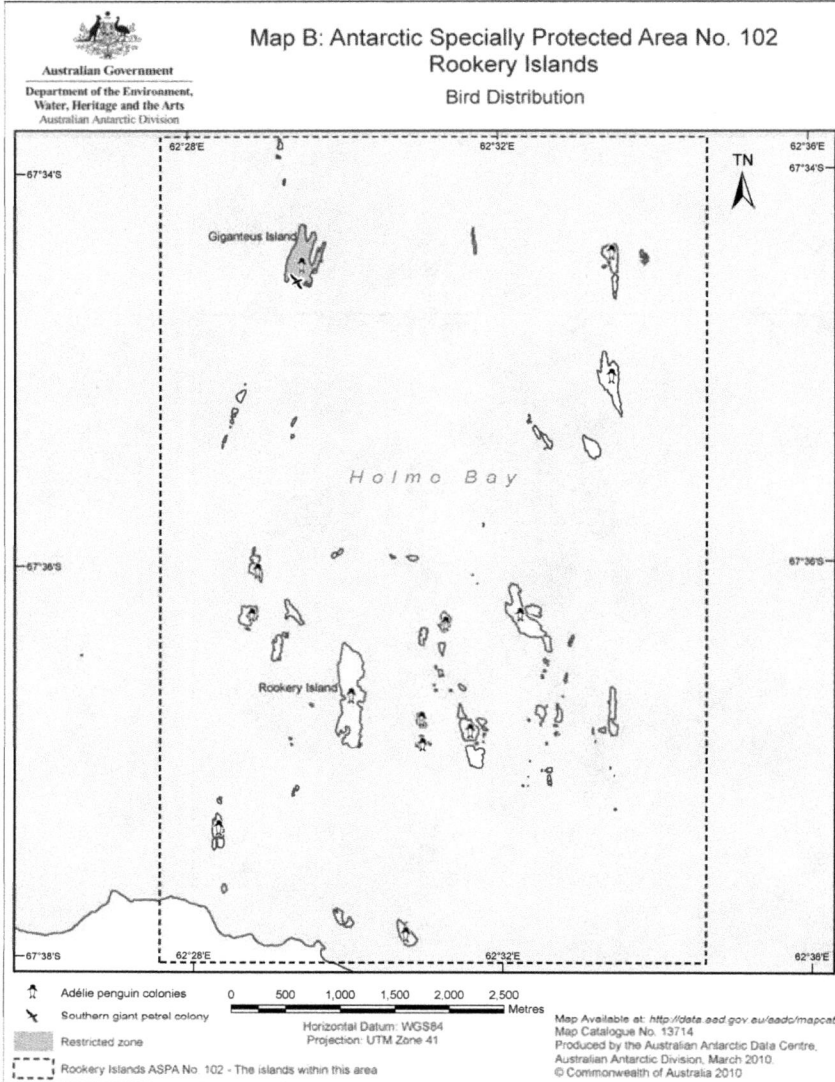

Map B: Antarctic Specially Protected Area No. 102
Rookery Islands
Bird Distribution

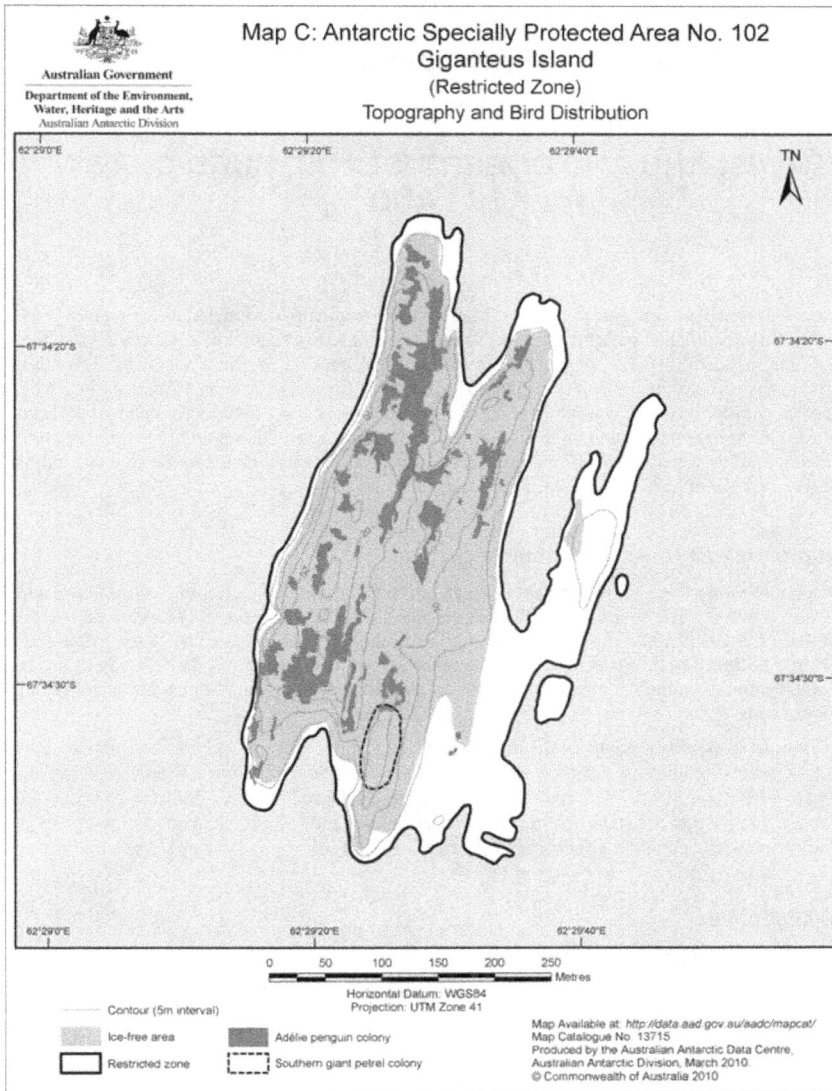

Map C: Antarctic Specially Protected Area No. 102
Gianteus Island
(Restricted Zone)
Topography and Bird Distribution

Australian Government
Department of the Environment,
Water, Heritage and the Arts
Australian Antarctic Division

Horizontal Datum: WGS84
Projection: UTM Zone 41

Contour (5m interval)
Ice-free area
Restricted zone
Adélie penguin colony
Southern giant petrel colony

Map Available at: http://data.aad.gov.au/aadc/mapcat/
Map Catalogue No. 13715
Produced by the Australian Antarctic Data Centre,
Australian Antarctic Division, March 2010.
© Commonwealth of Australia 2010

Management Plan for Antarctic Specially Protected Area No. 103

ARDERY ISLAND AND ODBERT ISLAND, BUDD COAST, WILKES LAND

Introduction

Ardery Island and Odbert Island (66°22'S; 110°28'E, Map A) were originally designated as Specially Protected Area No. 3 in accordance with the Agreed Measures for the Conservation of Antarctic Fauna and Flora, through Recommendation IV-III (1966), after a proposal by Australia. In accordance with Resolution XX-5 (1996), the site was redesignated and renumbered as Antarctic Specially Protected Area (ASPA) No. 103. A management plan for the Area was adopted under Recommendation XVII-2 (1992) and revised under Measure 2 (2005). The Area is designated on the grounds that the islands provide several breeding species of petrel, and an example of their habitat. The Antarctic petrel (*Thalassoica antarctica*) and the southern fulmar (*Fulmarus glacialoides*) are of particular scientific interest.

1. Description of values to be protected

The Area is designated primarily to protect the assemblage of the four fulmaine petrels at Ardery Island and Odbert Island (Map B and C). The four genera of fulmarine petrels are Antarctic petrel (*Thalassoica antarctica*), southern fulmars (*Fulmarus glacialoides*), Cape petrels (*Daption capense*) and snow petrels (*Pagodroma nivea*). All breed in the Area in sufficient numbers to allow comparative study. Study of these four genera at one location is of high ecological importance in understanding their responses to changes in the Southern Ocean ecosystem.

Ardery Island is unique insofar as it might be the only area in the Antarctic which harbours two different subspecies of snow petrels. Studies on morphological or ecological differences between these two subspecies are not possible anywhere else. In addition, both islands have breeding populations of Wilson's storm petrels (*Oceanites oceanicus*) and Antarctic skuas (*Catharacta maccormicki*) and Odbert Island also supports a breeding population of Adélie penguins (*Pygoscelis adeliae*).

2. Aims and Objectives

Management of Ardery Island and Odbert Island aims to:

- avoid degradation of, or substantial risk to, the values of the Area by preventing unnecessary human disturbance;
- allow scientific research on the ecosystem and physical environment, particularly on the avifauna, provided it is for compelling reasons which cannot be served elsewhere;
- minimise the possibility of introduction of pathogens which may cause disease in bird populations within the Area;
- minimise the possibility of introduction of alien plants, animals and microbes to the Area;
- allow for the gathering of data on the population status of the bird species on a regular basis; and
- allow visits for management purposes in support of the aims of the management plan.

3. Management activities

The following management activities shall be undertaken to protect the values of the Area:

- a copy of this Management Plan shall be made available at Casey station and to ships visiting the vicinity;

- the Area shall be visited as necessary, preferably no less than once every five years, to assess whether it continues to serve the purposes for which it was designated, and to ensure that management activities are adequate: and

- the Management Plan shall be reviewed at least every five years.

4. Period of designation

Designation is for an indefinite period.

5. Maps

Map A: Antarctic Specially Protected Area No 103, Ardery Island and Odbert Island, Budd Coast, Wilkes Land. The inset map indicates the location in relation to the Antarctic continent.

Map B: Antarctic Specially Protected Area No 103, Ardery Island: Topography and Bird Distribution.

Map C: Antarctic Specially Protected Area No 103, Odbert Island: Topography and Bird Distribution.

Map D: Antarctic Specially Protected Area No 103: Helicopter approach and landing sites.

Specifications for all maps: Horizontal Datum: WGS84; Vertical Datum: Mean Sea Level

6. Description of the Area

6(i) Geographical co-ordinates, boundary markers and natural features

Ardery Island (66°22'S, 110°28'E) and Odbert Island (66°22'S, 110°33'E) are among the southernmost of the Windmill Islands in the south of Vincennes Bay, off the Budd Coast of Wilkes Land, Eastern Antarctica. The Area comprises both islands down to low water mark.

Topography

Ardery Island and Odbert Island are located 5 km and 0.6 km, respectively, to the west of Robinson Ridge, south of Casey station.

Odbert Island is approximately 2.5 km long and 0.5 km wide. It has a rocky coast which rises steeply from the sea to a plateau. The highest point is 100 m altitude. The plateau is dissected by a series of valleys which run to the south from the high flat rim on the northern side. These valleys are snow covered in winter. The hill tops remain essentially ice and snow free. In some years, the island remains joined to Robinson Ridge on the mainland by sea ice.

Ardery Island is a steep, ice free island approximately 1 km long and 0.5 km wide, with an east-west orientation. The highest point is 113 m above sea level.

The terrain on both islands is rugged and dissected by fissures. The cliffs are fractured and have narrow exposed ledges which in summer are occupied by nesting sea birds. On the hillsides and plateau region, the exposed rock is ice-smoothed and the valley floors are covered with moraine. The islands have undergone isostatic rebound. Moraine and solifluction debris is abundant at heights in excess of 30 metres above mean sea level but considerably less at lower altitudes.

Geology

The Windmill Islands region represent one of the eastern most outcrops of a Mesoproterozoic low-pressure granulite facies terrain that extends west to the Bunger Hills and further to the Archaean complexes in Princess Elizabeth Land, to minor exposures in the east in the Dumont d'Urville area and in Commonwealth Bay. The total outcrop areas do not exceed more than a few square kilometres. The Mesoproterozoic outcrop of the Windmill Islands and the Archaean complexes of Princess Elizabeth Land are two of the few major areas in East Antarctica that can be directly correlated with an Australian equivalent in a Gondwana reconstruction. The Mesoproterozoic facies terrain comprise a series of migmatitic metapelites and metapsammites interlayered with mafic to ultramafic and felsic sequences with rare calc-silicates, large partial melt bodies (Windmill Island supacrustals), undeformed granite, charnockite, gabbro, pegmatite, aplites and cut by easterly-trending late dolerite dykes.

Ardery Island and Odbert Island are part of the southern gradation of a metamorphic grade transition which separates the northern part of the Windmill Islands region from the southern part. The metamorphic grade ranges from amphibolite facies, sillimanite-biotite orthoclase in the north at Clark Peninsula, through biotite-cordierite-almandine granulite, to hornblende-orthopyroxene granulite at Browning Peninsula in the south.

Ardery Island and Odbert Island together with Robinson Ridge, Holl Island, Peterson Island and the Browning Peninsula are similar geologically and are composed of Ardery charnockite. Charnockites are of granitic composition but were formed under anhydrous conditions. The Ardery Charnockite of Ardery Island and Odbert Island intrudes the Windmill metamorphics and consists of a modal assemblage of quartz + plagioclase + microline + orthopyroxene + biotite + clinopyroxene hornblende with opaques and minor zircon and apatite. An isotopic age of about 1200 million years for the Ardery charnockite has been established. The charnockite is prone to deep weathering and crumbles readily because of its mineral assemblage, whereas the metamorphic sequences of the northerly parts of the region have a much more stable mineral assemblage and crystalline structure. This difference has a significant influence on the distribution of vegetation in the Windmill Islands region with the northern rock types providing a more suitable substrate for slow growing lichens.

Soils on the islands are poorly developed and consist of little more than rock flour, moraine and eroded material. Some soils contain small amounts of organic matter derived from excreta and feathers from the seabirds.

Glaciation

The Windmill Islands region was glaciated during the Late Pleistocene. The southern region of the Windmill Islands was deglaciated by 8000 corr. yr B.P., and the northern region, including Bailey Peninsula deglaciated by 5500 corr. yr B.P. Isostatic uplift has occurred at a rate of between 0.5 and 0.6 m/100 yr, with the upper mean marine limit, featured as ice-pushed ridges, being observed at nearby Robinson Ridge at approximately 28.5 metres.

Climate

The climate of the Windmill Islands region is frigid-Antarctic. Conditions at Ardery Island and Odbert Island are probably similar to those of the Casey station area approximately 12 km to the north. Meteorological data for the period 1957 to 1983 from Casey station (altitude 32 m) on Bailey Peninsula show mean temperatures for the warmest and coldest months of 0.3 and -14.9°C, respectively, with extreme temperatures ranging from 9.2 to -41°C. Mean annual temperature for the period was –9.3°C.

The climate is dry with a mean annual snowfall of 195 mm year^{-1} (rainfall equivalent), precipitation as rain has been recorded in the summer. However, within the last 10 to 15 years the mean annual temperature has decreased to –9.1°C and the mean annual snowfall has increased to 230 mm year^{-1} (rainfall equivalent).

There is an annual average of 96 days with gale-force winds, which are predominantly easterly in direction, off the polar ice cap. Blizzards are frequent especially during winter. Snowfall is common during the winter, but the extremely strong winds scour the exposed areas. On most hill crests in the area snow gathers in the lee of rock outcrops and in depressions in the substratum. Further down the slopes snow forms deeper drifts.

Environmental domains analysis

Based on the Environmental Domains Analysis for Antarctica (Resolution 3(2008)) Ardery Island and Odbert Island are located within Environment L *Continental coastal-zone ice sheet.*

Biological Features

Terrestrial

The flora of Odbert Island consists of three moss species, eleven lichen species (Table 1) and an unknown number of terrestrial and freshwater algae. The most extensive development of lichens is towards the highest elevations of the southern parts of the island in an area of ice-fractured bedrock. The algae occur in tarns, soil seepage areas and soil. Stands of *Prasiola* and other green algae and cyanobacteria occur below snow drifts downslope from penguin colonies towards the western part of the island.

The flora of Ardery Island comprises several species of lichen similar to those found on Odbert Island.

The only recorded invertebrates are ectoparasites of birds. Ardery Island is the type locality for the Antarctic flea *Glaciopsyllus antarcticus*, associate with southern fulmars.

MOSSES

Bryum pseudotriquetrum Hedw.) Gaertn., Meyer & Scherb.
Ceratodon purpureus (Hedw.) Brid.
Schistidium antarcticum (= Grimmia antarctici) (Card.) L.I.Savicz & Smirnova

LICHENS

Buellia frigida (Darb.)
Buellia soredians Filson
Buellia sp.
Caloplaca athallina Darb.
Caloplaca citrina (Hoffm.) Th. Fr.
Candelariella flava (C.W.Dodge & Baker) Castello & Nimis
Rhizoplaca melanophthalma (Ram.) Leuck. et Poelt
Rinodina olivaceobrunnea Dodge & Baker
Umbilicaria decussata (Vill.) Zahlbr.
Xanthoria mawsonii Dodge.
Usnea antarctica Du Rietz

ALGAE

Prasiola crispa (Lightfoot) Kützing
Prasiococcus sp.

Table 1. List of mosses, lichens and algae recorded from Odbert Island.

Lakes

Cold monomictic lakes and ponds occur throughout the Windmill Islands region in bedrock depressions and are usually ice-free during January and February. Nutrient rich lakes are found near the coast in close proximity to penguin colonies or abandoned colonies. Sterile lakes are located further inland and are fed by melt water and local precipitation. On Ardery Island and Odbert Island there are a number of small tarns which are frozen in winter and filled with melt water in summer. Many of the tarns are ephemeral, drying out towards the end of summer. Other tarns located below snow banks are fed continuously by melt water.

Birds and seals

Odbert Island has breeding populations of Adélie penguins (*Pygoscelis adeliae*), Cape petrels (*Daption capensis*), snow petrels (*Pagodroma nivea*), southern fulmars (*Fulmarus glacialoides*), Wilson's storm petrels (*Oceanites oceanicus*), and south polar skuas (*Catharacta maccormicki*). Ardery Island supports a similar species composition, except for Adélie penguins. The southern giant petrel (*Macronectes giganteus*) which breeds on the Frazier Islands approximately 23 km to the north-west is the only species breeding in the Windmill Islands which breeds neither at Ardery Island nor at Odbert Island.

No seals inhabit Ardery Island and Odbert Island although Weddell seals (*Leptonychotes weddellii*) are frequently observed on the sea ice around them. The main pupping area is about 3 km to the south-east between Herring Island and the Antarctic mainland. In this area disturbance of the sea ice caused by movement of the Peterson Glacier ensures open water and easy access to food. About 100 pups are born annually in the region. Elephant seals (*Mirounga leonina*) haul out a little farther to the south on Petersen Island and on the Browning Peninsula. Up to 100 of these seals are seen annually with most being mature males. A few females have also been observed.

Adélie penguin (Pygoscelis adeliae)

Two large colonies of Adélie penguins are present on Odbert Island. In 1985, an estimated 5,000 -10,000 breeding pairs were present in the two colonies on the island. Egg laying usually commences before the middle of November, the first chicks hatch around mid-December, and juveniles start leaving the colony in early February. Although Adélie penguins regularly come ashore on Ardery Island, none nest there.

Southern fulmar (Fulmarus glacialoides)

The total population of southern fulmars in the Area is about 5000 breeding pairs. There are approximately 3000 occupied southern fulmar sites on Ardery Island; the largest colonies are located on the northern cliffs and around the eastern tip of the island. On Odbert Island, most of the 2000 sites are concentrated in two large colonies on Haun Bluff and in the central north.

Southern fulmars breed colonially on or near the cliffs and ravines. Nests are situated on small cliff ledges but also on large nearly flat terraces, some birds nest in the open, others in deep crevices or between loose rocks. First eggs appear in early December and most are laid within 10 days. Hatching commences in the third week of January and chicks fledge by mid-March.

Antarctic petrel (Thalassoica antarctica)

On Ardery Island, about 280 apparently occupied Antarctic petrel nest sites have been located. The largest colony, on the Northern Plateau, contains at least 150 sites in the main area and some 25 sites in smaller groups nearby. On Odbert Island, some 30 nests are located in a small area off the central northern cliffs. The total population has been estimated at just over 300 breeding pairs.

Most nests of Antarctic petrels are situated on plateau-like areas or gently sloping sections of steep cliffs on the Northern Plateau, and smaller colonies around Soucek Ravine. Nests are very close together; isolated nesting on small ledges appears to be avoided. In late November, the first Antarctic petrels return from their pre-laying exodus and a week later most birds have returned to lay their eggs. First hatchlings appear in the second week of January, fledging commences in late February to early March, and all chicks have left before the middle of March.

Cape petrel (Daption capense)

Approximately 600 Cape petrel sites have been located on Ardery Island, mostly in small colonies on the northern cliffs. Scattered nests are present on both sides of Snowie Mountain. There are approximately 100 to 200 nesting sites on Odbert Island mostly located around the fulmar colonies. The total population of the Cape petrel in the Area is about 750 breeding pairs.

Cape petrels prefer nesting sites sheltered by slightly overhanging rocks and substantial cover from the back and if possible the sides. Most nests are in less steep parts of cliffs or along the top edges of cliffs both in colonies and small scattered groups. After returning from the pre-laying exodus, eggs are laid in late November, and hatching commences in the second week of January. Most chicks have fledged by the first week of March.

Snow petrel (Pagodroma nivea)

The number of snow petrels in the Area is estimated at over 1,100 breeding pairs. Approximately 1000 snow petrel nesting sites were located on Ardery Island in 1990, mostly on the slopes of Snowie Mountain. Snow petrels appear to be less abundant on Odbert Island than on Ardery with 100 – 1000 nesting sites. In 2003, 752 active nests were found on Ardery Island and 824 on Odbert Island.

The snow petrels breed in crevices or in holes between loose rocks. Although the level of protection of nests varies considerably, these specific requirements prevent colonial nesting in many cases. Isolated nests may be found anywhere, and within colonies of other species. Suitable snow petrel habitat also harbours colonies of Wilson's storm petrels. The onset of egg laying varies between concentrations of nests, with laying occurring within the first three weeks of December, and chicks hatching from the middle of January onwards. All are fledged in the first two weeks of March.

Wilson's storm petrel (Oceanites oceanicus)

Wilson's storm petrels are widely distributed, and nest in all suitable rocky areas within the Area. Approximately 1000 nesting sites have been documented for Ardery Island. Odbert Island has 1000 – 2000 nesting sites, at a lower density than that of Ardery Island because of the general spread of suitable rock nesting areas.

Wilson's storm petrels breed in deep, narrow holes. First eggs are usually observed in the third week of December.

South polar skua (Catharacta maccormicki)

In 1984/85, ten pairs of south polar skua bred on Ardery Island and possibly three more pairs held territories. A similar number was present in 1986/87, although only seven pairs produced eggs. Odbert Island probably had between 10 and 20 pairs. The distribution of south polar skua nests on Ardery Island reflects their dependence on petrels. Most pairs have observation points close to petrel nests, from which they can observe their food territory on the bird cliffs. On Odbert Island most nests were near the penguin rookeries.

Nests are shallow hollows in gravel, either fully in the open on flat ground or slightly protected by surrounding rocks. Territories and nest locations appear to be stable from year to year; near a nest there are usually several depressions of previous nests. Egg laying dates vary considerably, though most are concentrated around late November to early December. The first chicks are observed in the last days of December, and juveniles begin to fly by mid February.

Non-breeding bird species

Emperor penguins (*Aptenodytes forsteri*) do not breed in the immediate Casey area but individual birds have been observed near Casey station and even far inland. A chinstrap penguin (*Pygoscelis antarctica*) was observed in January 1987 in the Adélie penguin rookery on Whitney Point, north of Casey. Southern giant petrels (*Macronectes giganteus*), both adults and immatures, are regular visitors to Ardery Island. In favourable winds they fly along the bird cliffs in search of food. An emaciated juvenile blue petrel (*Halobaena caerulea*) arrived at Casey in March 1987. In November 1984, an adult Dominican gull (*Larus dominicanus*) was sighted in the Casey area. Groups of terns, possibly Arctic tern (*Sterna paradisea*), have been observed in the Casey area in 1984/ 85 and in 1986/87, when a few groups of up to 100 birds were seen and heard high in the air in March.

6(ii) Access to the Area

Access to the Area is covered under section 7(ii) of this plan.

6(iii) Location of structures within or adjacent to the Area

There are no permanent structures within or adjacent to the Area.

6(iv) Location of other protected areas within close proximity

The following Protected Areas are located in the vicinity of Ardery Island and Odbert Island (see Map A):

- North-east Bailey Peninsula (66°17'S, 110°32'E) (ASPA No 135) approximately 12 km north of Ardery Island and Odbert Island;
- Clark Peninsula (66°15'S, 110°36'E) (ASPA No 136), approximately 16 km north of Ardery Island and Odbert Island;
- Frazier Islands (66°13'S 110°11'E) (ASPA No 160), approximately 23 km north-east of Ardery Island and Odbert Island.

6(v) Special zones within the Area

There are no special zones within the Area.

7. Permit conditions

7(i) General permit conditions

Entry into the Area is prohibited except in accordance with a permit issued by an appropriate national authority. Conditions for issuing a permit to enter the Area are that:

- it is issued only for compelling scientific reasons that cannot be served elsewhere, in particular for scientific study of the avifauna and ecosystem of the Area, or for essential management purposes consistent with plan objectives such as inspection, maintenance or review;

- the actions permitted will not jeopardise the values of the Area;

- the actions permitted are in accordance with the management plan;

- the permit, or an authorised copy, shall be carried within the Area;

- a visit report shall be supplied to the authority named in the permit;

- permits shall be issued for a stated period;

- the appropriate national authority shall be notified of any activities/measures undertaken that were not included in the authorised permit.

7(ii) Access to, and movement within or over the Area

Travel to the Area may be by vehicle over sea ice, by boat or by aircraft. Vehicles and boats used to visit the islands must be left at the shoreline. Movement within the area is by foot only.

Landing sites for access by sea and helicopter to Ardery Island and Odbert Island are shown on Map D. On Ardery Island, the preferred boat landing site is at Robertson Landing where there are three rock anchors present to tie down a boat or other equipment. The boat landing site marked for Ardery Island on Map D is within 200 metres of seabird colonies. However, it represents the preferred safe landing site on the island. All landings must be undertaken carefully to avoid disturbance to the birds. There are no defined pedestrian routes within the Area; however, pedestrians should avoid disturbance of the birds at all times.

If access to the islands is not possible by boat or by vehicle over sea ice, then fixed wing aircraft or helicopters may be used subject to the following conditions:

- disturbance of the colonies by aircraft shall be avoided at all times;

- sea ice landings shall be encouraged (where practicable);

- overflight of the islands should be avoided at all times, except where it is considered essential for scientific or management purposes as authorised in a permit. In these instances, overflight must be at a vertical or horizontal distance of no less than 930 metres (3050 feet) for single-engined aircraft and 1500 metres (5000 feet) for twin-engined aircraft;

- during the breeding season of penguins and petrels, defined here as the period from 1 November to 1 April, helicopter movement to the islands should be kept to the minimum;

- the use of twin-engined helicopters to land on Ardery Island or Odbert Island is prohibited;

- the single-engined helicopter approach to Ardery Island should be at a high altitude and from a southern direction as the lowest densities of birds are on the southern cliffs (see Maps B and D);

- the single-engined helicopter approach to Odbert Island should preferably be from the south, avoiding cliff areas because of the nesting petrels (see Maps C and D); and

- when utilising the single-engined helicopter landing sites marked on Map D, pilots shall ensure that disturbance of breeding colonies is avoided.

- only personnel who are required to carry out work in the Area should leave the helicopter;

- refuelling of aircraft is prohibited within the Area.

7(iii) Activities which are, or may be conducted within the Area

The following activities may be conducted within the Area as authorised in a permit;

- compelling scientific research consistent with the Management Plan for the Area which cannot be undertaken elsewhere and will not jeopardise the values for which the Area has been designated or the ecosystems of the Area;

- essential management activities, including monitoring; and

- sampling, which should be the minimum required for approved research programs.

7(iv) Installation, modification, or removal of structures

- No permanent structures are to be erected in the Area.

- Any structures erected or installed within the Area are to be specified in a permit.

- Scientific markers and equipment must be secured and maintained in good condition, clearly identifying the permitting country, name of principal investigator and year of installation. All such items should be made of materials that pose minimum risk of contamination of the Area.

- A condition of the permit shall be the removal of equipment associated with scientific research before the permit for that research expires. Details of markers and equipment temporarily left in situ (GPS locations, description, tags, etc. and expected "use by date") shall be reported to the permitting Authority.

- When permitted, the installation of a field hut on Ardery Island must take place before 1 November when the breeding season commences, and removal after 1 April when fledglings have departed. Installation and removal should be supported by vehicle over sea ice unless sea ice conditions prevent this.

7(v) Location of field camps

- Camping is prohibited on Odbert Island except in emergency.

- If required for field work, a hut may be erected on Ardery Island at the point specified on Map D. There are eight solid rock anchors available at this location. There is a refuge hut "Robinson Ridge Hut", on the mainland, located on Robinson Ridge (66°22.4'S 110°35.2'E), approximately 800 m west of Odbert Island.

7(vi) Restrictions on materials and organisms that may be brought into the Area

- No poultry products, including dried food containing egg powder, are to be taken into the Area.

- No depots of food or other supplies are to be left within the Area beyond the season for which they are required.

- No living animals, plant material or microorganisms shall be deliberately introduced into the Area and precautions shall be taken against accidental introductions.

- No herbicides or pesticides shall be brought into the Area. Any other chemicals, including radio-nuclides or stable isotopes, which may be introduced for scientific or management purposes specified in a permit, shall be removed from the Area at or before the conclusion of the activity for which the permit was granted.

- Fuel is not to be stored in the Area unless required for essential purposes connected with the activity for which the permit has been granted. Permanent fuel depots are not permitted.

- All material introduced shall be for a stated period only, shall be removed at or before the conclusion of that stated period, and shall be stored and handled so as to minimise the risk of environmental impact.

7(vii) Taking of or harmful interference with native flora and fauna

- Taking of or harmful interference with native flora and fauna is prohibited, except in accordance with a permit.

- Where taking or harmful interference with animals is involved this should, as a minimum standard, be in accordance with the *SCAR Code of Conduct for the Use of Animals for Scientific Purposes in Antarctica*.

- Ornithological research on the breeding birds present within the Area shall be limited to activities that are non-invasive and non-disruptive. Surveys shall have a high priority. If the capture of individuals is required, capture should occur at nests on the periphery of the Area if at all possible to reduce disturbance.

7(viii) Collection or removal of anything not brought into the Area by the permit holder

- Material may only be collected or removed from the Area as authorised in a permit and should be limited to the minimum necessary to meet scientific or management needs.

- Material of human origin likely to compromise the values of the Area, which was not brought into the Area by the permit holder or otherwise authorised, may be removed unless the impact of the removal is likely to be greater than leaving the material *in situ*. If such material is found, the appropriate Authority must be notified and approval obtained prior to removal.

7(ix) Disposal of waste

- All wastes, including human wastes, shall be removed from the Area.

7(x) Measures that may be necessary to continue to meet the aims of the management plan

- Permits may be granted to enter the Area to carry out biological monitoring and Area inspection activities, which may involve the collection of samples for analysis or review; the erection or maintenance of scientific equipment, structures, and signposts; or for other protective measures.

- Any specific sites of long-term monitoring shall be appropriately marked and a GPS position obtained for lodgement with the Antarctic Data Directory System through the appropriate National Authority.

- To help maintain the ecological and scientific values of the Area, visitors shall take special precautions against introductions. Of particular concern are pathogenic, microbial or vegetation introductions sourced from soils, flora and fauna at other Antarctic sites, including research stations, or from regions outside Antarctica. To minimise the risk of introductions, before entering the Area, visitors shall thoroughly clean footwear and any equipment, particularly sampling equipment and markers to be used in the Area.

7(xi) Requirement for reports

Parties should ensure that the principal permit holder for each permit submits to the appropriate National Authority a report on activities undertaken. Such reports should include, as appropriate, the information identified in the Visit Report form contained in Appendix 4 of the Guide to the Preparation of Management Plans for Antarctic Specially Protected Areas appended to Resolution 2 (1998). Parties should maintain a record of such activities and, in the Annual Exchange of Information, should provide summary descriptions of activities conducted by persons subject to their jurisdiction, which should be in sufficient detail to allow evaluation of the effectiveness of the Plan of Management. Parties should, wherever possible, deposit originals or copies of such original reports in a publicly accessible archive to maintain a record of usage, to be considered in any review of the Plan of Management and in organising the use of the Area. A copy of the report should be forwarded to the Party responsible for development of the Management Plan (Australia) to assist in management of the Area, and monitoring of bird populations. Additionally visit reports should provide detailed information on census data, locations of any new colonies or nests not previously recorded, a brief summary of research findings and copies of photographs taken of the Area.

7(xii) Emergency provision

Exceptions to restrictions outlined in the management plan are in emergency as specified in Article 11 of Annex V of the Protocol on Environmental Protection to the Antarctic Treaty (the Madrid Protocol).

8. Supporting documentation

Australian Antarctic Division. 2005. *Environmental Code of Conduct for Australian Field Activities*, Environmental Management and Audit Unit, Australian Antarctic Division.

Blight, D.F. & Oliver, R.L. 1977. The metamorphic geology of the Windmill Islands, Antarctica, a preliminary account. *Journal of the Geological Society of Australia* 22: 145-158.

Blight, D.F. & Oliver, R.L. 1982. Aspects of the history of the geological history of the Windmill Islands, Antarctica. In: *Antarctic Geoscience* (ed. C.C. Craddock), pp. 445-454, Madison: University of Wisconsin Press.

Cowan, A.N. 1979. Ornithological studies at Casey, Antarctica, 1977-1978. *Australian Bird Watcher*, 8:69.

Cowan, A.N. 1981. Size variation in the snow petrel. *Notornis* 28: 169-188.

Creuwels, J.C.S , van Frenker, J.A. 2001. Do two closely related petrel species have a different breeding strategy in Antarctica. *Proceedings of the VIIIth SCA International Biology Symposium*, 27 August-1 September 2001, Vrije Univesiteit, Amsterdam

Creuwels, J.C.S., Poncet S., Hodum, P.J, van Frenker, J.A. 2007. Distribution and abundance of the southern fulmars *Fulmarus glacialoides*, *Polar Biology* 30: 1083-1097.

Creuwels, J.C.S., van Frenenker, J.a., Doust, S.J., Beinssen A., Harding, B., Hentschel, O. 2008. Breeding strategies of Antarctic petrels *Thalassoica antarctica* and southern fulmars *Fulmarus glacialoides* in the high Antarctic and implications for reproductive success, *Ibis* 150: 160-171

Croxall, J.P., Steele, W.K., McInnes, S.J., Prince, P.A. 1995. Breeding distribution of the snow petrel *Pagodroma nivea*. *Marine Ornithology* 23: 69-99.

Filson, R.B. 1974. Studies on Antarctic lichens II: Lichens from the Windmill Islands, Wilkes Land. *Muelleria*, 3:9.

Goodwin, I.D. 1993. Holocene deglaciation, sea-level change, and the emergence of the Windmill Islands, Budd Coast, Antarctica. *Quaternary Research* 40: 70-80.

Horne, R. 1983. The distribution of penguin breeding colonies on the Australian Antarctic Territory, Heard Island, the McDonald Islands and Macquarie Island. *ANARE Research Notes* No. 9.

Jouventin, P., Weimerskirch, H. 1991. Changes in the population size and demography of southern seabirds: management implications. In: Perrins, C.M., Lebreton, J.-D. and Hirons, G.J.M. *Bird population studies: Relevance to conservation and management*. Oxford University Press: 297-314.

Keage, P. 1982. Location of Adélie penguin colonies, Windmill Islands. *Notornis*, 29, 340-341.

Luders, D.J. 1977. Behaviour of Antarctic petrels and Antarctic fulmars before laying. *Emu*, 77, 208.

McLeod, I.R. & Gregory, C.M. 1967. Geological investigations for along the Antarctic coast between longitudes 108°E and 166°E. Report of the Bureau for Mineral Resources, Geology and. Geophysics. Australia No. 78, pp. 30-31.

Melick, D.R., Hovenden. M.J., Seppelt, R.D. 1994. Phytogeography of bryophyte and lichen vegetation in the Windmill Islands, Wilkes Land, Continental Antarctica. *Vegetatio* 111: 71-87.

Murray, M.D., Orton, M.N. & Penny, R.L. 1972. Recoveries of silver-grey petrels banded on Ardery Island, Windmill Islands, Antarctica. *Australian Bird Bander* 10, 49-

Murray M.D., Luders D.J. 1990. Faunistic studies at the Windmill Islands, Wilkes Land, East Antarctica, 1959-80. *ANARE Research Notes* 73: 1-45.

Orton, M. R. 1963. A brief survey of the fauna of the Windmill Islands, Wilkes Land, Antarctica. *Emu*, 63, 14.

Paul, E., Stüwe, K., Teasdale, J., Worley, B. 1995. Structural and metamorphic geology of the Windmill Islands, east Antarctica: field evidence for repeated tectonothermal activity. *Australian Journal of Earth Sciences* 42: 453-469.

Phillpot, H.R. 1967. Selected surface climate data for Antarctic stations. Commonwealth of Australia: Bureau of Meteorology.

Robertson, R. 1961. Geology of the Windmill Islands, Antarctica. *IGY Bulletin* 43: 5-8.

Robertson , R. 1961. Preliminary report on the bedrock geology of the Windmill Islands. In: Reports on the Geological Observations 1956-60. IEY Glaciology Report No. 4, (IEY World Data Centre 4: Glaciology). New York, American Geographical Society.

Schwerdtfeger, W. 1970. The climate of the Antarctic. In: *Climate of polar regions* (ed. S. Orvig), pp. 253-355 Amsterdam: Elsevier.

Schwerdtfeger, W. 1984. Weather and climate of the Antarctic, 261 pp Amsterdam: Elsevier.

Smit, F.G.A.M. & Dunnet, G.M. 1962. A new genus and species of flea from Antarctica,(Siphonaptera: Ceratophyllidae). Pacific Insect4: 895-903.

van Franeker, J.A.; Bell, P.J.; Montague, T.L. 1990. Birds of Ardery and Odbert islands, Windmill Islands, Antarctica. Emu 90: 74-80.

van Franeker, J.A., Gavrilo, M., Mehlum, F., Veit, R.R., Woehler, E.J. 1999. Distribution and abundance of the Antarctic petrel. Waterbirds 22: 14-28.

Williams, I.S., Compston W., Collerson K.D., Arriens, P.A. & Lovering J.F. 1983. A Reassessment of the age of the Windmill metamorphics, Casey area. In: Antarctic Earth Science (ed. R.L. Oliver, P.R. James & J.B. Jago), pp. 73-76. Canberra: Australian Academy of Sciences.

Woehler E.J., Croxall J.P. 1997. The status and trends of Antarctic and subantarctic seabirds. *Marine Ornithology* 25: 43-66.

Woehler, E.J., Johnstone, G.W. 1991. Status and conservation of the seabirds of the Australian Antarctic Territory. In Croxall, J.P. (ed.) Seabird status and conservation: A Supplement. ICBP Technical Publication No. 11: 279-308.

Woehler, E.J., Slip, D.J., Robertson, L.M., Fullagar, P.J., Burton, H.R. 1991. The distribution, abundance and status of Adélie penguins *Pygoscelis adeliae* at the Windmill Islands, Wilkes Land, Antarctica. *Marine Ornithology* 19(1): 1-17.

Woehler, E.J., Cooper, J., Croxall, J.P., Fraser, W.R., Kooyman, G.L., Miller, G.D., Nel, D.C., Patterson, D.L., Peter, H-U, Ribic, C.A., Salwicka, K., Trivelpiece, W.Z., Wiemerskirch, H. 2001. *A Statistical Assessment of the Status and Trends of Antarctic and Subantarctic Seabirds.* SCAR/CCAMLR/NSF, 43pp.

Map A: Antarctic Specially Protected Area No 103, Ardery Island and Odbert Island, Budd Coast, Wikes Land, East Antarctica

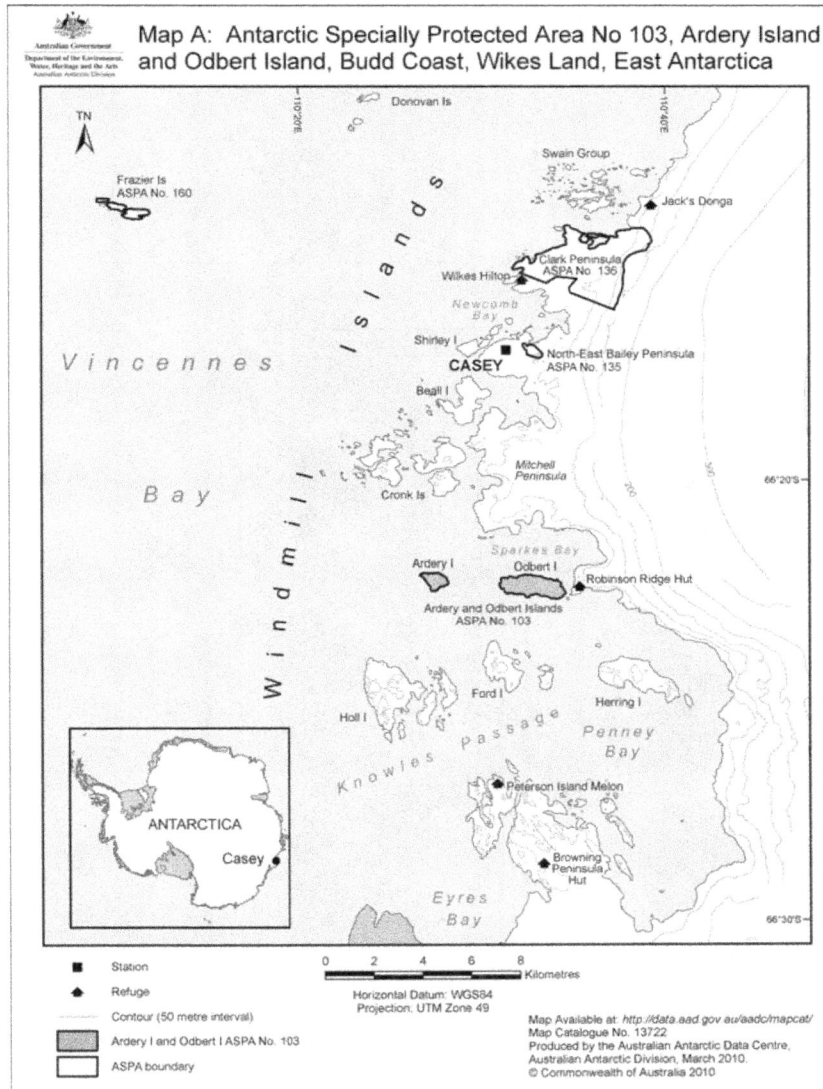

Map B: Antarctic Specially Protected Area No. 103
Ardery Island
Topography and Bird Distribution

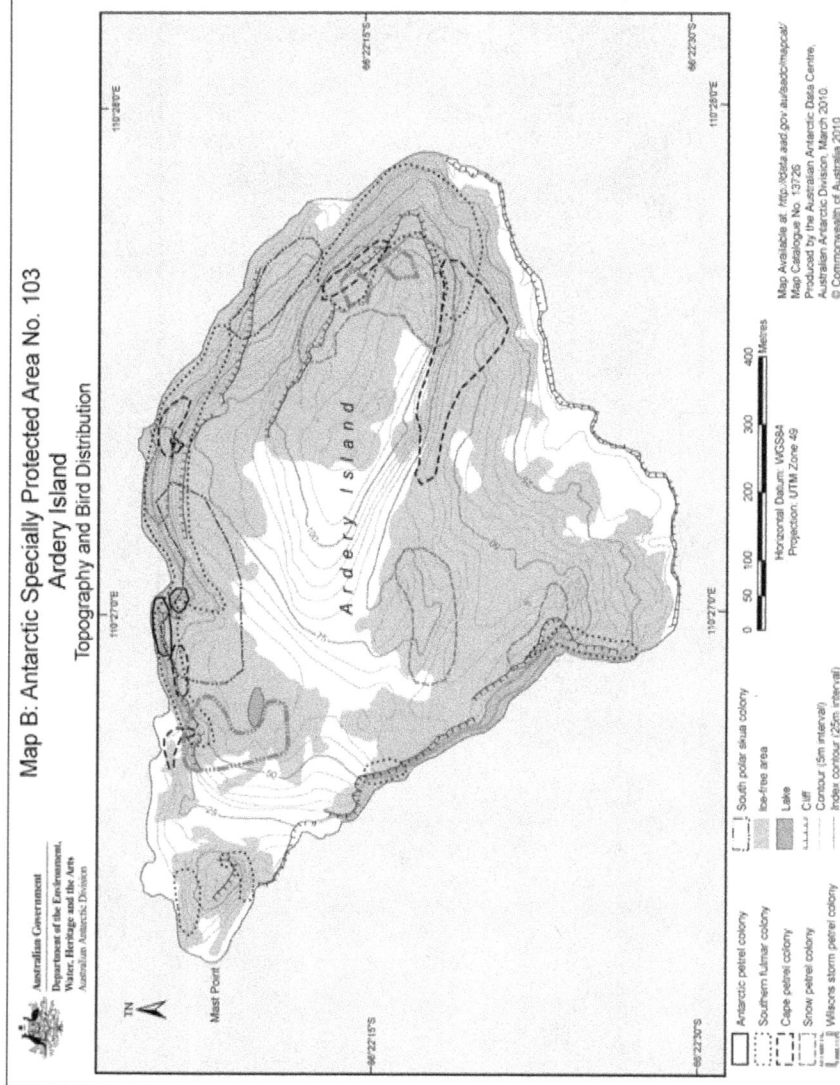

Australian Government
Department of the Environment,
Water, Heritage and the Arts
Australian Antarctic Division

TN

Mast Point

Ardery Island

Antarctic petrel colony
Southern fulmar colony
Cape petrel colony
Snow petrel colony
Wilsons storm petrel colony

South polar skua colony
Ice-free area
Lake
Cliff
Contour (5m interval)
Index contour (25m interval)

Horizontal Datum: WGS84
Projection: UTM Zone 49

0   50   100   200   300   400
Metres

Map Available at: http://data.aad.gov.au/aadc/mapcat/
Map Catalogue No. 13726
Produced by the Australian Antarctic Data Centre,
Australian Antarctic Division March 2010
© Commonwealth of Australia 2010

13

Australian Government
Department of the Environment,
Water, Heritage and the Arts
Australian Antarctic Division

Map C: Antarctic Specially Protected Area No. 103
Odbert Island
Topography and Bird Distribution

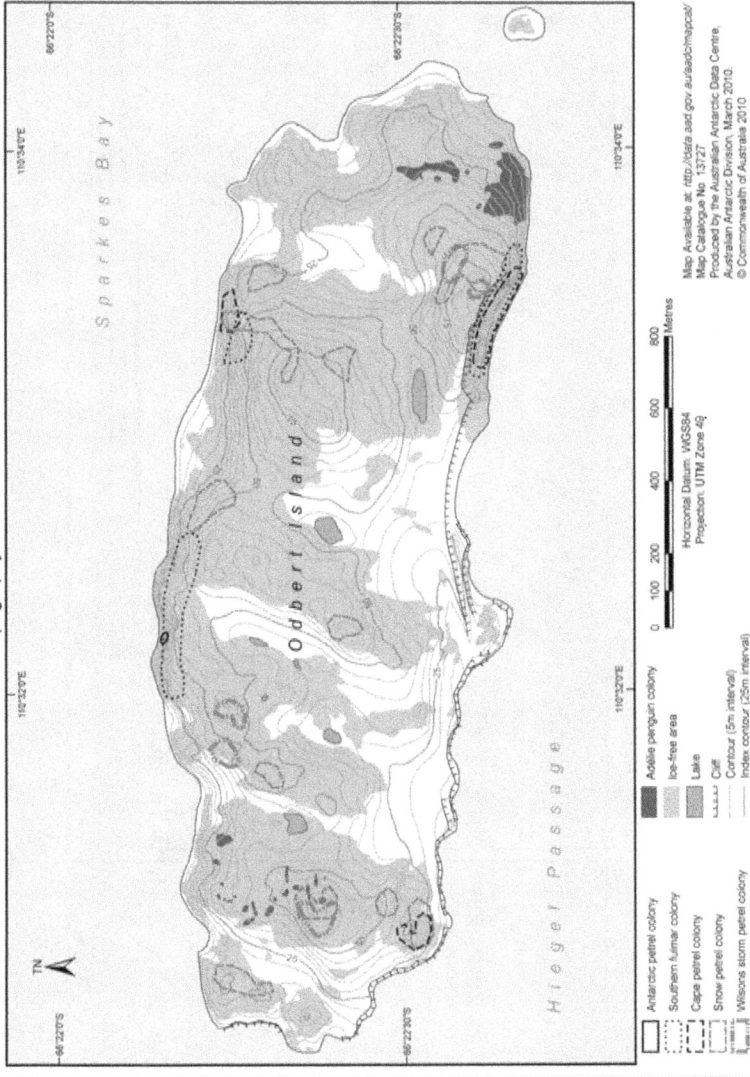

TN

Hieger Passage

Odbert Island

Sparkes Bay

66°22'0"S

110°32'0"E   110°34'0"E

66°22'30"S

66°22'0"S

66°22'30"S

Adélie penguin colony
Ice-free area
Lake
Cliff
Contour (5m interval)
Index contour (25m interval)

Antarctic petrel colony
Southern fulmar colony
Cape petrel colony
Snow petrel colony
Wilsons storm petrel colony

0   100   200   400   600   800   Metres

Horizontal Datum: WGS84
Projection: UTM Zone 49j

Map Available at: http://data.aad.gov.au/aadc/mapcat/
Map Catalogue No 13727
Produced by the Australian Antarctic Data Centre,
Australian Antarctic Division March 2010.
© Commonwealth of Australia 2010

14

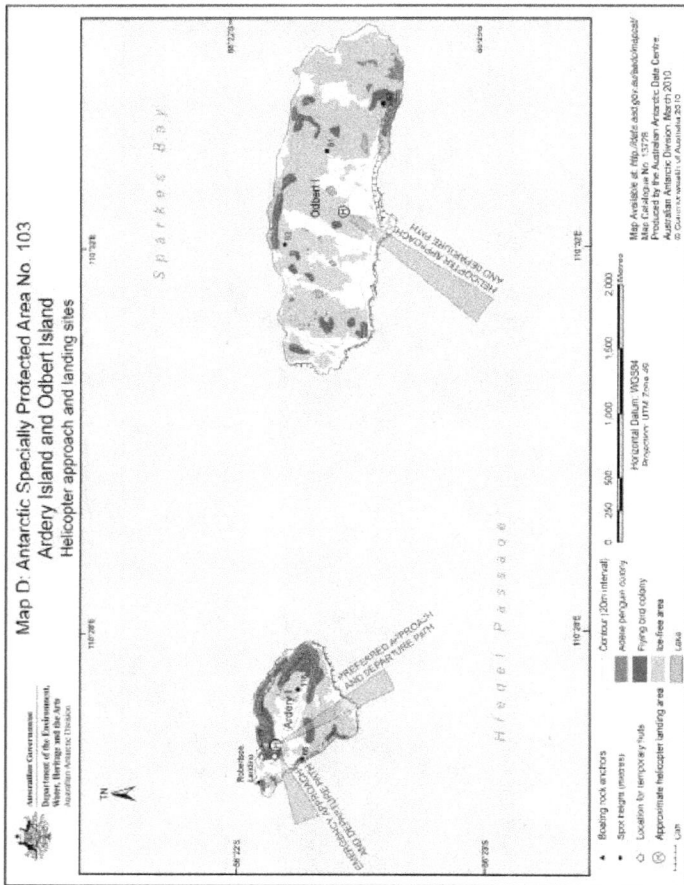

Map D: Antarctic Specially Protected Area No 103
Ardery Island and Odbert Island
Helicopter approach and landing sites

Management Plan For
Antarctic Specially Protected Area No. 105
BEAUFORT ISLAND, McMURDO SOUND, ROSS SEA

1. Description of Values to be Protected

Beaufort Island was originally designated as Specially Protected Area No. 5 in
Recommendation IV-5 (1966) on the grounds that it "contains substantial and varied
avifauna, that it is one of the most important breeding grounds in the region, and that it
should be protected to preserve the natural ecological system as a reference area." The Area
was re-designated by Decision 1 (2002) as Antarctic Specially Protected Area (ASPA) No.
105 and a revised Management Plan was adopted through Measure 2 (2003). The Area is an
island relatively untouched by human activity, set aside primarily to protect the ecological
values of the site from human interference.

Beaufort Island is the northern most feature of the Ross Archipelago, lying 19 kilometres
north of Cape Bird, Ross Island. It is a portion of the rim of a volcanic cone, the remainder of
which was eroded away and is now submerged to the east of the island. The island, and the
remains of the submerged caldera, block the predominantly westward drift of pack ice and ice
bergs calving from the nearby Ross Ice Shelf. Icebergs ground on these peaks which in turn
facilitate fast ice growth. Beaufort Island is predominantly rock but portions are ice and snow
covered. On the south west side of the island there is a broad ice-free shelf with raised
beaches behind which summer ponds form, fed by small meltwater streams draining to the
coast. Sloping ice fields (about 12° to 15°) cover much of the west and north side of the
island but the ice has been receding in recent years. An extensive flat area of less than 50 m
elevation is at the north end of the island, where the ice cap of the island drains to a boulder
beach, fringing that portion of the shore. Near vertical cliffs compose the eastern side of the
island facing the centre of the caldera.

The avifauna is the most varied in the southern Ross Sea. There exists a large Adélie penguin
(*Pygoscelis adeliae*) colony on the broad shelf of the southwest side of the island, and a
smaller newly formed subcolony, established in 1995, on the beach along the northwest coast.
The dating of Adélie penguin remains goes back 45,000 years. A breeding colony of Emperor
penguins (*Aptenodytes forsteri*) exists in variable locations on the fast ice to the north and
east of the island where grounded icebergs facilitate fast ice establishment. There is a dense
colony of South polar skua (*Catharacta maccormicki*) on both the north and south coasts and
Snow petrels (*Pagodroma nivea*) have been seen nesting in cavities on the cliffs at the south
of the island (no more than a half-dozen pairs). The boundaries of the Area, which previously
excluded the Emperor colony, have been extended to include the fast-ice that could
potentially be occupied by breeding birds. Weddell seals (*Leptonychotes weddellii*) haul out
and pup on the fast ice adjacent to the various grounded icebergs and Leopard seals (*Hydruga
leptonyx*) and Ross sea killer whales (Type C) but also the form known as Type B, occur in

the vicinity. The Ross sea killer whales are attracted by fish, and the Leopard seals and Type B killer whales are attracted by the penguins and seals. Crabeater seals (*Lobodon carcinophagus)*, Minke whales (*Balaenoptera acutorostrata*) and Arnoux's beaked whales (*Berardius arnuxii*) have also been seen in the surrounding waters.

As an isolated island difficult to access, most of the Area is known to have been visited only infrequently. Other than the penguins, Beaufort Island has not been comprehensively studied and is largely undisturbed by direct human activity. However, recent observations indicate that the snow and ice fields are receding. The ecological, scientific and aesthetic values derived from the isolation and relatively low levels of human impact are important reasons for special protection at Beaufort Island.

2. Aims and Objectives

The aim of the Management Plan is to provide protection for the Area and its features so that its values can be preserved. The objectives of the Management Plan are to:

- avoid degradation of, or substantial risk to, the values of the Area by preventing unnecessary human disturbance to the Area;
- preserve the natural ecosystem as a reference area largely undisturbed by direct human activities;
- allow scientific research on the natural ecosystems, plant communities, avifauna, invertebrate communities and soils in the Area provided it is for compelling reasons which cannot be served elsewhere;
- minimise human disturbance to these communities by preventing unnecessary sampling;
- minimise the possibility of introduction of alien plants, animals and microbes to the Area;
- allow visits for management purposes in support of the aims of the Management Plan.

3. Management Activities

The following management activities will be undertaken to protect the values of the Area:

- Copies of this Management Plan including maps of the Area, shall be made available at adjacent operational research/field stations.
- Markers, signs or structures erected within the Area for scientific or management purposes shall be secured and maintained in good condition, and removed when no longer necessary.

- Visits shall be made as necessary to assess whether the Area continues to serve the purposes for which it was designated and to ensure management and maintenance measures are adequate.
- National Antarctic Programmes operating in the region shall consult together with a view to ensuring these steps are carried out.

4. Period of Designation

Designated for an indefinite period.

5. Maps and Photographs

Map A: Beaufort Island topographic map. This map is derived from the orthophotograph used in Map B and C, using Map B and C specification. Inset: McMurdo Sound, showing Ross Island and the location of McMurdo Station (USA) and Scott Base (NZ).

Map B: Northern Beaufort Island orthophotograph. Orthophotograph specifications; Projection: Lambert Conformal Conic; Standard Parallel 1: 76.6°S; Standard Parallel 2: 79.3°S; Datum: WGS84; Includes material (c) METI and NASA 2006.

Map C: Southern Beaufort Island orthophotograph. Orthophotograph specifications as for Map B.

6. Description of the Area

6(i) Geographical coordinates, boundary markers and natural features
The designated Area encompasses the whole of Beaufort Island (76° 56'S, 166° 56'E) above the mean high water mark, and includes adjacent fast-ice occupied by breeding Emperor penguins (Map A). The coordinates include:

- From the northern coast of Beaufort Island at 76 ° 55' 44" S, 166° 52' 42" E north to 76° 55' 30" S, 166° 52' 49" E;
- From 76° 55' 30" S, 166° 52' 49" E east to 76° 55' 30" S, 167° 00' E;
- From 76° 55' 30" S, 167° 00' E south along the 167° longitude parallel to where it intersects with the coastline of Beaufort Island at 76° 55' 30"S, 167° E (Map A).

The island is part of the late Tertiary volcanic vents that developed in a series along a line of weakness in the Ross Sea floor. The island is the remains of a basaltic cone of about the Last Interglacial age, and is one portion of the caldera. More than three quarters of the cone now comprises a circular series of submerged peaks to the east of Beaufort Island. These submerged peaks, along with the island, block the predominant westward drift of pack ice and cause icebergs to ground here which in turn allows fast ice to establish in this area. It is upon this fast ice that the Emperor penguins breed. The location of the breeding colony varies with the fast ice distribution and therefore the protected area boundary has been extended to account for the location of the colony in any given season.

The geology of the island is typical of an eroded, sub-aerially produced basaltic complex, with lava flows and explosion breccias and tuffs evident. Many of the volcanic rocks have been intruded by a series of late stage basaltic dikes, and there is evidence of layered ash-fall tuffs and welded spatter flows from local subsidiary cinder and spatter cones. The island is roughly 7 km long and 3.2 km wide rising to a highest point of 771 m at Paton Peak. The west and northwest side of the island is predominantly an ice field with ice cliffs along the northwest edge of about 20 m on the coast, while the east and south sides of the island are largely ice-free, with almost vertical, inaccessible cliffs rising straight from the sea. On the south west shore is Cadwalader Beach which comprises a beach foreland and cuspate spit, backed by steep basaltic cliffs and several talus cones. A series of beach ridges, which are generally occupied by the breeding Adélie penguins, have trapped meltwater ponds and mark the growth of the beach face away from the cliffs with time and isostatic uplift. A series of raised beaches is evident at the northern side of the island, some with evidence (quills and guano) of former and apparently substantial penguin occupation (to 45,000 years). Sub-tidal (abrasion) platforms and massive boulders are found below the highly weathered southern cliffs. The eastern cliffs descend directly into the sea. Beaufort Island is relatively inaccessible by sea, except on the south and north shores, due to the steep cliff nature of the island and owing to the submerged peaks and grounded icebergs. Shipping, therefore, gives the island a wide berth. In view of the isolation of Beaufort Island and the current low levels of shipping activity in the region, boundary markers and signs have not been installed to mark the Area. The need for marking should be re-evaluated at each Management Plan review.

There is one main Adélie penguin colony and newly formed subcolony on Beaufort Island. The main colony of 48,276 breeding pairs (2006-07) occupies the flat area at Cadwalader Beach (Map A and C). The number of Adélie penguins breeding on Beaufort Island peaked at 53,733 pairs in 1986. Since then the population has ranged from 23,512 breeding pairs (in 1998) to 48,276 (in 2006). In 1995 a sub-colony established at the west end of the ice-free beach on the northern coast (76° 55' S, 166° 52'E) comprising 2 pairs with 3 chicks and approximately 10-15 non breeders. In the 2005-06 breeding season there were 525 breeding pairs and 677 breeding pairs in the 2008-09 season. Since 1996, scientists from the USA and NZ programmes have been banding a sample of 400 near-to-fledging Adélie penguin chicks at the Cadwalader Beach area. A few hundred banded adults, survivors of their juvenile years, now reside in the colony. Penguins banded at Cape Royds, Cape Bird and Cape Crozier have been sighted especially at the sub-colony on the north beach. Beaufort Island not long ago provided many emigrants to Ross Island colonies, but with recession of the ice fields and increased availability of nesting space, this is no longer the case. Above the beach, a raised ice-cored moraine terrace (5–20 m elevation, ranging from 2-3 metres wide over most of its length but broadening to 50 metres at its eastern end) extends for 550 m before rising more steeply toward the unstable basaltic cliffs which persist around the entire eastern side of the island. At least three sub-fossil penguin colony deposits have been identified within the moraine terrace, each layer vertically separated by around 50–100 cm of gravels and sand, suggesting this part of the island had been occupied by a sizable breeding penguin colony.

South polar skuas nest (roughly 150 pairs, but not specifically known) on the steep talus accumulating below the cliffs that rise behind the Adélie penguin colony at Cadwalader beach. Another population of approximately 50 pairs of skuas (1995 count) breed on the terrace and ice-free slopes on the northern shore. The proportion of breeders to non-breeders in this population is not known, but approximately 25 and 50 chicks were counted in January 1995 and 1997 respectively. Several snow petrels have also been seen in the cliffs above the Adélie colony at Cadwalader Beach.

On the fast-ice extending out from the northern and eastern coasts of Beaufort Island, a small colony of Emperor penguins (live chick counts from 1962 to 2005 range from 131 to 2,038 individuals; aerial photo of adult abundance was 1,312 in 2006) is present annually between the months of approximately April to January. Chick counts minimally represent the number of breeding pairs. The size of the colony is limited by the areal extent and condition of the fast-ice, which affects the availability of breeding sites in the lee of the northern slopes of Beaufort Island. The precise location of the colony varies from year to year and the colony moves within a breeding season, but the general area of occupation is on the fast ice at the foot of the cliffs off the north-eastern corner of the island, indicated on Map A and B. A higher coefficient of variation in chick abundance found at this small colony suggests that it occupies a marginal habitat and may be susceptible to environmental change.

The ice-cored moraine terrace above the beach on the north end of the island (Map A and B) supports the growth of vegetation. Little can grow in the thick guano covering the Cadwalader beach area and all other areas of the island are either cliffs or ice covered. An area of vegetation, 50 meters wide and 5-7 meters above the beach on the north of the island, was described from site visits in January 1995 and 1997, consisting of an extensive (approximately 2.5 ha), continuous area of a single moss species *Bryum argenteum*. A second species of moss, *Hennediella heimii*, is also found among the *B.argenteum*. The moss community is known to support significant populations of mites (Acari) and springtails (Collembola). Although a detailed survey of invertebrates has not been conducted, *Gomphiocephalus hodgsoni* (Collembola) and *Stereotydeus mollis* (Acari) were found to be very abundant in moss samples taken from Beaufort Island. Recent genetic analysis of these populations has found unique genetic mitochondrial DNA haplotypes at Beaufort Island not found in other invertebrate populations in the Ross Sea region.

A diverse community of algae, also prolific on the south-shore shelf, is found at this site and while a detailed algal survey has not yet been undertaken, several species of algae have been found including the red snow algae *Chlamydomonas sp.*, *Chloromonas sp.*, and *Chlamydomonas nivalis*, representing one of the most southerly locations where red snow algae have been observed and *Prasiola crispa* is particularly abundant at the north beach site. A number of unicellular chlorophytes and xanthophytes (including *Botrydiopsis* and *Pseudococcomyxa* species) and cyanobacteria (particularly scillatorians) were found mixed with *P. crispa*. Green snow algae, noticeable as a green band at the lower levels of snow banks above the beach and below the ice cliffs, contained a mixture of *Chloromonas* and *Klebsormidium* species.

6(ii) Restricted zones within the Area
None.

6(iii) Structures within and near the Area
The only structure known to exist on the island is a signpost on a prominent rock in the Adélie penguin colony at Cadwalader Beach (Map A and C). The sign, erected in 1959–60, bears the names and home towns of the seamen and the Captain of the HMNZS *Endeavour*. The sign is set in concrete and was in good condition in November 2008. The sign is of potential historic value and should remain *in situ* unless there are compelling reasons for its removal, which should be kept under review.

An astronomical survey station is recorded on a map of the island compiled in 1960, but it is unknown whether any associated permanent marker exists. The station is recorded as located at the south end of the main island ridge-line divide at an altitude of 549 m (Map C).

6(iv) Location of other protected areas within close proximity of the Area
The nearest protected area to Beaufort Island is New College Valley, Caughley Beach, Cape Bird (ASPA 116) located 35 km to the south at Cape Bird, Ross Island. Cape Royds and Backdoor Bay (ASPAs 121 and 157) are a further 35 km to the south on Ross Island. Cape Crozier (ASPA 124) is about 40 km to the east. (Refer to the inset: Map A).

7. Terms and Conditions for Entry Permits

Entry into the Area is prohibited except in accordance with a Permit issued by appropriate national authorities. Conditions for issuing a Permit to enter the Area are that:
- it is issued only for essential management purposes or compelling scientific reasons that cannot be served elsewhere;
- the actions permitted will not jeopardise the ecological or scientific values of the Area;
- any management activities are in support of the aims of the Management Plan;
- the actions permitted are in accordance with the Management Plan;

- the Permit, or an authorized copy, shall be carried within the Area;
- a visit report shall be supplied to the authority named in the Permit;
- Permits shall be issued for a stated period.

7(i) Access to and movement within the Area

Land vehicles are prohibited within the Area and access shall be by small boat or by aircraft. Aircraft should land on the island only at the designated site (166° 52' 31" E, 76° 55' 49" S: Maps A and B) on the large flat toe of ice on the north end of the island. Should snow conditions at the designated landing site at the time of visit militate against a safe aircraft landing, a suitable mid- to late-season alternative to the designated landing site may be found at the nominated northern camp site at the western end of the northern beach on Beaufort Island. It is preferred that aircraft approach and depart from the designated landing site from the south or west (Map A). When it is found necessary to use the alternative site at the northern beach campsite, practical considerations may dictate a northern approach. When this is the case, aircraft shall avoid over flight of the area east of this site indicated on Maps A and B. Use of smoke grenades when landing within the Area is prohibited unless absolutely necessary for safety and all grenades should be retrieved. There are no special restrictions on where access can be gained to the island by small boat. Pilots, air or boat crew, or other people on aircraft or boats, are prohibited from moving on foot beyond the immediate vicinity of the landing site unless specifically authorised by a Permit.

Over flight of bird breeding areas lower than 750 m (or 2500 ft) is normally prohibited. The areas where these special restrictions apply are shown on Maps A and B. When required for essential scientific or management purposes (e.g. aerial photography to assess colony size), transient over flights down to a minimum altitude of 300 m (1000 ft) may be allowed over these areas. Conduct of such over flights must be specifically authorised by a Permit.

Visitors should avoid unnecessary disturbance to birds, or walking on visible vegetation. Pedestrian traffic should be kept to the minimum consistent with the objectives of any permitted activities and every reasonable effort should be made to minimise effects.

7(ii) Activities that are or may be conducted in the Area, including restrictions on time or place

- Scientific research that will not jeopardise the ecosystem of the Area and which cannot be served elsewhere;
- Essential management activities, including monitoring.

7(iii) Installation, modification or removal of structures

No scientific equipment or structures are to be erected within the Area except as specified in a Permit. All markers, structures or scientific equipment installed in the Area must be approved by Permit and clearly identified by country, name of the principal investigator and year of installation. All such items should be made of materials that pose minimal risk of contamination of the Area. Removal of specific equipment for which the Permit has expired shall be a condition of the Permit.

7(iv) Location of field camps

Camping is permitted only at two designated sites (Maps A–C). The north camping site is located on the flat area north of the designated landing site, on a more sheltered location at the NW end of the beach, 200 m from where several pair of Adélie penguins and skuas nest (if present). The second site is located 100 m from the northern edge of the large Adélie penguin colony at Cadwalader Beach.

7(v) Restrictions on materials and organisms which can be brought into the Area

No living animals, plant material or microorganisms shall be deliberately introduced into the Area and the precautions listed in 7(ix) below shall be taken against accidental introductions. No herbicides or pesticides shall be brought into the Area. Any other chemicals, including radio-nuclides or stable isotopes, which may be introduced for scientific or management purposes specified in the Permit, shall be removed from the Area at or before the conclusion of the activity for which the Permit was granted. Fuel is not to be stored in the Area, unless required for essential purposes connected with the activity for which the Permit has been granted. All materials introduced shall be for a stated period only, shall be removed at or before the conclusion of that stated period, and shall be stored and handled so that risk of their introduction into the environment is minimised.

7(vi) Taking or harmful interference with native flora or fauna

Taking or interfering with native flora or fauna is prohibited, except in accordance with a Permit issued under Article 3 of Annex II by the appropriate national authority specifically for that purpose. Where animal taking or harmful interference is involved, this should, as a minimum standard, be in accordance with the *SCAR Code of Conduct for the Use of Animals for Scientific Purposes in Antarctica.*

7(vii) Collection or removal of anything not brought into the Area by the Permit holder

Material may be collected or removed from the Area only in accordance with a Permit and should be limited to the minimum necessary to meet scientific or management needs. Material of human origin likely to compromise the values of the Area, which was not brought into the Area by the Permit holder or otherwise authorised, may be removed unless the impact of removal is likely to be greater than leaving the material *in situ.* If this is the case the appropriate national authority should be notified.

7(viii) Disposal of waste

All wastes, including all human wastes, shall be removed from the Area.

7(ix) Measures that are necessary to ensure that the aims and objectives of the Management Plan can continue to be met

1. Permits may be granted to enter the Area to carry out biological monitoring and site inspection activities, which may involve the collection of small samples for analysis or review, or for protective measures.

2. Any specific sites of long-term monitoring shall be appropriately marked.

3. To help maintain the ecological and scientific values of the isolation and historically low level of human impact at Beaufort Island visitors shall take special precautions against introductions. Of particular concern are microbial or vegetation introductions sourced from soils at other Antarctic sites, including stations, or from regions outside Antarctica. Visitors shall take the following measures to minimise the risk of introductions:

a) Any sampling equipment or markers brought into the Area shall be sterilised and, to the maximum extent practicable, maintained in a sterile condition before being used within the Area. To the maximum extent practicable, footwear and other equipment used or brought into the Area (including backpacks, carry-bags, tent pegs, tarps and any other camping equipment) shall be thoroughly cleaned or sterilised and maintained in this condition before entering the Area;

b) Sterilisation should be by an acceptable method, such as by UV light, autoclave or by washing exposed surfaces in 70% ethanol solution in water.

7(x) Requirements for reports
Parties should ensure that the principal holder for each Permit issued, submit to the appropriate authority a report describing the activities undertaken. Such reports should include, as appropriate, the information identified in the Visit Report form suggested by SCAR. Parties should maintain a record of such activities and, in the Annual Exchange of Information, should provide summary descriptions of activities conducted by persons subject to their jurisdiction, which should be in sufficient detail to allow evaluation of the effectiveness of the Management Plan. Parties should, wherever possible, deposit originals or copies of such original reports in a publicly accessible archive to maintain a record of usage, to be used both in any review of the Management Plan and in organising the scientific use of the Area.

Bibliography

Ainley, D.G., Ballanrd, G., Barton, K.J., Karl, B.J., Rau, G.H., Ribic, C.A. and Wilson, P.R. 2003. Spatial and temporal variation of diet within a presumed metapopulation of Adélie penguins. *Condor*, 105, 95-106.

Barber-Meyer, S.M., Kooyman, G.L. and Ponganis, P.J. 2007. Estimating the relative abundance of emperor penguins at inaccessible colonies using satellite imagery. *Polar Biology*, 30, 1565-1570.

Barber-Meyer, S.M., Kooyman, G.L. and Ponganis, P.J. 2008. Trends in western Ross Sea emperor penguin chick abundances and their relationships to climate. *Antarctic Science*, 20 (1), 3-11.

Barry, J.P., Grebmeier, J.M., Smith, J. and Dunbar, R.B. 2003. Oceanographic versus seafloor-habitat control of ebnthic megafaunal communities in the S.W. Ross Sea, Antarctica. *Antarctic Research Series*, 76, 335-347.

Caughley, G. 1960. The Adélie penguins of Ross and Beaufort Islands. *Records of Dominion Museum*, 3 (4), 263-282.

Centro Ricera e Documetazione Polare, Rome, 1998. *Polar News*, 13 (2), 8-14.

Denton, G.H., Borns, H.W. Jr., Grosval's, M.G., Stuiver, M., Nichols, R.L. 1975. Glacial history of the Ross Sea. *Antarctic journal of the United States*, 10 (4), 160-164.

Emslie, S.D., Berkman, P.A., Ainley, D.G., Coats, L. and Polito, M. 2003. Late-Holocene initiation of ice-free ecosystems in the southern Ross Sea, Antarctica. *Marine Ecology Progress Series*, 262, 19-25.

Emslie, S.D., Coats, L., Licht, K. 2007. A 45,000 yr record of Adélie penguins and climate change in the Ross Sea, Antarctica. *Geology*, 35 (1), 61–64.

Harrington, H.J. 1958. Beaufort Island, remnant of Quaternary volcano in the Ross Sea, Antarctica. *New Zealand journal of geology and geophysics*, 1 (4), 595-603.

Kooymna, G.L., Ainley, D.G., Ballard, G. and Ponganis, P.J. 2007. Effects of giant icebergs on two emperor penguin colonies in the Ross Sea, Antarctica. *Antarctic Science* 19 (1), 31-38.

McGaughran, A., Torricelli, G., Carapelli, A., Frati, F., Stevens, M.I., Convey, P. and Hogg, I.D. 2009. Contrasting phylogenetic patterns for spring tails reflect different evolutionary histories between the Antarctic Peninsula and continental Antarctica. *Journal of Biogeography*, doi:10.1111/j.1365-2699.2009.02178.x

McGaughran, A., Hogg, I.D. and Stevens, M.I. 2008. Phylogeographic patterns for springtails and mites in southern Victoria Land, Antarctica suggests a Pleistocene and Holocene legacy of glacial refugia and range expansion. *Molecular Phylogenetics and Evolution,* 46, 606-618.

Schwaller, M.R. Olson, C.E. Jr., Ma, Z., Zhu, Z., Dahmer, P. 1989. Remote sensing analysis of Adélie penguin rookeries. *Remote sensing of environment*, 28, 199-206.

Seppelt, R.D., Green, T.G.A., Skotnicki, M.L. 1999. Notes on the flora, vertebrate fauna and biological significance of Beaufort Island, Ross Sea, Antarctica. *Polarforschung*, 66, 53-59.

Stevens, M.I. and Hogg, I.D. 2002. Expanded distributional records of Collembola and Acari in southern Victoira Land, Antarctica. *Pedobiologia,* 46, 485-495.

Stonehouse, B. 1966. Emperor penguin colony at Beaufort Island, Ross Sea, Antarctica. *Nature*, 210 (5039), 925-926.

Todd, F.S. 1980. Factors influencing Emperor Penguin mortality at Cape Crozier and Beaufort Island, Antarctica. *Biological Sciences*, 70 (1), 37-49

Map A - Beaufort Island, Antarctic Specially Protected Area 105: Topographic map

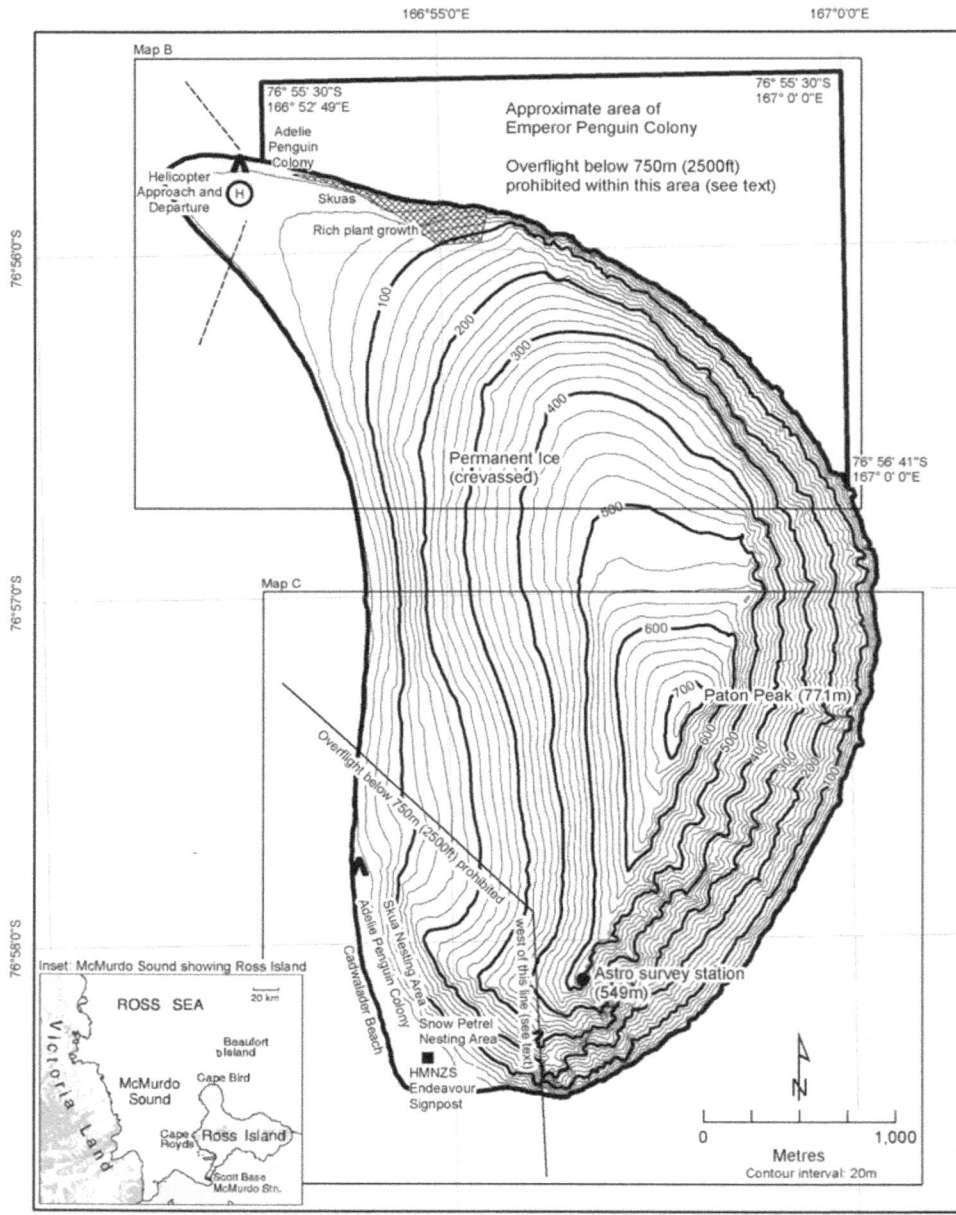

166°55'0"E

167°0'0"E

Map B

76° 55' 30"S
166° 52' 49"E

76° 55' 30"S
167° 0' 0"E

Adelie
Penguin
Colony

Approximate area of
Emperor Penguin Colony

Overflight below 750m (2500ft)
prohibited within this area (see text)

Helicopter
Approach and
Departure

Skuas

Rich plant growth

100

200

300

400

76° 56' 41"S
167° 0' 0"E

Permanent Ice
(crevassed)

500

Map C

600

700

Paton Peak (771m)

Overflight below 750m (2500ft) prohibited

west of this line (see text)

Adelie Penguin Colony

Skua Nesting Area

Cadwalader Beach

Astro survey station
(549m)

Snow Petrel
Nesting Area

HMNZS
Endeavour
Signpost

Inset: McMurdo Sound showing Ross Island

ROSS SEA

20 km

Beaufort
Island

Cape Bird

McMurdo
Sound

Cape
Royds

Ross Island

Scott Base
McMurdo Stn.

Victoria Land

0   1,000
Metres
Contour interval: 20m

Rich plant growth

H Designated helicopter pad

Protected area boundary
(includes fast ice occupied
by breeding Emperor penguins)

A Designated camp site

Projection: Lambert Conformal Conic
Standard Parallel 1: 76.6°S
Standard Parallel 2: 79.3°S
Datum: WGS84
Source: Beaufort Island Management Plan

76°56'0"S

76°57'0"S

76°58'0"S

Map B - North Beaufort Island, Antarctic Specially Protected Area 105: Site Orthophotograph

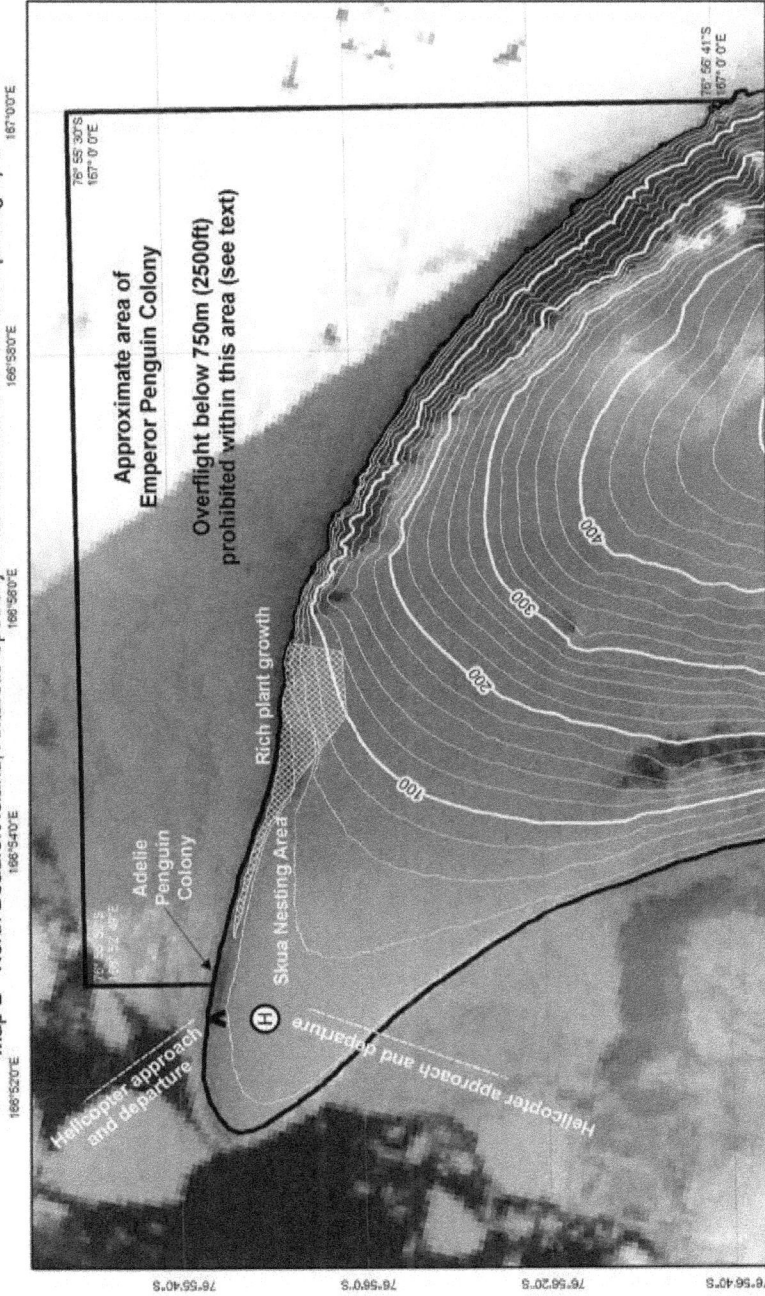

Approximate area of Emperor Penguin Colony

Overflight below 750m (2500ft) prohibited within this area (see text)

Rich plant growth

Adelie Penguin Colony

Skua Nesting Area

Helicopter approach and departure

Helicopter approach and departure

76° 55' 30"S
167° 0' 0"E

76° 55' 41"S
167° 0' 0"E

Imagery: 26 November 2006
Includes material (c) METI and NASA 2006
Projection: Lambert Conformal Conic
Standard Parallel 1: 76.6°S
Standard Parallel 2: 79.3°S

Datum: WGS84
Source: Beaufort Island Management Plan

▨ Rich plant growth

━ Protected area boundary
(includes fast ice occupied
by breeding Emperor penguins)

Ⓗ Designated helicopter pad

◄ Designated camp site

100
200
300
400

N

0   500
Metres
Contour interval: 20m

Map C - South Beaufort Island, Antarctic Specially Protected Area 105: Site Orthophotograph

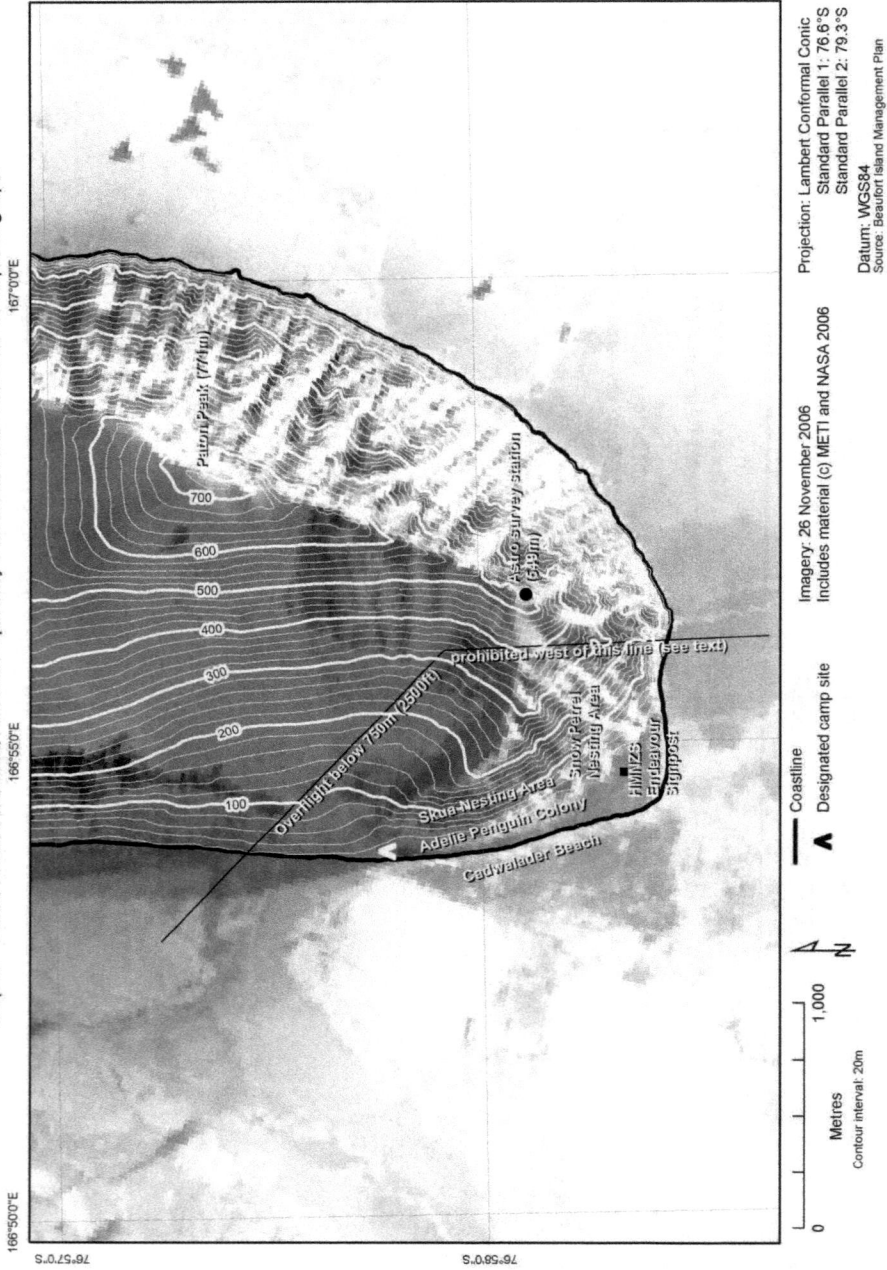

166°50'0"E

166°55'0"E

167°0'0"E

76°57'0"S

76°56'0"S

Patum Peak (744m)

700

600

500

400

300

200

100

prohibited west of this line (see text)

Astro Survey station (549m)

Overflight below 750m (2500ft)

Snow Petrel Nesting Area

Skua Nesting Area

Adelie Penguin Colony

Cadwalader Beach

HMNZS Endeavour Signpost

Coastline

Designated camp site

N

0   1,000

Metres

Contour interval: 20m

Projection: Lambert Conformal Conic
Standard Parallel 1: 76.6°S
Standard Parallel 2: 79.3°S

Datum: WGS84
Source: Beaufort Island Management Plan

Imagery: 26 November 2006
Includes material (c) METI and NASA 2006

Management Plan for

Antarctic Specially Protected Area (ASPA) No. 106

CAPE HALLETT, NORTHERN VICTORIA LAND, ROSS SEA

(170° 14' E, 72° 19' S)

Introduction

The Cape Hallett Antarctic Specially Protected Area is situated at the northern extremity of the Hallett Peninsula, northern Victoria Land at 170°13'25" E, 72°19'11" S. Approximate area: 0.53 km². The primary reason for designation of the Area is that it provides an outstanding example of biological diversity, in particular a rich and diverse terrestrial ecosystem. It includes a small area of particularly rich vegetation that represents a valuable scientific resource for monitoring of vegetation change in Antarctica. The Area contains the most diverse arthropod community known in the Ross Sea region, which is of scientific interest. Furthermore, the Area contains a substantial Adélie penguin (*Pygoscelis adeliae*) breeding colony comprising around 64,000 pairs in 2009-10, which is recolonizing the site of the former Hallett Station (NZ / US) and is therefore of particular scientific interest. Cape Hallett is the only protected area in northern Victoria Land designated on the grounds of its terrestrial ecosystem or which includes a substantial bird colony, providing an important representation of the ecosystem in this region of Antarctica. The Area was proposed by the United States of America and adopted through Recommendation IV-7 [1966, Specially Protected Area (SPA) No. 7]; boundaries were extended by Recommendation XIII-13 (1985); the Area was renamed and renumbered through Decision 1 (2002), and the boundaries were further extended through Measure 1 (2002) to include the Adélie penguin colony, increasing the size of the Area to 75 ha. A further adjustment of the boundary has been made in the present plan to delete the Managed Zone and replace this with two alternative sites outside of the protected area, to be managed by Antarctic Treaty Site Guidelines for Visitors. One of the sites identified for visitor access is on the northern / NW coast of Seabee Hook and the second is on the SE coast. In addition, a revision has been made to the eastern boundary to follow features apparent in recent mapping. The boundary revisions have reduced the size of the Area to 53 ha.

1. Description of values to be protected

An area of approximately 12 ha at Cape Hallett was originally designated in Recommendation IV-7 (1966, SPA No. 7) after a proposal by the United States of America on the grounds that the Area provided an outstanding example of biological diversity, containing "a small patch of particularly rich and diverse vegetation which supports a variety of terrestrial fauna". The proposal gave special mention to the rich avifauna in the Area, which was noted as being of "outstanding scientific interest". The boundaries of the Area were enlarged in Recommendation XIII-13 (1985) to include extensive stands of vegetation to the south and north of the Area, increasing the Area to approximately 32 ha. The boundaries were further extended in Measure 1 (2002) to include scientific values related to the Adélie penguin (*Pygoscelis adeliae*) colony on Seabee Hook, increasing the size of the Area to 75 ha. Boundary revisions and zoning changes in the present plan, particularly in the east, have reduced the size of the Area to 53 ha.

The eastern part of the Area contains a variety of habitats with plant communities that are considered important as they include most extensive, representative, and outstanding examples known near the northern extremity of the latitudinal gradient of Victoria Land and the Ross Sea. Vegetation surveys have recorded five species of moss in the Area, dominated by *Bryum subrotundifolium*, and 18 species of lichen. Although few algal species have been identified numerous species are expected to be present. The terrestrial habitats have been extensively studied, most recently as part of the international Latitudinal Gradient Project (LGP) (Italy, New Zealand, and United States). A vegetation plot in the eastern part of the Area is particularly valuable as a scientific resource for monitoring vegetation change in Antarctica, and this is designated a Restricted Zone. This site was first surveyed in detail in 1961-62 and provides a valuable baseline against which vegetation changes can be measured at a fine scale.

Detailed information on the distribution and abundance of arthropod species in the Area is available, which also represents a valuable scientific resource. In terms of species richness, Cape Hallett represents the most diverse arthropod community known in the Ross Sea region, with eight species of mites (Acari) and three of springtails (Collembola) identified within the Area. Of these, two (*Coccorhagidia gressitti* and *Eupodes wisei*) have their type localities at Cape Hallett.

A large number of markers were placed during early scientific studies conducted within the Area to mark sites of plant and bird studies. Many of these markers remain *in situ* and now represent a highly valuable resource for scientific studies that may wish to make repeat measurements.

Hallett Station was established by New Zealand and the United States on Seabee Hook in 1956 as part of the International Geophysical Year (IGY), and operated continuously until it closed in 1973. Although all structures have been removed, the site continues to possess enduring historic and heritage values relating to its former human use. In recognition of these values, many of the structures and artefacts from the former station are now held at the Canterbury Museum, Christchurch. In 2010, the only known remaining item of potential historical value and /or scientific value is the well-preserved body of a husky that died in 1964, which is contained in an enclosed wooden box located in the eastern part of the Area.

Adélie penguins have started to recolonize the site where the station was previously located. The history of human impact on the Adélie penguin colony and the subsequent station closure, together with the availability of reliable and repetitive historical data on Adélie population changes, make this site unique and ideal for scientific study of impacts on, and recovery of, the colony following substantial ecosystem disturbance. As such, the site has high scientific value, and in order to maintain this value it is desirable that any further human presence be carefully controlled and monitored.

In addition to the ecological and scientific values described, the Area possesses outstanding aesthetic values, with its combination of prolific biological resources and the impressive surrounding scenery of Edisto Inlet and Mt. Herschel (3335 m). Seabee Hook is one of only a few such sites that are relatively accessible in the northern Ross Sea. The site also has high educational value as an example of a station that was decommissioned and removed, with the site now showing evidence of recovery.

2. Aims and objectives

Management at Cape Hallett aims to:

- avoid degradation of, or substantial risk to, the values of the Area by preventing unnecessary human disturbance to the Area;
- allow scientific research, in particular on terrestrial and seabird ecology and on environmental recovery, while preventing unnecessary sampling and human disturbance in the Area;
- allow other scientific research provided it will not jeopardize the values of the Area;
- prevent the removal of, or disturbance to, markers used in previous scientific research that could be valuable for future comparative studies;
- allow environmental clean-up and remediation activities associated with the decommissioning and removal of the former Hallett Station as required and appropriate, provided the impacts of these activities are not greater than those arising from leaving material *in situ*;
- take into account the potential historic and heritage values of any artifacts before their removal and/or disposal, while allowing for appropriate clean-up and remediation;
- minimize the possibility of introduction of alien plants, animals and microbes into the Area; and
- allow visits for management purposes in support of the aims of the Management Plan.

3. Management activities

- Markers should be installed to identify areas requiring specific management activities, such as scientific monitoring sites;
- Markers, signs or structures erected within the Area for scientific or management purposes shall be secured and maintained in good condition, and removed when no longer necessary;
- National Antarctic programs operating in the Area should maintain a record of all new markers, signs and structures erected within the Area;
- To the extent practicable, efforts shall be made to remove any small waste debris still present within the Area following the removal of Hallett Station, although this shall be undertaken in consultation with an appropriate authority to ensure that potentially important historic or heritage values of any artifacts are not lost;
- Visits shall be made as necessary (preferably at least once every five years) to assess whether the Area continues to serve the purposes for which it was designated and to ensure that management and maintenance measures are adequate;
- National Antarctic programs operating in the region shall consult together for the purpose of ensuring that the above provisions are implemented.

4. Period of designation

Designated for an indefinite period.

5. Maps

Map 1: Cape Hallett Antarctic Specially Protected Area No. 106: Regional map.

Map specifications: Projection: Lambert Conformal Conic; Standard parallels: 1st 72° 20' S; 2nd 72° 30' S; Central Meridian: 170° 00'E; Latitude of Origin: 72° 00'S; Spheroid and horizontal datum: WGS84; Contour interval 200 m.

Map 2: Cape Hallett Antarctic Specially Protected Area No. 106: Air access guidance.

Map specifications: Projection: Lambert Conformal Conic; Standard parallels: 1st 72° 19' S; 2nd 72° 19' 30" S; Central Meridian: 170° 13' 30" E; Latitude of Origin: 72° 00' S; Spheroid: WGS84; Datum: USGS 'Fisher' geodetic station 1989-90: ITRF93 Coordinates 170° 12' 39.916" E, 72° 19' 06.7521" S;

Map 3: Cape Hallett Antarctic Specially Protected Area No. 106: Topographic map.

Specifications for Map 3 are the same as for Map 2. Contour interval 5 m: contours derived from a digital elevation model used to generate an orthophotograph at 1:2500 with a positional accuracy of ±1 m (horizontal) and ±2 m (vertical) with an on-ground pixel resolution of 0.25 m.

Map 4: Cape Hallett Antarctic Specially Protected Area No. 106: Former Hallett Station area.

Specifications for Map 4 are the same as for Map 2.

6. Description of the Area

6(i) Geographical coordinates, boundary markers and natural features

Boundaries and coordinates

Cape Hallett is located at the southern end of Moubray Bay, Northern Victoria Land, in the western Ross Sea (Map 1). The protected area occupies most of the ice-free ground of a cuspate spit of low elevation known as Seabee Hook and includes the adjacent western slopes of the northern extremity of Hallett Peninsula, extending east of Willett Cove to the margin of the permanent glaciers (Maps 1 – 3).

The northern boundary of the Area extends along the northern coast of Seabee Hook from 170° 14' 25.5"E, 72° 19' 05.0"S to the eastern limit of the Adélie colony at 170° 14' 19.3" E, 72° 19' 04.9" S (Map 3). The boundary then follows the edge of the nesting area of the Adélie colony (as defined in 2009), maintaining a distance of at least 5 m from the colony, extending to the coordinate 170° 12' 25.3" E, 72° 19' 07.9" S (Map 4).

From 170° 12' 25.3" E, 72° 19' 07.9" S the boundary extends 33 m due west to the coast at 170° 12' 21.8" E, 72° 19' 07.9" S (Map 4). From this coastal position, the boundary of the Area continues southward to follow the western and southern coastline of Seabee Hook to the position 170° 12' 54.3" E, 72° 19' 19.1" S, which is near the southeastern extremity of the spit (Map 3). From this location the boundary extends northward, following around the edge of the nesting area, maintaining a distance of at least 5 m from the colony, in the southeastern part of Seabee Hook to the position 170° 12' 58.7" E, 72° 19' 15.3" S (Map 3). From this coastal position, the boundary of the Area continues northward to follow the low water shoreline along the eastern coast of Seabee Hook, and then follows the low water coastline around Willett Cove to the southern boundary at 170° 13' 24.9" E, 72° 19' 28.0" S (Map 3).

From 170° 13' 24.9" E, 72° 19' 28.0" S the boundary extends eastward to the Bornmann Glacier, following a seasonal stream which descends from the glacier. The eastern boundary of the Area then follows the glacier and permanent ice margin northward at elevations approximately between 120 – 150 m, crossing the steep western slopes of Hallett Peninsula and following the upper outcrops of a series of rocky ridges dissecting the slope. The boundary then descends to join the northern coastline of Seabee Hook at the base of a rock buttress at 170° 14' 25.5" E, 72° 19' 05.0" S (Map 3).

Climate

Seabee Hook is surrounded by sea ice for approximately eight months of the year. Sea ice usually breaks out annually, beginning in late December to early January, and re-forms in early March. Summer temperatures range from 4°C to -8°C, with a mean annual temperature of -15.3°C, and winds are predominantly from the south. Precipitation in the form of snow is common during the summer, with annual precipitation approximately 18.3 cm of water equivalent.

Geology, geomorphology and soils

The topography of the Area comprises the large flat area of the spit and adjoining steep scree forming part of the western slopes of northern Hallett Peninsula. Seabee Hook is composed of coarse volcanic material deposited in a series of beach ridges, with gently undulating terrain of hummocks and depressions and a number of level areas. Many of the depressions contain melt water in the summer, and are colonized by dense mats of algae. In the northeastern part of the Area a small meltwater stream flows from the western slopes of the Hallett Peninsula down to Willett Cove. There is higher moisture availability in soils at Cape Hallett compared to sites in Southern Victoria Land. Sub-surface soils are typically saturated after snowfall, with groundwater at between 8 and 80 cm below the soil surface during summer.

Vegetation

In wetter parts of the Area, the algal component is comprised mainly of the sheet-like green alga *Prasiola crispa* and *Protococcus* sp., with associated filamentous and blue-green forms (*Ulothrix* sp.) and cyanobacteria (e.g. *Nostoc*). It is expected that a number of other algal species may be present, but few have been identified.

The vegetation within the Area, with the exception of algae such as *Prasiola*, is largely confined to the ice-free ground not occupied by breeding Adélie penguins, which is to the east of Willett Cove and south of 72° 19' 10" S. This area includes a 100-200 m strip of relatively level ground adjacent to Willett Cove and steeper slopes up to the crest of the Hallett Peninsula ridge. The strip of flat ground comprises a number of dry, gravel hummocks up to 1.5 m high, many of which are occupied by nesting skuas, and in the northern part old guano deposits indicate former occupation by Adélie penguins. Small patches of moss and algae may be found at the base of these hummocks but the upper parts are devoid of vegetation. Substantial beds of moss colonize stable gravel flats in the north part of the flat ground where there is a high water table, while scattered patches of moss, algae and lichen occur on coarser, more angular, loose rocks in the south. The moss becomes more sparse as the ground slopes upwards, with the notable exception of a particularly dense and extensive patch covering approximately 3900 m² with almost complete coverage of the substratum occupying a shallow valley on a scree slope in the south of the Area (Map 3). Only the most prolific areas are illustrated on Map 3.

Bryum subrotundifolium is the dominant moss within the Area. The presence of *Bryum subrotundifolium* in such a bird enriched area, makes the Area an excellent example of a bird affected vegetation site. Also, the presence of almost mono-specific stands of *Bryum pseudotriquetrum* at the site is unusual for the region.

The steep scree slope adjoining the largely flat area is dissected by shallow gullies and small ridges, with a number of prominent rock outcrops. These rock outcrops, particularly in the north of the Area, support large stands of lichens and scattered moss, with cover of 70 – 100% in many places. Table 1 lists moss and lichen species recorded within the Area.

Table 1: Moss, lichen and invertebrate species recorded within ASPA No. 106, Cape Hallett

Mosses [a]	Lichens [a]	Invertebrates [b]
Bryum subrotundifolium (formerly *Bryum argenteum*)	*Acarospora gwynnii*	**Mites**
	Amandinea petermannii	*Coccorhagidia gressittii*
Bryum pseudotriquetrum	*Buellia frigida*	*Eupodes wisei*
	Caloplaca athallina	*Maudheimia petronia*
Ceratodon purpureus	*Caloplaca citrina*	*Nanorchestes* sp.,
Grimmia sp *Sarconeurum glaciale*	*Candelaria murrayi*	*Stereotydeus belli*
	Candelariella flava	*S. puncatus*
	Lecanora chrysoleuca	*Tydeus setsukoae*
	Lecanora expectans	*T. wadei*
	Lecidea cancriformis	
	Physcia caesia	**Springtails**
	Pleopsidium chlorophanum	*Cryptopygus cisantarcticus*
	Rhizocarpon geographicum	*Friesea grisea*
	Rhizoplaca chrysoleuca	*Desoria klovstadi* (formerly
	Rhizoplaca melanophthalma	*Isotoma klovstadi*)
	Usnea sphacelata	
	Xanthoria elegans	
	Xanthoria mawsonii	

Sources:
a T.G.A. Green, University of Waikato, New Zealand and R. Seppelt, Australian Antarctic Division, 2002; b Sinclair *et al.* (2006).

Eight species of mites and three species of springtails have been recorded from within the Area (Table 1) (Sinclair *et al.* 2006). *F. grisea* occurs mainly on the scree slopes and adjacent level areas, *C. cisantarcticus* was reported to be associated with moss, occurring plentifully on level ground, while *D. klovstadi* was abundant under stones on the slopes.

Birds

Seabee Hook is the site of one of the largest Adélie penguin colonies in the Ross Sea region, numbering approximately 64,041 breeding pairs in 2009-10. Seabee Hook is also the site of the former Hallett Station, a joint United States and New Zealand station that was open from 1956-73. During operation the station and associated infrastructure occupied an area of 4.6 ha on land that had formerly been occupied by breeding Adélie penguins. Establishment of Hallett Station in 1956 required eviction of 7580 penguins, including 3318 chicks, in order to clear the 0.83 ha required for bulldozing and erection of buildings. The colony was subjected to substantial impacts from the establishment and operation of Hallett Station, and declined from 62,900 pairs in 1959 to a low of 37,000 pairs in 1968, although increased again to 50,156 by 1972. Fluctuations in populations may have been exacerbated by changes in sea ice cover documented for the entire region. By 1987, after the closure of the station in 1973, the colony had increased to near its 1959 population; however, few areas modified by humans had by that time been fully recolonized. The area formerly occupied by the station has now been partly recolonized, although numbers were estimated at 39,014 breeding pairs in 1998-99, and an aerial census in 2006-07 (conducted as part of a long-term program) recorded only 19,744 breeding pairs (Lyver and Barton 2008, unpublished data). Using a combination of ground counts and aerial and ground photography data gathered 26 November – 3 December 2009, the Adélie colony had recovered to around 64,041 breeding pairs, which is close to the numbers recorded on Seabee Hook around the time Hallett Station was built.

South Polar skuas (*Catharacta maccormicki*) breed within the Area. The population declined from 181 breeding pairs in 1960-61 to 98 breeding birds recorded in both 1968-69 and 1971-72. In January 1983 there was a population of 247 birds (84 breeding pairs and 79 non-breeding birds). A survey conducted between 27 November – 02 December 2009 recorded 14 breeding pairs and 66 individuals on Seabee Hook. An additional 23 breeding pairs and 92 individuals were counted in the area east of Willett Cove, giving a total of 37 breeding pairs and 158 individuals, and a grand total of 232 birds in 2009-10. Approximately 250 skua nest sites are marked and numbered within the Area; markers should not be disturbed or removed.

Emperor penguins (*Aptenodytes forsteri*) have been recorded in the vicinity in late December, and solitary Chinstrap penguins (*Pygoscelis antarctica*) have been recorded in late January and February. Wilson's Storm petrels (*Oceanites oceanicus*) and Snow petrels (*Pagodroma nivea*) breed close to Cape Hallett across Edisto Inlet; numerous Snow petrels were observed around the cliffs of Cape Hallett in December 2009, suggesting they may breed in this area. Southern Giant petrels (*Macronectes giganteus*) have been sighted frequently in the vicinity of the Area, although numbers have dropped in recent years, possibly due to declining populations further to the north. Weddell seals (*Leptonychotes weddellii*) are commonly seen; these seals breed in Edisto Inlet, and have been recorded ashore on Seabee Hook. Other mammals commonly seen offshore include Leopard seals (*Leptonyx hydrurga*) and Minke whales (*Balaenoptera acutorostrata*).

Human activities and impact

Hallett Station was established by New Zealand and the United States on Seabee Hook in December 1956 as part of the IGY. The base operated continuously until its closure in February 1973 and supported a range of activities including the 1967-68 Mt. Herschel expedition led by Sir Edmund Hilary. Station construction had significant impacts on the environment, with almost 8000 Adélie penguins removed from the site. Beginning in 1984, the station was progressively cleaned up, and a joint NZ / US multi-year remediation plan for the station and surrounding area was formulated in 2001. Remediation continued in 2003-04 and 2004-05, when most remaining structures were demolished and removed, and the last remaining substantial items were removed at the end of January 2010. Many of the buildings and artefacts from the former Hallett Station are now held at the Canterbury Museum, Christchurch.

Some material associated with the former station still remains dispersed throughout the Area, including small pieces of wood and metal, wire, and metal drums, much of which is firmly embedded in the ground. In addition, the well-preserved body of a husky that died in 1964 remains contained within an enclosed wooden box covered by rocks in the east of the Area (Map 3).

As part of the clean up operation, mounds were constructed within the old station footprint to encourage Adélie penguin recolonization, and substantial parts of these areas have now been occupied (Map 4). The history of human impact on the Adélie colony and its subsequent recovery make the site of high scientific value for research into the impacts on and recovery of the colony following significant ecosystem disturbance.

6(ii) Access to the Area

Access to the Area may be made by air, from the sea or by pedestrians over sea ice. Break out of sea ice at Cape Hallett usually begins between late December and early January and sea ice generally reforms in early March. Areas of sea ice that are potentially more stable and better suited to aircraft landing may be found at sites southwest of Seabee Hook in the enclosure of Edisto Inlet. However, sea ice within Edisto Inlet can break out rapidly, even early in the season, so care is needed.

The breeding season for Adélie penguins and skuas within the Area is between October and March. During this period and when suitable sea ice is present, fixed wing aircraft may land at any site outside of the 1/2 nautical mile (~930 m) guideline distance described in Section 7(i) and shown on Map 2. When landings beyond 1/2 nautical mile are unsafe or impractical, fixed wing landings may be made at any site beyond 1/4 nautical mile (~460m) of the Adélie colony on Seabee Hook. Access to the Area from fixed wing landing locations may be by helicopter or on foot over sea ice.

Helicopters may land at any site outside of the 1/2 nautical mile (~930m) guideline distance, except when such landings are unsafe or impractical, in which case the designated helicopter landing site within the Area in Willett Cove at 170° 13.579' E, 72° 19.228' S may be used. Helicopter access to the designated landing site should be from the south and follow the eastern coastline of Willett Cove (Map 2). Occasionally the designated helicopter landing site at Willett Cove may be susceptible to inundation by high tides.

When access to the Area is made from the sea, small boats may land anywhere within the Area, although small boat landings with the purpose of camping should be made to Willett Cove. Strong currents and eddies have been reported on the seaward margins of Seabee Hook, which may prove difficult for small boat landings. Ocean conditions are generally calmer in Willett Cove and in the lee of Seabee Hook.

Access to the Area on foot may be made over sea ice.

6(iii) Restricted and managed zones within the Area

Restricted Zone

A small zone directly below the scree slopes in the northeast of the Area is designated a Restricted Zone in order to preserve part of the Area as a reference site for future comparative vegetation studies. The remainder of the Area is more generally available for research programs and sample collection.

A vegetation study plot of approximately 28 m by 120 m was mapped in detail by Rudolph (1963), which was relocated and re-mapped by Brabyn *et al.* (2006) to provide a quantification of vegetation change at the site over a 42-year period. This site established by Rudolph represents an extremely valuable resource for monitoring vegetation change. Markers used in both studies remain *in situ* and define the extent of the vegetation monitoring plot. The NE corner of the monitoring plot is indicated by a large boulder with a cairn built on top, located at 170°14'2.55" E 72°19'11.37" S. Detailed descriptions of the plot are given in Rudolph (1963) and Brabyn *et al.* (2006). Rudolph also photographed stones colonized by lichens, which Brabyn *et al.* (2006) re-photographed to measure lichen growth rates. One of these sites (shown on Map 3) is within the Restricted Zone and should not be disturbed.

The Restricted Zone provides a buffer around the monitoring plot of 20 m on the NW side and 10 m on the other three sides, making a rectangle of 58 m in width and 140 m in length. The corner coordinates of the Restricted Zone are defined in Table 2. A series of cairns has been constructed (on existing rocks where possible) to indicate the extent of the Restricted Zone (Map 3).

Table 2. Restricted Zone corner coordinates

Corner	Latitude (S)	Longitude (E)
Northeast	72°19'11.219"	170°14'4.012"
Northwest	72°19'10.43"	170°13'58.341"
Southwest	72°19'14.479"	170°13'51.901"
Southeast	72°19'15.299"	170°13'57.338"

Access to the Restricted Zone is allowed only for compelling reasons that cannot be served elsewhere in the Area.

6(iv) Structures within and near the Area

Hallett Station was established on Seabee Hook in December 1956 and closed in February 1973. By 1960 the buildings of Hallett Station occupied 1.8 ha and the associated roads, refuse dumps, fuel caches and radio aerials a further 2.8 ha. The station was occupied year-round until 1964, from when summer-only operation continued until closure. The station was progressively dismantled after 1984 and in 1996 only six structures, including a large 378,500 liter (100,000 gallon) fuel tank remained. Liquid fuel remaining in the large fuel tank was removed in February 1996. Further clean-up work was undertaken in 2003-04 and 2004-05, to remove all remaining structures including the fuel tank, and to remove contaminated soil from the area. All remaining substantial items were removed from the Area on 30-31 January 2010.

Two Automatic Weather Stations (AWS) operated by the United States (McMurdo Dry Valleys Long Term Ecological Research) and New Zealand (National Institute of Water and Atmospheric Research) are located 10 m apart approximately 50 m north of the designated campsite (Map 3). New Zealand maintains a bunded fuel cache of several drums approximately 50 m south of the designated campsite. An enclosed box containing the remains of a husky dog that died in 1964 is located near a large rock in the eastern part of the Area, covered by loose rocks (Map 3).

The USGS geodetic station 'FISHER' (Maps 3 & 4) consists of a standard USGS Antarctic brass tablet stamped with "FISHER 1989-90" and is set flush on the top of a large concrete block (2x1x1 m) at an elevation of 2.15 m. The benchmark is located approximately 80 m south of the emergency cache and 140 m inland from the NW coast of Seabee Hook. Following recolonization of the old station area, the benchmark now lies within a small Adélie subcolony, and is therefore likely to be surrounded by breeding birds during the summer. An emergency cache, comprising a large box (~1.5 m square and 1 m in height) painted bright red on top with smaller box alongside, is located on the site of the former station (Map 4).

Markers from a number of scientific studies are present within the Area, including those delineating the vegetation monitoring plot within the Restricted Zone. It should be noted that not all historical markers have been documented.

6(v) Location of other protected areas within close proximity of the Area

The nearest protected areas to Cape Hallett are Cape Adare (ASPA No.159) 115 km to the north, and Mt. Melbourne (ASPA No.118) and Edmonson Point (ASPA No.165), both approximately 240 km to the south.

7. Permit conditions

Entry into the Area is prohibited except in accordance with a permit issued by an appropriate national authority. Conditions for issuing a permit to enter the Area are that:

- it is issued only for scientific purposes, or for educational purposes that cannot be served elsewhere, or for essential management purposes consistent with plan objectives such as assessment or remediation of impacts, inspection, maintenance or review;
- the actions permitted will not jeopardize the ecological, scientific, educational, historic or aesthetic values of the Area;
- access to the Restricted Zone is allowed only for compelling reasons that cannot be served elsewhere in the Area;
- any management activities are in support of the objectives of the Management Plan;
- the actions permitted are in accordance with the Management Plan;
- the permit, or a copy, shall be carried within the Area;
- a visit report shall be supplied to the authority named in the permit;
- permits shall be issued for a stated period.

7(i) Access to and movement within the Area

- Access into the Area shall be by small boat, helicopter, or on foot.
- Vehicles are prohibited in the Area;
- Restrictions on aircraft operations apply during the period between 01 October and 31 March, when aircraft shall operate and land within the Area according to strict observance of the following conditions:
    - Overflight of the Area below 2000 feet (~610 m) is prohibited, unless authorized by permit for purposes allowed for by the Management Plan;
    - Overflight and landings within ½ nautical mile (~930 m) of the Adélie colony on Seabee Hook for tourism is strongly discouraged;
    - Landings within ½ nautical mile (~930 m) of the Adélie colony on Seabee Hook should be avoided wherever possible;
    - Landings beyond ½ nautical mile (~930 m) of the Adélie colony may select landing sites according to visit needs and local conditions;
    - The Primary Landing Site (170° 11.460' E, 72° 19.686' S) shown on Map 2 represents the location where access to the designated camping site is shortest by traverse over sea ice. Landings at this site may be made as local conditions allow; and
    - When landings beyond ½ nautical mile (~930 m) of the Adélie colony are considered unsafe or impractical (e.g. because sea ice is absent or poor, if weather conditions are unfavorable, or because there is an important logistic need such as to move heavy equipment), the following conditions apply:

        FIXED WING
        - Fixed wing aircraft may land beyond ¼ nautical mile (~460 m) of the Adélie colony;
        - Fixed wing aircraft landings should not be made in Willett Cove.

        HELICOPTERS
        - Helicopters shall land at the designated site at Willett Cove (170° 13.579' E, 72° 19.228' S) (Map 2), either on land or on sea ice adjacent to the campsite;
        - On occasions the landing site is susceptible to inundation by high tides: if this occurs landings may made on nearby dry ground, avoiding vegetated sites and preferably remaining on beach gravels

> south of the designated landing site, keeping as close to the shore as possible. Landings closer to the Adélie penguin colony shall be avoided;
>
> - Helicopters should follow the designated approach route to the maximum extent practicable. The preferred helicopter approach route is from the south and extends from the primary landing site to the designated landing site following a route along the southern and eastern coastline of Willett Cove (Map 2).

- There are no special restrictions on where access can be gained to the Area by small boat, although small boat landings with the purpose of camping should be made to Willett Cove in order to avoid the need to haul camp equipment through the Adélie colony.
- It is important that all visitors are careful to restrict their movements around the campsite, keeping to the area along the shoreline to avoid trampling inland areas that are seasonally moist and richly colonized by a variety of plants and invertebrates, which are the subject of on-going research.
- Within the Adélie colony, visitors should not enter sub-groups of nesting penguins unless required for research or management purposes: visitors should walk around the coastal strip of Seabee Hook when possible, and/or around or between sub-groups. Traces of the old station road extend from the NW corner of Willett Cove through to the former station site, and remains a comparatively wide corridor where pedestrians can maintain a reasonable distance from nesting birds.
- Visitors should avoid walking on the scree slopes in the eastern part of the Area unless necessary for essential scientific or management purposes; screes are a sensitive and easily damaged habitat for a diverse community of flora and fauna.
- All pedestrian traffic should be kept to the minimum necessary consistent with the objectives of any permitted activities and every reasonable effort should be made to minimize effects. Visitors should avoid walking on visible vegetation. Care should be exercised when walking in areas of moist ground and on screes, where foot traffic can easily damage sensitive soils and plant communities.

7(ii) Activities that may be conducted in the Area

- Scientific research that will not jeopardize the values of the Area;
- Essential management activities, including assessment or remediation of impacts, and monitoring;
- Activities with educational aims (such as documentary reporting (photographic, audio or written), the production of educational resources or services, or educating program personnel about clean-up methods) that cannot be served elsewhere. Educational aims do not include tourism; and
- Activities with the aim of preserving or protecting historic resources within the Area.

7(iii) Installation, modification or removal of structures

- No structures are to be erected within the Area except as specified in a permit;
- All structures and scientific equipment installed in the Area must be authorized by permit and clearly identified by country, name of the principal investigator and year of installation. All such items should be made of materials that pose minimal risk of contamination of the Area;
- Installation (including site selection), maintenance, modification or removal of structures shall be undertaken in a manner that minimizes disturbance to flora and fauna;
- Respect the emergency cache and only use it in genuine emergency, reporting any such use to an appropriate authority so the cache can be restocked; and
- Removal of specific equipment for which the permit has expired shall be the responsibility of the authority which granted the original Permit, and shall be a condition of the permit.

7(iv) Location of field camps

Permanent field camps are prohibited within the Area. When conditions allow, temporary camping should preferably be located on sea ice in Willett Cove, which is outside of the Area. When this is not practical, temporary camping is permitted at a designated site on the eastern shore and 100 m south of the head of Willett Cove (72° 19' 13" S, 170° 13' 34" E). This site comprises unconsolidated beach gravels, is not colonized by birds or significant plant communities (although these are present nearby) and lies on the site of a former station road (Map 3). Stakes have been driven into the hard, stony ground at the campsite for tent guys; these should be used wherever possible.

The campsite is located immediately adjacent to areas rich in terrestrial fauna and flora and visitors should restrict their movements around the campsite to the area along the shoreline unless required for research purposes. On occasions the site is susceptible to inundation by high tides: if this occurs the camp may be moved to dry ground, avoiding vegetated sites to the maximum extent practicable and preferably remaining on beach gravels south of the designated campsite, keeping as close to the shore as possible.

7(v) Restrictions on materials and organisms that can be brought into the Area

- No living animals, plant material, microorganisms or soils shall be deliberately introduced into the Area, and the precautions listed below shall be taken against accidental introductions;

- To help maintain the ecological and scientific values of the Area visitors shall take special precautions against non-native species introductions. Of particular concern are microbial, invertebrate and vegetation introductions from soils at other Antarctic sites, including stations, or from regions outside Antarctica. Visitors shall ensure that sampling equipment and markers brought into the Area are clean. To the maximum extent practicable, footwear and other equipment used or brought into the area (including backpacks, carry-bags and tents) shall be thoroughly cleaned before entering the Area;

- In view of the presence of breeding bird colonies at Cape Hallett, no poultry products, including products containing uncooked dried eggs, and wastes from such products, shall be released into the Area;

- No herbicides or pesticides shall be brought into the Area;

- Any other chemicals, including radio-nuclides or stable isotopes, which may be introduced for scientific or management purposes specified in the permit, shall be removed from the Area at or before the conclusion of the activity for which the permit was granted;

- Fuel, food, and other materials are not to be stored in the Area, unless required for essential purposes connected with activities for which a permit has been granted or are contained within an emergency cache authorized by an appropriate authority;

- All materials introduced shall be for a stated period only, shall be removed at or before the conclusion of that stated period, and shall be stored and handled so that risk of their introduction into the environment is minimized; and

- If release occurs which is likely to compromise the values of the Area, removal is encouraged only where the impact of removal is not likely to be greater than that of leaving the material *in situ*.

7(vi) Taking or harmful interference with native flora or fauna

Taking or harmful interference of native flora and fauna is prohibited, except in accordance with a separate permit issued under Article 3 of Annex II by the appropriate national authority specifically for that purpose.

7(vii) Collection or removal of anything not introduced by a visitor.

- Material may be collected or removed from the Area only in accordance with a permit and should be limited to the minimum necessary to meet scientific or management needs;

- Removal of, or disturbance to, markers left by previous scientific work within the Area is prohibited unless specifically authorized by permit;

- Other than scientific markers as noted above, material of human origin likely to compromise the values of the Area, which was not brought into the Area by a permit holder, and is clearly of no historic value or otherwise authorized, may be removed from any part of the Area unless the impact of removal is likely to be greater than leaving the material *in situ*. If this is the case the appropriate authority should be notified;

- Material found that is likely to possess important historic or heritage values should not be disturbed, damaged, removed or destroyed. Any such artifacts should be recorded and referred to the appropriate authority for a decision on conservation or removal. Relocation or removal of artifacts for the purposes of preservation, protection, or to re-establish historical accuracy is allowable by permit;

- The well-preserved body of a husky is contained in an enclosed wooden box located in the eastern part of the Area and should not be disturbed while options for its future management remain under consideration; and

- The appropriate national authority should be notified of any items removed from the Area that were not introduced by the permit holder.

7(viii) Disposal of waste

All wastes, including all human wastes, shall be removed from the Area.

7(ix) Measures that may be necessary to ensure that the aims and objectives of the plan continue to be met

- Any specific sites of long-term monitoring should be appropriately marked.

7(x) Requirements for reports

- Parties should ensure that the principal holder for each permit issued submits to the appropriate authority a report describing the activities undertaken. Such reports should include, as appropriate, the information identified in the Visit Report form contained in Appendix 4 of Resolution 2 (1998)(CEP I).

- Parties should maintain a record of such activities and, in the Annual Exchange of Information, should provide summary descriptions of activities conducted by persons subject to their jurisdiction, which should be in sufficient detail to allow evaluation of the effectiveness of the Management Plan. Parties should, wherever possible, deposit originals or copies of such original reports in a publicly accessible archive to maintain a record of usage, to be used both in any review of the Management Plan and in organizing the scientific use of the Area.

- The appropriate authority should be notified of any activities/measures undertaken, and/or of any materials released and not removed, that were not included in the authorized permit.

Selected References

Brabyn, L., C. Beard, R.D. Seppelt, E.D. Rudolph, R. Türk & T.G.A. Green. 2006. Quantified vegetation change over 42 years at Cape Hallett, East Antarctica. *Antarctic Science* **18**(4): 561–72.

Brabyn, L., T.G.A. Green, C. Beard & R.D. Seppelt. 2005. GIS goes nano: Vegetation studies in Victoria Land, Antarctica. *New Zealand Geographer* **61**: 139–147.

Rudolph, E.D. 1963. Vegetation of Hallett Station area, Victoria Land, Antarctica. *Ecology* **44**: 585–86.

Sinclair, B.J., M.B. Scott, C.J. Klok, J.S. Terblanche, D.J. Marshall, B. Reyers & S.L. Chown. 2006. Determinants of terrestrial arthropod community composition at Cape Hallett, Antarctica. *Antarctic Science* **18**(3): 303-12.

(An extensive bibliography is available through the Latitudinal Gradient Project at www.lgp.aq)

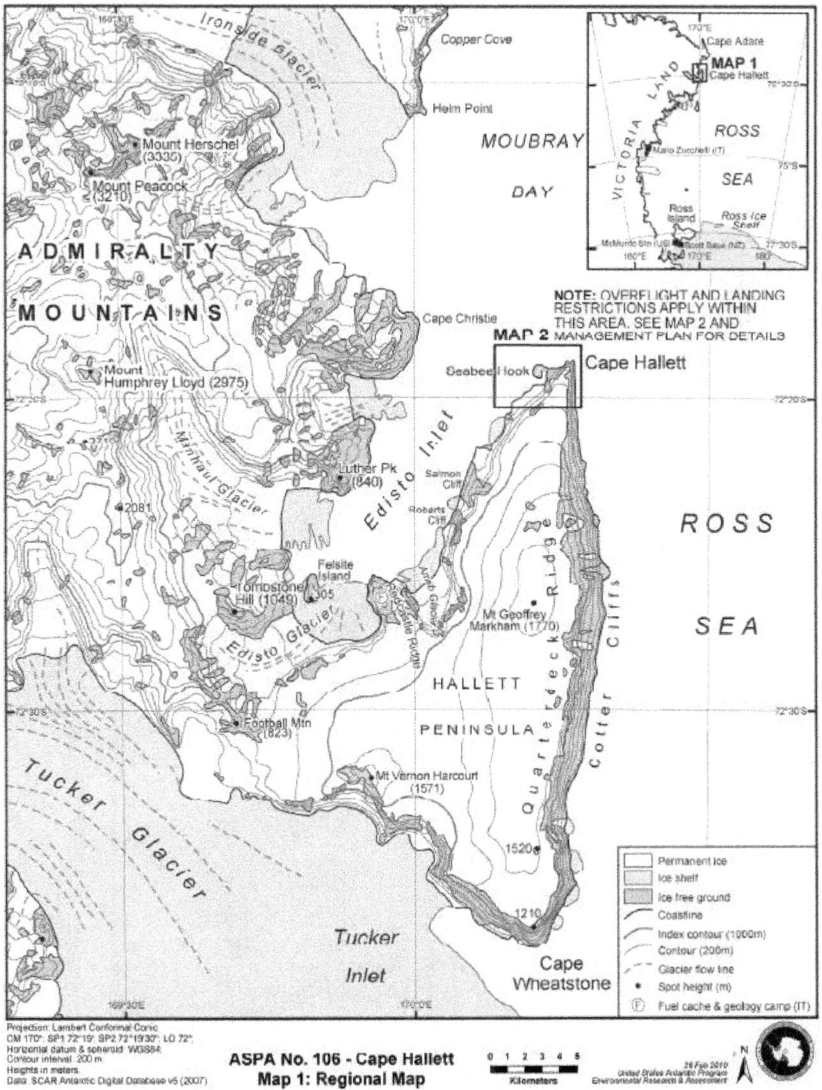

Projection: Lambert Conformal Conic
CM 170°; SP1 72°19'; SP2 72°19'30"; LO 72°;
Horizontal datum & spheroid: WGS84;
Contour interval: 200 m
Heights in meters.
Data: SCAR Antarctic Digital Database v5 (2007)

ASPA No. 106 - Cape Hallett
Map 1: Regional Map

0 1 2 3 4 5 Kilometers

25 Feb 2010
United States Antarctic Program
Environmental Research & Assessment

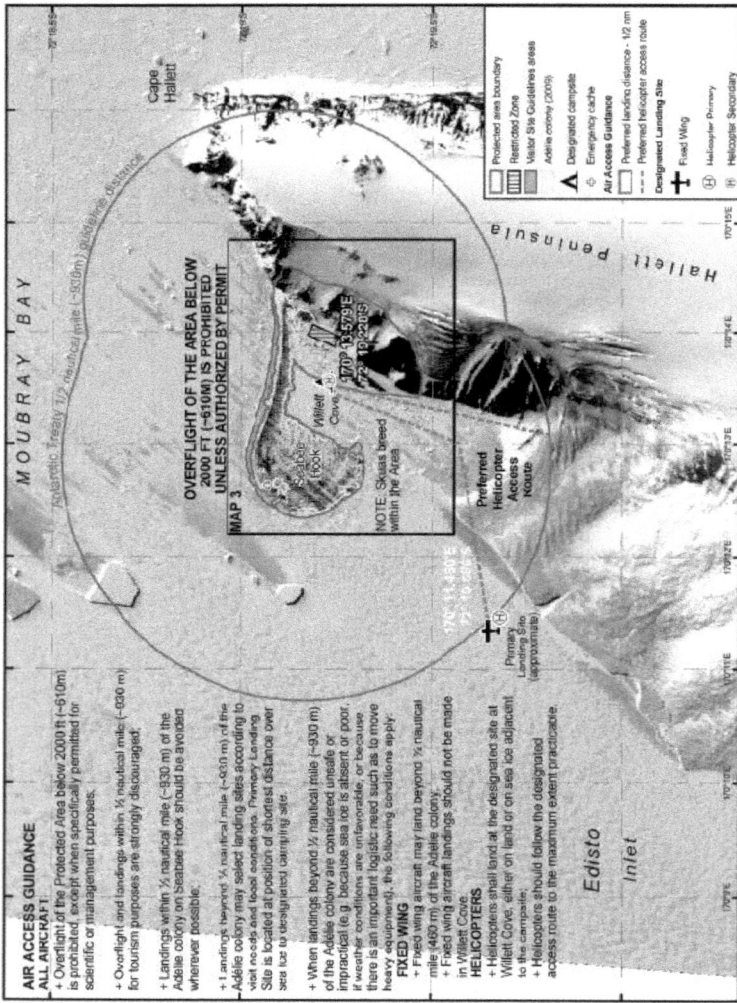

AIR ACCESS GUIDANCE

ALL AIRCRAFT

+ Overflight of the Protected Area below 2000 ft (~610m) is prohibited, except when specifically permitted for scientific or management purposes.

+ Overflight and landings within ½ nautical mile (~930 m) for tourism purposes are strongly discouraged.

+ Landings within ½ nautical mile (~930 m) of the Adélie colony on Seabee Hook should be avoided wherever possible.

+ Landings beyond ½ nautical mile (~930 m) of the Adélie colony may select landing sites according to visit needs and local conditions. Primary Landing Site is located at position of shortest distance over sea ice to designated camping site.

+ When landings beyond ½ nautical mile (~930 m) of the Adélie colony are considered unsafe or impractical (e.g. because sea ice is absent or poor, if weather conditions are unfavorable, or because there is an important logistic need such as to move heavy equipment, the following conditions apply.

FIXED WING

+ Fixed wing aircraft may land beyond ½ nautical mile (460 m) of the Adélie colony.

+ Fixed wing aircraft landings should not be made in Willett Cove.

HELICOPTERS

+ Helicopters shall land at the designated site at Willett Cove, either on land or on sea ice adjacent to the campsite;

+ Helicopters should follow the designated access route to the maximum extent practicable.

ASPA No.106 Cape Hallett
Map 2: Air access guidance

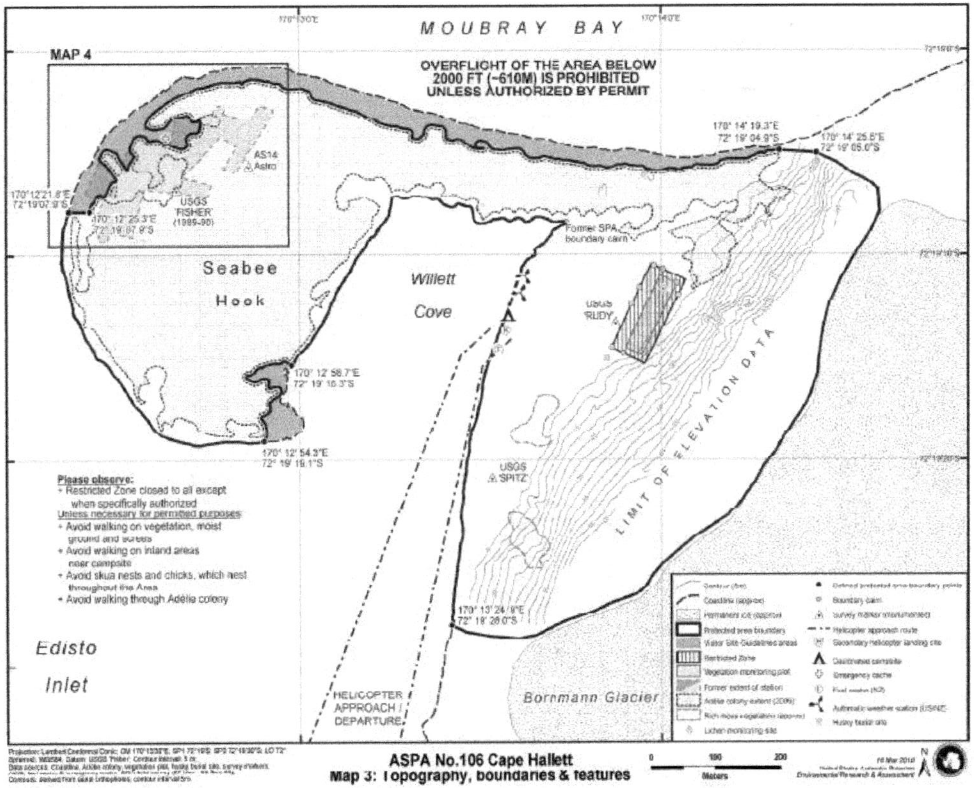

ASPA 106 - Cape Hallett

ASPA No.106 Cape Hallett
Map 3: Topography, boundaries & features

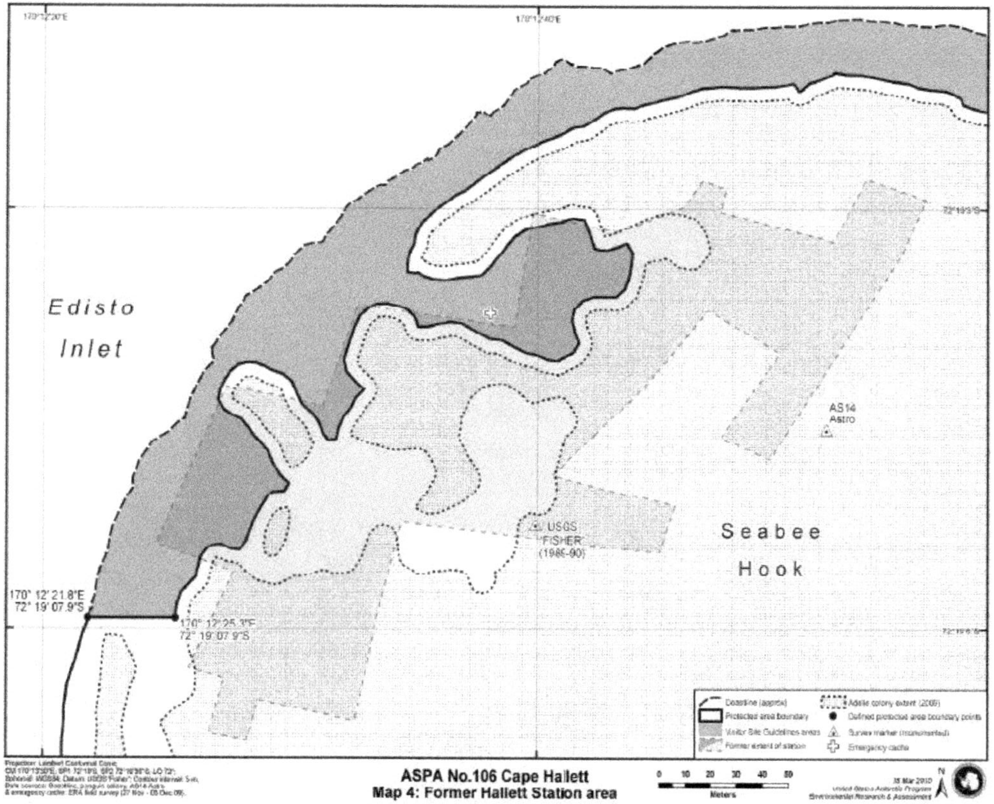
Edisto
Inlet
Seabee
Hook
170° 12' 21.8'E
72° 19' 07.9'S
170° 12' 25.3'E
72° 19' 07.9'S
USGS
FISHER
(1986-90)
AS14
Astro
ASPA No.106 Cape Hallett
Map 4: Former Hallett Station area
Meters

Management Plan for

Antarctic Specially Protected Area (ASPA) No. 119

DAVIS VALLEY AND FORLIDAS POND,

DUFEK MASSIF, PENSACOLA MOUNTAINS

(51° 05' W, 82° 29' S)

Introduction

Davis Valley and Forlidas Pond Antarctic Specially Protected Area (ASPA) is situated within the Dufek Massif, Pensacola Mountains at 51°4'53"W, 82°29'21"S. Approximate area: 57.3 km^2. The primary reason for the designation of the Area is that it contains some of the most southerly freshwater ponds with plant life known to exist in Antarctica, which represent unique examples of near-pristine freshwater ecosystems and their catchments. The geomorphology of the Area represents a unique scientific resource for the reconstruction of previous glacial and climatic events. As a consequence of its extreme remoteness and inaccessibility, the Area has experienced very little human activity and with the total number of visitors estimated to be less than 50 people. As a result, the Area has outstanding potential as a scientific reference site. Furthermore, the Area possesses outstanding wilderness and aesthetic values. The Area is one of the most southerly 'dry valley' systems in Antarctica and, as of March 2010, is the most southerly Antarctic Specially Protected Area (ASPA) in Antarctica. The Area was originally proposed by the United States of America and adopted through Recommendation XVI-9 (1991, SPA No. 23) and included Forlidas Pond (82°27'28"S, 51°16'48"W) and several ponds along the northern ice margin of the Davis Valley. The boundaries of the Area were extended to include the entire ice-free region centered on the Davis Valley through Measure 2 (2005). The boundaries of the Area have not been changed in the current management plan.

1. Description of Values to be Protected

Forlidas Pond (82°27'28" S, 51°16'48" W) and several ponds along the northern ice margin of the Davis Valley (82°27'30" S, 51°05' W), in the Dufek Massif, Pensacola Mountains, were originally designated as a Specially Protected Area through Recommendation XVI-9 (1991, SPA No. 23) after a proposal by the United States of America. The Area was designated on the grounds that it "contains some of the most southerly freshwater ponds known in Antarctica containing plant life" which "should be protected as examples of unique near-pristine freshwater ecosystems and their catchments". The original Area comprised two sections approximately 500 metres apart with a combined total area of around 6 km^2. It included Forlidas Pond and the meltwater ponds along the ice margin at the northern limit of the Davis Valley. The site has been rarely visited and until recently there has been little information available on the ecosystems within the Area.

This Management Plan reaffirms the original reason for designation of the Area, recognizing the ponds and their associated plant life as pristine examples of a southerly freshwater habitat. However, following a field visit made in December 2003 (Hodgson and Convey, 2004) the values identified for special protection and the boundaries for the Area have been expanded as described below.

The Davis Valley and the adjacent ice-free valleys is one of the most southerly 'dry valley' systems in Antarctica and, as of March 2010, is the most southerly Antarctic Specially Protected Area in Antarctica. While occupying an area of only 53 km^2, which is less than 1% of the area of the McMurdo Dry Valleys, the Area nevertheless contains the largest ice-free valley system found south of 80°S in the 90°W-0°-90°E half of Antarctica. Moreover, it is the only area known in this part of Antarctica where the geomorphology preserves such a detailed record of past glacial history. Some ice-free areas around the Weddell Sea region have scattered erratics and sometimes moraines, but the assemblage of drift limits, moraines, and abundant quartz-bearing erratics in the Davis Valley and associated valleys is unique and rare. The location of the Dufek Massif close to the junction between the western and the eastern Antarctic ice sheets also makes this site particularly valuable for the collection of data that can be used to constrain parameters such as the past thickness and dynamics of this sector of the Antarctic ice sheet. Such data are potentially extremely valuable for understanding the response of the Antarctic ice sheet to climate change. The Area therefore has exceptional and unique scientific value for the interpretation of past glacial events and climate in this part of Antarctica and it is important that this value is maintained.

The terrestrial ecology of the Area is impoverished but is also highly unusual, with lake and meltwater stream environments and their associated biota being rare this far south in Antarctica. As such, they provide unique opportunities for the scientific study of biological communities near the extreme limit of the occurrence of these environments. Vegetation appears to be limited to cyanobacterial mats and a very sparse occurrence of small crustose lichens. The cyanobacterial mat growth in the terrestrial locations is surprisingly extensive, and represents the best examples of this community type known this far south. The cyanobacterial community appears to survive in at least three distinct environments:

- in the permanent water bodies;
- in exposed terrestrial locations, particularly at the boundaries of sorted polygons; and
- in a series of former or seasonally dry pond beds on ice-free ground in the Davis Valley.

No arthropods or nematodes have thus far been detected in samples taken from within the Area, and the invertebrate fauna in the Area is unusually sparse. This characteristic distinguishes the Area from more northerly ice-free valley systems such as those at the Ablation Valley – Ganymede Heights (ASPA No. 147), Alexander Island, or at the McMurdo Dry Valleys (ASMA No. 2), where such communities are present. Rotifers and tardigrades have been extracted from samples taken within the Area, with the greatest numbers occurring within the former pond beds in the Davis Valley, although their diversity and abundance is also extremely limited compared with more northerly Antarctic sites (Hodgson and Convey, 2004). Further analyses of the samples obtained and identification of all taxa present are being published (Hodgson *et al.*, in press) and are expected to make an important contribution to the understanding of biogeographical relationships between the different regions of Antarctica.

The Area is extremely isolated and difficult to access, and as a result has been visited by only a small number of people. Reports indicate that small field parties visited the Area in December 1957, in the 1965-66 and 1973-74 austral summer seasons, in December 1978 and in December 2003. The total number of people having visited probably numbers less than 50, with visits generally limited to a period of a few weeks or days. No structures or installations have been built within the Area, and as far as is known all equipment brought into the Area has subsequently been removed. While Hodgson and Convey (2004) reported evidence of a very limited number of human footprints and several old soil pit excavations, the Area has been exposed to few opportunities for direct human impact. The Area is believed to be one of the most pristine ice-free valley systems in Antarctica, and is therefore considered to possess outstanding potential as a reference area for microbiological studies, and it is important that these values receive long-term protection.

The site possesses outstanding wilderness and aesthetic values. The dry and weathered brown valleys of the Area are surrounded by extensive ice-fields, the margins of which fringe the valleys with dry based glacial ice of a deep blue hue. This abrupt and dramatic blue-ice margin stands in stark contrast to the stony and barren ice-free landscape of the valleys, and aesthetically is extremely striking in appearance. One of the original explorers of this area in 1957 recalled "the excitement we felt at being the first people to view and enter this magnificently scenic, pristine area." (Behrendt, 1998: 354). Further examples of descriptions of the Area by visitors are: "[the blue ice] was towering over us ~ 150 feet – a large wave of blue. It was like being in a tidal wave that was held in suspension as we walked under it…" (Reynolds, field notes, 1978), and "I still cannot find adequate superlatives to describe the features, whether large or small, biologic or physical… [Of the] many settings that stretch the imagination…in my experience none match the northern side of the Dufek Massif, with Davis Valley as its crown jewel." (Reynolds, pers. comm., 2000); "the most unusual [landscape] I have ever seen on any of the seven continents." (Boyer, pers. comm., 2000); "Probably the single most remarkable environment I've been, either in Antarctica or elsewhere" (Convey, pers. comm., 2004). Burt (2004) described the region simply as "inspiringly awesome".

The boundaries of the Area have been revised to include the entire ice-free region centered on the Davis Valley, including the adjacent valleys and Forlidas Pond. In general, the margins of the surrounding ice sheets form the new boundary of the Area, resulting in special protection of the region as an integrated ice-free unit that more closely approximates the valley catchments. The full catchments of the surrounding glaciers that flow into these valleys extend considerable distances from the ice-free area and do not possess many of the values related to the purpose of special protection, and are therefore excluded from the Area.

2. Aims and Objectives

Management at Forlidas Pond and Davis Valley ponds aims to:

- avoid degradation of, or substantial risk to, the values of the Area by preventing unnecessary human disturbance and sampling in the Area;
- preserve the ecosystem as an area largely undisturbed by human activities;
- preserve the almost pristine ecosystem for its potential as a biological reference area;
- allow scientific research on the natural ecosystem and physical environment within the Area provided it is for compelling reasons which cannot be served elsewhere;
- minimize the possibility of introduction of alien plants, animals and microbes to the Area; and
- allow visits for management purposes in support of the aims of the Management Plan.

3. Management Activities

The following management activities shall be undertaken to protect the values of the Area:

- Markers, signs or other structures erected within the Area for scientific or management purposes shall be secured and maintained in good condition and removed when no longer necessary.
- Visits shall be made as necessary to assess whether the Area continues to serve the purposes for which it was designated and to ensure management and maintenance measures are adequate.

4. Period of Designation

Designated for an indefinite period of time.

5. Maps

Map 1: Davis Valley and Forlidas Pond, ASPA No. 119, Dufek Massif, Pensacola Mountains: Location Map.

Map Specifications: Projection: Lambert Conformal Conic; Standard parallels: 1st 82°S; 2nd 83°S; Central Meridian: 51°W; Latitude of Origin: 81°S; Spheroid: WGS84.

Inset: the location of the Pensacola Mountains and Map 1 in Antarctica.

Map 2: Davis Valley and Forlidas Pond, ASPA No. 119: Topographic map and protected area boundary.

Map Specifications: Projection: Lambert Conformal Conic; Standard parallels: 1st 82°S; 2nd 83°S; Central Meridian: 51°W; Latitude of Origin: 81°S; Spheroid: WGS84; Vertical datum: WGS84. EGM96 MSL height differential –21 m. Contour interval 25 m. Topographic data generated by digital orthophoto and photogrammetric techniques from USGS aerial photography (TMA400, TMA908, TMA909 (1958) and TMA1498 (1964)) by the Mapping and Geographic Information Centre, British Antarctic Survey (Cziferszky *et al.* 2004). Accuracy estimates: horizontal: ±1 m; vertical: ±2 m, declining towards the south away from available ground control points. Area beyond orthophoto coverage northwest of Forlidas Pond is mapped from a georectified Terra ASTER satellite image acquired 9 November 2002. Elevation data are unavailable in this region and it is therefore of reduced spatial accuracy.

6. Description of the Area

6(i) Geographical coordinates, boundary markers and natural features

General description

Davis Valley (82°28'30"S, 51°05'W) and Forlidas Pond (82°27'28"S, 51°16'48"W) are situated in the north-eastern Dufek Massif, Pensacola Mountains, part of the Transantarctic Mountain range. The Dufek Massif is situated approximately mid-way between the Support Force Glacier and the Foundation Ice Stream, two of the major glaciers draining northwards from the Polar Plateau into the Ronne and Filchner Ice Shelves. Approximately 60 km to the southeast is the Forrestal Range (also part of the Pensacola Mountains), which is separated from the Dufek Massif by the Sallee Snowfield. The Ford Ice Piedmont separates the Dufek Massif from the Ronne and Filchner Ice Shelves, about 50 km to the northwest and 70 km to the northeast respectively.

The Davis Valley is approximately five kilometers wide and seven kilometers long, with its northern extent defined by the blue ice lobes that form part of the southern margin of the Ford Ice Piedmont. It is bounded in the east by Wujek Ridge and Mount Pavlovskogo (1074 m), flanked on the outer side by a glacier draining north from the Sallee Snowfield to the Ford Ice Piedmont. The western extent of the valley is defined by Clemons Spur, Angels Peak (964 m) and Forlidas Ridge. The Edge Glacier extends approximately 4 km into the Davis Valley from the Sallee Snowfield. The southern Davis Valley is dominated by Mount Beljakova (1240 m), on the northwestern margin of the Sallee Snowfield. Several smaller valleys exist in the west of the Area, adjacent to the prominent Preslik Spur and Forlidas Ridge. Almost 75% of the region enclosed by the large surrounding ice fields is ice-free, comprising 39 km2 of ice-free ground in total, with the remainder of the area covered by the Edge Glacier, other permanent bodies of snow / ice and several small ponds.

Forlidas Pond is landlocked and occupies a small unnamed dry valley separated from the Davis Valley by a tributary ridge extending north from Forlidas Ridge. Other pro-glacial lakes and ponds occur within the Area at various locations along the blue ice margin of the Ford Ice Piedmont, at the terminus of the Edge Glacier, and along the ice margin west of Forlidas Ridge.

Boundary

The Area comprises all of the Davis Valley and the immediately adjacent ice-free valleys, including several of the valley glaciers within these catchments. The boundary predominantly follows the margins of the surrounding ice fields of the Ford Ice Piedmont and Sallee Snowfield, which enclose the ice-free area that is considered to be of outstanding value. The northern boundary extends parallel to and 500 metres north from the southern margin of the Ford Ice Piedmont in the Davis Valley and in the adjacent valley containing Forlidas Pond. This is in order to provide an additional buffer of protection around the freshwater bodies of value along this glacier margin. The eastern boundary follows the ice margin east of Wujek Ridge from the Ford Ice Piedmont to Mount Pavlovskogo. The southeastern boundary extends from Mount Pavlovskogo across the Sallee Snowfield and the upper slopes of the Edge Glacier, following areas of outcrop where they exist, and again across the Sallee Snowfield to Mount Beljakova. The southern and western boundaries of the Area follow the margins of the permanent ice. The boundary encompasses a total area of 57.2 km2.

Boundary markers have not been installed in the Area because of its remoteness, the limited opportunities for visits and the practical difficulties of maintenance. Moreover, the margins of the permanent ice fields are generally sharply defined and form a visually obvious boundary around most of the Area.

Meteorology

Several estimates of mean annual surface air temperature have been made in the Dufek Massif region from measurements taken in ice bores or crevasses at around 10 metres depth. A measurement of –24.96°C was obtained 32 km due north of Forlidas Pond on the Ford Ice Piedmont in December 1957 (Pit 12, Map 1) (Aughenbaugh et al., 1958). Another estimate of -9°C was made in December 1978 in the Enchanted Valley 26 km to the south (Map 1), measured in a crevasse at 8 metres depth (Boyer, pers. comm., 2000).

Detailed meteorological data for the Area itself are limited to records collected over two weeks in 2003. Hodgson and Convey (2004) measured temperature and relative humidity over snow and rock surfaces at their sampling sites within the Area from 3-15 December 2003, with data recorded at 30-minute intervals, though sensors were not shielded with a Stevenson screen. Temperatures over snow ranged from a maximum of +12.8°C to a minimum of –14.5°C, with an average over the period of –0.56°C. Temperatures over rock ranged from a maximum of +16.0°C to a minimum of –8.6°C, with an average over the period of +0.93°C (data over rock were only recorded from 3-11 December 2003). Relative humidity recorded over snow ranged from a maximum of 80.4% to a minimum of 10.8%, with an average over the period of 42.6%. Over rock surfaces (from 3-11 December 2003), relative humidity ranged from a maximum of 80.9% to a minimum of 5.6%, with an average over the period of 38.7%.

Directly measured data on windspeeds and directions within the Area are not available, but models suggest near surface winds are predominantly from the west-north-west with mean winter velocities of c. 10m s[-1] (van Lipzig et al., 2004). While the older exposed ice-free areas above the glacial drift limit possess many features related to long-term wind erosion, there is some evidence to suggest that windspeeds within the locality are currently not especially high. For example, ice and snow surfaces were observed as largely free of wind-blown debris, and terrestrial cyanobacterial mats exist in-tact in exposed locations in the bottom of dry valleys (Hodgson and Convey, 2004). No precipitation data are available, although the bare ice and rock surfaces and low average relative humidity recorded by Hodgson and Convey (2004) attest to a dry environment of low precipitation. This is consistent with a Type 2 dominated ablation area where sublimation-driven ablation occurs at the foot of the steep topographic barriers, with individual glacier valleys serving as gates for air drainage from the plateau to the Ronne-Filchner Ice Shelf. Strongest sublimation rates occur on these localized glaciers in the Transantarctic Mountains, where widespread blue ice areas are present (van den Broeke et al., 2006).

Geology, geomorphology and Soils

The Dufek Massif is characterized by layered bands of cumulate rock belonging to the Dufek intrusion, thought to be one of the largest layered gabbro intrusions in the world (Behrendt et al., 1974; 1980; Ferris et al., 1998). This is exposed in the Davis Valley as the light- to medium-gray, medium-grained Aughenbaugh gabbro, which is the lowest exposed part of the Middle Jurassic Dufek intrusion (Ford et al., 1978).

The Davis Valley primarily consists of minimally weathered talus and glacial till of both local and exotic origin. In particular there appears to be an abundance of erratics of Dover Sandstone, one of several metasedimentary layers disrupted by the Dufek intrusion. An extensive glacial geomorphological record is evident. Features include overlapping valley-glacier moraines, ice sheet moraines, lake shoreline, lateral glacial channels, ice eroded surfaces, well-developed patterned ground and erratics. Boyer (1979) identified at least three major glacial and two major interglacial events and recent work by Hodgson et al. (in prep) maps geomorphological features derived from up to seven glacial stages. From oldest to youngest, these stages were: alpine glaciation of the escarpment edge; over-riding warm-based glaciation; glacier advance to an upper limit (760 m); two ice-sheet advances to closely parallel limits in the valleys; advance of the plateau outlet glacier (Edge Glacier) to merge with the ice sheet; and finally an advance and retreat of the main ice sheet margin. Attempts to provide age constraints for some of these glacial events have been carried out using paired cosmogenic ^{10}Be-^{26}Al exposure ages on erratic boulders, composed of Dover Sandstone. These suggest that some parts of the valley have been exposed for > 1.0-1.8 Ma and experienced only a minor ice sheet advance at the Last Glacial Maximum, consistent with an emerging dataset from around the Weddell Sea rim that implies only rather modest ice thickening at this time.

Soils are not well-developed in the Area and generally lack a significant organic component. Parker et al. (1982) collected a soil that was light brown in color, resulting from gravel weathering predominantly to muscovite. The soil comprised sand (81%) with silt (14%) and clay (5%), a composition different from other sites in the Pensacola Mountains where the clay proportions of six samples ranges from 0.4% to 1.6%. The soil sample from the Davis Valley had a pH of 6.4 (Parker, et al., 1982).

Lakes, ponds and streams

Forlidas Pond is a perennially frozen, shallow, round landlocked pond that was estimated to be approximately 100 metres in diameter in 1957 (Behrendt, 1998). In December 2003 the lake was measured by Hodgson and Convey (2004) as 90.3 metres in diameter from shoreline to shoreline on a transect azimuth of 306° (magnetic). At this time it was frozen almost completely to its base, with a thin layer of hypersaline slush at the lake bottom, and a freshwater meltwater moat that was partly ice free and partly covered by 10-15 cm of ice (Hodgson and Convey, 2004). Depth was measured at 1.83 m and the thickness of the ice between 1.63 and 1.83 metres. The conductivity and temperature in the brine layer was 142.02 mS cm-1 and -7.67°C respectively, compared with 2.22 mS cm-1 and 0.7 C in the freshwater moat (Hodgson et al. in press). The salinity of the bottom-water in Forlidas Pond is thus around four times greater than seawater. This concentration of salts is the result of the pond being the evaporated remnant of a much larger lake, which evaporated from about 2200 years ago and can be identified by a series of lake terraces and a high shoreline 17.7 m above the present water level (Hodgson in prep.).

Hodgson and Convey (2004) also report a small remnant pro-glacial pond near the margin of the Ford Ice Piedmont, 900 metres north of Forlidas Pond. Two pro-glacial meltwater ponds also occur to the west of Forlidas Ridge and a series of similar pro-glacial meltwater ponds also occur along the blue-ice margin of the northern Davis Valley, located at 82° 27.5' S, 51° 05.5'W wand, 82° 27.55' S, 51° 07' W. The pro-glacial lake at the terminus of the Edge Glacier is the largest within the Area. This is permanently frozen to the bottom apart from at the eastern margins where seasonal meltwater has been observed.

Dry stream channels and water erosion features are evident within the ice-free area, although only the small glacial melt streams on the eastern margin of the Edge Glacier have thus far been reported as flowing in December (Hodgson and Convey, 2004). The apparent lack of melt streams may be because all visits to date have been made in the month of December, possibly before streams become more active. The presence of lake moats, the positive temperatures recorded by Hodgson and Convey (2004), as well as the biological and the geomorphological evidence, suggest that it is probable that at least some streams become active later in the season from melting snow, although perhaps not on an annual basis.

Biology

Visible biota is dominated by cyanobacterial mats, found both in lakes and in patches on the surface of ice-free ground, and a very sparse occurrence of small crustose lichens. Neuburg *et al.* (1959) observed yellow and black lichens growing sparsely in sheltered places in the Davis Valley, while Hodgson and Convey (2004) observed several lichen forms growing deep within the crevices of boulders. These have been identified as *Lecidea cancrioformis* Dodge & Baker (Hodgson *et al.*, in press, and see Appendix 1: Table A1 for a list of taxa identified in the Area). The British Antarctic Survey Plant Database also reports *Blastenia succinea* Dodge & Baker and *Xanthoria elegans* (Link.) Th. Fr. in samples from elsewhere in the Dufek Massif, although these have not been independently verified. Previous anecdotal reports of the possible occurrence of mosses within the Area could not be substantiated by Hodgson and Convey (2004), and it is probable that the rich cyanobacterial mat growth was earlier mistaken for bryophytes by non-specialists. The cyanobacterial community is the most abundant biota and is present in at least three distinct environments:

(1) In the permanent water bodies; particularly in the moat of Forlidas Pond, at the bottom and littoral zones of the Davis Valley Ponds, and in the seasonally wetted perimeter of Edge Lake. These habitats are extensively covered by red-brown cyanobacterial mats. These are actively photosynthesizing, as evidenced by gas bubbles trapped against the lower ice surfaces, and bubbles incorporated into the ice. Because perennially ice covered lakes have elevated concentrations of dissolved O_2 gas, the microbial mats growing on the bottom can become buoyant and start to float off the bottom as 'lift-off' mats, or become incorporated into the base of the lake ice when it makes contact with the bed. In Forlidas Pond and the Davis Valley Ponds lift off mats frozen into the base of the lake ice eventually migrate up through the ice profile. In the Davis Valley, this appears to take place over several years with each summer marked by the development of a 2-3 cm melt-cavity formed by the upward progression of the clump thorough the lake ice due to preferential heating of its upper surface. These clumps eventually break out at the surface and are dispersed by wind onto the shoreline, or further afield. Cyanobacteria were also present in the hypersaline brine of Forlidas Pond as single cells and as small flakes. A strain corresponding to the morphology of *Leptolyngbya antarctica* was isolated from the saline slush of TM1 (Fernandez-Carazo *et al.* in prep.).

(2) In exposed terrestrial locations, particularly at the edge of larger rocks and within the boundary crevices of frost sorted polygons. These are generally very foliose in form, mid brown in colour, and best developed at the edge of larger rocks with depths of at least 10-15 cm. Nearly all clumps were completely dry on discovery, although those near to melting snow were damp and some had lower thalli that were often deep green in colour. Particularly good examples of this growth form were found in the mid valley floor of Forlidas Valley and in Davis Valley (near a large snow gully where it meets the second major terrace above Edge Lake).

(3) In a series of dry pond beds in the Davis Valley, two of up to 50 m diameter, which have extensive areas of almost continuous cyanobacterial mat on the former pond floors. These pond beds and gullies occupy depressions and therefore may accumulate snow in winter, permitting the cyanobacteria to take advantage of the wet and protected environment within the snow patches.

The growth form also occurs in many of the adjacent small gullies between polygons or other cryoturbation features, which often have the appearance of temporary drainage features.

Analyses of the cyanobacterial molecular diversity from four samples collected in and around Forlidas Pond show a depleted diversity, with only 2 - 5 Operational Taxonomic Units (OTUs) per sample (Hodgson *et al*, in press). This is likely a product of geographical isolation combined with multiple environmental stressors such as salinity and seasonal desiccation, and UV radiation. Some of the cyanobacteria, for example from the brine of Forlidas Pond, are related to sequences from other hypersaline Antarctic lakes, whilst others are found almost exclusively in glacial regions. The six cyanobacterial OTUs described from the Dufek Massif are all distributed in more than one location within the continent and are found outside Antarctica.

The invertebrate fauna within the area is equally impoverished, with both the diversity and abundance of organisms being extremely limited compared with lower latitude and coastal Antarctic sites. No nematodes arthropods have been found but there are three species of the tardigrade present from two Classes: *Echiniscus* (cf) *pseudowendti* Dastych, 1984 (Heterotardigrada), *Acutuncus antarcticus* (Richters, 1904) and *Diphascon sanae* Dastych, Ryan and Watkins, 1990 (Eutardigrada) and a few unidentified bdelloid rotifers (Hodgson *et al* in press). *Acutuncus antarcticus* is an Antarctic species that occurs in semi-permanent damp/wet habitats throughout the Antarctic continent and sub-Antarctic islands, but has not been reported from any of the close neighbour continents. *Echiniscus* (cf) *pseudowendti* and *Diphascon sanae* found in samples from Forlidas Pond are also endemic to the Antarctic, with restricted distributions.

The most productive sites for these organisms were not the aquatic environments of the permanent lakes, but the former pond beds in the Davis Valley, showing these areas to be biologically productive, which necessitates a source of liquid water. In December 2003 very little snow was evident on the valley floor, prompting Hodgson and Convey (2004) to reason that the source of moisture may be from a considerable increase in melt later in the season flowing off the local ice sheet in the upper valley, or from local ice-cored moraines. Although this process was not occurring during their visit, footprints and shallow soil survey pits remaining from one of the previous parties (i.e. 25-46 years old) indicated that some ground was moist or waterlogged at the time of the earlier visit. Seasonal inundation by liquid water would explain the extensiveness and integrity of this cyanobacterial community, and its apparent resilience to the potential ravages of polar winds, as well as the relative abundance of invertebrates extracted from samples taken from within these areas.

Viable yeast species have been recorded in the soil, along with the algae *Oscillatoria* sp., *Trebouxia* sp. and *Heterococcus* sp. (Parker *et al.*, 1982). Chasmoendolithic microorganisms have been recorded in rocks in the Dufek Massif (Friedmann, 1977), although Hodgson and Convey (2004) found no evidence of their presence within the Area and noted that rock-types most favorable for the occurrence of endolithic organisms are not widespread.

Avifauna is sparse: in December 2003 a single snow petrel (*Pagadroma nivea*) was noted flying around one of the peaks above Davis Valley.

Human activities and impact

There have been few visits to the Area and human impacts are believed to be minimal (Table A2 Appendix 1). Because of its remoteness and the infrequency of visits, it is one of the few ice-free areas of Antarctica where the compiled record of past human activity at the site is almost complete. The almost pristine condition of the environment contributes to the extremely high value of the Area and is an important reason for its special protection.

The key characteristics of visits recorded to the Area are summarized in Table A2 (Appendix 1), which should be updated as required (see Section 7(x)). Past camps have generally been on the ice sheet outside of the Area. Previous parties removed all wastes from the Area, with the possible exception of small quantities of human wastes. In 2003 all wastes including all human wastes were removed, both from within the Area and from the party's adjacent campsite on the Ford Ice Piedmont (Map 2). Hodgson and Convey (2004) noted that in December 2003 the evidence of previous visits was limited to a number of footprints and several shallow soil excavations in the Davis Valley.

6(ii) Access to the Area

Access to the Area may be made only on foot. Access to the icefields surrounding the Area may be made by aircraft or via land routes. Access to the Area should be made as close as practicable to the intended study site, in order to minimize the amount of the Area that needs to be crossed. Due to the surrounding terrain and crevasse patterns, the most practical access routes into the Area are from the Ford Ice Piedmont to the north of the Area.

6(iii) Restricted and managed zones within the Area

None.

6(iv) Structures within and near the Area

No structures, installations or caches are known to exist within the Area.

6(iv) Location of other protected areas within close proximity of the Area

There are no other protected areas nearby, with the nearest being Ablation Valley – Ganymede Heights (ASPA No. 147), Alexander Island, which is approximately 1300 km to the north-west.

7. Permit conditions

Entry into the Area is prohibited except in accordance with a Permit issued by an appropriate national authority. Conditions for issuing a Permit to enter the Area are that:

- it is issued only for compelling scientific or educational reasons that cannot be served elsewhere, or for essential management purposes consistent with plan objectives such as inspection or review;
- the actions permitted will not jeopardize the physical, ecological, scientific or aesthetic and wilderness values of the Area, nor the pristine value of the Area and its potential as a largely undisturbed biological reference site;
- any management activities are in support of the objectives of the Management Plan;
- the actions permitted are in accordance with the Management Plan;
- the Permit, or a copy, shall be carried within the Area;
- a visit report shall be supplied to the authority, or authorities, named in the Permit;
- Permits shall be issued for a stated period.

7(i) Access to and movement within the Area

- Landing of aircraft is prohibited within the Area and overflight of the Area at less than 100 metres above ground level is prohibited.
- Vehicles are prohibited within the Area.
- Access into and movement within the Area shall be on foot.
- No special restrictions apply to the means of access, or air or land routes used, to move to and from the icefields surrounding the boundaries of the Area.
- Access into the Area should be at a practicable point close to sites of study in order to minimize the amount of the Area that needs to be traversed. The terrain and crevassing generally makes such access most practical from the Ford Ice Piedmont to the north of the Area.
- Pedestrian routes should avoid lakes, ponds, former pond beds, stream beds, areas of damp ground and areas of soft sediments or sedimentary features. Care should be exercised to avoid damage to any areas of cyanobacterial mat growth, in particular to the extensive areas found in former pond beds in Davis Valley.
- Pedestrian traffic should be kept to the minimum necessary consistent with the objectives of any permitted activities and every reasonable effort should be made to minimize effects.

7(ii) Activities that are or may be conducted in the Area, including restrictions on time or place

- Scientific research that will not jeopardize the scientific or ecosystem values of the Area, or its pristine value and potential as a reference site, and which cannot be served elsewhere;
- Essential management activities, including monitoring;
- Activities with educational aims that are undertaken for compelling reasons which cannot be served elsewhere. Activities may include documentary reporting (photographic, audio or written) or the production of educational resources or services. Educational activities shall not compromise the values for which the Area is protected, in particular its value as a near-pristine reference site. Educational aims do not include tourism.
- The appropriate authority should be notified of any activities/measures undertaken that were not included in the authorized Permit.

7(iii) Installation, modification or removal of structures

- No structures are to be erected within the Area except as specified in a Permit.
- Permanent structures are prohibited.

- All scientific equipment installed in the Area must be approved by Permit.
- Should equipment be intended to remain within the Area for a duration of more than one season it shall clearly be identified by country, name of the principal investigator and year of installation. All such items should be made of materials that pose minimal risk of contamination of the Area.
- Installation (including site selection), maintenance, modification or removal of structures shall be undertaken in a manner that minimizes disturbance to the physical, ecological, scientific or aesthetic and wilderness values of the Area;
- Removal of structures, equipment or markers for which the period specified in the Permit has expired shall be a condition of the Permit.

7(iv) Location of field camps

- Camping within the Area is prohibited.
- Suitable camp sites have been proven to the north and west of the Area on the Ford Ice Piedmont (Map 2), and also in the Enchanted Valley (Map 1).

7(v) Restrictions on materials and organisms which can be brought into the Area

- No living animals, plant material or microorganisms shall be deliberately introduced into the Area and the precautions listed in 7(ix) below shall be taken against accidental introductions.

To help maintain the ecological, scientific and wilderness values of the Area visitors shall take special precautions against non-native species introductions. Of particular concern are pathogenic, microbial, invertebrate and vegetation introductions from soils at other Antarctic sites, including stations, or from regions outside Antarctica. Visitors shall ensure that sampling equipment and markers brought into the Area are clean. To the maximum extent practicable, footwear and other equipment used or brought into the area (including backpacks, carry-bags and tents) shall be thoroughly cleaned before entering the Area;To reduce the risk of microbial contamination, the exposed surfaces of footwear, sampling equipment and markers should be sterilized before use within the Area. Sterilization should be by an acceptable method, such as by washing in 70% ethanol solution in water or in a commercially available solution such as 'Virkon'.

- No herbicides or pesticides shall be brought into the Area;
- Any other chemicals, including radio-nuclides or stable isotopes, which may be introduced for scientific or management purposes specified in the Permit, shall be removed from the Area at or before the conclusion of the activity for which the Permit was granted.
- Fuel, food, and other materials are not to be stored in the Area, unless required for essential purposes connected with the activity for which the permit has been granted or are contained within an emergency cache authorized by an appropriate authority;
- All materials introduced shall be for a stated period only, shall be removed at or before the conclusion of that stated period, and shall be stored and handled so that risk of their introduction into the environment is minimized;
- If release occurs which is likely to compromise the values of the Area, removal is encouraged only where the impact of removal is not likely to be greater than that of leaving the material *in situ*; and
- The appropriate authority should be notified of any materials released and not removed that were not included in the authorized Permit.

7(vi) Taking or harmful interference with native flora or fauna

- Taking or harmful interference with native flora or fauna is prohibited, except in accordance with a separate permit issued under Article 3 of Annex II to the Madrid Protocol by the appropriate national authority specifically for that purpose.

7(vii) Collection or removal of anything not brought into the Area by the Permit Holder

- Material may be collected or removed from the Area only in accordance with a Permit and should be limited to the minimum necessary to meet scientific or management needs. Permits shall not be granted if there is a reasonable concern that the sampling proposed would take, remove or damage such quantities of soil, native flora or fauna that their distribution or abundance within the Area would be significantly affected.

- Material of human origin likely to compromise the values of the Area, which was not brought into the Area by the Permit Holder or otherwise authorized, may be removed unless the impact of removal is likely to be greater than leaving the material *in situ*. If this is the case the appropriate authority should be notified.

- The appropriate national authority should be notified of any items removed from the Area that were not introduced by the permit holder.

7(viii) Disposal of waste

All wastes, including water used for any human purpose and including all human wastes, shall be removed from the Area. Individuals or groups shall carry appropriate containers for human waste and gray water so that they may be safely transported and removed from the Area.

7(ix) Measures that are necessary to ensure that the aims and objectives of the Management Plan can continue to be met

- Permits may be granted to carry out biological monitoring and site inspection activities within the Area, which may involve the collection of limited samples for analysis or review, or for protective measures.

- Any specific sites of long-term monitoring shall be appropriately marked;

- A comprehensive Code of Conduct and *Guidelines for Conduct of Scientific Research* have been developed for use within the McMurdo Dry Valleys (ASMA No. 2), much of which is relevant as guidance for activities within the dry valley system in this region. Visitors shall consult these guidelines and should apply them where appropriate to the conduct of scientific research and other activities within the Area.

7(x) Requirements for reports

- Parties should ensure that the principal holder for each Permit issued submits to the appropriate authority a report describing the activities undertaken. Such reports should include, as appropriate, the information identified in the Visit Report form contained in Appendix 4 of Resolution 2 (1998)(CEP I).

- Parties should maintain a record of such activities and, in the Annual Exchange of Information, should provide summary descriptions of activities conducted by persons subject to their jurisdiction, which should be in sufficient detail to allow evaluation of the effectiveness of the Management Plan.

- Parties should, wherever possible, deposit originals or copies of such original reports in a publicly accessible archive to maintain a record of usage, to be used both in any review of the Management Plan and in organizing the scientific use of the Area.

- The appropriate authority should be notified of any activities/measures undertaken, and/or of any materials released and not removed, that were not included in the authorized permit.

8. References

Aughenbaugh, N., Neuburg, H. and Walker P. 1958. Report 825-1-Part I, October 1958, USNC-IGY Antarctic Glaciological Data Field Work 1957 and 1958. Ohio State University Research Foundation. Source: World Data Center for Glaciology at Boulder, Colorado. (ftp://sidads.colorado.edu/pub/DATASETS/AGDC/antarctic_10m_temps/ells-filchner_57.txt).

Behrendt, J.C. 1998. *Innocents on the Ice; a memoir of Antarctic Exploration, 1957*. University Press of Colorado, Boulder.

Behrendt, J.C., Drewry, D.J., Jankowski, E., and Grim, M.S. 1980. Aeromagnetic and radio echo ice-sounding measurements show much greater area of the Dufek intrusion, Antarctica. *Science 209*: 1014-1017.

Behrendt, J.C., Henderson, J.R., Meister, L. and Rambo, W.K. 1974. Geophysical investigations of the Pensacola Mountains and Adjacent Glacierized areas of Antarctica. *U.S. Geological Survey Professional Paper* 844.

Boyer, S.J. 1979. Glacial geologic observations in the Dufek Massif and Forrestal Range, 1978-79. *Antarctic Journal of the United States* **14**(5): 46-48.

Burt, R. 2004. Travel Report - Sledge Bravo 2003-2004. SAGES-10K & BIRESA: Field trip to the lakes and dry valleys in the Dufek Massif and the Shackleton Mountains. Unpublished BAS Internal Report Ref. R/2003/K1. British Antarctic Survey, Cambridge

Cziferszky, A., Fox, A., Hodgson, D. and Convey, P. 2004. Unpublished topographic base map for Davis Valley, Dufek Massif, Pensacola Mountains. Mapping and Geographic Information Centre, British Antarctic Survey, Cambridge.

England, A.W. and Nelson, W.H. 1977. Geophysical studies of the Dufek Instrusion, Pensacola Mountains, Antarctica, 1976-1977. *Antarctic Journal of the United States* **12**(5): 93-94.

Ferris, J., Johnson, A. and Storey, B. 1998. Form and extent of the Dufek intrusion, Antarctica, from newly compiled aeromagnetic data. *Earth and Planetary Science Letters* 154: 185-202.

Ford, A.B. 1976. Stratigraphy of the layered gabbroic Dufek intrusion, Antarctica. *Contributions to stratigraphy: Geological Survey Bulletin* 1405-D.

Ford, A.B. 1990. *The Dufek intrusion of Antarctica. Antarctic Research Series* **51**. American Geophysical Union, Washington D.C.: *15-32.*

Ford, A.B., Schmidt, D.L. and Boyd, W.W. 1978. Geologic map of the Davis Valley quadrangle and part of the Cordiner Peaks quadrangle, Pensacola Mountains, Antarctica. *U.S Geological Survey Antarctic Geological Map A-10.*

Ford, A.B., Carlson, C., Czamanske, G.K., Nelson, W.H. and Nutt, C.J. 1977. Geological studies of the Dufek Instrusion, Pensacola Mountains, 1976-1977. *Antarctic Journal of the United States* 12(5): 90-92.

Friedmann, E.I. 1977. Microorganisms in Antarctic desert rocks from dry valleys and Dufek Massif. *Antarctic Journal of the United States* **12**(5): 26-29.

Hodgson, D.A., Convey, P., Verleyen, E., Vyverman, W., McIntosh, W., Sands, C.J., Fernández-Carazo, R., Wilmotte, A., DeWever, A., Peeters, K., Tavernier, I. and Willems, A. *in press*. The limnology and biology of the Dufek Massif, Transantarctic Mountains 82° South. *Polar Science.*

Hodgson, D. and Convey, P. 2004. Scientific Report - Sledge Bravo 2003-2004. BAS Signals in Antarctica of Past Global Changes: Dufek Massif – Pensacola Mountains; Mount Gass – Shackleton Mountains. Unpublished BAS Internal Report Ref. R/2003/NT1. British Antarctic Survey, Cambridge.

Neuburg, H., Theil, E., Walker, P.T., Behrendt, J.C and Aughenbaugh, N.B. 1959. The Filchner Ice Shelf. *Annals of the Association of American Geographers* **49**: 110-119.

Parker, B.C., Boyer, S., Allnutt, F.C.T., Seaburg, K.G., Wharton, R.A. and Simmons, G.M. 1982. Soils from the Pensacola Mountains, Antarctica: physical, chemical and biological characteristics. *Soil Biology and Biochemistry* **14**: 265-271.

Parker, B.C., Ford, A.B., Allnutt, T., Bishop, B. and Wendt, S. 1977. Baseline microbiological data for soils of the Dufek Massif. *Antarctic Journal of the United States* **12**(5): 24-26.

Schmidt, D.L. and Ford, A.B. 1967. Pensacola Mountains geologic project. *Antarctic Journal of the United States* **2**(5): 179.

Van den Broeke, M., van de Berg, W.J., van Meijgaard, E. and Reijmer, C. 2006. Identification of Antarctic ablation areas using a regional atmospheric climate model. *Journal of Geophysical Research* **111**:D18110. doi: 10.1029/2006JD007127

Van Lipzig, N.P.M., Turner, J., Colwell, S.R. and van Den Broeke, M.R. 2004. The near-surface wind field over the Antarctic continent. *International Journal of Climatology* **24**(15): 1973-82.

Appendix 1: Table A1. Biological sampling program in the Davis and Fortidas Valleys: groups of taxa identified and the methods used (Hodgson *et al.*, in press).

Description	Method	No. samples	No. taxa	Taxa
Bryophyta	Observational survey	0	0	n/a
Lichens	Observational survey	1	1	*Lecidea cancriformis* Dodge & Baker
Bacillariophyceae / Diatoms	Survey under light microscope	2	1	*Pinnularia microstauron* (Ehr.) Cl.††
Cyanobacteria	Clone library, DGGE + band sequencing, isolation of strains+ sequencing (microscopy)	3	6	Sample TM1: 16ST63, 16ST14 Sample TM2: 16ST63, 16ST14, 16ST44, 16ST49, 16ST80 Sample TM3: 16ST44, 16ST49, 16ST80, 16ST07
Chlorophyta /Green algae	DGGE + band sequencing	2	1	*Urospora* sp.
Rhizaria/ Cercozoa	DGGE + band sequencing	2	2	Heteromitidae, *Paulinella* sp.
Bacteria	DGGE + band sequencing	2	32	Cyanobacteria: Nostocales, Oscillatoriales, Chroococcales, Gloeobacteriales** Bacteroidetes: Sphingobacteriales, Flavobacteriales Firmicutes: Clostridiales Gammaproteobacteria: Pseudomonadales, Psychrobacter
Bacteria	Isolation of strains + sequencing	1	330 isolates	*Firmicutes* 33%, *Bacteroidetes* 23%, *Alphaproteobacteria* 25%, *Actinobacteria* 9%, *Betaproteobacteria.* 8%, *Gammaproteobacteria* 1.5%, Deinococci 0.3%
Arthropods	Tullenberg	50	0	n/a
Invertebrates	Baermann extractions	130	3	See Tardigrades (below)
Tardigrades	Light microscope (Molecular†)	14 20	3 1	*Echiniscus* (cf) *pseudowendti* Dastych, 1984 (Heterotardigrada), *Acutuncus antarcticus* (Richters, 1904) *Diphascon sanae* Dastych, Ryan and Watkins, 1990 (Eutardigrada)
Rotifers	Tullenberg and light microscope	130	present	Bdelloid rotifers
Soil bacteria and algae	Cultured (Parker *et al.,* 1982)*	1	3	Cyanobacteria: *Oscillatoria* sp. Algae: *Trebouxia* sp., *Heterococcus* sp. (viable yeasts present)
Avifauna	Observation	n/a	1	Snow petrel (*Pagadroma nivea*)

*previously published, ** tentative identification based on about 100 bases, †analyses carried out on morphologically congruent samples from the Shackleton Range, †† not considered as evidence of an extant community

Appendix 1: Table A2. Known visits to the Davis Valley and adjacent ice-free valleys within and near the Area.

Party	No. pers	Org	Purpose	Dates	Duration (days)	Locations visited	Camp	Transport

ASPA 119 – Davies Valley and Forlidas Pond

Party	No. pers	Org	Purpose	Dates	Duration (days)	Locations visited	Camp	Transport
Aughenbaugh, Behrendt, Neuburg, Thiel, Walker	5	IGY (US)	Geology Geophysics	Dec 1957	?	FIP, DV, FP, FR	FIP west of FR	Sno-Cat traverse to FIP, then on foot
Ford, Schmidt, Nelson, Boyd, Rambo (?)	5	USGS	Geology	Dec 1965 – Jan 1966	?	?	Base camp in Neptune Range	Numerous helicopter landings in Dufek Massif
Ford & team	?	USGS	Geology	Summer 1973-74	?	?	?	?
Ford, Carlson, Czamanske, Nutt, England, Nelson	6	USGS	Geology	30 Nov – 30 Dec 1976 (expedition dates)	?	?	Base camp close to Walker Peak (southwest Dufek Massif)	Numerous helicopter landings in Dufek Massif. Motor toboggans and ski traverses used on ground.
Russian team led by Shuljatin, O. G. Accompanied by Ford (and Gnue?) from the USA and Paech from Germany.	11	Soviet Antarctic Expedition (22)	Geology Geophysics	Summer 1976-77	49 (total expedition)	Dufek Massif and other locations in the Pensacola Mountains	Field camps on Provender Mountain, Read Mountain and Skidmor Mountain. Druznaja Station used as base camp.	Helicopter landings, snowmobile 'Buran', thence on foot
Russian team led by Kamenev, E. N.	6	Soviet Antarctic Expedition (23)	Geology Geophysics	06 Feb – 17 Feb 1978	11	Dufek Massif	Field camp in Schmidt Hills. Druznaja Station used as base camp.	Airplane, snowmobile 'Buran', thence on foot
Boyer, Reynolds	2	USGS	Geology	12 Dec 1978	2	FIP, DV	EV	Toboggan from EV to ice margin, thence on foot
Ford, Boyer. Reynolds Carl?	4	USGS	Geology	14 Dec 1978	4	FIP, DV, FR, AP	EV	Toboggan from EV to ice margin, thence on foot
Hodgson, Convey, Burt	3	BAS (UK)	Biology, Limnology, Glacial geo-morphology	3-15 Dec 2003	13	FIP, DV, FP, FR, AP	FIP 1.9km north of FP	Twin Otter to FIP, thence on foot.
TOTALS	~30				~40??	(numbers approximate owing to incomplete data)		

Key: FIP – Ford Ice Piedmont; DV – Davis Valley; FP – Forlidas Pond; FR– Forlidas Ridge; AP – Angels Peak; CS – Clemons Spur; PS – Preslik Spur; MB– Mt Beljakova; MP–Mt Pavlovskogo; EV–Enchanted Valley.

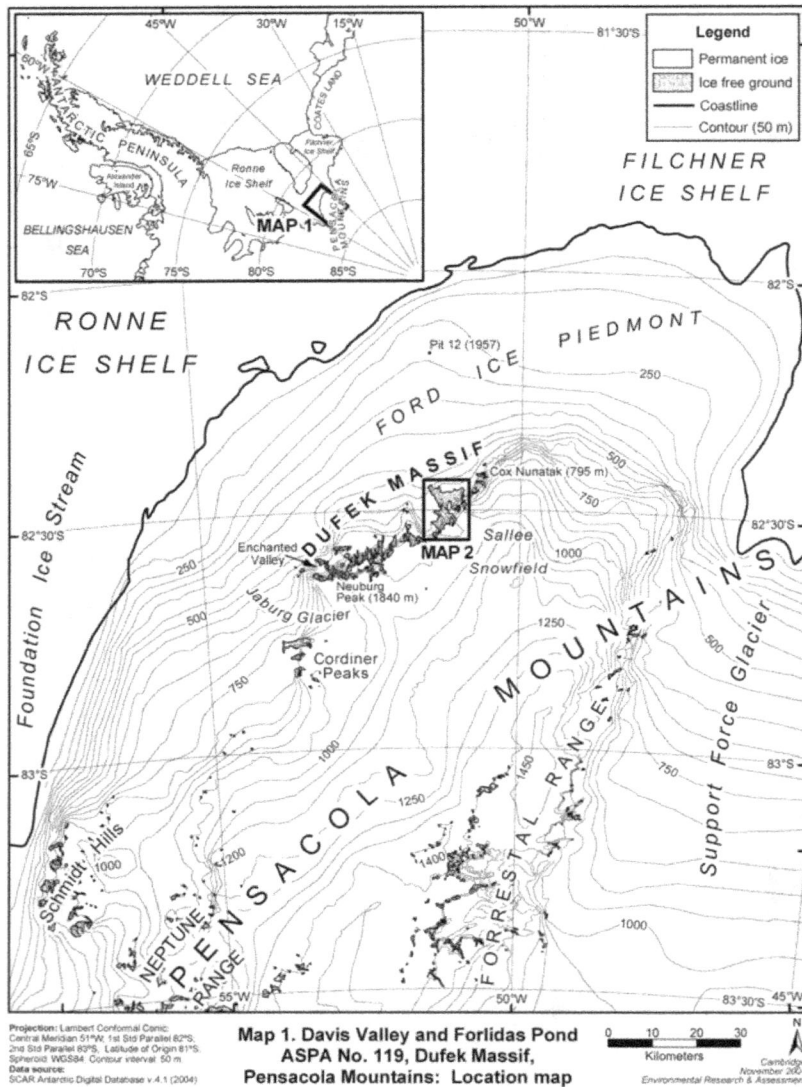

Map 1. Davis Valley and Forlidas Pond
ASPA No. 119, Dufek Massif,
Pensacola Mountains: Location map

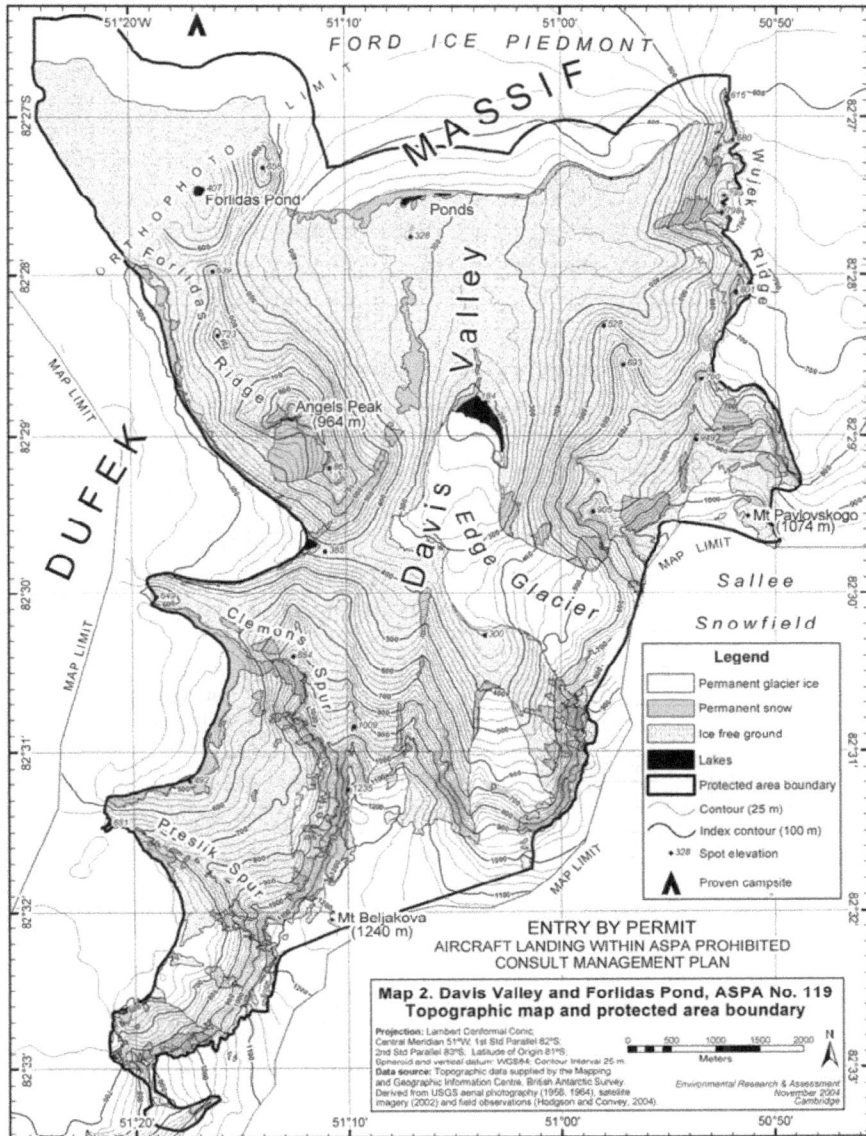

FORD ICE PIEDMONT

MASSIF

Forlidas Pond

Ponds

DUFEK

Forlidas Ridge

Angels Peak
(964 m)

Davis Valley

Edge Glacier

Wujek Ridge

Mt Pavlovskogo
(1074 m)

Sallee
Snowfield

Clemons Spur

Presiik Spur

Mt Beljakova
(1240 m)

Legend

	Permanent glacier ice
	Permanent snow
	Ice free ground
	Lakes
	Protected area boundary
	Contour (25 m)
	Index contour (100 m)
•328	Spot elevation
	Proven campsite

ENTRY BY PERMIT
AIRCRAFT LANDING WITHIN ASPA PROHIBITED
CONSULT MANAGEMENT PLAN

Map 2. Davis Valley and Forlidas Pond, ASPA No. 119
Topographic map and protected area boundary

Projection: Lambert Conformal Conic,
Central Meridian 51°W, 1st Std Parallel 82°S,
2nd Std Parallel 83°S, Latitude of Origin 81°S.
Spheroid and vertical datum: WGS84. Contour Interval 25 m.
Data source: Topographic data supplied by the Mapping
and Geographic Information Centre, British Antarctic Survey.
Derived from USGS aerial photography (1958, 1964), satellite
imagery (2002) and field observations (Hodgson and Convey, 2004).

0 500 1000 1500 2000
Meters

Environmental Research & Assessment
November 2004
Cambridge

Document	Figure	Source	Term	Translation	Proper Name	Translation
Davis Map 1	First	Legend	Permanent ice			
			Ice free ground			
			Coastline			
			Contour			
		Map	Ice Shelf		Filchner	
			Ice Shelf		Ronne	
			Ice Piedmont		Ford	
			Pit			
			Foundation Ice Stream			
			Massif		Dufek	
			Snowfield		Salle	
			Mountains		Pensacola	
			Enchanted Valley			
			Peak		Neuburg	
			Map			
			Glacier		Jaburg	
			Peaks		Cordiner	
			Hills		Schmidt	
			Range		Neptune	
			Range		Forrestal	
			Support Force Glacier			
					Cox Nunatak	
		Inset Map	Sea		Wendell	
			Penninsula		Antarctic	
			Sea		Bellinghausen	
			Map			
			Ice Shelf		Ronne	
			Mountains		Pensacola	
			Ice Shelf		Filchner	
			Coates land			
		Title	Map 1. Davis Valley and Forlidas Pond ASPA No. 119, Dufek Massif, Pensacola Mountains: Location map			
			Projection: Lambert Conformal Conic; Central Meridian 51°W; 1st Std Parallel 82°S; 2nd Std Parallel 83°S; Latitude of Origin 81°S; Spheroid: WGS84; Contour interval: 50 m. Data source: SCAR Antarctic Digital Database v.4.1 (2004)			

			Cambridge November 2004 Environmental Research & Assessment			
			Kilometers			

Document	Figure	Source	Term	Translation	Proper Name	Translation
Davis Map 2		Legend	Permanent glacier ice			
			Permanent snow			
			Ice free ground			
			Lakes			
			Protected area boundary			
			Contour			
			Index contour			
			Spot elevation			
			Proven campsite			
		Map	Ice Piedmont		Ford	
			Massif		Dufek	
			Orthophoto Limit			
			Pond		Forlidas	
			Ridge		Forlidas	
			Map Limit			
			Valley		Davis	
			Ridge		Wujek	
			Mount (Mt)		Pavlovskogo	
			Snowfield		Salle	
			Glacier		Edge	
			Angels Peak			
			Spur		Clemons	
			Spur		Preslik	
			Mount (Mt)		Beljakova	
			Entry by permit Aircraft landing within ASPA prohibited Consult Management Plan			
		Title	Map 2. Davis Valley and Forlidas Pond, ASPA No. 119 Topographic map and protected area boundary			

			Projection: Lambert Conformal Conic; Central Meridian 51°W; 1st Std Parallel 82°S; 2nd Std Parallel 83°S; Latitude of Origin 81°S; Spheroid and vertical datum: WGS84; Contour Interval 25 m. Data source: Topographic data supplied by the Mapping and Geographic Information Centre, British Antarctic Survey. Derived from USGS aerial photography (1956, 1964), satellite imagery (2002) and field observations (Hodgson and Convey, 2004).	
			Environmental Research & Assessment November 2004 Cambridge	
			Meters	

Management Plan for

Antarctic Specially Protected Area (ASPA) No. 139

BISCOE POINT, ANVERS ISLAND, PALMER ARCHIPELAGO

(64° 48' S, 63° 47' W)

Introduction

The Biscoe Point Antarctic Specially Protected Area is located near the south-west coast of Anvers Island, in the Palmer Archipelago, Antarctic Peninsula, at 64°48'40"S, 63°46'27"W. Approximate area: 0.63 km². The primary reason for the designation of the Area is its extensive vegetation communities, soils and terrestrial ecology. The Area contains the most extensive stands of Antarctic hair grass (*Deschampsia antarctica*) and Antarctic pearlwort (*Colobanthus quitensis*) in the Anvers Island region, as well as numerous species of mosses and lichens. The Area is a breeding site for several bird species, including Adélie (*Pygoscelis adeliae*) and Gentoo (*Pygoscelis papua*) penguins, Brown (*Catharacta loennbergi*), South Polar (*C. maccormicki*) and hybrid skuas, which have been the subject of long-term monitoring and ecological research. Furthermore, the long history of protection of the Area makes it a valuable reference site for comparative studies and long-term monitoring. The Area was proposed by the United States of America and adopted through Recommendation XII-8 [1985, Site of Special Scientific Interest (SSSI) No. 20]; date of expiry was extended by Resolution 3 (1996) and through Measure 2 (2000); and the Area was renamed and renumbered through Decision 1 (2002). The boundary of the Area was revised through Measure 2 (2004) to remove its marine component, and following the collapse of the ice ramp joining the island to Anvers Island. The boundaries of the Area have not been changed in the current management plan.

1. Description of values to be protected

Biscoe Point (64°48'47"S, 63°47'41"W), 0.63 km², Anvers Island, Palmer Archipelago, Antarctic Peninsula, was originally designated as a Site of Special Scientific Interest through Recommendation XIII-8 (1985, SSSI No. 20) after a proposal by the United States of America. It was designated on the grounds that the "Site contains a large (approximately 5000 m²) but discontinuous stand of the two native vascular plants, Antarctic hair grass (*Deschampsia antarctica*) and, less commonly, Antarctic pearlwort (*Colobanthus quitensis*). A relatively well developed loam occurs beneath closed swards of the grass and contains a rich biota, including the apterous midge *Belgica antarctica*. Long-term research programs could be jeopardised by interference from nearby Palmer Station and from tourist ships."

The present management plan reaffirms the exceptional ecological and scientific values associated with the rich flora and invertebrate fauna within the Area. In addition, it is noted that the first observation of *C. quitensis* growing south of 60°S was made at Biscoe Point, reported by Jean-Baptiste Charcot from the Expédition Antarctiques Française in 1903-05. The island on which Biscoe Point lies contains the most extensive communities of *D. antarctica* and *C. quitensis* in the Anvers Island vicinity, and they are of unusual abundance for this latitude. The abundance is much greater than previously described, with almost half of the island of Biscoe Point, and much of the ice-free area of the peninsula to the north, possessing significant stands of vegetation. The communities extend over a large proportion of the available ice-free ground, with a discontinuous cover of *D. antarctica*, *C. quitensis* and bryophytes and lichens of several species varying in density over an area of approximately 250,000 m². One stand of mosses in the prominent valley on the northern side of the main island extends almost continuously for 150 m along the valley floor, covering an area of approximately 6500 m². Individual, near-continuous stands of *D. antarctica* and *C. quitensis* reach a similar size, both on the main island and, to a lesser extent, on the promontory to the north.

Several plant community studies were in progress when the Area was designated in 1985. Although these studies were discontinued soon after site designation, botanical research at the site has continued. For example, *D. antarctica* and *C. quitensis* seeds have been collected from Biscoe Point for plant studies examining the influence of climate change and enhanced UV-B radiation (Day, pers. comm. 1999). Biscoe Point was valuable for these studies because of the amount and quality of seeds available within the Area. Cores containing plant material and soils have been collected within the Area to investigate carbon and nitrogen fluxes within the ecosystem and to evaluate the influence of increased temperature and precipitation on the ecosystem (Park *et al.*, 2007, Day *et al.*, 2009). In addition, Biscoe Point is one of the few low-lying vegetated sites that has not yet been substantially damaged by Antarctic fur seals, and as such the Area has been identified as a potential control site for assessing Antarctic fur seal impacts on vegetation and soils in this region.

Biscoe Point is also valuable for ornithological research. Research into seabird ecology and long-term monitoring studies are being conducted on Adélie (*Pygoscelis adeliae*) and Gentoo (*Pygoscelis papua*) penguin colonies, as well as Brown (*Catharacta loennbergi*) and hybrid skuas (Patterson-Fraser, pers. comm., 2010).The Gentoo colony became established at Biscoe Point some time around 1992 and, as a recently founded colony, is of particular value for monitoring long-term ecological changes to the local bird population structure and dynamics (Fraser, pers. comm., 1999). The Adélie colony is valuable for long-term monitoring and comparison with other colonies in Arthur Harbor that are subjected to higher levels of human influence. In this respect, the fact that the Area has been protected from significant human use, and that use allowed has been regulated by permit, for such a long period of time is of particular value. The Adélie colony is one of the oldest in the southern Anvers Island region (more than 700 years), and as such is valuable for paleoecological studies. The site is also the only site in the region where Brown (*Catharacta loennbergi*), south polar (*C. maccormicki*) and hybrid skuas are known to occur annually.

Until recently, Biscoe Point was on a peninsula joined to Anvers Island by an ice ramp extending from the adjacent glacier. The ice ramp disappeared as the glacier retreated, and a narrow channel now separates Anvers Island from the island on which Biscoe Point lies. The original boundary of the Area was of geometric shape and extended to include a separate ice-free promontory 300 m to the north of this island, and also included the intervening marine environment. The Area is now defined to include all land above the low tide water level of the main island on which Biscoe Point is situated (0.53 km^2), all offshore islets and rocks within 100 m of the shore of the main island, and most of the predominantly ice-free promontory 300 m to the north (0.1 km^2). The marine component has now been excluded from the Area because of the lack of information on its values. The Area in total is now approximately 0.63 km^2.

In summary, the Area at Biscoe Point therefore has high value for its outstanding:

- examples of vegetation communities, soils and associated terrestrial ecology;

- ornithological interest, with several of the resident breeding bird species and associated paleoecological features possessing unusual properties, and which are the subject of long-term studies; and

- utility as a reference site for comparative studies and monitoring.

In order to protect the values of the Area, it is important that visitation continue to remain low and be carefully managed.

2. Aims and Objectives

Management at Biscoe Point aims to:

- avoid degradation of, or substantial risk to, the values of the Area by preventing unnecessary human disturbance and sampling in the Area;

- allow scientific research on the ecosystem and physical environment associated with the values for which the Area is protected, while ensuring protection from over-sampling;

- allow other scientific research within the Area provided it is for compelling reasons which cannot be served elsewhere and provided it will not compromise the values for which the Area is protected;

- minimize the possibility of introduction of alien plants, animals and microbes to the Area;

- allow visits for management purposes in support of the aims of the management plan.

3. Management activities

The following management activities shall be undertaken to protect the values of the Area:

- Signs showing the location of the Area (stating the special restrictions that apply) shall be displayed prominently, and copies of this management plan, including maps of the Area, shall be made available at Palmer Station (US) on Anvers Island and at Yelcho Station (Chile) on Doumer Island.

- Markers, signs or other structures erected within the Area for scientific or management purposes shall be secured and maintained in good condition, and removed when no longer necessary.

- Visits shall be made as necessary (at least once every five years) to assess whether the Area continues to serve the purposes for which it was designated and to ensure management and maintenance measures are adequate.

4. Period of designation

Designated for an indefinite period.

5. Maps and photographs

Map 1: ASPA No. 139 Biscoe Point, in The context of ASMA No. 7 SW Anvers Island and Palmer Basin, showing the location of nearby stations (Palmer Station, US; Yelcho Station, Chile; and Port Lockroy, UK), and the location of nearby protected areas. Projection Lambert Conformal Conic: Standard parallels: 1st 64° 45' S; 2nd 65° 00' S; Central Meridian: 64° 06' W; Latitude of Origin: 63° 45' S, Spheroid WGS84, Data source SCAR Antarctic Digital Database V4.1. Inset: the location of Anvers Island and the Palmer Archipelago in relation to the Antarctic Peninsula.

Map 2: ASPA No. 139 Biscoe Point: Physical features, boundaries and access guidelines. Map specifications: Projection: Lambert Conformal Conic: Standard parallels: 1st 64° 48' S; 2nd 64° 50' S; Central Meridian: 63° 46' W; Latitude of Origin: 63° 48' S; Spheroid: WGS84; Vertical datum: mean sea level; Horizontal Datum: USGS BIS1 (1999); Contour interval: 5 m. The coastline of the island on which Biscoe Point lies is derived from USGS digital orthophotography with a horizontal and vertical accuracy of ± 2 m (Sanchez and Fraser, 2001). The peninsula to the north of Biscoe Point, several offshore islands and Anvers Island are beyond the limits of this orthophotograph. These features are digitized from an orthophotograph covering the wider area (ERA, 2010) and are estimated as accurate to ± 1 m.

Map 3: Biscoe Point, ASPA No. 139: Penguin colonies, approximate vegetation extent, and known contaminated sites. Map specifications as for Map 2.

6.   Description of the Area

6(i) Geographical coordinates, boundary markers and natural features

General description

Biscoe Point (64°48'47" S, 63°47'41" W) is at the western extremity of a small island (0.53 km^2), located close to the southern coast of Anvers Island (2700 km^2) about 6 km south of Mount William (1515 m), in the region west of the Antarctic Peninsula known as the Palmer Archipelago (Map 1). Until recently, this island was joined to Anvers Island by an ice ramp extending from the adjacent southward-flowing glacier, and many maps (now incorrectly) show Biscoe Point as lying on a peninsula. A narrow, permanent, marine channel of approximately 50 m in width now separates the island on which Biscoe Point lies from Anvers Island. This mostly ice-free island lies south-east of Biscoe Bay and to the north of Bismarck Strait. A smaller extent of mostly ice-free land about 300 m to the north remains joined as a peninsula to Anvers Island by an ice ramp.

The island on which Biscoe Point lies is approximately 1.8 km long in an east-west direction and of up to about 450 m in width (Map 2). Topography consists of a series of low-lying hills, with the main east-west oriented ridge rising to a maximum altitude of about 24 m. A small ice cap (0.03 km^2) previously rising to 12 m at the eastern end of the island no longer exists and has wasted to a series of small snow patches. The coastline is irregular and generally rocky, studded by offshore islets and rocks, and pitted by numerous bays. A number of the more sheltered bays harbor gentle and accessible gravel beaches. The unnamed promontory to the north is approximately 750 m in length (east-west) by 150 m wide and is of similar character, although of lower topography.

Palmer Station (US) is located 13.8 km north-west of the Area at Arthur Harbor, Yelcho Station (Chile) is located approximately 12 km to the southeast at Doumer Island, while 'Base A' (UK, Historic Site No. 61) is located at Port Lockroy, Goudier Island (off Wiencke Island) approximately 13 km to the east (Map 1).

Boundaries

The original boundary of the Area was of geometric shape to include the land associated with Biscoe Point, the separate ice-free promontory 300 m to the north, and also the intervening islands and marine environment. A recent detailed review revealed little information to substantiate special values associated with the local marine environment. The marine area is not the subject of current or planned scientific studies, nor is it being subjected to specific pressures or threats requiring management. For these reasons, the boundary has been revised to exclude the marine environment. The Area is now defined to include all land above the low tide water level of the main island on which Biscoe Point is situated (0.53 km^2), all offshore islets and rocks within 100 m of the shore of this main island, and most of the predominantly ice-free promontory 300 m to the north (0.1 km^2) (Map 2). The landward (eastern) boundary on the northern promontory bisects the peninsula at the point where it protrudes from Anvers Island, distinguished by a small bay cutting into the glacier in the south and a similar, although less pronounced, coastline feature in the north. The total area including the main island and the northern promontory is approximately 0.63 km^2.

Climate

No meteorological data are available for Biscoe Point, although data are available for Palmer Station (US), where conditions are expected to be broadly similar. Monthly air temperature averages recorded for Palmer Station over a 22-year period range from -7.8°C in August (the coldest month) to 2.5°C in January (the warmest) (Baker, 1996). The minimum recorded temperature is -31°C and the maximum is 9°C, while the annual mean is -2.3°C. During the same period, the average annual precipitation was 75cm and snowfall averaged 387 cm. Storms and precipitation at Palmer

Station are frequent, with winds being persistent but generally light to moderate in strength, prevailing from the northeast. Cloud cover is frequently extensive, often with a ceiling of less than 300 m. While these broad patterns are expected to be reflected at Biscoe Point, the Area is in a more exposed position that is open to weather particularly from the west and south, which may result in some minor climatic differences.

Geology and Soils

Specific descriptions are not available of the geology of island on which Biscoe Point lies, or of the peninsula to the north. However, the bedrock appears to be composed mainly of gabbros and adamellites of Late Cretaceous to Early Tertiary age belonging to the Andean Intrusive Suite, which dominate the composition of southeastern Anvers Island (Hooper, 1958). Gabbro is a dark, coarse-grained plutonic rock that is mineralogically similar to basalt, and which is composed mainly of calcium-rich plagioclase feldspar and pyroxene. Adamellite is a granitic rock composed of 10-50% quartz and which contains plagioclase feldspar. A fine mineral soil is present on the gentle terrain, although precise soil characteristics have yet to be described. A relatively well-developed, loamy soil is associated with the closed swards of *Deschampsia*. Cores extracted in the south of the island, close to the Adélie penguin colony, consisted of an organic horizon, overlying a sandy loam glacial drift or bedrock (Day *et al.* 2009).

Freshwater Habitat

A number of small seasonal streams and ponds are present on the island on which Biscoe Point lies, although they have not been scientifically described. A small pond (perhaps the largest, at approximately 30 m x 8 m) and stream occur in a valley on the southern side of the principal ridge of the island, 50 m NE of the southern small boat landing site (Map 2). The presence of a long rubber hose suggests that at one time visitors may have collected fresh water from this site. The hose was removed in 2009-10 and disposed of at Palmer Station. Another freshwater pond of similar size (approximately 25 m x 6 m) is found in the prominent east-west trending valley on the northern side of the island. A small associated stream drains this pond to the west. The freshwater environment has thus far escaped significant disturbance from seals. Information on the hydrology of the separate promontory to the north is not available.

Vegetation

The most significant aspect of the vegetation at Biscoe Point is the abundance and reproductive success of the two native Antarctic flowering plants, the Antarctic hair grass *Deschampsia antarctica* and Antarctic pearlwort *Colobanthus quitensis*. The communities of *D. antarctica* and *C. quitensis* at Biscoe Point are the most extensive in the Anvers Island vicinity and are considered particularly abundant for such a southerly location (Greene and Holtom 1971; Komárková 1983, 1984; Komárková, Poncet and Poncet 1985). The first observation of *C. quitensis* growing south of 60°S was made near Biscoe Point, recorded (as *C. crassifolius*) by the biologist Turquet on Jean-Baptiste Charcot's Expédition Antarctiques Française (1903-05). More recently, seeds from both flowering plants within the Area have been collected for propagation in studies on the effects of climate change and UV-B exposure on these species being conducted out of Palmer Station (Day, pers. comm., 1999; Xiong, 2000). In January 2004, cores of plant material and soils were collected from Biscoe Point and were used in multi-year experiments into the tundra ecosystem. The cores were used in combination with precipitation and surface runoff samples to measure pools and fluxes of carbon and nitrogen within the Biscoe Point ecosystem and to evaluate the role of nitrogen inputs from the nearby penguin colony (Park *et al.*, 2007). Cores were also used in climate manipulation experiments at Palmer Station, which investigated the influence of increased temperature and precipitation on plant productivity and the abundance of the springtail *Cryptopygus* (Day *et al.*, 2009).

The abundance of *D. antarctica* and *C. quitensis* is much greater than previously described, and almost half of the island on which Biscoe Point lies, and much of the ice-free area of the peninsula to the north, possess significant stands of these species and a wide range of bryophytes and lichens. The approximate distribution of the most substantial stands of vegetation on the main island has been estimated from air and ground photography (Map 3). The distribution illustrated in Map 3 is intended as a general guide to the main areas of vegetation cover, rather than as a definitive description, and is not based on a precise ground survey. However, it does serve to indicate the scale of the vegetated communities, which comprise a discontinuous cover of varied composition and density over an area of approximately 250,000 m^2. Komárková (1983) noted a discontinuous stand of *D. antarctica* and *C. quitensis* reaching approximately 5000 m^2 on the main island. One particularly extensive stand of mosses in the principal valley on the northern side of the main island extends almost continuously for 240 m along the valley floor, occupying an area of approximately 8000 m^2 (Harris, 2001). Stands of lesser extent are present elsewhere on the island and on the separate promontory 300 m to the north. Colonization has been observed occurring on recently deglaciated material.

Mosses tend to dominate on valley floors, close to streams and ponds, and in moist depressions. Mosses specifically recorded at Biscoe Point include *Bryum pseudotriquetrum* and *Sanionia uncinata* (Park *et al.*, 2007). On valley sides, mixed communities of moss and *C. quitensis* are frequent on lower north-facing slopes, with an increasing prevalence of *D. antarctica* with elevation. Mixed *D. antarctica* and *C. quitensis* communities are particularly prolific on northern slopes between 10-20 m, while *D. antarctica* tends to be more frequent on the higher exposed sites above 20 m. Mosses and lichens are frequently co-dominants or subordinate taxa. In some habitats *C. quitensis* may occur in small patches alone. Plant communities are commonly found on snow-free benches below the ridgelines on which Adélie (*Pygoscelis adeliae*) and Gentoo (*Pygoscelis papua*) penguins nest (Park and Day, 2007).Patches of dead vascular plants of up to 20 m² have been observed within the Area, believed to result from the effects of desiccation, flooding and frost during some summers (Komárková, Poncet and Poncet 1985).

Unlike many other low-lying coastal sites in the region, the vegetation at Biscoe Point does not appear to have been severely affected by the recent substantial increase in numbers of Antarctic fur seals (*Arctocephalus gazella*). As such, the Area has been identified as a potential control site for assessing Antarctic fur seal impacts on vegetation and soil (Day, pers. comm., 1999).

Invertebrates, Bacteria and Fungi

The apterous midge *Belgica antarctica* has been observed associated with the well-developed loam and closed swards of grass. Cores collected at Biscoe Point contained several species of microarthropod, including several species or genera of Acrai, one species of Diptera and three species of Collembola. The springtail *Cryptopygus antarcticus* was the most abundant microarthropod (Day *et al.*, 2009) No further information is available on the invertebrate assemblages in the Area, although in view of the well-developed plant communities a rich invertebrate fauna might be expected. There is no information available on local bacterial or fungal communities.

Breeding Birds and Mammals

At least six species of birds breed on the island on which Biscoe Point lies. The most numerous colony is of Adélie penguins (*Pygoscelis adeliae*), located on the ridge of a promontory on the south side of the island, above a narrow cove on the southern coast (Map 3). A Gentoo penguin (*Pygoscelis papua*) colony was discovered on slopes on the northern side of this cove, on the southern side of the main island ridge, in 1992-93 (Fraser, pers. comm., 1999) (Map 3) and Gentoo numbers have increased significantly in recent years with 2401 breeding pairs in the 2009-10 season (Patterson-Fraser, pers. comm., 2010). Data on numbers of breeding pairs are presented in Table 1.

Table 1. Numbers of breeding Adélie (*Pygoscelis adeliae*) and Gentoo (*Pygoscelis papua*) penguins on the island on which Biscoe Point lies 1971-2002.

Year	*Pygoscelis adeliae*			*Pygoscelis papua*		
	Breeding pairs	Count type[1]	Source	Breeding pairs	Count type[1]	Source
1971-72	3020	N3	2	0	N3	2
1983-84	3440	C3	3	0	C3	3
1984-85	2754	N1	3	0	N1	3
1986-87	3000	N4	4			
...						
1994-95				14	N1	5
1995-96				33	N1	5
1996-97	1801	N1	5	45	N1	5
1997-98				56	N1	5
1998-99				26	N1	5
1999-2000	1665	N1	5	149	N1	5
2000-01	1335	N1	5	296	N1	5
2001-02	692	N1	5	288	N1	5
2002-03	1025	N1	5	639	N1	5
2009-10	594	N1	6	2401	N1	6

1. N = Nest, C = Chick, A = Adults; 1 = < ± 5%, 2 = ± 5-10%, 3 = ± 10-15%, 4 = ± 25-50% (classification after Woehler, 1993)
2. Müller-Schwarze and Müller-Schwarze, 1975
3. Parmelee and Parmelee, 1987
4. Poncet and Poncet 1987 (note: the number of 3500 given in Woehler (1993) appears to be in error).
5. Fraser data supplied February 2003, based on multiple published and unpublished sources.
6. Patterson-Fraser data supplied March 2010 based on census at time of peak egg presence.

The Adélie colonies are some of the oldest in the region (more than 700 years), and have been the subject of paleoecological studies (Emslie, 2001), while the Gentoo colony is considered particularly interesting because it has been recently established (Fraser, pers. comm., 1999). Long-term studies are being conducted on the population structure and dynamics of the penguin colonies within the Area, which make a useful comparison with other colonies in Arthur Harbor that are subjected to higher levels of human influence (Fraser, pers. comm., 1999). The number of Adélie breeding pairs at Biscoe Point has declined from a high of around 3000-3500 in the 1980s to less than 600 in the most recent count made in 2009-10 (Patterson-Fraser pers. comm. 2010).

South Polar skuas (*Catharacta maccormicki*) and Brown skuas (*C. loennbergi*) breed within the Area annually, and hybrids also occur. On the island on which Biscoe Point lies, 132 pairs of South Polar skuas and one pair of Brown skuas were counted on 26-27 February 2001 (Harris, 2001). Concurrently, 15 pairs of South Polar skuas, usually with one or two chicks, were counted on the promontory 300 m to the north. Kelp gulls (*Larus dominicanus*) and Antarctic terns (*Sterna vittata*) breed within the Area (Fraser, pers. comm., 2000), although data on numbers are not available. Information on other bird species that breed within the Area, or that transiently visit, is not available.

Small numbers of non-breeding Antarctic Fur seals (*Arctocephalus gazella*) (several counted on the island in late-February 2001 – Harris, 2001), Weddell seals (*Leptonychotes weddellii*) and Southern Elephant seals (*Mirounga leonina*) have been observed on beaches in summer. Despite the presence of beaches and terrain suitable for haul-out, relatively few seals are typically observed within the Area. This may be a result of the observed frequent persistence of dense brash ice originating from glaciers calving from nearby Anvers Island (Fraser, pers. comm., 1999). Further information on numbers and breeding status, or on other seal species, is not available. No information is available on the local marine environment.

Human Activities and Impact

Human activity within the Area appears to have been minimal, but few details have been recorded. The first documented human activity in the vicinity of Biscoe Point occurred over 150 years ago, when John Biscoe, Royal Navy, entered the bay now named after him on 21 February 1832. Biscoe recorded a landing on Anvers Island, probably near Biscoe Point, to take formal possession for the United Kingdom of what he believed to be part of the mainland of Antarctica (Hattersley-Smith, 1991). The next recorded visit to Biscoe Point was in 1903-05, when Turquet made observations of *C. quitensis* at the site on the Première Expédition Antarctiques Française led by Charcot.

More recently, formal plots for plant studies were established on the island near Biscoe Point in 1982 (Komárková, 1983), although the long-term research originally planned was discontinued soon thereafter. Komárková used welding rods inserted into the soil to mark study sites. A partial survey accurately mapped the positions ($\pm$ 2 m) of 44 welding rods found in soils and vegetation during a systematic search made on the northeastern side of the island in February 2001 (Map 3) (Harris, 2001). The rods were located in an area of some of the richest vegetation on the island, and distributed over an area of at least 8000 m^2. In general, they had been inserted into soil or vegetation with chemically coated ends downwards. Contaminants from the rods appeared to kill all vegetation up to 20 cm from where the rods lay. Numerous rods have been found in previous seasons, possibly numbering in the hundreds (Fraser, Patterson, Day: pers. comms., 1999-2002). Additional welding rods were found on and near the beach during the 2009-10 season, which were collected and disposed of at Palmer Station (Patterson-Fraser, pers. comm., 2010). The Area is not considered suitable as a reference site for measuring chemical contamination, because there remains uncertainty over contaminant types and concentrations, which sites have been affected, and the extent to which contaminants may have moved through soil, water and biological systems.

Fraser (pers. comm., 2001) also reported markers made of lead present in the Gentoo colony. In addition, seaborne litter (mostly wood) may be found on beaches, and there remains a rubber hose (15 m long, ~15 cm diameter) in a small valley near the southern small boat landing site, which may once have been used for water supply purposes.

Recent scientific studies within the Area have focused on monitoring the breeding status of penguins and skuas The Area has also been used for the collection of seeds of *Deschampsia* and *Colobanthus* and cores of soil and plant material for ecological research in the Palmer Station region. Permits have been required to visit the Area since the site was specially protected in 1985.

6(ii) Access to the Area

Access to the Area may be made by small boat, by aircraft or across sea ice by vehicle or on foot. The seasonal cycle of sea ice formation in the Palmer area is highly variable, with sea ice formation beginning between March and May. For the period 1979 to 2004, the seasonal duration of sea ice in the Palmer area varied between five and 12 months (Stammerjohn *et al.*, 2008).

Aircraft access restrictions to the Area apply for the period 01 October to 15 April inclusive. During this time, helicopters may land at either of the two designated landing sites (Map 2). Landing site (A) is located on the northern coast of the main island on which Biscoe Point lies (64°48'35" S, 63°46'49" W). Landing site (B) is situated on the promontory 300 m north of the main island and is on the permanent snow slope approximately 50-100 m east of the ice-free ground (64°48'22" S, 63°46'24" W). Helicopter access to the Area should be within the Helicopter Access Zone. The zone allows helicopter access from two main directions: from the north and west, from the region of Biscoe Bay towards landing site (A) and from the north and east, across the Anvers Island coastline towards landing site (B).

When access to the Area is made by sea, two landing sites are recommended although small boats may land anywhere within the Area. The first recommended landing site is located on the southern coast of the island, on the beach on the northern shore of the elongated cove (Map 2) and is the site most likely to be free of sea ice. The second recommended landing site is on the beach in the small cove mid-way along the northern coast of the island and is adjacent to the designated camp and helicopter landing sites. Dense brash ice is frequently found in the vicinity of the island and originates from calving glaciers on Anvers Island.

When sea ice conditions allow, the Area may be accessed over sea ice on foot or by vehicle. However, movement within the Area is by foot only and vehicles may not be taken onto land within the Area. Persons entering the Area may not move beyond the immediate vicinity of their landing site unless specifically authorised by Permit.

6(iii) Restricted and managed zones within the Area

A Helicopter Access Zone (Maps 2 and 3) has been defined within the Management Plan for Antarctic Specially Managed Area No. 7, which applies to aircraft accessing the designated landing sites within the Area. The Helicopter Access Zone extends in northwesterly and northeasterly directions from the designated landing sites out to a distance of 2000 feet (610 m) from the edges of known bird colony breeding locations within the Area.

6(iv) Structures within and near the Area

No structures or instruments are known to be present within the Area. A permanent survey marker, consisting of a 5/8" stainless steel threaded rod, was installed on the island on which Biscoe Point lies by the USGS on 31 January 1999. The marker is located at 64°48'40.12"S, 63°46'26.42"W at an elevation of 23 m (Maps 2 & 3). It is sited approximately midway along the principal ridgeline of the island, about 100 m north of the southern small boat landing site. The marker is set in bedrock and marked by a red plastic survey cap.

6(v) Location of other protected areas within close proximity of the Area

The nearest protected areas to Biscoe Point are: Litchfield Island (ASPA No. 113) which is 16 km west of the Area in Arthur Harbor; South Bay (ASPA No. 146), which is approximately 12 km to the southeast at Doumer Island; and Eastern Dallmann Bay (ASPA No. 153) which is approximately 85 km to the northeast, adjacent to Brabant Island (Map 1).

7.   Permit conditions

Entry into the Area is prohibited except in accordance with a Permit issued by an appropriate national authority. Conditions for issuing a Permit to enter the Area are that:

- it is issued for scientific purposes, or for educational purposes that cannot be served elsewhere, or for essential management purposes consistent with plan objectives such as inspection, maintenance or review;

- the actions permitted will not jeopardize the ecological, scientific, or educational values of the Area;

- any management activities are in support of the objectives of the Management Plan;

- the actions permitted are in accordance with the Management Plan ;

- the Permit, or an copy, shall be carried within the Area;

- a visit report shall be supplied to the authority named in the Permit;

- permits shall be issued for a stated period.

7(i) Access to and movement within the Area

Access to the Area shall be by small boat, by aircraft, or over sea ice by vehicle or on foot.

Boat access

The recommended landing sites for small boats are at either of the following locations (Maps 2&3):

1) on the beach on the northern shore of the elongated cove on the southern coast of the island, which is the site most likely to be free of sea ice;
2) on the beach in the small cove mid-way along the northern coast of the island, adjacent to the designated camp and helicopter landing sites.

Access by small boat at other locations around the coast is allowed, provided this is consistent with the purposes for which a Permit has been granted.

Aircraft access and overflight

Restrictions on aircraft operations apply during the period between 01 October and 15 April inclusive, when aircraft shall operate and land within the Area according to strict observance of the following conditions:

1) Overflight of the Area below 2000 ft (~610 m) is prohibited outside of the Helicopter Access Zone (Map 2), except when specifically permitted for purposes allowed for by the Management Plan. It is recommended that aircraft maintain a 2000 ft (~610 m) horizontal separation distance from the edges of bird colonies breeding within the Area as shown in Map 2, unless accessing the designated landing sites through the Helicopter Access Zone;

2) Helicopter landing is permitted at two designated sites (Map 2), the first (A) on the main island on which Biscoe Point lies, and the second (B) on the separate promontory 300 m further to the north. The landing sites with their coordinates are described as follows:

(A) on beach gravels a few meters above sea level 35 m east of the beach on the eastern shore of a small cove on the northern coast of the island (64°48'35" S, 63°46'49" W). A small tidal pool of about 25 m in diameter is located 30 m east of the landing site; and

(B) on the lower (western) slopes of a permanent snow / ice ramp extending from Anvers Island towards the northern promontory at a site approximately 50-100 m east of the ice-free ground (64°48'22" S, 63°46'24" W). Care should be exercised on this snow slope, which is likely to be crevassed further towards the east and up-slope on Anvers Island.

3) Aircraft landing within the Area should approach within the Helicopter Access Zone to the maximum extent practicable. The Helicopter Access Zone allows access from the north and west, from the region of Biscoe Bay, to landing site (A), and from the north and east to landing site (B) (Map 2). The Helicopter Access Zone extends over the open water between landing sites (A) and (B).

4) Use of smoke grenades to indicate wind direction is prohibited within the Area unless absolutely necessary for safety, and any grenades used should be retrieved.

Vehicle access and use

When access over sea ice is viable, there are no special restrictions on the locations where such access may be made, although vehicles are prohibited from being taken on land within the Area.

Foot access and movement within the Area

Movement on land within the Area shall be on foot. All people in aircraft, boats, or vehicles are prohibited from moving on foot beyond the immediate vicinity of their landing site unless specifically authorised by Permit. Visitors should move carefully so as to minimize disturbance to flora, fauna, and soils, and should walk on snow or rocky terrain if practical, but taking care not to damage lichens. Pedestrians should walk around the penguin colonies and should not enter sub-groups of nesting penguins unless required for research or management purposes. Pedestrian traffic should be kept to the minimum consistent with the objectives of any permitted activities and every reasonable effort should be made to minimize effects.

7(ii) Activities that are or may be conducted in the Area, including restrictions on time or place

- Scientific research that will not jeopardize the ecosystem or values of the Area;

- Essential management activities, including monitoring;

- Activities with educational aims (such as documentary reporting (photographic, audio or written) or the production of educational resources or services) that cannot be served elsewhere.

- The appropriate authority should be notified of any activities/measures undertaken that were not included in the authorised Permit.

7(iii) Installation, modification or removal of structures

No structures are to be erected within the Area except as specified in a permit and, with the exception of permanent survey markers and signs, permanent structures or installations are prohibited;

All structures, scientific equipment or markers installed in the Area must be authorized by permit and clearly identified by country, name of the principal investigator and year of installation. All such items should be made of materials that pose minimal risk of contamination of the Area;

Installation (including site selection), maintenance, modification or removal of structures shall be undertaken in a manner that minimizes disturbance to flora and fauna.

Removal of specific equipment for which the permit has expired shall be the responsibility of the authority which granted the original Permit, and shall be a condition of the permit.

7(iv) Location of field camps

Temporary camping is allowed within the Area at the designated site located approximately 50 m north-east of helicopter landing site (A), on the northern coast of the main island on which Biscoe Point lies. The camp site is located on beach gravels and rocky ground a few meters above sea level, immediately north of a transient tidal pool, and is separated from the sea further to the north by a low rocky ridge of about 8 m. When necessary for essential purposes specified in the Permit, temporary camping is allowed on the separate peninsula 300 m to the north, although a specific camping site has not been determined. Camping on surfaces with significant vegetation cover is prohibited.

7(v) Restrictions on materials and organisms which can be brought into the Area

No living animals, plant material, microorganisms or soils shall be deliberately introduced into the Area, and the precautions listed below shall be taken against accidental introductions;

To help maintain the ecological and scientific values at Biscoe Point visitors shall take special precautions against introductions. Of concern are pathogenic, microbial, invertebrate or plant introductions sourced from other Antarctic sites, including stations, or from regions outside Antarctica. Visitors shall ensure that sampling equipment and markers brought into the Area are clean. To the maximum extent practicable, footwear and other equipment used or brought into the area (including backpacks, carry-bags and tents) shall be thoroughly cleaned before entering the Area;

In view of the presence of breeding birds at Biscoe Point, no poultry products, including products containing uncooked dried eggs, including wastes from such products, shall be released into the Area;

No herbicides or pesticides shall be brought into the Area;

Any other chemicals, including radio-nuclides or stable isotopes, which may be introduced for scientific or management purposes specified in the permit, shall be removed from the Area at or before the conclusion of the activity for which the permit was granted;

Fuel, food, and other materials are not to be stored in the Area, unless required for essential purposes connected with the activity for which the permit has been granted;

All materials introduced shall be for a stated period only, shall be removed at or before the conclusion of that stated period, and shall be stored and handled so that risk of their introduction into the environment is minimized;

If release occurs which is likely to compromise the values of the Area, removal is encouraged only where the impact of removal is not likely to be greater than that of leaving the material *in situ.*

7(vi) Taking or harmful interference with native flora or fauna

Taking or harmful interference of native flora and fauna is prohibited, except in accordance with a separate permit issued under Article 3 of Annex II by the appropriate national authority specifically for that purpose.

7(vii) Collection or removal of anything not brought into the Area by the Permit holder

Material may be collected or removed from the Area only in accordance with a permit and should be limited to the minimum necessary to meet scientific or management needs.

Material of human origin likely to compromise the values of the Area, which was not brought into the Area by the permit holder or otherwise authorized, may be removed from any part of the Area, unless the impact of removal is likely to be greater than leaving the material *in situ.* If this is the case the appropriate authority should be notified.

The appropriate national authority should be notified of any items removed from the Area that were not introduced by the permit holder.

7(viii) Disposal of waste

All wastes, including all human wastes, shall be removed from the Area.

7(ix) Measures that are necessary to ensure that the aims and objectives of the management plan can continue to be met

1) Permits may be granted to enter the Area to carry out biological monitoring and site inspection activities, which may involve the collection of limited samples for analysis or review, or for protective measures.
2) Any specific sites of long-term monitoring shall be appropriately marked.

7(x) Requirements for reports

Parties should ensure that the principal holder of each permit issued submit to the appropriate authority a report describing the activities undertaken. Such reports should include, as appropriate, the information identified in the Visit Report form contained in Appendix 4 of Resolution 2 (1998)(CEP I).

Parties should maintain a record of such activities, and, in the annual Exchange of Information, should provide summary descriptions of activities conducted by persons subject to their jurisdiction, in sufficient detail to allow evaluation of the effectiveness of the Management Plan. Parties should, wherever possible, deposit originals or copies of such original reports in a publicly accessible archive to maintain a record of usage, to be used both in any review of the Management Plan and in organizing the scientific use of the Area.

The appropriate authority should be notified of any activities/measures undertaken, and / or of any materials released and not removed, that were not included in the authorized permit.

References

Baker, K.S. 1996. Palmer LTER: Palmer Station air temperature 1974 to 1996. *Antarctic Journal of the United States* **31** (2): 162-64.

Day, T.A., Ruhland, C.T., Strauss, S., Park, J-H., Krieg, M.L., Krna, M.A., and Bryant, D.M. 2009. Response of plants and the dominatn microarthropod *Cryptopygus antarcticus*, to warming and constrasting precipitation regimes in Antarctic tundra. *Global Change Biology* **15**: 1640-1651.

Emslie, S.D., Fraser, W., Smith, R.C. and Walker, W. 1998. Abandoned penguin colonies and environmental change in the Palmer Station area, Anvers Island, Antarctic Peninsula. *Antarctic Science* **10**(3): 257-268.

Emslie, S.D. 2001. Radiocarbon dates from abandoned penguin colonies in the Antarctic Peninsula region. *Antarctic Science* **13**(3):289-295.

ERA. 2010. Biscoe Point Orthophoto 2010. Digital orthophotograph of Biscoe Point and adjacent areas of coast on Anvers Island. Ground pixel resolution 8 cm and horizontal / vertical accuracy of ± 1 m. MSL heights, 5 m^2 DTM. Aerial photography acquired by BAS on 29 Nov 2009 BAS/4/10. Unpublished data, Environmental Research & Assessment, Cambridge.

Greene, D.M. and Holtom, A. 1971. Studies in *Colobanthus quitensis* (Kunth) Bartl. and *Deschampsia antarctica* Desv.: III. Distribution, habitats and performance in the Antarctic botanical zone. *British Antarctic Survey Bulletin* **26**: 1-29.

Harris, C.M. 2001. Revision of management plans for Antarctic protected areas originally proposed by the United States of America and the United Kingdom: Field visit report. Internal report for the National Science Foundation, US, and the Foreign and Commonwealth Office, UK. Environmental Research and Assessment, Cambridge.

Hattersley-Smith, M.A. 1991. The history of place-names in the British Antarctic Territory. British Antarctic Survey Scientific Reports **113** (Part 1).

Hooper, P.R. 1958. Progress report on the geology of Anvers Island . Unpublished report, British Antarctic Survey Archives Ref AD6/2/1957/G3.

Hooper, P.R. 1962. The petrology of Anvers Island and adjacent islands. *FIDS Scientific Reports* **34**.

Komárková, V. 1983. Plant communities of the Antarctic Peninsula near Palmer Station. *Antarctic Journal of the United States* **18**: 216-218.

Komárková, V. 1984. Studies of plant communities of the Antarctic Peninsula near Palmer Station. *Antarctic Journal of the United States* **19**: 180-182.

Komárková, V, Poncet, S and Poncet, J. 1985. Two native Antarctic vascular plants, *Deschampsia antarctica* and *Colobanthus quitensis*: a new southernmost locality and other localities in the Antarctic Peninsula area. *Arctic and Alpine Research* **17**(4): 401-416.

Müller-Schwarze, C. and Müller-Schwarze, D. 1975. A survey of twenty-four rookeries of pygoscelid penguins in the Antarctic Peninsula region. In *The biology of penguins*, Stonehouse, B. (ed). Macmillan Press, London.

National Science Foundation, Office of Polar Programs, 1999. Palmer Station. OPP World Wide Web site address http://www.nsf.gov/od/opp/support/palmerst.htm

Park, J-H. and Day, T.A. 2007. Temperature response of CO2 exchange and dissolved organic carbon release in a maritime Antarctic tundra ecosystem. *Polar Biology* 30: 1535–1544. DOI 10.1007/s00300-007-0314-y.

Park, J-H., Day, T.A., Strauss, S., and Ruhland, C.T. 2007. Biogeochemical pools and fluxes of carbon and nitrogen in a maritime tundra near penguin colonies along the Antarctic Peninsula. *Polar Biology* **30**:199–207.

Parmelee, D.F. and Parmelee, J.M. 1987. Revised penguin numbers and distribution for Anvers Island, Antarctica. *British Antarctic Survey Bulletin* **76**: 65-73.

Poncet, S. and Poncet, J. 1987. Censuses of penguin populations of the Antarctic Peninsula, 1983-87. *British Antarctic Survey Bulletin* **77**: 109-129.

Rundle, A.S. 1968. Snow accumulation and ice movement on the Anvers Island ice cap, Antarctica: a study of mass balance. *Proceedings of the ISAGE Symposium, Hanover, USA, 3-7 September, 1968*: 377-390.

Sanchez, R. and Fraser, W. 2001. *Biscoe Point Orthobase*. Digital orthophotograph of island on which Biscoe Point lies, 6 cm pixel resolution and horizontal / vertical accuracy of ± 2 m. Geoid heights, 3 m^2 DTM, derived contour interval: 2 m. Data on CD-ROM and accompanied by USGS Open File Report 99-402 "GPS and GIS-based data collection and image mapping in the Antartcic Peninsula". Science and Applications Center, Mapping Applications Center. Reston, USGS.

Smith, R.I.L. 1996. Terrestrial and freshwater biotic components of the western Antarctic Peninsula. In Ross, R.M., Hofmann, E.E and Quetin, L.B. (eds). Foundations for ecological research west of the Antarctic Peninsula. *Antarctic Research Series* **70**: 15-59.

Smith, R.I.L. and Corner, R.W.M. 1973. Vegetation of the Arthur Harbour – Argentine Islands region of the Antarctic Peninsula. *British Antarctic Survey Bulletin* **33 & 34**: 89-122.

Stammerjohn, S.E., Martinson, D.G., Smith, R.C. and Iannuzzi, R.A. 2008.Sea ice in the western Antarctic Peninsula region: Spatio-temporal variabilityfrom ecological and climate change perspectives. *Deep-Sea Research II* **55:** 2041– 2058.

Woehler, E.J. (ed) 1993. *The distribution and abundance of Antarctic and sub-Antarctic penguins.* SCAR, Cambridge.

Xiong, F.S., Mueller, E.C. and Day, T.A. 2000. Photosynthetic and respiratory acclimation and growth response of Antarctic vascular plants to contrasting temperature regimes. *American Journal of Botany* **87**: 700-10.

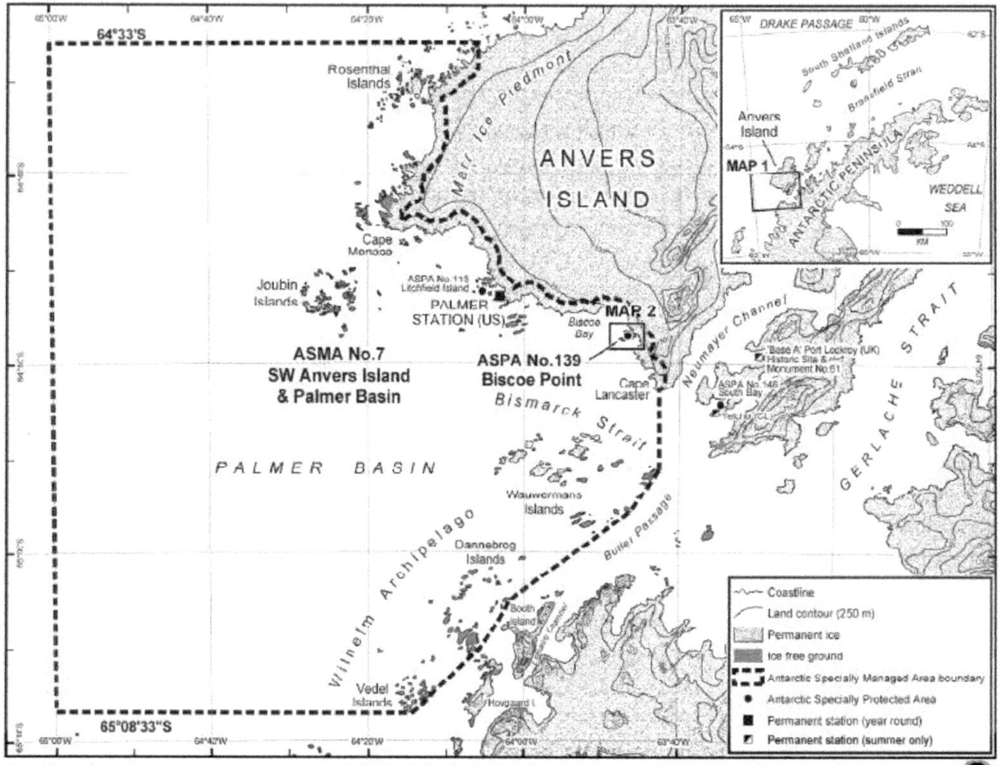

ASPA No. 139: Biscoe Point
Map 1: Biscoe Point, Anvers Island, Palmer Archipelago

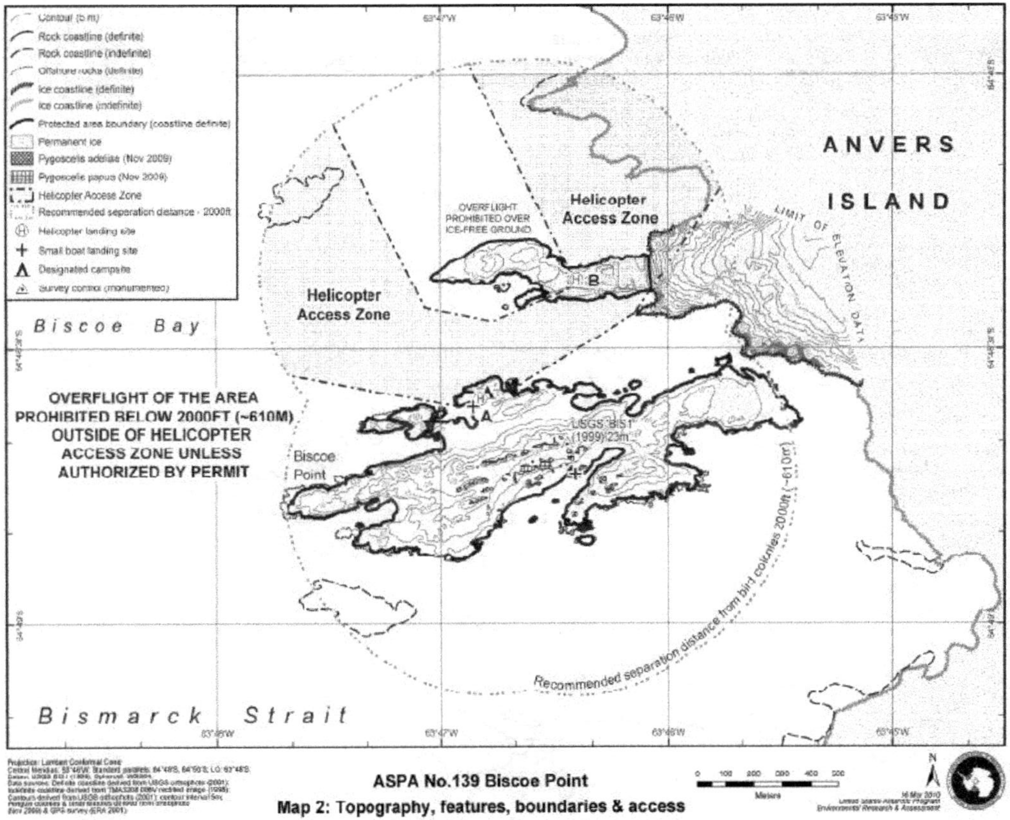

ASPA No.139 Biscoe Point

Map 2: Topography, features, boundaries & access

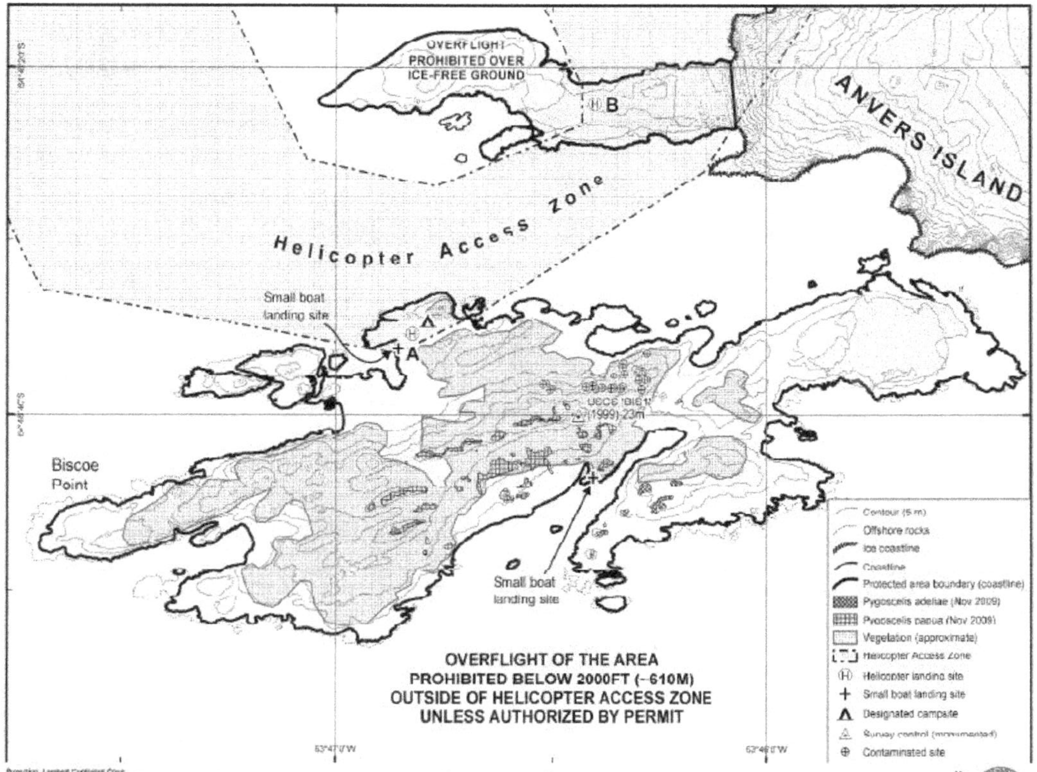

ASPA No.139 Biscoe Point

Map 3: Penguin colonies, approximate vegetation extent & known contaminated sites

Management Plan For
Antarctic Specially Protected Area No. 155
CAPE EVANS, ROSS ISLAND
(including Historic Site and Monument Nos. 16 and 17, the historic *Terra Nova* hut of Captain Robert Falcon Scott and its precincts and the Cross on Wind Vane Hill)

1. Description of Values to be Protected

The significant historic value of this Area was formally recognised when it was listed as Historic Site and Monument Nos. 16 and 17 in Recommendation 9 (1972). An area containing both sites was designated as Specially Protected Area No. 25 in Measure 2 (1997) and redesignated as Antarctic Specially Protected Area 155 in Decision 1 (2002).

The *Terra Nova* hut (Historic Site and Monument No. 16) is the largest of the historic huts in the Ross Sea region. It was built in January 1911 by the British Antarctic *Terra Nova* Expedition of 1910-1913, led by Captain Robert Falcon Scott, RN. It was subsequently used as a base by the Ross Sea party of Sir Ernest Shackleton's Imperial Trans-Antarctic Expedition of 1914-1917.

Historic Site and Monument No. 17 consists of the Cross on Wind Vane Hill, erected in the memory of three members of Shackleton's Ross Sea party who died in 1916. In addition to this, two anchors from the ship *Aurora* of the Imperial Trans-Antarctic Expedition, two instrument shelters (one on Wind Vane Hill and the other near the *Terra Nova* hut), several supply dumps and numerous artefacts are distributed around the site.

Cape Evans is one of the principal sites of early human activity in Antarctica. It is an important symbol of the Heroic Age of Antarctic exploration and, as such, has considerable historical significance. Some of the earliest advances in the study of earth sciences, meteorology, flora and fauna in Antarctica are associated with the *Terra Nova* Expedition based at this site. The data collected can provide a bench mark against which to compare current measurements. The history of these activities and the contribution they have made to the understanding and awareness of Antarctica therefore contribute to both the historic and scientific value of the site.

A revised version of the Management Plan was adopted by means of Measure 2 (2005) and changes to the access and movement provisions were adopted by means of Measure 12 (2008).

2. Aims and Objectives

The aim of the Management Plan is to provide protection for the Area and its features so that its values can be preserved. The objectives of the Management Plan are to:
- avoid degradation of, or substantial risk to, the values of the Area;
- maintain the historic values of the area through planned conservation work which may include:
  a. an annual 'on-site' maintenance programme,

    b. a programme of monitoring the condition of artefacts and structures, and the factors which affect them, and

    c. a programme of conservation of artefacts to be conducted on and off site;

- allow management activities which support the protection of the values and features of the Area including:

    a. mapping and otherwise recording the disposition of historic items in the hut environs, and

    b. recording other relevant historic data; and

- prevent unnecessary human disturbance to the Area, its features and artefacts through managed access to the *Terra Nova* hut.

3. Management Activities

The following management activities will be undertaken to protect the values of the Area:

- A regular programme of conservation work shall be undertaken on the *Terra Nova* hut and associated artefacts in the Area.
- Visits shall be made as necessary for management purposes.
- Systematic monitoring shall be put in place to assess the impacts of present visitor limits, and the results and any related management recommendations included in reviews of this Management Plan.
- National Antarctic Programmes operating in, or those with an interest in, the Area shall consult together with a view to ensuring the above management activities are implemented.
- Copies of this Management Plan, including maps of the Area, shall be made available at adjacent operational research/field stations.

4. Period of Designation

Designated for an indefinite period.

5. Maps

Map A: Cape Evans regional map. This map shows the boundaries of the Area with significant topographical features, field camp sites and helicopter landing sites. It also shows the approximate location of significant historical items within the area. Inset: Ross Island showing sites of nearby protected areas and stations.

Map B: Cape Evans site map. This map shows the approximate location of specific historic artefacts and sites within the Area.

6. Description of the Area

6(i) Geographical co-ordinates, boundary markers and natural features
Cape Evans is a small, triangular shaped, ice-free area at the south west of Ross Island, 10 kilometres to the south of Cape Royds and 22 kilometres to the north of Hut Point Peninsula on Ross Island. The ice-free area is composed of till-covered basalt bedrock. The designated

Area is located on the north western coast of Cape Evans adjacent to Home Beach and centered on Scott's *Terra Nova* hut. The boundaries of the ASPA are:

- South: a line extending east from a point at 77° 38' 15.47" S, 166° 25' 9.48" E – 20 metres south of the cross on Wind Vane Hill;
- South-west: a line from the reference point above extended to follow the crest of the small ridge descending in a north westerly direction to the shoreline at 77° 38' 11.50" S, 166° 24' 49.47" E;
- North-west: by the shoreline of Home Beach;
- North-east: by the line of the outlet stream from Skua Lake to Home Beach at 77° 38' 4.89" S, 166° 25' 13.46" E;
- East: by the line extending south from the western edge of Skua Lake at 77° 38' 5.96" S, 166° 25' 35.74" E – to intersect with the southern boundary at 77° 38' 15.48" S, 166° 25' 35.68" E.

Skua (*Catharacta maccormicki*) nest at Cape Evans and Adelie penguins (*Pygoscelis adeliae*) from the colony at Cape Royds may occasionally transit the Area. Weddell seals (*Leptonychotes weddellii*) have also been seen hauled out on Home Beach.

6(ii) Access to the Area
When safe conditions exist, vehicle approach to the Area can be made across the sea ice. Vehicles are prohibited from entering the Area, unless approved to do so for management activities in accordance with 7(i) below. During open water, landings by boat may be made directly in front of the hut at Home Beach. Helicopter landings may be made at either of the existing designated landing sites marked on Maps A and B. One site is approximately 100 metres to the north of the hut, just outside the Area. The other is located adjacent to the New Zealand refuge hut approximately 250 metres beyond the south western boundary of the Area.

6(iii) Location of structures within and adjacent to the Area
All structures located within the Area are of historic origin, although a temporary, modern protective enclosure around the magnetic hut remains in place. A major feature of the Area is Scott's *Terra Nova* hut located on the north western coast of Cape Evans at Home Beach. The hut is surrounded by many historic relics including the two anchors from the *Aurora*, dog skeletons, an instrument shelter, two dog lines, meteorological screen, fuel dump, magnetic hut, coal stores, a flag pole and the experimental rock hut/rubbish dump which is an historic rock structure linked with the 'Worst Journey in the World' to Cape Crozier (1911) containing a small collection of artefacts. A memorial cross to three members of Shackleton's Ross Sea party of 1914-1917 stands on Wind Vane Hill. All these features are included within the boundaries of the Area.

A New Zealand refuge hut, camp site and helicopter landing site are situated approximately 250m to the south west of the Area.

The former Greenpeace year-round World Park Base was sited to the north east of Scott's *Terra Nova* hut from 1987 to 1992. No visible sign of the base remains.

6(iv) Location of other Protected Areas in the vicinity
- ASPA 121 (previously SSSI No. 1), Cape Royds, and
- ASPA 157 (SPA No. 27), Backdoor Bay, Cape Royds are 10 kilometres north of Cape Evans.

- ASPA 122 (SSSI No. 2), Arrival Heights and
- ASPA 158 (SPA No. 28), Hut Point are approximately 22 kilometres south of Cape Evans at Hut Point Peninsula.
- ASPA 130 (SSSI No. 11), Tramway Ridge is approximately 20 kilometres east of Cape Evans.

All sites are located on Ross Island.

6(v) Special Zones within the Area
There are no special zones within the Area.

7. Terms and Conditions for Entry Permits

Entry to the Area is prohibited except in accordance with a Permit. Permits shall be issued only by appropriate national authorities and may contain both general and specific conditions. A Permit may be issued by a national authority to cover a number of visits in a season. Parties operating in the Area shall consult together and with groups and organisations interested in visiting the Area to ensure that visitor numbers are not exceeded. Permits to enter the site may be issued for a stated period for:
- activities related to conservation, research and/or monitoring purposes;
- management activities in support of the objectives of this Plan;
- activities related to educational or recreational activities including tourism, providing they do not conflict with the objectives of this Plan; and
- any other activity specifically provided for in this Plan.

7(i) Access to and movement within or over the Area
- Control of movement within the Area is necessary to prevent damage caused by crowding around the many vulnerable features within the Area. The maximum number in the Area at any time (including guides and those within the hut) shall be: **40 people**.
- Control of numbers within the hut is necessary to prevent damage caused by crowding around the many vulnerable features within the hut. The maximum number within the hut at any time (including guides) shall be: **12 people**.
- Avoidance of cumulative impacts on the interior of the hut requires an annual limit on visitor numbers. The effects of the current visitor levels (average 1127 per year between 1998 and 2009) suggest that a significant increase could cause significant adverse impacts. The maximum annual number of visitors shall be: **2,000 people**.
- These limits have been set based on current visitor levels and on the best advice available from conservation advisory agencies (which include conservators, archaeologists, historians, museologists and other heritage protection professionals). The limits are based on the proposition that any significant increase in the current level of visitor numbers would be detrimental to the values to be protected. An ongoing monitoring programme to assess the effects of visitors is required to provide the basis for future reviews of the Management Plan, in particular whether the current limits on numbers of visitors are appropriate.
- Adequate supervision of visits to the Area is necessary to prevent damage caused by crowding and by actions inconsistent with the Code of Conduct set out in section

7(ii). All tourism, educational and recreational visits must be supervised by an experienced guide nominated by the operator (refer section 7(ix)).

- Helicopter landings are prohibited within the Area as they have the potential to damage the site by blowing scoria and ice particles and to accelerate the abrasion of the hut and surrounding artefacts. Refer to section 6(ii) for recommended approaches and landing sites.
- Vehicles are prohibited from entering the Area except where it is necessary to use vehicles for management activities. This may include, but is not limited to activities such as clearing snow and ice that is judged to be a threat to the historic hut or other artefacts. In all such cases consideration shall be given to:
  - i. using the minimum sized vehicle required for the job;
  - ii. ensuring the vehicle operator is fully trained and aware of the provisions of this Plan, and of the sensitivities at the site of operation of the vehicle;
  - iii. careful planning and monitoring of all vehicle movements within the site so as to avoid damage to either the hut or artefacts buried beneath accumulated snow and ice.

7(ii) Activities which may be conducted within the Area
Activities which may be conducted within the Area include:
- visits for conservation purposes;
- educational and/or recreational visits including tourism; and
- scientific activity which does not detract from the values of the Area.

Visitors should adhere to the following Code of Conduct, except where conservation, research, monitoring or management activities specified in the Permit require otherwise:
- Thoroughly clean grit and scoria, ice and snow from boots using the brushes provided before entering the hut to reduce floor abrasion and only use tripods or monopods with flat bottomed rubber bases as opposed to those with metal spikes which can damage the floor;
- Remove any clothing made wet by sea water, and any sea ice crystals from boots, as salt particles accelerate corrosion of metal objects;
- Do not touch, move or sit on any items or furniture in the huts - handling artefacts causes damage;
- As many areas are cramped and artefacts can be accidentally bumped, do not wear packs inside and when the maximum number of visitors (12) are in the hut at one time the use of tripods or monopods is prohibited;
- When moving around the sites, take great care not to tread on any items which may be obscured by snow and remain on established walking tracks;
- Use of combustion style lanterns, naked flames or smoking in or around the hut is strictly forbidden as fire is a major risk; and
- Visits should be recorded in the book provided. This allows times and levels of visitation to be correlated with temperature and humidity data automatically logged inside the hut.

7(iii) Installation, modification or removal of structures
- No new structures are to be erected in the Area, or scientific equipment installed, except for conservation activities as specified in section 1.
- No historic structure shall be removed from the Area, unless specified in a Permit issued in accordance with the provisions of section 7(vii).

7(iv) Location of field camps
- Use of the historic hut for living purposes is not permitted. Camping is prohibited in the Area under any circumstances.
- An existing field camp site is associated with the two New Zealand field shelters located 250m south west of the Area and should be used by all parties intending to camp in this area. A second alternative field camp site is located to the north of the Area near the helicopter pad on Home Beach (Map A and B).

7(v) Restrictions on materials and organisms which may be brought to the Area
- No living animals, plant material, micro-organisms or soil shall be introduced to the Area. No food products shall be taken into the Area.
- Chemicals may only be introduced for permitted scientific or conservation purposes. Chemicals (including fuel) or other materials are not to be left in the Area, unless required for essential purposes connected with the conservation of the historic structures or associated relics.
- All introduced materials are to be removed when no longer required and before a date to be specified in the relevant Permit.

7(vi) Taking or harmful interference with native flora and fauna
- This activity is prohibited except in accordance with a Permit issued by the appropriate national authority specifically for that purpose under Article 3, Annex II to the Protocol on Environmental Protection.
- Where animal taking or harmful interference is involved, this should, as a minimum standard, be in accordance with the SCAR Code of Conduct for the Use of Animals for Scientific Purposes in Antarctica.

7(vii) Collection or removal of anything not imported by the Permit holder
- Material may be collected and removed from the Area for conservation reasons consistent with the objectives of this Management Plan only when specified in a Permit issued by the appropriate national authority.
- Materials which pose a threat to the environment or human health may be removed from the Area for disposal, in accordance with a Permit, where they meet one or more of the following criteria:
i. the artefact presents a threat to the environment, wildlife or human health and safety;
ii. it is in such poor condition that it is not reasonably possible to conserve it;
iii. it does not contribute in any significant way to our understanding of the hut, its occupants or the history of Antarctica;
iv. it does not contribute to, or it detracts from, the visual qualities of the site or the hut, and/or;
v. it is not a unique or rare item;

and where such action is:

i. undertaken by parties with appropriate heritage conservation expertise; and
ii. part of an overall plan for conservation work at the site.

- National authorities should ensure that any removal of artefacts and assessment against the above criteria is carried out by personnel with appropriate heritage conservation expertise.

- Artefacts judged to be of high historic value, which cannot be conserved on site with currently available techniques, may be removed in accordance with a Permit for storage in a controlled environment until such time as they can safely be returned to the Area.
- Except with respect to any part of, or the contents of, an historic site or monument, samples of soil and other natural materials may be removed for scientific purposes. Such removal must be in accordance with an appropriate Permit.

7(viii) Disposal of waste

All human waste, grey water and other waste generated by work parties or visitors shall be removed from the Area.

7(ix) Measures that may be necessary to ensure that the aims and objectives of the Management Plan continue to be met

- The Permit, or an authorised copy, shall be carried within the Area.
- Information on the requirements of this Plan shall be provided to all visitors.
- The Code of Conduct set out in section 7(ii) shall be followed by all visitors, except where conservation, research, monitoring or management purposes require otherwise.
- Operators facilitating educational and recreational visits (including tourism) to the Area shall, prior to commencement of the summer season, nominate people with a working knowledge of both the site and this Management Plan to act as guides during visits.
- All educational and recreational visits (including tourism) shall be supervised by a nominated guide, who is responsible for briefing visitors on the Code of Conduct and the requirements of this Management Plan and ensuring they are complied with.
- Parties shall consult and coordinate to develop skills and resources, particularly those related to conservation techniques, to assist with the protection of the Area's values.

7(x) Requirements for reports

Parties shall ensure that the principal holder for each Permit issued submits to the appropriate authority a report describing the activities undertaken. Such reports shall include, as appropriate, the information identified in the Visit Report provided in Appendix 4 of Resolution 2 (1998). In addition, any removal of materials in accordance with section 7(vii) shall be detailed, including the reason for removal and the current location of the items or the date of disposal. Any return of such items to the site shall also be reported.

Parties shall maintain a record of activities within the Area and, in the Annual Exchange of Information, shall provide summary descriptions of activities conducted by persons subject to their jurisdiction, in sufficient detail to allow an evaluation of the effectiveness of the Management Plan. Parties should wherever possible deposit originals or copies of such reports in a publicly accessible archive to maintain a record of visitation, to be used both for review of the Management Plan and in managing further visitation to the site.

Map A - Cape Evans, Ross Island, Antarctic Specially Protected Area 155: Regional Map

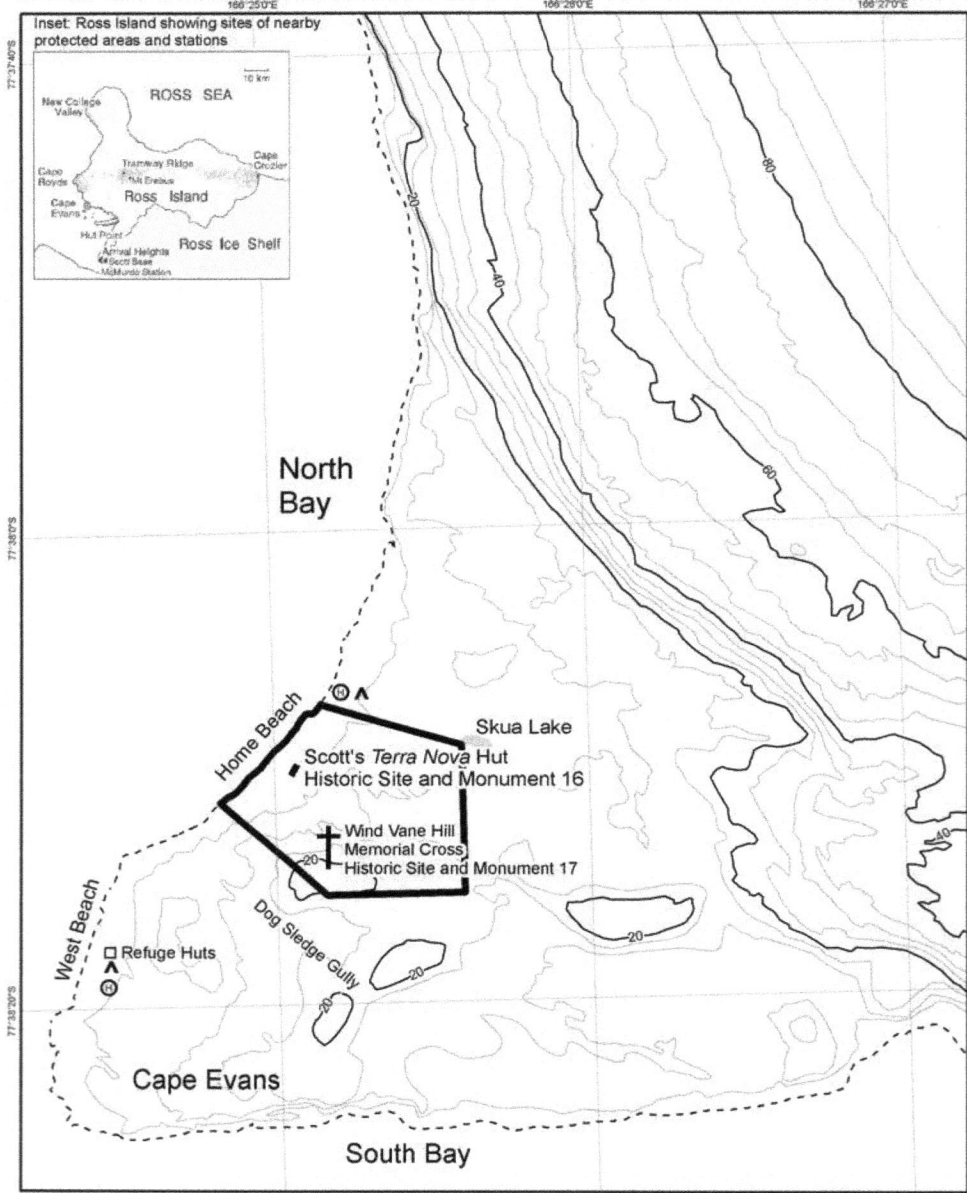

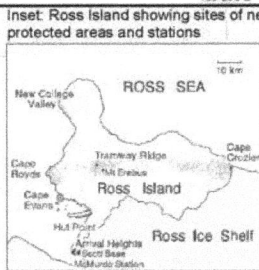

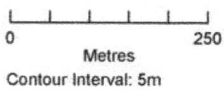

Inset: Ross Island showing sites of nearby protected areas and stations

ROSS SEA

New College Valley

ROSS SEA

Tramway Ridge
Mt Erebus

Cape
Royds

Ross Island

Cape
Crozier

Cape
Evans

Hut Point

Arrival Heights
Scott Base
McMurdo Station

Ross Ice Shelf

North
Bay

Skua Lake

Home Beach

Scott's *Terra Nova* Hut
Historic Site and Monument 16

Wind Vane Hill
Memorial Cross
Historic Site and Monument 17

Dog Sledge Gully

West Beach

Refuge Huts

Cape Evans

South Bay

0 ____ 250
Metres
Contour Interval: 5m

N

- - - Estimated position of coastline
Protected area boundary
Historic structures
⊕ Helicopter pad
Λ Campsite

Projection: Lambert conformal conic
Standard Parallel 1: 76.6°S
Standard Parallel 2: 79.3°S
Spheroid: WGS84

Source: Cape Evans historic area
management plan

Map B - Cape Evans, Ross Island, Antarctic Specially Protected Area 155: Site Map

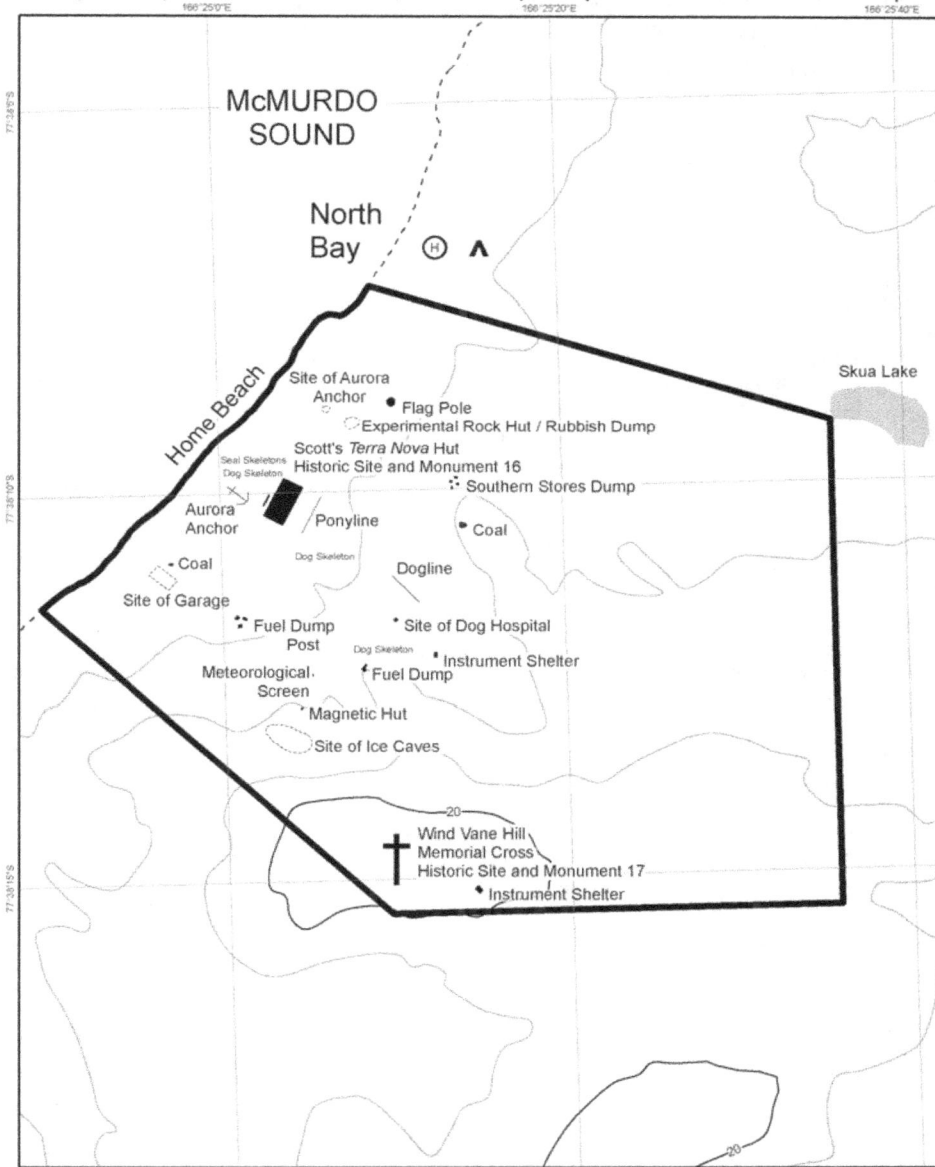

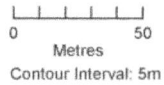

McMURDO
SOUND

North
Bay Ⓗ ∧

Skua Lake

Home Beach

Site of Aurora
Anchor   ● Flag Pole
            ⊙ Experimental Rock Hut / Rubbish Dump

Scott's *Terra Nova* Hut
Seal Skeletons   Historic Site and Monument 16
Dog Skeleton
                  ⊡ Southern Stores Dump

Aurora
Anchor   Ponyline   ● Coal

· Coal   Dog Skeleton
Site of Garage   Dogline

              ⁙ Fuel Dump   · Site of Dog Hospital
                 Post   Dog Skeleton
Meteorological   · Instrument Shelter
Screen   ● Fuel Dump

          · Magnetic Hut

          Site of Ice Caves

                     20
                  Wind Vane Hill
              † Memorial Cross
                  Historic Site and Monument 17
                  · Instrument Shelter

	- - -	Estimated position of coastline
	⸺	Protected area boundary
	▮	Historic structures
	Ⓗ	Helicopter pad
	∧	Campsite

0   50
Metres
Contour Interval: 5m

Projection: Lambert conformal conic
          Standard Parallel 1: 76.6°S
          Standard Parallel 2: 79.3°S
Spheroid: WGS84

Source: Cape Evans historic area
management plan

Management Plan For
Antarctic Specially Protected Area No. 157
BACKDOOR BAY, CAPE ROYDS, ROSS ISLAND
(including Historic Site and Monument No. 15, the historic hut of Sir Ernest Shackleton and its precincts)

1. Description of Values to be Protected

The significant historic value of this Area was formally recognised when it was listed as Historic Site and Monument No. 15 in Recommendation 9 (1972). It was designated as Specially Protected Area No. 27 in Measure 1 (1998) and redesignated as Antarctic Specially Protected Area 157 in Decision 1 (2002).

The hut (Historic Site and Monument No. 15) on which this Area is centered was built in February 1908 by the British Antarctic *Nimrod* Expedition of 1907-1909 which was led by Sir Ernest Shackleton. It was also periodically used by the Ross Sea party of Shackleton's Imperial Trans-Antarctic Expedition of 1914-1917.

Structures associated with the hut include stables, kennels, a latrine and a garage created for the first motor vehicle in Antarctica. Other significant relics in the Area include an instrument shelter, supply depots, and a rubbish site. Numerous additional artefacts are distributed around the Area.

Cape Royds is one of the principal areas of early human activity in Antarctica. It is an important symbol of the Heroic Age of Antarctic exploration and, as such, has considerable historical significance. Some of the earliest advances in the study of earth sciences, meteorology, flora and fauna in Antarctica are associated with the *Nimrod* Expedition which was based at this site. The history of these activities and the contribution they have made to the understanding and awareness of Antarctica give this Area significant scientific, aesthetic and historic value.

The Management Plan was reviewed and a revised version with additional visitor management provisions was adopted by means of Measure 2 (2005).

2. Aims and Objectives

The aim of the Management Plan is to provide protection for the Area and its features so that its values can be preserved. The objectives of the Management Plan are to:
- avoid degradation of, or substantial risk to, the values of the Area;
- maintain the historic values of the Area through planned conservation work which may include:
  a. an annual 'on-site' maintenance programme,
  b. a programme of monitoring the condition of artefacts and structures, and the factors which affect them, and
  c. a programme of conservation of artefacts conducted on and off site;
- allow management activities which support the protection of the values and features of the Area including:

a. mapping and otherwise recording the disposition of historic items in the hut environs, and
b. recording other relevant historic data; and
- prevent unnecessary human disturbance to the Area, its features and artefacts through managed access to the *Nimrod* hut.

3. Management Activities

The following management activities will be undertaken to protect the values of the Area:
- A regular programme of conservation work shall be undertaken on the *Nimrod* hut and associated artefacts in the Area.
- Visits shall be made as necessary for management purposes.
- Systematic monitoring shall be put in place to assess the impacts of present visitor limits, and the results and any related management recommendations included in reviews of this Management Plan.
- National Antarctic Programmes operating in or those with an interest in, the Area shall consult together with a view to ensuring the above management activities are implemented.
- Copies of this Management Plan, including maps of the Area, shall be made available at adjacent operational research/field stations.

4. Period of Designation

Designated for an indefinite period.

5. Maps

Map A: Backdoor Bay, Cape Royds regional topographic map. This map shows the location of the Area in relation to ASPA 121 and significant topographic features in the vicinity. Inset 1: shows the location of Ross Island in the Ross Sea region. Inset 2: shows the position of the site in relation to other protected areas on Ross Island.

Map B: Backdoor Bay, Cape Royds area topographic map. This map shows the boundaries of the Area and the adjacent ASPA 121. Also shown are the approaches, field camp and helicopter landing sites.

6. Description of the Area

6(i) Geographical coordinates, boundary markers and natural features
Cape Royds is an ice free area at the western extremity of Ross Island, approximately 40 kilometres to the south of Cape Bird and 35 kilometres to the north of Hut Point Peninsula on Ross Island. The ice free area is composed of till covered basalt bedrock. The designated Area is located to the north east of Cape Royds adjacent to Backdoor Bay. It is immediately to the east of ASPA 121, an Adélie penguin colony. The Area is centered on Shackleton's *Nimrod* Expedition hut.

The boundaries of the Area are:

- South and East, by the shoreline of the eastern coast of Cape Royds including Arrival and Backdoor Bays;
- West, by a line following the boundary of ASPA 121 from the coastline at Arrival Bay to a signpost (77°31′ 12.6" S, 166° 10′ 01.3" E) and then continuing to follow the boundary of ASPA 121 for 40 m in a northeast direction;
- Northwest, by a line extending in a northwest direction from the boundary of ASPA 121 and following the shore of a small lake to the NW of Pony Lake and then along a gully leading to a point at 77° 33′ 7.5" S, 166° 10′ 13" E; and
- North, by a line extended due east from a point at 77° 33′ 7.5" S, 166° 10′ 13" E to the coastline of Backdoor Bay.

Skua (*Catharacta maccormicki)* nest in the vicinity of the Area and Adelie penguins (*Pygoscelis adeliae)* from the adjacent colony at Cape Royds often transit the Area.

6(ii) Access to the Area

Access to the Area should be made on foot from Backdoor Bay or the helicopter landing sites using the routes shown in Map B. Landings by boat (when there is open water), or vehicle (when safe sea ice conditions exist), may be made in Backdoor Bay. Care should be taken to avoid the marine extent of ASPA 121 (see Map A and B). Helicopter landings may be made at the designated landing sites marked on Map B. The primary (and preferred) site is approximately 100 meters north of the Area. A secondary landing site is located 30 meters north of the Area and should be avoided from the start of November until the start of March, when the nearby Adélie penguin colony is occupied.

6(iii) Location of structures within and adjacent to the Area

Apart from a Treaty plaque, all structures within the Area are of historic origin. A major feature of the Area is Shackleton's *Nimrod* Expedition hut located in a sheltered basin. The hut is surrounded by many other historic relics including an instrument shelter, supply depots, and a dump site. Numerous additional artefacts are distributed around the site.

A New Zealand refuge hut and camp site are located at the northwest corner of the ASPA.

6(iv) Location of other Protected Areas in the vicinity

- ASPA 121 (previously SSSI No. 1), Cape Royds is immediately adjacent to this Area.
- ASPA 122 (SSSI No. 2), Arrival Heights and
- ASPA 158 (SPA No. 28), Hut Point are approximately 35 kilometres south of Cape Royds at Hut Point Peninsula.
- ASPA 130 (SSSI No. 11), Tramway Ridge is 20 kilometres east of Cape Royds.
- ASPA 116 (SSSI No. 10, SPA No. 20), New College Valley is located 35 kilometres north in the vicinity of Cape Bird.
- ASPA 155 (SPA No. 25), Cape Evans is 12 kilometres south.
- ASPA 156 (SPA No. 26), Lewis Bay is 36 kilometres to the north east.

All sites are located on Ross Island.

6 (v) Special Zones within the Area
There are no special zones within the Area.

7. Terms and Conditions for Entry Permits

Entry to the Area is prohibited except in accordance with a Permit. Permits shall be issued only by appropriate national authorities and may contain both general and specific conditions. A Permit may be issued by a national authority to cover a number of visits in a season. Parties operating in the Area shall consult together and with groups and organisations interested in visiting the Area to ensure that visitor numbers are not exceeded.

Permits to enter the site may be issued for a stated period for:
- activities related to conservation, research and/or monitoring purposes;
- management activities in support of the objectives of this Management Plan;
- activities related to educational or recreational activities including tourism, providing they do not conflict with the objectives of this Management Plan; and
- any other activity specifically provided for in this Plan.

7(i) Access to and movement within or over the Area
- Control of movement within the Area is necessary to prevent damage caused by crowding around the many vulnerable features within the Area. The maximum number in the Area at any time (including guides and those within the hut) shall be: **40 people.**
- Control of numbers within the hut is necessary to prevent damage caused by crowding around the many vulnerable features within the hut. The maximum number within the hut at any time (including guides) shall be: **8 people.**
- Avoidance of cumulative impacts on the interior of the hut requires an annual limit on visitor numbers. The effects of current visitor levels (average 833 per year between 1998 and 2009) suggest that a significant increase could cause significant adverse impacts. The annual maximum number of visitors shall be: **2,000 people.**
- These limits have been set based on current visitor levels and on the best advice available from conservation advisory agencies (which include conservators, archaeologists, historians, museologists and other heritage protection professionals). The limits are based on the proposition that any significant increase in the current level of visitors would be detrimental to the values to be protected. An ongoing monitoring programme to assess the effect of visitors is required to provide the basis for future reviews of the Management Plan, in particular whether the current limits on numbers of visitors are appropriate.
- Adequate supervision of visits to the Area is necessary to prevent damage caused by crowding and by actions inconsistent with the Code of Conduct set out in section 7(ii). All tourism, educational and recreational visits must be supervised by an experienced guide nominated by the operator (refer section 7(ix)).
- Helicopter landings are prohibited within the Area as they have the potential to damage the site by blowing scoria and ice particles and to accelerate the abrasion of the hut and surrounding artefacts. Vehicles are prohibited within the Area. Refer to 6(ii) for recommended approaches and landing sites near the Area.

7(ii) Activities which may be conducted within the Area
Activities which may be conducted within the Area include:
- visits for conservation purposes;
- educational and/or recreational visits including tourism;
- scientific activity which does not detract from the values of the Area.

Visitors should adhere to the following Code of Conduct, except where conservation, research, monitoring or management activities specified in the Permit require otherwise:

- Thoroughly clean grit and scoria, ice and snow from boots using the brushes provided before entering the hut to reduce floor abrasion and only use tripods or monopods with flat bottomed rubber bases as opposed to those with metal spikes which can damage the floor;
- Remove any clothing made wet by sea water, and any sea ice crystals from boots, as salt particles accelerate corrosion of metal objects;
- Do not touch, move or sit on any items or furniture in the huts - handling artefacts causes damage;
- As many areas are cramped and artefacts can be accidentally bumped, do not wear packs inside and when the maximum number of visitors (8) are in the hut at one time the use of tripods or monopods is prohibited;
- When moving around the sites, take great care not to tread on any items which may be obscured by snow and remain on established walking tracks;
- Use of combustion style lanterns, naked flames or smoking in or around the hut is prohibited, as fire is a major risk; and
- Visits should be recorded in the book provided. This allows times and levels of visitation to be correlated with temperature and humidity data automatically logged inside the hut.

7(iii) Installation, modification or removal of structures
- No new structures are to be erected in the Area, or scientific equipment installed, except for conservation or scientific activities that do not detract from the values of the Area as specified in section 1.
- No historic structure shall be removed from the Area, unless specified in a Permit issued in accordance with the provisions of section 7(vii).

7(iv) Location of field camps
- Use of the historic hut for living purposes is not permitted. Camping is prohibited within the Area under any circumstances.
- An existing field camp site and a New Zealand shelter are located at the north western boundary of the Area (see Map B).

7(v) Restrictions on materials and organisms which may be brought into the Area
- No living animals, plant material, soil or micro-organisms shall be introduced to the Area. No food products shall be taken into the Area.
- Chemicals may only be introduced for permitted scientific or conservation purposes. Chemicals (including fuel) or other materials are not to be left in the Area, unless required for essential purposes connected with the conservation of the historic structures or the associated relics.
- All introduced materials are to be removed when no longer required and before a date to be specified in the relevant Permit.

7(vi) Taking or harmful interference with native flora and fauna
- This activity is prohibited except in accordance with a Permit issued by the appropriate national authority specifically for that purpose under Article 3, Annex II to the Protocol on Environmental Protection.

- Where animal taking or harmful interference is involved, this should, as a minimum standard, be in accordance with the SCAR Code of Conduct for the Use of Animals for Scientific Purposes in Antarctica.

7(vii) Collection of anything not imported by the Permit Holder
- Material may be collected and removed from the Area for conservation reasons consistent with the objectives of this Management Plan only when specified in a Permit issued by the appropriate national authority.
- Materials which pose a threat to the environment or human health may be removed from the Area for disposal, in accordance with a Permit, where they meet one or more of the following criteria:
  i. the artefact presents a threat to the environment, wildlife or human health and safety;
  ii. it is in such poor condition that it is not reasonably possible to conserve it;
  iii. it does not contribute in any significant way to our understanding of the hut, its occupants or the history of Antarctica;
  iv. it does not contribute to, or it detracts from, the visual qualities of the site or the hut; and/or
  v. it is not a unique or rare item;

and where such action is:

  i. undertaken by parties with appropriate heritage conservation expertise; and
  ii. part of an overall plan for conservation work at the site.

- National authorities should ensure that any removal of artefacts and assessment against the above criteria is carried out by personnel with appropriate heritage conservation expertise.
- Artefacts judged to be of high historic value, which cannot be conserved on site with currently available techniques, may be removed in accordance with a Permit for storage in a controlled environment until such time as they can safely be returned to the Area.

7(viii) Disposal of waste

All human waste, grey water and other waste generated by work parties or visitors shall be removed from the Area.

7(ix) Measures that may be necessary to ensure that the aims and objectives of the Management Plan continue to be met
- The Permit, or an authorised copy, shall be carried within the Area.
- Information on the requirements of this Management Plan shall be provided to all visitors.
- The Code of Conduct set out in section 7(ii) shall be followed by all visitors, except where conservation, research, monitoring or management purposes require otherwise.
- Operators facilitating educational and recreational visits (including tourism) to the Area should, prior to commencement of the summer season, nominate people with a working knowledge of both the site and this Management Plan to act as guides during visits.

- All educational and recreational visits (including tourism) shall be supervised by a nominated guide, who is responsible for briefing visitors on the Code of Conduct and the requirements of this Management Plan and ensuring they are complied with.
- Parties should consult and coordinate to develop skills and resources, particularly those related to conservation techniques, to assist with the protection of the Area's values.

7(x) Requirements for reports

Parties shall ensure that the principal holder for each Permit issued submits to the appropriate authority a report describing the activities undertaken. Such reports shall include, as appropriate, the information identified in the Visit Report Form provided in Appendix 4 of Resolution 2 (1998). In addition, any removal of materials in accordance with section 7(vii) shall be detailed, including the reason for removal and the current location of the items or the date of disposal. Any return of such items to the site shall also be reported.

Parties shall maintain a record of activities within the Area and, in the Annual Exchange of Information, shall provide summary descriptions of activities conducted by persons subject to their jurisdiction, in sufficient detail to allow evaluation of the effectiveness of the Management Plan. Parties should wherever possible deposit originals or copies of such reports in a publicly accessible archive to maintain a record of visitation, to be used both for review of the Management Plan and in managing further visitation to the site.

Map A - Historic Hut, Backdoor Bay, Cape Royds, Ross Island, Antarctic Specially Protected Area 157: Regional Topographic Map

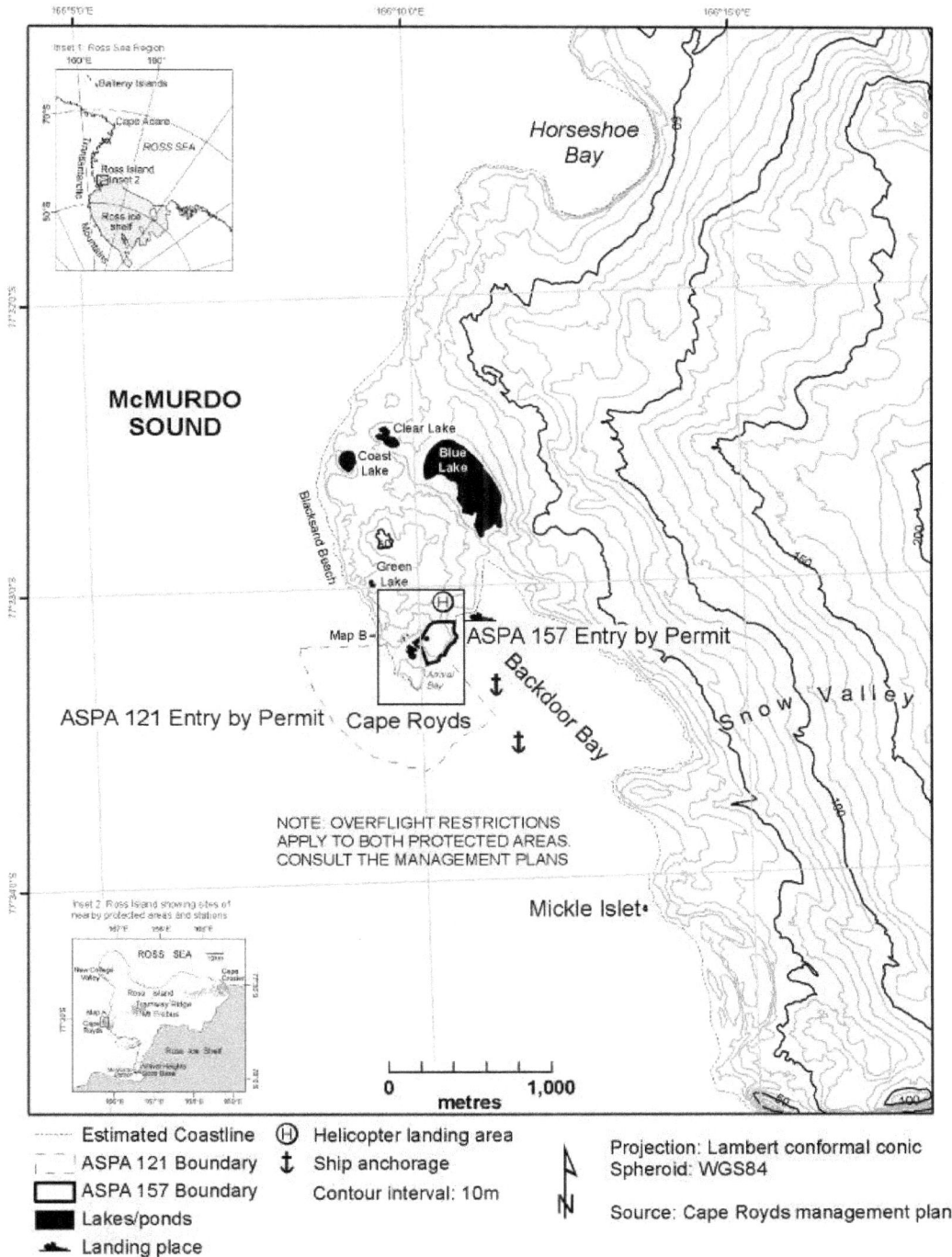

**Map B - Historic Hut, Backdoor Bay, Cape Royds, Ross Island,
Antarctic Specially Protected Area 157: Site Topographic Map**

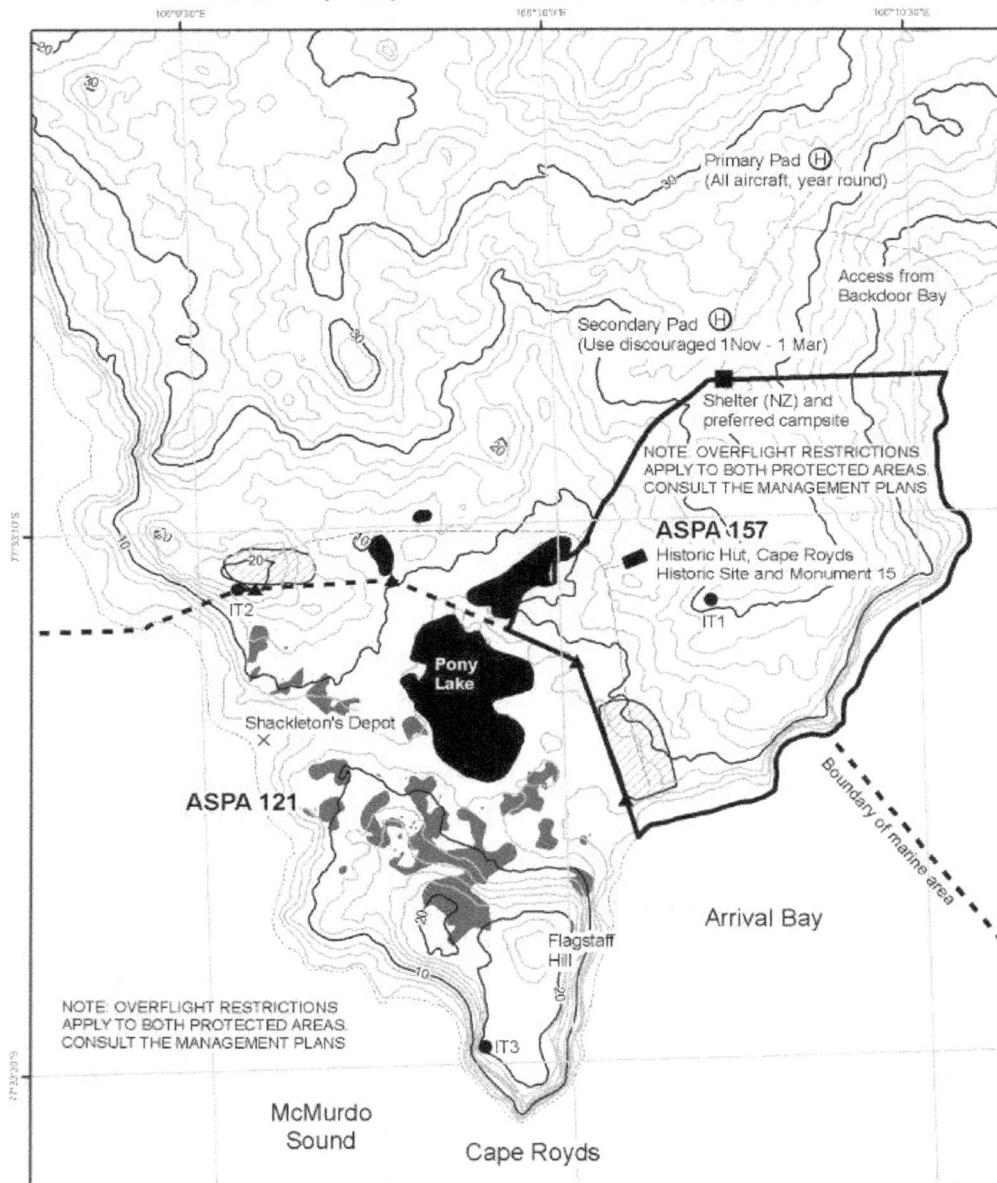

Primary Pad (H)
(All aircraft, year round)

Access from
Backdoor Bay

Secondary Pad (H)
(Use discouraged 1 Nov - 1 Mar)

Shelter (NZ) and
preferred campsite

NOTE: OVERFLIGHT RESTRICTIONS
APPLY TO BOTH PROTECTED AREAS.
CONSULT THE MANAGEMENT PLANS

ASPA 157
Historic Hut, Cape Royds
Historic Site and Monument 15

IT1

Pony
Lake

Shackleton's Depot
×

ASPA 121

IT2

Boundary of marine area

Arrival Bay

Flagstaff
Hill

NOTE: OVERFLIGHT RESTRICTIONS
APPLY TO BOTH PROTECTED AREAS.
CONSULT THE MANAGEMENT PLANS

IT3

McMurdo
Sound

Cape Royds

Lakes/ponds
Penguin nesting areas (1990)
Areas suitable for viewing penguins
Buildings
Survey Marks
Signposts

(H) Designated helicopter pads
...... Estimated position of coastline
ASPA 121 Boundary
ASPA 157 Boundary
---- Preferred walking routes

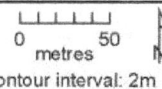

0   50
metres

Contour interval: 2m

Projection: Lambert conformal conic
Spheroid: WGS84

Source: Cape Royds management plan

Management Plan For
Antarctic Specially Protected Area No. 158
HUT POINT, ROSS ISLAND
(including Historic Site and Monument No. 18, the historic *Discovery* hut of Captain Robert Falcon Scott)

1. Description of Values to be Protected

The significant historic value of this Area was formally recognised when it was designated as Historic Site and Monument No. 18 in Recommendation 9 (1972). It was designated as Specially Protected Area No. 28 in Measure 1 (1998) and redesignated as Antarctic Specially Protected Area 158 in Decision 1 (2002).

The hut was built in February 1902 during the National Antarctic *Discovery* Expedition of 1901-1904, led by Captain Robert Falcon Scott who later found it a valuable advance staging point for journeys on the "Barrier" during his 1910-1913 expedition. It was also used by Sir Ernest Shackleton during the 1907-1909 British Antarctic *Nimrod* Expedition and later by his stranded Ross Sea party during the Imperial Trans-Antarctic Expedition of 1914-1917. This building was prefabricated in Australia to an 'outback' design with verandas on three sides.

The Hut Point site is one of the principal sites of early human activity in Antarctica. It is an important symbol of the Heroic Age of Antarctic exploration and, as such, has considerable historical significance. Some of the earliest advances in the study of earth sciences, meteorology, flora and fauna in Antarctica are associated with the *Discovery* Expedition based at this site. The history of these activities and the contribution they have made to the understanding and awareness of Antarctica give this Area significant scientific, aesthetic and historic value.

The Management Plan was reviewed and a revised version with additional visitor management provisions was adopted by means of Measure 2 (2005).

2. Aims and Objectives

The aim of the Management Plan is to provide protection for the Area and its features so that its values can be preserved. The objectives of the Management Plan are to:

- avoid degradation of, or substantial risk to, the values of the Area;
- maintain the historic values of the Area through planned conservation work which may include:
a. an annual 'on-site' maintenance programme,
b. a programme of monitoring the condition of artefacts and structures, and the factors which affect them, and
c. a programme of conservation of artefacts conducted on and off site;
- allow management activities which support the protection of the values and features of the Area including recording of any relevant historic data; and
- prevent unnecessary human disturbance to the Area, its features and artefacts through managed access to the *Discovery* hut.

3. Management Activities

The following management activities shall be undertaken to protect the values of the Area:

- A regular programme of conservation work shall be undertaken on the *Discovery* hut and associated artefacts in the Area;
- Visits shall be made as necessary for management purposes;
- Systematic monitoring shall be put in place to assess the impacts of present visitor limits, and the results and any related management recommendations included in reviews of this Management Plan;
- National Antarctic Programmes operating in, or those with an interest in, the Area shall consult together with a view to ensuring the above management activities are implemented.
- Copies of this Management Plan, including maps of the Area, shall be made available at adjacent operational research/field stations.

4. Period of Designation

Designated for an indefinite period.

5. Maps

Map A: Hut Point regional topographic map. This map shows the wider environs of the Area with significant topographic features and the adjacent US McMurdo Station. Inset: shows the position of the site in relation to other protected sites on Ross Island.

Map B: Hut Point site topographic map. This map shows the location of the historic hut, Vince's cross and other detail of the immediate environs.

6. Description of the Area

6(i) Geographical coordinates, boundary markers and natural features
Hut Point is a small ice free area protruding south west from Hut Point Peninsula and situated to the west of the United States McMurdo Station. The designated Area consists solely of the structure of the hut (77° 50'S, 166° 37'E) which is situated near the south western extremity of Hut Point.

6(ii) Access to the Area
There are no designated helicopter landings sites in the vicinity of the hut as helicopters have the potential to damage the hut by blowing scoria and ice particles and to accelerate the abrasion of the hut and surrounding artefacts. Vehicles may approach the hut along the road leading from the United States McMurdo Station, or from the sea ice when safe conditions exist. During open water, landings by boat may be made to the north of the hut.

6(iii) Location of structures within and adjacent to the Area
The designated Area consists solely of the structure of the historic *Discovery* hut (Historic Site and Monument No. 18). Historic Site and Monument No. 19, a cross to the memory of

George T. Vince (a member of the *Discovery* Expedition who died in the vicinity), is situated approximately 75 metres west of the hut.

6(iv) Location of other Protected Areas in the vicinity
- ASPA 121 (previously SSSI No. 1) Cape Royds and
- ASPA 157 (SPA No. 28), Backdoor Bay, Cape Royds, are 32 kilometres north of Hut Point.
- ASPA 122 (SSSI No. 2), Arrival Heights, is 2 kilometres north of Hut Point on Hut Point Peninsula.
- ASPA 155 (SPA No. 25), Cape Evans, is 22 kilometres to the north of Hut Point.

All sites are located on Ross Island.

6(v) Special Zones within the Area
There are no special zones within the Area.

7. Terms and Conditions for Entry Permits

Entry to the Area is prohibited except in accordance with a Permit. Permits shall be issued only by appropriate national authorities and may contain both general and specific conditions. A Permit may be issued by a national authority to cover a number of visits in a season. Parties operating in the Area shall consult together and with groups and organisations interested in visiting the Area to ensure that visitor numbers are not exceeded.

Permits to enter the site may be issued for a stated period for:
- activities related to conservation, research and/or monitoring purposes;
- management activities in support of the objectives of this Management Plan;
- activities related to educational or recreational activities including tourism, providing they do not conflict with the objectives of this Management Plan; and
- any other activity specifically provided for in this Plan.

7(i) Access to and movement within or over the Area
- Control of numbers within the hut is necessary to prevent damage caused by crowding around the many vulnerable features within the hut. The maximum number within the hut at any time (including guides) shall be: **8 people**
- Avoidance of cumulative impacts on the interior of the hut requires an annual limit on visitor numbers. The effects of current visitor levels (average 992 per year between 1998 and 2009) suggest that a significant increase could cause significant adverse impacts. The annual maximum number of visitors shall be: **2,000 people**
- These limits have been based on current visitor levels and on the best advice available from conservation advisory agencies (which include conservators, archaeologists, historians, museologists and other heritage protection professionals). The limits are based on the proposition that any significant increase in the current level of visitors would be detrimental to the values to be protected. An ongoing monitoring programme to assess the effect of visitors is required to provide the basis for future reviews of the Management Plan, in particular whether the current limits on numbers of visitors to the Area are appropriate.
- Adequate supervision of visits to the Area is necessary to prevent damage caused by crowding and by actions inconsistent with the Code of Conduct set out in section

7(ii). All tourism, educational and recreational visits must be supervised by an experienced guide nominated by the operator (refer section 7(ix)).

7(ii) Activities which may be conducted within the Area

Activities which may be conducted within the Area include:

- visits for conservation purposes;
- educational and/or recreational visits including tourism;
- scientific activity which does not detract from the values of the Area.

Visitors should adhere to the following Code of Conduct, except where conservation, research, monitoring or management activities specified in the Permit require otherwise:

- Thoroughly clean grit and scoria, ice and snow from boots using the brushes provided before entering the hut to reduce floor abrasion and only use tripods or monopods with flat bottomed rubber bases as opposed to those with metal spikes which can damage the floor;
- Remove any clothing made wet by sea water, and any sea ice crystals from boots, as salt particles accelerate corrosion of metal objects;
- Do not touch, move or sit on any items or furniture in the huts - handling artefacts causes damage;
- As many areas are cramped and artefacts can be accidentally bumped, do not wear packs inside and when the maximum number of visitors (8) are in the hut at one time the use of tripods or monopods is prohibited;
- When moving around the sites, take great care not to tread on any items which may be obscured by snow;
- Use of combustion style lanterns, naked flames or smoking in or around the hut is prohibited, as fire is a major risk; and
- Visits should be recorded in the book provided. This allows times and levels of visitation to be correlated with temperature and humidity data automatically logged inside the hut.

7(iii) Installation, modification or removal of structures

- No alteration to the structure shall be made, except for conservation purposes or scientific activities that do not detract from the values of the Area as specified in section 1.
- No historic structure shall be removed from the Area, unless specified in a Permit issued in accordance with the provisions of section 7(vii).

7(iv) Location of field camps

Use of the historic hut for living purposes is not permitted.

7(v) Restrictions on materials and organisms which may be brought into the Area

- No living animals, plant material, micro-organisms or soil shall be introduced to the Area. No food products shall be taken into the Area.
- Chemicals may only be introduced for permitted scientific or conservation purposes. Chemicals (including fuel) or other materials are not to be left in the Area, unless required for essential purposes connected with the conservation of the historic structure or the associated relics.
- All introduced materials are to be removed when no longer required and before a date to be specified in the relevant Permit.

7(vi) Taking or harmful interference with native flora and fauna
There are no native flora or fauna within the designated Area.

7(vii) Collection of anything not imported by the Permit Holder
- Material may be collected and removed from the Area for conservation reasons consistent with the objectives of this Management Plan only when specified in a Permit issued by the appropriate national authority.
- Materials which pose a threat to the environment or human health may be removed from the Area for disposal, in accordance with a Permit, where they meet one or more of the following criteria:
  i.   the artefact presents a threat to the environment, wildlife or human health and safety;
  ii. it is in such poor condition that it is not reasonably possible to conserve it;
  iii. it does not contribute in any significant way to our understanding of the hut, its occupants or the history of Antarctica;
  iv. it does not contribute to, or it detracts from, the visual qualities of the site or the hut, and/or;
  v.   it is not a unique or rare item;

and where such action is:

  i.   undertaken by parties with appropriate heritage conservation expertise; and
  ii. part of an overall plan for conservation work at the site.

- National authorities should ensure that any removal of artefacts and assessment against the above criteria is carried out by personnel with appropriate heritage conservation expertise.
- Artefacts judged to be of high historic value, which cannot be conserved on site with currently available techniques, may be removed in accordance with a Permit for storage in a controlled environment until such time as they can safely be returned to the Area.

7(viii) Disposal of waste
All human waste, grey water and other waste generated by work parties or visitors shall be removed from the Area.

7(ix) Measures that may be necessary to ensure that the aims and objectives of the plan continue to be met
- The Permit, or an authorised copy, shall be carried within the Area.
- Information on the requirements of this Management Plan shall be provided to all visitors.
- The Code of Conduct set out in section 7(ii) shall be followed by all visitors, except where conservation, research, monitoring or management purposes require otherwise.
- Operators facilitating educational and recreational visits (including tourism) to the Area shall, prior to commencement of the summer season, nominate people with a working knowledge of both the site and this Management Plan to act as guides during visits.
- All educational and recreational visits (including tourism) shall be supervised by a nominated guide, who is responsible for briefing visitors on the Code of Conduct and the requirements of this Management Plan and ensuring it is complied with.

- Parties shall consult and coordinate to develop skills and resources, particularly those related to conservation techniques, to assist with the protection of the Area's values.

7(x) Requirements for reports

Parties shall ensure that the principal holder for each Permit issued submits to the appropriate authority a report describing the activities undertaken. Such reports shall include, as appropriate, the information identified in the Visit Report Form provided in Appendix 4 of Resolution 2 (1998). In addition, any removal of materials in accordance with section 7 (vii) shall be detailed, including the reason for removal and the current location of the items or the date of disposal. Any return of such items to the site shall also be reported.

Parties shall maintain a record of activities within the Area and, in the Annual Exchange of Information, shall provide summary descriptions of activities conducted by persons subject to their jurisdiction, in sufficient detail to allow evaluation of the effectiveness of the Management Plan. Parties should wherever possible deposit originals or copies of such reports in a publicly accessible archive to maintain a record of visitation, to be used both for review of the Management Plan and in managing further visitation to the site.

Map A - Historic Hut, Hut Point, Ross Island, Antarctic Specially Protected Area 158:
Regional Topographic Map

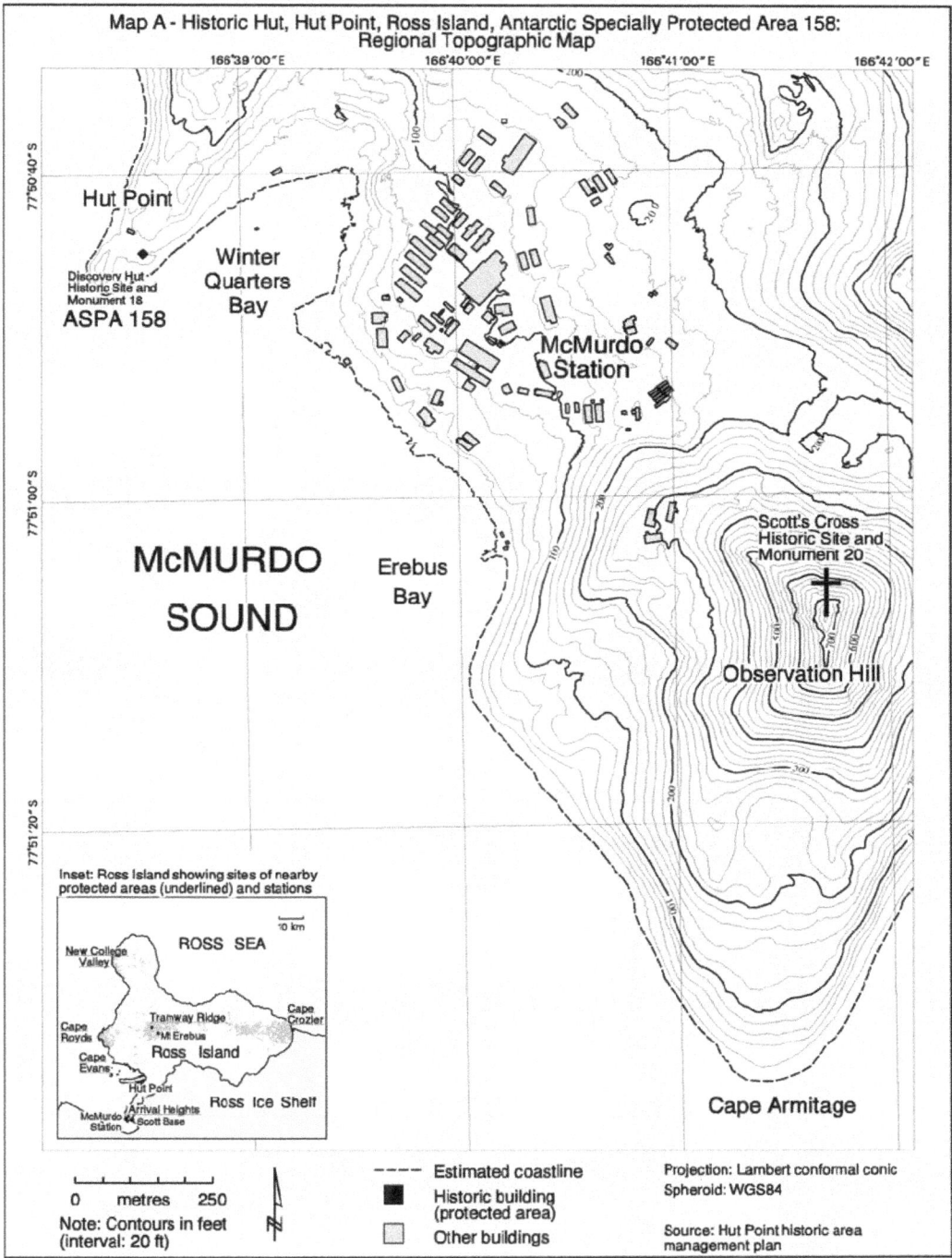

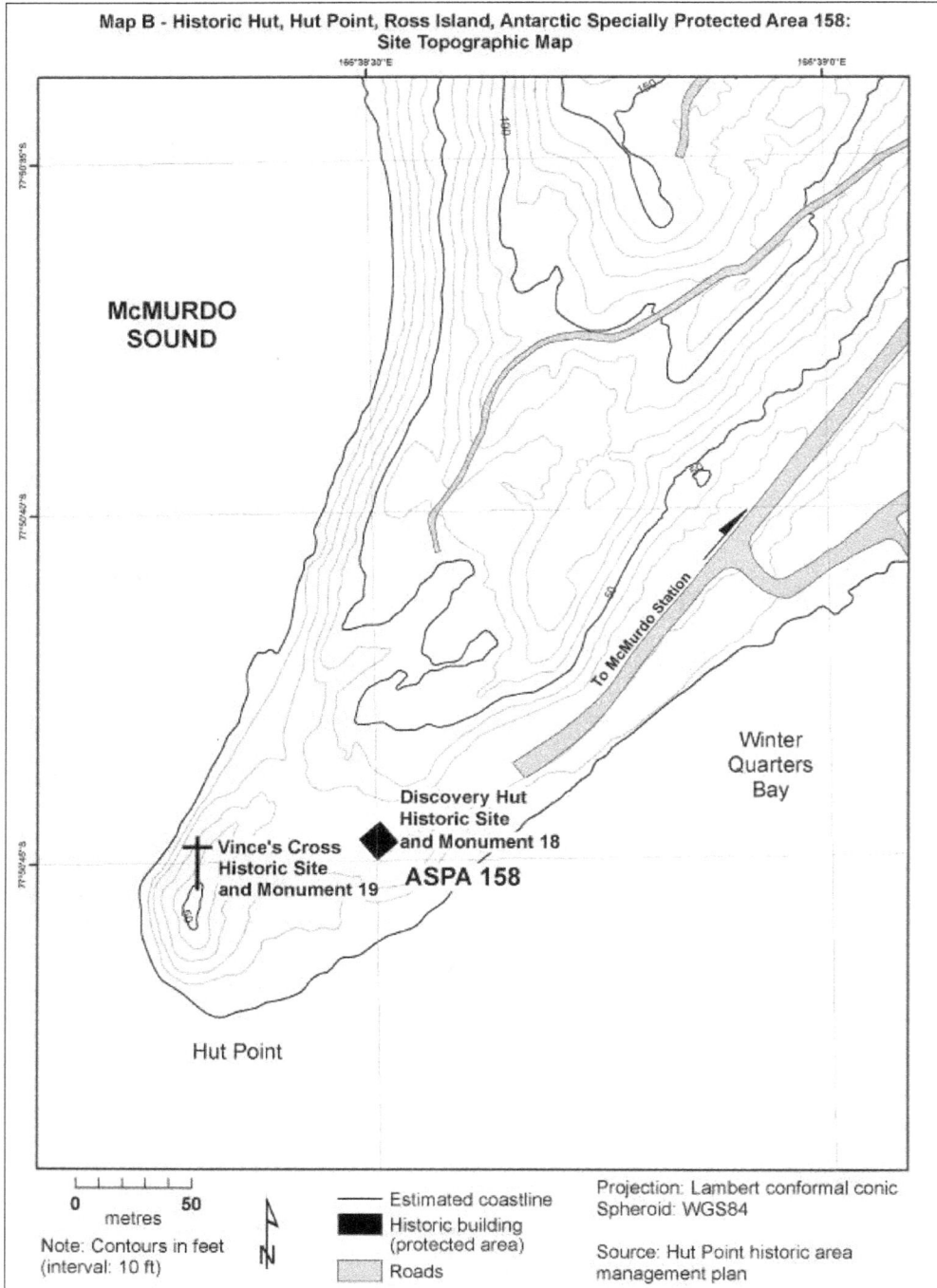

Map B - Historic Hut, Hut Point, Ross Island, Antarctic Specially Protected Area 158: Site Topographic Map

Management Plan For
Antarctic Specially Protected Area No. 159
CAPE ADARE, BORCHGREVINK COAST
(including Historic Site and Monument No. 22, the historic huts of Carsten Borchgrevink and Scott's Northern Party and their precincts)

1. Description of Values to be Protected

The historic value of this Area was formally recognized when it was listed as Historic Site and Monument No. 22 in Recommendation VII-9 (1972). It was designated as Specially Protected Area No. 29 in Measure 1 (1998) and redesignated as Antarctic Specially Protected Area 159 in Decision 1 (2002).

There are three main structures in the Area. Two huts were built in February 1899 during the British Antarctic *Southern Cross* Expedition led by Carsten E. Borchgrevink (1898-1900). One hut served as a living hut and the other as a store. They were used for the first winter spent on the Antarctic continent. The collapsing remains of a third hut built in February 1911 for the Northern party led by Victor L.A. Campbell of Robert Falcon Scott's British Antarctic *Terra Nova* Expeditions (1910-1913), is situated 30 meters to the north of Borchgrevink's hut. The Northern party wintered in this hut in 1911.

In addition to these features there are numerous other historic relics located in the Area. These include stores depots, a latrine structure, two anchors from the ship *Southern Cross*, an ice anchor from the ship *Terra Nova*, and supplies of coal briquettes. Other historic items within the Area are buried in guano. Collectively, the three huts and associated historic relics are listed as Historic Site and Monument No. 22.

Cape Adare is one of the principal sites of early human activity in Antarctica as it includes the first building erected on the continent. It is an important symbol of the Heroic Age of Antarctic exploration and, as such, has considerable historical significance. Some of the earliest advances in the study of earth sciences, meteorology, flora and fauna in Antarctica are associated with the two earliest expeditions based at this site. The history of these activities and the contribution they have made to the understanding and awareness of Antarctica give this Area significant scientific, aesthetic and historic value.

The Management Plan was reviewed and a revised version was adopted by means of Measure 2 (2005).

2. Aims and Objectives

The aim of the Management Plan is to provide protection for the Area and its features so that its values can be preserved. The objectives of the Plan are to:

- avoid degradation of, or substantial risk to, the values of the Area;
- maintain the historic values of the Area through planned conservation work which may include:
a. 'on-site' maintenance,

b. monitoring the condition of artefacts and structures, and the factors which affect them, and

c. conservation of artefacts to be conducted on and off site;

- allow management activities which support the protection of the values and features of the Area including:

a. mapping and otherwise recording the disposition of historic items in the hut environs, and

b. recording other relevant historic data; and

- prevent unnecessary human disturbance to the Area, its features and artefacts through managed access to Borchgrevink's hut.

3. Management Activities

- A programme of conservation work shall be undertaken on the historic huts and associated structures and artefacts in the Area.
- Visits shall be made as necessary for management purposes.
- Systematic monitoring shall be put in place to assess the impacts of present visitor limits, and the results and any related management recommendations included in reviews of this Management Plan.
- National Antarctic Programmes operating in, or those with an interest in, the Area shall consult together with a view to ensuring the above management activities are implemented.
- Copies of this Management Plan, including maps of the Area, shall be made available at adjacent operational research/field stations.

4. Period of Designation

Designated for an indefinite period.

5. Maps

Map A: Cape Adare regional map. This map shows the Cape Adare region along with the boundaries of the Area with significant topographic features. It also shows the approximate location of significant historical items within the Area.

Map B: Cape Adare site map. This map shows the approximate location of specific historic relics and structures within the Area.

6. Description of the Area

6(i) Geographical coordinates, boundary markers and natural features
Cape Adare is a generally ice free, prominent volcanic headland, at the northern extremity of Victoria Land, which marks the western approaches to the Ross Sea. The Area is located to the south west of the Cape on the southern shore of Ridley Beach, which encloses a large, flat, triangular area of shingle.

The whole of the flat area and the lower western slopes of the Adare Peninsula are occupied by one of the largest Adélie penguin (*Pygoscelis adeliae*) colonies in Antarctica. The penguins have almost completely occupied the Area and the need to avoid disturbance often restricts access to the huts.

The boundaries of the ASPA are:
- North, an east-west line drawn 50 metres north of the Northern Party Hut;
- East, a north-south line drawn 50 metres to the east of Borchgrevink's stores hut. The north east corner of the boundary is 71° 18.502'S, 170° 11.735'E and the south east corner of the boundary is 71° 18.633'S 170°11.735'E;
- West, a north-south line drawn 50 metres to the west of Borchgrevink's living hut. The north west corner of the boundary is 71° 18.502'S, 170° 11.547'E and the south west corner of the boundary is 71° 18.591'S, 170° 11.547'E; and
- South, the high tide mark of Ridley Beach.

Skuas (*Catharacta maccormicki*) nest in the vicinity and Weddell seals (*Leptonychotes weddellii*) also haul up along the beach.

6(ii) Access to the Area
There are no designated helicopter pads in the vicinity of the Area. Helicopter landings should be avoided as for most of the summer season it is difficult to operate helicopters without causing disturbance to penguins and skuas. Landings from the sea by boat, or vehicles travelling on the sea ice, may be made directly onto the beach as ice and surf conditions allow. From the beach, access to the Area is by foot. Care must be taken to avoid damage to artefacts in the Area and disturbance to birds nesting on and around the structures.

6(iii) Location of structures within and adjacent to the Area
Apart from a Treaty plaque all structures within the Area are of historic origin. Major features of the Area include Borchgrevink's *Southern Cross* Expedition living hut and the unroofed stores hut. Scott's Northern Party hut is situated 30 metres to the north of Borchgrevink's living hut and is in a state of collapse.

In addition to these structures there are many other historic relics distributed around the Area. These include stores depots, a latrine structure, two anchors from the ship *Southern Cross*, an ice anchor from the ship *Terra Nova*, and supplies of coal. Many of these items are either partly or completely covered in the guano of the Adélie penguins which also occupy the Area.

The grave (Historic Site and Monument No. 23) of Nicolai Hanson (biologist with the *Southern Cross* Expedition) is located approximately 1.5 km north east of historic huts. It is marked by a large boulder with an iron cross, a brass plaque and a white cross marked out in quartz pebbles.

6(iv) Location of other Protected Areas in the vicinity
The nearest Protected Area is ASPA 106 (previously SPA No. 7), approximately 115 km to the south, on the western side of Cape Hallett.

6(v) Special Zones within the Area
There are no special zones within the Area.

7. Terms and Conditions for Entry Permits

Entry to the Area is prohibited except in accordance with a Permit. Permits shall be issued only by appropriate national authorities and may contain both general and specific conditions. A Permit may be issued by a national authority to cover a number of visits in a season. Parties operating in the Area shall consult together and with groups and organisations interested in visiting the Area to ensure that visitor numbers are not exceeded.

Permits to enter the site may be issued for a stated period for:
- activities related to conservation, research and/or monitoring purposes;
- management activities in support of the objectives of this Management Plan;
- activities related to educational or recreational activities including tourism, providing they do not conflict with the objectives of this Management Plan; and
- any other activity specifically provided for in this Plan

7(i) Access to and movement within the Area
- Control of movement within the Area is necessary to prevent disturbance to wildlife and damage caused by crowding around the many vulnerable historic features within the Area. The maximum number in the Area at any time (including guides and those within the hut) shall be: **40 people.**
- Control of numbers within Borchgrevink's hut is necessary to prevent damage caused by crowding around the many vulnerable features within the hut. The maximum number within the hut at any time (including guides) shall be: **4 people.**
- Avoidance of cumulative impacts on the interior of Borchgrevink's hut requires an annual limit on visitor numbers. The number of visitors to the hut varies considerably from year to year (average 193 per year between 1998 and 2009) but the effect of visitors to other historic huts in the Ross Sea region suggests that similar limits should apply. The annual maximum number of visitors shall be: **2,000 people.**
- These limits have been based on current visitor levels and on the best advice available from conservation advisory agencies (which include conservators, archaeologists, historians, museologists and other heritage protection professionals). The limits are based on the proposition that any significant increase in the current level of visitors would be detrimental to the values to be protected. An ongoing monitoring programme to assess the effect of visitors is required to provide the basis for future reviews of the Management Plan, in particular whether the limits on number of visitors are appropriate.
- Adequate supervision of visits to the Area is necessary to prevent damage caused by crowding and by actions inconsistent with the Code of Conduct set out in section 7(ii). All tourism, educational and recreational visits must be supervised by an experienced guide nominated by the operator (refer section 7(ix)).
- Helicopter landings are prohibited within the Area.
- Vehicles are prohibited within the Area.

7(ii) Activities which may be conducted within the Area
Activities which may be conducted within the Area include:
- visits for conservation purposes;
- educational and/or recreational visits including tourism; and
- scientific activity which does not detract from the values of the Area.

Visitors should adhere to the following Code of Conduct, except where conservation, research, monitoring or management activities specified in the Permit require otherwise:

- Thoroughly clean grit and scoria, ice and snow from boots using the brushes provided before entering the hut to reduce floor abrasion and only use tripods or monopods with flat bottomed rubber bases as opposed to those with metal spikes which can damage the floor;
- Remove any clothing made wet by sea water, and any sea ice crystals from boots, as salt particles accelerate corrosion of metal objects;
- Do not touch, move or sit on any items or furniture in the huts - handling artefacts causes damage;
- As many areas are cramped and artefacts can be accidentally bumped, do not wear packs inside and when the maximum number of visitors (4) are in the hut at one time the use of tripods or monopods is prohibited;
- When moving around the sites, take great care not to tread on any items which may be obscured by snow and remain on established walking tracks;
- Use of combustion style lanterns, naked flames or smoking in or around the huts is prohibited, as fire is a major risk; and
- Visits should be recorded in the book provided. This allows times and levels of visitation to be correlated with temperature and humidity data automatically logged inside the hut.

7(iii) Installation, modification or removal of structures
- No new structures are to be erected in the Area, or scientific equipment installed, except for conservation or scientific activities that do not detract from the values of the Area as specified in section 1.
- No historic structure shall be removed from the Area, unless specified in a Permit issued in accordance with the provisions of section 7(vii).

7(iv) Location of field camps
- Use of the historic hut, or other structures in the Area, for living purposes is not permitted.
- Camping is prohibited within the Area under any circumstances.

7(v) Restrictions on materials and organisms which may be brought into the Area
- No living animals, plant material, soil or micro-organisms shall be introduced to the Area.
- No food products shall be taken into the Area.
- Chemicals may only be introduced for permitted scientific or conservation purposes. Chemicals (including fuel) or other materials are not to be left in the Area, unless required for essential purposes connected with the conservation of the historic structures or the associated relics.
- All introduced materials are to be removed when no longer required and before a date to be specified in the Permit.

7(vi) Taking or harmful interference with native flora and fauna
- This activity is prohibited except in accordance with a Permit issued by the appropriate national authority specifically for that purpose under Article 3, Annex II to the Protocol on Environmental Protection.

- Where animal taking or harmful interference is involved, this should, as a minimum standard, be in accordance with the SCAR Code of Conduct for the Use of Animals for Scientific Purposes in Antarctica.

7(vii) Collection of anything not imported by the Permit Holder
- Material may be collected and removed from the Area for conservation reasons consistent with the objectives of this Management Plan only when specified in a Permit issued by the appropriate national authority.
- Materials which pose a threat to the environment or human health may be removed from the Area for disposal, in accordance with a Permit, where they meet one or more of the following criteria:
i. the artefact presents a threat to the environment, wildlife or human health and safety;
ii. it is in such poor condition that it is not reasonably possible to conserve it;
iii. it does not contribute in any significant way to our understanding of the hut, its occupants or the history of Antarctica;
iv. it does not contribute to, or it detracts from, the visual qualities of the site or the hut, and/or;
v. it is not a unique or rare item;

and where such action is:

i. undertaken by parties with appropriate heritage conservation expertise; and
ii. part of an overall plan for conservation work at the site.

- National authorities should ensure that any removal of artefacts and assessment against the above criteria is carried out by personnel with appropriate heritage conservation expertise.
- Artefacts judged to be of high historic value, which cannot be conserved on site with currently available techniques, may be removed in accordance with a Permit for storage in a controlled environment until such time as they can safely be returned to the Area.

7(viii) Disposal of waste
All human waste, grey water and other waste generated by work parties or visitors shall be removed from the Area.

7(ix) Measures that may be necessary to ensure that the aims and objectives of the plan continue to be met
- The Permit, or an authorised copy, shall be carried within the Area.
- Information on the requirements of this Management Plan shall be provided to all visitors.
- The Code of Conduct set out in section 7(ii) shall be followed by all visitors, except where conservation, research, monitoring or management purposes require otherwise.
- Operators facilitating educational and recreational visits (including tourism) to the Area shall, prior to commencement of the summer season, nominate people with a working knowledge of both the site and this Management Plan to act as guides during visits.
- All educational and recreational visits (including tourism) shall be supervised by a nominated guide, who is responsible for briefing visitors on the Code of Conduct and ensuring it is complied with.

- Parties shall consult and coordinate to develop skills and resources, particularly those related to conservation techniques, to assist with the protection of the Area's values.

7(x) Requirements for reports

Parties shall ensure that the principal holder for each Permit issued submits to the appropriate authority a report describing the activities undertaken. Such reports shall include, as appropriate, the information identified in the Visit Report Form provided in Appendix 4 of Resolution 2 (1998). In addition, any removal of materials in accordance with section 7 (vii) shall be detailed, including the reason for removal and the current location of the items or the date of disposal. Any return of such items to the site shall also be reported.

Parties shall maintain a record of such activities and, in the Annual Exchange of Information, shall provide summary descriptions of activities conducted by persons subject to their jurisdiction, in sufficient detail to allow evaluation of the effectiveness of the Management Plan. Parties should wherever possible deposit originals or copies of such reports in a publicly accessible archive to maintain a record of visitation, to be used both for review of the Management Plan and in managing further visitation to the site.

Map A - Historic Hut, Cape Adare, Antarctic Specially Protected Area 159: Regional Map

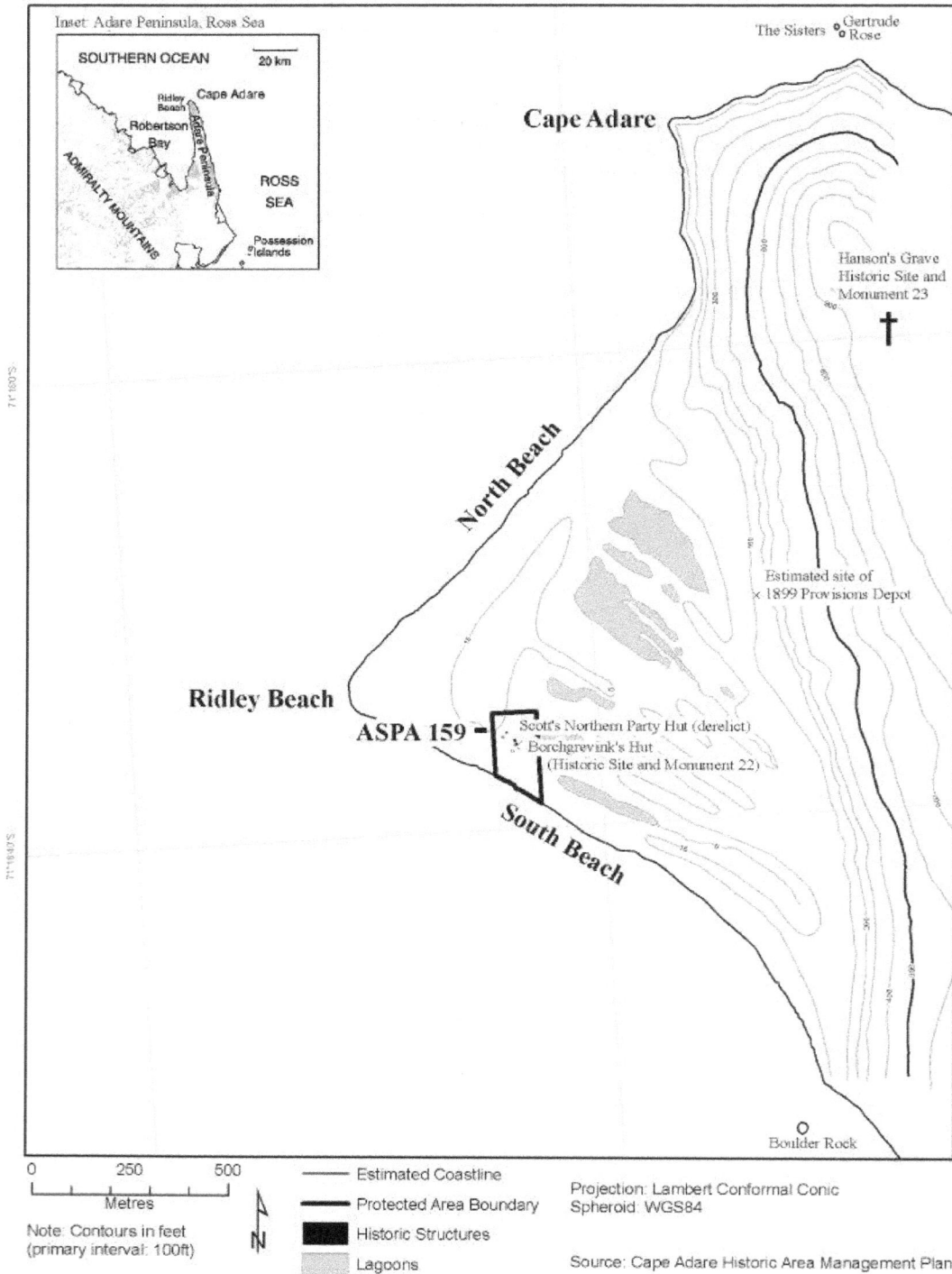

Inset: Adare Peninsula, Ross Sea

SOUTHERN OCEAN   20 km

Ridley Beach   Cape Adare

Robertson Bay

ADMIRALTY MOUNTAINS

Adare Peninsula

ROSS SEA

Possession Islands

The Sisters   Gertrude Rose

Cape Adare

Hanson's Grave Historic Site and Monument 23

North Beach

Estimated site of 1899 Provisions Depot

Ridley Beach

ASPA 159

Scott's Northern Party Hut (derelict)
Borchgrevink's Hut
(Historic Site and Monument 22)

South Beach

Boulder Rock

0   250   500

Metres

N

Note: Contours in feet
(primary interval: 100ft)

—— Estimated Coastline

—— Protected Area Boundary

■ Historic Structures

Lagoons

Projection: Lambert Conformal Conic
Spheroid: WGS84

Source: Cape Adare Historic Area Management Plan

Map B - Historic Hut, Cape Adare, Antarctic Specially Protected Area 159: Site Map

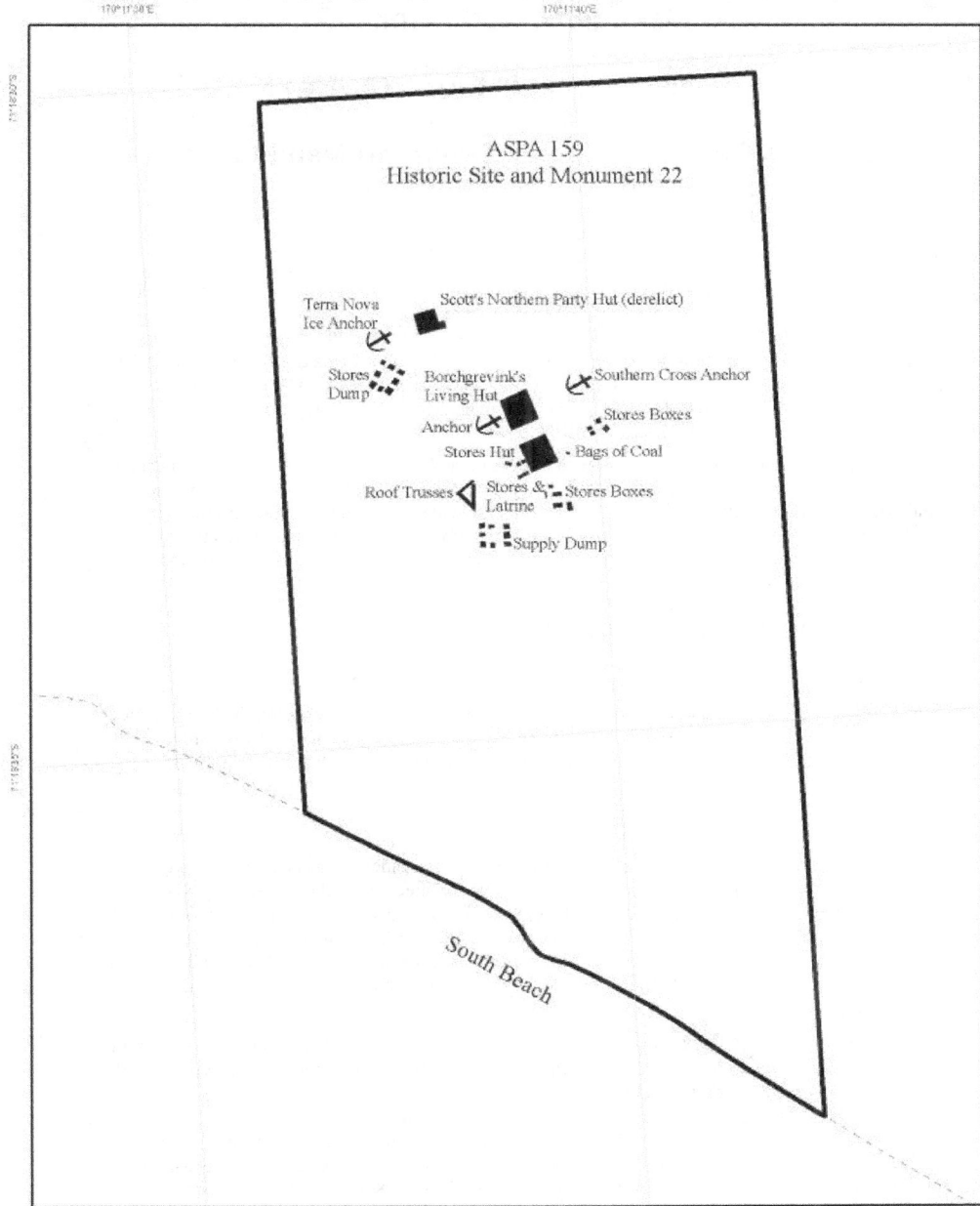

ASPA 159
Historic Site and Monument 22

Terra Nova
Ice Anchor

Scott's Northern Party Hut (derelict)

Stores
Dump

Borchgrevink's
Living Hut

Southern Cross Anchor

Stores Boxes

Anchor

Stores Hut

Bags of Coal

Roof Trusses

Stores &
Latrine

Stores Boxes

Supply Dump

South Beach

0   20
Metres

N

- - - Estimated Coastline

—— Protected Area Boundary

■ Historic Structures

Projection: Lambert Conformal Conic
Spheroid: WGS84

Source: Cape Adare Historic Area Management Plan

Management Plan for

Antarctic Specially Protected Area (ASPA) No 163:

Dakshin Gangotri Glacier, Dronning Maud Land

1. Introduction

India introduced a Working Paper at XXV ATCM (WP47) on a draft management plan for a proposed site of Special Scientific Interest for snout of Dakshin Gangotri Glacier, Schirmacher Hills (also known as Vassfjellet), Dronning Maud Land. The Committee noted that this should be termed an ASPA rather than SSSI. Accordingly, during XXVI ATCM India submitted a draft management plan for Antarctica Specially Protected Area (XXVI ATCM/WP-38) and thereafter submitted revised management plan during XXVII-ATCM (WP 33). The management plan was adopted by Measure 2 (2005) and designated ASPA 163 during XXVIII ATCM (WP 25).

Dakshin Gangotri glacier has significant value in terms of glacier retreat monitoring. A snout is being monitored since 1983 to understand the effect of climate change on glacier. This area is also important for study of algae, moss, cynobacteria and lichen which are wide spread in Schirmacher Hills and especially within the ASPA site. Cynobacteria contribute significantly to the nitrogen fixation, and many species have been identified so far from this area. Many species of lichens are also indentified in this area according to study conducted since 2003.

2. Description of values to be protected

i. Historic Value

Dakshin Gangotri Glacier is a small tongue of polar continental ice sheet, overriding the Schirmacher Hills in central Dronning Maud Land (CDML). It was identified by the second Indian Antarctic Expedition in 1982-83 and since then its snout is being monitored regularly for fluctuation w.r.t. retreat/advance.

ii. Scientific Value

With the availability of the vast amount of data for the past two decades, it has become a valuable site for observing the changes in the movement of the Antarctic ice sheet under the impact of global warming. The area has primary scientific importance for glaciologists and environmental scientists. Due to The scientific values of the Area and the nature of the research, the area is protected as an Antarctic Specially Protected Area consistent with Articles 2, 3, 5 and 6 of Annex V of the Protocol on Environmental Protection to the Antarctic Treaty; to prevent interference with ongoing planned scientific investigations.

Global positioning system (GPS) campaigns were conducted during the 2003 and 2004 austral summer seasons to obtain insight into the velocity and strain-rate distribution on the margin of the continental ice sheet overriding southern part of Schirmacher Hills in CDML. GPS data were collected for two years at 21 sites and analyzed to estimate the site coordinates baselines and velocities. Horizontal velocities of the glacier sites lie between 1.89 ± 0.01 and 10.88 ± 0.01 m a-1 to the north-northeast, with an average velocity of 6.21 ± 0.01 m a-1. The principal strain rates provide a quantitative measurement of extension rates, which range from (0.11 ± 0.01) &times 10-3 to $(1.48\pm0.85) \times$ 10-3 a-1, and shortening rates, which range from $(0.04\pm0.02) \times$ 10-3 to $(0.96\pm0.16) \times$ 10-3 a-1 (Sunil et al., 2007).

iii. Environmental Value

At the designated area, exploration showed abundant faunal diversity of the moss-inhabiting terrestrial invertebrate fauna. Schirmacher Hills is also an important area for the algae and cyanobacterial diversity. Terrestrial mosses are quite widespread in the Schirmacher Hills colonizing on a wide range of habitats. The mosses, because of their poikilohydric nature and alternative strategy of adaptation, are one of the plant groups which grow in Antarctica. Mosses play role in habitat modification, nutrient cycling and providing shelter and security to associated invertebrate animals. Studies on mosses in Schirmacher Hills revealed that distribution of mosses is significant at central part and at designated area as compare to eastern and western part.

Distribution of algae and cyanobacteria and flora of fresh water streams of the Hills at the designated area have been studied. The species reported are *G.magma, Chaemosiphon subglobosus, Oscillatoria limosa, O.limnetica,P. frigidum, P. autumnale, Nostoc commune, N.punctiforme, Calothrix gracilis, C.brevissima, Uronema sp.,and Cosmarium leave*. Among the cyanobacteria encountered in the stream of Schirmacher Hills, N_2 –fixing species might play a significant role in nitrogen economy of the ecosystem through N_2 –fixation. Studies on polar Skuas were also conducted at Schirmacher Hills and their nesting and breeding success have been reported around the designated place.

Further study on the Lichens carried out since 2003-04 within the protected area site, revealed occurance of species such as; *Acarospora geynnii* , C.W.Dodge & E.D.Rudolph, *Acarospora williamsii*, Filson, *Amandinea punctata*,(Hoffm.) Coppins & Scheid, *Buellia frigida*, Darb., *Buellia grimmiae*, Filson, *Candelaria murrayi*, Poelt, *Candelariella flava* , (C.W.Dodge & G.E. Baker), Castello & Nimis, *Carbonea vorticsa*, (Florke) Hertel, *Lecanora expectans* , Darb., *Lecanora fuscobrunnea* , C.W. Dodge & G.E. Baker, *Lecanora geophila* (Th. Fr.) Poelt, *Lecidea andersonii*, Filson, *Lecidea cancriformis* , C.W.Dodge & G.E. Baker, *Lecidella siplei* , (C.W. Dodge & G.E. baker) May., *Lepraria cacuminum* , (A. Massal.) Lohtander, *Physcia caesia* , (Hoffm.) Furnr., *Pseudephebe minuscule* , (Nyl. Ex Arnold) Brodo & D. Hawksw., and *Rhizoplaca melanophtalma*, (Ram.) Luckert & Poelt (Olech et al., 2010).

3. Aims and Objectives

Management of Dakshin Gangotri Glacier is aimed to:

- avoid degradation of values of the Area by preventing undue human interference

- allow glaciological and environmental scientific research, while ensuring protection of observational accuracy from any sort of man-made inputs

- ensure that peripheral points along the snout are not adversely affected by human activity in the Area

- maintain the Area as a reference marker for studying the movement patterns of this part of the Antarctic ice-sheet under the influence of global warming

- allow visits for management purposes in support of the aims of the Management Plan for the Area

- minimize the possibility of introduction of alien plants, animals and microbes into the Area

4. Management Activities

The following management activities will be undertaken to protect the values of the Area:

- A detailed map showing the location and boundaries of the Area and stating the special restrictions that apply would be displayed prominently at Maitri (India) and Novolazarevskaya (Russia) research stations; copies of this management plan will also be made available at both the stations.

- Two signs displaying the location and boundaries of the Area with clear statements of entry restrictions will be placed on prominent rocks near both the entrance points to the valley, the eastern end and the south-eastern end; to help avoid inadvertent entry.

- Copies of this management plan along with location and boundary maps of the Area will be provided to all the visiting ships/aircraft.

- Markers, signs, cairns and other structures erected within the Area for scientific and management purposes will be secured and maintained in good condition, and will be removed when no longer necessary.

- Visits shall be made as necessary (at least once every year) to assess whether the Area continues to serve the purposes for which it was designated and to ensure that maintenance and management are adequate.

- The management plan shall be reviewed no less than once every five years and updated as required.

5. Period of Designation

The ASPA is designated for an indefinite period.

6. Maps

The following maps and photographs are enclosed for illustrating the Area and the proposed plan:

Map 1: Location of Schirmacher Hills in central Dronning Maud Land, East Antarctica.

Map2: Map of Schirmacher Hills, showing locations of Maitri Research Station (India) and Novolazarevskaya Research Station (Russia).

Map 3: Classification and Numbering of Lakes of Schirmacher Hills. (after Ravindra et al, 2001)

Map 4: Topographic map of the Area. (contour interval 10 m)

Map 5: Paths of Fossil Glaciers in Schirmacher Hills. (after Beg et al, 2000)

Map 6: Aerial view of the Snout of Dakshin Gangotri Glacier.

Figure 1: Image showing the markers showing boundary location of ASPA

7. Description of the Area

i. Geographical coordinates, Boundary markers and Natural features

Schirmacher Hills is a rocky hill range, about 17 km long in E-W trend (bounded by Eastern longitudes 11° 22' 40" and 11° 54' 20") and about 0.7 km to 3.3 km wide (bounded by Southern latitudes 70° 43' 50" and 70° 46' 40"). Its elevation varies from 0 to 228 m above the msl. It is a part of central Dronning Maud Land in Eastern Antarctica. The proposed area is a fragment of the western part of Schirmacher Hills.

The Area proposed under ASPA is bounded by Eastern longitudes 11° 33' 30" and 11° 36' 30" and by the Southern latitudes 70° 44' 10" and 70° 45' 30". The Area is 4.53 sq. km in aerial extent. The northeastern and northwestern corners of the Area are on shelf-ice, while the southwestern extremity is on polar ice-sheet. The southeastern end lies on a rocky outcrop.

Topographically, the Area can be divided into four distinct units- the southern continental ice-sheet, rocky hill slopes, a vast central proglacial lake (Lake-B7, Sbrosovoye Lake) and northern undulatory shelf ice.

The southernmost ice-sheet is bare 'blue ice', descending from 180 m contour to 10 m contour at the snout of the Glacier. It is crevassed and crisscrossed by NE-SW to NNE-SSW trending fractures. Two small and ephemeral supraglacial streams flow over the snout in a NNE direction.

The rocky terrain is uneven and has the minimum width of the Schirmacher Hills at the snout point;

less than 50 m only. The eastern and western sides of the hills slope towards the snout, making a wide valley. The contours descend from 150 m to msl at the northern margin of the rock outcrops.

The central part of the Area is occupied by Lake B7. It is a lake of glacial origin. The dimensions of the lake are about 500 m x 300 m.

The northernmost part of the Area comprises shelf ice with pressure ridges, fractures and crevasses. The contact between shelf ice and eastern rocky slopes is marked by a prominent 3-km long, NNE-SSW trending lineament. The fractures in the ice are also aligned parallel to this lineament.

Schirmacher Hills exposes a granulite to amphibolite facies metamorphic terrain. The rock types are represented by charnockites, enderbites, garnet-sillimanite, gneisses, garnet-biotite gneisses, quartzofeldspathic augen gneisses with some foliated lamprophyres, amphibolites, dolerite, metagabbro and metabasalt. The rock suites dominantly fall under Grenvillean (1000 Ma) and Pan-African (550 Ma) events. Three phases of deformation are distinct.

The Area comprises mostly charnockite-Khondalite type of rocks (quartz-garnet-sillimanite-perthite±graphite gneisses) with some interlayering of garnet-sillimanite quartzites, calc silicate gneisses and mafic granulites. Two sets of faults (N30E and N50E) are quite prominent. One such major fault runs from the north-eastern corner of the Area; cutting all the three geomorphological units- shelf ice, rocks and continental ice-sheet.

Meteorological data from the nearby Indian Research Station Maitri shows that the Area has a dry polar climate. The extreme temperatures for the warmest and the coldest months range between 7.4 to -34.8°C. The mean annual temperature is -10.2°C. December is the warmest month of the year and August is the coldest. The blizzards touch a gale speed of 90 to 95 knots; the mean annual wind speed is 18 knots. The dominant wind direction is E-SE. Snowfall is quite frequent during the winter months, but gale force winds scrub the rocky surfaces clean and snow deposition is widespread on the leeward side of the hillocks.

Glaciological observations from 1983 to 1996 were carried out by surveys from two fixed points ('G' and 'H') using EDM or theodolite. The results showed that the Glacier is steadily receding every year at an average recession rate of 70 cm per annum.

In 1996, to enhance the accuracy of the observations, 19 peripheral points were marked encircling the snout of the Glacier. The average annual recession in the years 1997 to 2002 was 48.7 cm, 74.9 cm, 69.5 cm, 65.8 cm and 62.7 cm, respectively. This translates into an overall average recession of 65.3 cm per annum for the period 1996-2002; which is in conformity with the observations for the previous period (1983 – 1996) of a recession rate of 7 meters per decade.

Further monitoring were carried out and data revealed that average yearly recession for 2003, 2004, 2005 and 2006, gradually increased to 68.0, 69.4, 71.3, 72.8 cm per annum. However during the year 2006-2007, the average retreat of the Dakshin Gangotri polar ice front was only 0.6 m, but the data collected from the western margin of Schirmacher Hills showed an average annual retreat of around 1.4 m during the year 2006-07. The average annual retreat of the snout of Dakshin Gangotri was recorded to be about 1m in 2008, whereas the average annual retreat for the western extension of polar ice front was recorded to be about 2m. The maximum recession was observed at observation-point-14, which recorded a cumulative recession of 17.21 meters in ten years (1996-2006).

ii. Restricted and Managed Zones within the Area

Along the periphery of the Dakshin Gangotri Glacier, 19 observation points have been marked in February 1996. With reference to these points it was possible to record the movement of the Glacier with an accuracy of 1 cm. Precise monitoring on cm-scale is also available for the years 1996-2002. Access to this zone should be restricted. To protect the accuracy of scientific observations,it is proposed that a 100 m radius all along the periphery of the Glacier should have limited admittance.

iii. Structures within and near the Area

There are no structures present in the Area, apart from two cairns ('G' and 'H') marking the sites used for glaciological and topographical surveys.

In future, some signs and cairns will be erected notifying the protected status of the Area.

iv. Location of other Protected Areas within close proximity of the Area

In the entire Schirmacher Hills, there are no other protected areas.

8. Permit Conditions

a)   Access to and movement within the Area

Entry into the Area would be prohibited except in accordance with a permit issued by an appropriate National Authority as designated under Annex V, Article 7 of the Protocol on Environmental Protection to the Antarctic Treaty.

A permit to enter the Area may only be issued for scientific research, or for essential management purposes consistent with the Management Plan's objectives and provisions; with the condition that the actions permitted will not jeopardize the scientific and environmental values of the Area and will not interfere with ongoing scientific studies. Access to the area is permitted only by foot, access to site using land vehicle or helicopter landing is prohibited within the area.

b)   Activities that are or may be conducted within the Area, including restrictions on time or place

The following activities may be conducted within the Area:

- Scientific research programmes consistent with the management Plan for the Area, including the values for which the Area has been designated; which can not be carried out elsewhere and which will not jeopardize the ecosystem of the Area.

- Essential management activities, including monitoring.

c)   Installation, modification or removal of structures

No structures are to be erected within the Area except as specified in a permit. Any equipment should not be installed if it is not essential for scientific research or for management activities, and it must be authorized in a permit. All scientific equipment installed in the Area must be clearly identified by country with name of principal investigator, year of installation and expected date of completion of the study. Details are to be included in the visit report. All such equipment should be made of materials that pose minimum risk of contamination and must be removed immediately after completion of the study. Removal of specific equipment for which the permit has expired shall be a condition of the permit.

d)   Location of field camps

Camping is not allowed in the Area. The field parties can camp either 1000 meters away from the eastern edge of Lake B7 (Sbrosovoye Lake) or 500 meters away from the western edge of same lake

e)   Restriction on materials and organisms, which can be brought into the Area

No living animals, plant material or microorganism shall be deliberately introduced into the Area and precautions shall be taken against accidental introductions.

- No pesticides, herbicides, chemicals, radio-isotopes shall be brought into the Area, other than those permitted for scientific or management purposes. These authorized agents shall be removed from the Area at the conclusion of the activity.

- Fuel is not to be stored in the Area unless connected with authorized activity. Permanent depots are not to be built in the Area.

- All material taken into the Area shall be for a stated period only and shall be removed at or before the conclusion of that stated period.

f)   Taking or harmful interference with native flora and fauna

Any interference with the native flora and fauna of the Area shall be in accordance with the requirements of the Protocol on Environmental Protection to the Antarctic Treaty, 1991, annex II, Article 3. Where taking or harmful interference with animals is involved, SCAR Code of Conduct for Use of Animals for Scientific Purposes in Antarctica shall be used as a minimum standard.

g)   Collection or removal of anything not brought into the Area by the Permit holder

Material may only be collected or removed from the Area as specified in the permit and shall be limited to the minimum necessary to meet scientific or management requirements.

Material of human origin, not brought into the Area by the permit holder, but which is likely to compromise the values of the Area may be removed from the Area unless the impact of removal is likely to be greater than leaving the material in situ. If this is the case the appropriate authority should be notified.

h)   Disposal of Waste

All wastes, including human wastes, shall be removed from the Area.

i)   Measures that are necessary to ensure that the aims and objectives of the management plan can continue to be met

- Permits may be granted to enter the Area to carry out biological monitoring and area inspection activities.

- Specific sites of long-term monitoring shall be appropriately marked and GPS positions will be obtained for records with the Antarctic Data Directory System through the appropriate National Authority.

j)   Requirements for Reports

The principal permit holder would submit to the appropriate National Authority a visit report describing the activities undertaken by those issued permit. Reports are due and shall be submitted as soon as possible after the expiration of the permit, and include the types of information contained in SCAR visit report form or as required by national laws. The Authority will maintain a record of such activities and make this accessible to interested Parties.

Supporting Bibliography

ASTHANA R., GAUR M.P., CHATURVEDI, A. (1996): Notes on Pattern of Snow Accumulation/ablation on ice shelf and Secular Movement of Dakshin Gangotri Glacier Snout in Central Dronning Maud Land, East Antarctica. *In: scientific Report of the Twelfth Indian Scientific Expedition to Antarctica,* Tech. Pub. No. 10 D.O.D., Govt. of India, New Delhi, pp.111-122.

BEG M.J., PRASAD A.V.K., CHATURVEDI, A. (2000): Interim Report on Glaciological Studies in the Austral Summer of 19th Indian Antarctic Expedition. In: *Scientific Report of Nineteenth Indian Expedition to Antarctica,* Tech. Pub. No. 17, D.O.D., Govt. of India, New Delhi, pp. 121-126.

BEJARNIYA B.R., RAVIKANT V., KUNDU A. (2000): Glaciological Studies in Schirmacher Hill and on Ice Shelf during XIV Antarctica Expedition. In: *Scientific Report of Sixteenth Indian Expedition to Antarctica,* Tech. Pub. No. 14, D.O.D., Govt. of India, New Delhi, pp. 121-126.

CHATURVEDI A., SINGH A., GAUR M.P., KRISHNAMURTHY, K.V., BEG M.J. (1999): A confirmation of Polar Glacial Recession by Monitoring the Snout of Dakshin Gangotri Glacier in Schirmacher Range. In: *Scientific Report of Fifteenth Indian Expedition to Antarctica,* Tech. Pub. No. 13, D.O.D., Govt. of India, New Delhi, pp. 321-336.

D'SOUZA M.J., KUNDU A. (2000): Glaciological studies during the Seventeenth Antarctic Expedition. In: *Scientific Report of Seventeenth Indian Expedition to Antarctica,* Tech. Pub. No. 15, D.O.D., Govt. of India, New Delhi, pp.67-72.

KASHYAP A.K. (1988.): Studies on Algal flora of Schirmacher Oasis, Dronning Maud land, Antarctica . In: *Proceedings of Workshop on Antarctic Studies,* D.O.D.,CSIR, Govt. of India, New Delhi, pp.435-439

KAUL M.K., CHAKRABORTY S.K., RAINA V.K. (1985): A Note on the snout of the Dakshin Gangotri Glacier, Antarctica. In: *Scientific Report of Second Indian Expedition to Antarctica,* Tech. Pub. No. 2, D.O.D., Govt. of India, New Delhi, pp. 91-93.

KAUL M.K., SINGH R.K., SRIVASTAVA D., MUKERJI S., JAYARAM S. (1998): Observations on the Changes in the Snout of Dakshin Gangotri Glacier, Antarctica. In: *Scientific Report of the Fifth Indian Expedition to Antarctica,* Tech. Pub. No. 5, D.O.D., Govt. of India, New Delhi, pp. 205-209.

MUKERJI S., RAVIKANT V., BEJARNIYA B.R., OBEROI L.K., NAUTIYAL S.C. (1995): A Note on the Glaciological Studies Carried Out During Eleventh Indian Expedition to Antarctica. In: *Scientific Report of Eleventh Indian Expedition to Antarctica,* Tech. Pub. No. 9, D.O.D., Govt. of India, New Delhi, pp. 153-162.

OLECH M., SINGH S.M. (2010) : Lichens and Lichenicolous Fungi of Schirmacher Oasis, Antarctica. *Monograph,* National Centre for Antarctic and Ocean Research, India. NISCAIR, New Delhi (In press).

PANDEY K.D., KASHYAP A.K. (1995): Diversity of Algal Flora in Six Fresh Water Streams of Scirmacher Oasis, Antarctica. In: *Scientific Report of Tenth Indian Expedition to Antarctica,* Tech. Pub. No. 8, D.O.D., Govt. of India, New Delhi, pp. 218-229.

RAVINDRA R., CHATURVEDI A. AND BEG M.J. (2001): Melt Water Lakes of Schirmacher Oasis - Their Genetic Aspects and Classification. In: *Advances in Marine and Antarctic Science,* Ed. Sahu, DB and Pandey, PC, Dariyaganj, New Delhi, pp. 301-313.

RAVINDRA R., SRIVASTAVA V.K., SHARMA B.L., DEY A., BEDI, A.K. (1994): Monitoring of Icebergs in Antarctic Waters and a Note on the Secular Movement of Dakshin Gangotri Glacier. In: *Scientific Report of Ninth Indian Expedition to Antarctica,* Tech. Pub. No. 6, D.O.D., Govt. of India, New Delhi, pp. 239-250.

RAVINDRA, R. (2001): Geomorphology of Schirmacher Oasis, East Antarctica. *Proc. Symp. on Snow, Ice and Glaciers*, Geol. Sur. India, Spl. Pub. No. 53, pp. 379-390.

SINGH D.K., SEMWAL R.C. (2000): Bryoflora of Schirmacher Oasis,East Antarctica: A Preliminary Study. In: *Scientific Report of Sixteenth Indian Expedition to Antarctica,* Tech. Pub. No. 14, D.O.D., Govt. of India, New Delhi, pp.173-186

SUNIL P.S., REDDY C.S., PONRAJ M., DHAR A., JAYAPAUL D. (2007) : GPS Determination of the Velocity and Strain-Rate Fields on Schirmacher Glacier, Central Dronning Maud Land, Antarctica. *Journal of Glaciology*, vol. 53, pp. 558-564.

VENKATARAMAN K. (1998): Studies on Phylum Tardigrada and Other Associated Fauna, South Polar Skua and Bird and Mamal Ligging during 1994-1995 Expedition. In: *Scientific Report of Fourteenth Indian Expedition to Antarctica,* Tech. Pub. No. 12, D.O.D., Govt. of India, New Delhi, pp.220-243

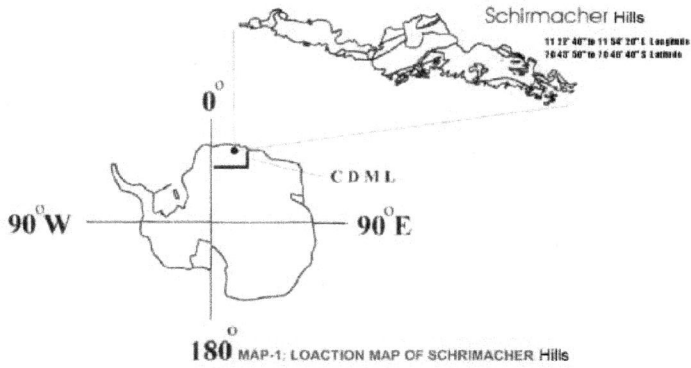

Schirmacher Hills

MAP-1: LOACTION MAP OF SCHRIMACHER Hills

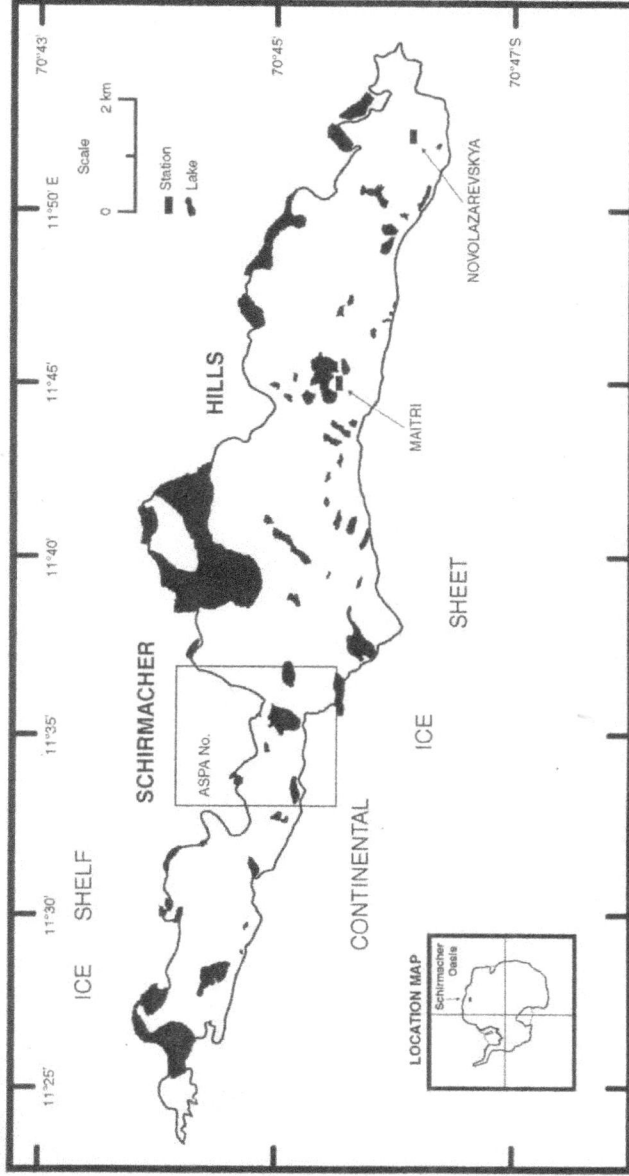

MAP-2: MAP SHOWING LOCATION OF MAITRI (INDIA) & NOVOLAZAREVSKAYA RUSSIA

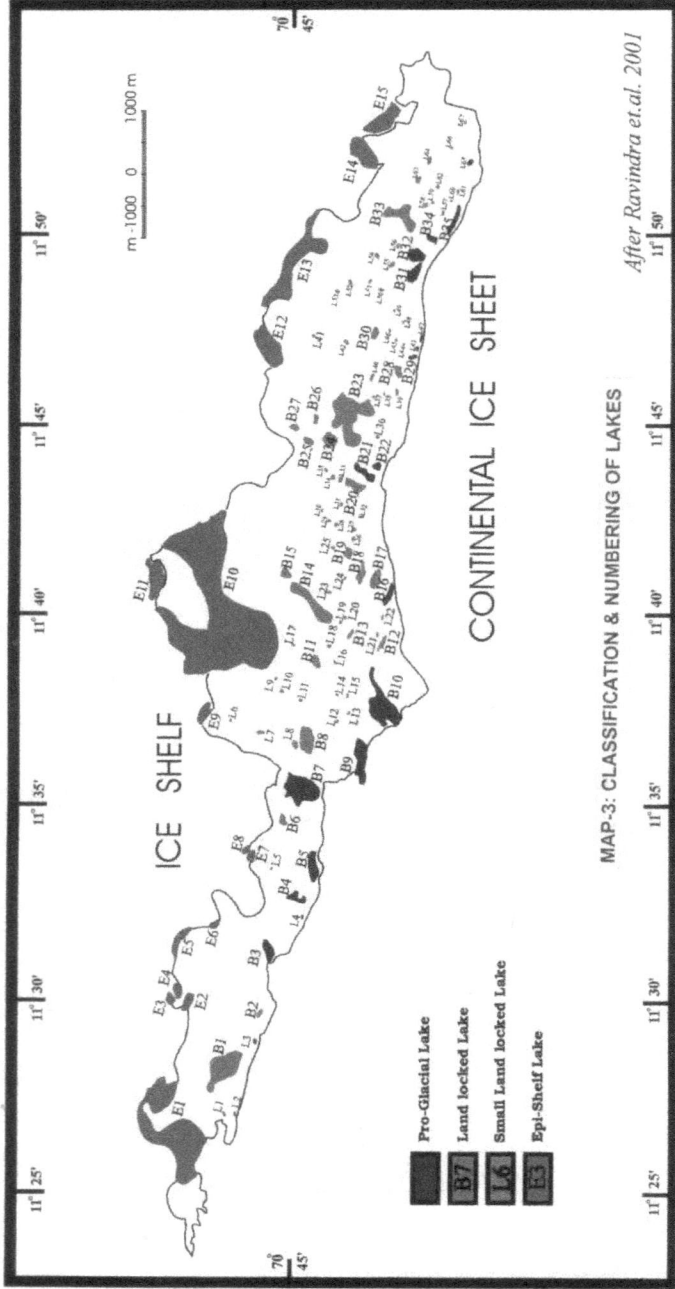

MAP-3: CLASSIFICATION & NUMBERING OF LAKES

After Ravindra et.al. 2001

ICE SHELF

CONTINENTAL ICE SHEET

Pro-Glacial Lake

B7 Land locked Lake

L6 Small Land locked Lake

E3 Epi-Shelf Lake

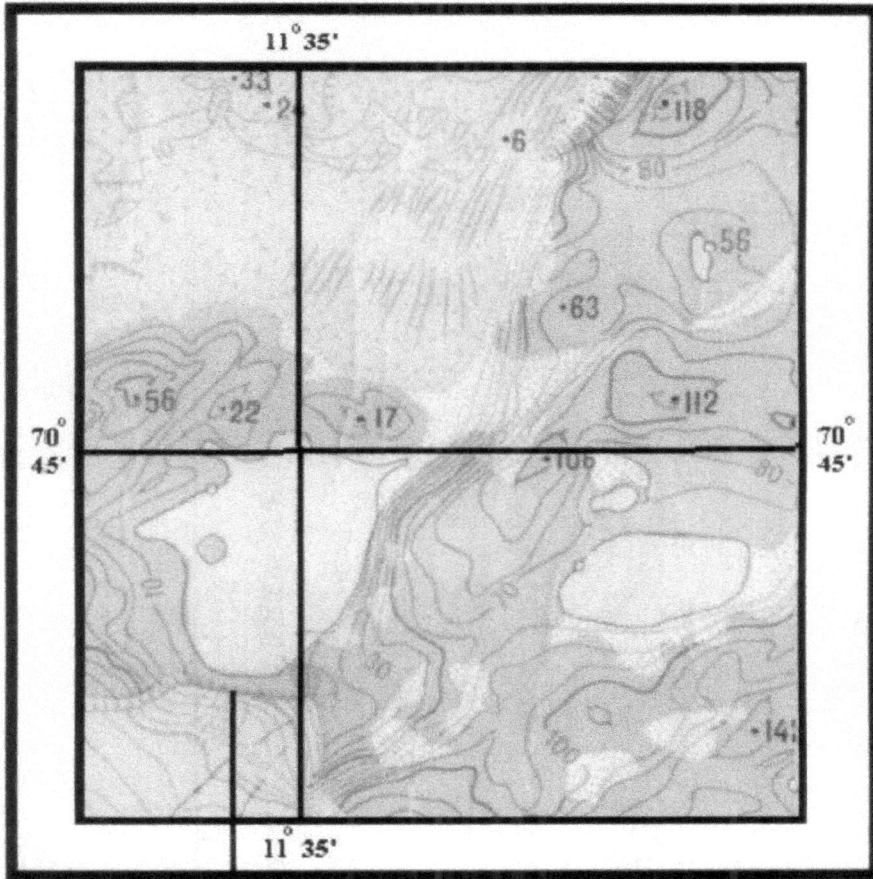

Plate - 4

Snout of Dakshin Gangotri

MAP-4: TOPOGRAPHIC MAP OF THE AREA

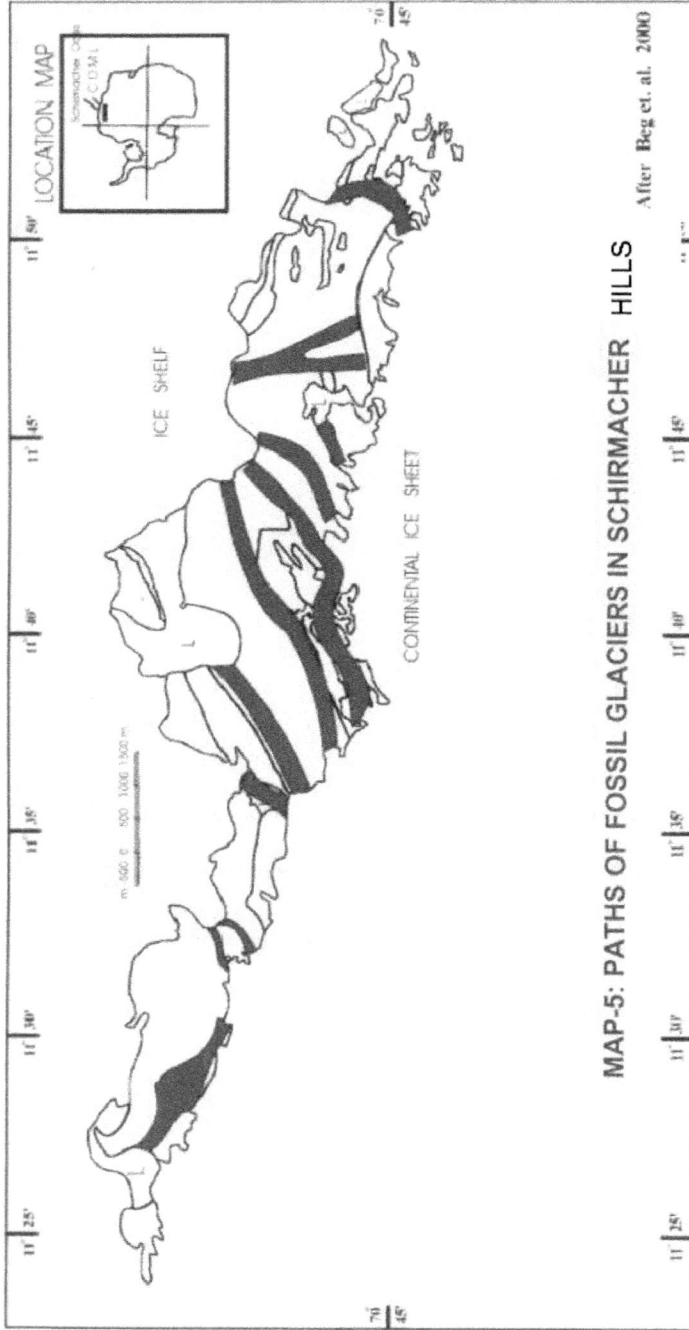

MAP-5: PATHS OF FOSSIL GLACIERS IN SCHIRMACHER HILLS

After **Beg** et. al. 2000

MAP-6: Snout of Dakshin Gangotri Glacier

Figure 1 : Images of secured marker at two different locations at the boundary of ASPA 163

Management Plan
for Antarctic Specially Protected Area No. 164

SCULLIN AND MURRAY MONOLITHS, MAC.ROBERTSON LAND

Introduction

Scullin Monolith (67° 47'S, 66° 42'E) and Murray Monolith (67° 47'S, 66° 53'E) (Map A) were designated as Antarctic Specially Protected Area (ASPA) No 164 under Measure 2(2005), following a proposal by Australia. The Area is designated to protect the greatest concentration of breeding colonies of seabirds in East Antarctica. Seven species occupy territories in the Area: five species of petrel (Antarctic petrels *Thalassoica antarctica*, Cape petrels *Daption capense*, southern fulmars *Fulmarus glacialoides*, snow petrels *Pagodroma nivea*, Wilson's storm petrel *Oceanites oceanicus*), one penguin (Adelie penguin *Pygoscelis adeliae*) and one larid (south polar skua *Catharacta maccormicki*).

Compared to some other sites in East Antarctica, Scullin and Murray Monoliths have been visited infrequently, and with the one known exception, all visits have been brief (less than a day). Scullin and Murray Monoliths were first visited during the second British, Australian and New Zealand Antarctic Research Expedition (BANZARE) voyage in 1930-31, on 13 February 1931. Sir Douglas Mawson named both monoliths during this visit. Murray Monolith was named after Sir George Murray, Chief Justice of South Australia, Chancellor of the University of Adelaide and a patron of the Expedition, while Scullin Monolith was named after James H. Scullin, Prime Minister of Australia from 1929-31.

A brief landing was made at Scullin Monolith on 26 February 1936 from the R.R.S. William Scoresby, when an ascent was made to a height of several hundred metres. The Norwegian Lars Christensen landed on 30 January 1937 and visited Scullin Monolith. Australian Antarctic program personnel have made a few visits to the Area from Mawson station, approximately 160 km to the west. The only recorded stay within the Area was a six-day visit (1 to 6 February 1987), when comprehensive ornithological surveys were conducted. The first visit by a commercial tourist vessel to the Area was made on 10 December 1992, and a small number of brief visits have been made in subsequent years.

With little activity conducted during previous visits the Area, particularly with regard to the avifauna, the Area is of particular value as a relatively undisturbed area suitable as a reference site for other areas that experience a greater level of human visitation and extent of activities.

1. Description of values to be protected

The Area is primarily designated to protect the outstanding ecological and scientific values associated with the important assemblage of seabirds found at Scullin Monolith and Murray Monolith.

With at least 160,000 pairs, the Antarctic petrel colony on Scullin Monolith is second in population size only to the colony at Svarthameren in the Mühlig Hofmannfjella, in Dronning Maud Land. Thus, about a third of the estimated global population of approximately half a million pairs breeds at Scullin Monolith.

Adélie penguin colonies occupy the lower slopes of both monoliths, extending almost to the foreshore. Approximately 50,000 pairs nest on Scullin Monolith and a further 20,000 pairs on Murray Monolith. This represents approximately 10% of the Adélie penguin breeding population for East Antarctica and approximately 3% of the global population.

Many of the ocean-facing slopes of both monoliths are occupied by the other petrel species. Extensive breeding colonies occur on many of the steeper, higher-altitude slopes of both monoliths. South polar skuas nest throughout the Area, making use of the high density of breeding seabirds as prey during their breeding season.

Some larger colonies of seabirds are known from elsewhere in East Antarctica (e.g. the Rauer Group). However, the combined breeding population conservatively estimated at 230,000 pairs and the rich species diversity within the two very small ice-free areas of Scullin and Murray Monoliths (about 1.9 and 0.9 km2, respectively) mean that the monoliths support the greatest concentration of breeding seabirds and one of the most diverse seabird breeding localities in East Antarctica (Appendix 1).

In addition to the outstanding ecological and scientific values, the Area possesses outstanding aesthetic values arising from the geomorphology of the two monoliths, which are occupied by a large number of nesting seabirds, and have as a spectacular backdrop of glaciers that descend from the continental plateau and flow around the monoliths to end in calving glaciers.

The very large and diverse breeding assemblage of seabirds in a setting of high aesthetic and wilderness values warrants the highest level of protection.

2. Aims and Objectives

Management of Scullin and Murray Monoliths aims to:

- avoid degradation of, or substantial risk to, the values of the Area by preventing unnecessary human disturbance to the Area;
- maintain the undisturbed nature of the Area to permit its future use as a reference area;
- allow scientific research on the ecosystem and values of the Area, providing it is for compelling reasons which cannot be served elsewhere and will not impact on the values of the Area, particularly ornithological values;
- accord high priority to the collection of seabird census data from representative sample areas, reference breeding groups (RBGs) or of whole breeding populations. These census data will be major determinants in, and contributions to, future revisions of the management strategy for the Area;
- accord high priority to the collection of other biological survey data, in particular flora and invertebrate surveys. These survey data will be incorporated into future revisions of the management strategy for the Area;
- allow visits for management purposes in support of the aims of the management plan; and
- minimise the potential for introduction of non-native plants, animals and micro-organisms, particularly avian pathogens.

3. Management Activities

The following management activities will be undertaken to protect the values of the Area:

- where practical, the Area shall be visited as necessary, and preferably no less than once every five years, to conduct censuses of seabird breeding populations, including mapping of colonies and nest sites;
- information on the Scullin and Murray Monoliths ASPA, including copies of this management plan, will be made available at both Davis and Mawson stations and to all visitors;
- national Antarctic programs operating in the vicinity or intending to visit the Area shall consult with other national programs to ensure that research projects do not overlap or conflict; and
- where practical, management visits will be made to remove unnecessary materials currently located within the Area.

4. Period of Designation

The Area is designated for an indefinite period.

5. Maps and Photographs

Map A: Antarctic Specially Protected Area No 164, Scullin and Murray Monoliths, Mac.Robertson Land, East Antarctica. The inset map indicates the location in relation to the Antarctic continent.

Map B: Antarctic Specially Protected Area No. 164, Scullin Monolith: Topography and Bird Distribution.

Map C: Antarctic Specially Protected Area No. 164, Murray Monolith: Topography.

Map D: Antarctic Specially Protected Area No. 164: Scullin Monolith: Helicopter approach and landing site.

Specifications for all maps: Horizontal Datum: WGS84; Vertical Datum: Mean Sea Level.

6. *Description of the Area*

6(i) Geographical coordinates, boundary markers and natural features

Scullin Monolith (67° 47'S, 66° 42'E) and Murray Monolith (67° 47'S, 66° 53'E) are situated on the coast of Mac.Robertson Land some 160 km east of Mawson station (Map A). The monoliths are approximately seven kilometres apart and abut the sea at the edge of the continental ice sheet. The coastline to the west and east, and between the monoliths, consists of ice cliffs 30 – 40 m high; the Antarctic plateau rising steeply from there to the south. Scullin Monolith is a crescent-shaped massif whose highest point is 433 m above sea level. It encloses a broad north-facing cove with an entrance approximately two kilometres wide. All upper slopes of the monolith are precipitous, but in the lower 100 m the slope eases in many parts and these areas are strewn with boulders and large stones. Elsewhere in the lower parts the rock face falls sheer to the sea, and there are some scree slopes.

The walls of Murray Monolith rise from the sea to a dome-shaped summit at 243 m above sea level. On the western side of Murray Monolith, the lower slopes drop to a coastal platform. The Area extends over all ice-free areas associated with the two monoliths, and includes a portion of the adjacent continental ice. There are no boundary markers delimiting the site.

The Scullin and Murray Monoliths ASPA comprises two sectors (see Map B and Map C):

- Scullin Monolith: the boundary commences at a coordinate on the coastline at 67°47'01"S, 66°40'31"E , then in a southerly direction to a coordinate at 67°48'03"S, 66°40'26"E, east to a coordinate at 67°48'06"S, 66° 44'33"E then north to a coordinate on the coast at 67°46'41"S, 66°44'37"E, then west following the coast line at the low tide mark to the coordinate 67°48'03"S,66° 40'26"E.

- Murray Monolith: the boundary commences on the coastline at 67°46'29"S, 66°51'01"E, then continuous in a southerly direction to 67°48'03"S, 66° 50'55"E, extends east to 67°48'05"S, 66°53'51"E, and north to 67°46'42"S, 66°53'59"E, then west following the coast line at the low tide mark to the coordinate 67°46'29"S, 66°51'01"E.

Birds

Seven species occupy territories in the Area: five species of petrel (Antarctic petrels *Thalassoica antarctica*, Cape petrels *Daption capense*, southern fulmars *Fulmarus glacialoides*, snow petrels *Pagodroma nivea*, Wilson's storm petrel *Oceanites oceanicus*), one penguin (Adelie penguin *Pygoscelis adeliae*) and one larid (south polar skua *Catharacta maccormicki*). Scullin Monolith hosts the second largest colony of Antarctic petrels with a population of at least 160,000 pairs and significant Adélie penguin colonies of approximately 50,000 pairs. Less is known about the species diversity of Murray Monolith; however approximately 20,000 Adélie penguins have been observed (Appendix 1).

There are no data on population trends available, and census and survey data collected in 1986/87 serve as baseline data for all future ornithological work in the Area. Some limited census data were collected from Reference Breeding Groups (RBGs) established in the mid 1980s to monitor the Antarctic petrel population but there have been no surveys of these RBGs for more than a decade. Many breeding populations of Adélie penguin have increased throughout East Antarctica in the last 20 or so years; it is possible that the Adélie penguin population at the Scullin and Murray Monoliths is greater than the 70,000 pairs reported in 1986/87. Further, it is likely that the 1986/87 census under-estimated the breeding population of Antarctic petrels, given the census occurred late in the breeding season.

Geology

The geology of the two monoliths is poorly understood, as they have been neither the subject of dedicated study nor specific geological mapping. The geology of the monoliths appears to be similar in general terms to that of the region around Mawson station. The rocks consist dominantly of high grade granulite facies gneisses of metasedimentary origin, including some sapphirine bearing rocks. The metamorphism occurred in anhydrous conditions probably at about 1000Ma. An age range of between 1254Ma and as young as 625Ma have been documented for the gneisses from Scullin Monolith. Metamorphism involved sedimentary rocks initially of Proterozoic age. These metamorphic basement rocks were intruded at about 920-985Ma by the Mawson Charnockite a form of granite characterised by presence of orthopyroxene, and common in this region. It forms the faces of the monoliths. The recorded an age of 433 and 450Ma which may reflect a later influence of the '500 Ma or Pan-African event' recorded widely throughout Gondwana. The margins of the monoliths contain some sediment carried by the icesheet and deposited by melting ice. The source cannot be specified but it may contain recycled material from farther inland and could perhaps provide evidence of some of the geology beneath the ice.

Environmental domains analysis

Based on the Environmental Domains Analysis for Antarctica (Resolution 3(2008)) Scullin and Murray Monoliths are located within Environments D *East Antarctic coastal geologic* and L *Continental coastal-zone ice sheet.*

Vegetation

The flora reported from Scullin Monolith is given in Appendix 3, based on visits in 1972 and 1987. All species of lichens and moss found on Scullin Monolith occur elsewhere in Mac.Robertson Land (Appendix 2). Vegetation on Scullin Monolith is restricted mainly to the western plateau and associated nunataks. The coastal slopes are generally void of vegetation due to high levels of seabird guano. The distribution of vegetation on the western plateau is influenced by microtopography that controls the extent of exposure and moisture availability. Although not recorded, it is likely that vegetation at Murray Monolith is similar to that found at Scullin Monolith.

Other biota

There have been no comprehensive invertebrate studies at Scullin or Murray Monoliths. A leopard seal *Hydrurga leptonyx* was sighted during a visit in 1936 and several Weddell seals *Leptonychotes weddellii* were observed during visits in 1997 and 1998; no further observations of biota have been reported.

6(ii) Access to the Area

Access to the Area is covered under section 7(ii) of this plan.

6(iii) Structures within and adjacent to the Area

At the time of writing (March 2010), a fibreglass 'Apple' refuge is situated on the south western summit ridge of Scullin Monolith (approximately 67° 47.2'S, 66° 41.5'E) (Map B and Map D). There are four 200-litre drums of helicopter fuel and one empty 200-litre drum as well as the (reported) remains of a food cache (1985/86 vintage). It is intended that all of this material be removed from the Area at the first suitable opportunity. It is unknown if this refuge is still suitable for use.

6(iv) Location of other protected areas within close proximity of the Area

There are two ASPAs located to the west of Scullin and Murray; ASPA No. 102, Rookery Islands, is approximately 180 km to the west (c.20 km west of Mawson), and ASPA No. 101, Taylor Rookery, is located approximately 75 km further west of the ASPA No. 102.

6(v) Special zones within the Area

There are no special zones within the Area.

7. Permit conditions

7(i) General permit conditions

Entry to the Area is prohibited except in accordance with a permit issued by an appropriate national authority. General conditions for issuing a permit to enter the Area are that:

- it is issued only for compelling scientific or management purposes that cannot be served elsewhere, in particular for scientific study of the avifauna and ecosystem of the Area, or for essential management purposes consistent with plan objectives, such as inspection, maintenance or review;
- the actions permitted are in accordance with this management plan and will not jeopardise the values of the Area;
- it is issued for a specified period;
- it will authorise the entry into the Area of no more than 10 people at any one time during the seabird breeding season, and no more than 15 people at any one time during the remainder of the year;
- the permit or an authorised copy shall be carried at all times when within the Area;
- a visit report shall be supplied to the appropriate national authority at the conclusion of the permitted activity; and
- the appropriate national authority shall be notified of any activities/measures undertaken that were not included in the authorised permit.

7(ii) Access to and movement within or over the Area

- Travel to the Area is possible by small boat, by over-snow/ice vehicles or by aircraft.
- Any movement within and around the Area shall observe the minimum specified wildlife approach distances (Appendix 3); closer approach may be allowed specifically under permit.
- Movement by visitors within the Area shall be by foot only.
- Small boats used to approach the Area must be operated at or below five knots within 500 m of the shore.
- It is recommended that visitors not permitted to enter the Area do not approach within 50 m of the shoreline.
- To reduce disturbance to wildlife, noise levels including verbal communication are to be kept to a minimum. The use of motor-driven tools and any other activity likely to generate loud noise and thereby cause disturbance to nesting birds shall not be allowed within the Area during the summer seabird breeding season (1 October to 31 March).

Aircraft may be used to enter the Area subject to the following conditions:

- disturbance of the colonies by aircraft shall be avoided at all times
- during the breeding season (1 October to 31 March) there shall be no overflights of the Area below 1500 m (5000 ft) for twin-engined helicopters and below 930 m (3050 ft)for single-engined helicopters and fixed-wing aircraft;
- landings within the Area shall only occur at the designated landing site at Scullin monolith (Map D) and only by single-engined helicopters;
- single-engined helicopters shall approach the landing site from the south-west (as shown by the approved flight corridor in Map D);
- during the breeding season, twin-engined helicopters shall not land, take off or fly within 1500 m of the Area;
- during the breeding season, fixed wing aircraft shall not land or take off within 930 m or fly within 750 m (2500 ft) of the Area;
- under no circumstances are aircraft to fly within the Scullin Monolith amphitheatre during the breeding season;
- twin-engined helicopters may land at the designated landing site outside the breeding season (1 October to 31 March); and

- refuelling of aircraft is not to take place within the Area.

7(iii) Activities that are, or may be conducted within the Area, including restrictions on time and place

The following activities may be conducted within the Area as authorised by permit:

- compelling scientific research that cannot be undertaken elsewhere, including the initiation or continuance of ongoing monitoring programmes; and
- other scientific research and essential management activities consistent with this Management Plan that will not affect the values of the Area or its ecosystem integrity.

7(iv) Installation, modification or removal of structures

No permanent structures or semi-permanent structures (in place beyond the end of the seabird breeding season) are to be erected within the Area.

Markers, signs and other indicators of the Area's extent shall not be erected, to maintain the aesthetic values and undisturbed nature of the Area.

7(v) Location of field camps

Temporary camps for field parties are permitted within the Area, but must be placed as far from seabird colonies and nesting sites as is practicable without compromising visitor safety. Camps shall be established for the minimum time necessary to undertake approved activities and shall not be allowed to remain from one seabird breeding season to the next.

7(vi) Restrictions on materials and organisms that may be brought into the Area

- A small amount of fuel is permitted within the Area for cooking purposes while field parties are present. Otherwise, fuel is not to be stored within the Area.
- No poultry products, including dried foods containing egg powder, are to be taken into the Area.
- No herbicides or pesticides are to be taken into the Area.
- All chemicals required for research purposes must be approved by permit, and shall be removed at or before the conclusion of the permitted activity to which they relate. The importation and use of radio-nucleides and stable isotopes within the Area is prohibited.
- The highest level precautions shall be employed to prevent the introduction to the Area of micro-organisms, including pathogens. No living organisms shall be deliberately introduced to the Area. Clothing (and in particular all footwear) and field equipment shall be cleaned before entering and after leaving the Area. Research equipment shall be disinfected, to prevent possible contamination of the Area.

7(vii) Taking of or harmful interference with native flora and fauna

Taking of, or harmful interference with, native flora and fauna is prohibited, except in accordance with a permit. Where taking or harmful interference with animals is involved this should, as a minimum standard, be in accordance with the *SCAR Code of Conduct for the Use of Animals for Scientific Purposes in Antarctica*. Disturbance to wildlife should be avoided at all times.

7(viii) Collection or removal of anything not brought into the Area by the permit holder

Material of human origin likely to compromise the values of the Area, which was not brought into the Area by the permit holder or was otherwise authorised, may be removed unless the impact of the removal is likely to be greater than leaving the material in situ. If such material is found the permit issuing authority shall be notified if possible while the field party is present within the Area.

Specimens of natural material may only be collected or removed from the Area as authorised in a permit and should be limited to the minimum necessary to meet scientific or management needs.

7(ix) Disposal of waste

All wastes, including human wastes, shall be removed from the Area. Wastes from field parties shall be stored in such a manner to prevent scavenging by wildlife (e.g. skuas) until such time as the wastes can be disposed or removed. Wastes are to be removed no later than the departure of the field party. Human wastes and grey water may be disposed into the sea outside the Area.

7(x) Measures that may be necessary to ensure that the aims and objectives of the Management Plan continue to be met

- Permits may be granted to enter the Area to carry out biological monitoring and Area inspection activities, which may involve the collection of samples for analysis or review.
- Ornithological surveys, including aerial photographs for the purposes of population census, shall have a high priority.
- All GPS, survey and census data collected by field parties visiting the Area shall be made available to the permit issuing authority and the Party responsible for developing the management plan (if different).
- These data shall be lodged in the Antarctic Master Data Directory.
- Visitors shall take special precautions against the introduction of alien organisms to the Area. Of particular concern are pathogenic, microbial or vegetation introductions sourced from soils, flora or fauna at other Antarctic sites, including research stations, or from regions outside Antarctica. To minimise the risk of introductions, before entering the Area, visitors shall thoroughly clean footwear and any equipment to be used in the Area, particularly sampling equipment and markers.

7(xi) Requirements for reports

The principal permit holder for each visit to the Area shall submit a report to the appropriate national authority as soon as practicable, and no later than six months after the visit has been completed.

Such visit reports should include, as applicable, the information identified in the recommended visit report form contained in Appendix 4 of the Guide to the Preparation of Management Plans for Antarctic Specially Protected Areas appended to Resolution 2 (1998).

The national authority should also forward a copy of the visit report to the Party that proposed the Management Plan, to assist in managing the Area and reviewing the Management Plan.

Parties should, wherever possible, deposit originals or copies of such original visit reports in a publicly accessible archive to maintain a record of usage, for the purpose of any review of the Management Plan and in organising the scientific use of the Area.

All visit reports shall provide detailed information on all census data, locations of any new colonies or nests not previously recorded, as texts and maps. A brief summary of research findings and copies of relevant photographs taken of the Area should also be included.

7(xii)   Emergency provision

Exceptions to restrictions outlined in the management plan are in an emergency as specified in Article 11 of Annex V of the Protocol on Environmental Protection to the Antarctic Treaty (the Madrid Protocol).

8. *Supporting documentation*

Alonso J.C., Johnstone G.W., Hindell M., Osborne P. & Guard R. (1987): Las aves del Monolito Scullin, Antártida oriental (67° 47'S, 66° 42'E). In: Castellvi J (ed) *Actas del Segundo symposium Espanol de estudios antarcticos*, pp. 375-386, Madrid.

Bergstrom, D.M., Seppelt, R.D. (1990): The lichen and bryophyte flora of Scullin Monolith Mac.Robertson Land. *Polar Record* 26, 44

Christensen L. (1938): My last expedition to the Antarctic 1936 - 1937. JG Tanum, Oslo. Christensen L 1939. Charting the Antarctic. *Polar Times* 8, 7-10.

Filson R.B. (1966): The lichens and mosses of Mac.Robertson Land. *ANARE Scientific Reports* B(II) Botany.

Funaki, M., Saito, K. (1992): Paleomagnetic and Ar-40/Ar-39 dating studies of the Mawson charnockite and some rocks from the Christensen Coast., In Y. Yoshida (ed) *Recent progress in Antarctic earth science.* pp191-201, Terra Scientific Publishing Company, Tokyo

Johnstone, G. (1987): Visit to Scullin Monotlith. *ANARE News*, June 1987, 3

Klages, N. T.W., Gales, R., Pemberton, D. (1990): The stomach contents of Antarctic petrels Thalassoica antarctica feeding young chicks at Scullin Monolith, Mawson Coast, Antarctica. *Polar Biology* 10, 545-547

Rayner, G.W. & Tilley C.E. (1940): Rocks from Mac Robertson Land and Kemp Land, Antarctica. *Discovery Reports*, XIX, 165-184.

Takigami, Y., Funaki M. & Tokieda K. (1992): 40Ar-39Ar geochronological studies on some paleomagnetic samples of East Antarctica. in Y. Yoshida et al. (editors) *Recent Progress in Antarctic Earth Science*, pp 61-66, Tokyo, Terra Scientific Publishing Co.

Tingey R.J. (1991): The regional geology of Archaean and Proterozoic rocks in Antarctica. In Tingey RJ (ed) *The Geology of Antarctic*, pp 1-73, Oxford, Oxford Science Publications.

van Franeker J.A., Gavrilo M., Mehlum F., Veit R.R. & Woehler E.J. (1999): Distribution and abundance of the Antarctic Petrel. *Waterbirds* 22, 14-28.

Appendix 1: Breeding populations (pairs) of seabirds at Scullin and Murray Monoliths

Species	Scullin Monolith	Murray Monolith
Adélie penguin *Pygoscelis adeliae*	49,500	20,000
Southern fulmar *Fulmarus glacialoides*	1,350	150
Antarctic petrel *Thalassoica antarctica*	157,000	3,500
Cape petrel *Daption capense*	14	ND
Snow petrel *Pagodroma nivea*	1,200	ND
Wilson's storm petrel *Oceanites oceanicus*	ND	ND
South polar skua *Catharacta maccormicki*	30	ND

Note: ND indicates no census data are available

Appendix 2: Flora recorded at Scullin Monolith

The following taxa were collected at Scullin Monolith in 1972 (R Seppelt) and in 1987 (D Bergstrom), and were published in Bergstrom & Seppelt 1990).

LICHENS **Acarosporaceae**	**Teloschistaceae**
Biatorella cerebriformis (Dodge) Filson	*Caloplaca citrina* (Hoffm.) Th. Fr.
Acarospora gwynii Dodge & Rudolph	*Xanthoria elegans* (Link.) Th. Fr.
Lecanoraceae *Lecanora expectans* Darb *Rhizoplaca melanophthalma* (Ram.) Leuck.	*Xanthoria mawsonii* Dodge **Candelariaceae** *Candellariella hallettensis* Murray
Lecideaceae	**Umbilicariaceae**
Lecidea phillipsiana Filson	*Umbilicaria decussata* (Vill.) Zahlbr.
Lecidea woodberryi Filson **Physciaceae** *Physcia caesia* (Hoffm.) Hampe	**Usneaceae** *Usnea antarctica* Du Rietz *Pseudophebe miniscula* (Nyl. Ex Arnold) Brodo et Hawksw.
Buellia frigida Darb	
Buellia grimmiae Filson *Buellia lignoides* Filson	**BRYOPHYTES**
Rinodina olivaceobrunnea Dodge & Baker	**Grimmiaceae** *Grimmia lawiana* Willis **Pottiaceae** *Sarconeurum glaciale (C. Muell.) Card. Et Bryhn*

Appendix 3: Approach distances guide: minimum distances (m) to maintain when approaching wildlife without permit.

Species	People on foot/ski	Quad/skidoo	Hagglunds
Southern Giant Petrel	100	150	250
Emperor penguins in colonies	30		
Other penguins in colonies Moulting penguins Seals with pups Seal pups on their own Prions and petrels on nest South Polar Skua on nest	15		
Penguins on sea ice Non-breeding adult seals	5		

Notes:

1. These distances are a guide, and should you find that your activity is disturbing wildlife, a greater distance is to be maintained.

2. 'Prions and petrels' comprises Cape petrels, Antarctic petrels, Wilson's storm petrels, snow petrels and southern fulmars.

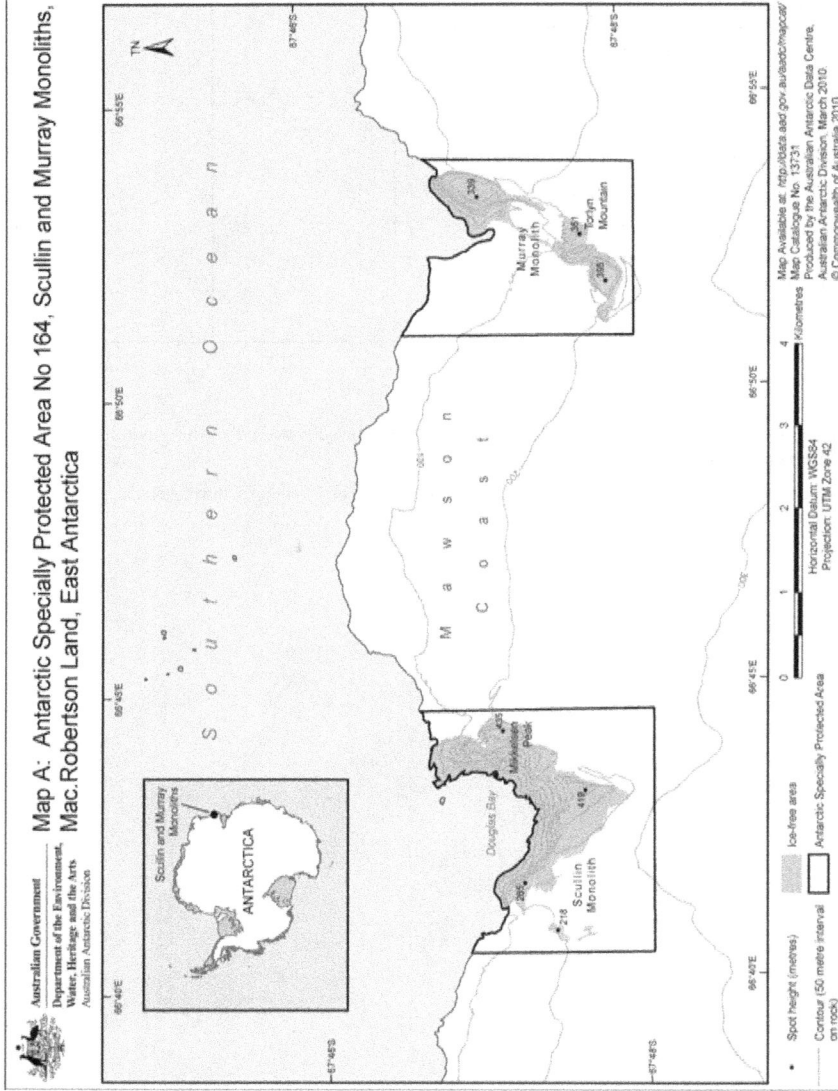

Map A: Antarctic Specially Protected Area No 164, Scullin and Murray Monoliths, Mac.Robertson Land, East Antarctica

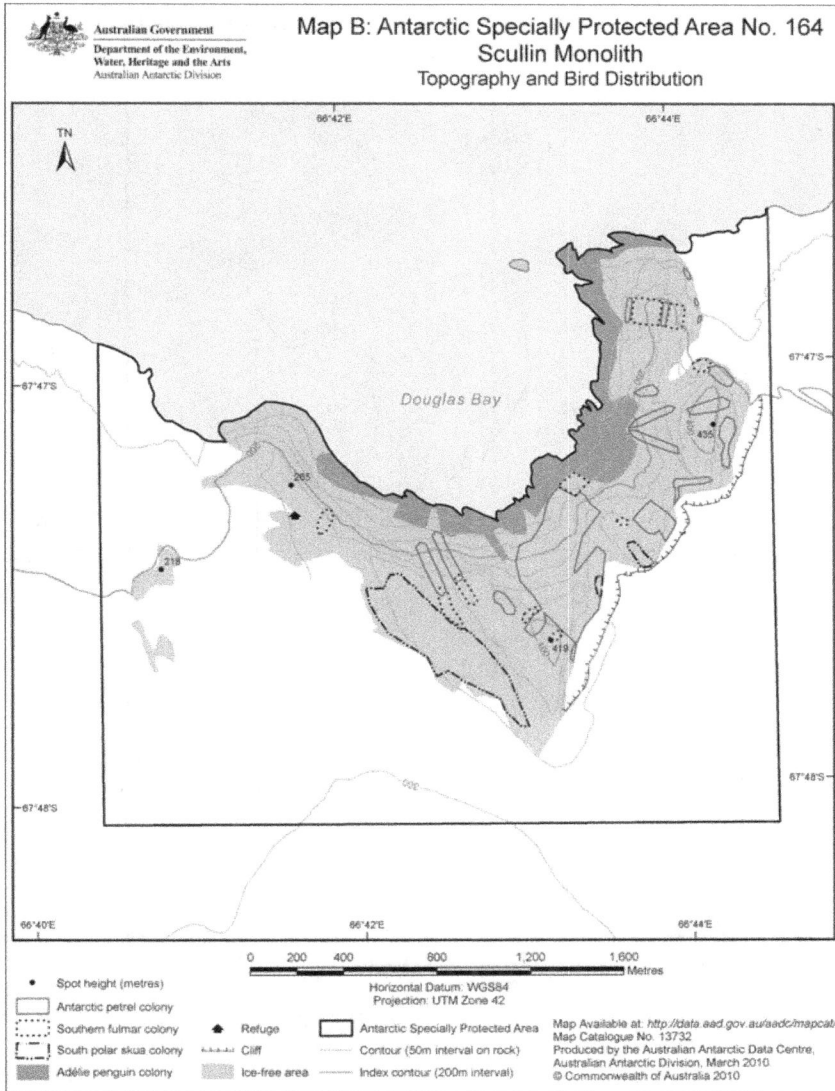

Map B: Antarctic Specially Protected Area No. 164
Scullin Monolith
Topography and Bird Distribution

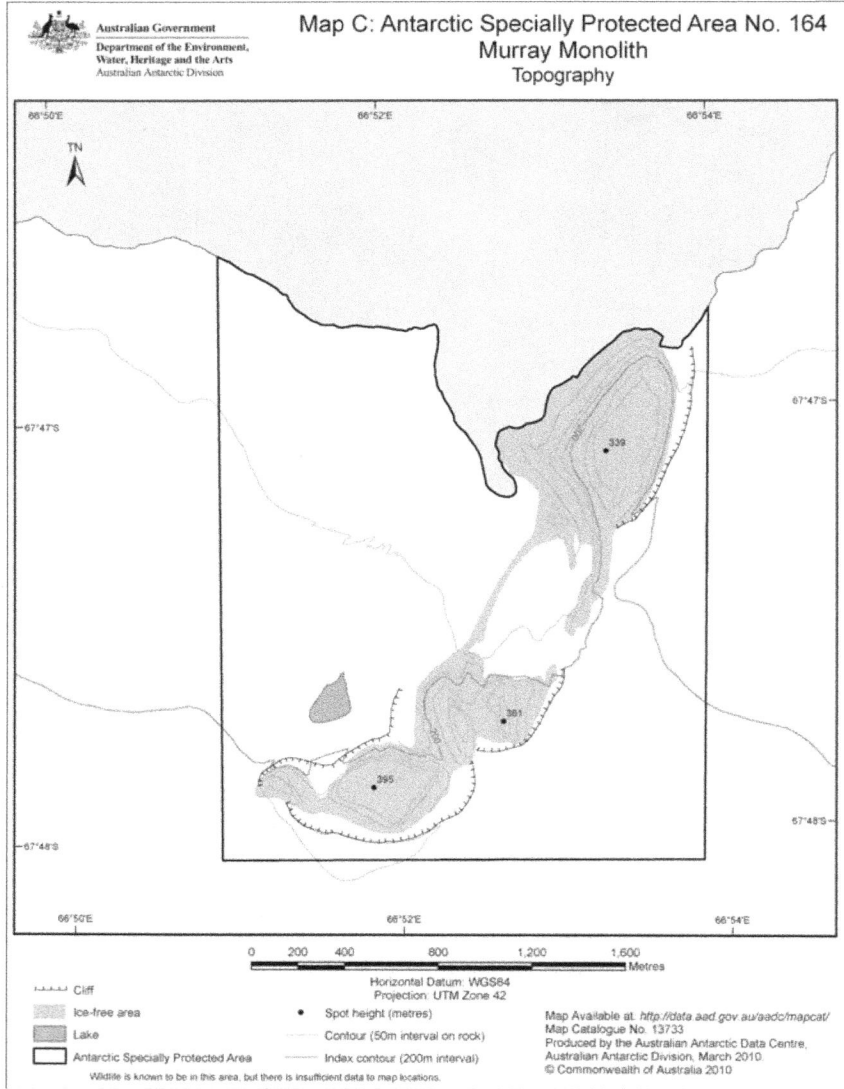

Map C: Antarctic Specially Protected Area No. 164
Murray Monolith
Topography

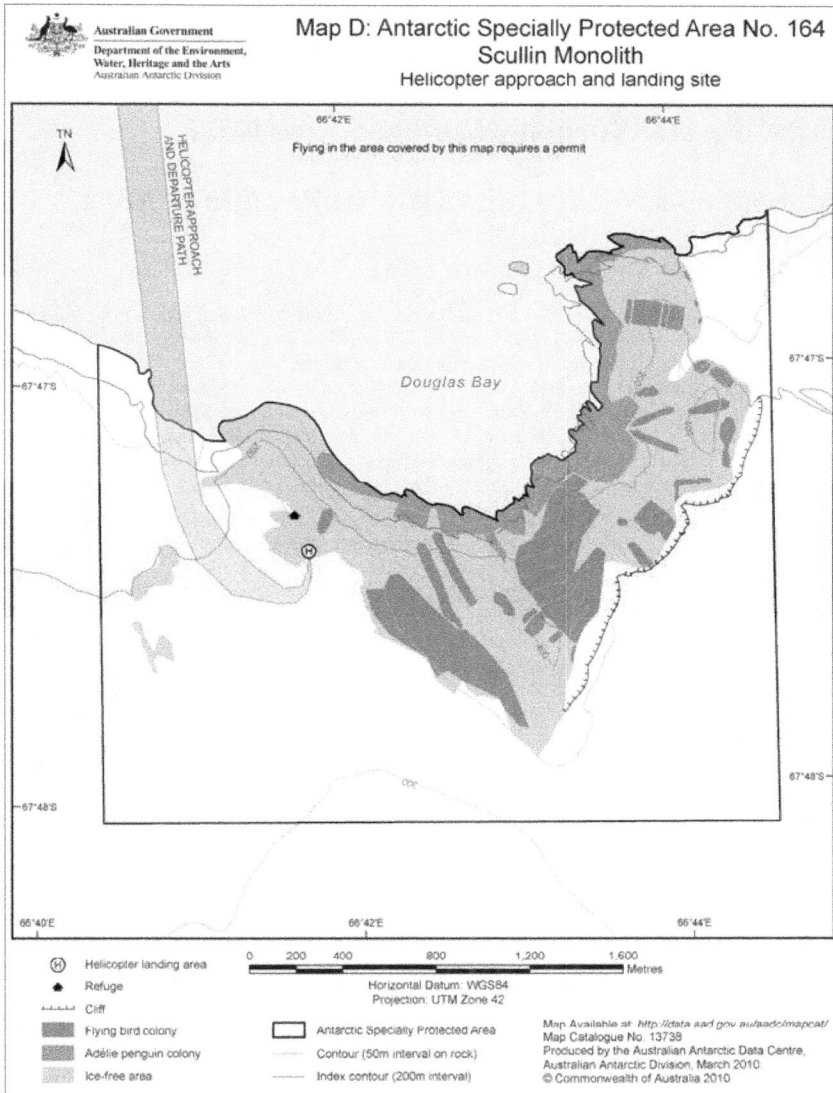

Map D: Antarctic Specially Protected Area No. 164
Scullin Monolith
Helicopter approach and landing site

Australian Government
Department of the Environment,
Water, Heritage and the Arts
Australian Antarctic Division

Flying in the area covered by this map requires a permit

TN

HELICOPTER APPROACH AND DEPARTURE PATH

Douglas Bay

66°42'E
66°44'E
67°47'S
67°48'S
66°40'E

Helicopter landing area
Refuge
Cliff
Flying bird colony
Adélie penguin colony
Ice-free area

Antarctic Specially Protected Area
Contour (50m interval on rock)
Index contour (200m interval)

0   200   400   800   1,200   1,600   Metres

Horizontal Datum: WGS84
Projection: UTM Zone 42

Map Available at: http://data.aad.gov.au/aadc/mapcat/
Map Catalogue No. 13738
Produced by the Australian Antarctic Data Centre,
Australian Antarctic Division, March 2010.
© Commonwealth of Australia 2010

15

Management Plan for

Antarctic Specially Managed Area No. 7

SOUTHWEST ANVERS ISLAND AND PALMER BASIN

Introduction

The region that includes southwest Anvers Island and the Palmer Basin and its fringing island groups has a wide range of important natural, scientific and educational values and is an area of considerable and increasing scientific, tourist and logistic activities. The importance of these values and the need to provide an effective means to manage the range of activities was recognised with adoption of the area as a Multiple-Use Planning Area for voluntary observance at the XVIth Antarctic Treaty Consultative Meeting (1991). With the acquisition of new data and information and changes to logistics and the pressures arising from human activities in the region, the original plan has been comprehensively revised and updated to meet current needs as an Antarctic Specially Managed Area (ASMA).

In particular, scientific research being undertaken within the Area is important for considering ecosystem interactions and long-term environmental changes in the region, and how these relate to Antarctica and the global environment more generally. This research is important to the work of the Committee for Environmental Protection, the Commission for the Conservation of Antarctic Marine Living Resources (CCAMLR) and the Antarctic Treaty System as a whole. There is a risk that these globally important research programs and long-term datasets could be compromised if activities were to occur in the marine area that were not appropriately managed to avoid potential conflicts and possible interference. While marine harvesting activities are not currently being conducted within the Area, and the marine component of the Area represents only 0.5% of CCAMLR Subarea 48.1, it is important that should harvesting be undertaken within the Area then it should be carried out in such a way that it would not impact on the important scientific and other values present within the Area.

Important values present in the proposed ASMA in the vicinity of Palmer Station and key activities to be managed are summarised as follows:

1. Values to be protected and activities to be managed

(i) Scientific values

The diverse and easily accessible assemblages of marine and terrestrial flora and fauna in the southwest Anvers Island and Palmer Basin area are particularly valuable for science, with some datasets spanning the past 100 years and intensive scientific interest beginning in the 1950s. Studies have been carried out on a wide variety of topics, including long-term monitoring of seal and bird populations, surveys of plants and animals in both the terrestrial and sub-tidal environments, investigations of the physiology and biochemistry of birds, seals, terrestrial invertebrates and zooplankton, the behavior and ecology of planktonic marine species, physical oceanography, and marine sedimentology and geomophology. While the United States (US) maintains the only permanent research station within the Area, research in these fields has been undertaken by scientists from a broad range of Antarctic Treaty Parties, often as collaborative projects with US scientists. Some important recent examples from the Palmer Long Term Ecological Research (LTER) program are described below.

The southwest Anvers Island and Palmer Basin area has exceptional importance for long-term studies of the natural variability in Antarctic ecosystems, the impact of world-wide human activities on Antarctica and on the physiology, populations and behaviour of its plants and animals. Research in this region is essential for understanding the linkages among avifauna, krill dynamics and the changing marine habitat.

In particular, the United States Antarctic Program (USAP) has a major and ongoing commitment to ecosystem research in the Antarctic Peninsula region, which was formalized through the designation in 1990 of the area around Palmer Station (US) as a Long Term Ecological Research (LTER) site. The Palmer LTER (PAL-LTER) site is part of a wider network of LTER sites, and one of only two in the Antarctic, designed specifically to address important research questions related to environmental change over a sustained period spanning more than several decades. Since 1991, the PAL-LTER program has included spatial sampling during annual and seasonal cruises within a large-scale (200,000 km²) regional grid along the west coast of the Antarctic Peninsula, as well as temporal sampling from October to March in the local area adjacent to Palmer Station. The Palmer LTER and the British Antarctic Survey are collaborating on research comparing the marine ecosystem in the Palmer Basin region with that in Marguerite Bay approximately 400 km further to the south. In the Palmer region, the ecosystem is changing in response to the rapid regional warming first documented by BAS scientists. In addition, recent collaboration has been established as part of the International Polar Year with scientists from France and Australia using metagenomic tools to understand microbial community adaptations to the polar winter.

A major theme in the PAL-LTER is the study of sea-ice dynamics and related impacts on all aspects of the ecosystem (Smith *et al.* 1995). The annual advance and retreat of sea-ice is a major physical determinant of spatial and temporal changes in the structure and function of the Antarctic marine ecosystem, from total and annual primary production to breeding success in seabirds. The Western Antarctic Peninsula (WAP) is a premier example of a region experiencing major changes in species abundance, range and distribution, in response to regional climate change. This change is manifested primarily as a southern migration of regional climate characteristics (Smith *et al.* 1999, 2001). Paleoecological records on sea-ice, diatom stratigraphy and penguin colonization have also placed the current LTER data into a longer-term context (Smith *et al.* 1999, 2001). In particular, the Palmer Basin has been the site of extensive paleoecological and climate change studies. The Palmer Basin also exhibits a variety of geomorphological features of value.

Extensive seabird research has focused on the ecology of Adélie penguins and their avian predators and scavengers within the inshore 50 km² PAL-LTER grid close to Palmer Station. Colonies on 18 islands in this area are visited every 2-7 days in the summer season, and three more distant control sites within the ASMA are also visited infrequently to assess the extent of possible disturbance from activities around Palmer Station. Sea ice forms a critical winter habitat for Adélie penguins, and interdisciplinary research has focused on the impacts of changes in the frequency, timing and duration of sea-ice on the life histories of this and other bird species, as well as on prey populations.

Torgersen Island is the site of a study on the impacts of tourism, and has been divided into two areas, one open to visitors and the other closed as a site for scientific reference. This site together with other nearby islands not visited by tourists provide a unique experimental setting to examine the relative effects of natural versus human-induced variability on Adélie penguin populations. The long-term data sets obtained from this site are of particular value in understanding the impacts of tourism on birds.

The southwest Anvers Island and Palmer Basin region also hold particular scientific interest in terms of newly-exposed terrestrial areas that have been subject to vegetation colonization after glacial retreat. With continuing trends of glacial retreat, these areas are likely to be of increasing scientific value.

Seismic monitoring at Palmer Station contributes to a global seismic monitoring network, and the remote location of the station also makes it a valuable site for long-term monitoring of global levels of radionuclides.

It is important that the region is carefully managed so that these scientific values can be maintained and the results of the long-term research programs are not compromised.

(ii) Flora and fauna values

The southwest Anvers Island and Palmer Basin region is one of the most biologically diverse in Antarctica, with numerous species of bryophytes, lichens, birds, marine mammals and invertebrates (Appendix C). These organisms are dependent on both the marine and terrestrial ecosystems for food and habitat requirements, with the Palmer Basin exerting a substantial influence on regional ecological processes.

Breeding colonies of birds and seals are present on ice-free areas along the coast of Anvers Island, as well as on many of the offshore islands within the region. Eleven species of birds breed in the Area, with Adélie penguins (*Pygoscelis adeliae*) the most abundant, and several other species are frequent non-breeding visitors. Five species of seals are commonly found in the Area, but are not known to breed there. Palmer Basin is an important foraging area for birds, seals and cetaceans.

The two native Antarctic vascular plants, *Deschampsia antarctica* and *Colobanthus quitensis*, are commonly found on surfaces with fine soil in the area around Arthur Harbor, although they are relatively rare along the Antarctic Peninsula (Komárková *et al.* 1985). The vascular plant communities found at Biscoe Point (ASPA No. 139) and on the Stepping Stones are some of the largest and most extensive in the Anvers Island region, and are particularly abundant for such a southerly location. Dense communities of mosses and lichens are also found on Litchfield Island (ASPA No. 113) – a site specially protected for exceptional vegetation values – and at several other locations around Arthur Harbor.

The soils and plant communities provide an important habitat for invertebrates, and the ice-free islands and promontories close to Palmer Station are particularly valuable for their abundant populations of the endemic wingless midge *Belgica antarctica*, the southernmost, free-living true insect. This is also of significant value for scientific studies, since this species has not been found to the same extent close to other research stations on the Antarctic Peninsula.

(iii) Educational and visitor values

The southwest Anvers Island area holds a special attraction to tourists because of its biological diversity, accessibility and the presence of Palmer Station. These features offer tourists the opportunity to observe wildlife, and gain an appreciation of Antarctic environments and scientific operations. Outreach to tourists via local tours and shipboard lectures given by scientists is a valuable educational tool, and information is also made available to high school students in the US by initiatives through the LTER program.

2. Aims and objectives

The aim of this Management Plan is to conserve and protect the unique and outstanding environment of the southwest Anvers Island and Palmer Basin region by managing the variety of activities and interests in the Area. The Area requires special management to ensure that these important values are protected and sustained in the long-term, especially the extensive scientific data sets collected over the last 100 years. Increasing human activity and potentially conflicting interests have made it necessary to manage and coordinate activities more effectively within the Area.

The specific objectives of management in the Palmer Basin region are to:

- Facilitate scientific research while maintaining stewardship of the environment;
- Assist with the planning and coordination of human activities in the region, managing potential or actual conflicts of interest among different values, activities and operators, including between different areas of scientific research;
- Ensure that any marine harvesting activities are coordinated with scientific research and other activities taking place within the Area. This coordination could include the development of a plan for harvesting within the Area in advance of any such activities taking place.
- Ensure the long-term protection of scientific, ecological, and other values of the Area through the minimization of disturbance to or degradation of these values, including disturbance to fauna and flora, and to minimize the cumulative environmental impacts of human activities;
- Minimize the footprint of all facilities and scientific experiments established in the Area, including the proliferation of field camps and boat landing sites;
- Promote the use of energy systems and modes of transport that have the least environmental impact, and minimize the use of fossil fuels for the conduct of activities in the Area;
- Encourage communication and co-operation between users of the Area, in particular through dissemination of information on the Area and the provisions that apply.

3. Management activities

To achieve the aims and objectives of this Management Plan, the following management activities are to be undertaken:

- National Programs operating within the Area should establish a Southwest Anvers Island and Palmer Basin Management Group to oversee coordination of activities in the ASMA. The Management Group is established to:
    - facilitate and ensure effective communication among those working in or visiting the Area;
    - provide a forum to resolve any potential conflicts in uses;
    - maintain a record of activities and, where practical, impacts in the Area;
    - develop strategies to detect and address cumulative impacts;
    - evaluate the effectiveness of management activities; and
    - disseminate information on the values and objectives of the ASMA to those working in or visiting the Area.

The Management Group should convene on an annual basis to review past, existing, and future activities and to make recommendations on the implementation of this Management Plan, including its revision when necessary.

- To guide activities in the Area, a general Code of Conduct for activities is included in this Management Plan (see Section 7) and further Guidelines relating to specific activities and zones are included in the Appendices.
- National Programs operating within the Area and tour operators visiting should ensure that their personnel (including staff, crew, visiting scientists and passengers) are briefed on, and are aware of, the requirements of this Management Plan;
- The USAP determines annually the number of tourist vessel visits to Palmer Station (approximately 12 per season) through a pre-season scheduling and approval process;
- Signs and markers shall be erected where necessary and appropriate to show the boundaries of Antarctic Specially Protected Areas (ASPAs) and other zones within the Area. Signs shall be secured and maintained in good condition, and removed when no longer necessary;
- Copies of this Management Plan and supporting documentation will be made available at Palmer Station (US). In addition, the Management Group shall make this information freely available in electronic form to enable visitors to consult plan requirements in advance and to enable them to carry a copy when visiting;
- Visits should be made to the Area as necessary (no less than once every 5 years) to evaluate the effectiveness of the Management Plan, and to ensure that management and maintenance measures are adequate. The Management Plan, Code of Conduct and Guidelines will be revised and updated as necessary.

Note: any activity planned inside an ASPA within the Area requires a permit and must refer to the appropriate management plan for guidance.

4. Period of Designation

Designated for an indefinite period.

5. Maps and photographs

Map 1. Regional map and ASMA boundary.

Map 2. SW Anvers Island Restricted Zones: Rosenthal, Joubin and Dream islands.

Map 3. Arthur Harbor & Palmer Station access.

Map 4. Palmer Station Operations Zone.

Map 5. Torgersen Island Zones.

Map 6. Dream Island Restricted Zone.

Map 7. Litchfield Island, ASPA No.113.

Map 8. Biscoe Point, ASPA No.139.

6. Description of the Area

(i) Geographical co-ordinates, boundary markers and natural features

General description

Anvers Island is the largest and most southerly island in the Palmer Archipelago, located approximately 25 km west of the Antarctic Peninsula. It is bounded by Neumayer Channel and Gerlache Strait in the southeast and Bismarck Strait to the south (Map 1). Anvers Island is heavily glaciated, the southwestern half being dominated by the Marr Ice Piedmont, a broad expanse of permanent ice rising gently from the coast to around 1000 m elevation. The southern and western coastlines of Anvers Island within the Area comprise mainly ice cliffs on the edge of the Marr Ice Piedmont, punctuated by small rocky outcrops, ice-free promontories and numerous small near-shore islands. Other prominent land features within the Area include ice-free Cape Monaco at the southwestern extremity of Anvers Island, and Cape Lancaster in the southeast. These ice-free areas form important sites for animal and plant colonisation.

Six main island groups exist within the Area: in the north are the Rosenthal Islands (~22 km NW of Palmer Station). Fringing the Palmer Basin are the Joubin Islands, the Arthur Harbor island group (location of Palmer Station), the Wauwermans Islands, the Dannebrog Islands and the Vedel Islands. These island groups are of low relief, generally of less than 100 m in elevation, although local topography can be rocky and rugged together with small relict ice-caps.

Palmer Station (US) (64°46'27"S, 64°03'15"W) is located within Arthur Harbor on Gamage Point, an ice-free promontory on the southwestern coast of Anvers Island at the edge of the Marr Ice Piedmont (Maps 3 & 4). Immediately to the south of the station are Hero Inlet and Bonaparte Point. Norsel Point lies 2.7 km from Palmer Station at the NW extremity of the largest island in Arthur Harbor, which until recently was joined to Anvers Island by an ice-bridge. Other islands within a few km west of the station include Torgersen (Map 5), Humble, Breaker and Litchfield (Map 7) islands, the latter designated as ASPA No. 113. Those nearby to the southeast include Shortcut, Christine, Hermit, Limitrophe, Laggard and Cormorant islands (Map 3). More distant, Biscoe Point, ASPA No. 136, lies on a small island ~14 km to the southeast that was until recently also joined by an ice-bridge to Anvers Island (Map 8). To the west, Fraser, Halfway (Map 2) and Dream (Map 6) islands lie 5.9, 6.4 and 9.4 km respectively NW of Palmer Station in Wylie Bay.

There are three dominant marine features in the Palmer Basin region:

1. Shallow shelves: extend from Anvers Island and the adjacent island groups to depths of 90-140 m.

2. Bismarck Strait: located south of Palmer Station and north of the Wauwermans Islands on an east–west axis, with depths generally between 360 to 600 m, connecting the southern entrances to Gerlache Strait and Neumayer Channel to Palmer Basin.

3. Palmer Basin: the only deep basin in the area, located 22 km southwest of Palmer Station and with a maximum depth of ~1400 m. It is bordered by the Joubin Islands to the north, the Wauwermans Islands to the east, and the Dannebrog and Vedel island groups in the southeast, and is surrounded by shelves shallower than 165 m. A channel of ~460 m depth connects Palmer Basin to the continental shelf edge west of the Area.

Boundaries of the Area

The Southwest Anvers Island and Palmer Basin ASMA encompasses an area of approximately 3275 km^2, including both terrestrial and marine components. For ease of navigation, the boundaries of the Area follow geographic features where practical and latitude/longitude lines in open ocean areas remote from prominent land features. The northeastern boundary of the Area is defined as a line extending parallel to and approximately one kilometre inland from the southwest Anvers Island coastline. This terrestrial boundary extends from a northerly location at 64°33'S, 64°06'03"W, ~3.1 km north of Gerlache Island, to 64°51'21"S, 63°42'36"W at Cape Lancaster in the south. From Cape Lancaster, the eastern boundary is defined as the 63°42'36"W line of longitude extending 7.9 km across Bismarck Strait to 64°55'36"S on Wednesday Island, the most easterly of the Wauwermans Islands. The boundary then follows a general southwesterly direction to 65°08'33"S, 64°14'22"W at the southern extremity of the Vedel Islands, following the eastern coastlines of the Wauwermans, Dannebrog and Vedel island groups. The southern boundary of the area is defined as the 65°08'33"S line of latitude extending due west from 64°14'22"W in the Vedel Islands to 65°00'W.

The northern boundary is defined as the line of latitude extending from 64°33'S, 64°06'03"W to the coast (~3.1 km north of Gerlache Island) and thence due west to the 65°00'W line of longitude. The western boundary of the Area is defined as the 65°00'W line of longitude, extending between 64°33'S in the north and 65°08'33"S in the south.

The boundaries of the Area have been designed to include areas of high ecological value while also maintaining a practical configuration for ease of use and navigation. The original Multiple-use Planning Area boundary has been extended northwards to include the Rosenthal Islands, which contain several large colonies of chinstrap and gentoo penguins that may function as source populations for other colonies in the southwest Anvers Island region (W. Fraser *pers. comm.* 2006). The original boundary has also been extended westwards and southwards to include the full extent of the Palmer Basin, because of the biological, palaeoecological and oceanographic importance of this feature.

The extent of the terrestrial component has been revised from the original Multiple-use Planning Area boundary to exclude extensive ice fields on the Marr Ice Piedmont, which do not possess values related to the core objectives of the management plan. The boundary encompasses all ice-free coastal areas, the Palmer Basin which plays a key role in regional ecosystem processes, and the nearby associated island groups, which are biologically important and also the focus of most human activity in the region.

Climate

The western Antarctic Peninsula is experiencing the most rapid warming of any marine ecosystem on the planet (Ducklow *et al.* 2007). The mean annual temperature at Palmer Station between 1974-96 was –2.29° C, with an average minimum monthly air temperature over this period of –7.76° C in August, and a maximum of 2.51° C in January (Baker 1996). Data from Faraday / Vernadsky Station 53 km to the south demonstrate a statistically significant trend of annual average temperature rise, from –4.4° in 1951 to –2.0° in 2001, an average rate of 0.057° C per annum (Smith *et al.* 2003). The minimum recorded temperature at Palmer Station as of 2006 is –31° C, and the maximum is 9° C. Storms and precipitation are frequent, with approximately 35-50 cm water equivalent of precipitation received annually in the form of snow and rain (Smith *et al.* 1996). Winds are persistent but generally light to moderate in strength, prevailing from the northeast.

Glaciology, geology and geomorphology

The dominant glacial feature within the Area is the Marr Ice Piedmont. Smaller glaciers and ice-caps are found on many of the islands and promontories, the largest of which is located on Gerlache Island in the Rosenthal Islands (Map 2). Recent observations show the local glaciers to be retreating by approximately 10 m annually, with a number of ice-bridges between the Marr Ice Piedmont and offshore islands having collapsed.

Anvers Island and the numerous small islands and rocky peninsulas along its southwestern coast are composed of late-Cretaceous to early-Tertiary age granitic and volcanic rocks belonging to the Andean Intrusive Suite. These rocks dominate the Anvers Island area (Hooper 1962) and similar rock types extend into the island groups further south.

The main marine geomorphological feature within the Area is Palmer Basin, an erosional, inner-shelf trough located at the convergence of former ice-flows that once drained across the continental shelf from three distinct accumulation centers on the Antarctic Peninsula and Anvers Island (Domack *et al.* 2006). Seafloor features include relict terraces, sub-glacial lake deltas, channels, debris slopes and morainal banks. These remain as evidence of the development of a sub-glacial lake within the Palmer Basin during, or prior, to the last glacial maximum, its subsequent drainage, and the recession of the Palmer Basin ice stream system (Domack *et al.* 2006).

Freshwater habitat

Throughout the Area there are no significant lakes or streams, although there are numerous small ponds and temporary summer melt streams (Lewis Smith 1996). These are mainly on Norsel Point and some of the offshore islands in Arthur Harbor: notably on Humble Island, and also found on Breaker, Shortcut, Laggard, Litchfield and Hermit islands, and at Biscoe Point (W. Fraser, *pers. comm.* 2006), although many are heavily contaminated by neighboring penguin colonies and groups of non-breeding skuas. The streams possess few biota other than marginal mosses (e.g. *Brachythecium austrosalebrosum*, *Sanionia uncinata*), which are a favored habitat for the larvae of the Antarctic wingless midge, *Belgica antarctica*. However, the ponds support a diverse micro-algal and cyanobacterial flora, with over 100 taxa being recorded, although numbers vary considerably between ponds (Parker 1972, Parker & Samsel 1972). Of the freshwater fauna there are numerous species of protozoans, tardigrades, rotifers, and nematodes, and a few free-swimming crustaceans of which the anostracan *Branchinecta gaini* (Antarctic fairy shrimp) and copepods *Parabroteus sarsi* and *Pseudoboeckella poppii* are the largest and most conspicuous (Heywood 1984).

Flora

The Area lies within the cold maritime Antarctic environment of the western Antarctic Peninsula, where conditions of temperature and moisture availability are suitable to support a high diversity of plant species, including the two native flowering plants Antarctic hairgrass (*Deschampsia antarctica*) and Antarctic pearlwort (*Colobanthus quitensis*) (Longton 1967; Lewis Smith 1996, 2003). In Antarctica these flowering plants occur only in the western Peninsula region, South Shetland and South Orkney Islands, occurring most frequently on sheltered, north-facing slopes, especially in gullies and on ledges near sea level. In a few favourable sites the grass has developed locally extensive closed swards (Lewis Smith 1996), notably at Biscoe Point (ASPA No. 139), where closed swards cover up to 6500 m^2. Throughout the maritime Antarctic, and especially in the Arthur Harbor area, the warming trend since the early 1980s has resulted in populations of both species rapidly increasing in number and extent, and numerous new colonies becoming established (Fowbert & Lewis Smith 1994; Day *et al.* 1999).

Vegetation within the Area is otherwise almost entirely cryptogamic (Lewis Smith 1979), with bryophytes dominating moist to wet habitats and lichens and some cushion-forming mosses occupying the drier soils, gravels and rock surfaces (Komárková *et al.* 1985). Dense communities of mosses and lichens are found at several locations around Arthur Harbor, including Norsel Point, Bonaparte Point and Litchfield Island, as well as some of the outer islands and Cape Monaco. In particular, sheltered north-facing slopes support locally extensive communities of the moss turf sub-formations up to 30 cm in depth, with stands of the *Polytrichum strictum–Chorisodontium aciphyllum* association predominating (Lewis Smith 1982). In Arthur Harbor large banks of these mosses can be found overlying an accumulation of peat exceeding a meter in depth and radio-carbon dated at almost 1000 years old. These are particularly apparent on Litchfield Island (ASPA No. 113), which is protected principally because of its outstanding vegetation values. Smaller examples are found on Laggard Island, Hermit Island and on Norsel Point, with small banks occurring on coastal promontories and islands throughout the Area. The largest of the Joubin Islands has a peat bank composed solely of *Chorisodontium* (Fenton & Lewis Smith 1982). From the late 1970s relictual patches of centuries-old peat formed by these mosses became exposed below the receding ice cliffs of Marr Ice Piedmont, notably on Bonaparte Point (Lewis Smith 1982). Wet level areas and seepage slopes usually support communities of the moss carpet and mat sub-formation in which *Sanionia uncinata*, *Brachythecium austrosalebrosum* and *Warnstorfia* spp. are usually dominant. One exceptionally extensive stand on Litchfield Island was destroyed by the increasing summer influx of fur seals during the 1980s.

Lichen-dominated (e.g. species of *Usnea*, *Pseudephebe*, *Umbilicaria* and many crustose forms) communities of the fruticose and foliose lichen sub-formation (often referred to as fellfield) are widespread on most stable, dry stony ground and exposed rock surfaces, often with associated cushion-forming mosses (e.g. species of *Andreaea*, *Hymenoloma*, *Orthogrimmia* and *Schistidium*) (Lewis Smith & Corner 1973). Rocks and boulders close to the shore, especially where influenced by nutrient (nitrogen) input from nearby penguin and petrel colonies, usually support various communities of the crustose and foliose lichen sub-formation. Many of the species (e.g. *Acarospora*, *Amandinea*, *Buellia*, *Caloplaca*, *Haematomma*, *Lecanora*, *Lecidea*, *Xanthoria*) are brightly coloured (orange, yellow, gray-green, brown, white).

The green foliose alga *Prasiola crispa* develops a conspicuous zone on the highly nutrient enriched soil and gravel around penguin colonies. In late summer melting ice fields and permanent snow patches develop a reddish hue as huge aggregations of unicellular snow algae accumulate in the melting firn. Elsewhere, green snow algae give the surface a distinctive coloration.

A checklist of flora observed in the Area is included in Appendix C.

Invertebrates

The vegetation communities found within the Area serve as important habitat for invertebrate fauna. As is common elsewhere on the Antarctic Peninsula, springtails and mites are especially prominent. Colonies of the mite *Alaskozetes antarcticus* are frequently observed on the sides of dry rocks, while other species are associated with mosses, fruticose lichens and Antarctic hairgrass. The most common springtail, *Cryptopygus antarcticus*, is found in moss beds and under rocks. Springtails and mites are also found in other habitats, including bird nests and limpet accumulations (Lewis Smith 1966).

The islands near Palmer Station are notable for their abundant populations of the wingless midge *Belgica antarctica*, a feature not found to the same extent close to other research stations on the Antarctic Peninsula. This endemic species is significant because it is the southernmost, free-living true insect. It inhabits a wide range of habitats including moss, the terrestrial alga *Prasiola crispa* and nutrient-enriched microhabitats adjacent to elephant seal wallows and penguin colonies. Larvae are exceptionally tolerant of freezing, anoxia, osmotic stress and desiccation.

Colonies of the seabird tick *Ixodes uriae* are frequently found beneath well-drained rocks adjacent to seabird nests and especially Adélie penguin colonies. This tick has a circumpolar distribution in both hemispheres and exhibits the greatest range of thermal tolerance (-30 to 40°C) of any Antarctic terrestrial arthropod. The abundance of this tick has decreased during the past three decades concomitantly with observed decreases in Adélie penguin populations (R. Lee *pers. comm.* 2007).

Birds

Three species of penguins, Adélie (*Pygoscelis adeliae*), chinstrap (*P. antarctica*) and gentoo (*P. papua*), breed in the southwest Anvers Island area (Parmelee & Parmelee 1987, Poncet & Poncet 1987, Woehler 1993). The most abundant species is the Adélie penguin, which breeds on Biscoe Point, Christine, Cormorant, Dream, Humble, Litchfield and Torgersen islands, as well as the Joubin and Rosenthal islands (Maps 2-8). Numbers of Adélie penguins have declined significantly over the last 30 years, thought to be linked to the effects of the changing climate on sea-ice conditions, snow accumulation and prey availability (Fraser & Trivelpiece 1996, Fraser & Hofmann 2003, Fraser & Patterson 1997, Trivelpiece & Fraser 1996). Numbers of Adélie penguins breeding on Litchfield Island declined from 884 pairs to 143 pairs between 1974/75 and 2002/03, with no pairs breeding in 2006/07 (W. Fraser *pers. comm.* 2007). Chinstrap penguins are present on Dream Island, on small islands near Gerlache Island, and on the Joubin Islands. The Rosenthal Islands contain source populations of chinstrap and gentoo penguins that are likely to be closely linked to other colonies in the southwest Anvers Island region. Gentoo penguins are thought to be increasing in the region in response to the regional warming, and may be colonising new sites in recently deglaciated areas or sites vacated by Adélie penguins. In particular, small glaciers on the Wauwermans Islands are retreating and may provide important habitat for new gentoo colonies (W. Fraser *pers. comm.* 2006).

Southern giant petrels (*Macronectes giganteus*) breed at numerous locations within the Area. Blue-eyed shags (*Phalacrocorax* [atriceps] *bransfieldensis*) breed on Cormorant Island, Elephant Rocks and in the Joubin Islands. Other breeding bird species occurring in the Area include kelp gulls (*Larus dominicanus*), Wilson's storm petrels (*Oceanites oceanicus*), sheathbills (*Chionis alba*), south polar skuas (*Catharacta maccormicki*), brown skuas (*C. loennbergi*) and Antarctic terns (*Sterna vittata*). Common non-breeding visitors include southern fulmars (*Fulmarus glacialoides*), Antarctic petrels (*Thalassoica antarctica*), cape petrels (*Daption capense*) and snow petrels (*Pagadroma nivea*). A full list of breeding, frequent and less common or transient visitors recorded in the Area is provided in Appendix C.

Marine mammals

There are few published data on the marine mammals within the area. Cruises conducted in Gerlache Strait have observed fin (*Balaenoptera physalus*), humpback (*Megaptera novaeangliae*) and southern bottlenose (*Hyperoodon planifrons*) whales (Thiele 2004). Anecdotal observations by Palmer Station personnel and visitors have noted fin, humpback, sei (*Balaenoptera borealis*), southern right (*Eubalaena australis*), minke (*Balaenoptera bonaerensis*) and killer (*Orcinus orca*) whales within the Area, as well as hourglass dolphins

(*Lagenorhynchus cruciger*) (W. Fraser *pers. comm.* 2007). Non-breeding Weddell (*Leptonychotes weddellii*) and southern elephant seals (*Mirounga leonina*) haul out on accessible beaches, and crabeater (*Lobodon carcinophagus*) and leopard seals (*Leptonyx hydrurga*) are also commonly seen at sea and on ice floes within the Area. Numbers of non-breeding Antarctic fur seals (*Arctocephalus gazella*), mainly juvenile males, have increased in recent years, and depending on the time of year hundreds to thousands of individuals may be found on local beaches throughout the Area. Their increasing abundance is damaging vegetation at lower elevations (Lewis Smith 1996, Harris 2001). Despite the lack of published data concerning marine mammals within the Area, their presence is likely to be related to foraging for Antarctic krill, which forms an important component in their diets (Ducklow *et al.* 2007). A list of marine mammals observed within the Area is provided in Appendix C.

Oceanography

The Western Antarctic Peninsula is unique as the only region where the Antarctic Circumpolar Current (ACC) is adjacent to the continental shelf. The ACC flows in a northeasterly direction off the shelf, and there is also some southward flow on the inner part of the shelf (Smith *et al.* 1995). Circumpolar Deep Water (CDW) transports macronutrients and warmer, more saline water onto the shelf, which has significant implications for heat and salt budgets in the southwest Anvers Island and Palmer Basin region. Circulation patterns and the presence of the CDW water mass may also affect the timing and extent of sea ice (Smith *et al.* 1995). The extent of sea ice cover and the timing of the appearance of the marginal ice zone (MIZ) in relation to specific geographic areas have high interannual variability (Smith *et al.* 1995), although Smith and Stammerjohn (2001) have shown a statistically significant reduction in overall sea-ice extent in the Western Antarctic Peninsula region over the period for which satellite observations are available. The ice edge and the MIZ form major ecological boundaries, and are of particular interest in the region because of their interaction with many aspects of the marine ecosystem, including phytoplankton blooms and seabird habitat. Within the Area, the Palmer Basin is a focal point of biological and biogeochemical activity and an important area of upwelling.

Marine ecology

The marine ecosystem west of the Antarctic Peninsula is highly productive, with dynamics that are strongly coupled to the seasonal and interannual variations in sea ice. The rapid climate changes occurring on the western Antarctic Peninsula, with resultant changes in sea ice, is affecting all levels of the food web (Ducklow *et al.* 2007). Marine flora and fauna within the Area are strongly influenced by factors including low temperatures, a short growing season, high winds influencing the depth of the mixed layer, proximity to land with the potential for input of micronutrients, and the varying sea-ice coverage. It is a high-nutrient, low-biomass environment.

High levels of primary production are observed within the region, maintained by topography-induced upwellings and stratification by fresh water input from glaciers (Prézelin *et al.* 2000, 2004; Dierssen *et al.* 2002). In terms of biomass, the phytoplankton communities are dominated by diatoms and cryptomonads (Moline & Prezelin 1996). Species distribution and composition varies with water masses, fronts and the changing position of the ice edge.

Salps and Antarctic krill (*Euphausia* sp.) often dominate the total zooplankton biomass (Moline & Prezelin 1996). Dominant organisms in the neritic province on the shelf southwest of Anvers Island are *E. superba, E. crystallorophias,* and fish larvae (Ross *et al.* 1996). The distribution and abundance of zooplankton is variable over time, and Spiridonov (1995) found krill in the Palmer Archipelago to exhibit a highly variable life cycle as compared with other areas of the western Antarctic Peninsula.

There is a high level of endemism among fish species sampled on the Antarctic continental shelf as compared with other isolated marine communities, with new species still being regularly discovered (Eastman 2005). Examples of fish collected within the Area are six species of Nototheniidae (*Notothenia coriiceps neglecta, N. gibberifrons, N. nudifrons, Trematomus bernachii, T. hansoni* and *T. newnesi*), one of Bathydraconidae (*Parachaenichthys charcoti*) and one of Channichthydae (*Chaenocephalus aceratus*) (De Witt & Hureau 1979, Detrich 1987, McDonald *et al.* 1992).

The soft-bottomed macrobenthic community of Arthur Harbor is characterised by high species diversity and abundance, being dominated by polychaetes, peracarid crustaceans and molluscs (Lowry 1975, Richardson

& Hedgpeth 1977, Hyland *et al.* 1994). Samples collected during a study of UV effects on marine organisms carried out close to Palmer Station during the austral spring (Karentz *et al.* 1991) yielded 57 species (1 fish, 48 invertebrates, and 8 algae). Sampling was from a combination of rocky intertidal areas (yielding 72% of organisms), subtidal and planktonic habitats. Of the marine invertebrates collected, the greatest number of species was found in the phylum Arthropoda (12 species). The Antarctic limpet (*Nacella concinna*) is common in Arthur Harbor (Kennicutt *et al.* 1992b).

Human activities and impact

'Base N' (UK) was built on Norsel Point (Map 3) in 1955 and operated continuously until 1958. The United States established 'Old Palmer' Station nearby on Norsel Point in 1965, although in 1968 transferred the main US operations to the present site of Palmer Station on Gamage Point. 'Base N' was used as a biological laboratory by US scientists from 1965-71, although this burnt to the ground in 1971. 'Old Palmer' station was removed by the US in 1991, and all that remains of both 'Old Palmer' and 'Base N' are the original concrete footings.

On 28 January 1989, the Argentine vessel *Bahia Paraiso* ran aground 750 m south of Litchfield Island, releasing more than 600,000 liters (150,000 gallons) of petroleum into the surrounding environment (Kennicutt 1990, Penhale *et al.* 1997). Contamination was lethal to some of the local biota including krill, intertidal invertebrates and seabirds, particularly Adélie penguins and blue-eyed shags (Hyland *et al.* 1994, Kennicutt *et al.* 1992a&b, Kennicutt & Sweet 1992). A summary of the spill, research on the environmental impact, and the joint 1992/1993 clean-up by Argentina –and The Netherlands can be found in Penhale *et al.* (1997).

All fin-fishing is currently prohibited in the western Antarctic Peninsula region (CCAMLR Statistical Subarea 48.1) under CCAMLR Conservation Measure 32-02 (1998) (CCAMLR 2006a). Krill fishing occurs in the offshore region to the northwest of the Palmer Archipelago, and is currently concentrated mainly around the South Shetland Islands further to the north. The total krill catch for Subarea 48.1 was reported at 7095 tonnes in the 2004/05 season (CCAMLR 2006b), and there has been some limited historical activity in the vicinity of the ASMA. However, fine-scale data show krill catches in the southwest Anvers Island region during only one 3-month period between 2000 and 2005, with a total catch of less than 4 tonnes (Q2, 2002/03)(CCAMLR 2006b: 187). CCAMLR-related activities are therefore occurring within or close to the Area, but are currently minimal.

Current human activities in the Area are mainly related to science and associated logistic activities, and tourism. Palmer Station (US) serves as the base for scientific research and associated logistic operations conducted in the western Antarctic Peninsula and Palmer Archipelago by the United States Antarctic Program (USAP) and collaborators from a number of other Antarctic Treaty Parties. Scientific and logistic support is received from ships operated or chartered by the USAP, which visit the station approximately 15 times per year. Aircraft are not operated routinely from Palmer Station, although helicopters may visit occasionally in summer. Local scientific transport and support is provided using small inflatable boats, which are operated throughout the 3-mile (~5 km) 'safe boating limit' area during the summer season (Map 3). Frequent visits are made to islands within the safe boating limit for scientific research, and also for recreation by base personnel.

Published information on the impacts of science (for example from sampling, disturbance or installations) within the Area is limited. However, numerous welding rods inserted into soil to mark vegetation study sites (Komárková 1983) were abandoned at Biscoe Point (ASPA No. 139) and Litchfield Island (ASPA No. 113) in 1982. Where these remained, surrounding vegetation had been killed as an apparent result of highly localised contamination by chemicals from the rods (Harris 2001).

Between 1984/85 and 1990/91, the number of tour ship visits each season at Palmer Station increased from 4 visits (340 visitors) to 12 (1300 visitors). Since 1991 the number of tour ship visits to Palmer Station has been maintained at approximately 12 vessels annually, with visits arranged prior to the start of the season. Tourists typically land at the station itself for a tour of the facilities, visit the Visitor Zone on Torgersen Island (Map 5), and make short cruises around the nearshore islands using inflatable boats. Yachts also visit Palmer Station and the surrounding area, with 17 vessels visiting during the 2007/08 season. Studies of changes in penguin populations on Torgersen Island and nearby islands suggest that the impacts of visits by tourists, base personnel, and scientists on breeding performance have been small compared to longer-term climate-related forcing factors (Fraser & Patterson 1997, Emslie *et al.* 1998, Patterson 2001).

(ii) Structures within the Area

Modern Palmer Station (Map 4) consists of two main buildings, a laboratory facility and several ancillary structures including an aquarium, small boathouse, workshops, storage and communications facilities. The station is powered by one diesel-electric generator, the fuel for which is stored in two double-walled tanks. A pier has been constructed adjacent to the station at the entrance to Hero Inlet, which may accommodate medium-sized scientific and logistic support ships. The station is operated year-round and can accommodate approximately 44 people, with a summer occupancy of at least 40, and a winter complement of around 10.

(iii) Restricted and managed zones within the Area

Three types of management zones (Restricted, Visitor and Operations) are designated within the Area. Two ASPAs are also located within the Area.

(a) Restricted Zones

Sixteen sites of special ecological and scientific value are designated as Restricted Zones (Maps 2-6). These sites are particularly sensitive to disturbance during the summer months, and are listed as follows:

Table 1: Restricted Zones within the Southwest Anvers Island and Palmer Basin ASMA

Bonaparte Point (incl. 'Diana's Island' and 'Kristie Cove')	Laggard Island
Christine Island	Limitrophe Island
Cormorant Island	Norsel Point
Dream Island	Rosenthal Islands
Elephant Rocks	Shortcut Island
Hermit Island	Shortcut Point
Humble Island	Stepping Stones
Joubin Islands	Torgersen Island (SW half of island)

The Restricted Zones include a buffer extending 50 m from the shore into any adjacent marine area (Map 2). A 50 m Restricted Zone buffer also extends around Litchfield Island (ASPA No. 113). In order to protect sensitive bird colonies throughout the breeding season to the maximum extent possible, and also plant communities, access to Restricted Zones between 1 October to 15 April inclusive is restricted to those conducting essential scientific research, monitoring or maintenance. All non-essential small boat traffic should avoid transit of or cruising within the 50 m marine buffers of Restricted Zones.

Specific guidelines for scientific research activities within Restricted Zones are included in the Scientific Guidelines for the ASMA (Appendix A).

(b) Visitor Zone

The northeastern half of Torgersen Island is designated as a Visitor Zone (Map 5). Visitors are currently directed to this part of the island, while access to the Restricted Zone in the southwest part of the island, which is set aside as a scientific reference area, is restricted to those conducting essential scientific research, monitoring or maintenance. Specific guidelines for activities within the Visitor Zone are included in the Visitor Guidelines for the ASMA (Appendix B).

(c) Operations Zone

Palmer Station facilities are largely concentrated within a small area on Gamage Point. The Operations Zone is designated as the area of Gamage Point encompassing the station buildings, together with adjacent masts, aerials fuel storage facilities and other structures and extending to the permanent ice edge of the Marr Ice Piedmont (Map 4).

(d) Antarctic Specially Protected Areas (ASPAs)

Two Antarctic Specially Protected Areas, ASPA No. 113 Litchfield Island and ASPA No. 139 Biscoe Point, are located within the ASMA (Maps 7 and 8). Revised management plans for both sites were adopted by the Antarctic Treaty Parties in 2004. All entry is prohibited unless in accordance with a Permit issued by an appropriate national authority.

(iv) Location of other protected areas within close proximity of the Area

In addition to ASPA No. 113 and ASPA No. 139 within the Area, the only other protected area within close proximity is ASPA No. 146, South Bay, Doumer Island, 25 km southeast of Palmer Station (Map 1). There are no Historic Sites and Monuments within the Area, with the nearest being HSM No. 61, Base A, Port Lockroy, Goudier Island, 30 km east of Palmer Station (Map 1).

7. General Code of Conduct

The Code of Conduct in this section is the main instrument for the management of activities in the Area. It outlines the overall management and operational principles for the Area. More specific environmental, scientific and visitor guidelines are provided in the appendices.

(i) Access to and movement within the Area

Access to the Area is generally by ship (Map 4), with occasional access by helicopter. There are no special restrictions on the transit of vessels through the Area, with the exception of seasonal buffer zones extending 50 m from the shore at a small number of islands designated as Restricted Zones (see Section 6(iii)(a)). Prior to visiting Palmer Station, radio contact should always be made to obtain guidance on local activities being conducted in the region (Map 3).

Tour ships, yachts and National Program vessels may stand offshore and access Palmer Station and the surrounding coast and islands by small boat, taking into account the access restrictions applying within designated zones. The region of safe small boat operations and preferred small boat landing sites within the area local to Palmer Station are shown on Map 3 (see also Appendix A).

Access to Restricted Zones between 1 October – 15 April inclusive is restricted to those conducting essential scientific research, monitoring or maintenance, including the nearshore marine area within 50 m of the coast of these zones (see Section 6(iii)(a) for details). Access to ASPAs is prohibited except in accordance with a Permit issued by an appropriate national authority.

Aircraft operating within the Area should follow the 'Guidelines for the operation of aircraft near concentrations of birds in Antarctica' (Resolution 4, XXVII Antarctic Treaty Consultative Meeting). The primary helicopter landing site at Palmer Station is a flat, rocky area approximately 400 m east of Palmer Station. Helicopter approach should be high over the peninsula east of Palmer Station or up the channel from SE (refer to Palmer Station page in the Anvers Island section of the *Wildlife Awareness Manual* (Harris 2006)). Overflight of wildlife colonies should be avoided throughout the Area, and specific overflight restrictions apply at Litchfield Island (ASPA No.113) and Biscoe Point (ASPA No.139) (Maps 7 & 8 and specific provisions in the ASPA management plans).

Movement on land within the Area is generally on foot, although vehicles are used in the Operations Zone. A route leading from Palmer Station up onto the Marr Ice Piedmont is marked by flags to avoid crevassed areas. The precise route varies according to conditions and visitors should obtain the latest information on the route from Palmer Station. In the winter, snowmobiles are sometimes used on this route. All movement should be undertaken carefully to minimise disturbance to animals, soil and vegetated areas.

(ii) Activities that are or may be conducted within the Area

Activities that may be conducted in the Area include:

- scientific research, or the logistical support of scientific research, that will not jeopardise the values of the Area;
- management activities, including the maintenance or removal of facilities, clean-up of abandoned work-sites, and monitoring the implementation of this Management Plan; and
- tourist or private expedition visits consistent with the provisions of this Management Plan and the Visitor Guidelines (Appendix B);
- media, arts, education or other official national program visitors;
- harvesting of marine living resources, which should be conducted in accordance with the provisions of this Management Plan and with due recognition of the important scientific and environmental values of the Area. Any such activities should be conducted in coordination with research and other activities taking place, and could include development of a plan and guidelines that would help to ensure that harvesting activities did not pose a significant risk to the other important values of the Area.

All activities in the Area should be conducted in such a manner so as to minimize environmental impacts. Specific guidelines on the conduct of activities within the Area, including within specific zones, can be found in the Appendices.

(iii) Installation, modification or removal of structures

Site selection, installation, modification or removal of temporary refuges or tents should be undertaken in a manner that does not compromise the values of the Area. Installation sites should be re-used to the greatest extent possible and the location recorded. The footprint of installations should be kept to the minimum practical.

Scientific equipment installed in the Area should be clearly identified by country, name of principal investigator, contact details, and date of installation. All such items should be made of materials that pose minimal risk of contamination to the area. All equipment and associated materials should be removed when no longer in use.

(iv) Location of field camps

Temporary field camps may be made where required for research, and in accordance with the Restricted Zone and ASPA provisions. Field camps should be located on non-vegetated sites, or on thick snow or ice cover when practical, and should avoid concentrations of mammals or breeding birds. The location of field camps should be recorded, and previously occupied campsites should be re-used where appropriate. The footprint of campsites should be kept to the minimum practical.

Emergency caches are located on several islands within the Area for safety purposes, and are identified on Map 3. Please respect the caches and only use them in a genuine emergency, reporting any such use to Palmer Station so the cache can be restocked.

(v) Taking or harmful interference with native flora and fauna

Taking (including killing or capturing) or harmful interference with native flora or fauna is prohibited, except by Permit issued in accordance with Annex II to the *Protocol on Environmental Protection to the Antarctic Treaty* (1998).

(vi) Collection or removal of anything not brought into the Area

Material not covered by 7(v) above should only be removed from the area for scientific and associated educational purposes or essential management or conservation purposes, and should be limited to the minimum necessary to fulfill those needs. Material of human origin likely to compromise the values of the Area may be removed unless the impact of removal is likely to be greater than leaving the material in place. If this is the case the appropriate authority should be notified. Do not disturb experimental sites or scientific equipment.

(vii) Restrictions on materials and organisms which can be brought into the Area

Visitors should seek to minimize the risk of introduction of non-native species to the maximum extent practical.

(viii) Waste disposal / management

All wastes other than human wastes and domestic liquid waste shall be removed from the Area. Human and domestic liquid wastes from stations or field camps may be disposed of into the sea below the high water mark. In accordance with Article 4, Annex III of the Protocol on Environmental Protection, wastes shall not be disposed of into freshwater streams or lakes, onto ice-free areas, or onto areas of snow or ice which terminate in such areas or have high ablation.

(ix) Requirements for Reports

Reports of activities in the Area should be maintained by the Management Group to the greatest extent possible, and made available to all Parties. In accordance with Article 10 of Annex V of the Protocol on Environmental Protection, arrangements should be made for collection and exchange of reports of inspection visits and on any significant changes or damage within the Area.

Tour operators should record their visits to the Area, including the number of visitors, dates, and any incidents in the Area.

8. Exchange of information

In addition to the normal exchange of information by means of the annual national reports to the Parties of the Antarctic Treaty, and to SCAR and COMNAP, Parties operating in the Area should exchange information through the Management Group. All National Antarctic Programs planning to conduct scientific activities within the Area should, as far as practical, notify the Management Group in advance of their nature, location and expected duration, and any special considerations related to the deployment of field parties or scientific instrumentation within the Area.

All tour ships and yachts should, as far as practical, provide the Management Group with details of scheduled visits in advance.

All those planning to conduct marine harvesting activities within the Area should, as far as practical, notify the Management Group in advance of their nature, location and expected duration, and of any special considerations related to how these activities could impact on scientific investigations being carried out within the Area.

Information on the location of scientific activities within the Area should be disseminated as far as practical.

9. Supporting documentation

This Management Plan includes the following supporting documents as appendices:

- Appendix A: Scientific and Environmental Guidelines (including guidelines for Restricted Zones);
- Appendix B: Visitor Guidelines (including guidelines for the Visitor Zone);
- Appendix C: Plant, bird and mammal species recorded within the Southwest Anvers Island and Palmer Basin ASMA;
- Appendix D: References.

Appendices

Appendix A - Supporting Guidelines and Data

Scientific and Environmental Guidelines (including guidelines for Restricted Zones)

The coastal marine environmental of the West Antarctic Peninsula has become an important site for scientific research, with a history of study going back some fifty years. This code suggests how you can help to protect the values of the area for future generations and ensure that your presence in the region will have as little impact as possible.

- Everything taken into the field must be removed. Do not dump any unwanted material on the ground or in the water.
- Do not collect specimens or any natural material of any kind, including fossils, except for approved scientific and educational purposes.
- For those based at Palmer Station, stay within the safe boating limits: these are approximately 5 km (3 miles) from the station and no closer than 300 m from the glacier front along the Anvers Island coastline (Map 3).
- Visit only approved islands at approved times. Do not harass wildlife. Do not disturb mummified seals or penguins.
- When traveling on foot, stay on established trails whenever possible. Do not walk on vegetated areas or rock formations. Some of the biological communities in them have taken several thousand years to develop.
- Ensure that equipment and supplies are properly secured at all times to avoid dispersion by high winds. High velocity winds can arrive suddenly and with little warning.
- Avoid any activities that would result in the dispersal of foreign substances (e.g., food, fuel, reagents, litter). Do not leave any travel equipment behind.

Fuel and chemicals:
- Take steps to prevent the accidental release of chemicals such as laboratory reagents and isotopes (stable or radioactive). When permitted to use radioisotopes, precisely follow all instructions provided.
- Ensure you have spill kits appropriate to the volume of fuel or chemicals you have and are familiar with their use.

Sampling and experimental sites:
- All sampling equipment should be clean before being brought into the field.
- Once you have drilled a sampling hole in sea ice or dug a soil pit, keep it clean and make sure all your sampling equipment is securely tethered.
- Avoid leaving markers (e.g. flags) and other equipment for more than one season without marking them clearly with your event number and duration of your project.

Glaciers:
- Minimize the use of liquid water (e.g., with hot water drills) which could contaminate the isotopic and chemical record within the glacier ice.
- Avoid the use of chemical-based fluids on the ice.
- If stakes or other markers are placed on a glacier, use the minimum number of stakes required to meet the needs of the research; where possible, label these with event number and project duration.

Restricted Zones:

- Research in Restricted Zones should be carried out with particular care to avoid or minimize trampling of vegetation and disturbance of wildlife;
- Minimize any disturbance to birds during the breeding season (1 October to 15 April) except for compelling scientific reasons;
- Access to the mooring adjacent to the Restricted Zone on Bonaparte Point should be by small boat when ice and weather permit. If it is necessary to approach the mooring from within the Restricted Zone, walk as close to the coastline as possible to avoid south polar skua (*Catharacta* [skua] *maccormicki*) nesting territories on the ridge crest.
- All visits to and activities within Restricted Zones should be recorded, in particular records should be kept of the type and quantity of all sampling.

Appendix B- Visitor Guidelines (including guidelines for the Visitor Zone)

These guidelines are for commercial tour operators and private expeditions, as well as for National Antarctic Program staff when undertaking recreational activities within the Area.

- Visitor activities should be undertaken in a manner so as to minimize adverse impacts on the southwest Anvers Island and Palmer Basin ecosystem and/or on the scientific activities in the Area;
- Tour operators should provide visit schedules to National Programs operating in the Area in advance of their visits, which should be circulated to the Management Group as soon as they become available;
- In addition to the above, tour vessels and yachts planning to visit Palmer Station should make contact with the station at least 24 hours before arrival to confirm details of the visit;
- At Palmer Station, no more than 40 passengers should be ashore at any time;
- Small boat cruising should avoid any disturbance of birds and seals, and take account of the 50 m operation limit around Restricted Zones;
- Visitors should maintain a distance of 5 meters from birds or seals, to avoid causing them disturbance. Where practical, keep at least 15 meters away from fur seals;
- Visitors should avoid walking on any vegetation including mosses and lichens;
- Visitors should not touch or disturb scientific equipment, research areas, or any other facilities or equipment;
- Visitors should not take any biological, geological or other souvenirs, or leave behind any litter;
- Within the group of islands in Arthur Harbor, tourist landings should be confined to the designated Visitor Zone.

Visitor Zone (Torgersen Island)

Visits to Torgersen Island should be undertaken in accordance with the general visitor guidelines outlined above. Further site-specific guidelines are as follows:

- Landings on Torgersen Island should be made at the designated small boat landing site at 64°46'17.8"S, 64°04'31"W on the northern shore of the island;
- No more than 40 passengers should be ashore at any time;
- Visitors should limit their visit to the Visitor Zone portion of the island, as the Restricted Zone is a control site for scientific research (Map 5).

Appendix C- Plant, bird and mammal species recorded within the Southwest Anvers Island and Palmer Basin ASMA

Table C.1: Plant species recorded within the Area (extracted from British Antarctic Survey Plant Database (2007)).

Flowering plants	Lichens
Colobanthus quitensis	*Acarospora macrocyclos*
Deschampsia antarctica	*Amandinea petermannii*
Liverworts	*Buellia anisomera, B. melanostola, B. perlata, B. russa*
Barbilophozia hatcheri	*Catillaria corymbosa*
Cephaloziella varians	*Cetraria aculeata*
Lophozia excisa	*Cladonia carneola, C. deformis, C. fimbriata, C. galindezii, C. merochlorophaea var. novochloro, C.*
Mosses	*pleurota, C. pocillum, C. sarmentosa, C. squamosa*
Andreaea depressinervis, A. gainii var. gainii, A. regularis M	*Coelopogon epiphorellus*
Bartramia patens	*Haematomma erythromma*
Brachythecium austrosalebrosum	*Himantormia lugubris*
Bryum archangelicum, B. argenteum, B. boreale, B. pseudotriquetrum	*Lecania brialmontii*
Ceratodon purpureus	*Lecanora polytropa, L. skottsbergii*
Chorisodontium aciphyllum	*Leptogium puberulum*
Dicranoweisia crispula, D. dryptodontoides	*Massalongia carnosa*
Grimmia reflexidens	*Mastodia tessellata*
Hymenoloma grimmiaceum	*Melanelia ushuaiensis*
Kiaeria pumila	*Ochrolechia frigida*
Platydictya jungermannioides	*Parmelia cunninghamii, P. saxatilis*
Pohlia cruda, P. nutans	*Physcia caesia, P. dubia*
Polytrichastrum alpinum	*Physconia muscigena*
Polytrichum juniperinum, P.piliferum, P. strictum	*Pseudephebe minuscula, P. pubescens*
Sanionia uncinata	*Psoroma cinnamomeum, P. hypnorum*
Sarconeurum glaciale	*Rhizoplaca aspidophora*
Schistidium antarctici, S. urnulaceum	*Rinodina turfacea*
Syntrichia magellanica	*Sphaerophorus globosus*
Syntrichia princeps, S. sarconeurum	*Stereocaulon alpinum*
Warnstorfia laculosa	*Umbilicaria antarctica, U. decussata*
	Usnea antarctica, U. aurantiaco-atra
	Xanthoria candelaria
	Xanthoria elegans

Notes: The number of species recorded within the Area = 83

Table C.2: Bird and mammal species recorded within the Area (Parmelee et al. 1977; W. Fraser pers. comm. 2007).

Common name	Scientific name	Status within Area
Birds		
chinstrap penguin	*Pygoscelis antarctica*	Confirmed breeder
Adélie penguin	*Pygoscelis adeliae*	Confirmed breeder
gentoo penguin	*Pygoscelis papua*	Confirmed breeder
southern giant petrel	*Macronectes giganteus*	Confirmed breeder
blue-eyed shag	*Phalacrocorax* [atriceps] *bransfieldensis*	Confirmed breeder
kelp gull	*Larus dominicanus*	Confirmed breeder
Wilson's storm petrel	*Oceanites oceanites*	Confirmed breeder
sheathbill	*Chionis alba*	Confirmed breeder
south polar skua	*Catharacta maccormicki*	Confirmed breeder
brown skua	*Catharacta loennbergi*	Confirmed breeder
Antarctic tern	*Sterna vittata*	Confirmed breeder
southern fulmar	*Fulmarus glacialoides*	Frequent visitor
Antarctic petrel	*Thalassoica antarctica*	Frequent visitor
cape petrel	*Daption capense*	Frequent visitor
snow petrel	*Pagadroma nivea*	Frequent visitor
emperor penguin	*Aptenodytes forsteri*	Occasional visitor
king penguin	*A. patagonicus*	Occasional visitor
macaroni penguin	*Eudyptes chrysolophus*	Occasional visitor
rockhopper penguin	*Eudyptes chrysocome*	Occasional visitor
Magellanic penguin	*Spheniscus magellanicus*	Occasional visitor
black-browed albatross	*Diomedea melanophris*	Occasional visitor
gray-headed albatross	*D. chrystosoma*	Occasional visitor
northern giant petrel	*Macronectes halli*	Occasional visitor
black-bellied storm petrel	*Fregetta tropica*	Occasional visitor
red phalarope	*Phalaropus fulicarius*	Occasional visitor
South Georgia pintails	*Anas georgica*	Occasional visitor
black-necked swan	*Cygnus melancoryphus*	Occasional visitor
sandpiper	(sp. unknown)	Occasional visitor
cattle egret	*Bubulcus ibis*	Occasional visitor
Arctic tern	*Sterna paradisaea*	Occasional visitor
Seals (no data on breeding or numbers available)		
Weddell seal	*Leptonychotes weddellii*	Frequent visitor
southern elephant seal	*Mirounga leonina*	Frequent visitor
crabeater seal	*Lobodon carcinophagus*	Frequent visitor
leopard seal	*Leptonyx hydrurga*	Frequent visitor
Antarctic fur seals	*Arctocephalus gazella*	Frequent visitor
Whales and dolphins (no data on breeding or numbers available)		
fin whale	*Balaenoptera physalus*	Observed
humpback whale	*Megaptera novaeangliae*	Observed
sei whale	*Balaenoptera borealis*	Observed
southern right whale	*Eubalaena australis*	Observed
minke whale	*Balaenoptera bonaerensis*	Observed
killer whale	*Orcinus orca*	Observed
hourglass dolphins	*Lagenorhynchus cruciger*	Observed

Appendix D: References

Baker, K.S. 1996. Palmer LTER: Palmer Station air temperature 1974 to 1996. *Antarctic Journal of the United States* **31**(2): 162-64.

CCAMLR 2006a. Schedule of Conservation Measures in force 2006/07 season. CCAMLR, Hobart, Australia.

CCAMLR 2006b. Statistical Bulletin, Vol. 18 (1996*2005). CCAMLR, Hobart, Australia.

Day, T.A., C.T. Ruhland, C.W. Grobe & F. Xiong 1999. Growth and reproduction of Antarctic vascular plants in response to warming and UV radiation reductions in the field. *Oecologia* **119**: 24-35.

Detrich III, H.W. 1987. Formation of cold-stable microtubules by tubulins and microtubule associated proteins from Antarctic fishes. *Antarctic Journal of the United States* **22**(5): 217-19.

Domack E., D. Amblàs, R. Gilbert, S. Brachfeld, A. Camerlenghi, M. Rebesco, M. Canals & R. Urgeles 2006. Subglacial morphology and glacial evolution of the Palmer deep outlet system, Antarctic Peninsula. *Geomorphology* **75**(1-2): 125-42.

Ducklow, H.W., K.S. Baker, D.G. Martinson, L.B. Quetin, R.M. Ross, R.C. Smith, S.E. Stammerjohn, M. Vernet & W. Fraser 2007. Marine pelagic ecosystems: The West Antarctic Peninsula. Special Theme Issue, Antarctic Ecology: From Genes to Ecosystems. *Philosophical Transactions of the Royal Society of London* **362**: 67-94.

Eastman, J.T. 2005. The nature and diversity of Antarctic fishes. *Polar Biology* **28**(2): 93-107.

Emslie, S.D., W.R. Fraser, R.C. Smith & W. Walker 1998. Abandoned penguin colonies and environmental change in the Palmer Station area, Anvers Island, Antarctic Peninsula. *Antarctic Science* **10**(3): 257-68.

Fraser, W.R. & Trivelpiece, W.Z. 1996. Factors controlling the distribution of seabirds: winter-summer heterogeneity in the distribution of Adélie penguin populations. In: R. Ross, E. Hofmann, & L. Quetin (eds) *Foundations for ecological research west of the Antarctic Peninsula. Antarctic Research Series* **70**. American Geophysical Union, Washington, DC: 257-52.

Fraser, W.R. & Hofmann, E.E. 2003. A predator's perspective on causal links between climate change, physical forcing and ecosystem response. *Marine Ecology Progress Series* **265**: 1-15.

Fraser, W.R. & Patterson, D.L. 1997. Human disturbance and long-term changes in Adélie penguin populations: a natural experiment at Palmer Station, Antarctic Peninsula. In: B. Battaglia, J. Valencia & D. Walton (eds) *Antarctic communities: species, structure and survival.* Cambridge University Press, Cambridge: 445-52.

Fraser, W.R., W.Z. Trivelpiece, D.G. Ainley & S.G. Trivelpiece 1992. Increases in Antarctic penguin populations: reduced competition with whales or a loss of sea ice due to global warming? *Polar Biology* **11**: 525-31.

Fenton, J.H.C. & Lewis Smith, R.I. 1982. Distribution, composition and general characteristics of the moss banks of the maritime Antarctic. *British Antarctic Survey Bulletin* **51**: 215-36.

Fowbert, J.A. & Lewis Smith, R.I. 1994. Rapid population increases in native vascular plants in the Argentine Islands, Antarctic Peninsula. *Arctic and Alpine Research* **26**: 290-96.

Harris, C.M. 2001. Revision of management plans for Antarctic Protected Areas originally proposed by the United Kingdom and the United States of America: 2001 field visit report. Unpublished report, Environmental Research & Assessment, Cambridge.

Harris, C.M. (ed) 2006. *Wildlife Awareness Manual: Antarctic Peninsula, South Shetland Islands, South Orkney Islands.* First Edition. Wildlife Information Publication No. 1. Prepared for the UK Foreign & Commonwealth Office and HMS *Endurance.* Environmental Research & Assessment, Cambridge.

Heywood, R.B. 1984. Antarctic inland waters. In: R. Laws (ed) *Antarctic ecology* (Volume 1). Academic Press, London: 279-344.

Hooper, P.R. 1962. The petrology of Anvers Island and adjacent islands. *FIDS Scientific Reports* **34**.

Huiskes, A.H.L., D. Lud, T.C.W. Moerdijk-Poortviet, & J. Rozema 1999. Impact of UV-B radiation on Antarctic terrestrial vegetation. In: J. Rozema (ed) *Stratospheric ozone depletion; the effects of enhancing UV-B radiation on terrestrial ecosystems*. Blackhuys Publishers, Leiden: 313-37.

Kennicutt II, M.C. 1990. Oil spillage in Antarctica: initial report of the National Science Foundation-sponsored quick response team on the grounding of the *Bahia Paraiso*. *Environmental Science and Technology* **24**: 620-24.

Kennicutt II, M.C., T.J. McDonald, G.J. Denoux & S.J. McDonald 1992a. Hydrocarbon contamination on the Antarctic Peninsula I. Arthur Harbor – subtidal sediments. *Marine Pollution Bulletin* **24**(10): 499-506.

Kennicutt II, M.C., T.J. McDonald, G.J. Denoux & S.J. McDonald 1992b. Hydrocarbon contamination on the Antarctic Peninsula I. Arthur Harbor – inter- and subtidal limpets (*Nacella concinna*). *Marine Pollution Bulletin* **24**(10): 506-11.

Kennicutt II, M.C & Sweet, S.T. 1992. Hydrocarbon contamination on the Antarctic Peninsula III. The *Bahia Paraiso* – two years after the spill. *Marine Pollution Bulletin* **24**(9-12): 303-06.

Komárková, V. 1983. Plant communities of the Antarctic Peninsula near Palmer Station. *Antarctic Journal of the United States* **18**: 216-18.

Komárková, V. 1984. Studies of plant communities of the Antarctic Peninsula near Palmer Station. *Antarctic Journal of the United States* **19**: 180-82.

Komárková, V., S. Poncet & J. Poncet 1985. Two native Antarctic vascular plants, *Deschampsia antarctica* and *Colobanthus quitensis*: a new southernmost locality and other localities in the Antarctic Peninsula area. *Arctic and Alpine Research* **17**(4): 401-16.

Lascara, C.M., E.E. Hofmann, R.M. Ross & L.B. Quetin 1999. Seasonal variability in the distribution of Antarctic krill, *Euphausia superba*, west of the Antarctic Peninsula. *Deep Sea Research Part I: Oceanographic Research Papers* **46**(6): 951-84.

Lewis Smith, R.I. & Corner, R.W.M. 1973. Vegetation of the Arthur Harbour-Argentine Islands region of the Antarctic Peninsula. *British Antarctic Survey Bulletin* **33-34**: 89-122.

Lewis Smith, R.I. 1979. Peat forming vegetation in the Antarctic. In: E. Kivinen, L. Heikurainen & P. Pakarinen (eds), *Classification of peat and peatlands*. University of Helsinki, Helsinki: 58-67.

Lewis Smith, R.I. 1982. Plant succession and re-exposed moss banks on a deglaciated headland in Arthur Harbour, Anvers Island. *British Antarctic Survey Bulletin* **51**: 193-99.

Lewis Smith, R.I. 1996. Terrestrial and freshwater biotic components of the western Antarctic Peninsula. In: R. Ross, E. Hofmann, & L. Quetin (eds) *Foundations for ecological research west of the Antarctic Peninsula*. *Antarctic Research Series* **70**. American Geophysical Union, Washington, DC: 15-59.

Lewis Smith, R.I. 2003. The enigma of *Colobanthus quitensis* and *Deschampsia antarctica* in Antarctica. In A. Huiskes, W. Gieskes, J. Rozema, R. Schorno, S. van der Vies & W. Wolff (eds) *Antarctic biology in a global context*. Backhuys Publishers, Leiden: 234-39.

Longton, R.E. 1967. Vegetation in the maritime Antarctic. In: J. Smith (ed) A discussion on the terrestrial Antarctic ecosystem. *Philosophical Transactions of the Royal Society of London* **252B**(777): 213-35.

McDonald, S., M. Kennicutt II, K. Foster-Springer & M. Krahn 1992. Polynuclear aromatic hydrocarbon exposure in Antarctic fish. *Antarctic Journal of the United States* **27**(5): 333-35.

Moline, M.A. & Prezelin, B.B. 1996. Palmer LTER 1991-1994: long term monitoring and analysis of physical factors regulating variability in coastal Antarctic phytoplankton biomass, in situ productivity and taxanomic composition over subseasonal, seasonal and interannual time scales phytoplankton dynamics. *Marine Ecology Progress Series* **145**: 143-60.

Parker, B.C. 1972. Conservation of freshwater habitats on the Antarctic Peninsula. In: B. Parker (ed) *Conservation problems in Antarctica*. Allen Press Inc., Lawrence, Kansas: 143-162.

Parker, B.C. & Samsel, G.L. 1972. Fresh-water algae of the Antarctic Peninsula. 1. Systematics and ecology in the U.S. Palmer Station area. In: G. Llano (ed) *Antarctic terrestrial biology. Antarctic Research Series* **20**. American Geophysical Union, Washington, DC: 69-81.

Parmelee, D.F., W.R. Fraser & D.R. Neilson 1977. Birds of the Palmer Station area. *Antarctic Journal of the United States* **12**(1-2): 15-21.

Parmelee, D.F. & Parmelee, J.M. 1987. Revised penguin numbers and distribution for Anvers Island, Antarctica. *British Antarctic Survey Bulletin* **76**: 65-73.

Patterson, D.L. 2001. The effects of human activity and environmental variability on long-term changes in Adélie penguin populations at Palmer Station, Antarctica. Unpublished MSc thesis in Fish & Wildlife Management, Montana State University, Bozeman.

Patterson, D.L., E.H. Woehler, J.P. Croxall, J. Cooper, S. Poncet & W.R. Fraser (in press). Breeding distribution and population status of the northern giant petrel *Macronectes halli* and the southern giant petrel *M. giganteus. Marine Ornithology* (submitted).

Penhale, P.A., J. Coosen & E.R. Marshcoff 1997. The *Bahai Paraiso*: a case study in environmental impact, remediation and monitoring. In: B. Battaglia, J. Valencia & D. Walton (eds) *Antarctic Communities: species, structure and survival*. Cambridge University Press, Cambridge: 437-44.

Poncet, S. & Poncet, J. 1987. Censuses of penguin populations of the Antarctic Peninsula 1983-87. *British Antarctic Survey Bulletin* **77**: 109-29.

Smith, R.C. & Stammerjohn, S.E. 2001. Variations of surface air temperature and sea-ice extent in the western Antarctic Peninsula (WAP) region. *Annals of Glaciology* **33**(1): 493-500.

Smith, R.C., K.S. Baker, W.R. Fraser, E.E. Hofmann, D.M. Karl, J.M. Klinck, L.B. Quetin, B.B. Prézelin, R.M. Ross, W.Z. Trivelpiece & M. Vernet 1995. The Palmer LTER: A long-term ecological research program at Palmer Station, Antarctica. *Oceanography* **8**(3): 77-86.

Smith, R.C., S.E. Stammerjohn & K.S. Baker. 1996. Surface air temperature variations in the western Antarctic Peninsula region. In: R. Ross, E. Hofmann, & L. Quetin (eds) *Foundations for ecological research west of the Antarctic Peninsula. Antarctic Research Series* **70**. American Geophysical Union, Washington, DC: 105-12.

Smith, R.C., K.S. Baker & S.E. Stammerjohn. 1998. Exploring sea ice indexes for polar ecosystem studies. *BioScience* **48**: 83-93.

Smith, R.C., D. Ainley, K.S. Baker, E. Domack, S. Emslie, W.R. Fraser, J. Kennett, A. Leventer, E. Mosley-Thompson, S.E. Stammerjohn & M. Vernet. 1999. Marine Ecosystem Sensitivity to Climate Change. *BioScience* **49**(5): 393-404.

Smith, R.C., K.S. Baker, H.M. Dierssen, S.E. Stammerjohn, & M. Vernet 2001. Variability of primary production in an Antarctic marine ecosystem as estimated using a multi-scale sampling strategy. *American Zoologist* **41**(1): 40-56.

Smith, R.C., W.R. Fraser, S.E. Stammerjohn & M. Vernet 2003. Palmer Long-Term Ecological Research on the Antarctic marine ecosystem. In: E. Domack, A. Leventer, A. Burnett, R. Bindschadler, P. Convey & M. Kirby (eds) *Antarctic Peninsula climate variability: historical and paleoenvironmental perspectives. Antarctic Research Series* **79**. American Geophysical Union, Washington, DC: 131-44.

Stammerjohn, S.E. & Smith, R.C. 1996. Spatial and temporal variability of western Antarctic Peninsula sea ice coverage. In: R. Ross, E. Hofmann, & L. Quetin (eds) *Foundations for ecological research west of the Antarctic Peninsula. Antarctic Research Series* **70**. American Geophysical Union, Washington, DC: 81-104.

Stammerjohn, S.E. & Smith, R.C. 1997. Opposing Southern Ocean climate patterns as revealed by trends in regional sea ice coverage. *Climatic Change* **37**: 617-39.

Stammerjohn, S.E., M.R. Drinkwater, R.C. Smith & X. Liu 2003. Ice-atmosphere interactions during sea-ice advance and retreat in the western Antarctic Peninsula region. *Journal of Geophysical Research* **108** (C10) 10: 1029/2002JC001543.

Thiele D., K. Asmus, S. Dolman, C.D. Falkenberg, D. Glasgow, P. Hodda, M. McDonald, E. Oleson, A. Širovic, A. Souter, S. Moore & J. Hildebrand 2004. International Whaling Commission – Southern Ocean GLOBEC/CCAMLR collaboration: Cruise Report 2003-2004. *Journal of Cetacean Research & Management* SC/56/E24.

Trivelpiece W.Z. & Fraser, W.R. 1996. The breeding biology and distribution of Adélie penguins: adaptations to environmental variability. In: R. Ross, E. Hofmann, & L. Quetin (eds) *Foundations for ecological research west of the Antarctic Peninsula. Antarctic Research Series* **70**. American Geophysical Union, Washington, DC: 273-85.

Woehler, E.J. (ed) 1993. *The distribution and abundance of Antarctic and Subantarctic penguins.* SCAR, Cambridge.

Personal communications

Fraser, W. various personal communications 2003-08;
Patterson, D. 2006;
Lee, R. 2007;
Lewis Smith, R. 2007.

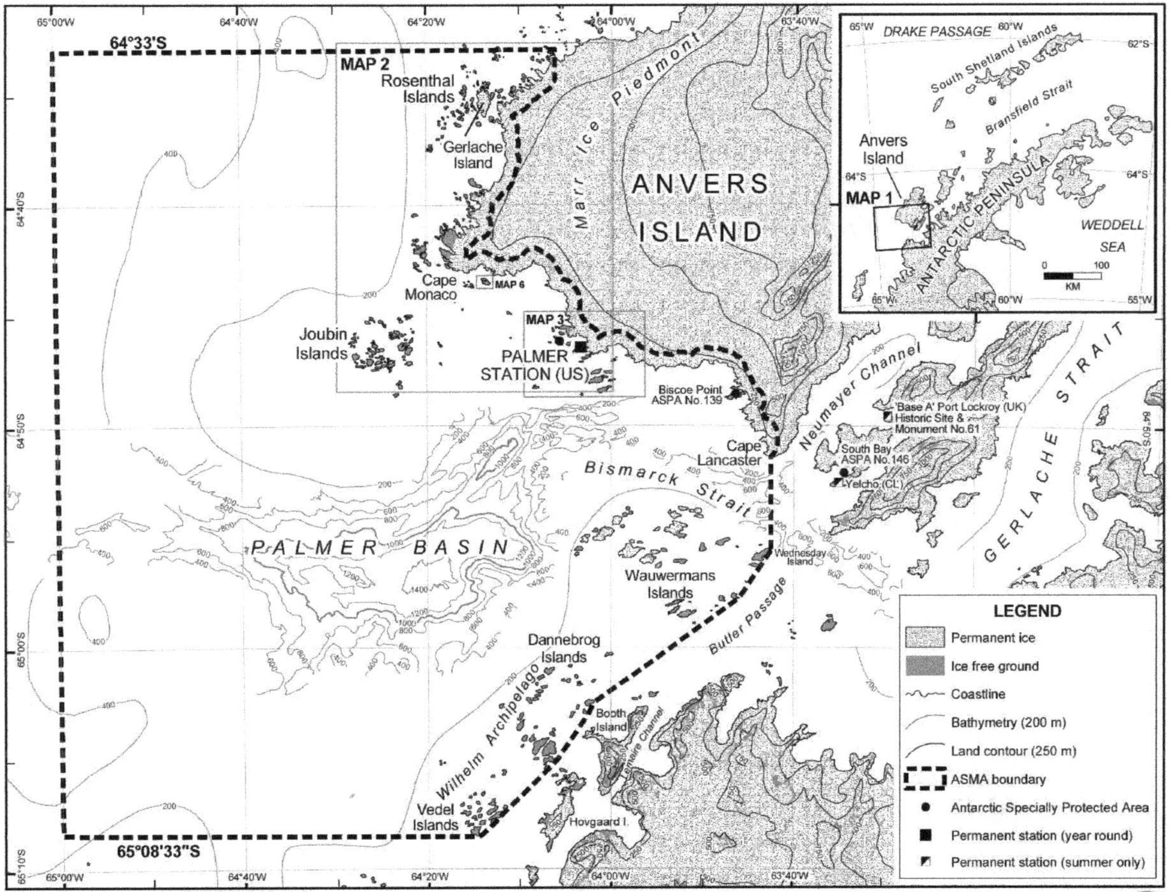

Projection: Lambert Conformal Conic - CM 64°06'; SP1 64°45'; SP2 65°; LO 63°45';
Spheroid: WGS84; Contour interval: Land - 250 m; Marine - 200 m
Data sources: Palmer Basin bathymetry: Domack et al. (2006);
Other bathymetry: GEBCO (2003);
Land features: SCAR ADD v4.1 SQ19-20 (2005)

ASMA No. 7: SW Anvers Island & Palmer Basin
Map 1: Regional map & ASMA boundary

0 5 10 15 Kilometers

06 April 2009
United States Antarctic Program
Environmental Research & Assessment

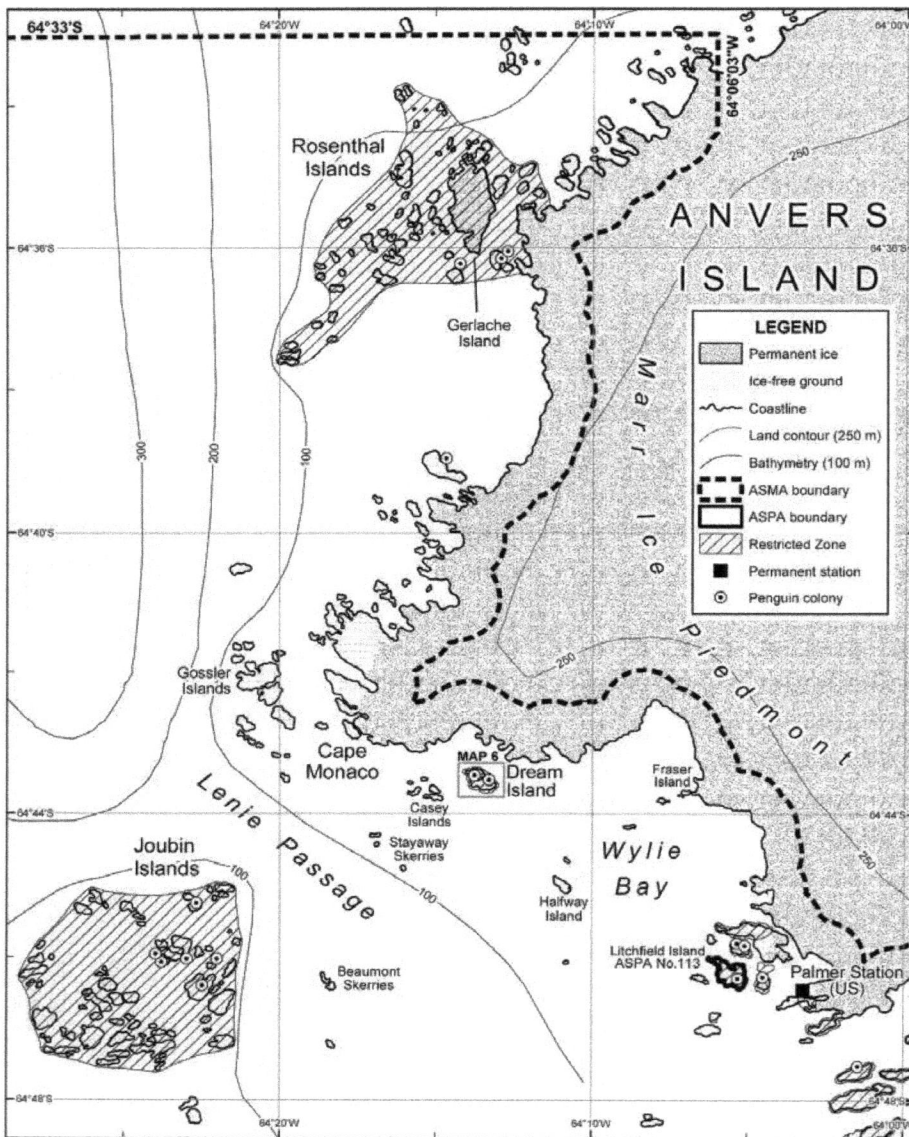

ASMA No. 7: SW Anvers Island & Palmer Basin
Map 2: SW Anvers Island Restricted Zones
Rosenthal, Joubin & Dream islands

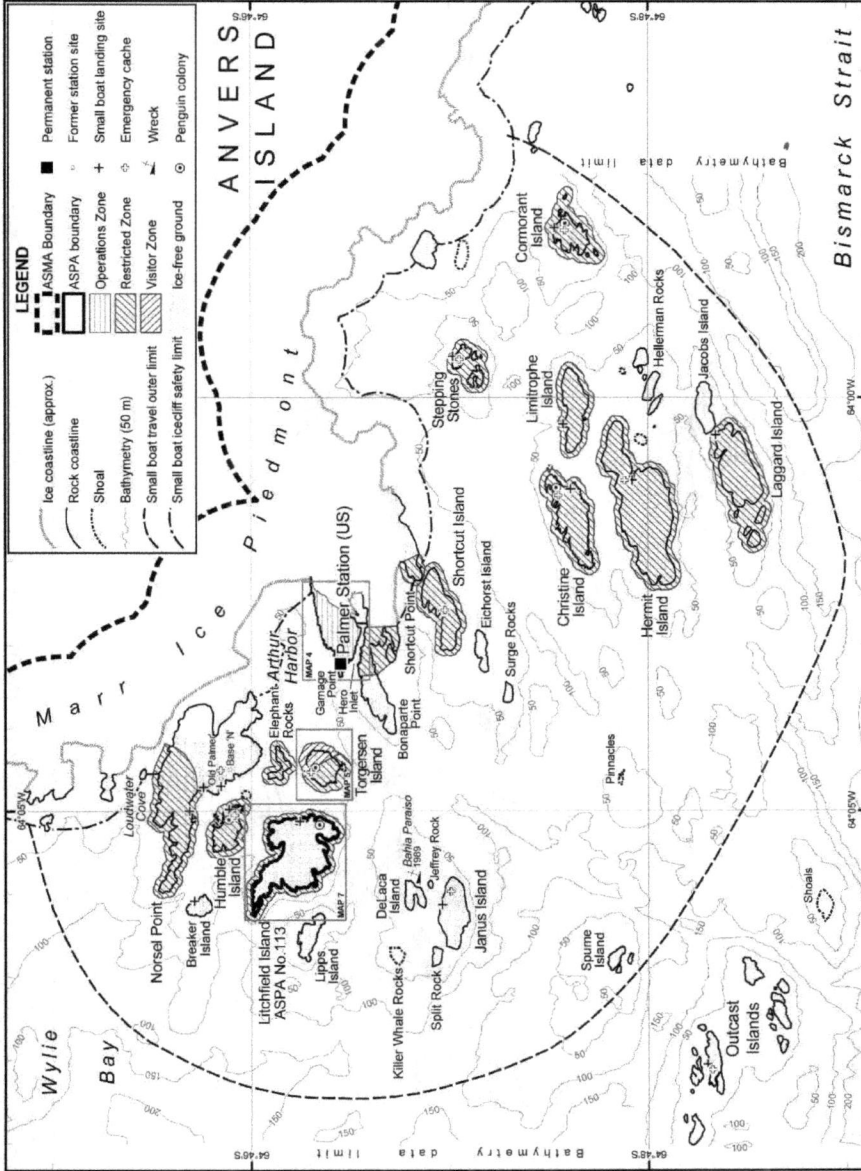

ASMA No. 7: SW Anvers Island & Palmer Basin

Map 3: Arthur Harbor & Palmer Station access

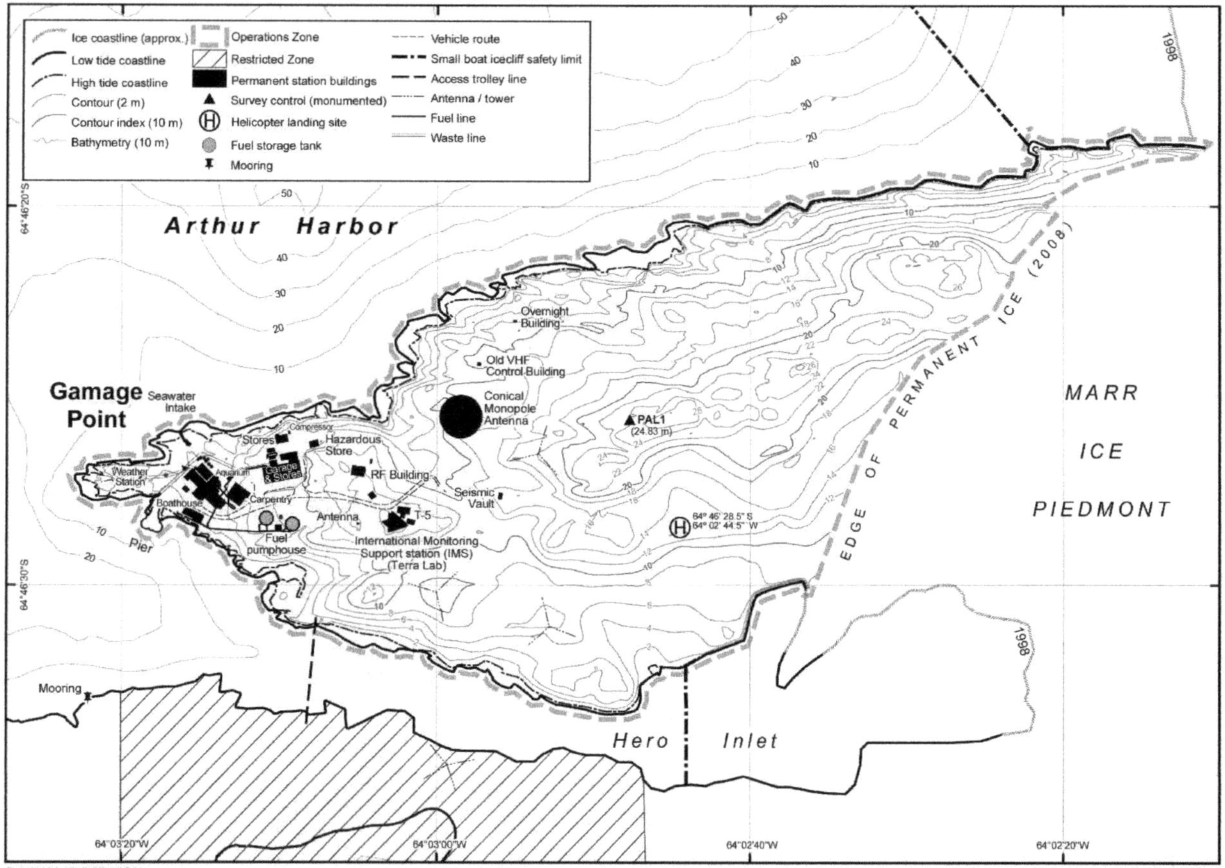

Projection: Lambert Conformal Conic
Central Meridian: 64°03'W; Standard parallels: 64°46'S, 64°48'S;
Datum: USGS PAL1; Spheroid: WGS84;
Bathymetry contour interval: 10 m
Data sources: Infrastructure RPSC CAD & Survey (2007);
Coastline: RPSC CAD & Survey (2004) & TMA3210 24v rectified image (1998);
Ice edge: TMA3210 24v rectified image (1998);
Bathymetry derived from Asper & Gallagher PRIMO survey (2004)

ASMA No. 7: SW Anvers Island & Palmer Basin

Map 4: Palmer Station Operations Zone

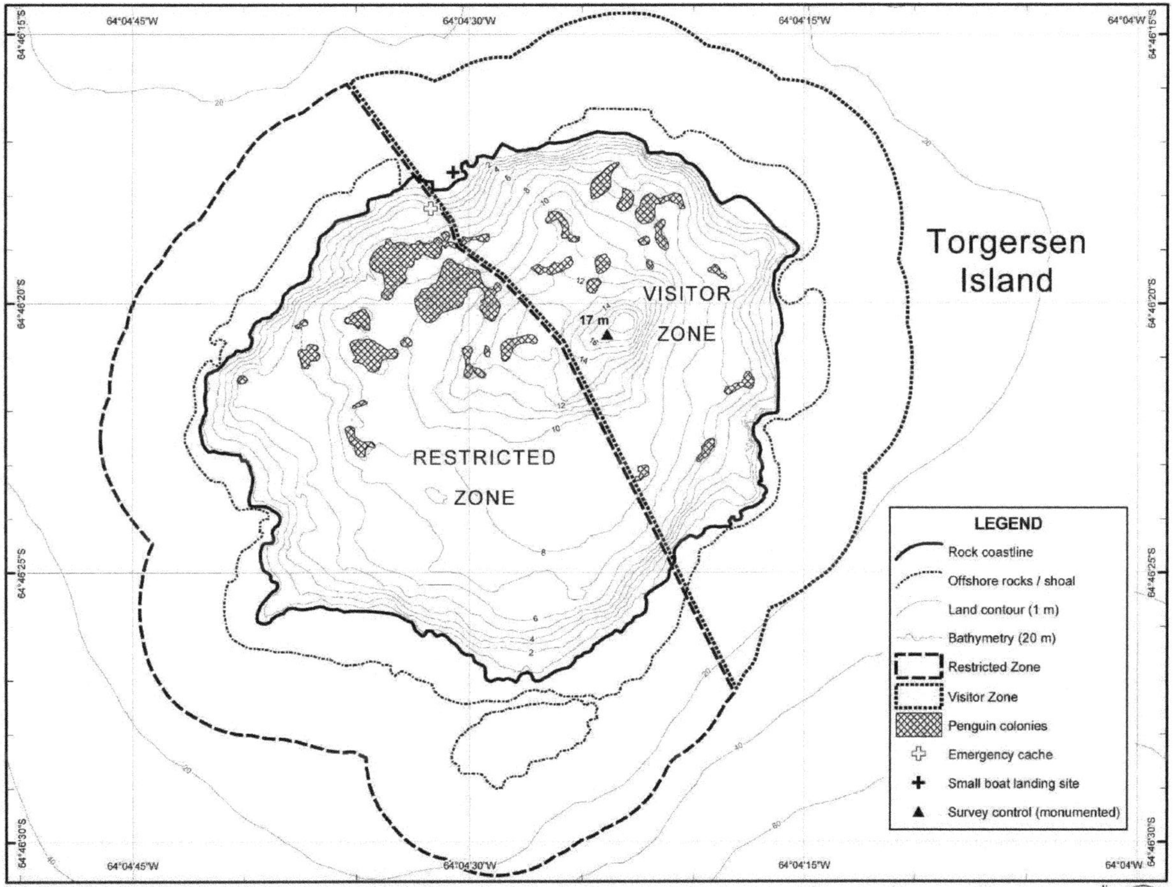

Projection: Lambert Conformal Conic; Central Meridian: 64°04'30"W;
Standard parallels: 64°46'S, 64°48'S; Datum: USGS TOR1; Spheroid: WGS84
Contour interval: Land - 1 m; Marine - 20 m
Data sources: Coastline & penguin colonies derived from USGS orthophoto (2001) & Patterson (2001).
Bathymetry derived from Asper & Gallagher PRIMO survey (2004).

ASMA No. 7: SW Anvers Island & Palmer Basin
Map 5: Torgersen Island Zones

11 December 2008
United States Antarctic Program
Environmental Research & Assessment

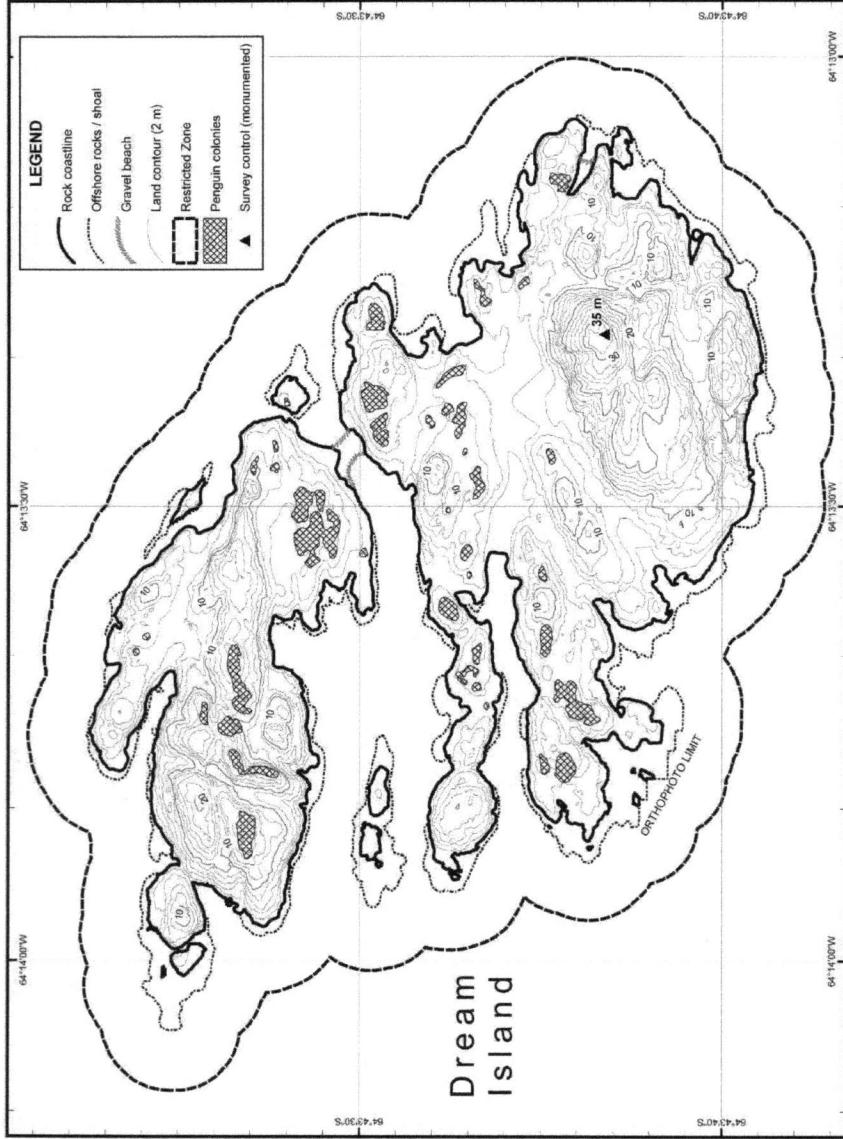

ASMA No. 7: SW Anvers Island & Palmer Basin

Map 6: Dream Island Restricted Zone

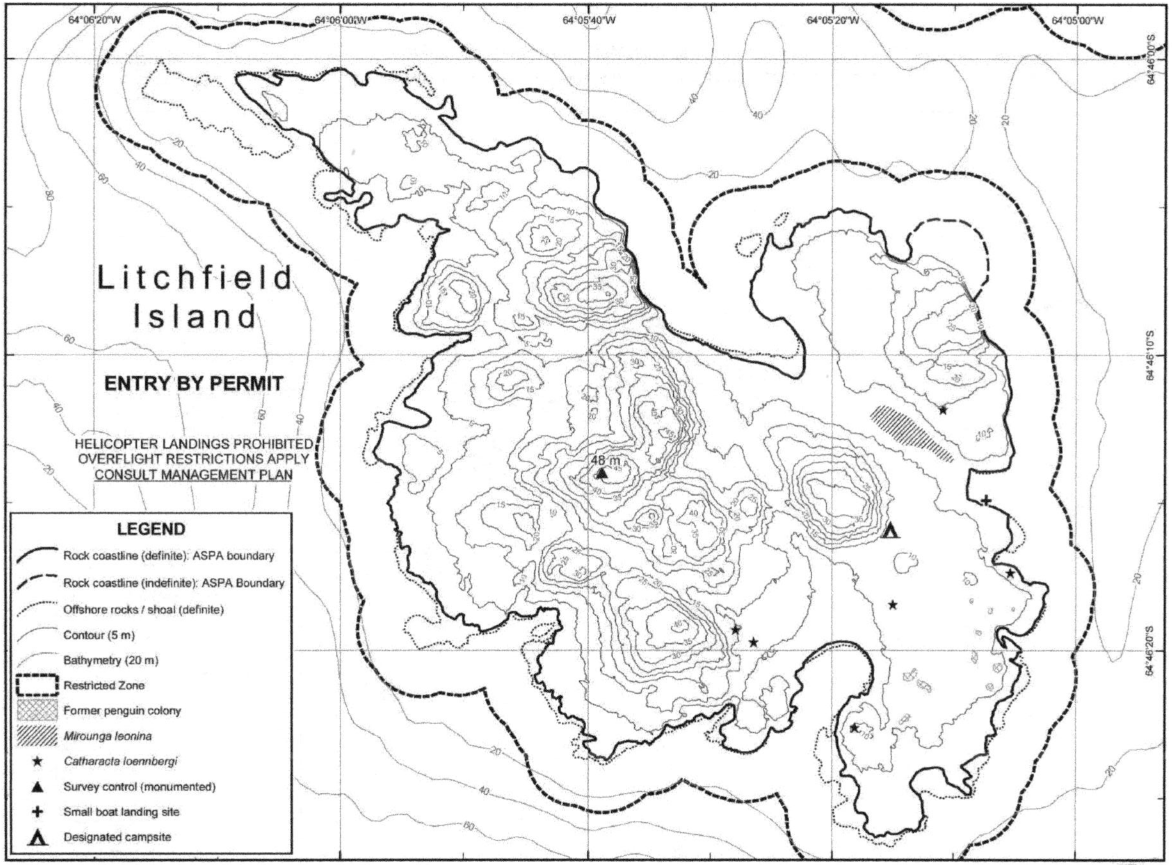
64°06'20"W
64°06'00"W
64°05'40"W
64°05'20"W
64°05'00"W
64°46'00"S
64°46'10"S
64°46'20"S
Litchfield Island
ENTRY BY PERMIT
HELICOPTER LANDINGS PROHIBITED
OVERFLIGHT RESTRICTIONS APPLY
CONSULT MANAGEMENT PLAN
48 m
LEGEND
Rock coastline (definite): ASPA boundary
Rock coastline (indefinite): ASPA Boundary
Offshore rocks / shoal (definite)
Contour (5 m)
Bathymetry (20 m)
Restricted Zone
Former penguin colony
Mirounga leonina
Catharacta loennbergi
Survey control (monumented)
Small boat landing site
Designated campsite
0 50 100 150 200
Meters
N
06 February 2009
United States Antarctic Program
Environmental Research & Assessment

Projection: Lambert Conformal Conic
Central Meridian: 64°06'W; Standard parallels: 64°46'S, 64°48'S;
Datum: USGS LIT1 (1999); Spheroid: WGS84;
Contour interval: Land - 5 m; Marine - 20 m.
Definite coastline & seal colony derived from USGS orthophoto (2001);
Indefinite coastline from TMA3210 24V rectified image (1998);
Bathymetry derived from Asper & Gallagher PRIMO survey (2004);
Bird data W. Fraser (2001-2009).

ASMA No. 7: SW Anvers Island & Palmer Basin

Map 7: Litchfield Island, ASPA No.113

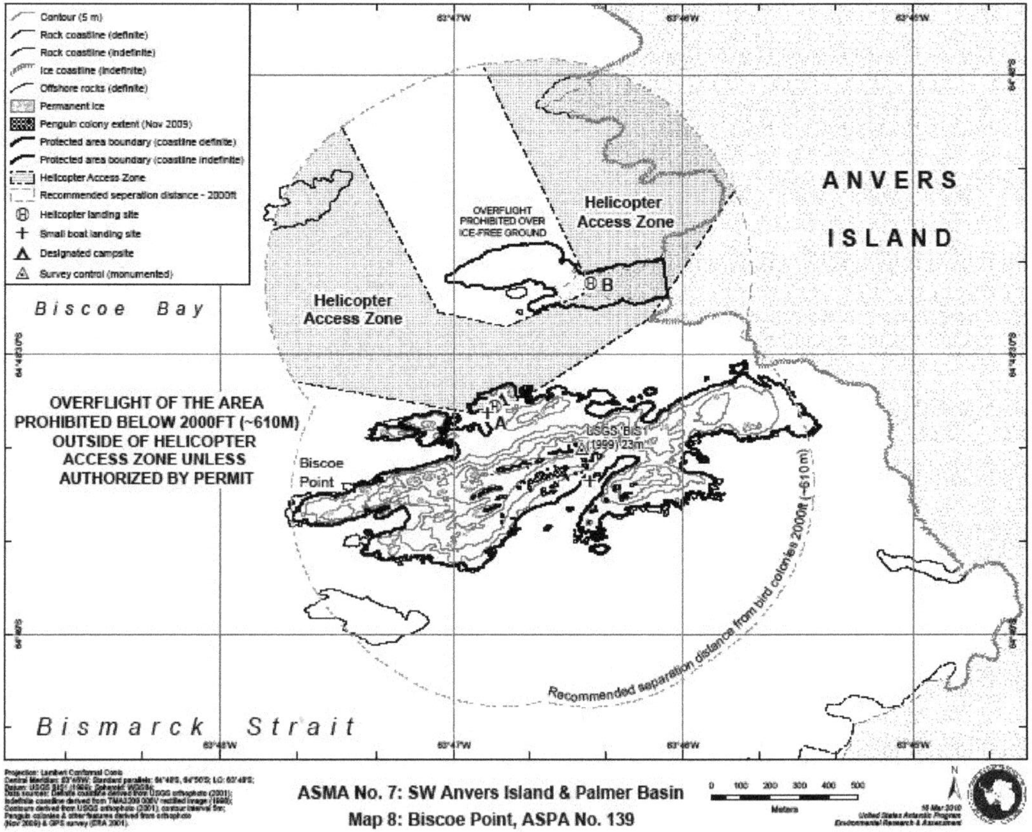
Contour (5 m)
Rock coastline (definite)
Rock coastline (indefinite)
Ice coastline (indefinite)
Offshore rocks (definite)
Permanent ice
Penguin colony extent (Nov 2009)
Protected area boundary (coastline definite)
Protected area boundary (coastline indefinite)
Helicopter Access Zone
Recommended seperation distance - 2000ft
Helicopter landing site
Small boat landing site
Designated campsite
Survey control (monumented)
Biscoe Bay
Bismarck Strait
ANVERS ISLAND
Helicopter Access Zone
Helicopter Access Zone
OVERFLIGHT PROHIBITED OVER ICE-FREE GROUND
OVERFLIGHT OF THE AREA PROHIBITED BELOW 2000FT (~610M) OUTSIDE OF HELICOPTER ACCESS ZONE UNLESS AUTHORIZED BY PERMIT
Biscoe Point
USGS BIS1 (1999) 23m
Recommended separation distance from bird colonies 2000ft (~610m)
63°48'W
63°47'W
63°46'W
63°45'W
ASMA No. 7: SW Anvers Island & Palmer Basin
Map 8: Biscoe Point, ASPA No. 139
0 100 200 300 400 500
Meters

PART III

Opening and Closing Addresses and Reports from ATCM XXXIII

1. Statements at the Signing of the Headquarters Agreement for the Secretariat of the Antarctic Treaty

Signature of the Headquarters agreement of the Antarctic Treaty Secretariat between Argentina and the Antarctic Treaty Consultative Meeting

Speech by Mr. Jorge Taiana, Minister of Foreign Affairs

(Punta del Este, Wednesday 12 May – 6 PM)

Mr. Jose Mujica, President of the Eastern Republic of Uruguay, Dr. Puceiro Ripoll, President of the Antarctic Treaty Consultative Meeting, Mr. Manfred Reinke, Executive Secretary, distinguished delegates, Ladies and Gentlemen:

First of all, allow me to thank the Eastern Republic of Uruguay for offering to host the XXXIII Antarctic Treaty Consultative Meeting here in the beautiful city of Punta del Este, the year before it will fall upon us to organize the next meeting, which will take place in Buenos Aires in June 2011.

It is an honor to be able to attend this meeting with all of you. On this occasion, the headquarters agreement is being signed between the Argentine Republic and the Antarctic Treaty Consultative Meeting represented by its President, Dr. Puceiro Ripoll. the Antarctic Treaty Secretariat was established in the city of Buenos Aires by Measure 1 (2003) and its formal framework was defined during the XXVI Antarctic Treaty Consultative Meeting in Madrid, Spain. Although for all practical purposes, the Secretariat began its work in 2004, its foundation is consolidated here today.

The Secretariat is the result of the joint efforts carried out for several years by all of the Consultative Parties, with the noble intent of making such an important international cooperation instrument more efficient, and to grant its Parties the necessary instruments and institutions to foster and further facilitate the development of science and international cooperation, two of the main pillars of all activities carried out in Antarctica.

As a result of the consensus reached in 2001 in Saint Petersburg to establish the Secretariat in Buenos Aires, the negotiations related to its functional aspects have traveled a long road. Stops along the way included Buenos Aires, Warsaw, Buenos Aires once again, and then Madrid and Cape Town where the negotiations finally concluded and where the first Executive Secretary, Mr. Johannes Huber, was elected. Mr. Huber recently finished a successful and productive first mandate as the head of the Secretariat.

More recently, in October of last year, Measure 1 (2003) entered into force, thereby concluding what we may consider the first stage of the Secretariat.

The growing complexity and variety of the demands of the Antarctic have convinced the parties of the need for an administrative tool that would assist in the organization of meetings of both the ATCM and the Committee for Environmental Protection. In view of the new challenges, the agendas of these two bodies have grown considerably over the past years.

In this framework, protecting the environment of the Antarctic is probably the most important common concern. This is what led the consultative Parties to establish the Secretariat so quickly, as they were convinced that in particular, the tasks of the Committee for Environmental protection would largely benefit from the Secretariat. I believe this has been the case.

Argentina has always been committed to the principles and goals of the Antarctic Treaty and has upheld them firmly in a framework of close and honest international cooperation in Antarctica. This cooperation has covered a wide range of science and logistics.

Argentina is also privileged and proud to have worked for more than 106 years at the oldest scientific station in Antarctica: Orcadas. Founded in 1904, it was the only permanent station in Antarctica for decades. Ever since, the station has been contributing meteorological data that are essential for many of today's scientific tasks related to climate change and global change, both of which are issues of analysis and concern.

But this is only part of my country's experience and commitment to Antarctica and science with regard to the white continent. In conjunction with this aim, our ultimate goal is to preserve its pristine environment.

I consider the choice of Buenos Aires as the Secretariat's headquarters as an acknowledgement of this commitment, and I am here today to express my appreciation to you for choosing us.

Therefore, and as evidence of the importance that Argentina places on its activities in the Antarctic, the Argentine Government, by signing the headquarters agreement, has decided to take advantage of this opportunity to formalize the operations of the Secretariat on the premises it has made available in Buenos Aires.

At the same time, it is only fair to acknowledge the efforts made by the Consultative Parties and their constructive approach throughout the negotiations in order to reach consensus. This reflects the strong spirit of cooperation that prevails between our countries in Antarctica. The Antarctic Treaty, with its goal of peace and its international cooperation in scientific research, has become an example of how states with common goals can leave aside their differences in order to work together. The ultimate goal is to protect a continent whose preservation is of the utmost importance for mankind.

Finally, I would like to give my regards to the newly appointed Executive Secretary, Dr. Manfred Reinke, at his first Consultative Meeting in this post, and to reiterate our warm welcome to Argentina. I wish to emphasize, Dr. Reinke, that you will always have our support in the tasks that await you at the helm of the Secretariat, thus continuing what Mr. Huber started with all the Secretariat's collaborators, who have performed so efficiently.

I am convinced that the Headquarters Agreement signed today constitutes a solid basis to complete the present tasks and face any challenges that may arise in the future.

I thus reiterate my Country's firm commitment to continue our cooperation to improve the Secretariat. We look forward to welcoming all of you in Buenos Aires next year.

Thank you very much.

Statement by Mr. Roberto Puceiro, Chair of the ATCM XXXIII

When the time came to evaluate this instrument, two things came to mind. First, a few memories, and then some reflections on these memories. The memories of students who continuously complain about the fact that in public international law, the process in which treaties are entered into is so complex that nobody understands it. As a result, although treaties are so important, their approval is difficult to understand.

This is true – to a certain extent. But we have to go beyond this question to address the metaphysics of the problem, because an agreement is, ultimately, a path towards harmony and to solutions that must be taken step by step. The way in which treaties are regulated was designed in order to avoid sending an ambassador and receiving a corpse in return. In other words, political groups gradually agreed on how to adopt treaties, and, like the agreement we are presently signing, the path is progressively cleared in order for parties to engage.

The document we are signing today follows this path, and if we look at the metaphysics of the issue, as it were, we understand that behind the agreement, there is a philosophy that protects and preserves this agreement.

At the heart of any valid and effective agreement that has a future, there is a philosophy about which the negotiating parties remain unaware. But therein lies the novel aspect, something different, something that goes beyond the words, the signatures and the difficulties that students may face when trying to understand the process of entering into treaties.

In this case, then, if we read between the lines of the agreement we have just signed on behalf of the Antarctic Treaty Consultative Meeting, we will discover its hidden values. The agreement we have entered into is a tribute to cooperation, peace, coordination and good faith: it allows for the free and effective development of the Antarctic Treaty Consultative Meeting.

Allow me then to insist: beyond this agreement, we see the light of the principles that lead to international understanding and concord. And for this reason, we must thank the Argentine Republic, and particularly its messenger, Minister Jorge Taiana. Because what we are actually doing here is historical in terms of establishing an instrument, but it is also historical because we are seeing how close our ties are each day. And the agreement we signed today proves that there are a number of values behind a simple agreement and that we often merely look at the outcome without stopping to look at the richness behind it.

With this agreement, the Argentine Republic and the Antarctic Treaty Consultative Meeting have laid down the path we will travel together to achieve what we have promised to achieve. We believe that the agreement has been signed in a climate of mutual understanding and goodwill, and with the aim of establishing the best possible agreement, one that will serve as an open bridge between the Antarctic Treaty Consultative Meeting and the Argentine Republic.

That is why, if you allow me to, I will once again thank the Argentine Republic, and namely its Minister of Foreign Affairs, on behalf of the other Consultative Parties, by saying how grateful we all are for everything Argentina has done in this field. The path has been laid and our expectations are high, and all that remains is for the parties to take the outstretched hands and do what they have promised to do.

Thank you very much.

2. Reports by Depositaries and Observers

Report of the Depositary Government of the Antarctic Treaty and its Protocol in accordance with Recommendation XIII-2

This report covers events with respect to the Antarctic Treaty and the Protocol on Environmental Protection.

In the past year, there has been one accession to the Antarctic Treaty and one accession to the Protocol on Environmental Protection. Portugal acceded to the Antarctic Treaty on January 29, 2010, and Monaco acceded to the Protocol on July 1, 2009. There are forty-eight (48) Parties to the Treaty and thirty-four (34) Parties to the Protocol.

The following countries have provided notification that they have designated the persons so noted as Arbitrators in accordance with Article 2(1) of the Schedule to the Protocol on Environmental Protection:

Bulgaria	Mrs. Guenka Beleva	30 July 2004
Chile	Amb. María Teresa Infante	June 2005
	Amb. Jorge Berguño	June 2005
	Dr. Francisco Orrego	June 2005
Finland	Amb. Holger Bertil Rotkirch	14 June 2006
India	Prof. Upendra Baxi	6 October 2004
	Mr. Ajai Saxena	6 October 2004
	Dr. N. Khare	6 October 2004
Japan	Judge Shunji Yanai	18 July 2008
Rep. of Korea	Prof. Park Ki Gab	21 October 2008
United States	Prof. Daniel Bodansky	1 May 2008
	Mr. David Colson	1 May 2008

Lists of Parties to the Treaty, to the Protocol, and of Recommendations/Measures and their approvals are attached.

The Antarctic Treaty

Done: Washington; December 1, 1959

Entry into force: June 23, 1961
In accordance with Article XIII, the Treaty was subject to ratification by the signatory States and is open for accession by any State which is a Member of the United Nations, or by any other State which may be invited to accede to the Treaty with the consent of all the Contracting Parties whose representatives are entitled to participate in the meetings provided for under Article IX of the Treaty; instruments of ratification and instruments of accession shall be deposited with the Government of the United States of America. Upon the deposit of instruments of ratification by all the signatory States, the Treaty entered into force for those States and for States which had deposited instruments of accession to the Treaty. Thereafter, the Treaty enters into force for any acceding State upon deposit of its instrument of accession.

Legend: (no mark) = ratification; a = accession; d = succession; w = withdrawal or equivalent action

Participant	Signature	Consent to be bound		Other Action	Notes
Argentina	December 1, 1959	June 23, 1961			
Australia	December 1, 1959	June 23, 1961			
Austria		August 25, 1987	a		
Belarus		December 27, 2006	a		
Belgium	December 1, 1959	July 26, 1960			
Brazil		May 16, 1975	a		
Bulgaria		September 11, 1978	a		
Canada		May 4, 1988	a		
Chile	December 1, 1959	June 23, 1961			
China		June 8, 1983	a		
Colombia		January 31, 1989	a		
Cuba		August 16, 1984	a		
Czech Republic		January 1, 1993	d		i
Denmark		May 20, 1965	a		
Ecuador		September 15, 1987	a		
Estonia		May 17, 2001	a		
Finland		May 15, 1984	a		
France	December 1, 1959	September 16, 1960			
Germany		February 5, 1979	a		ii
Greece		January 8, 1987	a		
Guatemala		July 31, 1991	a		
Hungary		January 27, 1984	a		
India		August 19, 1983	a		
Italy		March 18, 1981	a		
Japan	December 1, 1959	August 4, 1960			
Korea (DPRK)		January 21, 1987	a		
Korea (ROK)		November 28, 1986	a		
Monaco		May 31, 2008	a		
Netherlands		March 30, 1967	a		iii
New Zealand	December 1, 1959	November 1, 1960			

Norway	December 1, 1959	August 24, 1960			
Papua New Guinea		March 16, 1981	d		iv
Peru		April 10, 1981	a		
Poland		June 8, 1961	a		
Portugal		January 29, 2010	a		
Romania		September 15, 1971	a		v
Russian Federation	December 1, 1959	November 2, 1960			vi
Slovak Republic		January 1, 1993	d		vii
South Africa	December 1, 1959	June 21, 1960			
Spain		March 31, 1982	a		
Sweden		April 24, 1984	a		
Switzerland		November 15, 1990	a		
Turkey		January 24, 1996	a		
Ukraine		October 28, 1992	a		
United Kingdom	December 1, 1959	May 31, 1960			
United States	December 1, 1959	August 18, 1960			
Uruguay		January 11, 1980	a		viii
Venezuela		March 24, 1999	a		

---

[i] Effective date of succession by the Czech Republic. Czechoslovakia deposited an instrument of accession to the Treaty on June 14, 1962. On December 31, 1992, at midnight, Czechoslovakia ceased to exist and was succeeded by two separate and independent states, the Czech Republic and the Slovak Republic.

[ii] The Embassy of the Federal Republic of Germany in Washington transmitted to the Department of State a diplomatic note, dated October 2, 1990, which reads as follows:

"The Embassy of the Federal Republic of Germany presents its compliments to the Department of State and has the honor to inform the Government of the United States of America as the depositary Government of the Antarctic Treaty that, t[h]rough the accession of the German Democratic Republic to the Federal Republic of Germany with effect from October 3, 1990, the two German states will unite to form one sovereign state which, as a contracting party to the Antarctic Treaty, will remain bound by the provisions of the Treaty and subject to those recommendations adopted at the 15 consultative meetings which the Federal Republic of Germany has approved. From the date of German unity, the Federal Republic of Germany will act under the designation of "Germany" within the framework of the [A]ntarctic system.
"The Embassy would be grateful if the Government of the United States of America could inform all contracting parties to the Antarctic Treaty of the contents of this note.
"The Embassy of the Federal Republic of Germany avails itself of this opportunity to renew to the Department of State the assurances of its highest consideration."

Prior to unification, the German Democratic Republic deposited an instrument of accession to the Treaty, accompanied by a declaration, on November 19, 1974, and the Federal Republic of Germany deposited an instrument of accession to the Treaty, accompanied by a statement, on February 5, 1979.

[iii] The instrument of accession to the Treaty by the Netherlands states that the accession is for the Kingdom in Europe, Suriname and the Netherlands Antilles; as of January 1, 1986, Aruba as a separate entity.

[iv] Date of deposit of notification of succession by Papua New Guinea; effective September 16, 1975, the date of its independence.

[v] The instrument of accession to the Treaty by Romania was accompanied by a note of the Ambassador of the Socialist Republic of Romania to the United States of America, dated September 15, 1971, which reads as follows:
"Dear Mr. Secretary:
"Submitting the instrument of adhesion of the Socialist Republic of Romania to the Antarctic Treaty, signed at Washington on December 1, 1959, I have the honor to inform you of the following:
'The Council of State of the Socialist Republic of Romania states that the provisions of the first paragraph of the article XIII of the Antarctic Treaty are not in accordance with the principle according to which the multilateral treaties whose

object and purposes are concerning the international community, as a whole, should be opened for universal participation.'

"I am kindly requesting you, Mr. Secretary, to forward to all parties concerned the text of the Romanian instrument of adhesion to the Antarctic Treaty, as well as the text of this letter containing the above mentioned statement of the Romanian Government.

"I avail myself of this opportunity to renew to you, Mr. Secretary, the assurances of my highest consideration."

Copies of the Ambassador's letter and the Romanian instrument of accession to the Treaty were transmitted to the Antarctic Treaty parties by the Secretary of State's circular note dated October 1, 1971.

[vi] The Treaty was signed and ratified by the former Union of Soviet Socialist Republics. By a note dated January 13, 1992, the Russian Federation informed the United States Government that it "continues to perform the rights and fulfil the obligations following from the international agreements signed by the Union of Soviet Socialist Republics."

[vii] Effective date of succession by the Slovak Republic. Czechoslovakia deposited an instrument of accession to the Treaty on June 14, 1962. On December 31, 1992, at midnight, Czechoslovakia ceased to exist and was succeeded by two separate and independent states, the Czech Republic and the Slovak Republic.

[viii] The instrument of accession to the Treaty by Uruguay was accompanied by a declaration, a Department of State English translation of which reads as follows:

"The Government of the Oriental Republic of Uruguay considers that, through its accession to the Antarctic Treaty signed at Washington (United States of America) on December 1, 1959, it helps to affirm the principles of using Antarctica exclusively for peaceful purposes, of prohibiting any nuclear explosion or radioactive waste disposal in this area, of freedom of scientific research in Antarctica in the service of mankind, and of international cooperation to achieve these objectives, which are established in said Treaty.

"Within the context of these principles Uruguay proposes, through a procedure based on the principle of legal equality, the establishment of a general and definitive statute on Antarctica in which, respecting the rights of States as recognized in international law, the interests of all States involved and of the international community as a whole would be considered equitably.

"The decision of the Uruguayan Government to accede to the Antarctic Treaty is based not only on the interest which, like all members of the international community, Uruguay has in Antarctica, but also on a special, direct, and substantial interest which arises from its geographic location, from the fact that its Atlantic coastline faces the continent of Antarctica, from the resultant influence upon its climate, ecology, and marine biology, from the historic bonds which date back to the first expeditions which ventured to explore that continent and its waters, and also from the obligations assumed in conformity with the Inter-American Treaty of Reciprocal Assistance which includes a portion of Antarctic territory in the zone described in Article 4, by virtue of which Uruguay shares the responsibility of defending the region.

"In communicating its decision to accede to the Antarctic Treaty, the Government of the Oriental Republic of Uruguay declares that it reserves its rights in Antarctica in accordance with international law."

PROTOCOL ON ENVIRONMENTAL PROTECTION TO THE ANTARCTIC TREATY

Signed at Madrid on October 4, 1991*

State	Date of Signature	Date deposit of Ratification, Acceptance (A) or Approval (AA)	Date deposit of Accession	Date of entry into force	Date Acceptance ANNEX V**	Date of entry into force of Annex V
CONSULTATIVE PARTIES						
Argentina	Oct. 4, 1991	Oct. 28, 1993 [3]		Jan. 14, 1998	Sept. 8, 2000 (A) Aug. 4, 1995 (B)	May 24, 2002
Australia	Oct. 4, 1991	Apr. 6, 1994		Jan. 14, 1998	Apr. 6, 1994 (A) June 7, 1995 (B)	May 24, 2002
Belgium	Oct. 4, 1991	Apr. 26, 1996		Jan. 14, 1998	Apr. 26, 1996 (A) Oct. 23, 2000 (B)	May 24, 2002
Brazil	Oct. 4, 1991	Aug. 15, 1995		Jan. 14, 1998	May 20, 1998 (B)	May 24, 2002
Bulgaria			April 21, 1998	May 21, 1998	May 5, 1999 (AB)	May 24, 2002
Chile	Oct. 4, 1991	Jan. 11, 1995		Jan. 14, 1998	Mar. 25, 1998 (B)	May 24, 2002
China	Oct. 4, 1991	Aug. 2, 1994		Jan. 14, 1998	Jan. 26, 1995 (AB)	May 24, 2002
Ecuador	Oct. 4, 1991	Jan. 4, 1993		Jan. 14, 1998	May 11, 2001 (A) Nov. 15, 2001 (B)	May 24, 2002
Finland	Oct. 4, 1991	Nov. 1, 1996 (A)		Jan. 14, 1998	Nov. 1, 1996 (A) Apr. 2, 1997 (B)	May 24, 2002
France	Oct. 4, 1991	Feb. 5, 1993 (AA)		Jan. 14, 1998	Apr. 26, 1995 (B) Nov. 18, 1998 (A)	May 24, 2002
Germany	Oct. 4, 1991	Nov. 25, 1994		Jan. 14, 1998	Nov. 25, 1994 (A) Sept. 1, 1998 (B)	May 24, 2002
India	July 2, 1992	Apr. 26, 1996		Jan. 14, 1998	May 24, 2002 (B)	May 24, 2002
Italy	Oct. 4, 1991	Mar. 31, 1995		Jan. 14, 1998	May 31, 1995 (A) Feb. 11, 1998 (B)	May 24, 2002
Japan	Sept. 29, 1992	Dec. 15, 1997 (A)		Jan. 14, 1998	Dec. 15, 1997 (AB)	May 24, 2002
Korea, Rep. of	July 2, 1992	Jan. 2, 1996		Jan. 14, 1998	June 5, 1996 (B)	May 24, 2002
Netherlands	Oct. 4, 1991	Apr. 14, 1994 (A) [6]		Jan. 14, 1998	Mar. 18, 1998 (B)	May 24, 2002
New Zealand	Oct. 4, 1991	Dec. 22, 1994		Jan. 14, 1998	Oct. 21, 1992 (B)	May 24, 2002
Norway	Oct. 4, 1991	June 16, 1993		Jan. 14, 1998	Oct. 13, 1993 (B)	May 24, 2002
Peru	Oct. 4, 1991	Mar. 8, 1993		Jan. 14, 1998	Mar. 8, 1993 (A) Mar. 17, 1999 (B)	May 24, 2002
Poland	Oct. 4, 1991	Nov. 1, 1995		Jan. 14, 1998	Sept. 20, 1995 (B)	May 24, 2002
Russian Federation	Oct. 4, 1991	Aug. 6, 1997		Jan. 14, 1998	June 19, 2001 (B)	May 24, 2002

South Africa	Oct. 4, 1991	Aug. 3, 1995		Jan. 14, 1998	June 14, 1995 (B)	May 24, 2002
Spain	Oct. 4, 1991	July 1, 1992		Jan. 14, 1998	Dec. 8, 1993 (A) / Feb. 18, 2000 (B)	May 24, 2002
Sweden	Oct. 4, 1991	Mar. 30, 1994		Jan. 14, 1998	Mar. 30, 1994 (A) / Apr. 7, 1994 (B)	May 24, 2002
Ukraine			May 25, 2001	June 24, 2001	May 25, 2001 (A)	May 24, 2002
United Kingdom	Oct. 4, 1991	Apr. 25, 1995[5]		Jan. 14, 1998	May 21, 1996 (B)	May 24, 2002
United States	Oct. 4, 1991	Apr. 17, 1997		Jan. 14, 1998	Apr. 17, 1997 (A) / May 6, 1998 (B)	May 24, 2002
Uruguay	Oct. 4, 1991	Jan. 11, 1995		Jan. 14, 1998	May 15, 1995 (B)	May 24, 2002

** The following denotes date relating either
to acceptance of Annex V or approval of Recommendation XVI-10
(A) Acceptance of Annex V   (B) Approval of Recommendation XVI-10

NON-CONSULTATIVE PARTIES

State	Date of Signature	Ratification Acceptance or Approval	Date deposit of Accession	Date of entry into force	Date Acceptance ANNEX V**	Date of entry into force of Annex V
Austria	Oct. 4, 1991					
Belarus			July 16, 2008	Aug. 15, 2008		
Canada	Oct. 4, 1991	Nov. 13, 2003		Dec. 13, 2003		
Colombia	Oct. 4, 1991					
Cuba						
Czech Rep. [1,2]	Jan. 1, 1993	Aug. 25, 2004 [4]		Sept. 24, 2004		
Denmark	July 2, 1992					
Estonia				Jan. 14, 1998		
Greece	Oct. 4, 1991	May 23, 1995				
Guatemala						
Hungary	Oct. 4, 1991					
Korea, DPR of	Oct. 4, 1991					
Monaco						
Papua New Guinea			July 1, 2009	July 31, 2009		
Romania	Oct. 4, 1991	Feb. 3, 2003		Mar. 5, 2003	Feb. 3, 2003	Mar. 5, 2003
Slovak Rep. [1,2]	Jan. 1, 1993					
Switzerland	Oct. 4, 1991					
Turkey						
Venezuela						

• Signed at Madrid on October 4, 1991; thereafter at Washington until October 3, 1992.
The Protocol will enter into force initially on the thirtieth day following the date of deposit of instruments of ratification, acceptance, approval or accession by all States which were Antarctic Treaty Consultative Parties at the date on which this Protocol was adopted. (Article 23)

** Adopted at Bonn on October 17, 1991 at XVIth Antarctic Consultative Meeting.

1. Signed for Czech & Slovak Federal Republic on Oct. 2, 1992 - Czechoslovakia accepts the jurisdiction of the International Court of Justice and Arbitral Tribunal for the settlement of disputes according to Article 19, paragraph 1. On December 31, 1992, at midnight, Czechoslovakia ceased to exist and was succeeded by two separate and independent states, the Czech Republic and the Slovak Republic.
2. Effective date of succession in respect of signature by Czechoslovakia which is subject to ratification by the Czech Republic and the Slovak Republic.
3. Accompanied by declaration, with informal translation provided by the Embassy of Argentina, which reads as follows: "The Argentine Republic declares that in as much as the Protocol to the Antarctic Treaty on the Protection of the Environment is a Complementary Agreement of the Antarctic Treaty and that its Article 4 fully respects what has been stated in Article IV, Subsection 1, Paragraph A) of said Treaty, none of its stipulations should be interpreted or be applied as affecting its rights, based on legal titles, acts of possession, contiguity and geological continuity in the region South of parallel 60, in which it has proclaimed and maintained its sovereignty."
4. Accompanied by declaration, with informal translation provided by the Embassy of the Czech Republic, which reads as follows: "The Czech Republic accepts the jurisdiction of the International Court of Justice and of the Arbitral Tribunal under Article 19, paragraph 1, of the Protocol on Environmental Protection to the Antarctic Treaty, done at Madrid on October 4, 1991."
5. Ratification on behalf of the United Kingdom of Great Britain and Northern Ireland, the Bailiwick of Jersey, the Bailiwick of Guernsey, the Isle of Man, Anguilla, Bermuda, the British Antarctic Territory, Cayman Islands, Falkland Islands, Montserrat, St. Helena and Dependencies, South Georgia and the South Sandwich Islands, Turks and Caicos Islands and British Virgin Islands.

6. Acceptance is for the Kingdom in Europe. At the time of its acceptance, the Kingdom of the Netherlands stated that it chooses both means for the settlement of disputes mentioned in Article 19, paragraph 1 of the Protocol, i.e. the International Court of Justice and the Arbitral Tribunal. A declaration by the Kingdom of the Netherlands accepting the Protocol for the Netherlands Antilles was deposited on October 27, 2004 with a statement confirming that it chooses both means for the settlement of disputes mentioned in Article 19, paragraph 1 of the Protocol.

Department of State,
   Washington, April 2, 2010.

Approval, as notified to the Government of the United States of America, of measures relating to the furtherance of the principles and objectives of the Antarctic Treaty

	16 Recommendations adopted at First Meeting (Canberra 1961) Approved	10 Recommendations adopted at Second Meeting (Buenos Aires 1962) Approved	11 Recommendations adopted at Third Meeting (Brussels 1964) Approved	28 Recommendations adopted at Fourth Meeting (Santiago 1966)* Approved	9 Recommendations adopted at Fifth Meeting (Paris 1968) Approved	15 Recommendations adopted at Sixth Meeting (Tokyo 1970) Approved
Argentina	ALL	ALL	ALL	ALL	ALL	ALL
Australia	ALL	ALL	ALL	ALL	ALL	ALL
Belgium	ALL	ALL	ALL	ALL	ALL	ALL
Brazil (1983)+	ALL	ALL	ALL	ALL	ALL	ALL (except 10)
Bulgaria (1998)+						
Chile	ALL	ALL	ALL	ALL	ALL	ALL
China (1985)+	ALL	ALL	ALL	ALL	ALL	ALL (except 10)
Ecuador (1990)+						
Finland (1989)+						
France	ALL	ALL	ALL	ALL	ALL	ALL
Germany (1981)+	ALL	ALL	ALL (except 8)	ALL (except 16-19)	ALL (except 6)	ALL (except 9)
India (1983)+	ALL	ALL	ALL (except 8***)	ALL (except 18)	ALL	ALL (except 9 & 10)
Italy (1987)+	ALL	ALL	ALL	ALL	ALL	ALL
Japan	ALL	ALL	ALL	ALL	ALL	ALL
Korea, Rep. (1989)+						
Netherlands (1990)+	ALL (except 11 & 15)	ALL (except 3, 5, 8 & 10)	ALL (except 3, 4, 6 & 9)	ALL(except 20, 25, 26 & 28)	ALL (except 1, 8 & 9)	ALL (except 15)
New Zealand	ALL	ALL	ALL	ALL	ALL	ALL
Norway	ALL	ALL	ALL	ALL	ALL	ALL
Peru (1989)+	ALL	ALL	ALL	ALL	ALL	ALL
Poland (1977)+	ALL	ALL	ALL	ALL	ALL	ALL
Russia	ALL	ALL	ALL	ALL	ALL	ALL
South Africa	ALL	ALL	ALL	ALL	ALL	ALL
Spain (1988)+	ALL	ALL	ALL	ALL	ALL	ALL
Sweden (1988)+						
U.K.	ALL	ALL	ALL	ALL	ALL	ALL
Uruguay (1985)+	ALL	ALL	ALL	ALL	ALL	ALL
U.S.A.	ALL	ALL	ALL	ALL	ALL	ALL

* IV-6, IV-10, IV-12, and V-5 terminated by VIII-2

*** Accepted as interim guideline

+ Year attained Consultative Status. Acceptance by that State required to bring into force Recommendations or Measures of meetings from that year forward.

Approval, as notified to the Government of the United States of America, of measures
relating to the furtherance of the principles and objectives of the Antarctic Treaty

	9 Recommendations adopted at Seventh Meeting (Wellington 1972)	14 Recommendations adopted at Eighth Meeting (Oslo 1975)	6 Recommendations adopted at Ninth Meeting (London 1977)	9 Recommendations adopted at Tenth Meeting (Washington 1979)	3 Recommendations adopted at Eleventh Meeting (Buenos Aires 1981)	8 Recommendations adopted at Twelfth Meeting (Canberra 1983)
	Approved	**Approved**	**Approved**	**Approved**	**Approved**	**Approved**
Argentina	ALL	ALL	ALL	ALL	ALL	ALL
Australia	ALL	ALL	ALL	ALL	ALL	ALL
Belgium	ALL	ALL	ALL	ALL	ALL	ALL
Brazil (1983)+	ALL (except 5)	ALL	ALL	ALL	ALL	ALL
Bulgaria (1998)+						
Chile	ALL	ALL	ALL	ALL	ALL	ALL
China (1985)+	ALL (except 5)	ALL	ALL	ALL	ALL	ALL
Ecuador (1990)+						
Finland (1989)+						
France	ALL	ALL	ALL	ALL	ALL	ALL
Germany (1981)+	ALL (except 5)	ALL (except 2 & 5)	ALL	ALL (except 1 & 9)	ALL	ALL
India (1983)+	ALL	ALL	ALL	ALL (except 1 & 9)	ALL	ALL
Italy (1987)+	ALL (except 5)	ALL	ALL	ALL	ALL	ALL
Japan	ALL	ALL	ALL	ALL	ALL	ALL
Korea, Rep. (1989)+	ALL	ALL	ALL	ALL	ALL	ALL
Netherlands (1990)+	ALL	ALL	ALL (except 3)	ALL (except 9)	ALL (except 2)	ALL
New Zealand	ALL	ALL	ALL	ALL	ALL	ALL
Norway	ALL	ALL	ALL	ALL	ALL	ALL
Peru (1989)+	ALL	ALL	ALL	ALL	ALL	ALL
Poland (1977)+	ALL	ALL	ALL	ALL	ALL	ALL
Russia	ALL	ALL	ALL	ALL	ALL	ALL
South Africa	ALL	ALL	ALL	ALL	ALL	ALL
Spain (1988)+	ALL	ALL	ALL	ALL (except 1 & 9)	ALL (except 1)	ALL
Sweden (1988)+						
U.K.	ALL	ALL	ALL	ALL	ALL	ALL
Uruguay (1985)+	ALL	ALL	ALL	ALL	ALL	ALL
U.S.A.	ALL	ALL	ALL	ALL	ALL	ALL

* IV-6, IV-10, IV-12, and V-5 terminated by VIII-2

*** Accepted as interim guideline

+ Year attained Consultative Status. Acceptance by that State required to bring into force Recommendations or Measures of meetings from that year forward.

Approval, as notified to the Government of the United States of America, of measures relating to the furtherance of the principles and objectives of the Antarctic Treaty

	16 Recommendations adopted at Thirteenth Meeting (Brussels 1985)	10 Recommendations adopted at Fourteenth Meeting (Rio de Janeiro 1987)	22 Recommendations adopted at Fifteenth Meeting (Paris 1989)	13 Recommendations adopted at Sixteenth Meeting (Bonn 1991)	4 Recommendations adopted at Seventeenth Meeting (Venice 1992)	1 Recommendation adopted at Eighteenth Meeting (Kyoto 1994)
	Approved	**Approved**	**Approved**	**Approved**	**Approved**	**Approved**
Argentina	ALL	ALL	ALL	ALL	ALL	ALL
Australia	ALL	ALL	ALL	ALL	ALL	ALL
Belgium	ALL	ALL	ALL	ALL	ALL	ALL
Brazil (1983)+	ALL	ALL	ALL	ALL	ALL	ALL
Bulgaria (1998)+				XVI-10		
Chile	ALL	ALL	ALL	ALL	ALL	ALL
China (1985)+	ALL	ALL	ALL	ALL	ALL	ALL
Ecuador (1990)+				XVI-10		
Finland (1989)+			ALL	ALL	ALL	ALL
France	ALL	ALL	ALL	ALL	ALL	ALL
Germany (1981)+	ALL	ALL	ALL (except 3, 8, 10, 11&22)	ALL	ALL	ALL
India (1983)+	ALL	ALL	ALL	ALL	ALL	ALL
Italy (1987)+	ALL	ALL	ALL	ALL	ALL	ALL
Japan	ALL	ALL	ALL	XVI-10	ALL	ALL
Korea, Rep. (1989)+	ALL	ALL	ALL (except 1-11, 16, 18, 19)	ALL (except 12)	ALL (except 1)	ALL
Netherlands (1990)+	ALL	ALL (except 9)	ALL (except 22)	ALL	ALL	ALL
New Zealand	ALL	ALL	ALL	ALL	ALL	ALL
Norway	ALL	ALL	ALL	ALL	ALL	ALL
Peru (1989)+	ALL	ALL	ALL (except 22)	ALL (except 13)	ALL	ALL
Poland (1977)+	ALL	ALL	ALL	ALL	ALL	ALL
Russia	ALL	ALL	ALL	ALL	ALL	ALL
South Africa	ALL	ALL	ALL	ALL	ALL	ALL
Spain (1988)+	ALL	ALL	ALL	ALL	ALL	ALL
Sweden (1988)+	ALL		ALL	ALL	ALL	ALL
U.K.	ALL	ALL (except 2)	ALL (except 3, 4, 8, 10, 11)	ALL (except 4, 6, 8, & 9)	ALL	ALL
Uruguay (1985)+	ALL	ALL	ALL	ALL	ALL	ALL
U.S.A.	ALL	ALL	ALL (except 1-4, 10, 11)	ALL	ALL	ALL

* IV-6, IV-10, IV-12, and V-5 terminated by VIII-2

*** Accepted as interim guideline

+ Year attained Consultative Status. Acceptance by that State required to bring into force Recommendations or Measures of meetings from that year forward.

Approval, as notified to the Government of the United States of America, of measures relating to the furtherance of the principles and objectives of the Antarctic Treaty

	5 Measures adopted at Nineteenth Meeting (Seoul 1995) Approved	2 Measures adopted at Twentieth Meeting (Utrecht 1996) Approved	5 Measures adopted at Twenty-First Meeting (Christchurch 1997) Approved	2 Measures adopted at Twenty-Second Meeting (Tromso 1998) Approved	1 Measure adopted at Twenty-Third Meeting (Lima 1999) Approved
Argentina	ALL	ALL	ALL	ALL	ALL
Australia	ALL	ALL	ALL	ALL	ALL
Belgium	ALL	ALL	ALL	ALL	ALL
Brazil (1983)+	ALL	ALL	ALL	ALL	ALL
Bulgaria (1998)+					
Chile	ALL	ALL	ALL	ALL	ALL
China (1985)+	ALL	ALL	ALL	ALL	ALL
Ecuador (1990)+					
Finland (1989)+	ALL	ALL	ALL	ALL	ALL
France	ALL	ALL	ALL	ALL	ALL
Germany (1981)+	ALL	ALL	ALL	ALL	ALL
India (1983)+	ALL	ALL	ALL	ALL	ALL
Italy (1987)+	ALL	ALL	ALL	ALL	ALL
Japan					
Korea, Rep. (1989)+	ALL	ALL	ALL	ALL	ALL
Netherlands (1990)+	ALL	ALL	ALL	ALL	ALL
New Zealand	ALL	ALL	ALL	ALL	ALL
Norway	ALL	ALL	ALL	ALL	ALL
Peru (1989)+	ALL	ALL	ALL	ALL	ALL
Poland (1977)+	ALL	ALL	ALL	ALL	ALL
Russia	ALL	ALL	ALL	ALL	ALL
South Africa	ALL	ALL	ALL	ALL	ALL
Spain (1988)+	ALL	ALL	ALL	ALL	ALL
Sweden (1988)+	ALL	ALL	ALL	ALL	ALL
U.K.	ALL	ALL	ALL	ALL	ALL
Uruguay (1985)+	ALL (except 2, 3, 4 and 5)	ALL (except 2)	ALL (except 3, 4 and 5)	ALL (except 2)	ALL
U.S.A.	ALL	ALL	ALL	ALL	ALL

"+Year attained Consultative Status. Acceptance by that state required to bring into force Recommendations or Measures of meetings from that Year forward."

Approval, as notified to the Government of the United States of America, of measures relating to the furtherance of the principles and objectives of the Antarctic Treaty

	2 Measures adopted at Twelfth Special Meeting (The Hague 2000) Approved	3 Measures adopted at Twenty-Fourth Meeting (St. Petersburg 2001) Approved	1 Measure adopted at Twenty-Fifth Meeting (Warsaw 2002) Approved	3 Measures adopted at Twenty-Sixth Meeting (Madrid 2003) Approved	4 Measures adopted at Twenty-Seventh Meeting (Cape Town 2004) Approved
Argentina			*	XXVI-1, XXVI-2 *, XXVI-3 **	XXVII-1 *, XXVII-2 *, XXVII-3 **
Australia	ALL	ALL	ALL	XXVI-1, XXVI-2 *, XXVI-3 **	XXVII-1 *, XXVII-2 *, XXVII-3 **
Belgium	ALL	ALL	ALL	ALL	ALL
Brazil (1983)+	ALL	ALL	ALL	ALL	XXVII-1, XXVII-2, XXVII-3
Bulgaria (1998)+			*	XXVI-1, XXVI-2 *, XXVI-3 **	XXVII-1, XXVII-2 *, XXVII-3 **
Chile	ALL	ALL	ALL	ALL	ALL
China (1985)+	ALL	ALL	ALL	ALL	XXVII-1 *, XXVII-2 *, XXVII-3 **
Ecuador (1990)+			*	XXVI-1, XXVI-2 *, XXVI-3 **	XXVII-1 *, XXVII-2 *, XXVII-3 **
Finland (1989)+	ALL	ALL	*	XXVI-1, XXVI-2 *, XXVI-3 **	XXVII-1 *, XXVII-2 *, XXVII-3 **
France	ALL (except SATCM XII-2)		*		XXVII-1, XXVII-2 *, XXVII-3, XXVII-4
Germany (1981)+	ALL	ALL	ALL	ALL	XXVII-1 *, XXVII-2 *, XXVII-3 **
India (1983)+	ALL	ALL	ALL	ALL	XXVII-1 *, XXVII-2 *, XXVII-3 **
Italy (1987)+			*	ALL	XXVII-1 *, XXVII-2 *, XXVII-3 **
Japan			*	ALL	XXVII-1 *, XXVII-2 *, XXVII-3 **, XXVII-4
Korea, Rep. (1989)+	ALL	ALL	ALL	XXVI-1, XXVI-2 *, XXVI-3 **	XXVII-1 *, XXVII-2 *, XXVII-3 **
Netherlands (1990)+	ALL	ALL	ALL	ALL	ALL
New Zealand	ALL	ALL	*	XXVI-1, XXVI-2 *, XXVI-3 **	XXVII-1 *, XXVII-2 *, XXVII-3 **, XXVII-4
Norway		ALL	ALL	XXVI-1, XXVI-2 *, XXVI-3 **	XXVII-1 *, XXVII-2 *, XXVII-3 **
Peru (1989)+	ALL	ALL	ALL	XXVI-1, XXVI-2 *, XXVI-3 **	XXVII-1 *, XXVII-2 *, XXVII-3 **
Poland (1977)+		ALL	ALL		ALL
Russia	ALL	ALL	ALL	XXVI-1, XXVI-2, XXVI-3 **	XXVII-1 *, XXVII-2 *, XXVII-3 **
South Africa	ALL	ALL	ALL	ALL	ALL
Spain (1988)+			*	XXVI-1, XXVI-2 *, XXVI-3 **	XXVII-1 *, XXVII-2 *, XXVII-3 **
Sweden (1988)+	ALL	ALL	ALL	ALL	XXVII-1 *, XXVII-2 *, XXVII-3 **
Ukraine (2004)+					XXVII-1 *, XXVII-2 *, XXVII-3 **
U.K.	ALL (except SATCM XII-2)	ALL (except XXIV-3) ALL (except XXIV-1 and XXIV-2)	ALL	ALL	XXVII-1 *, XXVII-2 *, XXVII-3 **, XXVII-4
Uruguay (1985)+	ALL	ALL	*	XXVI-1, XXVI-2 *, XXVI-3	XXVII-1 *, XXVII-2 *, XXVII-3 **
U.S.A.	ALL	ALL	*	XXVI-1, XXVI-2 *, XXVI-3 **	XXVII-1 *, XXVII-2 *, XXVII-3 **

"+ Year attained Consultative Status. Acceptance by that state required to bring into force Recommendations or Measures of meetings from that Year forward."

* Management Plans annexed to this Measure were deemed to have been approved in accordance with Article 6(1) of Annex V to the Protocol on Environmental Protection to the Antarctic Treaty and the Measure not specifying a different approval method.

** Revised and updated List of Historic Sites and Monuments annexed to this Measure was deemed to have been approved in accordance with Article 8(2) of Annex V to the Protocol on Environmental Protection to the Antarctic Treaty and the Measure not specifying a different approval method.

Approval, as notified to the Government of the United States of America, of measures relating to the furtherance of the principles and objectives of the Antarctic Treaty

	5 Measures adopted at Twenty-Eighth Meeting (Stockholm 2005) Approved	4 Measures adopted at Twenty-Ninth Meeting (Edinburgh 2006) Approved	3 Measures adopted at Thirtieth Meeting (New Delhi 2007) Approved	14 Measures adopted at Thirty-first Meeting (Kyiv 2008) Approved	16 Measures adopted at Thirty-second Meeting (Baltimore 2009) Approved
Argentina	XXVIII-2*, XXVIII-3*, XXVIII-4*, XXVIII-5**	XXIX-1*, XXIX-2*, XXIX-3**, XXIX-4***	XXX-1*, XXX-2*, XXX-3**	XXXI-1*, XXXI-2*, ... XXXI-14*	XXXII-1*, XXXII-2*, ... XXXII-14**
Australia	XXVIII-2*, XXVIII-3*, XXVIII-4*, XXVIII-5**	XXIX-1*, XXIX-2*, XXIX-3**, XXIX-4***	XXX-1*, XXX-2*, XXX-3**	XXXI-1*, XXXI-2*, ... XXXI-14*	XXXII-1*, XXXII-2*, ... XXXII-14**
Belgium	ALL except Measure 1	ALL	ALL	XXXI-1*, XXXI-2*, ... XXXI-14*	XXXII-1*, XXXII-2*, ... XXXII-14**
Brazil (1983)+	ALL except Measure 1	XXIX-1*, XXIX-2*, XXIX-3**, XXIX-4***	XXX-1*, XXX-2*, XXX-3**	XXXI-1*, XXXI-2*, ... XXXI-14*	XXXII-1*, XXXII-2*, ... XXXII-14**
Bulgaria (1998)+	XXVIII-2*, XXVIII-3*, XXVIII-4*, XXVIII-5**	XXIX-1*, XXIX-2*, XXIX-3**, XXIX-4***	XXX-1*, XXX-2*, XXX-3**	XXXI-1*, XXXI-2*, ... XXXI-14*	XXXII-1*, XXXII-2*, ... XXXII-14**
Chile	ALL except Measure 1	XXIX-1*, XXIX-2*, XXIX-3**, XXIX-4***	XXX-1*, XXX-2*, XXX-3**	XXXI-1*, XXXI-2*, ... XXXI-14*	XXXII-1*, XXXII-2*, ... XXXII-14**
China (1985)+	XXVIII-2*, XXVIII-3*, XXVIII-4*, XXVIII-5**	XXIX-1*, XXIX-2*, XXIX-3**, XXIX-4***	XXX-1*, XXX-2*, XXX-3**	XXXI-1*, XXXI-2*, ... XXXI-14*	XXXII-1*, XXXII-2*, ... XXXII-14**
Ecuador (1990)+	XXVIII-2*, XXVIII-3*, XXVIII-4*, XXVIII-5**	XXIX-1*, XXIX-2*, XXIX-3**, XXIX-4***	XXX-1*, XXX-2*, XXX-3**	XXXI-1*, XXXI-2*, ... XXXI-14*	XXXII-1*, XXXII-2*, ... XXXII-14**
Finland (1989)+	XXVIII-2*, XXVIII-3*, XXVIII-4*, XXVIII-5**	XXIX-1*, XXIX-2*, XXIX-3**, XXIX-4***	XXX-1*, XXX-2*, XXX-3**	XXXI-1*, XXXI-2*, ... XXXI-14*	XXXII-1*, XXXII-2*, ... XXXII-14**
France	XXVIII-2*, XXVIII-3*, XXVIII-4*, XXVIII-5**	XXIX-1*, XXIX-2*, XXIX-3**, XXIX-4***	XXX-1*, XXX-2*, XXX-3**	XXXI-1*, XXXI-2*, ... XXXI-14*	XXXII-1*, XXXII-2*, ... XXXII-14**
Germany (1981)+	XXVIII-2*, XXVIII-3*, XXVIII-4*, XXVIII-5**	XXIX-1*, XXIX-2*, XXIX-3**, XXIX-4***	XXX-1*, XXX-2*, XXX-3**	XXXI-1*, XXXI-2*, ... XXXI-14*	XXXII-1*, XXXII-2*, ... XXXII-14**
India (1983)+	XXVIII-2*, XXVIII-3*, XXVIII-4*, XXVIII-5**	XXIX-1*, XXIX-2*, XXIX-3**, XXIX-4***	XXX-1*, XXX-2*, XXX-3**	XXXI-1*, XXXI-2*, ... XXXI-14*	XXXII-1*, XXXII-2*, ... XXXII-14**
Italy (1987)+	XXVIII-2*, XXVIII-3*, XXVIII-4*, XXVIII-5**	XXIX-1*, XXIX-2*, XXIX-3**, XXIX-4***	XXX-1*, XXX-2*, XXX-3**	XXXI-1*, XXXI-2*, ... XXXI-14*	XXXII-1*, XXXII-2*, ... XXXII-14**,
Japan	XXVIII-2*, XXVIII-3*, XXVIII-4*, XXVIII-5**	XXIX-1*, XXIX-2*, XXIX-3**, XXIX-4***	XXX-1*, XXX-2*, XXX-3**	XXXI-1*, XXXI-2*, ... XXXI-14*	XXXII-1*, XXXII-2*, ... XXXII-14**, XXXII-15
Korea, Rep. (1989)+	ALL except Measure 1	ALL	ALL	XXXI-1*, XXXI-2*, ... XXXI-14*	XXXII-1*, XXXII-2*, ... XXXII-14**
Netherlands (1990)+	XXVIII-2*, XXVIII-3*, XXVIII-4*, XXVIII-5**	XXIX-1*, XXIX-2*, XXIX-3**, XXIX-4***	XXX-1*, XXX-2*, XXX-3**	ALL	XXXII-1, XXXII-2*, ... XXXII-14
New Zealand	XXVIII-2*, XXVIII-3*, XXVIII-4*, XXVIII-5**	XXIX-1*, XXIX-2*, XXIX-3**, XXIX-4***	XXX-1*, XXX-2*, XXX-3**	XXXI-1*, XXXI-2*, ... XXXI-14*	XXXII-1*, XXXII-2*, ... XXXII-14**
Norway	XXVIII-1, XXVIII-2*, XXVIII-3*, XXVIII-4*, XXVIII-5**	XXIX-1*, XXIX-2*, XXIX-3**, XXIX-4***	XXX-1*, XXX-2*, XXX-3**	XXXI-1*, XXXI-2*, ... XXXI-14*	XXXII-1*, XXXII-2*, ... XXXII-14**
Peru (1989)+	XXVIII-1, XXVIII-2*, XXVIII-3*, XXVIII-4*, XXVIII-5**	ALL	ALL	XXXI-1*, XXXI-2*, ... XXXI-14*	XXXII-1*, XXXII-2*, ... XXXII-14**
Poland (1977)+	ALL	ALL	ALL	XXXI-1*, XXXI-2*, ... XXXI-14*	XXXII-1*, XXXII-2*, ... XXXII-14**
Russia	XXVIII-2*, XXVIII-3*, XXVIII-4*, XXVIII-5**	XXIX-1*, XXIX-2*, XXIX-3**, XXIX-4***	XXX-1*, XXX-2*, XXX-3**	XXXI-1*, XXXI-2*, ... XXXI-14*	XXXII-1*, XXXII-2*, ... XXXII-14**

		ALL			
South Africa	XXVIII-2*, XXVIII-3*, XXVIII-4*, XXVIII-5**		XXX-1*, XXX-2*, XXX-3**	XXXI-1*, XXXI-2*,....XXXI-14*	XXXII-1*, XXXII-2*,....XXXII-14**
Spain (1988)+	XXVIII-1, XXVIII-2*, XXVIII-3*, XXVIII-4*, XXVIII-5**	XXIX-1*, XXIX-2*, XXIX-3**, XXIX-4***	XXX-1*, XXX-2*, XXX-3**	XXXI-1*, XXXI-2*,....XXXI-14*	XXXII-1*, XXXII-2*,....XXXII-14**
Sweden (1988)+	XXVIII-1, XXVIII-2*, XXVIII-3*, XXVIII-4*, XXVIII-5**	XXIX-1*, XXIX-2*, XXIX-3**, XXIX-4***	XXX-1*, XXX-2*, XXX-3**	XXXI-1*, XXXI-2*,....XXXI-14*	XXXII-1*, XXXII-2*,....XXXII-14**
Ukraine (2004)+	XXVIII-2*, XXVIII-3*, XXVIII-4*, XXVIII-5**	XXIX-1*, XXIX-2*, XXIX-3**, XXIX-4***	XXX-1*, XXX-2*, XXX-3**	XXXI-1*, XXXI-2*,....XXXI-14*	XXXII-1*, XXXII-2*,....XXXII-14**
U.K.	XXVIII-2*, XXVIII-3*, XXVIII-4*, XXVIII-5**	XXIX-1*, XXIX-2*, XXIX-3**, XXIX-4***	XXX-1*, XXX-2*, XXX-3**	XXXI-1*, XXXI-2*,....XXXI-14*	XXXII-1*, XXXII-2*,....XXXII-14**
Uruguay (1985)+	XXVIII-2*, XXVIII-3*, XXVIII-4*, XXVIII-5**	XXIX-1*, XXIX-2*, XXIX-3**, XXIX-4***	XXX-1*, XXX-2*, XXX-3**	XXXI-1*, XXXI-2*,....XXXI-14*	XXXII-1*, XXXII-2*,....XXXII-14**
U.S.A.	XXVIII-2*, XXVIII-3*, XXVIII-4*, XXVIII-5**	XXIX-1*, XXIX-2*, XXIX-3**, XXIX-4***	XXX-1*, XXX-2*, XXX-3**	XXXI-1*, XXXI-2*,....XXXI-14*	XXXII-1*, XXXII-2*,....XXXII-14**

"+Year attained Consultative Status. Acceptance by that state required to bring into force Recommendations or Measures of meetings from that Year forward."

* Management Plans annexed to this Measure deemed to have been approved in accordance with Article 6(1) of Annex V to the Protocol on Environmental Protection to the Antarctic Treaty and the Measure not specifying a different approval method.

** Revised and updated List of Historic Sites and Monuments annexed to this Measure deemed to have been approved in accordance with Article 8(2) of Annex V to the Protocol on Environmental Protection to the Antarctic Treaty and the Measure not specifying a different approval method.

*** Modification of Appendix A to Annex II to the Protocol on Environmental Protection to the Antarctic Treaty deemed to have been approved in accordance with Article 9(1) of Annex II to the Protocol on Environmental Protection to the Antarctic Treaty and the Measure not specifying a different approval method.

Office of the Assistant Legal Adviser for Treaty Affairs
Department of State
Washington, April 2, 2010.

Report Submitted to Antarctic Treaty Consultative Meeting XXXIII by the Depositary Government for the Convention for the Conservation of Antarctic Seals in Accordance with Recommendation XIII-2, Paragraph 2(D)

Submitted by the United Kingdom

This report covers events regarding the Convention for the Conservation of Antarctic Seals (CCAS) for the reporting year 1 March 2008 to 28 February 2009.

The summary at Annex A lists all capturing and killing of Antarctic seals by Contracting Parties to CCAS during the reporting period. A report of events in the 2009 – 2010 year will be submitted to ATCM XXXIV, once the June 2010 deadline for exchange of information has passed.

The United Kingdom would like to remind Contracting Parties to CCAS that the reporting period for the Exchange of Information is from 1 March to the end of February each year. The reporting period was changed to the above dates during the September 1988 Meeting to Review the Operation of the Convention. This is documented in Paragraph 19(a) of the Report of that Meeting.

The Exchange of Information, referred to in Paragraph 6(a) in the Annex to the Convention, should be submitted to other Contracting Parties and to SCAR by **30 June** each year, including nil returns. The UK regrets that this is not a complete report of all Parties activities as, despite our best efforts, we were unable to obtain returns from all Parties. The UK continues to encourage all Contracting Parties to CCAS to submit returns on time to ensure that all relevant information has been provided.

Since ATCM XXIII there have been no accessions to CCAS. A list of countries which were original signatories to the Convention, and countries which have subsequently acceded is attached to this report (Annex B).

March 2010

CONVENTION FOR THE CONSERVATION OF ANTARCTIC SEALS (CCAS)

Synopsis of reporting in accordance with Article 5 and the Annex of the Convention: Capturing and killing of seals during the period 1 March 2008 to 28 February 2009.

Contracting Party	Antarctic Seals Captured	Antarctic Seals Killed
Argentina	191[a]	Nil
Australia	113[b]	Nil
Belgium	Nil	Nil
Brazil	No return	No return
Canada	Nil	Nil
Chile	Nil	Nil
France	100[c]	Nil
Germany	40[d]	Nil
Italy	Nil	Nil
Japan	Nil	Nil
Norway	Nil	Nil
Poland	Nil	Nil
Russia	Nil	Nil
South Africa	Nil	Nil
United Kingdom	10[e]	Nil
United States of America	1110[f]	Nil

[a] 170 Elephant Seals, 21 Leopard Seals
[b] 46 Southern Elephant Seals, 37 Leopard Seals, 30 Weddell Seals
[c] 100 Weddell Seals
[d] 40 Weddell Seals
[e] 10 Weddell Seals
[f] 530 Antarctic Fur Seals, 460 Weddell Seals, 50 Southern Elephant Seals, 35 Crabeater Seals, 30 Leopard Seals, 5 Ross Seals

All reported capturing was for scientific research.

CONVENTION FOR THE CONSERVATION OF ANTARCTIC SEALS (CCAS)

London, 1 June – 31 December 1972

(The Convention entered into force on 11 March 1978)

State	Date of Signature	Date of deposit (Ratification or Acceptance)
Argentina[1]	9 June 1972	7 March 1978
Australia	5 October 1972	1 July 1987
Belgium	9 June 1972	9 February 1978
Chile[1]	28 December 1972	7 February 1980
France[2]	19 December 1972	19 February 1975
Japan	28 December 1972	28 August 1980
Norway	9 June 1972	10 December 1973
Russia[1,2,4]	9 June 1972	8 February 1978
South Africa	9 June 1972	15 August 1972
United Kingdom[2]	9 June 1972	10 September 1974[3]
United States of America[2]	28 June 1972	19 January 1977

ACCESSIONS

State	Date of deposit of Instrument of Accession
Brazil	11 February 1991
Canada	4 October 1990
Germany, Federal Republic of	30 September 1987
Italy	2 April 1992
Poland	15 August 1980

[1] Declaration or Reservation
[2] Objection
[3] The instrument of ratification included the Channel Islands and the Isle of Man
[4] Former USSR

Report of the Depositary Government for the Convention on the Conservation of Antarctic Marine Living Resources (CCAMLR)

Summary

A report is provided by Australia as depositary of the Convention on the Conservation of Antarctic Marine Living Resources 1980 on the status of the Convention.

Depositary report

Australia, as depositary of the Convention on the Conservation of Antarctic Marine Living Resources 1980 (the Convention) is pleased to report to the Thirty-third Antarctic Treaty Consultative Meeting on the status of the Convention.

Australia advises the Antarctic Treaty Parties that, since the Thirty-second Antarctic Treaty Consultative Meeting, no States have acceded to the Convention.

A copy of the status list for the Convention is available upon request to the Treaties Secretariat of the Australian Government Department of Foreign Affairs and Trade. Requests could be conveyed through Australian diplomatic missions, or via the internet on the Australian Treaties Database at the following internet address: http://www.austlii.edu.au/au/other/dfat/treaty_list/depository/CCAMLR.html .

Report of the Depositary Government for the Agreement on the Conservation of Albatrosses and Petrels (ACAP)

Summary

A report is provided by Australia as depositary of the Agreement on the Conservation of Albatrosses and Petrels 2001 on the status of the Agreement.

Depositary report

Australia, as depositary of the Agreement on the Conservation of Albatrosses and Petrels 2001 (the Agreement) is pleased to report to the Thirty-third Antarctic Treaty Consultative Meeting on the status of the Convention.

Australia advises the Antarctic Treaty Parties that, since the Thirty-second Antarctic Treaty Consultative Meeting, no States have acceded to the Agreement.

A copy of the status list for the Agreement is available upon request to the Treaties Secretariat of the Australian Department of Foreign Affairs and Trade. Requests could be conveyed through Australian diplomatic missions, or via the internet on the Australian Treaties Database at the following internet address: http://www.austlii.edu.au/au/other/dfat/treaty_list/depository/consalbnpet.html.

Report by the CCAMLR Observer to the Thirty-Third Antarctic Treaty Consultative Meeting

Executive Summary

Introduction

1. The Twenty-Eighth Meeting of the Commission for the Conservation of Antarctic Marine Living Resources (CCAMLR)[1] was held in Hobart from 26 October to 6 November 2009. Emphasis in this report is given to items that are particularly relevant to the ATCM XXXIII agenda. Paragraph references for relevant discussions and decisions from CCAMLR XXVIII are provided in Appendix I.

CCAMLR Fisheries in 2008/09

Catches in 2009/098

2. The catches of the three main target species over the last three seasons are shown in Table 1

Table1. Catches of toothfish (*Dissostichus* spp.), icefish (*Champsocephalus gunnari*) and krill (*Euphausia superba*) reported from the CAMLR Convention Area during the seasons 2006/07 to 2008/09.

Target Species	Reported catch (tonnes)		
	2006/07	**2007/08**	**2008/09**
Toothfish	16328	15593	13381
Icefish	4347	2690	1936
Krill	104586	156521	125830

3. It is estimated that, in addition to these reported catches, some 938 tonnes of Toothfish. were taken as a result of IUU fishing in the Convention Area in 2008/09, compared with 1168 tonnes in 2007/08. The catch of krill in 2008/09 was taken from the Antarctic Peninsula and South Orkney regions with <1t taken from South Georgia.

Development of the krill fishery

4. In response to evidence of market-led changes in the krill fishery CCAMLR this year agreed to:

- spatially sub-divide the existing catch trigger level among subareas in Area 48.
- increase the reporting frequency of krill catches
- implement a process to obtain systematic observer coverage from all krill vessels.

Conservation Measures

5. CCAMLR introduced a requirement (CM 23-07) for daily catch and effort reporting from exploratory fisheries (with the exception of krill) to allow more accurate forecasting of the closure of fisheries, especially those with low catch limits.

6. Three new CCAMLR Resolutions were introduced at CCAMLR XXVIII:

- *Resolution 29/XXVIII Ratification of the Salvage Convention by Members of CCAMLR*

---

[1] The Convention on the Conservation of Antarctic Marine Living Resources is usually referred to as the "CAMLR-Convention"

- *Resolution 30/XXVIII Climate Change*
- Resolution 31/XXVIII Best Available Science

7. All measures and resolutions are published in the Schedule of Conservation Measures in Force 2008/09 available from the CCAMLR Secretariat or http://www.ccamlr.org/pu/e/e_pubs/cm/09-10/toc.htm.

Illegal, Unregulated and Unreported (IUU) Fishing

8. IUU fishing for *Dissostichus* spp. in the Convention Area has been a major issue for the Commission since 1997. CCAMLR affords high priority to eliminating such fishing and implements an integrated suite of administrative, political and enforcement-related measures to address the problem consistent with international best practice.

Ecosystem Monitoring and Management

9. The CCAMLR scientific community is continuing to develop procedures to allow data on the ecosystem, including those collected through CEMP, to be formally incorporated into precautionary management decisions. In this respect, the Commission has afforded high priority to:
- Ecosystem Effects of Fishing for krill,
- Spatial Management to Facilitate the Conservation of Marine Biodiversity including Marine Protected Areas and avoiding significant adverse impacts on vulnerable marine ecosystems
- Ecosystem models
- Climate change in relation to conservation of Antarctic marine living resources.

Deep-sea bottom fishing and Vulnerable Marine Ecosystems (VMEs)

10. CCAMLR received 30 VME indicator notifications of which seven consisted of at least 10 VME indicator units and resulted in seven Risk Areas being declared, and closed to fishing, in Subareas 88.1 and 88.2.

11. The Secretariat has also received a total of 30 notifications of encounters with VMEs made during the course of research surveys, following the procedure outlines in Conservation Measure 22-06, and these VMEs be recorded in the Secretariat's VME Register. CCAMLR agreed that the VMEs reported in Subarea 48.2 should be given protection in the experimental harvest regime for crabs in that subarea by closing experimental blocks A, C and E.

Incidental mortality in CCAMLR Fisheries

12. Compliance with seabird mitigation measures in CCAMLR managed fisheries has resulted in low or near zero incidental mortality. However, the levels of incidental mortality i of seabird species breeding in the Convention Area n adjacent fisheries remains a cause for concern.

Marine Protected Areas (MPAS)

13. CCAMLR and the CEP have concluded that a system of marine areas for biodiversity conservation in the Southern Ocean should be addressed as a matter of priority (CCAMLR XXIII, paragraph 4.13; CEP-IX, paragraph 94 to 101).

14. In 2009 CCAMLR endorsed the Scientific Committee recommendations on a proposal for a marine protected area in the South Orkney Islands and adopted Conservation Measure 91-03 (2009) 'Protection of the South Orkney Islands southern shelf'. This 94000km^2 MPA (Figure 1) was selected on the basis of a systematic conservation planning analysis and includes representative examples of two pelagic bioregions, incorporates an area of key importance for winter penguin foraging and unique oceanographic frontal systems.

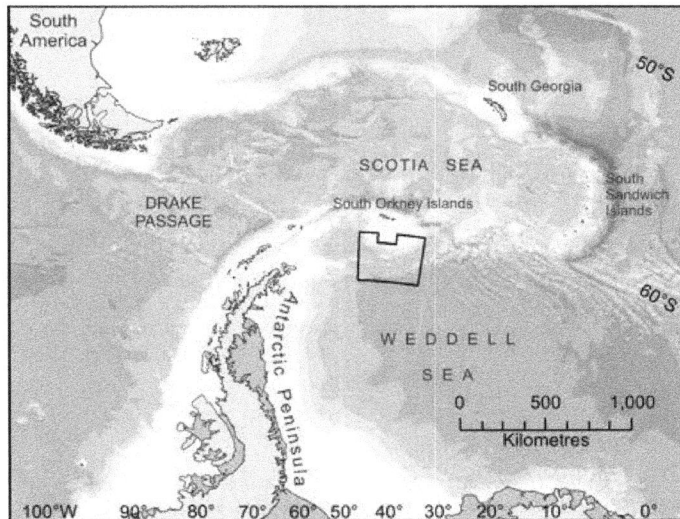

Figure 1. Map showing the location of the MPA on the southern shelf of the South Orkney Islands.

CCAMLR Performance Review

15. CCAMLR recognises the need to develop the capacity to ensure the long-term provision of high-quality scientific advice. Following the generous offer by Norway to provide A$100 000 CCAMLR established a 'General Science Capacity Special Fund' to facilitate the provision of the best scientific information available to the Commission by :

    i)   securing wider participation, not least from young scientists, in the work of the Scientific Committee,

    ii)   promoting burden sharing and build capacity within the Scientific Committee, through assistance with the collection, study and exchange of information.

    iii) encouraging and promoting the conduct of cooperative and collaborative research in order to extend knowledge of the marine living resources of the Antarctic marine ecosystem.

16. In response to the recommendations of the *CCAMLR Performance Review* to highlight obligations arising from connections between the CAMLR Convention and the Antarctic Treaty the CCAMLR Secretariat prepared an information pack (CCAMLR-XXVIII/BG/16) with a covering note prepared by Australia (as Depositary) (CCAMLR-XXVIII/BG/38). These documents outlined the nature of those connections, along with other information, to be provided to States wishing to accede to the Convention, as well as to Acceding States wishing to become Members of CCAMLR.

Co-operation with international organizations, particularly the ATCM.

ATCM

17. CCAMLR noted the importance of ATCM XXXII as it marked the 50th anniversary of the signing of the Antarctic Treaty. CCAMLR also recognised the importance of Ministerial Declarations on the Fiftieth Anniversary of the Antarctic Treaty and the International Polar Year and Polar Science. These declarations included an affirmation of the principles of the Antarctic Treaty System that are at the core of CCAMLR and the promotion of the science that underpins all of the Commission's work. In recognition of their importance, CCAMLR agreed to append the text of these Declarations to its report (CCAMLR XXVIII Annex 7).

18. CCAMLR endorsed the recommendations of the Joint SC-CAMLR–CEP Workshop report and agreed that this had been a very productive and timely meeting.

Non-Contracting Parties

19. As part of this policy CCAMLR approved expenditure to support a capacity building training event in Africa in order to prevent, deter and eliminate IUU fishing in the Convention Area which is undertaken by vessels flagged to NCPs in Africa and / or supported by activities and services found in the ports of NCPs in Africa.

Co-Operation with Other International Organizations

20. CCAMLR continues to urge its Members to accept and ratify a number of relevant international agreements, such as the Agreement on the Conservation of Albatrosses and Petrels (ACAP). In order to facilitate these interactions CCAMLR works closely with the Agreement on the Conservation of Albatrosses and Petrels and in April 2010 agreed an MOU with ACAP to formalise data sharing and other arrangements between the two bodies.

Appointment of the Executive Secretary

21. The Heads of Delegations of CCAMLR Members appointed Mr Andrew (Drew) Wright (Australia) to take over from the present Executive Secretary. Mr Wright is currently Executive Secretary of the WCPFC and will take up this appointment at CCAMLR in April 2010.
22. The Commission agreed that the outgoing Executive Secretary Dr Denzil Miller was the embodiment of CCAMLR and an asset to the Antarctic Treaty System and would be missed very much.

Appendix 1

CCAMLR-XXVII References for Topics & Decisions

The CCAMLR-XXVIII report is downloadable from:

(http://www.ccamlr.org/pu/e/e_pubs/cr/09/toc.htm).

1. Topics & Decisions	2. CCAMLR-XXVII Paragraphs
3. 1. General Fishery Matters	4.
5. 1.1 Fisheries Catches in 2007/08	6. 4.12-4.38
7. 1.2 Fishery Regulation Measures 2008/09	8. 12.17-12.84
9. 1.3 Bottom Fishing + VMEs	10. 5.3-5.10, 12.17-12.23
11. 1.4 Mitigation Measures	12. 12.26-12.28
13. 1.5 Scheme International Scientific Observation	14. 10.1-10.7
15. 1.6 Climate Change	16. 4.44-4.45, 12.88
17. 2. IUU fishing in Convention Area	18.
19. 2.1 Current Levels	20. 9.1-9.4
21. 2.2 IUU Vessel Lists	22. 9.13-9.20
23. 3. General Compliance	24.
25. 3.1 Compliance with Conservation Measures	26. 8.3-8.39
27. 3.2 Market-Related Measures	28. 12.94-12.105
29. 3.3 Compliance Evaluation Procedure	30. 8.37-8.39
31. 4. Ecosystem Approach to Fisheries Management	32.
33. 4.1 Krill Ecosystem-Based Management	34. 4.8-4.10
35. 4.2 Incidental Mortality Seabird/Mammals	36. 6.4-6.17
37. 4.3 Marine Debris	38. 6.1-6.3
39. 5. Marine Protected Areas	40.
41. 5.1 Protected Areas	42. 7.1-7.19
43. 6. Cooperation Antarctic Treaty System	44.
45. 6.1 ATCM	46. 14.1-14.12
47. 7. Cooperation Other International Organisations	48.
49. 7.1 ACAP	50. 15.2-15.12
51. 7.2 Other	52. 15.13-15.28
53. 8. CCAMLR Performance Review	54.
55. 7.1 General	56. 16.2 – 16.25

The Annual Report for 2009 of the Scientific Committee on Antarctic Research (SCAR) of the International Council for Science (ICSU)

SCAR is the foremost, non-governmental organisation that initiates, develops, and coordinates high quality international scientific research in the Antarctic region including the study of Antarctica's role in the earth system. SCAR's members currently include scientific academies of 35 nations and 9 of ICSU's scientific unions.

SCAR's scientific research adds value to national efforts by enabling national researchers to collaborate on large-scale scientific questions to accomplish objectives not easily obtainable by any single country or programme. SCAR's biennial Open Science Conference provides an important forum for polar scientists; the next one is in Buenos Aires (August 3-6, 2010). SCAR is also cosponsoring the 2nd IPY Open Science Conference, in Oslo (June 8-12, 2010). SCAR supports research Fellows and young scientists (in partnership with the Association for Polar Early Career Scientists – APECS), and provides a number of data and information products (Appendix I).

SCAR provides independent scientific advice in support of the wise management of the Antarctic environment, in partnership with the Antarctic Treaty Parties and CCAMLR, and works closely with COMNAP and ACAP. In 2010 SCAR is providing the ATCM and CEP with 4 Working Papers and 8 Information Papers covering a wide range of important topics. This represents a large effort in manpower and resources for which SCAR is not reimbursed.

SCAR's success depends on the quality and timeliness of its key scientific outputs, which in most cases are assessed through external peer-review. Descriptions of SCAR's research programmes and key scientific outputs are available at www.scar.org. In 2009, an external group reviewed the performance of SCAR, with favourable results. SCAR is now producing its Strategic Plan for 2011-2016.

SCAR Executive Director Colin Summerhayes retired on April 9 after 6 years service and was replaced by the Executive Officer Dr. Michael Sparrow, after an exhaustive international search. He was in turn replaced by Dr Renuka Badhe, a marine biologist and Indian citizen, who was selected from 44 international candidates.

During 2009, SCAR's research continued focusing on five main themes:

(i) the modern ocean-atmosphere-ice system;

(ii) the evolution of climate over the past 34 million years since glaciation began;

(iii) the response of life to change;

(iv) preparations to study subglacial aquatic environments; and

(v) the response of the Earth's outer atmosphere to the changing impact of the solar wind at both poles.

Highlights for 2009 include:

1. Publication of a major 560-page interdisciplinary review of "Antarctic Climate Change and the Environment (ACCE)" (http://www.scar.org/publications/occasionals/acce.html) showing how the climate has changed in the past and is likely to change in the future, with probable effects on the biota.

2. The discovery that increased growth in Antarctic sea ice during the past three decades results from strengthening of surface winds around Antarctica caused by development of the ozone hole; these winds limit the impact of global warming on Antarctic climate.

3. Published images of the aurora taken simultaneously in the Northern and the Southern hemispheres show that they can be totally asymmetric, contradicting the commonly held assumption that they should be mirror images of one another (Nature 460, 491-493, 2009).

4. A barcoding campaign extended the number of Antarctic DNA barcodes from 3,500 pre-2009 to over 10,000. The data show high numbers of cryptic species in the Antarctic benthos, especially in species previously thought to have circum-Antarctic distributions.

5. Recent research shows that terrestrial, shelf and deeper water biotas all have components that survived repeated glaciations in what appear to be temporary and shifting refugia, which likely also contributed to substantial radiation in the marine biota (reviewed in Quaternary Science Reviews vol. 28, 3035-3048).

6. The SCAR-supported ANDRILL Programme, which contributes to SCAR's Antarctic Climate Evolution (ACE) programme, recovered more than 20 million years of climate and ice sheet history from McMurdo Sound, providing numerical modellers with new constraints on ice sheet behaviour and Ross Sea conditions. The cores reveal periodical collapse of the West Antarctic ice sheet (WAIS) leading to open water in the Ross Sea embayment (Naish et al., Nature 2009).

7. Publication of the first SCAR Data and Information Strategy (DIMS), defining the direction for SCAR data management activities over the next 5 years, emphasises the need to leverage established regional, global and thematic data-centric networks to improve data management capability within the Antarctic science community as a whole.

8. SCAR successfully ran the first year of the Martha T Muse Prize for Science and Policy in Antarctica, a $100,000 unrestricted yearly prize given to an early to mid-career individual who has demonstrated excellence and the potential or leadership in Antarctic science or policy. Dr Steven Chown was the inaugural recipient. Presentation of the award and a lecture by Dr Chown will take place at the Oslo IPY Conference in June 2010.

Antarctica In The Global Climate System (AGCS)

Activities under this heading are jointly conducted with the World Climate Research Programme (WCRP) and its Climate and Cryosphere programme (CliC). Papers in press in Deep-Sea Research II discuss the development of empirical relationships between ice thickness and satellite-derived snow freeboard, and their application to IceSAT altimetry to determine, for the first time, an adequate baseline for ice thickness distribution for future monitoring of climatic changes in the Antarctic sea ice cover. AGCS has also recovered and archived additional Antarctic data in the Met-, Ice- and Southern Ocean- READER databases.

Antarctic Climate Evolution (ACE)

ACE activities are coordinated with the International Partnership in Ice Core Sciences (IPICS); the palaeoclimate community via the past climate change (PAGES) programme of the International Geosphere Biosphere Programme (IGBP); the IASC programme on Arctic Palaeoclimate and its Extremes (APEX); and drilling programmes such as the Antarctic Geological Drilling programme (ANDRILL) and the Integrated Ocean Drilling Program (IODP).

In 2009, ACE held its first Antarctic Climate Evolution conference in Granada, Spain (7-11 September) (http://www.acegranada2009.com/), with nearly 200 attendees. Review papers will be published by Elsevier. Planning is underway for site surveys preparing for the next ANDRILL Project on the Coulman High.

Evolution And Biodiversity In The Antarctic (EBA)

A wide range of national and multinational projects contributes to EBA, including CAML (Census of Antarctic Marine Life), SCAR-MarBIN (the Marine Biodiversity Information Network), MERGE (Microbiological and Ecological Responses to Global Environmental Changes in Polar Regions), the Latitudinal Gradient Project, and ICED (Integrating Climate and Ecosystem Dynamics in the Southern Ocean). Major meetings in 2009 included 10th SCAR Biology Symposium in Sapporo, Japan, 27-31 July 2009, attended by some 300 participants.

In part EBA's success relies on biological data being maintained, archived and exchanged, much of which is done through the Australian Antarctic Division's Biodiversity Database. EBA also relies on other databases including SCAR-MarBIN (www.scarmarbin.be). The ANTOBIS geodatabase (forming the Antarctic node of the Ocean Biogeographic Information System, OBIS) has now reached over 1 million records from 145 distributed databases. Since it started in 2005, the SCAR-MarBIN website has reached over 700,000 visitors, 5,000,000 hits, and a total of over 32,000,000 downloaded records. SCAR-MarBIN is funded by the

Belgian Science Policy office, with assistance from Australia, Germany, The Netherlands, the TOTAL Foundation and the ArcOD consortium.

In the last five years, CAML has coordinated the largest-ever survey of biota in the Southern Ocean, including 18 major voyages to Antarctica. The survey discovered hundreds of new species and published over 1,000 scientific papers. Main findings will be published in a special volume of *Deep-Sea Research II*. These achievements provide a robust benchmark against which future change in the Antarctic marine ecosystems may be measured.

Subglacial Antarctic Lake Environments (SALE)

The SALE programme has succeeded in stimulating funding for 3 major national projects to sample subglacial aquatic environments over the next 5 years, including: Subglacial Lake Ellsworth (direct exploration in 2012/13); Subglacial Lake Whillans and its associated watershed (drill testing in 2011-2012, lake sampling in 2012-2013, and sampling the lake's outflow in 2013-2014); and Subglacial Lake Vostok (plan to enter the lake in 2010-2011). In addition, Japanese scientists confirmed that liquid water was present at the base of the Dome Fuji ice core. Belgian scientists continue to improve numerical models of ice flow over subglacial lakes, and the influence of basal conditions on the dynamic behaviour of Antarctic glaciers and ice streams. A Chapman Conference on subglacial environments was held on 15-17 March 2010 in Baltimore, Maryland, USA, and a monograph is being produced (http://www.agu.org/meetings/chapman/2010/ccall/index.php).

Inter-Hemispheric Conjugacy Effects In Solar-Terrestrial And Aeronomy Research (ICESTAR).

ICESTAR is describing the upper atmosphere over Antarctica and its coupling to the global atmosphere and solar-terrestrial links. During periods of enhanced geomagnetic activity the surface temperatures in certain high-latitude regions are on average 4-5°C higher or lower than during quiet conditions. The ICESTAR team continue to develop and refine the Global Auroral Imaging Access (GAIA) data portal; see http://gaia-vxo.org, a virtual observatory for dealing with data from geospace optical and riometer systems, containing more than 10,000,000 summary images. At the XXXI SCAR meeting in August, ICESTAR will become an Expert Group and its place as a Scientific Research Programme will be taken by the Astronomy and Astrophysics from Antarctica Programme.

Other SCAR Research Areas are described in Appendix II.

Appendix 1. SCAR'S Products

For the benefit of the wider community SCAR provides several products underpinning the work SCAR scientists do. These can be useful to other communities too. The list includes:

- Antarctic Data Directory System (ADDS)
- REference Antarctic Data for Environmental Research (Meteo-READER)
- The Ocean READER database
- The Ice READER database
- Antarctic Digital Database (ADD)
- Antarctic Biodiversity Database
- Composite Gazetteer of Antarctica
- Seismic Data Library System (SDLS)
- Geodetic Data including: Master index for Antarctic positional control; Geophysical and geodetic observatories; and Geodectic Control Database
- Antarctic Map Catalogue (
- Antarctic Bedrock Mapping (BEDMAP)
- Tide gauge data
- Antarctic Digital Magnetic Anomaly Project
- The SCAR King George Island Geographical Information System
- The Continuous Plankton Recorder database
- The Feature Catalogue
- Sea Ice Database

Appendix II. Other SCAR Research Areas

SCAR carries out smaller scale investigations on a wide range of topics through the following groups (for more information see www.scar.org):

1. Expert Group on Birds and Marine Mammals;

2. Expert Group on Continuous Plankton Recorder Research

3. Action Group on Prediction of Changes in the Physical and Biological Environments of the Antarctic

4. Integrating Climate and Ecosystem Dynamics in the Southern Ocean

5. Southern Ocean Global Ocean Ecosystems Dynamics

6. Expert Group on Human Biology and Medicine

7. Action Group on Antarctic Fuel Spills

8. Expert Group on Geodetic Infrastructure of Antarctica

9. Solid Earth Response and influences on Cryospheric Evolution Scientific Programme Planning Group:

10. Expert Group on the International Bathymetric Chart of the Southern Ocean

11. Expert Group on Antarctic Permafrost and Periglacial Environments

12. Sub-Ice Geological Exploration Action Group:

13. Seeps and Vents Antarctica Action Group

14. International Partnership in Ice Coring Science Expert Group

15. Astronomy and Astrophysics from Antarctica Scientific Research Programme Planning Group

16. Operational Meteorology Expert Group

17. Environmental Contamination in Antarctica Action Group

18. Polar Atmospheric Chemistry at the Tropopause Action Group

19. Joint SCAR/SCOR Oceanography Expert Group

20. CLIVAR/CliC/SCAR Southern Ocean Implementation Panel (SOIP) and the WCRP/SCAR International Programme for Antarctic Buoys (IPAB)

21. Ice Sheet Mass Balance and Sea Level Expert Group

22. GPS For Weather and Space Weather Forecast Action Group

23. Prediction of Changes in the Physical and Biological Environment of the Antarctic

24. King George Island Cross SSG Action Group:

25. Antarctic Data Management (Standing Committee)

26. Antarctic Geographic Information (Standing Committee)

27. Antarctic Treaty System (Standing Committee)

28. History Action Group

29. Capacity Building, Education and Training Committee.

Council of Managers of National Antarctic Programs (COMNAP) Report to ATCM XXXIII

Executive Summary

1. Introduction

This report provides an overview of COMNAP's current activities. 2009 continued to be a year in transition for COMNAP under the new way of working and new constitution.

2. Supporting Science

There is often a misconception that COMNAP's sole focus is logistics. Today, COMNAP's mission is much broader, since the Managers of National Antarctic Programs control more than the logistics of their respective programs.

Increasingly complex science questions are being poised which can only be answered by multi-disciplinary and often multi-national science teams. This complexity, along with more demanding environmental measures and, in some cases, reduced funding, contribute to added pressure on National Antarctic Programs and to an even greater need for international collaboration. COMNAP works in support of greater collaboration between National Antarctic Programs and recognises the need for robust partnerships with organisations with similar goals.

3. Supporting the Antarctic Treaty System

COMNAP was, in 1991, given the status of Observer at ATCMs.

4. COMNAP Constitution

COMNAP's Constitution states that our purpose is "To develop and promote best practice in managing the support of scientific research in Antarctica". COMNAP membership is only open to those organisations with national responsibility for managing the support of scientific research in the Antarctic Treaty Area on behalf of their respective governments, which must have signed the Antarctic Treaty and ratified its Protocol on Environmental Protection.

For further information, see: ATCM XXXII IP078 *COMNAP's 20 years: a New Constitution and a New Way of Working to Continue Supporting Science and the Antarctic Treaty System.*

5. COMNAPs Restructure

In conjunction with the new Constitution, COMNAP adopted in St Petersburg, a new way of working. Development and implementation of this new way of working is still in progress. So that 2009/2010 is a year in transition for COMNAP. New rules of procedure have been developed and are in the process of review and will be discussed at the upcoming COMNAP Annual General Meeting in August 2010.

In support of the COMNAP objective to facilitate and promote international partnerships, there is recognition that strategic partnerships with other key Antarctic organizations are important to COMNAP as an organization. To support this, COMNAP has created standing items within the tasks of its Executive Committee (EXCOM) to develop and support key relationships with the CEP, SCAR and the Antarctic Treaty Secretariat.

6. 2009-2010 officers, topic-based information sharing and strategic projects

6.1 Executive Committee (EXCOM)

The COMNAP Chair and Vice-Chairs are elected officers of COMNAP. The elected officers plus the Executive Secretary, compose the COMNAP Executive Committee as follows:

Position	Officer	Term expires
Chair	José Retamales (Chile)	mid-2010
Vice-Chairs	Virginia Mudie (Australia)	mid-2012
	Maaike Vancauvenberghe (Belgium)	mid-2012
	Rasik Ravindra (India)	mid-2010
	Kazuyuki Shiraishi (Japan)	mid-2011
	Lou Sanson (New Zealand)	mid-2010
Executive Secretary	Michelle Rogan-Finnemore	30 Sept 2015

Table 1 – COMNAP Executive Committee.

6.2 Expert groups & topic-based information sharing

An important and valuable aspect of COMNAP is to allow exchange of information between National Antarctic Program staff on a range of relevant topics.

Exchange of information on each topic is coordinated and supported by a nominated Expert Group Leader. Each Principal Contact is overseen and supported by a designated EXCOM member.

For 2009-2010 expert groups are as follows:

Expert Group (topic)	Expert Group leader	EXCOM officer (oversight)
Science	Heinz Miller	Lou Sanson
Outreach	Linda Capper	Lou Sanson
Air	Giuseppe De Rossi	Virginia Mudie
Environment	Rodolfo Sanchez (confirmation pending)	Maaike Vancauwenberghe
Training		Rasik Ravindra
Medical	Iain Grant	Lou Sanson
Shipping	Juan Jose Danobeitia & David Blake	Jose Retamales
Safety	Robert Culshaw	Kazuyuki Shiraishi
Energy & Technology	David Blake	Rasik Ravindra
Data Management		Jose Retamales
External Relationships	Michelle Rogan-Finnemore	EXCOM
Strategic Framework	Michelle Rogan-Finnemore	Virginia Mudie

Table 2 – COMNAP expert groups (topics).

6.3 Strategic projects

COMNAP activity focuses on a small number of Strategic Projects, each managed by a Project Manager and overseen by a designated member of EXCOM. For 2009-2010, the Strategic Projects are:

Project	Project Manager	EXCOM officer (oversight)
COMNAP Symposium 2010 - organizing and review committee	Mariano Memolli	Kazuyuki Shiraishi
Framework for a 5-year Strategic Project Plan	Michelle Rogan-Finnemore	Virginia Mudie
Developing an action plan for a strategic partnership with SCAR	Michelle Rogan-Finnemore	Jose Retamales
Medical Contact Group & Workshop	Iain Grant	Lou Sanson
Outreach Workshop	Linda Capper	Lou Sanson
Energy & Technology Contact Group & Workshop	David Blake	Rasik Ravindra & Kazuyuki Shiraishi
Review issue of introduction of non-native species into Antarctica (Workshop) and determine practical remediation actions/quarantine management procedures	Yves Frenot	Maaike Vancauwenberghe
Antarctic glossary	Valerie Lukin	Virginia Mudie
AFIM – results of the review	Brian Stone & Giuseppe De Rossi	Virginia Mudie
IMO Proposal on the use of fuels and what that means for COMNAP Members	David Blake	Jose Retamales
AINMR System & implementation	Robert Culshaw	Kazuyuki Shiraishi
Surplus equipment buy/sell service	David Blake	Virginia Mudie
King George Island project	Michelle Rogan-Finnemore	Jose Retamales

Table 3 – COMNAP strategic projects.

7. An overview of COMNAP activities and services

7.1 COMNAP Ship Position Reporting System (SPRS)

The COMNAP SPRS is an optional, voluntary system for exchange of information about National Program ship operations and capabilities. Its primary purpose is to facilitate collaboration between National Programs.

7.2 Review of the Antarctic Flight Information Manual (AFIM)

The AFIM is a handbook of aeronautical information published by COMNAP as recommended by the ATCM Recommendation XV-20 *Air safety in Antarctica.*

An in-depth review of the AFIM was conducted in 2008-2009. Now, the results of that review are being considered as a strategic project for 2009-2010.

7.3 Antarctic Telecommunications Operators Manual (ATOM)

The ATOM is an evolution of the handbook of telecommunications practices that ATCM Recommendation X-3 *Improvement of Telecommunications in Antarctica and the Collection and Distribution of Antarctic Meteorological Data* refers to - it is no longer limited to stations and ships. It now also includes contact details for National Antarctic Programs, Search and Rescue (SAR) authorities and a number of other stakeholders. COMNAP members and SAR authorities have access to the latest version (August 2009) at http://www.comnap.aq/atom.

7.4 Accident, Incident and Near-Miss Reporting (AINMR)

Information on problems encountered in Antarctica has always been exchanged. The very first ATCM recommended in Recommendation I-VII Exchange *of Information on Logistics Problems* that this should be so.

COMNAP AGMs offer an opportunity for Members to exchange such information and also a new, comprehensive AINMR system is under development as one of COMNAP's strategic projects.

7.5   Hydrographic surveying using ships of opportunity

COMNAP worked with the Hydrographic Commission on Antarctica (HCA) to develop a "Collection and Rendering of Hydrographic Data Form" that can be used by ships of opportunity operating in the Antarctic. A presentation by the HCA was also made at the COMNAP AGM in August 2009 in Punta Arenas, Chile. A COMNAP representative, Henry Valentine (SANAP) attended the HCA9.

7.6   Information Exchange

The COMNAP infoX electronic information exchange system will manage a range of dynamic information on National Antarctic Program capabilities and activities.

There have been many delays to the completion and deployment of the COMNAP infoX system. It is currently still under development and not ready for implementation.

7.7   SCAR/COMNAP Action Group

As a result of the joint SCAR/COMNAP Executive Committee Meeting held in August in Punta Arenas, Chile, SCAR/COMNAP have formed an Action Group which met for the first time in March 2010.

Work on this important relationship will continue and will be reported at the COMNAP AGM and the SCAR Meetings in Buenos Aires, Argentina, in August 2010.

7.8   Collaboration with the Antarctic Treaty Secretariat

The COMNAP and Antarctic Treaty Secretariats have developed and maintained a close and constructive working relationship and discuss a number of practical matters as and when appropriate.

7.9   Antarctic Treaty Meeting of Experts (ATME) on the Management of Ship-bourne Tourism in the Antarctic Treaty Area

COMNAP attended the ATME and presented IP10 *Search and Rescue Coordination and Response in the Antarctic: Workshop Discussions*.

7.10   Antarctic Treaty Summit

The Chair and the Executive Secretary of COMNAP attended the Antarctic Treaty Summit in Washington D.C. The COMNAP Chair delivered a presentation entitled *The Role of COMNAP* as part of the Summit session entitled "International Cooperation in Antarctica".

8.   Meetings

August 2009 COMNAP AGM (COMNAP XXI) Punta Arenas, Chile; September 2009 COMNAP EXCOM, Christchurch, New Zealand; Antarctic Search and Rescue (SAR) Workshop II, Buenos Aires, Argentina; Upcoming: COMNAP Outreach Workshop (to be held on the margins of the IPY Oslo Science Conference, Norway); Upcoming: August 2010 COMNAP AGM (COMNAP XXII) & XIV Symposium, Buenos Aires, Argentina; Upcoming: 2011 COMNAP AGM (COMNAP XXIII) Sweden (dates and city to be confirmed).

9.   Secretariat

In 2009, the formal process to select the location of the COMNAP Secretariat was completed, with the appointment of Michelle Rogan-Finnemore as the new Executive Secretary and the selection of Christchurch, New Zealand, as the location of the COMNAP Secretariat.

3. Reports by Experts

Report of the Antarctic and Southern Ocean Coalition (ASOC)

1.   Introduction

ASOC is pleased to be in the Oriental Republic of Uruguay for this annual Antarctic Treaty meeting. This report briefly describes ASOC's work over the past year, and outlines some key issues for this ATCM, further discussed in our Information Papers.

The precedent of holding a meeting of experts on climate change, in Norway in April, was welcome and important. ASOC participated actively, submitting four papers. We fully support the recommendations made by the ATME to this ATCM.

The ATME on ship-borne tourism held in New Zealand last December also was an important event, at which ASOC participated actively. We have re-submitted for this ATCM some of our papers presented there because they are relevant to the CEP and Tourism Working Group.

2.   ASOC Worldwide

ASOC maintains its Secretariat office in Washington DC, USA. Our website (http://www.asoc.org) provides details about the organisation, including its governance, staff and associated experts, finances and history. It contains a document and photo archive, a blog, and other information about ASOC and its work.

ASOC has 30 full member groups, with member offices in most signatory countries to the Antarctic Treaty. ASOC campaigns are coordinated by teams of scientists, lawyers and policy experts located in Argentina, Australia, Brazil, Chile, France, Japan, Netherlands, New Zealand, Norway, Poland, South Africa, South Korea, Spain, Russia, Ukraine, United Kingdom and USA.

3.   ASOC Intersessional Activities Since XXXII ATCM

Since XXXII ATCM ASOC monitored all discussions in the ATCM and CEP Fora, and contributed actively to the discussions on biological prospecting, non-native species, revision of Recommendation XVIII-10, effects of tourism, and protected areas.

In addition, ASOC attended:

- 28th Meeting of CCAMLR in October-November 2009, introducing papers on Antarctic krill management, Marine Protected Areas, the Ross Sea, and impacts of climate change.
- International Maritime Organization (IMO) meetings, including the 59th and 60th Marine Environment Protection Committee sessions, and the 53rd session of the Ship Design and Equipment sub-committee regarding a Polar Code for ships operating in polar waters.
- Antarctic Treaty Meeting of Experts on Management of Ship-borne Tourism in Wellington, New Zealand, December 2009.
- Annual meeting of the International Whaling Commission in Santiago in June 2009 and the March 2010 IWC Working Group meeting in Florida as an accredited observer.
- Meeting of Parties to the Agreement on the Conservation of Albatrosses and Petrels in Norway, May 2009, as an accredited observer, and its Advisory Committee in Argentina, April 2010 by WWF as an accredited observer.
- Antarctic Treaty Meeting of Experts on Climate Change held in Svolvær, Norway, April 2010.

4.   Information Papers for XXXIII ATCM

ASOC has introduced 10 Information Papers, which suggest steps for the ATCM, CEP and CCAMLR that will help to better achieve effective protection of Antarctic ecosystems and wilderness values over the longer term. Several highlight the need for closer, more effective working relationships between the ATCM and CCAMLR and their respective CEP and SC-CAMLR, and between the Antarctic Treaty System and the IMO, ACAP and IWC.

- **IP 68: Working Towards A Polar Vessel Code** – This paper identifies critical issues related to Antarctic vessel operations. ASOC supports a mandatory, legally-binding instrument for <u>all</u> vessels operating in polar waters, which addresses both safety aspects and the full range of environmental impacts from vessels operating south of the Antarctic Polar Front.

- **IP 70: Comparison of Three Antarctic Treaty Meeting of Experts on Shipping and Tourism** – This paper compares the outcomes of the recent Antarctic Treaty Meeting of Experts on Ship-borne tourism (Wellington, 2009) with previous ATMEs on shipping (London, 2000) and tourism (Norway, 2004). Progress on regulation of shipping and tourism should continue at a more rapid pace, so that regulation has substantive effects on tourism developments and shipping standards.

- **IP73: Key Climate Change Actions in Antarctica: Emissions Reduction, Adaptation and Science** – Activities related to climate change need to take place in three areas: 1) Reduction of greenhouse gas emissions through use of energy efficiency and coordination of transport and logistics; 2) Implementation of climate adaptation strategies to reduce the vulnerability of climate-sensitive ecosystems; and 3) Continued timely dissemination of the findings of climate research in Antarctica to policy makers and the world population in general.

- **IP 74: Energy Efficiency And Renewable Energy Under Extreme Conditions: Case Studies From Antarctica** – This paper was recently published in the internationally peer-reviewed journal *Renewable Energy* and provides examples of energy efficiency and renewable energy systems in use at Antarctic research stations. Years of successful operation demonstrate that these can make a substantial contribution to reducing energy use.

- **IP 77: The Case for Inclusion of the Ross Sea Continental Shelf and Slope in a Southern Ocean Network of Marine Reserves** – ASOC proposes that the Ross Sea shelf and slope be protected as an MPA for a range of scientific and environmental reasons. It is the least affected large stretch of continental shelf remaining on Earth, a site of unique evolutionary significance, a region with exemplary benthic biodiversity and globally-significant populations of Adélie and emperor penguins, Antarctic petrels, Antarctic minke whales, Ross Sea killer whales and Weddell seals. It is projected to be the least affected large marine ecosystem in the face of global climate change, and thus an excellent climate reference zone and refugium.

- **IP 79: Tourism and Land-based Facilities in Antarctica: Analysis of a Questionnaire Distributed to Antarctic Treaty Parties at XXXII ATCM** – ASOC has continued updating information on land facilities used to support tourism in Antarctica, based on responses to a questionnaire distributed at XXXII ATCM. ASOC would appreciate the inputs of all Parties to the questionnaire attached to the paper.

- **IP 80: Making Tangible Progress on a Strategic Vision for Antarctic Tourism** – This paper recommends that key legally binding instruments that are still not in force become effective as soon as possible; that Parties adopt binding regulations in implementing the general principles of Resolution 7, 2009, by means of Measures; review and improve how EIA is applied to tourism; and use protected area instruments proactively as strategic tourism management tools.

- **IP 81: Coastal Hydrocarbon Pollution: A Case Study From Deception Island, Antarctica** - This paper updates results of monitoring activities conducted by ASOC at Deception Island in 2001-2002 jointly with the Institute of Chemical Physics of Materials, Environment and Energy, University of Buenos Aires, Argentina, as reported to the SCAR/IASC Open Science Conference, St. Petersburg, Russian Federation, July 2008.

- **IP 82: Antarctic Ship-borne Tourism and Inspections Under Article VII of the Antarctic Treaty and Article 14 of the Protocol on Environmental Protection** – This paper reviews official inspections of tourism cruise vessels in the Antarctic Treaty Area between 1959 and 2009. Tourism is a major Antarctic activity and should be the focus of inspections to a greater degree than hitherto. Purpose-made checklists for tourism would be useful.

- **IP 83: Rising to the challenge: Key steps to deliver a Comprehensive and Representative Marine Protected Areas Network in the Southern Ocean by 2012** – This elaborates on key outcomes required during 2010 to ensure that a representative network of marine protected areas and marine reserves is in place across the Southern Ocean by 2012, and the importance of close collaboration with CCAMLR by the ATCM and CEP in this endeavour.

In addition, ASOC has prepared a poster that explores the human footprint in Antarctica for display at XXXIII ATCM.

5.   *Other Important Issues for XXXIII ATCM*

- ASOC urges Parties to increase their efforts in implementing the **Environmental Protocol** to high standards. This includes addressing strategic environmental issues such as establishment of new stations, protection of wilderness values, and research on the subglacial environment.

- Bringing **Annex VI on Liability Arising from Environmental Emergencies** into force as rapidly as possible should be a high priority for all ATCPs. ASOC urges all Parties to redouble their efforts over the next year to solve the remaining implementation problems, so that Annex VI can be ratified and come into force in 2011.

- **Biological prospecting** represents a further penetration of commercial interests into the Antarctic, and is currently unregulated. ASOC supports a framework for managing it, including much more transparent sharing of data and information by Parties. ASOC remains surprised by the limited responses to Recommendation 2 of Resolution 7 (2005), which requires Parties to provide information annually on the nature and extent of their biological prospecting activities in the Antarctic Treaty Area by their scientists and companies.

Concluding Remarks

The Antarctic region is facing many new pressures from global climate change and a wide and expanding range of activities within the region. ASOC and its member groups around the world hope that the Antarctic Treaty Consultative Parties will take concrete actions and make decisions in Punta del Este that will protect the Antarctic over the longer term.

Report of the International Association of Antarctica Tour Operators 2009-10

Under Article III (2) of the Antarctic Treaty

Introduction

The International Association of Antarctica Tour Operators (IAATO) is pleased to present a report of its activities to ATCM XXXIII, under Article III (2) of the Antarctic Treaty.

IAATO continues to focus activities in support of its mission statement to ensure:
- Effective day-to-day management of member activities in Antarctica;
- Educational outreach, including scientific collaboration; and
- Development and promotion of Antarctic tourism industry best practices.

A detailed description of IAATO, its mission statement, primary activities and recent developments can be found on the IAATO website: www.iaato.org.

IAATO Membership and Activities during 2009-10

IAATO member offices are located worldwide, representing companies from 57% of the Antarctic Treaty Consultative Parties, and carrying nationals from nearly all Treaty Parties annually to Antarctica.

For visitation during the 2009-10 Antarctic tourism season, the overall number of visitors dropped 6.8% to 35,262 from the previous season (37,858 visitors in 2008-09). These numbers reflect only those traveling with IAATO member companies. Details on tourism statistics can be found in ATCM XXXIII IP *IAATO Overview of Antarctic Tourism: 2009-10 Season and Preliminary Estimates for 2010-11 and Beyond*. The Membership Directory and additional statistics on IAATO member activities can be found at ***www.iaato.org***.

IAATO Annual Meeting and Participation at Other Meetings during 2009-10

IAATO Secretariat staff and member representatives participated in internal and external meetings, liasing with National Antarctic Programs, governmental, scientific and environmental organizations during 2009-10.

- The IAATO 20th Annual Meeting (June 8-11, 2009, Providence, Rhode Island, USA) hosted 105 participants. Two full days were open to Treaty Party representatives. Several notable outcomes of the meeting included:
  - Adoption of additional industry best practice measures, including measures related to field staff training and accreditation, prevention of introduction of non-native species, and a strategic review of forthcoming priority areas;
  - *Actions to Enhance Marine Safety* and *Guidelines for Small Boat Operation in the Vicinity of Ice*, recommended by the IAATO Marine Committee, were approved by Members (see ATCM XXXIII IP061 *IAATO Further Recommendations to Tourism Vessel Operators to Enhance Marine Safety, and Guidelines for Small Boat Operations in the Vicinity of Ice*); and
  - Establishment of a climate change working group to: quantify members' carbon footprint, assess and ultimately augment current mitigation practices; and develop educational material for passengers on the implications of climate change in Antarctica;

  In addition, IAATO members and representatives from several Treaty Parties participated in an informal round table discussion on Antarctic tourism-related issues (see ATCM XXXIII IP084 *Establishing an Annual Round Table Discussion on Antarctic Tourism: Summary Report on June 2009 IAATO Meeting)*.

- Two IAATO representatives attended COMNAP XXI. IAATO welcomed occasions where its input was requested: refining methods of reporting major incidents to COMNAP; containment of potential H1N1 virus; clarification and likely outcome of pending IMO ban on use and carriage of HFO in Antarctic waters; and improved scientific and logistical collaboration. IAATO supports further cooperation and collaboration between its operators and National Antarctic Programs.

- Two IAATO representatives attended the 9th International Hydrographic Organization / Hydrographic Committee on Antarctica (IHO/HCA) Meeting. IAATO strongly supports the constructive work of the IHO/HCA and is pleased to continue to offer IAATO vessels as ships of opportunity for hydrographic data collection. During 2009-10, hydrographers visited several IAATO vessels in key ports to discuss directly with ships' officers the most effective means to collect data. The HCA will also make a presentation at the 2010 IAATO Annual Meeting to appraise members on the work of the HCA and discuss further assistance that can be provided by IAATO operators.

- Five IAATO representatives participated in the 2nd Annual *Workshop Towards Improved Search and Rescue (SAR) Coordination and Response in the Antarctic.* The workshop resulted in a number of key points and recommendations, some focusing on tourism-related activities. Attendees worked through four hypothetical SAR exercises, resulting in some realistic appraisals of SAR assets available to Maritime Rescue Coordination Centers (MRCCs) including the extent to which IAATO members can provide SAR assets. The IAATO vessel-tracking system was noted as an important tool in helping to "take the search out of search & rescue," and figured into some of the key points and recommendations. IAATO strongly supports the recommendation that National Antarctic Programs express to their countries the need for contingency planning to be outlined in all authorization applications or advance notifications.

- IAATO was pleased to participate in the 2009 ATME on Ship-borne Tourism, presenting three Information Papers: IP007 *IAATO Summary of Antarctic Ship-Based Tourism: Final Statistics for the 2008-09 Season and Revised Estimates for the 2009-10 Season and Projected Trends through the 2012-13 Season*; IP008 *IAATO Actions and Recommendations to Tourism Vessel Operators to Enhance Marine Safety*; and – jointly with the US – IP009 *Spatial Patterns of Tour Ship Traffic in the Antarctic Peninsula Region.* IAATO looks forward to continued discussions on tourism-related topics.

- IAATO sent a representative to the International Maritime Organization (IMO) Design and Equipment (D&E) Subcommittee's 53rd meeting (February 2010), as an advisor for Cruise Lines International Association (CLIA). Cognizant of the focus on the development of a mandatory Polar Code and the importance placed by the Secretary General and the Chair of the Subcommittee to produce prudent measures toward the protection of life and the polar environments, IAATO was pleased to make a presentation of a risk-based approach intended to inform the discussion and contribute to the development of the Code. A general description of the material provided in IAATO's presentation can be found in ATCM XXXIII IP060 *Developing a Risk Assessment Framework for IAATO Passenger Vessels.* Through CLIA, IAATO looks forward to actively participating in the discussions to develop the Code.

- IAATO sent a representative to the 2010 ATME on Climate Change, presenting IP003 *IAATO's Climate Change Working Group.* IAATO welcomes these discussions, noting their importance for the effective management of the Antarctic environment.

- The IAATO 21st Annual Meeting is scheduled for June 21-24, 2010 in Turin, Italy. Interested Treaty Parties that would like to attend or participate should contact IAATO at iaato@iaato.org.

Environmental Impact Assessment, Monitoring, Advance Notification and other Treaty Agreements

Most IAATO member operators are required to submit Environmental Impact Assessments (EIAs), Advance Notification and/or operational documents that substitute for EIAs to their national authorities pending each country's legal process. Not all governments require EIAs or yearly updates. A comparison of operators' EIAs, which they are required to submit to their respective national authorities, reflects some notable variations in requirements. IAATO endeavors to bridge these variations by building best-practice operating standards and guidelines, in particular to ensure that mitigation measures and procedures are in place to avoid environmental impacts.

In addition, Recommendation XVIII-1 (1994) *Guidance for Those Organizing and Conducting Tourism and Non-governmental Activities in the Antarctic* is provided to all members in order to inform them of key obligations and procedures to be followed. IAATO urges Parties to consider formally adopting Recommendation XVIII-1 for Visitors and Tour Organizers. IAATO remains concerned about visitors traveling as part of non-IAATO recreational operations that may not be aware of the Environmental Protocol and its obligations.

IAATO is pleased to be working collaboratively with Oceanites, Antarctic Site Inventory and University of Maryland on data collection and analysis regarding IAATO member activities for monitoring purposes. In addition, IAATO is pleased to have commenced collaboration with the University of Stellenbosch regarding pathways and vectors for non-native species, and looks forward to further collaborative efforts with other scientific bodies in the forthcoming year.

Update on Tourism Incidents 2008-09, and Tourism Incidents 2009-10

IAATO awaits final flag-state reports from Panama and Bahamas, respectively, for two marine incidents that occurred during the 2008-09 season: the December 4, 2008 grounding of *MV Ushuaia*, and February 17, 2009 grounding of *MV Ocean Nova*.

Three notable incidents occurred during the 2009-10 season: two medical evacuations from the South Pole, and a damaged propeller and shaft incurred when an expedition vessel, *Clelia II*, struck a rock during a routine landing operation at Petermann Island, Penola Strait, Antarctic Peninsula. Circular No. 1 / 2010, distributed by the Antarctic Treaty Secretariat on January 7, 2010, described all three incidents.

Scientific and Conservation Support

During the 2009-10 season, IAATO members cost-effectively transported scores of scientific, support and heritage trust staff, as well as equipment used by these personnel, to and from stations, field sites and gateway ports. In addition, IAATO members and their passengers continued the tradition of financial contributions to many scientific and conservation organizations active in Antarctica. A breakdown of monies raised and transport provided during 2009-10 will soon be available on the IAATO website under *Papers and Publications.*

With Thanks – Cooperation with National Programs, Antarctic Treaty Parties and all Stakeholders

IAATO appreciates the opportunity to work cooperatively with Antarctic Treaty Parties, COMNAP, SCAR, CCAMLR, IHO/HCA, ASOC and others towards the long-term protection of Antarctica.

Report by the International Hydrographic Organization (IHO) on "Cooperation in hydrographic surveying and charting of Antarctic waters"

Introduction

Through its Hydrographic Commission on Antarctica (HCA), the International Hydrographic Organization (IHO) plays an important role in contributing to safety of life at sea and the protection of the marine environment in Antarctica. This Report that provides a brief summary of the key coordination activities had since last ATCM; the status of hydrographic surveys and nautical chart production of Antarctic waters, conclusions and recommendations.

The IHO confirms its willingness to continue working closely with the AT System and other relevant international organizations to improve safety of life at sea, safety of navigation, and enhance its contribution to the efforts aimed at the protection of the marine environment and marine scientific research in Antarctica.

1.- Key Coordination Activities

1.1. Seminar on Hydrography at the Annual Meeting of COMNAP

On behalf of the IHO, the HCA participated in the Annual Meeting of COMNAP held in Punta Arenas, Chile, in August 2009 and delivered a short seminar on the "Importance of Hydrographic Activities in Antarctica".

26 COMNAP members and 4 international organizations were present with over 150 delegates. The IHO participated with its HCA Chairman and IHB Director, Captain Hugo Gorziglia, together with RAdm Ian Moncrieff and Commander Enrique Silva, representatives of UK and Chile to the HCA, respectively.

The objective of the seminar was: to raise awareness at the operational level on the importance of hydrographic activity in the Antarctica; to achieve a better understanding of COMNAP on the existing risks associated to the present status of charting in the region and to explore ways to jointly improve the situation.

Two concrete initiatives were proposed to and agreed by COMNAP. One was to put in practice the *"IHO Collection and Rendering of Hydrographic Data Form* and the second one was to review and provide comments to the HCA on the existing Hydrographic Survey Priority List developed by the Commission.

1.2. The 9th Meeting of the IHO Hydrographic Commission on Antarctica

This meeting took place in South Africa 12-14 October 2009. Twelve HCA Member States (Australia, Brazil, Chile, France, Germany, Korea (Rep of), New Zealand, Norway, South Africa, Spain, UK and Venezuela), were represented at this meeting, plus observers from COMNAP, IAATO, GEBCO/IBCSO and the South African DEAT. In total, 25 delegates were in attendance. The Republic of Korea and Venezuela were welcomed as new members of HCA, which brought its total number to 23.

The Commission reviewed the action list agreed at the last HCA meeting and decided: to nominate Dr. Schenke (Germany) as HCA representative to the International Bathymetric Chart of the Southern Ocean in order to improve coordination with the scientific community; to coordinate the visit of hydrographic surveyors from Argentina, Chile and New Zealand with at least one IAATO ship when calling in port on her way to Antarctica to advise on the collection and rendering of hydrographic data to ensure collected data can be used for charting purposes.

The ATCM Secretariat, COMNAP, IAATO and SCAR submitted reports for consideration by the HCA. The HCA would like to thank the international organizations for the cooperation and collaboration, as well as the joint work in progress. Outcomes from the discussion had were: the convenience to address environmental and scientific issues in addition to safety of navigation issues and that HCA members interested in making use of IAATO ships, to coordinate directly with IAATO.

The Commission examined the status of hydrographic surveys and nautical charts production, the details of which are provided under section 2 in this report.

Also it was discussed how the HCA could contribute to the ATME that will examine issues surrounding ship-borne tourism in the Antarctic Treaty Area, in New Zealand, in December 2009, details of which are provided in section 1.3 of this report.

Finally, the Commission decided to accept UK's proposal to host HCA10 in Cambridge, 20 to 22 of September 2010.

1.3. Antarctic Treaty Meeting of Experts (ATME)

Pursuant to Decision 7 (2009), the ATME on the Management of Ship-borne Tourism in the Antarctic Treaty Area took place in Wellington, New Zealand, 09-11 December 2009. The IHO was represented by HCA Chairman and IHB Director, Captain Gorziglia.

The IHO submitted two papers. One paper noted the role of IHO and the work so far undertaken by HCA. The second paper dealt with the existing cooperation between ATCM and IHO. The meeting agreed to continue inviting IHO HCA to the annual ATCM meetings and where appropriate to be represented at IHO HCA meetings.

In addition the Hydrographer of New Zealand submitted a working paper providing details on the hydro-cartographic activities New Zealand has conducted.

Out of the recommendations adopted by the Meeting of Experts, two had direct relation with the IHO. The texts are as follow:

 a) « *That the AT Parties should continue to contribute to hydrographic surveying and charting information and consider advising vessels intending to operate in the AT area that many areas have not been surveyed to modern standards* ».
 b) « *The IHO HCA should continue to be invited to annual ATCMs to report the status of hydrographic survey and nautical chart production in Antarctic waters. Parties also agreed that, as appropriate, the ATCM should be represented at IHO HCA meetings. Where an IHO HCA meeting was to be held in a country that was also Consultative Party, then that Consultative Party should consider attending the HCA meeting* ».

2.- Status of Hydrographic Surveys and Nautical Chart Production.

2.1 Hydrographic Surveys.

Out of the 15 National Reports submitted to the last HCA meeting, only 7 indicated that some systematic hydrographic surveys have taken place during the season 2008/2009. There is no assessment yet with respect to the 2009/2010 season.

As these surveys are associated to a particular INT Chart we can expect an improvement on data availability to produce new charts. Nevertheless the Commission is fully aware that it is urgent to assign a high priority to hydrographic survey activities as the "only way" to ensure the timely production of the INT charts.

It is expected that with the commission of new survey ships and modern equipment installed on hydrographic survey ships, in the near future there will be a better capacity to conduct surveys in Antarctica.

The contribution by IAATO ships and other Ships of Opportunity, in hydrographic data gathering shall be assessed at the next HCA meeting. For the time being there is no indication that special hydrographic teams have used the opportunity to embark on IAATO ships due to the complexity in the coordination and doubtful cost / benefit ratio.

Resolution 5 (2008) recommended AT Parties to clarify with HCA requirements for the collection of hydrographic data of sufficient quality for use in the development of electronic navigational charts and to identify priority areas for the collection of additional hydrographic and bathymetric data. The ATCM shall be aware that the *"IHO Collection and Rendering of Hydrographic Data Form"*, included as Annex B in this report, provides the minimum requirements that hydrographic data shall comply in order to be considered for cartographic purposes.

The HCA Hydrographic Survey Prioritizing Working Group with cooperation from COMNAP and IAATO continues to progress its mandate and the preparation of graphics reflecting the status of hydrographic surveys assets, in the short list priority areas and related INT Charts.

2.2 Nautical Chart Production.

The situation with regard to chart production is provided in detail in Annex C.

The INT Chart scheme includes 102 charts and 67 INT Charts have been produced or shall be finalized in 2010.

Resolution 5 (2008) recommends to cooperate with HCA to improve hydrographic surveying and charting in the Antarctic region and endeavour to find additional resources towards improving hydrographic surveying and charting in the Antarctic region. It is evident that there is a willingness to progress in the production of new INT charts. This sentiment requires to be translated in an effective increase in the priority assigned by Governments to conduct hydrographic surveying and allocate resources to nautical chart production.

With regard to the ENC production, the Commission confirms that small and medium scales have been agreed. Large scale scheme is under consideration. It was agreed that producers of ENCs should be those of the corresponding INT charts. The Commission congratulates the following countries for their progress in ENC production: Australia, Brazil, Chile, France, Germany, Italy, Norway and UK. 14 overview; 6 coastal; 9 approaches, 10 harbour, and one berthing ENC are available. Other 35 are in production.

3.- Conclusions.

1.-   The IHO/HCA recognizes the cooperation and contribution received from several international organizations to progress hydrographic surveying and nautical chart production of Antarctic waters, supporting the protection of the marine environment and the marine scientific research. It is expected that ATCM will soon provide HCA its view with regard to the identification of priority areas for the collection of additional hydrographic and bathymetric data.

2.-   Despite the willingness expressed by AT representatives at different meetings, hydrographic surveys and production of nautical charts of Antarctica does not hold, in the practice, the required priority. The IHO/HCA is concerned by the extremely low progress achieved in terms of nautical chart delivery covering an extremely vulnerable marine environment.

3.-   Contribution expected from Ships of Opportunity operations should not be seen as THE solution, but as an opportunity not to be missed. The *"IHO Collection and Rendering of Hydrographic Data Form"*, is a concrete step forward in this line.

4.- Recommendations.

It is recommended that the XXXIII ATCM:

9. Takes note of the IHO Report.

10. Considers providing HCA the identification of priority areas of which hydrographic surveys and availability of INT charts could support to the protection of the marine environment and facilitate marine scientific research.

11. Instructs the AT System to make use of the *"IHO Collection and Rendering of Hydrographic Data Form"* as a follow up of Resolution 5 (2008).

Monaco, March 2010.

ANNEX A

HCA MEMBERSHIP SITUATION

(March 2010)

MEMBERS:

Argentina

Australia

Brazil

Chile

China

Ecuador

France

Germany

Greece

India

Italy

Korea, Republic of

New Zealand

Norway

Peru

Russian Federation

South Africa

Spain

United Kingdom

Uruguay

USA

Venezuela

Japan

OBSERVER ORGANIZATIONS:

Antarctic Treaty Secretariat (ATS)

Council of Managers of National Antarctic Programmes (COMNAP)

Standing Committee on Antarctic Logistics and Operations (SCALOP)

International Association of Antarctic Tour Operators (IAATO)

Scientific Committee on Antarctic Research (SCAR)

International Maritime Organization (IMO)

Intergovernmental Oceanographic Commission (IOC)

General Bathymetric Chart of the Oceans (GEBCO)

International Bathymetric Chart of the Southern Ocean (IBCSO)

IHO Data Center for Digital Bathymetry (DCDB)

Australian Antarctic Division

Antarctica New Zealand.

ANNEX B

IHO Collection and Rendering of Hydrographic Data Form
(To be used by Ships of Opportunity-SOO[2] in Antarctica)

The objective of this IHO Form is to facilitate the provision of the essential information required by the appropriate National Hydrographic Office to make use of the hydrographic data collected by a SOO in Antarctica. The Form has four sections: General information, Hydrographic Surveying information, Navigational Aids and Ancillary information and Data Format.

This Form together with all the documentation should be completed and made available to the:

International Hydrographic Organization
4 quai Antoine 1er B.P. 445 MC 98011 Monaco Cedex, MONACO
Phone +377 93108100 Fax + 377 93108140 e-mail info@ihb.mc

SECTION 1 « General Information »

General Area	Antarctic Peninsula	☐[3]	South Georgia	☐	Other (Please specify)	☐
	South Orkneys	☐	South Shetlands	☐		
Location						
Name of Vessel				Draught : (in meters)		
Name of Captain				Date :		
OBSERVATIONS : (Note 1)						

SECTION 2 « Hydrographic Surveying Information »

Position Fixing (Note 2)	GPS	☐	Visual /Radar	☐	Other (Please	☐

---

[2]SOO for the purpose of this Form is any ship, with the exception of hydrographic and research platforms, volunteer to collect hydrographic data during routine transit utilizing her own equipment.

[3] To tick box, double click on box> default value > activate.

					specify)	
	Model of receiver					
	Datum setting (ie.WGS84)					
	Remarks: (eg Plotting errors between GPS and Chart)					
Echo Sounder (Note 3)	Manufacturer			Name /Type		
	Multibeam/Swathe	☐	Single Beam	☐	Survey line (spacing in metres)	
Stylus:	Revolutions per minute					
Scale Setting	Zero depth recorded from:	Sea Surface?	☐	Under Keel?	☐	
Sound Velocity	Correction made?	YES (if YES) Metres per second	☐	NO	☐	
Transducer displacement applied:	N/A	☐	YES	☐	NO	☐
Details of transducer displacement:						
X offset = Port (-) or Starboard (+) from GPS receiver		Y offset = Aft (-) or Fwd (+) from GPS receiver		Z offset = Above (-) or Below (+) from GPS receiver		
..........................metres		..........................metres		................metres		
Echo trace rendered: Note (4)		YES	☐		NO	☐
Speed of vessel		...................................knots				

SECTION 3 « Navigational Aids and Ancillary Information »

Lights report rendered			YES	☐	NO	☐
Name/Location	Position	Working ? YES or NO	Characteristics Checked ? YES or NO	Remarks:		
Buoys/beacons report rendered			YES	☐	NO	☐
Name/Location	Position	Condition: Good, bad, missing	Remarks:			

Conspicuous Objects report rendered:			YES ☐		NO ☐	
Name/Location	Position	Bearing from Seaward	Remarks:			
View report rendered: (Note 5)			YES ☐		NO ☐	
Location	Position/bearing from seaward	Panoramic	Pilotage	Portrait	Close up	Remarks

SECTION 4 « Data Format »

Data format (Note 6)	Chart/Chart cutting	☐	Corrected to NM (.........../...........)	Tracing	☐
	Plotting sheet	☐	Floppy disc/CD rom	Photographs	☐
	Other - please state	☐			

Recommended references: IHO. S-44, UK. NP100 & NP9, US MGD77
For further information on any of the above Sections, please contact info@ihb.mc

Note 1
Observations: Proposed amendments to the existing text of the Sailing Directions and/or Antarctic Pilot are always welcome. Comments or remarks that the mariner thinks would improve charting coverage or the Sailing Directions is always appreciated by the IHO. Examples of these include transit notes and tracings or chart cuttings delineating areas of kelp. Constructive comments on chart coverage or the lack of it are useful for the future planning of charts and surveying.

Note 2
1. Visual fixes: To ensure the greatest accuracy, a fix defined by compass bearings or ranges, should consist if possible of more than two observations. These observations should be taken as nearly as possible simultaneously, carefully recorded at the time and listed in the report with any corrections that have been applied to them.
2. GPS positions: The report should state which datum was set on the receiver outputting positions,(eg WGS84 Datum) and/or whether any shifts quoted on the chart have been applied.
3. Observed differences: Mariners are requested to report observed differences between positions referred to chart system and those from GPS, referenced to WGS84 Datum.

Note 3
1. The speed of sound in sea water in metres per second equivalent to the stylus speed.
2. Whether soundings have been corrected from *Echo-sounding correction tables*.
3. Zero Scale Setting. That is whether depths are recorded from the sea surface or from under the keel.
4. Where the displacement of the transducers from the position of the GPS receiver or other instrument used to fix is appreciable, the amount of this displacement and whether allowance has been made for it should be reported.

Note 4
If an echo trace is rendered it should be marked as follows:
1. A line drawn across it each time a fix is taken, and at regular intervals.
2. The times of each fix and alteration of course inserted, and times of interval marks at not more than 15 minute intervals.

3. The position of each fix and other recorded events inserted where possible, unless a GPS printout or separate list of times and corresponding positions is enclosed with the report.
4. The recorded depths of all peak soundings inserted.
5. The limits of the phase or scale change in which the set is running marked, noting particularly when a change is made.
6. Name of ship, date, zone time used and scale reading of the shoaling edge of the transmission line should be marked on the trace. (diagram 8.14 in NP100)

Note 5

Photographs should be obtained whenever possible and where such view would help the mariner. An imperfect photograph, correctly annotated, can often be used to produce a view of considerable help to the mariner.

The various types of views and examples are given the following names:

1. Panoramic. A composite view made up from a series of overlapping photographs. This type of view is intended to show the offshore aspect including hinterland.
2. Pilotage. A single or composite view from the approach course to a harbour or narrows showing any leading marks, transits or conspicuous fixing marks. It may be combined with a close-up of the mark if necessary for positive identification.
3. Portrait. The single view of a specific object set in its salient background.
4. Close-up. Single views of one object or feature with emphasis on clarity of the subject for its identification.

Note 6

The largest scale chart, a plotting sheet at a similar scale, a tracing or chart cutting should be used to plot the ships position during data collection.

If a chart cutting is used the additions and alterations should be marked in red. If a tracing is preferred, the additions should be marked in red, with adequate chart detail in black to enable fitting down. If a chart is rendered with data inserted, a replacement copy will be supplied free of charge.

Computer discs and CD Roms are also an easy way to render data and photographs, but must have easily readable formats.

ANNEX C

INT Chart Present Production Status (March 2010)

No.	INT No.	Name of the INT Charts	Scale	Producer	Status Publication	Status N. Edition
1	900	Ross Sea	2 000 000	NZ	1998	
2	901	De Cape Goodenough à Cape Adare	2 000 000	FR	2006	
3	902	Mawson Sea and Davis Sea	2 000 000	RU	2000	
4	903	Sodruzhestva Sea	2 000 000	RU	2001	
5	904	Dronning Maud Land	2 000 000	NO	2002	
6	905	South Sandwich Islands	2 000 000	DE	Proj. 2011	
7	906	Weddell Sea	2 000 000	GB	2005	
8	907	Antarctic Peninsula	2 000 000	GB	2000	
9	908	Bryan Coast to Martin Peninsula	2 000 000	GB	> 2015	
10	909	Martin Peninsula, Cape Colbeck	2 000 000	NO	Proj. 2011	
11	9000	Terra Nova Bay to Moubray Bay	500 000	IT	?	
12	9001	Cape Royds to Pram Point	60 000	NZ	2007	
13	9002	Scientific Stations McMurdo and Scott	5 000	NZ	2007	
14	9003	Approaches to Scott Island	75 000	NZ	2008	
		Plan A – Scott Island	25 000			
15	9004	Terra Nova Bay	250 000	IT	2007	2008
16	9005	Da Capo Russell a Campbell Glacier Tongue	50 000	IT	2000	
17	9006	Cape Adare and Cape Hallett	50 000	NZ	2003	2006
		Plan A – Cape Adare	50 000			
		Plan B – Cape Hallett	50 000			
		Plan C – Ridley Beach	15 000			
		Plan D – Seabee Hook	15 000			
18	9007	Possession Islands	60 000	NZ	2003	2006
19	9008	Cape Adare to Cape Daniell	200 000	NZ	2003	2006
20	9009	Cape Hooker to Coulman Island	500 000	NZ	2004	
21	9010	Matusevich Glacier to Ob' Bay	500 000	RU	2000	
22	9011	Mys Belousova to Terra Nova Island	200 000	RU	2000	
		Plan A – Leningradskaya Station	1 000			
23	9012	Balleny Islands	300 000	NZ	2006	
		Continuation: Balleny Seamount	300 000			
24	9014	Approaches to Commonwealth Bay	25 000	AU	2002	

No.	INT No.	Name of the INT Charts	Scale	Producer	Status Publication	Status N. Edition
		Plan A – Boat Harbour	5000			
25	9015	Du Glacier Dibble au Glacier Mertz	500 000	FR	2004	
26	9016	De la Pointe Ebba au Cap de la Découverte	100 000	FR	2004	
		Plan A – Archipel Max Douguet - Port-Martin	10 000			
		Plan B – Archipel Max Douguet	30 000			
27	9017	De l'Ile Hélène au Rocher du Débarquement - Archipel de Pointe Géologie	20 000	FR	2002	
		Plan A – Archipel de Pointe Géologie	7500			
28	9020	Mill Island to Cape Poinsett	500 000	AU	1998	
29	9021	Approaches to Casey	50 000	AU	1999	Proj. 2010
		Plan A – Newcomb Bay	12 500			
30	9025	Davis Sea	500 000	RU	1999	
31	9026	Approaches to Polar Station Mirny	200 000	RU	1999	
32	9027	Road Mirny	10 000	RU	1999	
33	9030	Sandefjord Bay to Cape Rundingen	500 000	AU	1992	
34	9031	Cape Rundingen to Cape Filchner	500 000	AU	2002	
35	9032	Approaches to Davis Anchorage	12 500	AU	2003	
36	9033	Cape Rouse to Sandefjord Bay	500 000	AU	1991	Proj. 2011
37	9035	Magnet Bay to Cape Rouse	500 000	AU	1993	Proj. 2011
38	9036	Approaches to Mawson	25 000	AU	2007	Proj. 2011
		Plan A - Horseshoe harbour	5000			
39	9037	Gibbney Island to Kista Strait	25 000	AU	Proj. 2011	
40	9040	Alasheyev Bight to Cape Ann	500 000	RU	2000	
41	9041	Alasheyev Bight	100 000	RU	1999	
42	9042	Approaches to Molodezhnaya Station	12 500	RU	1999	
43	9045	Vestvika Bay	500 000	JP	Proj. 2010	
44	9046	Eastern Part of Ongul	100 000	JP	2009	
45	9047	Western Part of Ongul	10 000	JP	2009	
46	9050	Sergei Kamenev Gulf to Neupokojevabukta	500 000	RU	1999	
47	9051	Approaches to Leningradbukta	200 000	RU	1998	
48	9055	Muskegbukta Bay to Atka Gulf	500 000	DE	2009	
49	9056	Approaches to Dronning Maud Land	300 000	ZA	2006	2009
50	9057	Approaches to Atka Iceport	200 000	DE	2009	

No.	INT No.	Name of the INT Charts	Scale	Producer	Status	
					Publication	N. Edition
51	9060	Cape Roule to Farell Bay	500 000	RU	2000	
52	9061	Approaches to Halley Base	200 000	GB	2005	
53	9062	*To be determined*	200 000	US	?	
54	9100	Isla Marambio	25 000	AR	?	
		Plan A – Base aéra Marambio	5000			
55	9101	Peninsula Trinidad	10 000	AR	Proj. 2012	
		Plan A – Base Esperanza, Caleta Choza	5000			
56	9102	Estrecho Bransfield, Rada Covadonga y Accesos	10 000	CL	2003	
57	9103	Gerlache Strait	50 000	CL	Proj. 2013	
58	9104	Gerlache Strait	50 000	CL	Proj. 2011	
59	9105	Bismarck strait, Approaches to Arthur Harbour	25 000	US	?	
		Plan A – Arthur Harbour	10 000			
60	9106	Argentine Islands and Approaches	60 000	GB	1996	
		Plan A – Argentine Islands	15 000			
61	9107	Pendleton Strait etc.	50 000	GB	> 2015	
62	9108	Hanusse Bay to Wyatt Island	50 000	CL	?	
63	9109	British Antarctic Survey Base Rothera	25 000	GB	1999	
64	9110	Adelaide Island, South Western Approaches	30 000	CL	?	
65	9111	Bahía Margarita	25 000	AR	Proj. 2012	
66	9112	Plans in Bransfield Strait		GB	> 2015	
		Plan A – Yankee Harbour	12 500			
		Plan B – Freud (Pampa) Passage	50 000			
		Plan C – Portal Point	25 000			
		Plan D – Penguin Island	20 000			
		Plan E – Hydrurga Rocks	10 000			
67	9113	Plans in Elephant Island		GB	?	
		Plan A – Cape Lookout	50 000			
		Plan B – Cape Valentine	10 000			
		Plan C – Point Wild	10 000			
68	9114	Antarctic Sound		GB	?	
		Plan A – Fridtjof Sound	50 000			
		Plan B – Brown Bluff	10 000			
		Plan C – Gourdin Island	15 000			
69	9115	Active Sound	50 000	AR	?	

No.	INT No.	Name of the INT Charts	Scale	Producer	Status Publication	N. Edition
70	9116	Plans in Paulet and Danger Islands		GB	?	
		Plan A – Paulet Island	50 000			
		Plan B – Danger Islands	50 000			
71	9120	Isla Decepción	50 000	AR	2004	2006 Proj. 2010
		Plan A - Fuelles de Neptuno	12 500			
72	9121	Isla Livingston, de Punta Band a la Bahía Brunow	35 000	ES	1998	
		Plan A – Isla de la Media Luna	25 000			
		Plan B – Base Juan Carlos I	5 000			
73	9122	Bahía Chile, Puerto Soberanía y Ensenadas Rojes e Iquique		CL	1998	
		Plan A - Bahía Chile	20 000			
		Plan B - Puerto Soberanía y Ensenadas Rojas e Iquique	5000			
74	9123	Caletas en Bahía Fildes		CL	2007	
		Plan A – Caleta Potter	10 000			
		Plan B – Caleta Ardley	10 000			
		Plan C – Caleta Marian	10 000			
75	9124	Bahia Fildes	30 000	CL	2007	
76	9125	Baia do Almirantado	40 000	BR & PE	Proj. 2010	
		Plan A – Ensenada Martel	20 000			
		Plan B – Estação Arctowski	10 000			
		Plan C – Ensenada Mackellar	15 000			
77	9126	Baia Rei George (Ilha Rei George)	40 000	BR	?	
78	9127	Baia Sheratt (Ilha Rei George)	40 000	BR	?	
79	9130	Crystal Hill to Devil Island	75 000	GB	?	
		Plan A - Bald Head	10 000			
		Plan B - View Point	10 000			
		Plan C - Matts Head	10 000			
		Plan D - Crystal Hill	10 000			
		Plan E - Camp Point	10 000			
		Plan F - Devil Island	10 000			
80	9131	Crystal Sound	75 000	GB	?	
81	9132	Grandidier Channel	75 000	GB	?	
82	9140	Islas Orcadas del Sur	150 000	AR	> 2015	
83	9141	Approaches to Signy Island	50 000	GB	2006	
		Plan A – Borge Bay and Approaches	10 000			

No.	INT No.	Name of the INT Charts	Scale	Producer	Status	
					Publication	N. Edition
84	9142	Bahía Scotia	10 000	AR	2006	
85	9150	Islas Elefante y Clarence	200 000	BR	1999	2009
86	9151	De Isla De Jorge a Isla Livingston	200 000	CL & BR	Proj. 2017	
87	9152	De Isla Livingston a Isla Low	200 000	CL & BR	Proj. 2017	
88	9153	Church Point to Cape Longing including James Ross Island	150 000	GB & AR	1999	2004 Proj. 2010
89	9154	Joinville Island to Cape Ducorps and Church Point	150 000	GB & AR	1996	2002 Proj. 2010
90	9155	Estrecho Bransfield - Rada Covadonga a Isla Trinidad	150 000	CL	2003	
91	9156	Archipiélago de Palmer, de Isla Trinidad a Isla Amberes	150 000	AR	2009	
92	9157	Gerlache Strait	150 000	CL	Proj. 2020	
93	9158	Anvers Island to Renaud Island	150 000	GB	2001	2003
		Plan A – Port Lockroy	12 500			
94	9159	Pendleton Strait & Grandidier Channel	150 000	GB	Proj. 2011	
95	9160	Crystal Sound	150 000	GB	Proj. 2013	
96	9161	Matha Strait to Pourquoi Pas Island	150 000	CL	?	
97	9162	Adelaide Island	150 000	CL	?	
98	9163	Marguerite Bay; Rothera	150 000	GB	2009	
99	9164	Margarita Bay	150 000	CL	?	
100	9170	Islas Shetland y Mar de la Flota	500 000	AR	1997	
101	9171	Brabant Island to Adelaide Island	500 000	GB	> 2015	
102	9172	Matha Strait to Rothschild Island	500 000	RU	1999	

Resume:

a) 67 out of 102 INT Charts have been produced (or shall be finalized in 2010).
b) 5 charts are planned for 2011
c) 2 chart is planned for 2012
d) 2 charts are planned for 2013
e) 0 chart is planned for 2014
f) 8 charts are planned for "no earlier than 2015"
g) 18 charts have not yet been considered in the planning.

========= THE END =========

PART IV

**Additional Documents
from XXXIII ATCM**

1. Additional Documents

Abstract of SCAR Lecture

Psychrophiles: a challenge for life

Prof. Charles Gerday, University of Liege-Laboratory of Biochemistry

Institute of Chemistry, B6, Sart-Tilman, B-4000, Liege, Belgium

Punta del Este, 06th May 2010

The word psychrophiles means, "loving cold" and these organisms have been found in all cold environments on Earth, including the naturally coldest place on Earth the Antarctic.

To fully appreciate the importance of the challenge faced by psychrophiles one has to remember that a drop of 30°C of the environmental temperature should induce an average decrease of the rate of the chemical reactions occurring in the organism by a factor close to 30. This will immediately lead to death or at best to a dormant state of an organism. To prevent this and to become independent of the daily or seasonally fluctuations of the temperature some organisms, like mammals and birds, have succeeded, in the course of evolution, to keep constant their internal temperature. However, because this is so costly energy wise most of the living organisms on Earth leave their temperature to fluctuate as a function of the environmental temperature, including the psychrophiles that cover a wide range of living creatures from microorganisms to fish via invertebrates and insects. They have colonized all cold environments on Earth and rather successfully. Recent investigations carried out on bacteria isolated from Antarctic sea ice and from Alaskan soils frozen down to –35°C have indicated that microbial growth and metabolic activities are still significant at temperatures as low as –20°C.

Psychrophiles, exposed to these extreme conditions, have successfully developed specific molecular adaptations by producing first cryoprotectants and second so-called ice structuring proteins and antifreezes. Many of these have commercial applications, for example antifreeze proteins offer a high potential in biotechnology. Intuitively they appear highly suitable as additive for the preservation of tissue and organs at sub-zero temperatures, for scar treatment and re-epithelization of wounds, but are also used in some cosmetic regeneration creams and even in several ice cream brands. It efficiently prevents ice recrystallisation that can lead to a reduction of taste and texture quality.

The ice-nucleating protein from psychrophiles is nowadays heavily used for the production of snow on ski tracks and is starting to be used in the field of Bioremediation. Bioremediation of polluted sites is increasingly considered as a potent tool to clean and detoxify soils and waters contaminated by unwanted residues mainly generated by human activities. Other uses on enzymes isolated from psychrophiles include improved detergents that work at lower temperatures, removing lactose from milk-based products and even for making better bread.

For copies of the talk and more detailed text please go to:

http://www.scar.org/communications/

2. List of Documents

2. List of Documents

Working Papers								
Number	Ag. Items	Title	Submitted By	E	F	R	S	Attachments
WP001	ATCM 11 ATCM 4 CEP 6b	Chairs Report - Antarctic Treaty Meeting of Experts on the Management of Ship-borne Tourism in the Antarctic Treaty Area	New Zealand	X	X	X	X	Appendix A. Environmental aspects of Antarctic ship-borne tourism
WP002	ATCM 17	Biological prospecting in the Antarctic region: a conservative overview of current research	SCAR	X	X	X	X	SCAR Bioprospecting Questionnaire for ATCM
WP003	CEP 7f	Biodiversity-based Evaluation of the Environmental Domains Analysis	SCAR	X	X	X	X	
WP004	CEP 8a	Preliminary Results from the International Polar Year Programme: Aliens in Antarctica	SCAR	X	X	X	X	
WP005	CEP 7b	Proposed addition of the Plaque Commemorating the PM-3A Nuclear Power Plant at McMurdo Station to the List of Historic Sites and Monument	United States	X	X	X	X	
WP006	CEP 8a	Current knowledge for reducing risks posed by terrestrial non-native species: towards an evidence-based approach	SCAR Australia	X	X	X	X	Appendices 1 and 2
WP007	CEP 11	Report of the CEP Observer to the twenty-eighth meeting of the Scientific Committee to CCAMLR; 26 – 30 October 2009	New Zealand	X	X	X	X	
WP008	CEP 8a	Draft procedures for vehicle cleaning to prevent transfer of non-native species into and around Antarctica	United Kingdom	X	X	X	X	
WP009	CEP 8a	Open-ended Intersessional Contact Group on "Non-Native Species" (NNS) - 2009-2010 Report	France	X	X	X	X	Annexes I to IV
WP010	CEP 7a	Guidelines for the Application of Management Zones within Antarctic Specially Managed Areas and Antarctic Specially Protected Areas	United States	X	X	X	X	Appendix I: Guidelines for the Application of Management Zones within Antarctic Specially Managed Areas and Antarctic Specially Protected Areas
WP011	ATCM 10 CEP 5	Forwarding of hydrographic data collected during the IPY	Uruguay	X	X	X	X	
WP012	CEP 6b	Guidelines on Minimising the Impact of Pollution by Light at Antarctic Stations and Ships	United Kingdom	X	X	X	X	
WP013	ATCM 17	Report of the ATCM Intersessional Contact Group to Examine the Issue of Biological Prospecting in the Antarctic Treaty Area	Netherlands	X	X	X	X	
WP014	CEP 8a	Intra-regional transfer of species in terrestrial Antarctica	United Kingdom	X	X	X	X	
WP015	CEP 8a	Guidance for visitors and environmental managers following the discovery of a suspected non-native species in the terrestrial and freshwater Antarctic environment	United Kingdom	X	X	X	X	A. Guidelines for visitors upon finding a suspected terrestrial or freshwater non-native species within the Antarctic Treaty

Working Papers								
Number	Ag. Items	Title	Submitted By	E	F	R	S	Attachments
								Area B. General guidelines for environmental managers upon finding a suspected terrestrial or freshwater non-native species within the Antarctic Treaty Area
WP016	CEP 7f	The Implications of Climate Change for the Antarctic Protected Areas System	United Kingdom	X	X	X	X	Appendix 1
WP017	CEP 7c	Antarctic Treaty Visitor Site Guide for Torgersen Island, Arthur Harbor, Southwest Anvers Island	United States	X	X	X	X	Visitor Site Guide Torgersen
WP018	CEP 7a	Revision of maps and text for the Management Plan for Antarctic Specially Managed Area No. 7: Southwest Anvers Island & Palmer Basin	United States	X	X	X	X	ASMA 7 - SW Anvers-Palmer Revised Map 8 ASMA 7 Revised Management Plan
WP019 rev.1	CEP 7a	Revised Management Plan for ASPA No. 119 Davis Valley and Forlidas Pond, Dufek Massif, Pensacola Mountains	United States	X	X	X	X	ASPA 119 Revised Management Plan
WP020	ATCM 5	Forwarding of recommendations on operational matters to COMNAP	Uruguay	X	X	X	X	
WP021	ATCM 12 CEP 10	Australian Antarctic Treaty and Environmental Protocol inspections, East Antarctica, 2010	Australia	X	X	X	X	
WP022	ATCM 11	Enhanced coordination of Antarctic Treaty proposals within the IMO	Australia	X	X	X	X	
WP023	CEP 7d	Assessing cumulative environmental impacts: identifying the distribution and concentration of national operator activities in Antarctica	United Kingdom	X	X	X	X	
WP024	ATCM 17	Principles for the Access to and Use of Biological Material in the Antarctic Treaty Area	Netherlands	X	X	X	X	
WP025	ATCM 11 CEP 7b	Report of an incident at Wordie House (HSM No. 62)	United Kingdom France Ukraine	X	X	X	X	
WP026	ATCM 12	Final Report of the Intersessional Contact Group on the revision of List A "Permanent Antarctic Stations and Associated Installations" appended to Resolution 5 (1995)	Argentina	X	X	X	X	Revised Checklist A
WP027	CEP 7a	Revised Management Plan for Antarctic Specially Protected Area No. 139 Biscoe Point, Anvers Island, Palmer Archipelago	United States	X	X	X	X	ASPA 139 Revised Management Plan
WP028	ATCM 14 CEP 6b	Environmental Aspects of Antarctic Ship-borne Tourism	Australia	X	X	X	X	Appendix A. Environmental aspects of Antarctic ship-borne tourism
WP029	CEP 7d	The concept of Human Footprint in the Antarctic	New Zealand	X	X	X	X	
WP030	CEP 7a	Subsidiary Group on Management Plans – Report on Term of Reference #4: Improving Management Plans and the Process for their Intersessional Review	Australia	X		X	X	

Working Papers								
Number	Ag. Items	Title	Submitted By	E	F	R	S	Attachments
WP031	CEP 7a	Revision of Management Plan for Antarctic Specially Protected Areas (ASPA) No. 105: Beaufort Island, Mc Murdo Sound, Ross Sea	New Zealand	X	X	X	X	
WP032	CEP 7a	Revision of Management Plans for Antarctic Specially Protected Areas No. 155: Cape Evans, Ross Island	New Zealand	X	X	X	X	ASPA 155 Revised Management Plan
WP033	CEP 7a	Revision of Management Plans for Antarctic Specially Protected Areas (ASPA) No. 157: Backdoor Bay, Cape Royds, Ross Island	New Zealand	X	X	X	X	ASPA 157 Revised Management Plan
WP034	CEP 7a	Revision of Management Plans for Antarctic Specially Protected Areas (ASPA) No. 158: Hut Point, Ross Island	New Zealand	X	X	X	X	ASPA 158 Revised Management Plan
WP035	CEP 7a	Revision of Management Plans for Antarctic Specially Protected Areas (ASPA) No. 159: Cape Adare, Borchgrevink Coast	New Zealand	X	X	X	X	ASPA 159 Revised Management Plan
WP036	CEP 6b	Environmental Aspects and Impacts of Tourism and Non-governmental Activities in Antarctica: Project Report	New Zealand	X	X	X	X	
WP037	ATCM 11	The Enhancement of Port State Control for Passenger Ships Departing to Antarctica	New Zealand	X	X	X	X	
WP038	CEP 7a	Review of Management Plans for Antarctic Specially Protected Areas (ASPAs) 101, 102, 103 and 164	Australia	X	X	X	X	ASPA 101 Revised Management Plan ASPA 102 Revised Management Plan ASPA 103 Revised Management Plan ASPA 164 Revised Management Plan
WP039	CEP 7c	Site Guidelines for Danco Island, Errera Channel, Antarctic Peninsula	United Kingdom United States	X	X	X	X	
WP040	CEP 7f	Third Progress Report on the Discussion of the International Working Group about Possibilities for Environmental Management of Fildes Peninsula and Ardley Island	Chile Germany	X	X	X	X	Annex I: Results of the Meeting of the International Working Group about Possibilities for Environmental Management of Fildes Peninsula Region Annex II: Revised Possible Modules of a Management Plan for Antarctic Specially Managed Area No. ***, Fildes Peninsula Region, South Shetland Islands
WP041	ATCM 16	Antarctic Treaty Information Exchange via the Electronic Information Exchange System (EIES): Current state and improvements for a consistent use	Germany	X	X	X	X	
WP042	CEP 7c	Antarctic Treaty Visitor Site Guidelines for Seabee Hook, Cape Hallett, Northern Victoria Land, Ross Sea	United States	X	X	X	X	Visitor Site Guidelines for Seabee Hook,

Working Papers								
Number	Ag. Items	Title	Submitted By	E	F	R	S	Attachments
								Cape Hallett, Northern Victoria Land, Ross Sea
WP043	CEP 7a	Management Plan for Antarctic Specially Protected Area No. 126, Byers Peninsula, Livingstone Island, South Shetland Islands	United Kingdom Chile Spain	X	X	X	X	ASPA 126 Revised Management Plan
WP044 rev.1	ATCM 4	Complementary protection for Marine Protected Areas designated by CCAMLR	United Kingdom Belgium	X	X	X	X	
WP045	ATCM 5	Rules governing the participation of experts in meetings of ATCM bodies	France	X	X	X	X	
WP046	ATCM 9	Improving the coordination of maritime search and rescue in the Antarctic Treaty area	France	X	X	X	X	
WP047	CEP 7b	Proposal for the discussion of aspects related to the management of Historic Sites and Monuments	Argentina	X	X	X	X	
WP048	ATCM 11	Supervision of Antarctic Tourism	Argentina	X	X	X	X	
WP049	ATCM 11	Proposal for the drafting of guidelines for bases that receive visitors	Argentina	X	X	X	X	
WP050	CEP 7a	Use of the Guidelines for the designation of Protected Areas	Argentina	X	X	X	X	
WP051	ATCM 5	A proposal to continue review of ATCM recommendations	Argentina Germany	X	X	X	X	
WP052	ATCM 11 CEP 6b	Data Collection and Reporting on Yachting Activity in Antarctica	United States United Kingdom	X	X	X	X	
WP053	ATCM 11	Public Availability of Information Concerning Life-saving Appliances Onboard Passenger Ships	United States	X	X	X	X	
WP054	CEP 7f	Enhancing the Antarctic Protected Areas Database to help assess and further develop the protected areas system	Australia	X	X	X	X	
WP055 rev.1	CEP 7a	Review of Management Plan for Antarctic Specially Protected Area (ASPA) No 163: Dakshin Gangotri Glacier, Dronning Maud Land	India	X	X	X	X	ASPA 163 Revised Management Plan
WP056	CEP 7c	Site Guidelines for Damoy Point, Wiencke Island, Antarctic Peninsula	United Kingdom Argentina	X	X	X	X	Site Guidelines for Damoy Point
WP057	ATCM 12 CEP 10	The 2009 Norwegian Antarctic Inspection under Article VII of the Antarctic Treaty	Norway	X	X	X	X	
WP058	CEP 7a	Subsidiary Group on Management Plans – Report on Terms of Reference #1 to #3: Review of Draft Management Plans	Australia	X	X	X	X	ASPA 106 Revised Management Plan
WP059	CEP 6a	Answers to comments on CEE for "Water Sampling the Subglacial Lake Vostok"	Russian Federation	X		X	X	
WP060	ATCM 13	Current tendencies of climatic changes based on data of Russian studies in the Antarctic	Russian Federation	X		X	X	
WP061	ATCM 11	Queen Maud Land – a new center of non-governmental activity in the Antarctic	Russian Federation	X		X	X	
WP062	CEP 9a	Environmental Monitoring and Ecological Activities in Antarctica, 2010-2012	Romania	X		X	X	
WP063	ATCM 4	Report from Antarctic Treaty Meeting of	Norway	X	X	X	X	Co-Chairs' Report

Working Papers								
Number	**Ag. Items**	**Title**	**Submitted By**	**E**	**F**	**R**	**S**	**Attachments**
	CEP 9a	Experts on Implications of Climate Change for Antarctic Management and Governance. Co-chairs' executive summary with advice for actions	United Kingdom					from Antarctic Treaty Meeting of Experts on Implications of Climate Change for Antarctic Management and Governance
WP064	CEP 7c	Site Guidelines for the Northeast beach of Ardley Peninsula (Ardley Island), King George Island (25 de Mayo Island), South Shetland Islands	Argentina Chile	X	X	X	X	Site Guidelines for Northeast beach of Ardley Island Toponyms table
WP065	ATCM 11	Report of the Intersessional Contact Group on Marathons and other large – scale Sporting Activities in Antarctica	Chile	X		X	X	
WP066	ATCM 5	Considerations of Chile on the Antarctic Treaty System Handbook	Chile	X	X	X	X	
WP067	CEP 7b	Proposed Modification to Historic Site Nº 37	Chile	X		X	X	
WP068 rev.1	ATCM 11	Recommendations for controlling yachts under a third flag navigating in the Antarctic Chilean SAR area	Chile	X			X	
WP069	ATCM 11	Recommendations for reducing risks that affects the safety of human life, considering the increase in tourism in Antarctica during the last decade	Chile	X			X	

Information Papers								
Number	Ag. Item	Title	Submitted By	E	F	R	S	Attachments
IP001	CEP 6b	Initial Environmental Evaluation for Development of Approach Path at Proposed New Indian Research Station at Larsemann Hills, East Antarctica	India	X				
IP002	ATCM 11 CEP 7f	Spatial Patterns of Tour Ship Traffic in the Antarctic Peninsula Region	United States IAATO	X				Lynch et al - Spatial patterns of tour ship traffic in the Antarctic Peninsula region
IP003	ATCM 13	The SCAR Lecture - Psychrophiles: a challenge for life	SCAR	X				SCAR Lecture slides
IP004	ATCM 4	Report by the CCAMLR Observer to the Thirty-Third Antarctic Treaty Consultative Meeting	CCAMLR	X	X	X	X	CCAMLR Full Report
IP005	ATCM 12 CEP 10	Inspection undertaken by Japan in accordance with Article VII of the Antarctic Treaty and Article XIV of the Protocol on Environmental Protection	Japan	X	X	X	X	
IP006	ATCM 12 CEP 6a	Update on the Comprehensive Environmental Evaluation (CEE) of New Indian Research Station at Larsemann Hills, Antarctica	India	X	X	X	X	
IP007	ATCM 11	Marine oil spills in the Antarctic Treaty Area – Environmental considerations regarding oil spill behaviour and potential for impacts	New Zealand	X				
IP008	ATCM 11	Oil Spill Response	New Zealand	X				
IP009	CEP 12	Belgian Antarctic Research Expedition BELARE 2009-2010	Belgium	X				
IP010	ATCM 4	The Annual Report for 2009 of the Scientific Committee on Antarctic Research (SCAR) of the International Council for Science (ICSU)	SCAR	X				
IP011	ATCM 11	International requirements for ships operating in polar waters	New Zealand	X				
IP012	CEP 11	Report by the SC-CAMLR Observer to the Thirteenth Meeting of the Committee for Environmental Protection	CCAMLR	X				
IP013	CEP 6b	Continued operation of Kohnen Base as a summer base in Dronning Maud Land including maintenance of a lab in the deep ice by the Alfred Wegener Institute for Polar and Marine Research (AWI)	Germany	X				
IP014	CEP 8a	Research Project "The role of human activities in the introduction of non-native species into Antarctica and in the distribution of organisms within the Antarctic"	Germany	X				
IP015	ATCM 4	Report Submitted to Antarctic Treaty Consultative Meeting XXXIII by the Depositary Government for the Convention for the Conservation of Antarctic Seals in Accordance with Recommendation XIII-2, Paragraph 2(D)	United Kingdom	X	X	X	X	
IP016	CEP 7a	Deception Island Antarctic Specially Managed Area (ASMA) Management Group report	Argentina Chile Norway Spain United Kingdom United States	X			X	
IP017	ATCM 13	1st India-Brazil-South Africa (IBSA)	Brazil	X				

Information Papers								
Number	Ag. Item	Title	Submitted By	E	F	R	S	Attachments
		Dialogue Forum Seminar on Antarctica: exchange amongst Antarctic programs	India South Africa					
IP018	CEP 7a	Bird populations on Deception Island	Spain	X			X	
IP019	CEP 7a	Volcanic risk on Deception Island	Spain	X			X	
IP020	CEP 7d	Possible human impact on Deception Island	Spain	X			X	
IP021	CEP 7b	Enhancement activities for HSM 38 "Snow Hill"	Argentina	X			X	
IP022	CEP 7b	Additional information for the discussion of aspects related to the management of Historic Sites and Monuments	Argentina	X			X	Tablas 1 y 2
IP023	ATCM 14	Report of clean-up efforts by the Argentinian National Antarctic Program in the area of the Neko Harbour refuge (north-west coast of the Antarctic Peninsula)	Argentina	X			X	
IP024	CEP 6b	IAATO Guidelines to Minimize Seabirds Landing on Ships	IAATO	X				
IP025	ATCM 11 CEP 6b	IAATO Online Field Staff Assessment & Logbook	IAATO	X				
IP026	ATCM 11 CEP 7c	Antarctic Site Inventory: 1994-2010	United States	X				
IP027 rev.1	ATCM 14 CEP 9b	Energy Management Strategies for U.S. Antarctic Research Stations	United States	X				Renewable Energy Use at Field Camps in Antarctica
IP028	ATCM 15	The Association of Polar Early Career Scientists (APECS): Shaping the Future of Polar Research	SCAR	X				
IP029	ATCM 15	The Uruguayan Antarctic Institute's educational and awareness-raising activities in 2009-2010	Uruguay	X			X	
IP030	ATCM 12 CEP 10	Report of the Norwegian Antarctic Inspection under Article VII of the Antarctic Treaty. February 2009	Norway	X				Inspection Report in PDF
IP031	CEP 7a	Revision of Maps for Antarctic Specially Managed Area No. 2 McMurdo Dry Valleys, Victoria Land	United States	X				Figure 1 Figure 2 Figure 3 Figure 4 Figure 5
IP032	CEP 7e	Identificación y evaluación de la acción antrópica de grupos poblacionales de mamíferos marinos pinnípedos en áreas de la costa del Estrecho de Drake	Uruguay				X	
IP033	CEP 7a	Blood Falls, Taylor Valley, Victoria Land: an initiative towards proposal of a new Antarctic Specially Protected Area	United States	X				Blood Falls - Boundary options
IP034	CEP 9a	Southern Ocean Sentinel: an international program to assess climate change impacts on marine ecosystems	Australia	X				
IP035	ATCM 9 CEP 9b	Report of a Joint Oil Spill Exercise: RV Laurence M. Gould at Rothera Research Station	United Kingdom United States	X				
IP036	ATCM 11	A Proposal to Enhance Port State Control for Tourist Vessels Departing to Antarctica	New Zealand	X				Draft questionnaire
IP037	ATCM 13	Ross Island Wind Energy Project: Sustainability through collaboration	New Zealand United States	X				
IP038	ATCM 13	The Meeting Report of the 10th AFoPS	China	X				

		Information Papers						
Number	Ag. Item	Title	Submitted By	E	F	R	S	Attachments
IP039	ATCM 9	Report on the Evacuation of an Injured Expeditioner at Zhongshan Station	China	X				
IP040	CEP 7a	Report of the Larsemann Hills Antarctic Specially Managed Area (ASMA) Management Group	Australia China India Romania Russian Federation	X				
IP041	CEP 8c	Southern giant petrel monitoring in ASPA 167, Hawker Island, using automated cameras	Australia	X				
IP042	CEP 8a	Colonisation status of known non-native species in the Antarctic terrestrial environment	United Kingdom	X				
IP043	CEP 8a	Eradication of a vascular plant species recently introduced to Whaler's Bay, Deception Island	United Kingdom Spain	X				
IP044	CEP 8a	Suggested framework and considerations for scientists attempting to determine the colonisation status of newly discovered terrestrial or freshwater species within the Antarctic Treaty Area	United Kingdom	X				
IP045	CEP 7e	Terra Nova Bay – Wood Bay Marine Protected Area inside a wider proposal for a Ross Sea MPA	Italy	X				
IP046	ATCM 13 CEP 9a	Antarctic Climate Change and the Environment – An Update	SCAR	X				
IP047	ATCM 13 CEP 8c	Census of Antarctic Marine Life (CAML)	SCAR Australia	X				
IP048	CEP 7d	Topic Summary: Footprint	Australia	X				
IP049	CEP 7d	The concept of Human Footprint in the Antarctic	New Zealand	X				
IP050	ATCM 13 CEP 5	The Southern Ocean Observing System (SOOS)	SCAR	X				
IP051	ATCM 4	Report by the International Hydrographic Organization (IHO) on "Cooperation in hydrographic surveying and charting of Antarctic waters"	IHO	X	X	X	X	Annexes A, B and C
IP052	ATCM 4	Report of the Depositary Government for the Agreement on the Conservation of Albatrosses and Petrels (ACAP)	Australia	X		X	X	
IP053	ATCM 4	Report of the Depositary Government for the Convention on the Conservation of Antarctic Marine Living Resources (CCAMLR)	Australia	X		X	X	
IP054	ATCM 14 CEP 6b	The Republic of Korea's contribution to Antarctic science by installing a new permanent station in Terra Nova Bay, Ross Sea	Korea (ROK)	X				
IP055	ATCM 13	Scientific and Science-related Collaborations with Other Parties During 2009-2010	Korea (ROK)	X				
IP056	ATCM 14	The First Antarctic Expedition of Araon	Korea (ROK)	X				
IP057	ATCM 15	Highlight of Korean Outreach Programmes 2009-2010	Korea (ROK)	X				
IP058	ATCM 4 CEP 7e	Designation of a new Marine Protected Area for the South Orkney Islands southern shelf	United Kingdom	X				
IP059	CEP 7a	Review of management plans under the Protocol: an example at Cape Hallett	United States	X				Appendix A: Identification of Issues

Information Papers								
Number	Ag. Item	Title	Submitted By	E	F	R	S	Attachments
								Appendix B - Stakeholder consultation Appendix C - Field visit report Appendix D - Boundary revisions Appendix E - Air Access
IP060	ATCM 11	Developing a Risk Assessment Framework for IAATO Passenger Vessels	IAATO	X				
IP061	ATCM 11	IAATO Further Recommendations to Tourism Vessel Operators to Enhance Marine Safety, and Guidelines for Small Boat Operations in the Vicinity of Ice	IAATO	X				
IP062	ATCM 11 CEP 7c	Report on IAATO Member use of Antarctic Peninsula Landing Site and ATCM Visitor Site Guidelines - 2008-09 Season	IAATO	X				
IP063	ATCM 13 CEP 6b	Preliminary Plan for Installation and Operation of the PANSY Atmospheric Radar System at Syowa Station	Japan	X				Full document in PDF
IP064	ATCM 10	Japan in IPY 2007–2008	Japan	X				
IP065	ATCM 13	Japan's Antarctic Research Highlights in 2009-2010	Japan	X				
IP066	ATCM 13 CEP 9b	SCAR Data and Information Strategy (DIMS)	SCAR	X				
IP067	CEP 7b	Actualización del estudio de los restos históricos del naufragio de Punta Suffield	Uruguay				X	
IP068	ATCM 14	Working Towards A Polar Vessel Code	ASOC	X				
IP069	CEP 9b	Benthic Marine Invertebrates as a Tool for the Monitoring of Fuel Transfer from Transport Ships in King George Island	Uruguay	X				
IP070	ATCM 11	Comparison of Three Antarctic Treaty Meeting of Experts on Shipping and Tourism	ASOC	X				
IP071	CEP 7f	Progress on Designation of Broad-scale Management System in the Vernadsky Station Area	Ukraine	X		X		
IP072	CEP 4	Annual Report Pursuant to Article 17 of the Protocol on Environmental Protection to the Antarctic Treaty	Ukraine	X		X		
IP073	ATCM 13 CEP 9a	Key Climate Change Actions in Antarctica: Emissions Reduction, Adaptation and Science	ASOC	X				
IP074	ATCM 14	Energy Efficiency And Renewable Energy Under Extreme Conditions: Case Studies From Antarctica	ASOC	X				Tin, et al. Energy efficiency and renewable energy under extreme conditions: Case studies from Antarctica.
IP075	ATCM 11 CEP 6b	Non-IAATO Tourism and Visitation in Antarctica	IAATO	X				
IP076	ATCM 9	Towards Improved Search and Rescue in the Antarctic	COMNAP	X				SAR Report in PDF
IP077	ATCM 13 CEP 7e	The Case for Inclusion of the Ross Sea Continental Shelf and Slope in a Southern Ocean Network of Marine Reserves	ASOC	X				
IP078	CEP 4	Annual report pursuant to Article 17 of	Italy	X				Annual Report in

		Information Papers						
Number	**Ag. Item**	**Title**	**Submitted By**	**E**	**F**	**R**	**S**	**Attachments**
		the Protocol on Environmental Protection to the Antarctic Treaty						PDF
IP079	ATCM 11 CEP 6b	Tourism and Land-based Facilities in Antarctica: Analysis of a Questionnaire Distributed to Antarctic Treaty Parties at XXXII ATCM	ASOC	X				
IP080	ATCM 11	Making Tangible Progress on a Strategic Vision for Antarctic Tourism	ASOC	X				
IP081	ATCM 11 CEP 7d	Coastal Hydrocarbon Pollution: A Case Study From Deception Island, Antarctica	ASOC	X				Poster (4 MB)
IP082	ATCM 11 CEP 10	Antarctic Ship-borne Tourism and Inspections Under Article VII of the Antarctic Treaty and Article 14 of the Protocol on Environmental Protection	ASOC	X				
IP083	ATCM 13 CEP 7e	Rising to the challenge: Key steps to deliver a Comprehensive and Representative Marine Protected Areas Network in the Southern Ocean by 2012	ASOC	X				
IP084	ATCM 11	Establishing an Annual Round Table Discussion on Antarctic Tourism: Summary Report on June 2009 IAATO Meeting	IAATO	X				
IP085	ATCM 15	The Chilean Antarctic scientific program: a leap forward	Chile	X				
IP086	ATCM 15	Three strategies to talk about Antarctica and science. When nobody knows what you are talking about	Chile	X				
IP087	ATCM 13	Two recent International Climate Change Scientific Events held in Chile	Chile	X				Declaración Magallanes
IP088	ATCM 4 CEP 11	Council of Managers of National Antarctic Programs (COMNAP) Report to ATCM XXXIII	COMNAP	X				COMNAP Full Report
IP089	ATCM 15	Training and education center at Bellingshausen station	Russian Federation	X		X		
IP090	ATCM 13	Results of Russian studies of subglacial lake Vostok in the season 2009/2010	Russian Federation	X		X		
IP091	ATCM 13	Russian research in the Antarctic in 2009	Russian Federation	X		X		
IP092	ATCM 11 CEP 7a	Amundsen-Scott South Pole Station, South Pole Antarctic Specially Managed Area (ASMA No. 5) 2010 Management Report	United States	X				Appendix A: Additional Guidelines for Non-Governmental Organizations at the South Pole ASMA 5 Revised Map 2 ASMA 5 Revised Map 3 ASMA 5 Revised Map 4
IP093	CEP 7b	Conservation and Management of Mawson's Huts, Cape Denison, King George V Land, ASPA 162, ASMA 4 and HSM 77	Australia	X				
IP094	ATCM 9	Amendments to MARPOL Annex I on Special requirements for the use or carriage of oils in the Antarctic Area	IMO	X			X	
IP095	ATCM 15 CEP 7a	Management Report of Narębski Point, ASPA No. 171 (2009-2010)	Korea (ROK)	X				
IP096	ATCM 17	The Role of Ex-Situ Collections in Antarctic Bioprospecting	Belgium UNEP	X				
IP097	ATCM 13	European and International Partnership in Polar Climate Science	Romania	X				

Information Papers								
Number	Ag. Item	Title	Submitted By	E	F	R	S	Attachments
IP098	CEP 9a	Climate Processes of Ocean, Ice and Atmosphere - ERICON AB Icebreaker FP7 Project	Romania	X				
IP099	CEP 5	Young Scientists Fully Aware of the Importance of Antarctic Environment	Romania	X				
IP100	ATCM 10	Romania contribution in IPY 2007-2008	Romania	X				
IP101	ATCM 13	Scientific Activities in the Law-Racovita Station with Logistic Support of India January-February 2009	Romania	X				
IP102	ATCM 4	Report of the Depositary Government of the Antarctic Treaty and its Protocol in accordance with Recommendation XIII-2	United States	X			X	Antarctic Treaty Status Table List of Recommendations/Measures and their approvals Protocol Status Table
IP103	ATCM 13	The Bulgarian Antarctica Project about Multimedia Installation	Bulgaria	X				
IP104	CEP 6b	An Environmental Management System for the Brazilian Antarctic Station "Comandante Ferraz"	Brazil	X				
IP105	ATCM 13 CEP 9a	Management implications of climate change in the Antarctic region – an initial Australian assessment	Australia	X				Attachments A and B
IP106	ATCM 14	New State of the Art Polar Research and Supply Vessel for South Africa	South Africa	X				
IP107	CEP 7e	Bioregionalisation and Spatial Ecosystem Processes in the Ross Sea Region	New Zealand	X				
IP108	ATCM 13	XXXI SCAR Meeting – XXXIII COMNAP Meeting Buenos Aires - 2010. (Argentine invitation for participants)	Argentina	X		X		
IP109	ATCM 13	Grants program to attend SCAR-OSC 2010	Argentina	X		X		
IP110	ATCM 14 CEP 12	Dismantling and subsequent use of Neumayer Station II for SANAP Summer Station and Russian Antarctic Expedition	Germany South Africa	X				
IP111	ATCM 11	Antarctic Waters Operations Course 2010	Chile	X		X		
IP112	ATCM 4	Report of the International Association of Antarctica Tour Operators 2009-10	IAATO	X				
IP113	ATCM 11	IAATO Overview of Antarctic Tourism: 2009-10 Season and Preliminary Estimates for 2010-11 and Beyond	IAATO	X				
IP114	ATCM 4	Report of the Antarctic and Southern Ocean Coalition (ASOC)	ASOC	X	X			
IP115	CEP 7a	Revisión del ASMA Nº 4. Isla Decepción. Bibliografía científica española	Spain				X	
IP116	ATCM 9	Antarctic Navigation Course (Offered by Argentina)	Argentina	X			X	
IP117	CEP 8c	Biodiversidad Microbiológica y Aplicaciones Biotecnológicas	Ecuador				X	
IP118	CEP 8c	Aislamiento e Identificación de Bacterias Antárticas Capaces de Biodegradar Hidrocarburos	Ecuador				X	
IP119	ATCM 13	Estimación del balance de masa sobre el Glaciar Quito en Punta Fort William	Ecuador				X	
IP120	ATCM 13	Ejes de Investigación del Instituto Antártico Ecuatoriano	Ecuador				X	
IP121	ATCM 13 CEP 9b	Estimación de riesgo al cambio climático y la variabilidad climática, en los ecosistemas terrestres circundantes y en	Ecuador				X	

Information Papers							
Number	Ag. Item	Title	Submitted By	E	F	R	S	Attachments
		la infraestructura física de la Estación Científica Maldonado						
IP122	CEP 6b	Informe preliminar del Estudio de Impacto Ambiental ex – post de la Estación Científica Pedro Vicente Maldonado	Ecuador				X	
IP123	ATCM 13	Desarrollo de Robots Submarinos Autónomos no Tripulados para exploración Antártica	Ecuador				X	
IP124	ATCM 15	Activities carried out in Chile to commemorate the Fiftieth Anniversary of the signing of the Antarctic Treaty	Chile	X			X	
IP125	ATCM 17	Informe de proyectos de bio-prospección impulsados por el Ecuador, 2009-2010	Ecuador				X	
IP126	ATCM 13	Informe del V Simposio Latinoamericano sobre Investigaciones Antárticas y II Simposio Ecuatoriano de Ciencia Polar, Ecuador 2009	Ecuador				X	
IP128	ATCM 13	The Czech research activities on the James Ross Island and Antarctic Peninsula in 2009/10	Czech Republic	X				
IP129	ATCM 11	Report on Antarctic tourist flows and cruise ships operating in Ushuaia during the 2009/2010 austral summer season	Argentina	X			X	
IP130	ATCM 11	The Antarctic voyage experience and visitors' satisfaction for the 2009/2010 season	Argentina	X			X	

Secretariat Papers							
Number	Ag. Item	Title	Submitted By	E	F	R	S	Attachments
SP001 rev.2	ATCM 3 CEP 2	ATCM XXXIII - CEP XIII Agenda and Schedule	ATS	X	X	X	X	
SP002 rev.1	ATCM 6	Secretariat Report 2009/10	ATS	X	X	X	X	Appendix 1 – Financial Report 2008/09 Appendix 2 - Provisional Financial Report 2009/10 Appendix 3 - Contributions 2009/10 Auditor´s report
SP003 rev.2	ATCM 6	Draft Secretariat Programme 2010/11	ATS	X	X	X	X	Appendix 1 - Prov. Report 2009/10, Budget 2010/11, Forecast Budget 2011/12 Appendix 2 - Contribution scale 2011/12 Appendix 3 - Salaries Scale Appendix 4 - CCAMLR letter regarding Regulation 10.4 of the ATS Staff Regulations
SP004	ATCM 6	Contributions Received by the Antarctic Treaty Secretariat 2008-2011	ATS	X	X	X	X	
SP005	ATCM 5	Review of the Status of ATCM Recommendations on Protected Areas and Monuments	ATS	X	X	X	X	

Secretariat Papers								
Number	Ag. Item	Title	Submitted By	E	F	R	S	Attachments
SP006	ATCM 5	Review of the Status of ATCM Recommendations on Operational Matters	ATS	X	X	X	X	
SP007	ATCM 5	Review of the Status of ATCM Recommendations on Environmental Issues other than Area Protection and Management	ATS	X	X	X	X	
SP008	ATCM 5	The Handbook of the Antarctic Treaty System	ATS	X	X	X	X	Proposal for the Volume 1 of the Handbook circulated by the Secretariat on August, 2009
SP009	ATCM 16 CEP 4	Electronic Information Exchange System (EIES): Report on the 2nd operational season and summary information examples	ATS	X	X	X	X	
SP010	CEP 7a	Register of the status of Antarctic Specially Protected Area and Antarctic Specially Managed Area Management Plans	ATS	X	X	X	X	Register updated January 2010
SP011 rev.1	CEP 6b	Annual list of Initial Environmental Evaluations (IEE) and Comprehensive Environmental Evaluations (CEE) prepared between April 1st 2009 and March 31st 2010	ATS	X	X	X	X	

3. List of Participants

3. List of Participants

Participants: Consultative Parties				
Party	Title	Contact	Position	Email
Argentina	Mr.	Barreto, Juan	Delegate	bat@mrecic.gov.ar
Argentina	Lic	Bunge, Carlos	Advisor	
Argentina	Mr	Costantino, Leonardo	Delegate	
Argentina	Dr	Curtosi, Antonio	Advisor	
Argentina	Mrs	Daverio, María Elena	Advisor	medaverio@arnet.com.ar
Argentina	Mr	Gowland, Máximo	Delegate	gme@mrecic.gov.ar
Argentina	Ms	Gucioni, Paola	Advisor	
Argentina	Mr	López Crozet, Fausto	Alternate	flc@mrecic.gov.ar
Argentina	Dr.	MacCormack, Walter	Advisor	
Argentina	Mr.	Mansi, Ariel	Head of Delegation	rpc@mrecic.gov.ar
Argentina	Dr.	Marenssi, Sergio	Delegate	smarenssi@dna.gov.ar
Argentina	Dr.	Memolli, Mariano A.	CEP Representative	mmemolli@dna.gov.ar
Argentina	Mrs.	Ortúzar, Patricia	Delegate	portuzar@dna.gov.ar
Argentina	Dr.	Quartino, Liliana	Advisor	
Argentina	Mr	Roballo, Jorge	Advisor	elroba@hotmail.com
Argentina	Mr	Sánchez, Rodolfo	Delegate	rsanchez@dna.gov.ar
Argentina	Ms	Vereda, Marisol	Advisor	
Argentina	Dr	Vlasich, Veronica	Advisor	
Australia	Mr	Gunn, John	CEP Representative	john.gunn@aad.gov.au
Australia	Ms	Maddock, Lyn	Alternate	lyn.maddock@aad.gov.au
Australia	Mr.	Maggs, Tom	Delegate	tom.maggs@aad.gov.au
Australia	Mr	McIvor, Ewan	CEP Representative	ewan.mcivor@aad.gov.au
Australia	Mr	Nicoll, Rob	Advisor	RNicoll@wwf.org.au
Australia	Mr	Palmisano, Edward	Delegate	Edward.Palmisano@dfat.gov.au
Australia	Ms	Richards, Penny	Head of Delegation	penny.richards@dfat.gov.au
Australia	Mr	Rowe, Richard	Delegate	Richard.Rowe@dfat.gov.au
Australia	Ms	Slocum, Gillian	Delegate	Gillian.Slocum@aad.gov.au
Australia	Dr	Tracey, Phillip	Delegate	phil.tracey@aad.gov.au
Australia	Ms	Trousselot, Chrissie	Advisor	Chrissie.trousselot@development. tas.gov.au
Belgium	Mr.	de Lichtervelde, Alexandre	CEP Representative	alexandre.delichtervelde@health.f gov.be
Belgium	Mrs.	Vancauwenberghe, Maaike	Delegate	vcau@belspo.be
Belgium	Mr	Vanden Bilcke, Christian	Head of Delegation	christian.vandenbilcke@diplobel.f ed.be
Belgium	Ms	Wilmotte, Annick	Delegate	awilmotte@ulg.ac.be
Brazil	Rear Admiral	de Carvalho Ferreira, Marcos José	Alternate	
Brazil	Comander	Ferreira da Cruz, Marcello	Delegate	marcello.cruz@secirm.mar.mil.br
Brazil	Comander	Leite, Márcio	Delegate	marcio.leite@secirm.mar.mil.br

Participants: Consultative Parties				
Party	Title	Contact	Position	Email
Brazil	Dr	Machado, Maria Cordélia	Delegate	mmachado@mct.gov.br
Brazil	Comander	Trad Souza, Haynnee	Delegate	haynnee@secirm.mar.mil.br
Brazil	Minister	Vaz Pitaluga, Fábio	Head of Delegation	dmae@itamaraty.gov.br
Brazil	Ms	Viana, Mariana de Sá	CEP Representative	mariana.viana@mma.gov.br
Bulgaria	Mr.	Chipev, Nesho	Delegate	chipev@ecolab.bas.bg
Bulgaria	Dr.	Dimitroff, Zlatko	Head of Delegation	zdimitroff@mfa.government.bg
Bulgaria	Prof.	Pimpirev, Christo	Alternate	polar@gea.uni-sofia.bg
Chile	Sra.	Alvarez, Laura	Advisor	lalvarezyercic@gmail.com
Chile	Amb.	Berguño, Jorge	Head of Delegation	jberguno@inach.cl
Chile	Cap. de Fragata IM	Budge, Jorge	Delegate	jbudge@emdn.cl
Chile	Ms.	Carvallo, María Luisa	Alternate	mlcarvallo@minrel.gov.cl
Chile	Coronel	Castillo, Rafael	Delegate	castillo.antartica@gmail.com
Chile	Coronel (A)	Madrid, Santiago	Delegate	smadrid@fach.cl
Chile	Dr.	Retamales, José	Head of Delegation	jretamales@inach.cl
Chile	Ms.	Sardiña, Jimena	Delegate	jsardina@inach.cl
Chile	Cap. de Navío	Sepulveda, Victor	Delegate	vsepulveda@armada.cl
Chile	Capitan de Navío	Valenzuela, Ivan	Delegate	ivalenzuela@directemar.cl
Chile	Ms.	Vallejos, Verónica	CEP Representative	vvallejos@inach.cl
Chile	Cap. Corbet LT. Mr.	Velásquez, Ricardo	Delegate	rvelasquezo@directemar.cl
China	Miss	Fang, Lijun	Advisor	
China	Mr.	Gou, Haibo	Delegate	gou_haibo@mfa.gov.cn
China	Ms.	Jiang, Mei	Delegate	
China	Mr.	Liu, Shaoqing	Delegate	
China	Mr.	Qu, Tanzhou	CEP Representative	qutanzhou@vip.sina.com
China	Mr.	Wang, Antao	Delegate	
China	Miss.	Yang, Fan	Advisor	yang_fan2@mfa.gov.cn
China	Mr	Zhou, Jian	Head of Delegation	zhou_jian@mfa.gov.cn
Ecuador	Licenciada	Burbano, Mónica	Delegate	inae@gye.satnet.net
Ecuador	Doctor	Cabrera, Arturo	Delegate	inae@gye.satnet.net
Ecuador	Captain	Olmedo Morán, José	Staff	pinguino.olmedo@gmail.com
Ecuador	Docto	Palacios, Patricio	Delegate	inae@gye.satnet.net

Participants: Consultative Parties				
Party	Title	Contact	Position	Email
	r			
Ecuador	Master	Rosero, Javier	CEP Representative	inae@gye.satnet.net
Ecuador	Contralmirante	Sarzosa, Angel	Head of Delegation	inae@gye.satnet.net
Finland	Ms	Luikku, Laura	Alternate	laura.luikku@formin.fi
Finland	Ms.	Mähönen, Outi	CEP Representative	outi.mahonen@ely-keskus.fi
Finland	Ambassador	Meres-Wuori, Ora	Head of Delegation	ora.meres-wuori@formin.fi
France	Mrs	Belna, Stéphanie	Delegate	stephanie.belna@developpement-durable.gouv.fr
France	Dr.	Choquet, Anne	Advisor	anne.choquet@univ-brest.fr
France		Dalmas, Dominique	Delegate	dominique.dalmas@interieur.gouv.fr
France	Dr	Frenot, Yves	CEP Representative	yves.frenot@ipev.fr
France	Mr	Montagut, Géraud	Delegate	geraud.montagut@diplomatie.gouv.fr
France	Mr	Reuillard, Emmanuel	Delegate	emmanuel.reuillard@taaf.fr
France	Mr.	Segura, Serge	Head of Delegation	serge.segura@diplomatie.gouv.fr
France	Mr	Tribon, Pierre	Delegate	pierre.tribon@agriculture.gouv.fr
Germany	Dr.	Gaedicke, Christoph	Advisor	
Germany	Dr.	Herata, Heike	Advisor	heike.herata@uba.de
Germany	Dr.	Läufer, Andeas	Advisor	andreas.laeufer@bgr.de
Germany		Liebschner, Alexander	Advisor	alexander.liebschner@bfn-vilm.de
Germany	Prof. Dr.	Miller, Heinrich	Advisor	heinrich.miller@awi.de
Germany	Dr.	Nixdorf, Uwe	Advisor	Uwe.Nixdorf@awi.de
Germany	Ms.	Reppe, Silvia	Delegate	silvia.reppe@bmu.bund.de
Germany	Ambassador	Winkelmann, Ingo	Head of Delegation	504-rl@diplo.de
India	Dr.	Chaturvedi, Sanjai	Advisor	
India	Dr	Rangreji, Luther	Delegate	rangreji@yahoo.com
India	Dr	Ravindra, Rasik	Head of Delegation	rasik@ncaor.org
India	Dr	Sharma, R K	Delegate	rks@nic.in
India	Mr	Singh, Taranjit	Delegate	waheguruji13@ymail.com
India	Mr.	Tiwari, Anoop	Delegate	anooptiwari@ncaor.org
Italy	Amb.	Fornara, Arduino	Head of Delegation	arduino.fornara@esteri.it
Italy	Dr.	Tamburelli, Gianfranco	Advisor	gtamburelli@pelagus.it
Italy	Ms.	Tomaselli, Maria Stefania	Advisor	tomaselli.stefania@minambiente.it
Italy	Dr.	Torcini, Sandro	Advisor	sandro.torcini@casaccia.enea.it
Italy	Ms.	Vigni, Patrizia	Alternate	vigni@unisi.it
Japan	Mr.	Akimoto, Meguru	Delegate	MEGURU_AKIMOTO@env.go.jp
Japan	Prof.	Fujii, Yoshiyuki	Delegate	fujii@nipr.ac.jp

Participants: Consultative Parties				
Party	Title	Contact	Position	Email
Japan	Ms.	Fujimoto, Masami	Delegate	masami.fujimoto@mofa.go.jp
Japan	Mr	Kawashima, Tetsuya	Delegate	tetsuya_kawashima@nm.maff.go.jp
Japan	Mr	Osumi, Yo	Head of Delegation	yo.osumi@mofa.go.jp
Japan	Prof.	Watanabe, Kentaro	Delegate	
Japan	Prof.	Yamanouchi, Takashi	Delegate	
Korea (ROK)	Dr	Ahn, In-Young	CEP Representative	iahn@kopri.re.kr
Korea (ROK)	Ms.	Cho, Ji I	Delegate	jicho07@mofat.go.kr
Korea (ROK)	Dr.	Choi, Jaeyong	Advisor	jaychoi@cnu.ac.kr
Korea (ROK)	Dr.	Jin, Dongmin	Alternate	dmjin@kopri.re.kr
Korea (ROK)	Mr.	Joo, Hyun-Jong	Delegate	joohj84@korea.kr
Korea (ROK)	Dr.	Kim, Yeadong	CEP Representative	ydkim@kopri.re.kr
Korea (ROK)	Dr.	Kim, Ji Young	Advisor	mythe@kei.re.kr
Korea (ROK)	Mr	Lee, Key Cheol	Head of Delegation	kclee85@mofat.go.kr
Korea (ROK)	Dr	Seo, Hyun kyo	Delegate	shkshk@kopri.re.kr
Netherlands	Dr.	Bastmeijer, Kees	Advisor	c.j.bastmeijer@uvt.nl
Netherlands		Elstgeest, Marlynda	Advisor	
Netherlands	Drs.	Gräber, Babette	CEP Representative	babette.graber@minvrom.nl
Netherlands	Drs	van der Kroef, Dick	Advisor	kroef@nwo.nl
Netherlands	Mr.	van Zeijst, Vincent	Head of Delegation	vincent-van.zeijst@minbuza.nl
New Zealand	Dr.	Gilbert, Neil	CEP Representative	n.gilbert@antarcticanz.govt.nz
New Zealand	Ms	Hooker, Jane	Advisor	jane.hooker@mfat.govt.nz
New Zealand	Mr.	Hughes, Trevor	Head of Delegation	trevor.hughes@mfat.govt.nz
New Zealand	Mr	Martin, Peter	Advisor	peter.martin@mfat.govt.nz
New Zealand	Ms	Newman, Jana	Advisor	j.newman@antarcticanz.govt.nz
New Zealand	Mr.	Walker, James	Advisor	james.walker@mfat.govt.nz
Norway	Mr.	Halvorsen, Svein Tore	CEP Representative	sth@md.dep.no
Norway	Ms.	Holten, Inger	Delegate	iho@mfa.no
Norway	Ms.	Ingebrigtsen, Hanne Margrethe	Alternate	hanne.margrethe.ingebrigtsen@jd.dep.no
Norway	Dr.	Jan-Gunnar, Winther	Delegate	
Norway	Mr.	Klepsvik, Karsten	Head of Delegation	karsten.klepsvik@mfa.no
Norway	Mr.	Koefoed, Jens Henning	Advisor	Jens.Koefoed@sjofartsdir.no
Norway	Mrs.	Korsvoll, Marie Helene	Delegate	mhk@md.dep.no
Norway	Ms.	Njaastad, Birgit	CEP Representative	njaastad@npolar.no
Norway	Mr.	Rosenberg, Stein Paul	Alternate	
Norway	Ms.	Sund, Tonje	Delegate	tonje.sund@NHD.dep.no
Peru	Ms.	Gagliuffi, Patricia	Delegate	pgagliuffi@rree.gob.pe
Peru	Amb.	Isasi-Cayo, Fortunato	Alternate	fisasi@rree.gob.pe
Peru	Mr.	Sandiga Cabrera, Luis	Head of Delegation	lsandiga@rree.gob.pe
Poland	Dr.	Tatur, Andrzej	CEP Representative	tatura@interia.pl
Poland	Ambassador	Wolski, Jakub T.	Head of Delegation	jakub.wolski@msz.gov.pl

Participants: Consultative Parties				
Party	Title	Contact	Position	Email
Romania	Masterand	Magdalin, Andreia	Delegate	negoita_antarctic@yahoo.com
Russian Federation	Mrs.	Bystramovich, Anna	Delegate	antarc@mcc.mecom.ru
Russian Federation	Mrs	Dunaeva, Elena	Staff	dp@mid.ru
Russian Federation	Mr.	Lukin, Valery	CEP Representative	lukin@aari.nw.ru
Russian Federation	Mr.	Masolov, Valery	Delegate	
Russian Federation	Mr.	Pomelov, Victor	Delegate	pom@aari.nw.ru
Russian Federation	Mr.	Timokhin, Konstantin	Delegate	dp@mid.ru
Russian Federation	Mr.	Titushkin, Vassily	Head of Delegation	tvj2000@mail.ru
South Africa	Ms	Jacobs, Carol	CEP Representative	cjacobs@deat.gov.za
South Africa	Mr	Maqungo, Sivu	Advisor	
South Africa	Mr.	Skinner, Richard	Delegate	Rskinner@deat.gov.za
South Africa	Mr	Smit, Danie	CEP Representative	dsmit@deat.gov.za
South Africa	Dr.	Thaoge-Lefyedi, Mathoto	Advisor	mathoto.thaoge-lefyedi@dst.gov.za
South Africa	Mr.	Valentine, Henry	Head of Delegation	hvalentine@deat.gov.za
Spain	Rear-Admiral (R)	Catalan, Manuel	CEP Representative	cpe@micinn.es
Spain	Ambassador	Martinez-Cattaneo, Juan Antonio	Head of Delegation	juan.mcattaneo@maec.es
Spain	Capitán de Navío	Perez Carrillo de Albornoz, Francisco Jose	Advisor	fperde@fn.mde.es
Spain	Mrs	Ramos, Sonia	Alternate	cpe@micinn.es
Sweden	Dr.	Bjork, Lars	Advisor	lars.bjork@ebc.uu.se
Sweden	Administrative Offic	Israelson, Ann-Sofi	CEP Representative	ann-sofi.israelson@naturvardsverket.se
Sweden	Dr.	Melander, Olle	Alternate	olle.melander@polar.se
Sweden	Ambassador	Ödmark, Helena	Head of Delegation	helena.odmark@foreign.ministry.se
Ukraine	Mr.	Fedchuk, Andrii	CEP Representative	andriyf@gmail.com
Ukraine	Dr.	Lytvynov, Valerii	Head of Delegation	uac@uac.gov.ua
United Kingdom	Mr.	Bowman, Rob	Alternate	rob.bowman@fco.gov.uk
United Kingdom	Ms.	Brazier, Rachel	Advisor	
United Kingdom	Ms	Clarke, Rachel	Delegate	racl@bas.ac.uk
United Kingdom	Mr	Culshaw, Robert	Delegate	r.culshaw@bas.ac.uk
United Kingdom	Mr.	Downie, Rod	Delegate	rhd@bas.ac.uk

Participants: Consultative Parties

Party	Title	Contact	Position	Email
United Kingdom	Ms	Hourigan, Eleanor	Advisor	eleanor.hourigan@fco.gov.uk
United Kingdom	Ms.	Piaggio, Carla	Advisor	
United Kingdom	Ms.	Rumble, Jane	Head of Delegation	Jane.Rumble@fco.gov.uk
United Kingdom	Dr.	Shears, John	Delegate	jrs@bas.ac.uk
United Kingdom	Ms.	St. Cooke, Lynda	Advisor	
United Kingdom	Dr	Walmsley, Simon	Delegate	SWalmsley@wwf.org.uk
United States	Ms.	Adkins, Jocelyn	Advisor	Adkins.Jocelyn@epamail.epa.gov
United States	Mr.	Bloom, Evan T.	Head of Delegation	bloomet@state.gov
United States	Ms.	Dahood-Fritz, Adrian	Advisor	adahood@nsf.gov
United States	Mr.	Edwards, David	Advisor	
United States	Mr.	Foster, Harold D.	Alternate	fosterhd@state.gov
United States	Ms.	Hessert, Aimee	Advisor	
United States	Dr.	Lyons, Berry	Advisor	
United States	Ms.	Markley, Erin	Advisor	markleyen@state.gov
United States	Mr.	McDonald, Samuel	Advisor	
United States	Mr.	Naveen, Ron	Advisor	
United States	Dr.	Penhale, Polly A.	CEP Representative	ppenhale@nsf.gov
United States	Ms.	Perrault, Michele	Advisor	
United States	Mr.	Rudolph, Lawrence	Advisor	lrudolph@nsf.gov
United States	Mr.	Spangler, Bryson	Advisor	Bryson.T.Spangler@uscg.mil
United States	Mr.	Stone, Brian	Advisor	
United States	Ms.	Toschik, Pamela	Advisor	
United States	Mr.	Watters, George	Advisor	George.Watters@noaa.gov
United States	Ms.	Wheatley, Victoria	Advisor	
Uruguay	Mr	Abdala, Juan	CEP Representative	jabdala@iau.gub.uy
Uruguay	CA	Alonso, Leonardo	Head of Delegation	presidente@iau.gub.uy
Uruguay	Dr.	Grillo, Bartolome	Delegate	cakrill@redfacil.com.uy
Uruguay		Pin, Oscar	Advisor	
Uruguay	Dr.	Puceiro Ripoll, Roberto	ATCM Chair	eliro@adinet.com.uy
Uruguay	Mr.	Schunk, Ricardo	Delegate	dirsecretaria@iau.gub.uy

Participants: Non-Consultative Parties

Party	Title	Contact	Position	Email
Canada	Mr.	Mudroch, Paul	CEP Representative	paul.mudroch@ec.gc.ca
Czech Republic	Mr.	Venera, Zdenek	Head of Delegation	zdenek.venera@geology.cz
Monaco	Del.	Van Klaveren, Céline	Delegate	cevanklaveren@gouv.mc
Monaco	Mr.	Van Klaveren, Patrick	Head of Delegation	pvanklaveren@gouv.mc
Romania	Dr.	Negoita, Teodor Gheorghe	Head of Delegation	negoita_antarctic@yahoo.com

Participants: Observers

Party	Title	Contact	Position	Email
CCAMLR	Dr	Agnew, David	CEP Representative	d.agnew@mrag.co.uk
CCAMLR	Dr	Reid, Keith	Advisor	keith@ccamlr.org

Participants: Observers

Party	Title	Contact	Position	Email
CCAMLR	Mr	Wright, Andrew	Head of Delegation	
COMNAP	Ms.	Rogan-Finnemore, Michelle	Head of Delegation	michelle.finnemore@comnap.aq
SCAR	Dr	Badhe, Renuka	Delegate	rb302@cam.ac.uk
SCAR	Dr	Gerday, Charles	Delegate	Ch.Gerday@ulg.ac.be
SCAR	Prof	Kennicutt, Mahlon (Chuck)	Head of Delegation	m-kennicutt@tamu.edu
SCAR	Dr.	Sparrow, Mike	Delegate	mds68@cam.ac.uk

Participants: Experts

Party	Title	Contact	Position	Email
ASOC	Mr.	Barnes, James	Head of Delegation	jimbo0628@mac.com
ASOC	Ms.	Christian, Claire	Advisor	Claire.Christian@asoc.org
ASOC	Ms.	Cirelli, Verónica	Advisor	oceanosaustrales@vidasilvestre.org.ar
ASOC	Mr.	Leiva, Sam	Advisor	
ASOC	Mr.	Page, Richard	Advisor	richard.page@uk.greenpeace.org
ASOC	Ms.	Prior, Judith Sian	Advisor	Karen.Sack@wdc.greenpeace.org
ASOC	Mr.	Roura, Ricardo	CEP Representative	ricardo.roura@worldonline.nl
ASOC	Dr.	Tin, Tina	Advisor	tinatintk@gmail.com
ASOC	Mr	Werner Kinkelin, Rodolfo	Advisor	rodolfo.antarctica@gmail.com
IAATO	Dr.	Crosbie, Kim	CEP Representative	kimcrosbie@iaato.org
IAATO	Ms.	Hohn-Bowen, Ute	Delegate	ute@antarpply.com
IAATO	Mr.	Rootes, David	Delegate	david.rootes@antarctic-logistics.com
IAATO	Ms.	Schillat, Monika	Delegate	Monika@antarpply.com
IAATO	Mr.	Wellmeier, Steve	Head of Delegation	swellmeier@iaato.org
IAATO	Mrs	Wikander, Erica	Delegate	ericawikander@aol.com
IHO	Capt.	Gorziglia, Hugo	Delegate	hgorziglia@ihb.mc

Participants: Invited guests

Party	Title	Contact	Position	Email
Malaysia	Dr	Hamzah, B.Ahmad	Advisor	bahamzah@pd.jaring.my
Malaysia	Dr	Mohd Nor, Salleh	Delegate	salleh.mohdnor@gmail.com
Malaysia	His Excellency	Yaacob, Dato´Zulkifli	Head of Delegation	aizzaty@kln.gov.my

Participants: Secretariats

Party	Title	Contact	Position	Email
ATS	Mr.	Acero, José Maria	Alternate	tito.acero@ats.aq
ATS	Mr.	Agraz, José Luis	Staff	pepe.agraz@ats.aq
ATS	Ms.	Barrett, Jill	Staff	Jill.barrett@btinternet.com
ATS	Mr.	Davies, Paul	Staff	littlewest2@googlemail.com
ATS	Ms	Guyomard, Ann-Isabelle	Staff	AnnGuyomard@hotmail.com
ATS	Dr.	Reinke, Manfred	Head of Delegation	manfred.reinke@ats.aq

Participants: Secretariats				
Party	Title	Contact	Position	Email
ATS	Mr.	Wainschenker, Pablo	Staff	pablo.wainschenker@ats.aq
ATS	Mr.	Wydler, Diego	Staff	diego.wydler@ats.aq
Translation & Interpretation	Mr.	Ponette, Bernard	Staff	bernardponette@gmail.com
HCS	Mrs.	Barcos, Beatriz	Staff	
HCS	Mr	Batista, Rubel	Staff	secretaria@atcm2010.gub.uy
HCS	Mr	Benavidez, Gary	Staff	secretaria@atcm2010.gub.uy
HCS	Mr	Bottaro, Hugo	Staff	secretaria@atcm2010.gub.uy
HCS	Mr	Caula, Nicole	Delegate	secretaria@atcm2010.gub.uy
HCS	Ms.	Cuadrado, Lara	Staff	
HCS		Dematteis, Sergio	Staff	
HCS	Mr	Denis, Andrés	Staff	secretaria@atcm2010.gub.uy
HCS	Mrs	Di Cristofaro, Mariela	Advisor	ambiente@iau.gub.uy
HCS	Mrs	Durán, Valeria	Staff	valeduran1@hotmail.com
HCS	Mr	Dutra, Hector	Staff	secretaria@atcm2010.gub.uy
HCS	Mrs	Eguren, Gabriela	Advisor	
HCS	Ms	Erceg, Diane	Staff	di_erceg@hotmail.com
HCS	Mrs	Escardo , Ines	Staff	i.escardo@perspectiva.com.uy
HCS	Mr	Escayola, Carlos	Delegate	secretaria@atcm2010.gub.uy
HCS	Mr.	Felici, Aldo	Advisor	ambiente@iau.gub.uy
HCS	Ms	Figueroa, Cristina	Delegate	secretaria@atcm2010.gub.uy
HCS	Mr	Fontes, Waldemar	Staff	secretaria@atcm2010.gub.uy
HCS	Mr	Fortunato, José	Staff	secretaria@atcm2010.gub.uy
HCS	Mr.	García, Federico	Staff	fede_riko1@hotmail.com
HCS		Garre, Anakaren	Staff	
HCS	Ms	Geisz, Heidi	Advisor	heidig@vims.edu
HCS	Mr	González, Joaquín	Staff	joaco@hotmail.com
HCS	Dr.	Grillo, Bartolome	Delegate	cakrill@redfacil.com.uy
HCS	Mr	Juri, Eduardo	Staff	secretaria@atcm2010.gub.uy
HCS	Ms	Kelly, Emily	Staff	emilylak@gmail.com
HCS	Ms	Lages, Carol	Staff	secretaria@atcm2010.gub.uy
HCS	Mr	Latorre, Leonardo	Staff	secretaria@atcm2010.gub.uy
HCS	Ms	Lebrato, Andrea	Staff	secretaria@atcm2010.gub.uy
HCS	Mr.	Lluberas, Albert	Staff	alexllub@iau.gub.uy
HCS	Mrs	Loperena, Lilian	Advisor	
HCS	Ms	Lynch, Heather	Staff	hiynch@umd.edu
HCS	Ms	Magano, Claudia	Staff	secretaria@atcm2010.gub.uy
HCS	Mr	Martinez, Andrés	Staff	secretaria@atcm2010.gub.uy
HCS		Nagy, José	Delegate	
HCS	Mr	Nobile, Javier	Delegate	secretaria@atcm2010.gub.uy
HCS		Orlando, Marcia	Staff	
HCS	Mr.	Pena, Ignacio	Staff	nacho_p_09@hotmail.com
HCS	Mr	Percy, Ian	Staff	santorpercy@gmail.com

Participants: Secretariats				
Party	Title	Contact	Position	Email
HCS		Pereyra, Ana María	Delegate	
HCS		Pin, Oscar	Advisor	
HCS	Dr.	Puceiro Ripoll, Roberto	Staff	eliro@adinet.com.uy
HCS		Radio, Waldemar	Staff	
HCS	Mr	Ricci, Marcelo	Staff	marce.ricci@gmail.com
HCS	Ms	Rodriguez, Sandra	Delegate	secretaria@atcm2010.gub.uy
HCS	Mrs	Rodriguez, Doris	Advisor	hcs@atcm2010.gub.uy
HCS	Ms	Saint Bois, Alejandra	Staff	secretaria@atcm2010.gub.uy
HCS	Mr	Santellán, Mauricio	Staff	secretaria@atcm2010.gub.uy
HCS	Mr.	Schunk, Ricardo	Delegate	dirsecretaria@iau.gub.uy
HCS		Scott, Edgar	Staff	
HCS	Mrs	Simonassi, María Victoria	Staff	mvss789@hotmail.es
HCS	Mr	Somma, Gustavo	Alternate	
HCS	Mrs	Sulikowski, Chavelli	Staff	chavelli.sulikowski@utas.edu.au
HCS	Mrs	Sutlovich, Veronica	Staff	v.sutlovich@perspectiva.com.uy
HCS	Mr	Sutlovich, Alberto	Staff	administracion@perspectiva.com.uy
HCS	Mr	Tuttle, Robin	Staff	robitut@yahoo.com
HCS	Ms	Vang, Sue	Staff	svang1802@yahoo.com
HCS	Amb.	Varela, Ricardo	Delegate	hcs@atcm2010.gub.uy
HCS	Ms	Vaz, Natalia	Staff	secretaria@atcm2010.gub.uy
HCS	Mr	Vignali, Daniel	Delegate	secretaria@atcm2010.gub.uy
HCS	Mrs	Volonterio , Odile	Advisor	ambiente@iau.gub.uy
HCS	Mr	Watson, Jordan Thomas	Staff	jordan.t.watson@gmail.com